MASS EFFECT

MASS EFFECT™

OMNIBUS
VOLUME 1

REDEMPTION
EVOLUTION
INVASION
HOMEWORLDS

STORY
MAC WALTERS
PATRICK WEEKES
JOHN DOMBROW
SYLVIA FEKETEKUTY

SCRIPT
JOHN JACKSON MILLER
JEREMY BARLOW
MAC WALTERS

ART
OMAR FRANCIA
EDUARDO FRANCISCO
CHRIS STAGGS WITH MARC DEERING
GARRY BROWN
JEAN DIAZ

COLORS
MICHAEL ATIYEH

LETTERING
MICHAEL HEISLER

DARK HORSE BOOKS

PUBLISHER
MIKE RICHARDSON

EDITOR
DAVE MARSHALL

ASSISTANT EDITORS
**SHANTEL LAROCQUE, IAN TUCKER,
BRENDAN WRIGHT,** AND **RACHEL ROBERTS**

COLLECTION DESIGNER
SARAH TERRY

DIGITAL ART TECHNICIAN
ALLYSON HALLER

MASS EFFECT OMNIBUS VOLUME 1

This volume collects the Dark Horse comic book series *Mass Effect: Redemption* #1–#4, *Evolution* #1–#4, *Invasion* #1–#4, and *Homeworlds* #1–#4, as well as the short stories "Incursion," "Inquisition," and "Conviction."

Special thanks to BioWare, including: Derek Watts, Art Director • Casey Hudson, Executive Producer • Aaryn Flynn, Studio GM, BioWare Edmonton • Ray Muzyka and Greg Zeschuk, BioWare Co-Founders

Published by Dark Horse Books
A division of Dark Horse Comics, Inc.
10956 SE Main Street | Milwaukie, OR 97222

DarkHorse.com | MassEffect.com

First edition: November 2016
ISBN 978-1-50670-276-6

1 3 5 7 9 10 8 6 4 2
Printed in China

Library of Congress Cataloging-in-Publication Data is available.

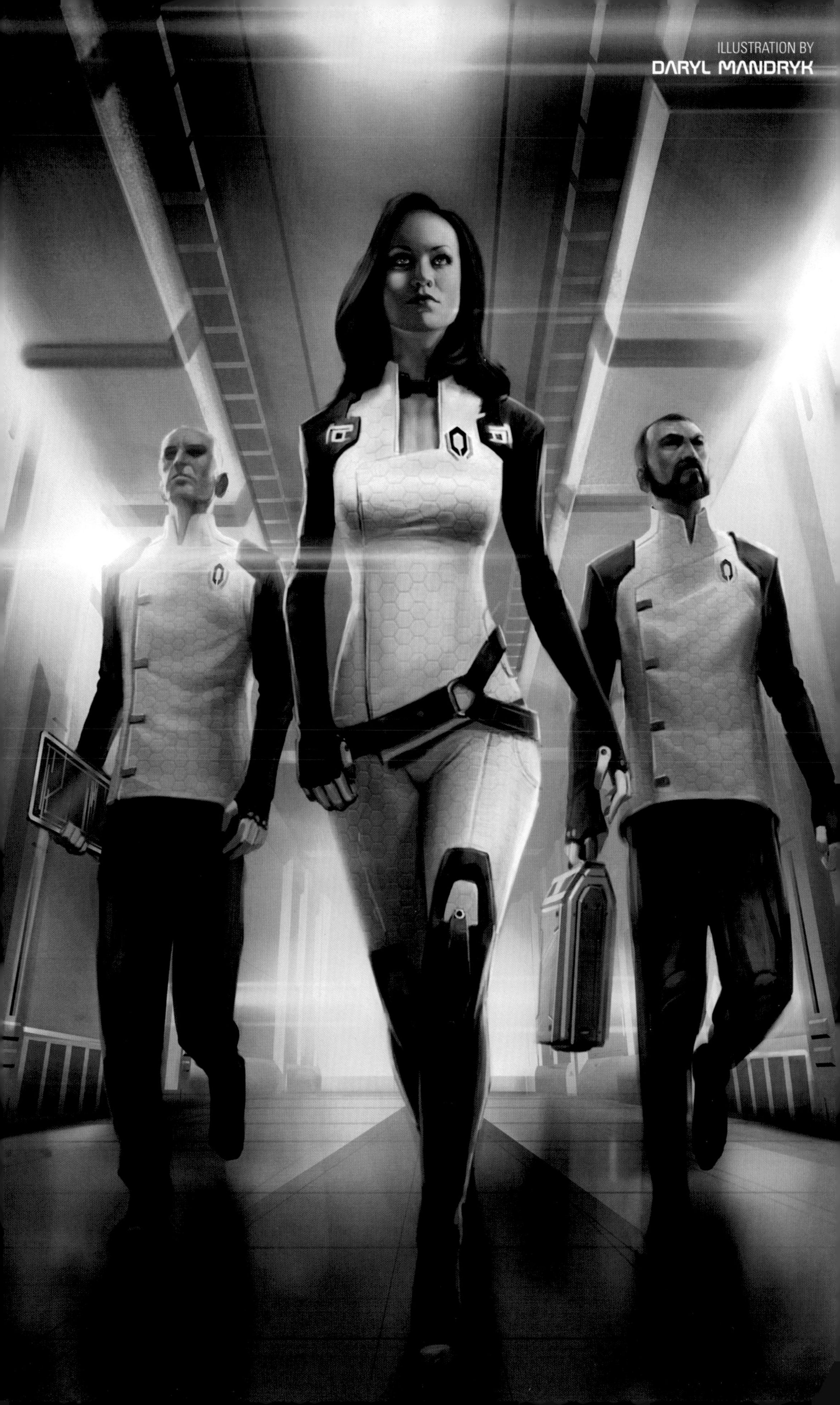
ILLUSTRATION BY
DARYL MANDRYK

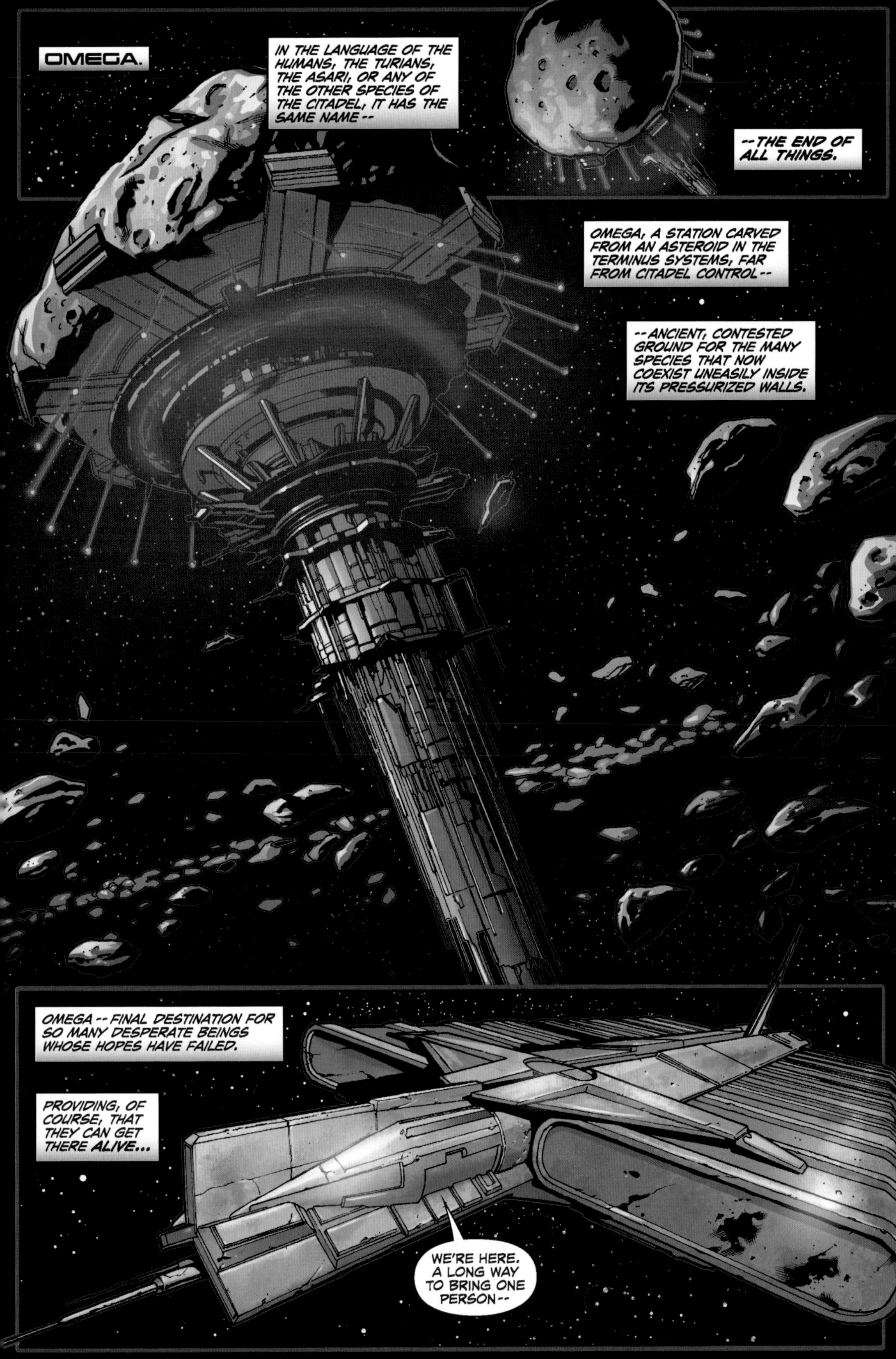
OMEGA.
IN THE LANGUAGE OF THE HUMANS, THE TURIANS, THE ASARI, OR ANY OF THE OTHER SPECIES OF THE CITADEL, IT HAS THE SAME NAME --
--THE END OF ALL THINGS.
OMEGA, A STATION CARVED FROM AN ASTEROID IN THE TERMINUS SYSTEMS, FAR FROM CITADEL CONTROL--
--ANCIENT, CONTESTED GROUND FOR THE MANY SPECIES THAT NOW COEXIST UNEASILY INSIDE ITS PRESSURIZED WALLS.
OMEGA -- FINAL DESTINATION FOR SO MANY DESPERATE BEINGS WHOSE HOPES HAVE FAILED.
PROVIDING, OF COURSE, THAT THEY CAN GET THERE ALIVE...
WE'RE HERE. A LONG WAY TO BRING ONE PERSON--

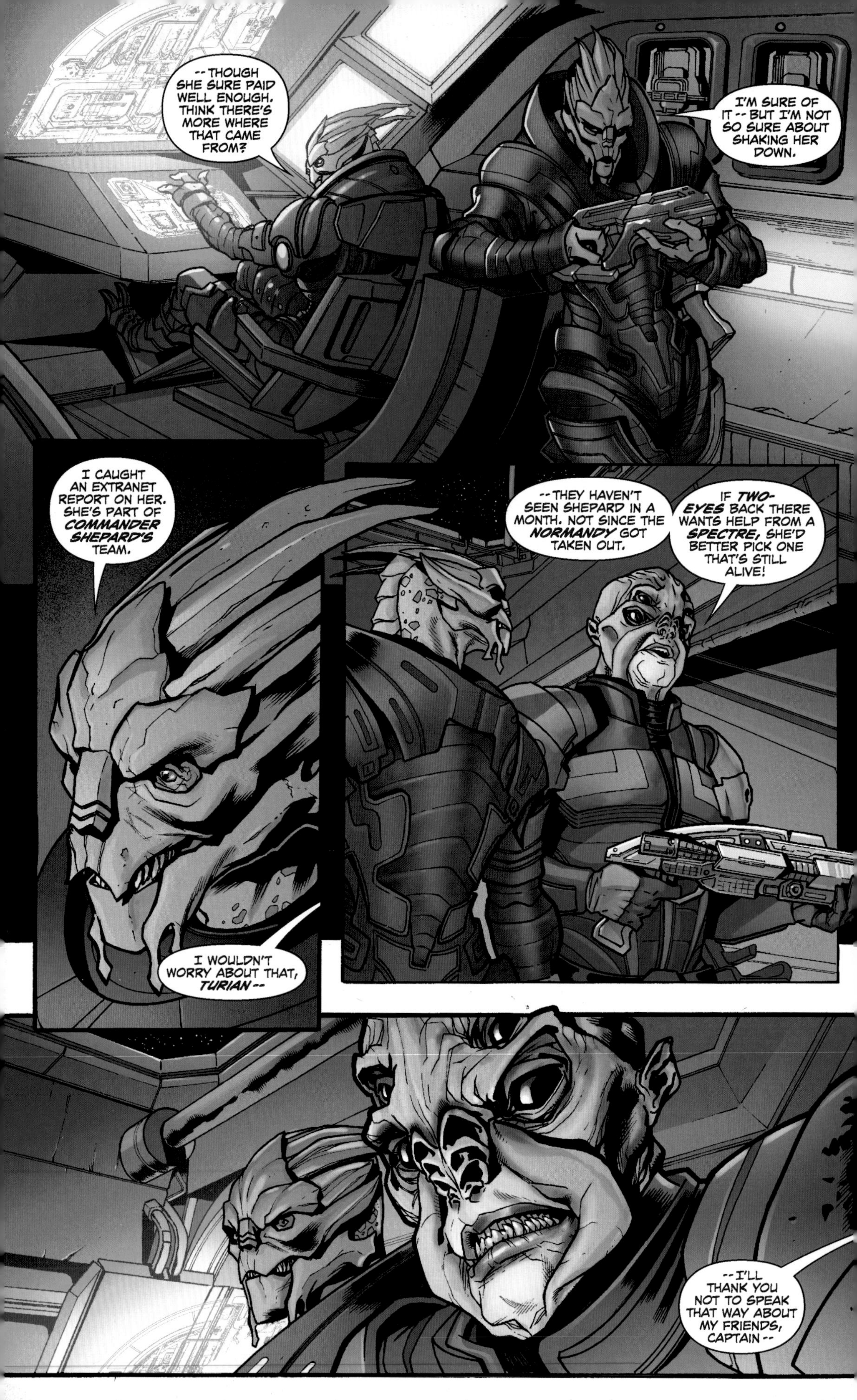
--THOUGH SHE SURE PAID WELL ENOUGH. THINK THERE'S MORE WHERE THAT CAME FROM?
I'M SURE OF IT--BUT I'M NOT SO SURE ABOUT SHAKING HER DOWN.
I CAUGHT AN EXTRANET REPORT ON HER. SHE'S PART OF *COMMANDER SHEPARD'S* TEAM.
I WOULDN'T WORRY ABOUT THAT, *TURIAN*--
--THEY HAVEN'T SEEN SHEPARD IN A MONTH. NOT SINCE THE *NORMANDY* GOT TAKEN OUT.
IF *TWO-EYES* BACK THERE WANTS HELP FROM A *SPECTRE,* SHE'D BETTER PICK ONE THAT'S STILL ALIVE!
--I'LL THANK YOU NOT TO SPEAK THAT WAY ABOUT MY FRIENDS, CAPTAIN--

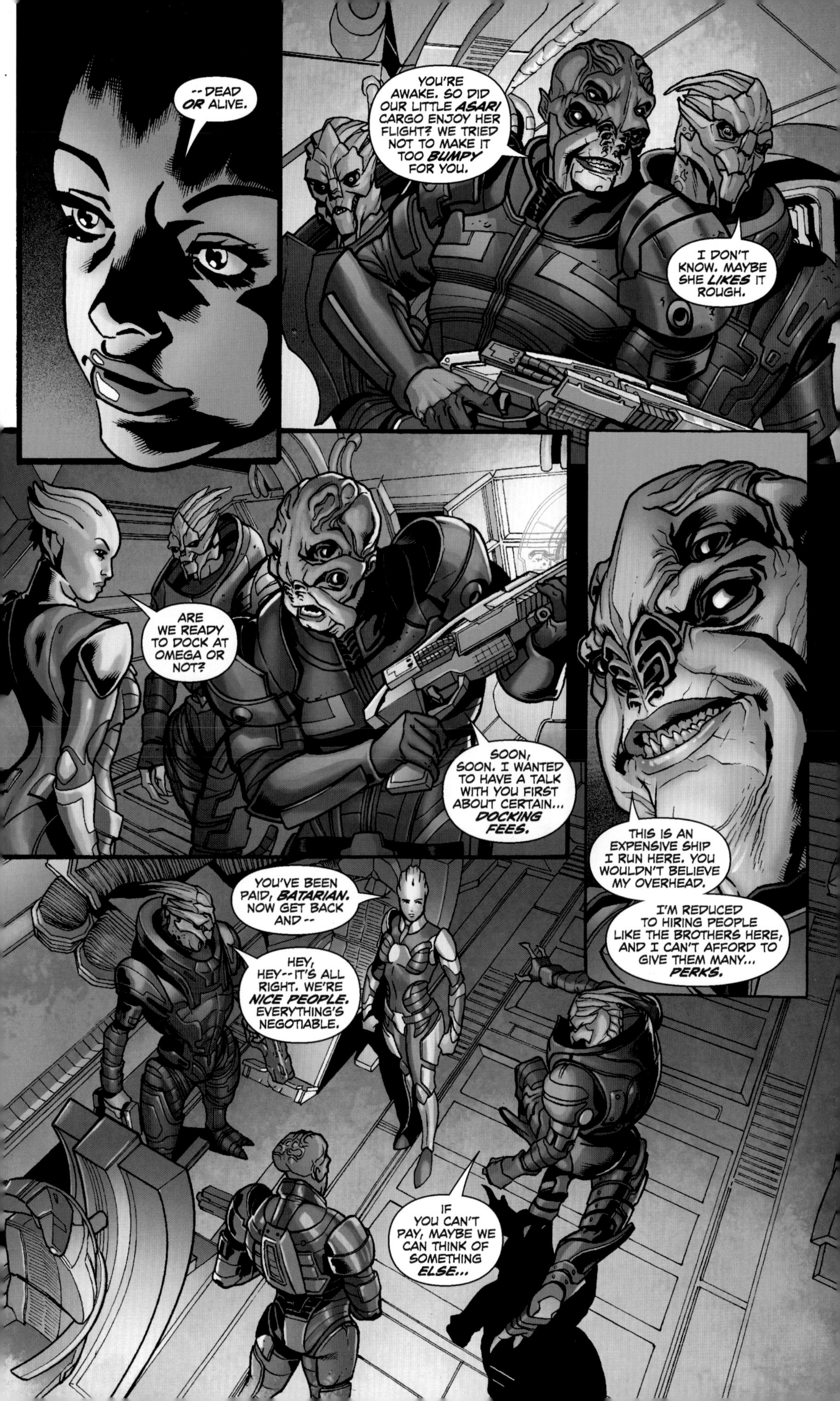

--DEAD OR ALIVE.
YOU'RE AWAKE. SO DID OUR LITTLE ASARI CARGO ENJOY HER FLIGHT? WE TRIED NOT TO MAKE IT TOO BUMPY FOR YOU.
I DON'T KNOW. MAYBE SHE LIKES IT ROUGH.
ARE WE READY TO DOCK AT OMEGA OR NOT?
SOON, SOON. I WANTED TO HAVE A TALK WITH YOU FIRST ABOUT CERTAIN... DOCKING FEES.
THIS IS AN EXPENSIVE SHIP I RUN HERE. YOU WOULDN'T BELIEVE MY OVERHEAD.
I'M REDUCED TO HIRING PEOPLE LIKE THE BROTHERS HERE, AND I CAN'T AFFORD TO GIVE THEM MANY... PERKS.
YOU'VE BEEN PAID, BATARIAN. NOW GET BACK AND--
HEY, HEY--IT'S ALL RIGHT. WE'RE NICE PEOPLE. EVERYTHING'S NEGOTIABLE.
IF YOU CAN'T PAY, MAYBE WE CAN THINK OF SOMETHING ELSE...

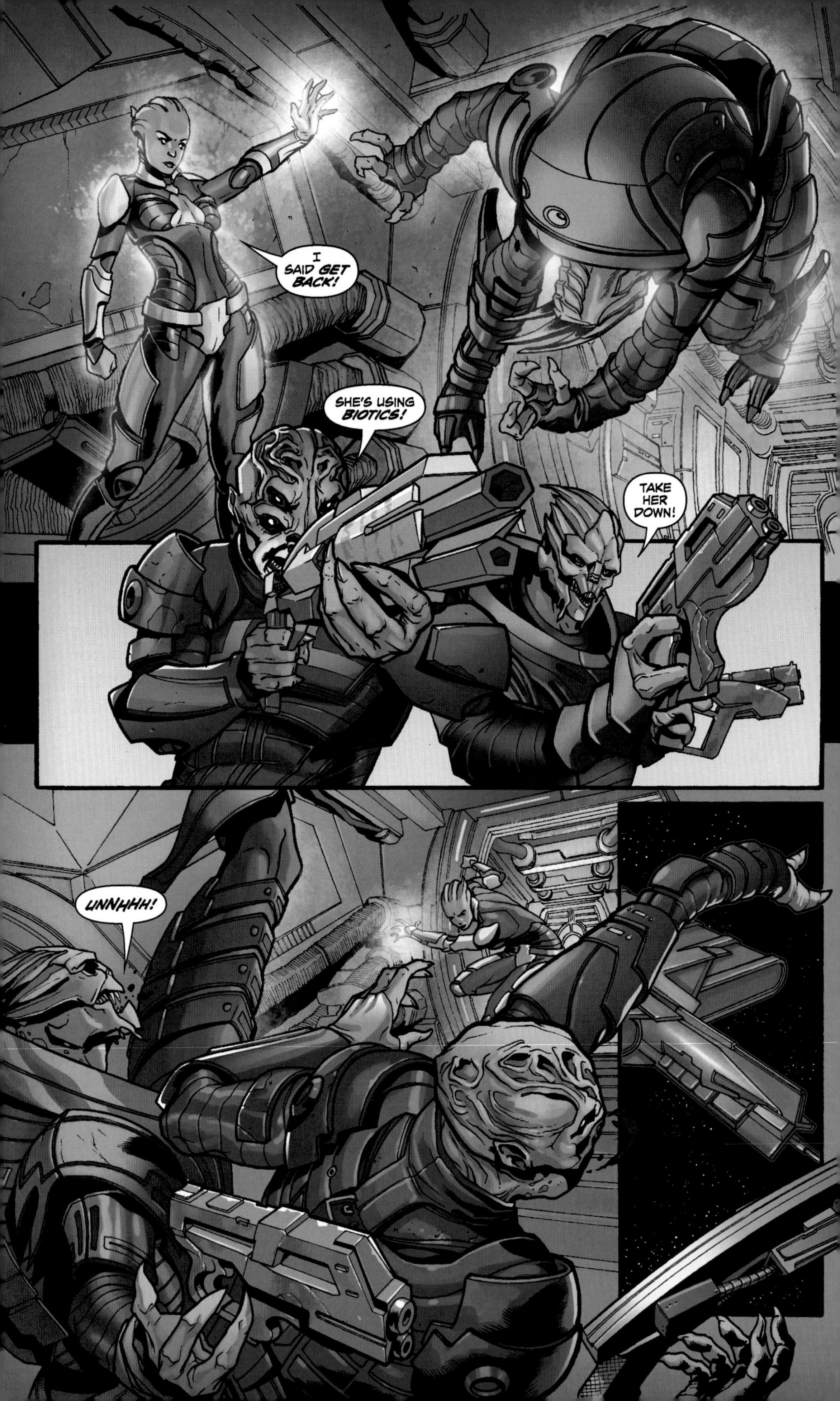

I SAID GET BACK!
SHE'S USING BIOTICS!
TAKE HER DOWN!
UNNHHH!

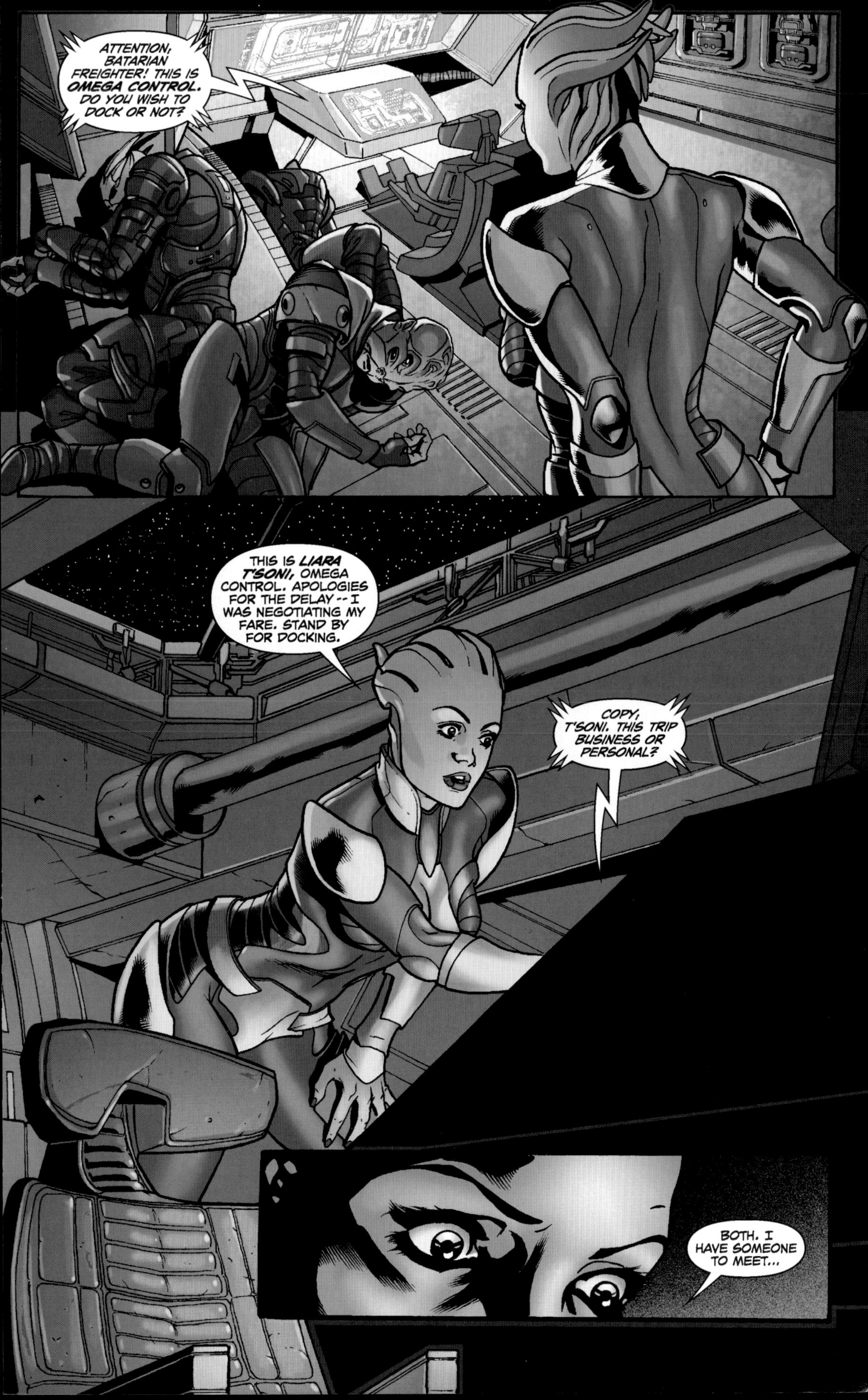
ATTENTION, BATARIAN FREIGHTER! THIS IS OMEGA CONTROL. DO YOU WISH TO DOCK OR NOT?
THIS IS LIARA T'SONI, OMEGA CONTROL. APOLOGIES FOR THE DELAY -- I WAS NEGOTIATING MY FARE. STAND BY FOR DOCKING.
COPY, T'SONI. THIS TRIP BUSINESS OR PERSONAL?
BOTH. I HAVE SOMEONE TO MEET...

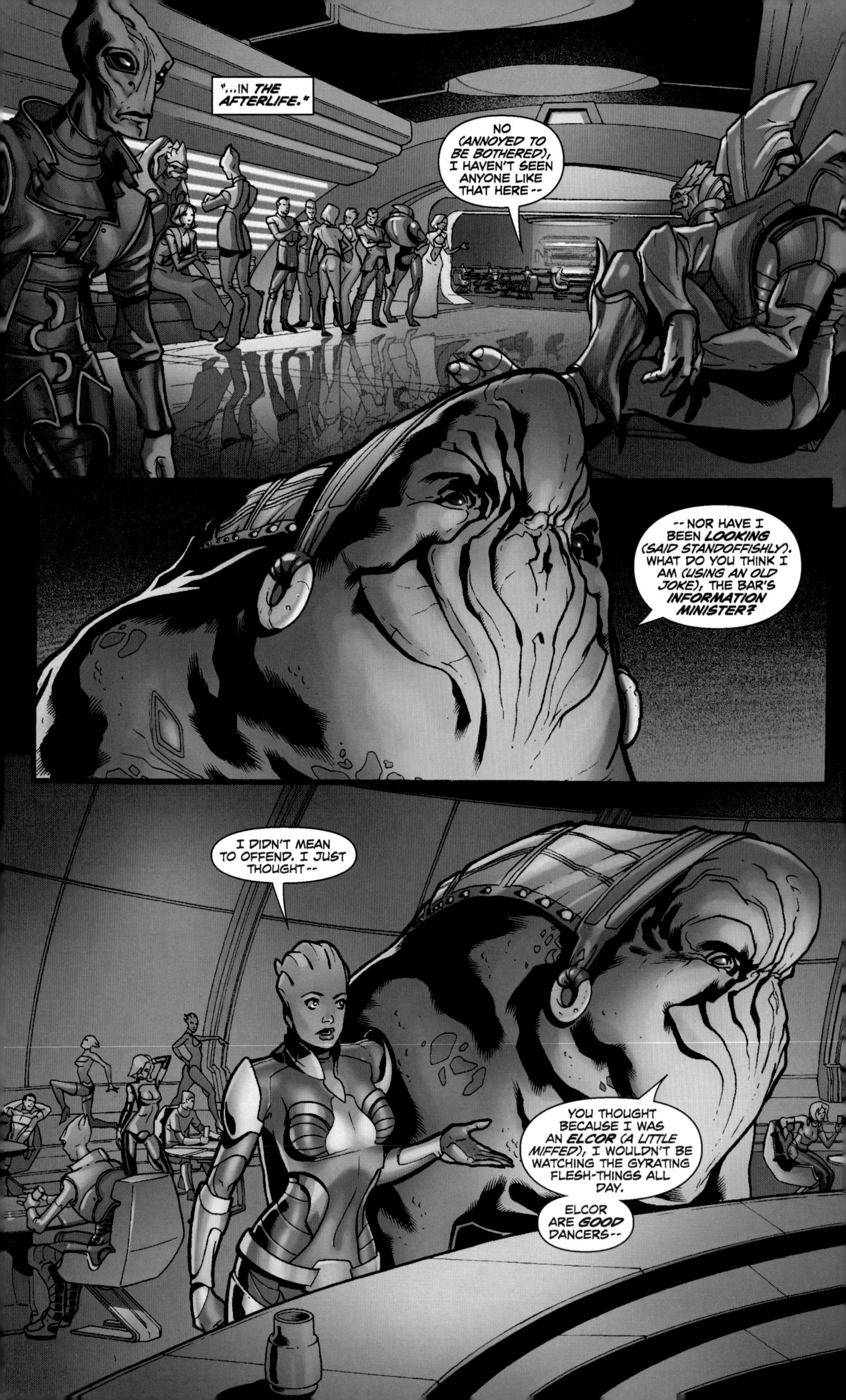
"...IN *THE AFTERLIFE.*"
NO *(ANNOYED TO BE BOTHERED)*, I HAVEN'T SEEN ANYONE LIKE THAT HERE--
--NOR HAVE I BEEN ***LOOKING*** *(SAID STANDOFFISHLY)*. WHAT DO YOU THINK I AM *(USING AN OLD JOKE)*, THE BAR'S ***INFORMATION MINISTER?***
I DIDN'T MEAN TO OFFEND. I JUST THOUGHT--
YOU THOUGHT BECAUSE I WAS AN ***ELCOR*** *(A LITTLE MIFFED)*, I WOULDN'T BE WATCHING THE GYRATING FLESH-THINGS ALL DAY.
ELCOR ARE ***GOOD*** DANCERS--

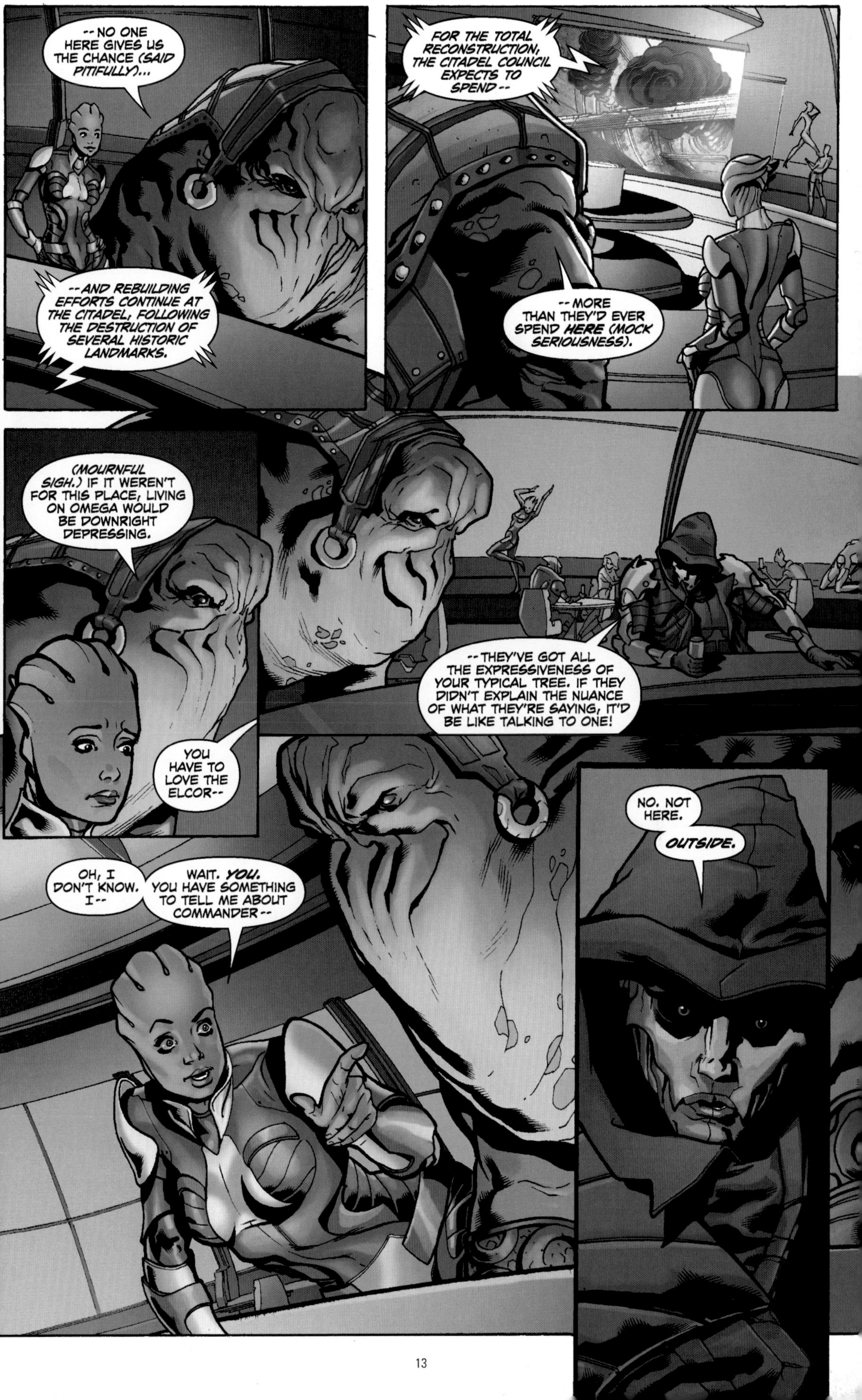
--NO ONE HERE GIVES US THE CHANCE (SAID PITIFULLY)...
--AND REBUILDING EFFORTS CONTINUE AT THE CITADEL, FOLLOWING THE DESTRUCTION OF SEVERAL HISTORIC LANDMARKS.
FOR THE TOTAL RECONSTRUCTION, THE CITADEL COUNCIL EXPECTS TO SPEND--
--MORE THAN THEY'D EVER SPEND HERE (MOCK SERIOUSNESS).
(MOURNFUL SIGH.) IF IT WEREN'T FOR THIS PLACE, LIVING ON OMEGA WOULD BE DOWNRIGHT DEPRESSING.
YOU HAVE TO LOVE THE ELCOR--
--THEY'VE GOT ALL THE EXPRESSIVENESS OF YOUR TYPICAL TREE. IF THEY DIDN'T EXPLAIN THE NUANCE OF WHAT THEY'RE SAYING, IT'D BE LIKE TALKING TO ONE!
OH, I DON'T KNOW. I--
WAIT. YOU. YOU HAVE SOMETHING TO TELL ME ABOUT COMMANDER--
NO. NOT HERE.
OUTSIDE.

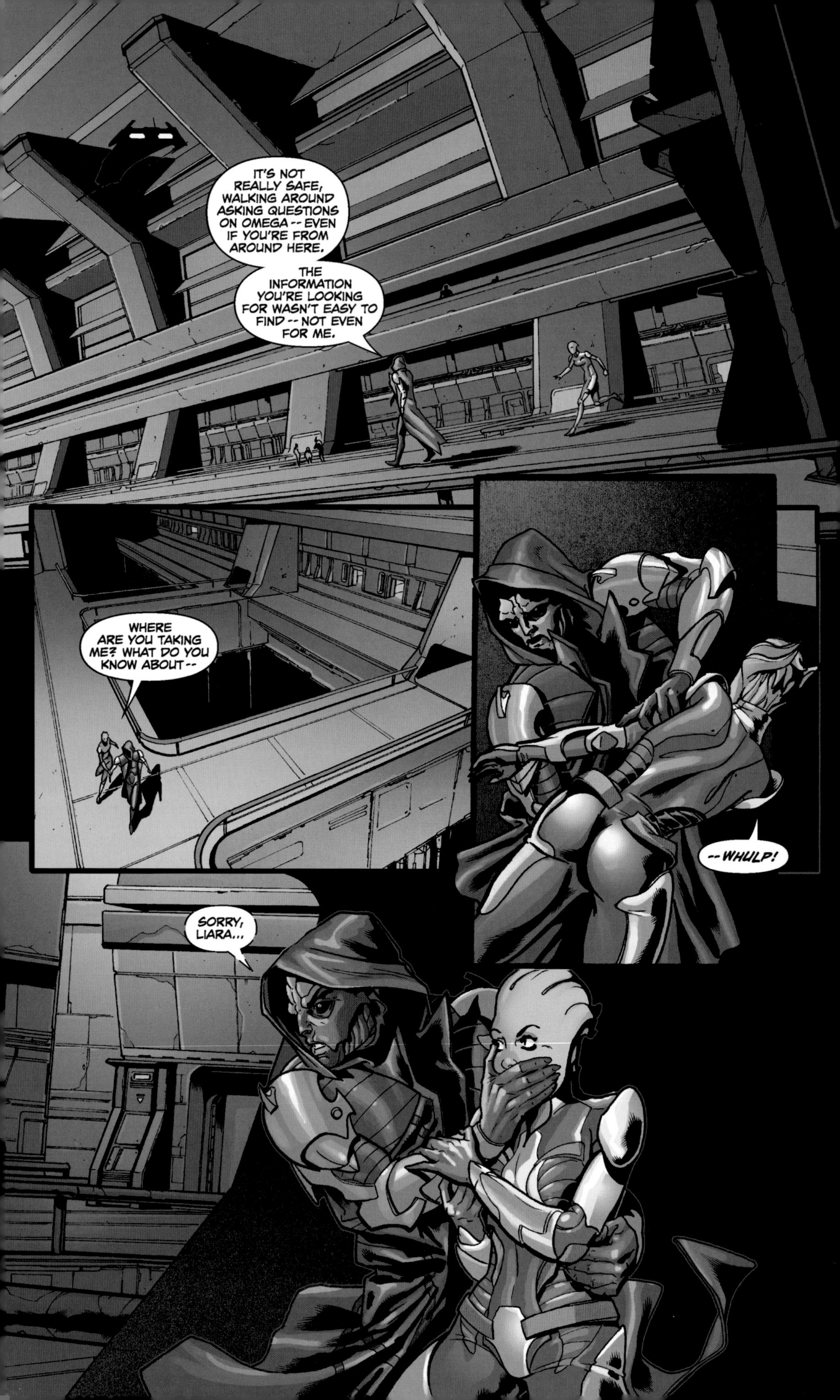
IT'S NOT REALLY SAFE, WALKING AROUND ASKING QUESTIONS ON OMEGA -- EVEN IF YOU'RE FROM AROUND HERE.
THE INFORMATION YOU'RE LOOKING FOR WASN'T EASY TO FIND -- NOT EVEN FOR ME.
WHERE ARE YOU TAKING ME? WHAT DO YOU KNOW ABOUT --
--WHULP!
SORRY, LIARA...

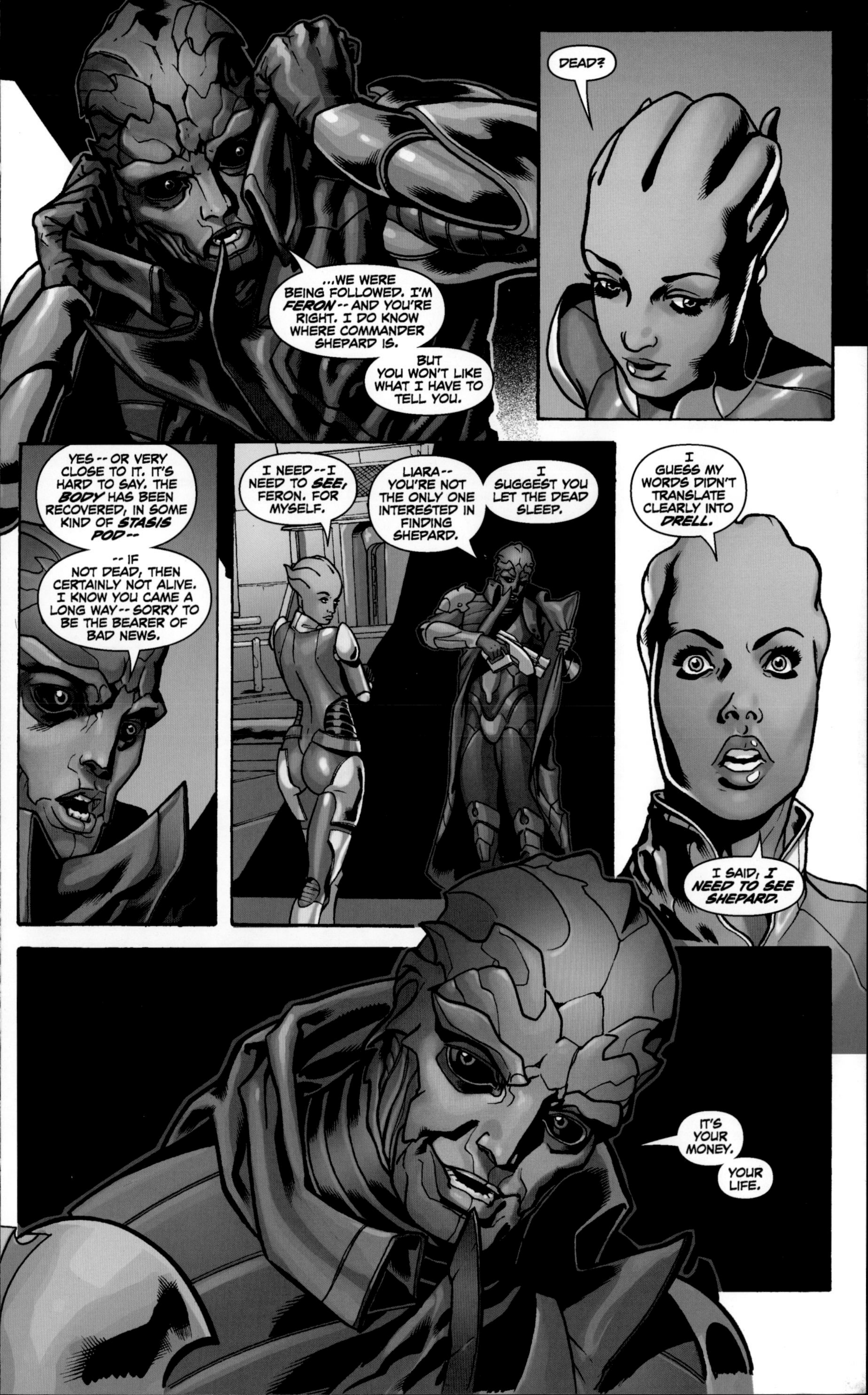
...WE WERE BEING FOLLOWED. I'M FERON -- AND YOU'RE RIGHT. I DO KNOW WHERE COMMANDER SHEPARD IS.
BUT YOU WON'T LIKE WHAT I HAVE TO TELL YOU.
DEAD?
YES -- OR VERY CLOSE TO IT. IT'S HARD TO SAY. THE BODY HAS BEEN RECOVERED, IN SOME KIND OF STASIS POD --
-- IF NOT DEAD, THEN CERTAINLY NOT ALIVE. I KNOW YOU CAME A LONG WAY -- SORRY TO BE THE BEARER OF BAD NEWS.
I NEED -- I NEED TO SEE, FERON. FOR MYSELF.
LIARA -- YOU'RE NOT THE ONLY ONE INTERESTED IN FINDING SHEPARD.
I SUGGEST YOU LET THE DEAD SLEEP.
I GUESS MY WORDS DIDN'T TRANSLATE CLEARLY INTO DRELL.
I SAID, I NEED TO SEE SHEPARD.
IT'S YOUR MONEY.
YOUR LIFE.

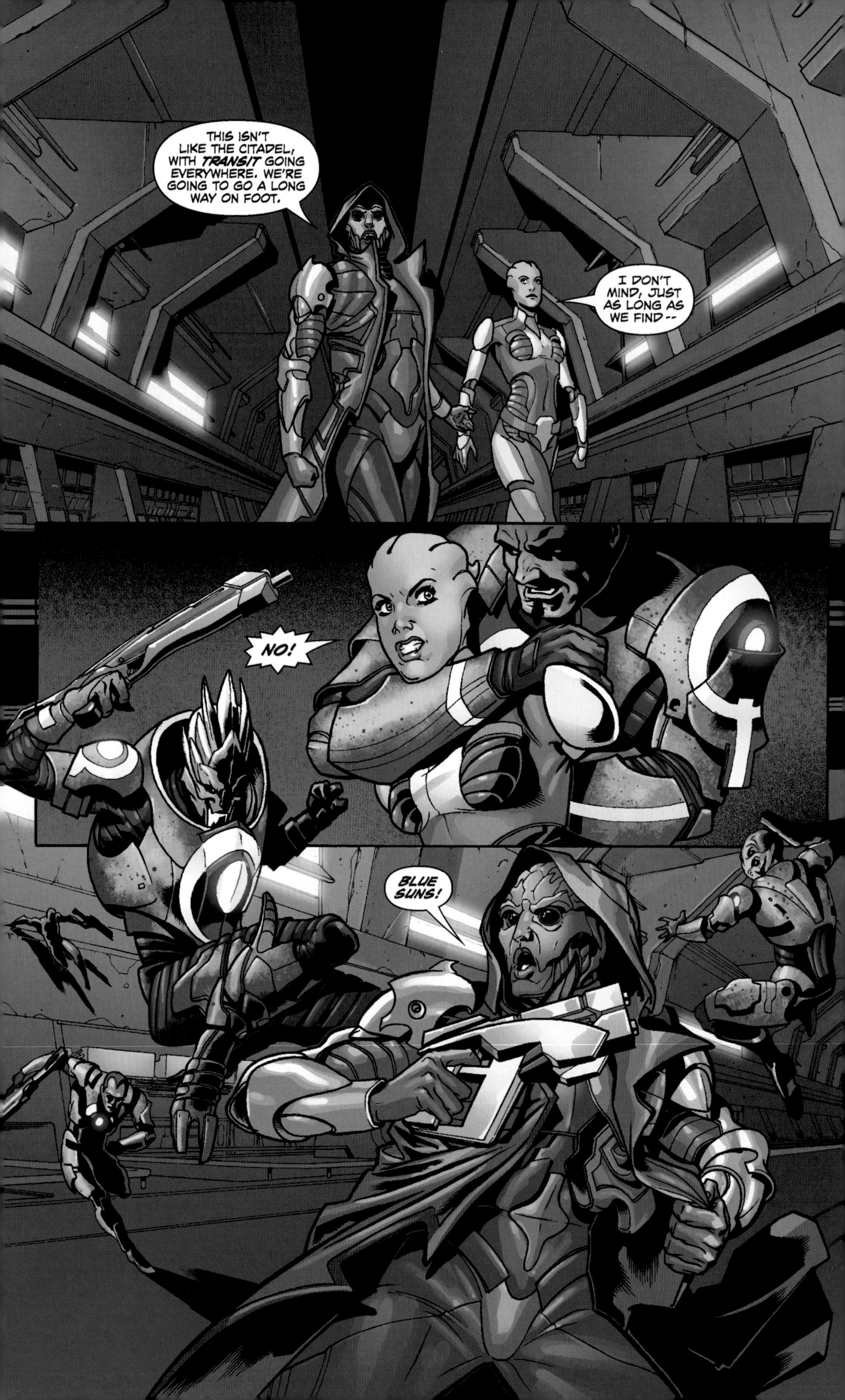
THIS ISN'T LIKE THE CITADEL, WITH *TRANSIT* GOING EVERYWHERE. WE'RE GOING TO GO A LONG WAY ON FOOT.
I DON'T MIND, JUST AS LONG AS WE FIND--
NO!
BLUE SUNS!

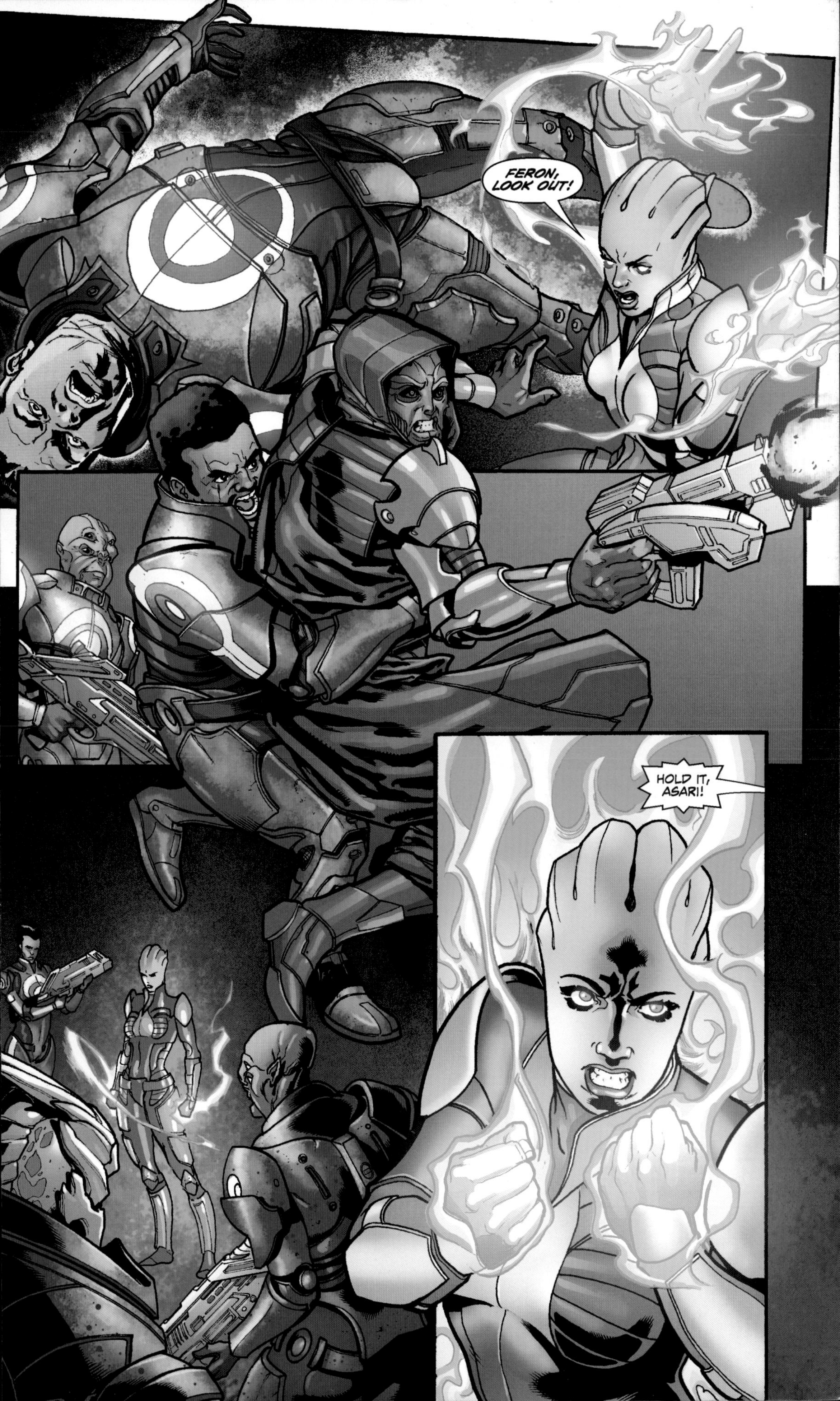
FERON, LOOK OUT!
HOLD IT, ASARI!

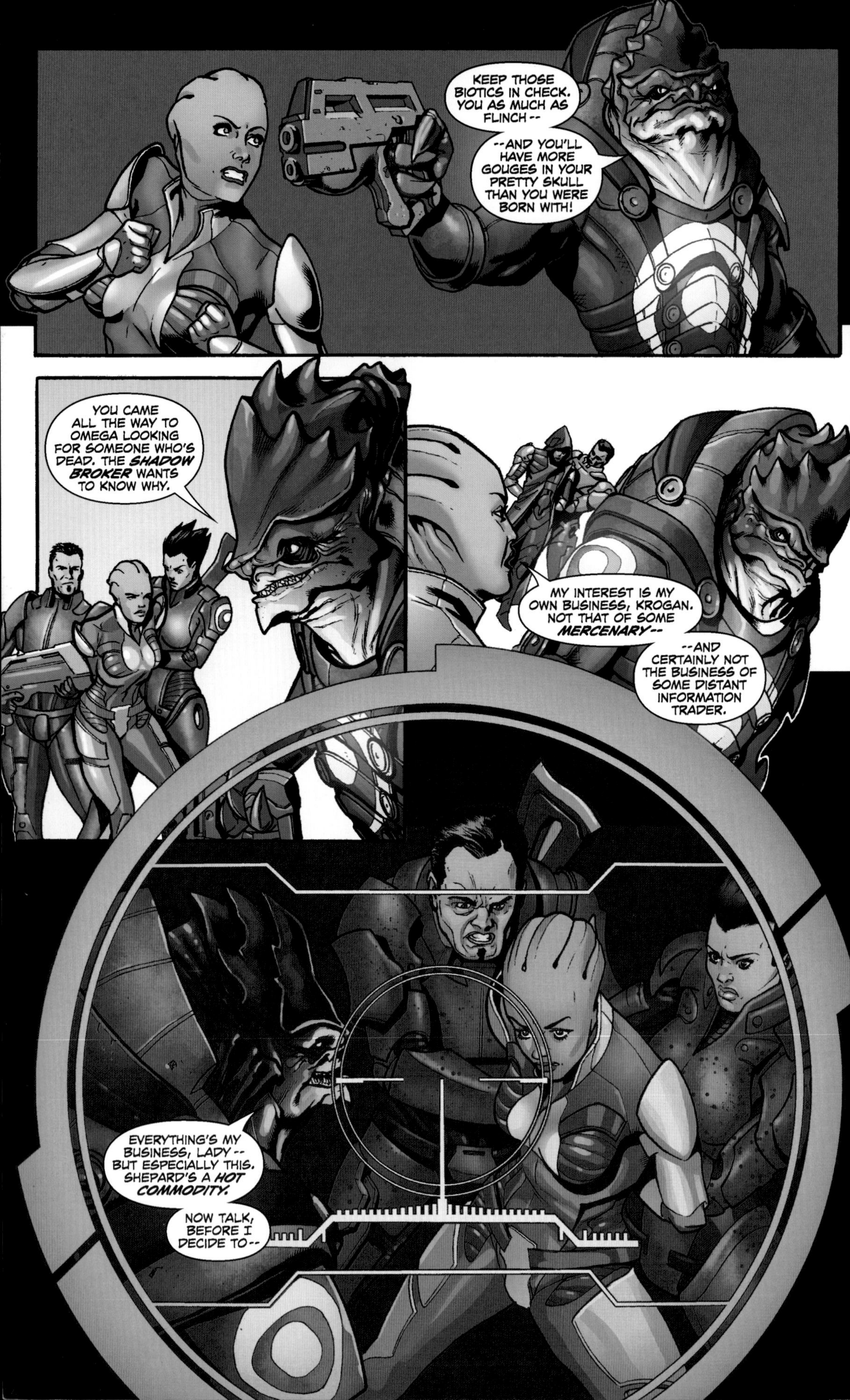
KEEP THOSE BIOTICS IN CHECK. YOU AS MUCH AS FLINCH --
--AND YOU'LL HAVE MORE GOUGES IN YOUR PRETTY SKULL THAN YOU WERE BORN WITH!
YOU CAME ALL THE WAY TO OMEGA LOOKING FOR SOMEONE WHO'S DEAD. THE SHADOW BROKER WANTS TO KNOW WHY.
MY INTEREST IS MY OWN BUSINESS, KROGAN. NOT THAT OF SOME MERCENARY--
--AND CERTAINLY NOT THE BUSINESS OF SOME DISTANT INFORMATION TRADER.
EVERYTHING'S MY BUSINESS, LADY -- BUT ESPECIALLY THIS. SHEPARD'S A HOT COMMODITY.
NOW TALK, BEFORE I DECIDE TO--

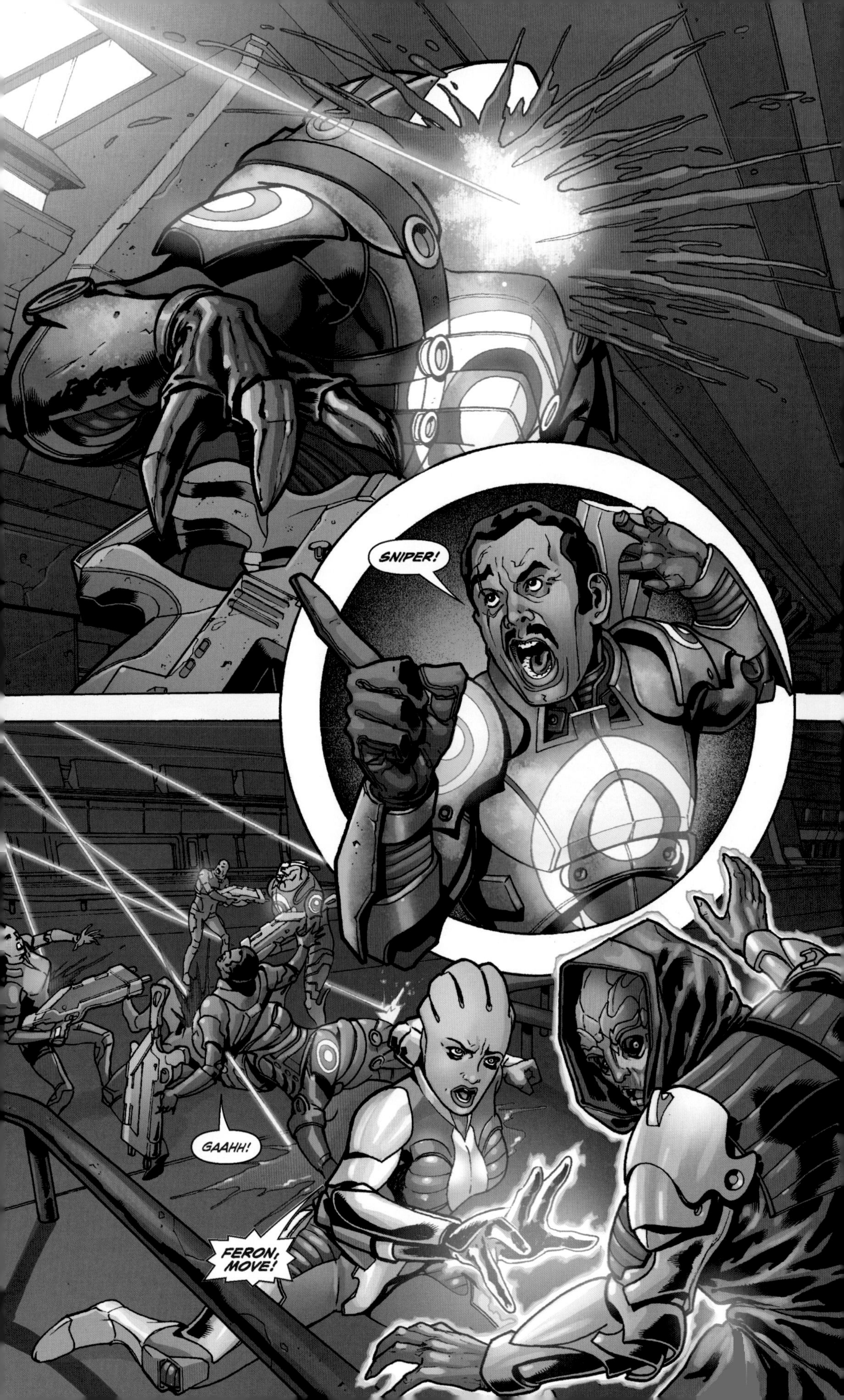
SNIPER!
GAAHH!
FERON, MOVE!

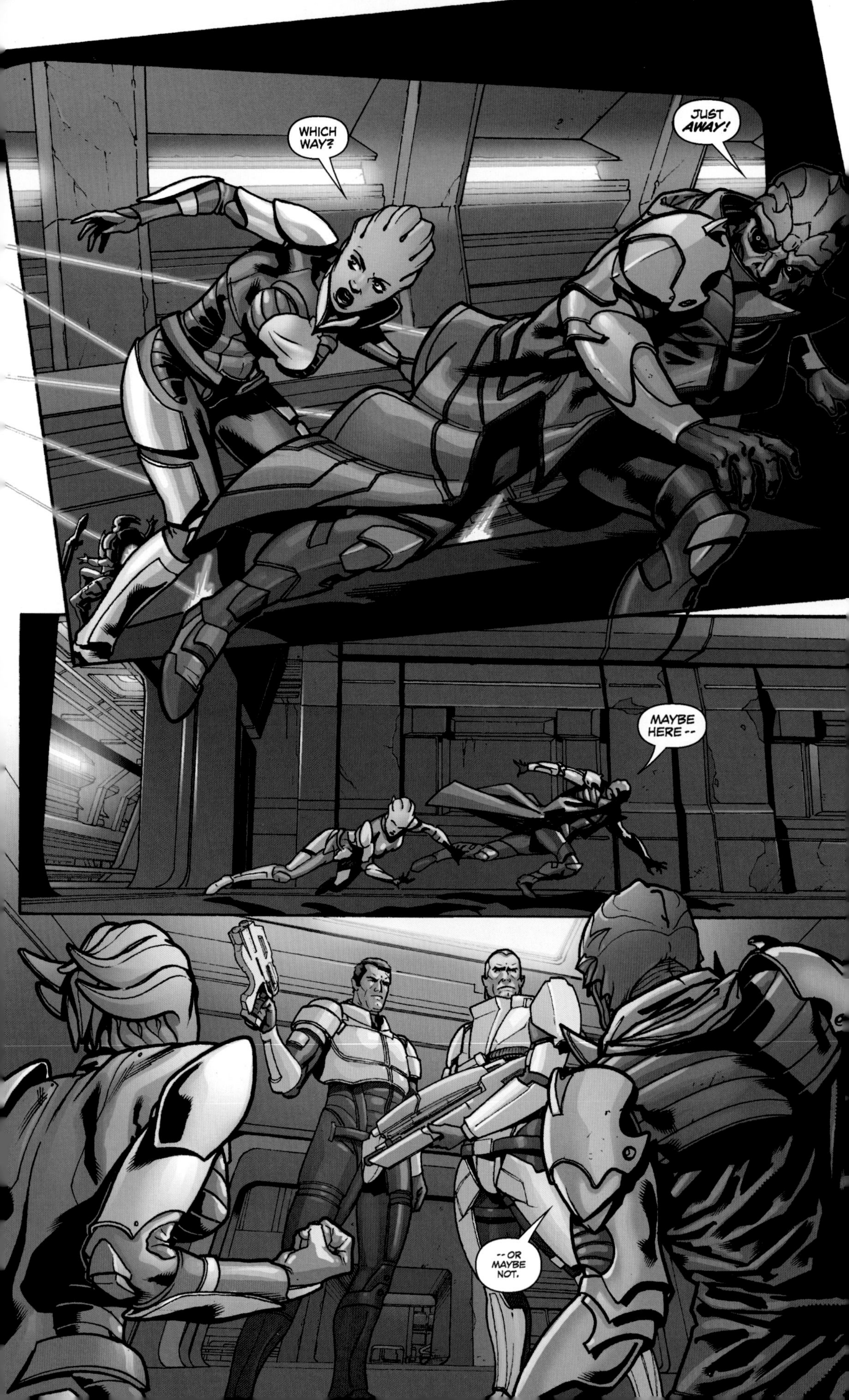
WHICH WAY?
JUST *AWAY!*
MAYBE HERE --
-- OR MAYBE NOT.

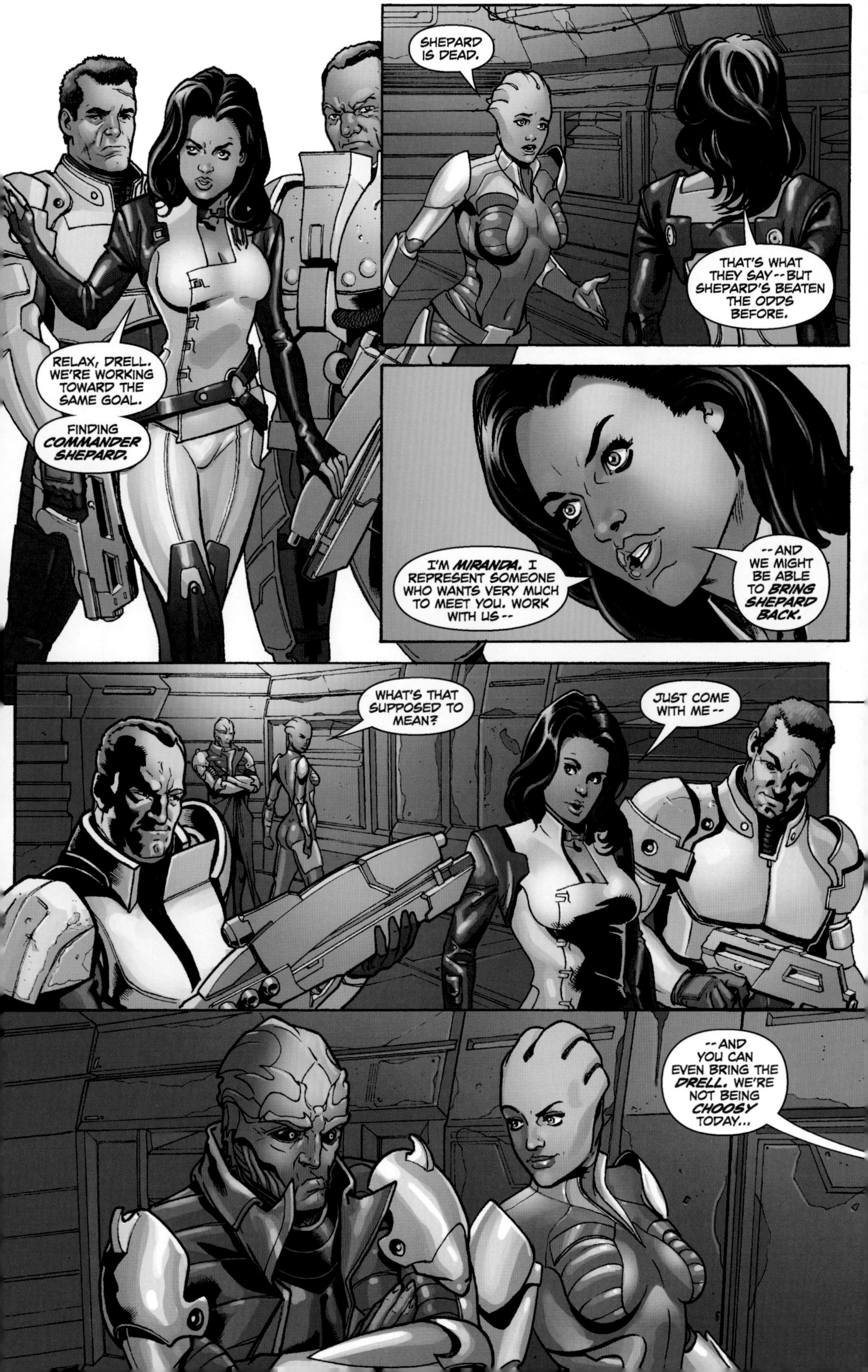
RELAX, DRELL. WE'RE WORKING TOWARD THE SAME GOAL.
FINDING COMMANDER SHEPARD.
SHEPARD IS DEAD.
THAT'S WHAT THEY SAY--BUT SHEPARD'S BEATEN THE ODDS BEFORE.
I'M MIRANDA. I REPRESENT SOMEONE WHO WANTS VERY MUCH TO MEET YOU. WORK WITH US--
--AND WE MIGHT BE ABLE TO BRING SHEPARD BACK.
WHAT'S THAT SUPPOSED TO MEAN?
JUST COME WITH ME--
--AND YOU CAN EVEN BRING THE DRELL. WE'RE NOT BEING CHOOSY TODAY...

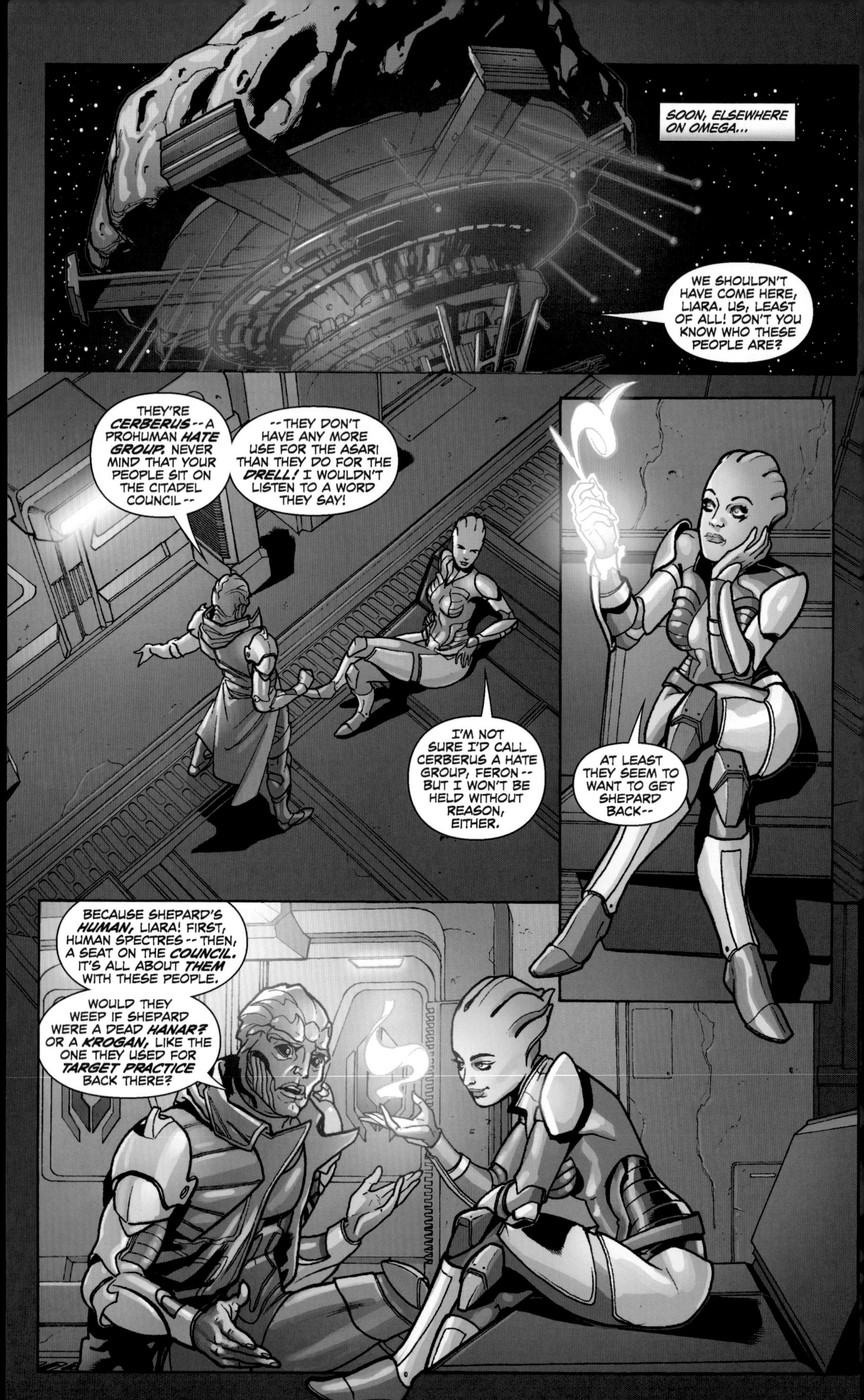
SOON, ELSEWHERE ON OMEGA...
WE SHOULDN'T HAVE COME HERE, LIARA. US, LEAST OF ALL! DON'T YOU KNOW WHO THESE PEOPLE ARE?
THEY'RE CERBERUS--A PROHUMAN HATE GROUP. NEVER MIND THAT YOUR PEOPLE SIT ON THE CITADEL COUNCIL--
--THEY DON'T HAVE ANY MORE USE FOR THE ASARI THAN THEY DO FOR THE DRELL! I WOULDN'T LISTEN TO A WORD THEY SAY!
I'M NOT SURE I'D CALL CERBERUS A HATE GROUP, FERON--BUT I WON'T BE HELD WITHOUT REASON, EITHER.
AT LEAST THEY SEEM TO WANT TO GET SHEPARD BACK--
BECAUSE SHEPARD'S HUMAN, LIARA! FIRST, HUMAN SPECTRES--THEN, A SEAT ON THE COUNCIL. IT'S ALL ABOUT THEM WITH THESE PEOPLE.
WOULD THEY WEEP IF SHEPARD WERE A DEAD HANAR? OR A KROGAN, LIKE THE ONE THEY USED FOR TARGET PRACTICE BACK THERE?

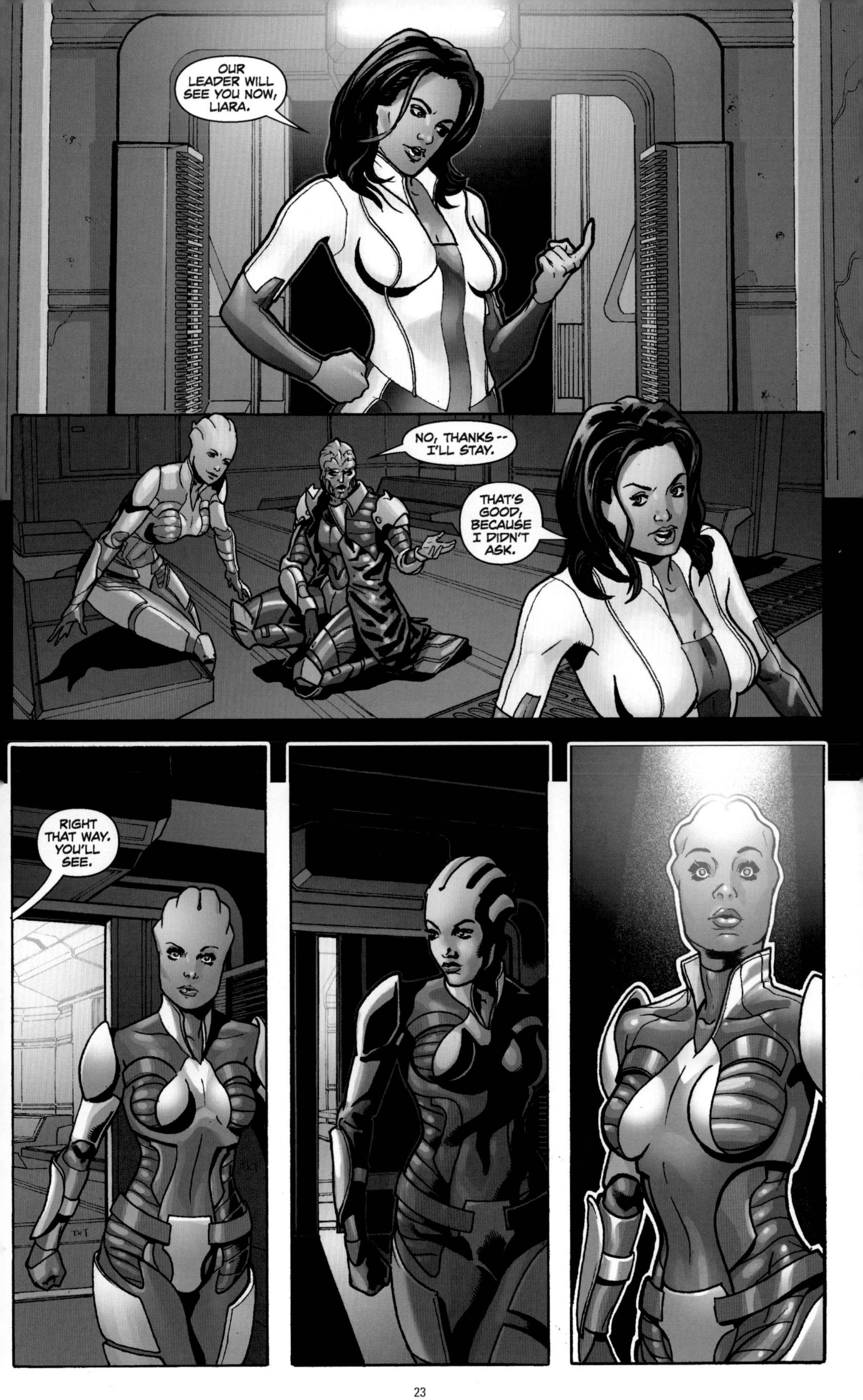
OUR LEADER WILL SEE YOU NOW, LIARA.
NO, THANKS -- I'LL STAY.
THAT'S GOOD, BECAUSE I DIDN'T ASK.
RIGHT THAT WAY. YOU'LL SEE.

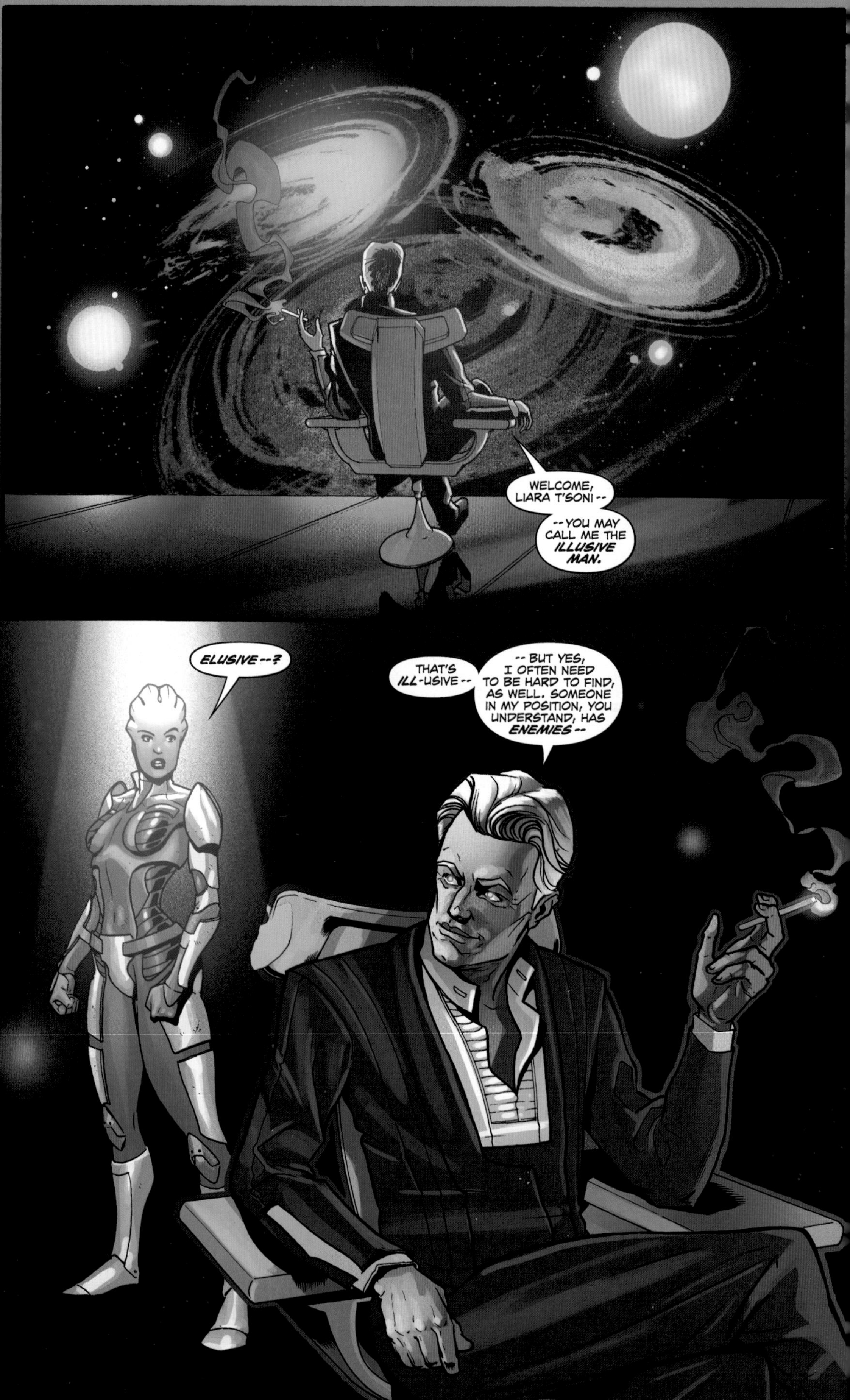
WELCOME, LIARA T'SONI --
-- YOU MAY CALL ME THE ***ILLUSIVE MAN.***
ELUSIVE --?
THAT'S ***ILL***-USIVE --
-- BUT YES, I OFTEN NEED TO BE HARD TO FIND, AS WELL. SOMEONE IN MY POSITION, YOU UNDERSTAND, HAS ***ENEMIES*** --

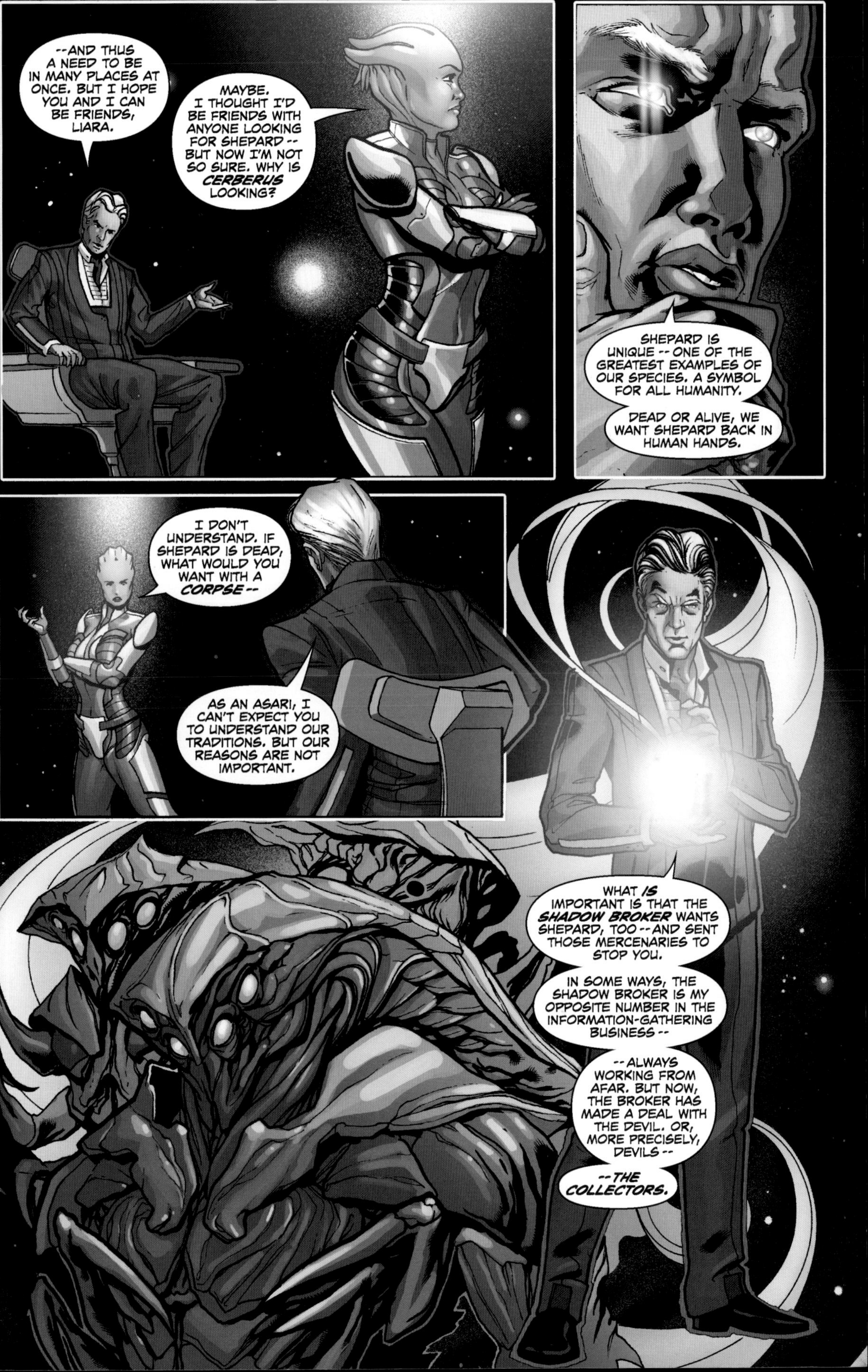
--AND THUS A NEED TO BE IN MANY PLACES AT ONCE. BUT I HOPE YOU AND I CAN BE FRIENDS, LIARA.
MAYBE. I THOUGHT I'D BE FRIENDS WITH ANYONE LOOKING FOR SHEPARD -- BUT NOW I'M NOT SO SURE. WHY IS CERBERUS LOOKING?
SHEPARD IS UNIQUE -- ONE OF THE GREATEST EXAMPLES OF OUR SPECIES. A SYMBOL FOR ALL HUMANITY.
DEAD OR ALIVE, WE WANT SHEPARD BACK IN HUMAN HANDS.
I DON'T UNDERSTAND. IF SHEPARD IS DEAD, WHAT WOULD YOU WANT WITH A CORPSE --
AS AN ASARI, I CAN'T EXPECT YOU TO UNDERSTAND OUR TRADITIONS. BUT OUR REASONS ARE NOT IMPORTANT.
WHAT IS IMPORTANT IS THAT THE SHADOW BROKER WANTS SHEPARD, TOO -- AND SENT THOSE MERCENARIES TO STOP YOU.
IN SOME WAYS, THE SHADOW BROKER IS MY OPPOSITE NUMBER IN THE INFORMATION-GATHERING BUSINESS --
-- ALWAYS WORKING FROM AFAR. BUT NOW, THE BROKER HAS MADE A DEAL WITH THE DEVIL. OR, MORE PRECISELY, DEVILS --
-- THE COLLECTORS.

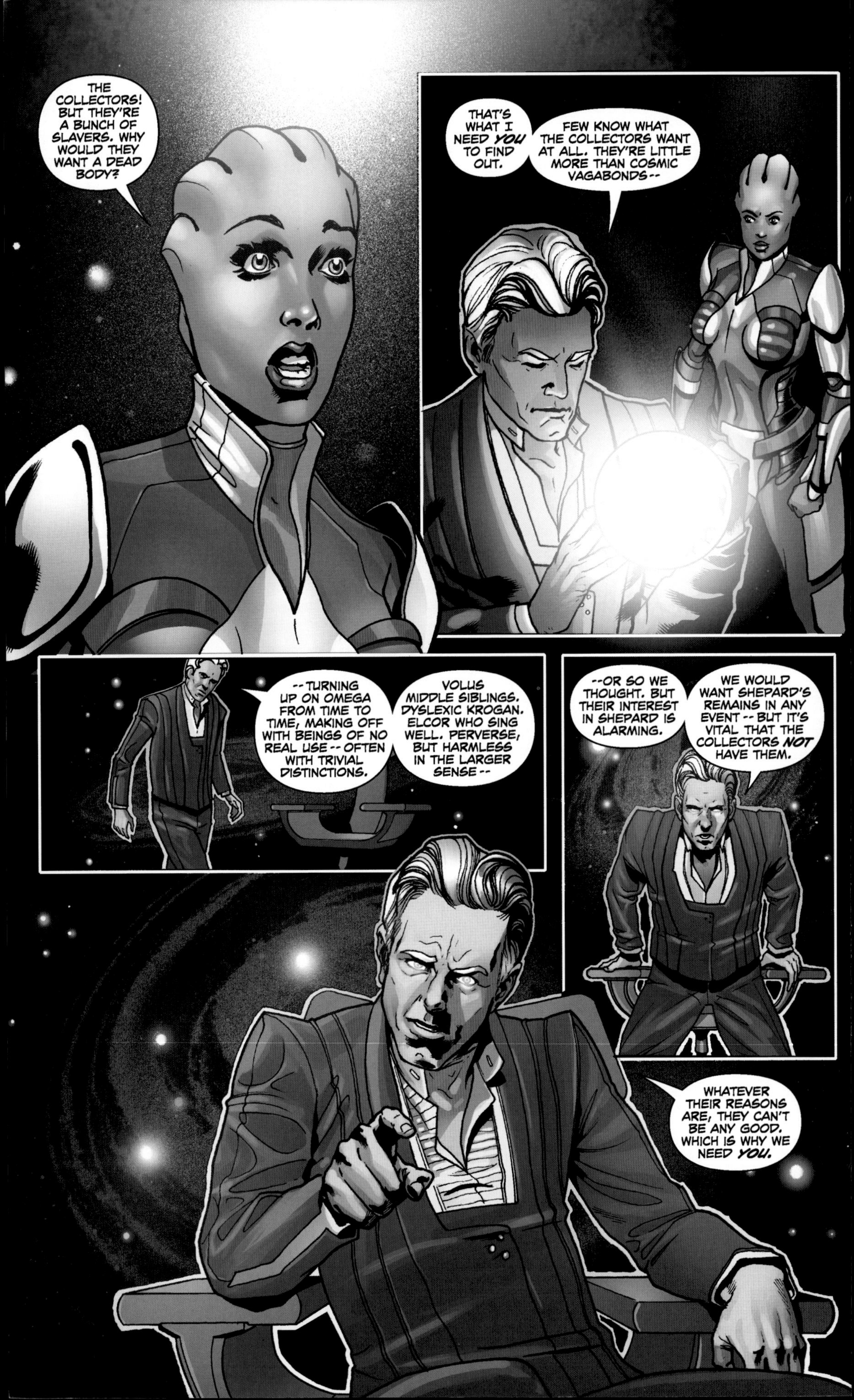
THE COLLECTORS! BUT THEY'RE A BUNCH OF SLAVERS. WHY WOULD THEY WANT A DEAD BODY?
THAT'S WHAT I NEED *YOU* TO FIND OUT.
FEW KNOW WHAT THE COLLECTORS WANT AT ALL. THEY'RE LITTLE MORE THAN COSMIC VAGABONDS--
--TURNING UP ON OMEGA FROM TIME TO TIME, MAKING OFF WITH BEINGS OF NO REAL USE--OFTEN WITH TRIVIAL DISTINCTIONS.
VOLUS MIDDLE SIBLINGS. DYSLEXIC KROGAN. ELCOR WHO SING WELL. PERVERSE, BUT HARMLESS IN THE LARGER SENSE--
--OR SO WE THOUGHT. BUT THEIR INTEREST IN SHEPARD IS ALARMING.
WE WOULD WANT SHEPARD'S REMAINS IN ANY EVENT--BUT IT'S VITAL THAT THE COLLECTORS *NOT* HAVE THEM.
WHATEVER THEIR REASONS ARE, THEY CAN'T BE ANY GOOD. WHICH IS WHY WE NEED *YOU.*

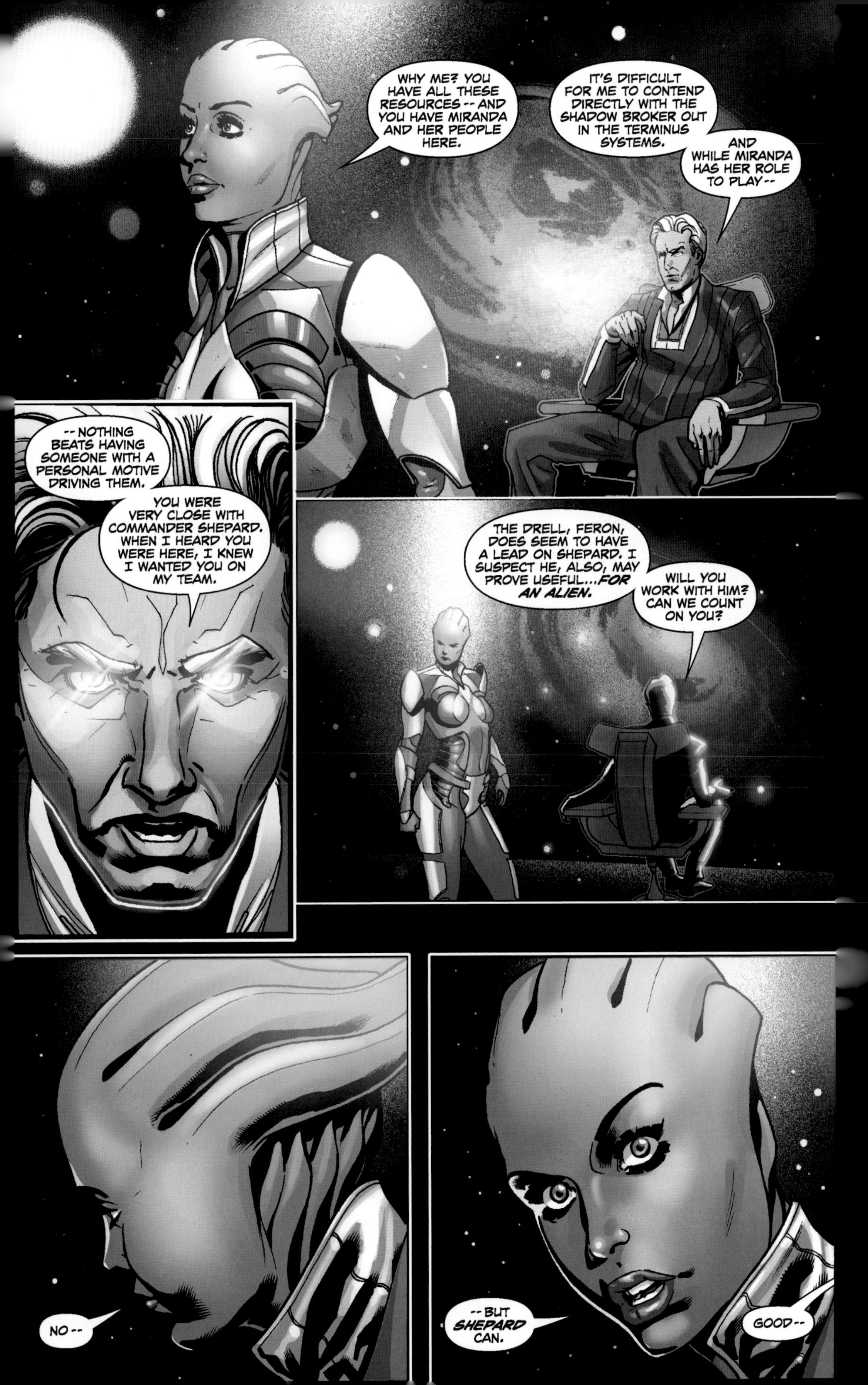
WHY ME? YOU HAVE ALL THESE RESOURCES -- AND YOU HAVE MIRANDA AND HER PEOPLE HERE.
IT'S DIFFICULT FOR ME TO CONTEND DIRECTLY WITH THE SHADOW BROKER OUT IN THE TERMINUS SYSTEMS.
AND WHILE MIRANDA HAS HER ROLE TO PLAY --
-- NOTHING BEATS HAVING SOMEONE WITH A PERSONAL MOTIVE DRIVING THEM.
YOU WERE VERY CLOSE WITH COMMANDER SHEPARD. WHEN I HEARD YOU WERE HERE, I KNEW I WANTED YOU ON MY TEAM.
THE DRELL, FERON, DOES SEEM TO HAVE A LEAD ON SHEPARD. I SUSPECT HE, ALSO, MAY PROVE USEFUL... ***FOR AN ALIEN.***
WILL YOU WORK WITH HIM? CAN WE COUNT ON YOU?
NO --
-- BUT ***SHEPARD*** CAN.
GOOD --

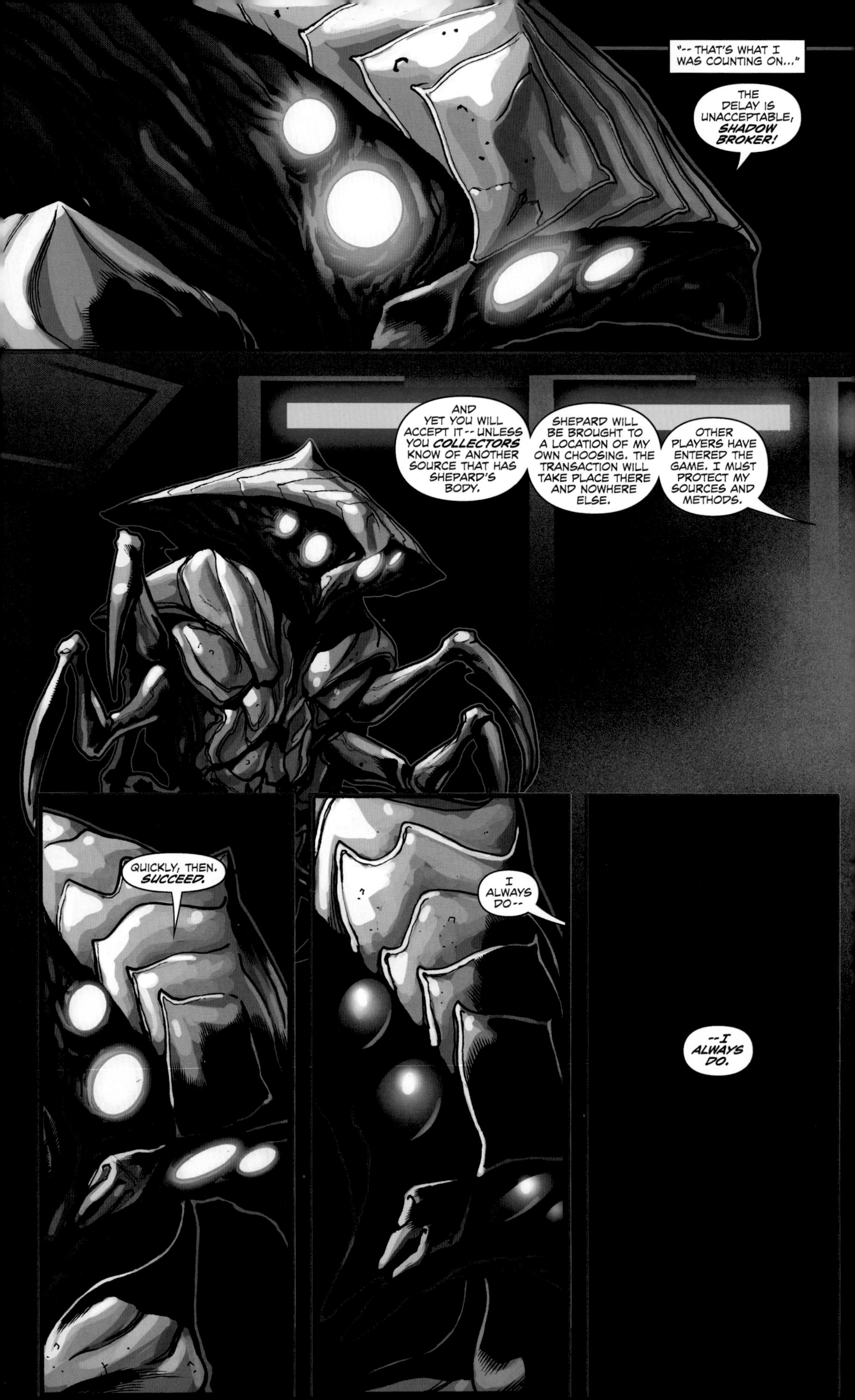
"-- THAT'S WHAT I WAS COUNTING ON..."
THE DELAY IS UNACCEPTABLE, *SHADOW BROKER!*
AND YET YOU WILL ACCEPT IT -- UNLESS YOU *COLLECTORS* KNOW OF ANOTHER SOURCE THAT HAS SHEPARD'S BODY.
SHEPARD WILL BE BROUGHT TO A LOCATION OF MY OWN CHOOSING. THE TRANSACTION WILL TAKE PLACE THERE AND NOWHERE ELSE.
OTHER PLAYERS HAVE ENTERED THE GAME. I MUST PROTECT MY SOURCES AND METHODS.
QUICKLY, THEN. *SUCCEED.*
I ALWAYS DO --
-- I ALWAYS DO.

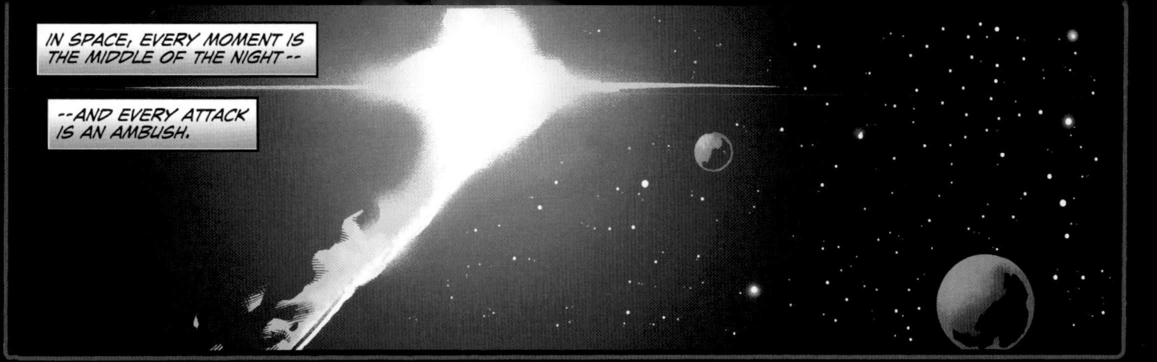
IN SPACE, EVERY MOMENT IS THE MIDDLE OF THE NIGHT --
--AND EVERY ATTACK IS AN AMBUSH.

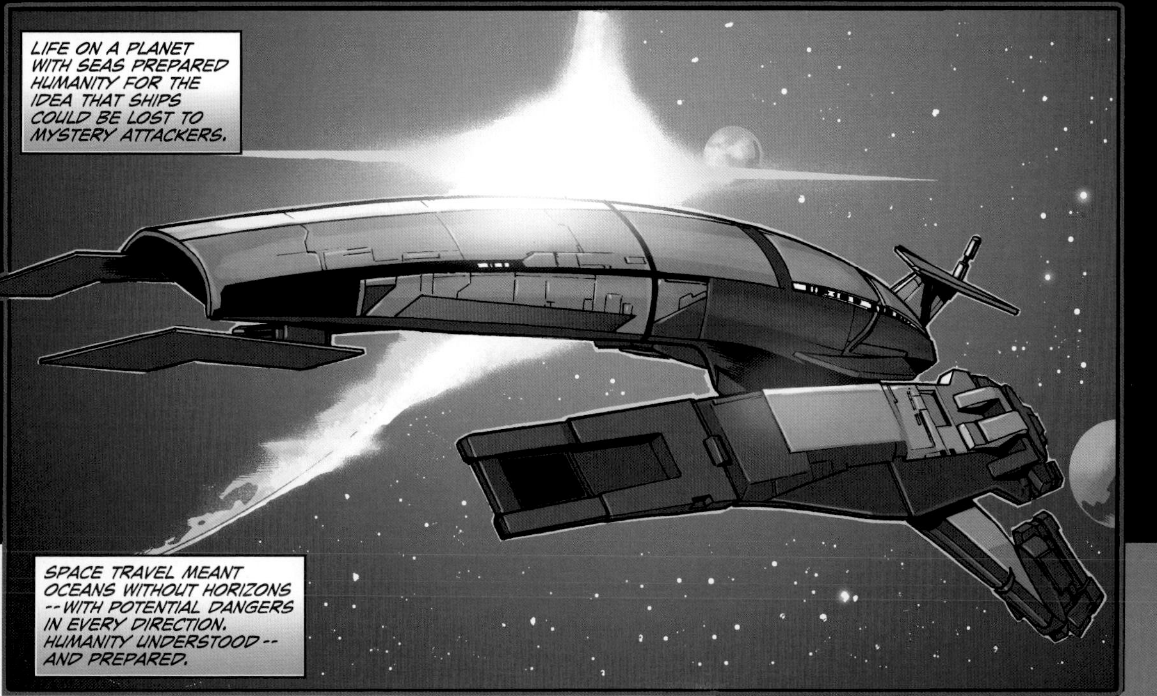
LIFE ON A PLANET WITH SEAS PREPARED HUMANITY FOR THE IDEA THAT SHIPS COULD BE LOST TO MYSTERY ATTACKERS.
SPACE TRAVEL MEANT OCEANS WITHOUT HORIZONS --WITH POTENTIAL DANGERS IN EVERY DIRECTION. HUMANITY UNDERSTOOD -- AND PREPARED.

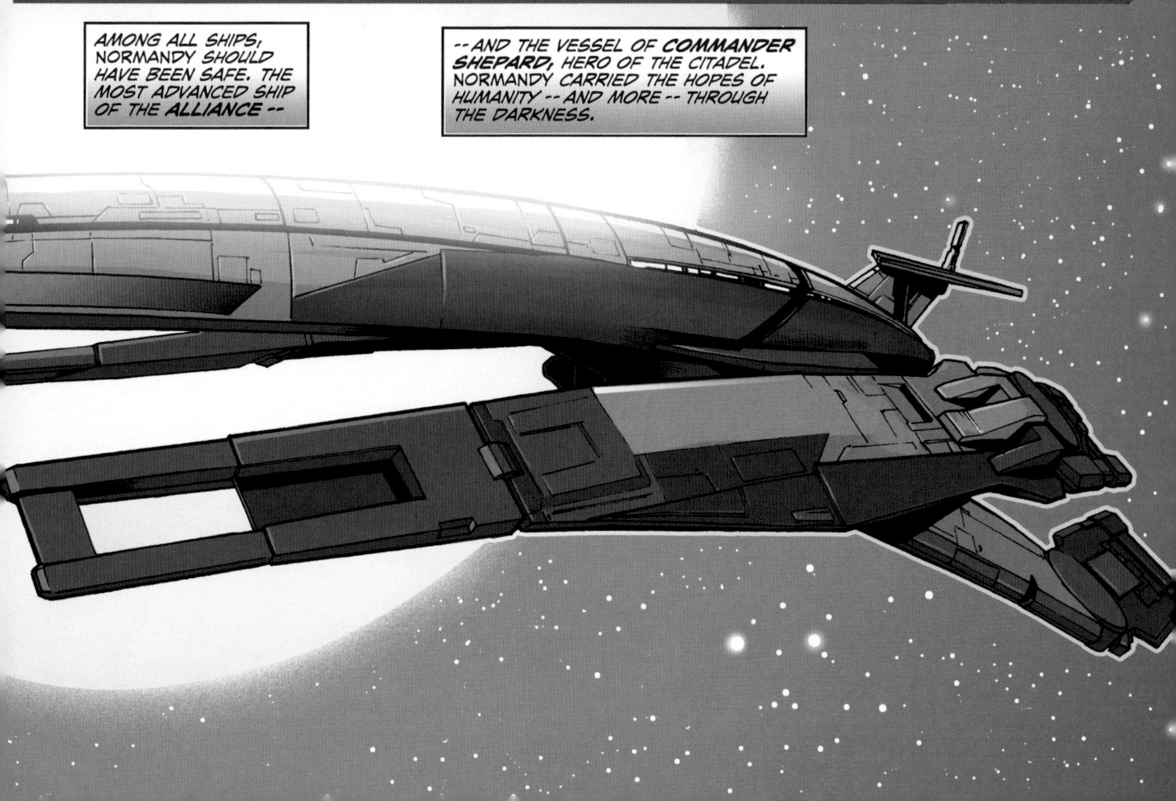
AMONG ALL SHIPS, NORMANDY SHOULD HAVE BEEN SAFE. THE MOST ADVANCED SHIP OF THE ALLIANCE --
--AND THE VESSEL OF COMMANDER SHEPARD, HERO OF THE CITADEL. NORMANDY CARRIED THE HOPES OF HUMANITY -- AND MORE -- THROUGH THE DARKNESS.

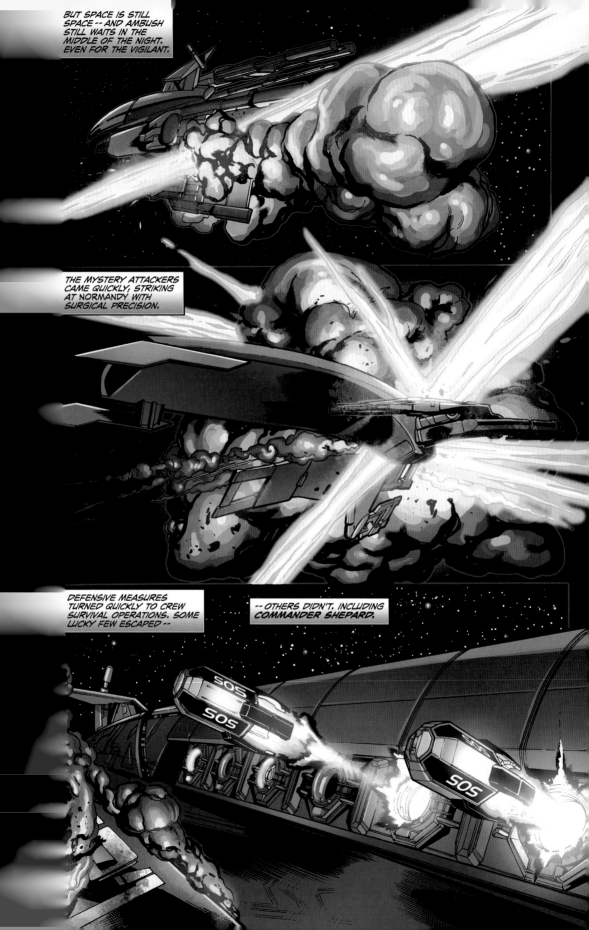

BUT SPACE IS STILL SPACE -- AND AMBUSH STILL WAITS IN THE MIDDLE OF THE NIGHT. EVEN FOR THE VIGILANT.

THE MYSTERY ATTACKERS CAME QUICKLY, STRIKING AT NORMANDY WITH SURGICAL PRECISION.

DEFENSIVE MEASURES TURNED QUICKLY TO CREW SURVIVAL OPERATIONS. SOME LUCKY FEW ESCAPED --

-- OTHERS DIDN'T. INCLUDING COMMANDER SHEPARD.

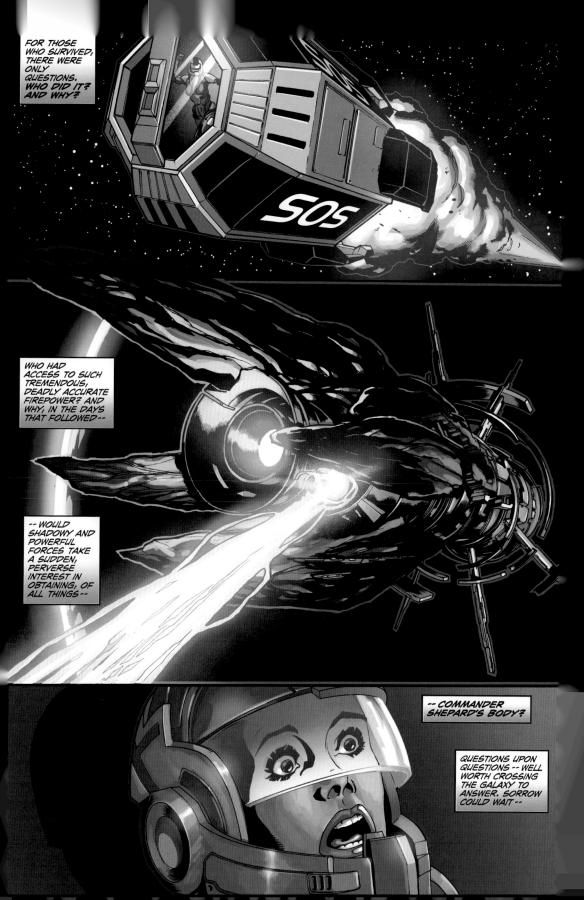

FOR THOSE WHO SURVIVED, THERE WERE ONLY QUESTIONS. WHO DID IT? AND WHY?

SOS

WHO HAD ACCESS TO SUCH TREMENDOUS, DEADLY ACCURATE FIREPOWER? AND WHY, IN THE DAYS THAT FOLLOWED--

-- WOULD SHADOWY AND POWERFUL FORCES TAKE A SUDDEN, PERVERSE INTEREST IN OBTAINING, OF ALL THINGS--

-- COMMANDER SHEPARD'S BODY?

QUESTIONS UPON QUESTIONS -- WELL WORTH CROSSING THE GALAXY TO ANSWER. SORROW COULD WAIT --

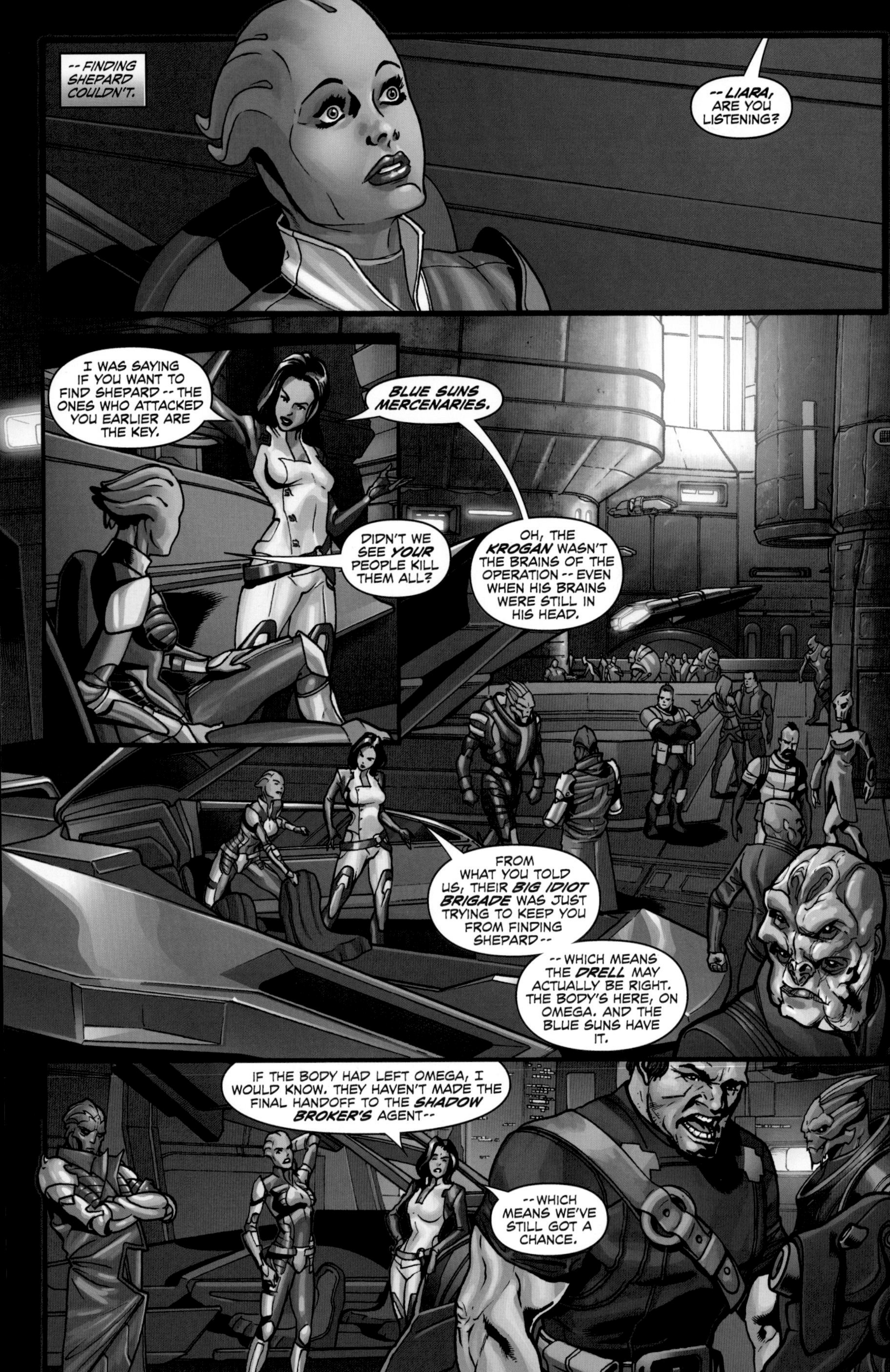
-- FINDING SHEPARD COULDN'T.
-- LIARA, ARE YOU LISTENING?
I WAS SAYING IF YOU WANT TO FIND SHEPARD -- THE ONES WHO ATTACKED YOU EARLIER ARE THE KEY.
BLUE SUNS MERCENARIES.
DIDN'T WE SEE YOUR PEOPLE KILL THEM ALL?
OH, THE KROGAN WASN'T THE BRAINS OF THE OPERATION -- EVEN WHEN HIS BRAINS WERE STILL IN HIS HEAD.
FROM WHAT YOU TOLD US, THEIR BIG IDIOT BRIGADE WAS JUST TRYING TO KEEP YOU FROM FINDING SHEPARD --
-- WHICH MEANS THE DRELL MAY ACTUALLY BE RIGHT. THE BODY'S HERE, ON OMEGA. AND THE BLUE SUNS HAVE IT.
IF THE BODY HAD LEFT OMEGA, I WOULD KNOW. THEY HAVEN'T MADE THE FINAL HANDOFF TO THE SHADOW BROKER'S AGENT --
-- WHICH MEANS WE'VE STILL GOT A CHANCE.

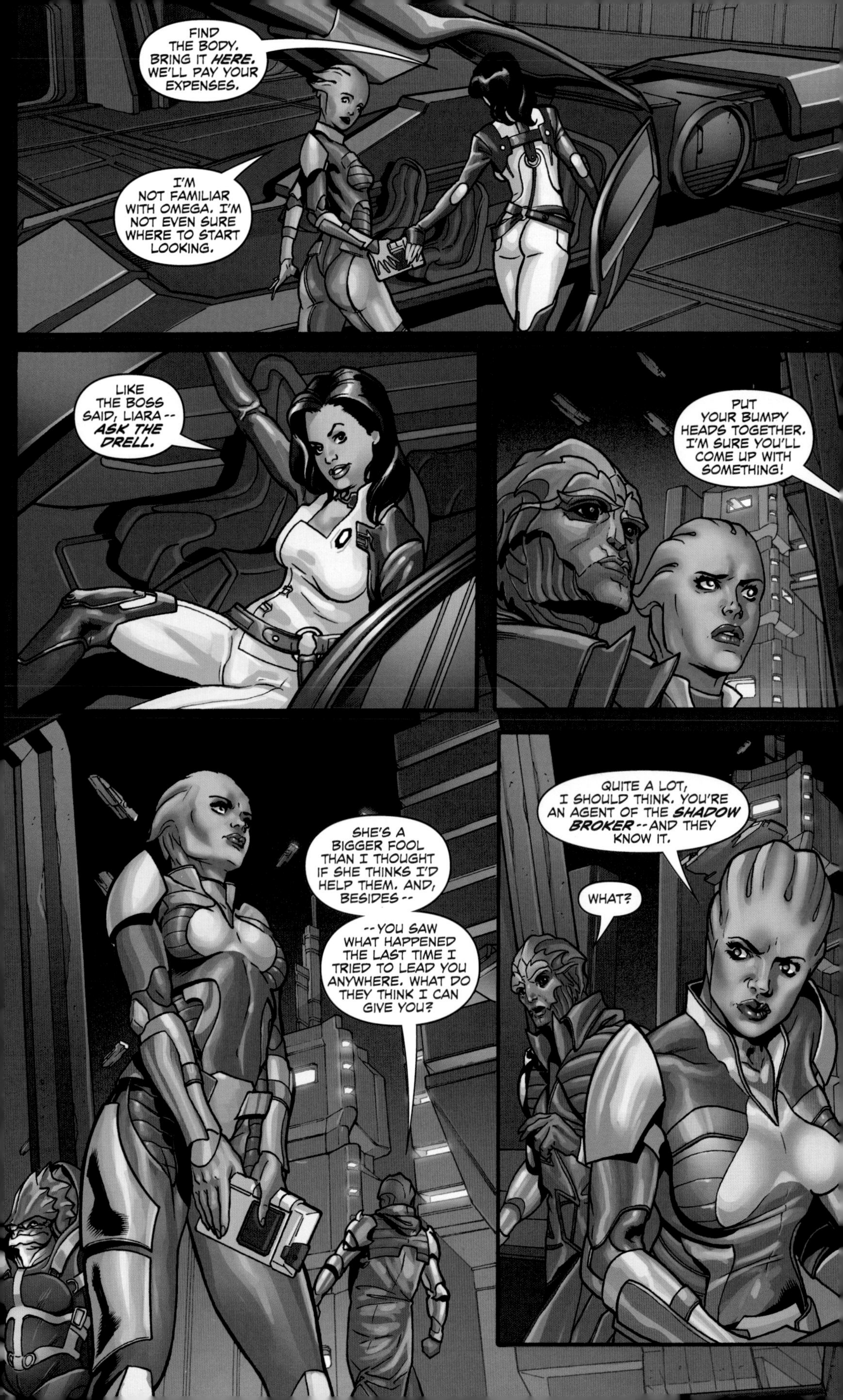
FIND THE BODY. BRING IT *HERE.* WE'LL PAY YOUR EXPENSES.
I'M NOT FAMILIAR WITH OMEGA. I'M NOT EVEN SURE WHERE TO START LOOKING.
LIKE THE BOSS SAID, LIARA-- ***ASK THE DRELL.***
PUT YOUR BUMPY HEADS TOGETHER. I'M SURE YOU'LL COME UP WITH SOMETHING!
SHE'S A BIGGER FOOL THAN I THOUGHT IF SHE THINKS I'D HELP THEM. AND, BESIDES--
--YOU SAW WHAT HAPPENED THE LAST TIME I TRIED TO LEAD YOU ANYWHERE. WHAT DO THEY THINK I CAN GIVE YOU?
QUITE A LOT, I SHOULD THINK. YOU'RE AN AGENT OF THE ***SHADOW BROKER***--AND THEY KNOW IT.
WHAT?

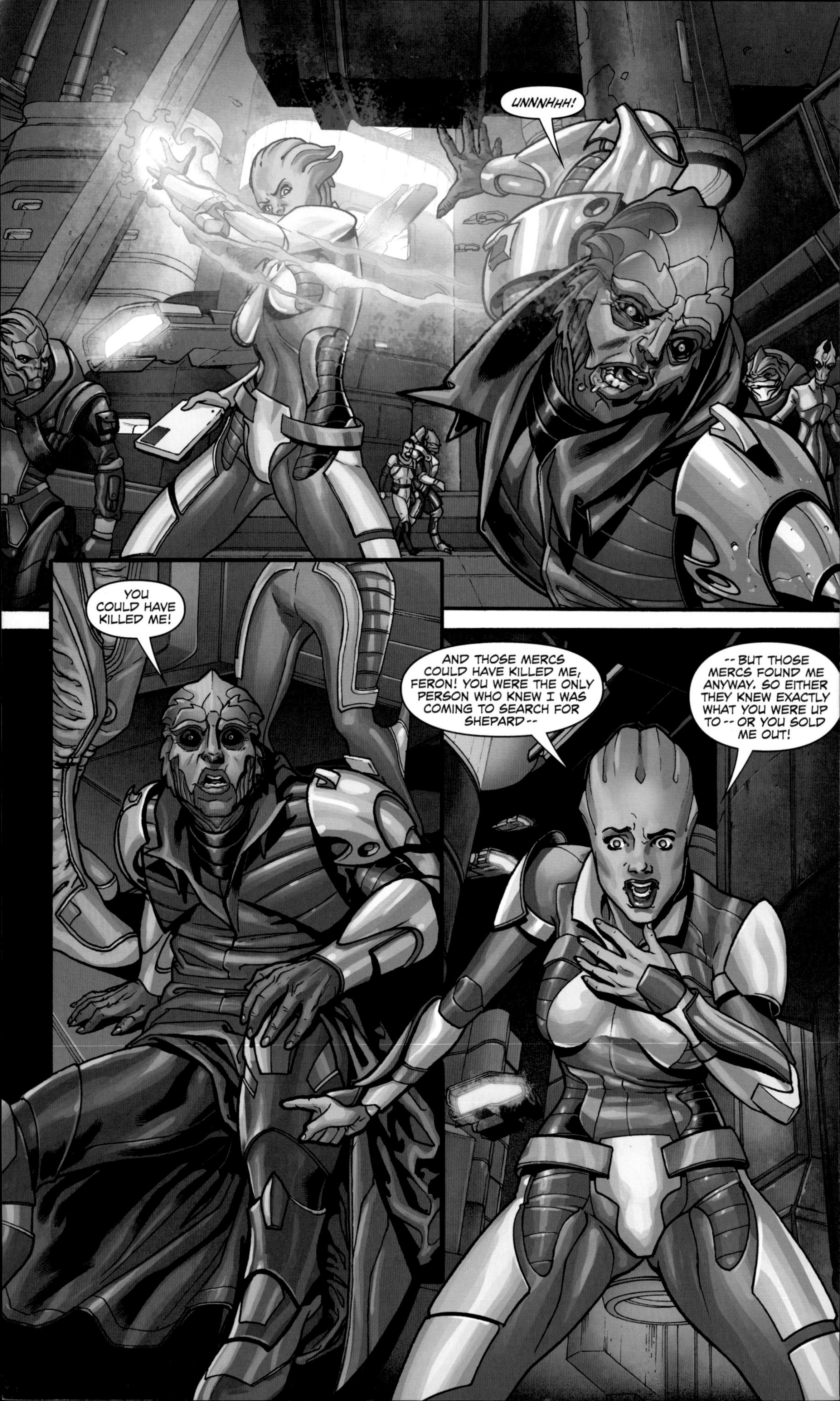
UNNNHHH!
YOU COULD HAVE KILLED ME!
AND THOSE MERCS COULD HAVE KILLED ME, FERON! YOU WERE THE ONLY PERSON WHO KNEW I WAS COMING TO SEARCH FOR SHEPARD--
--BUT THOSE MERCS FOUND ME ANYWAY. SO EITHER THEY KNEW EXACTLY WHAT YOU WERE UP TO--OR YOU SOLD ME OUT!

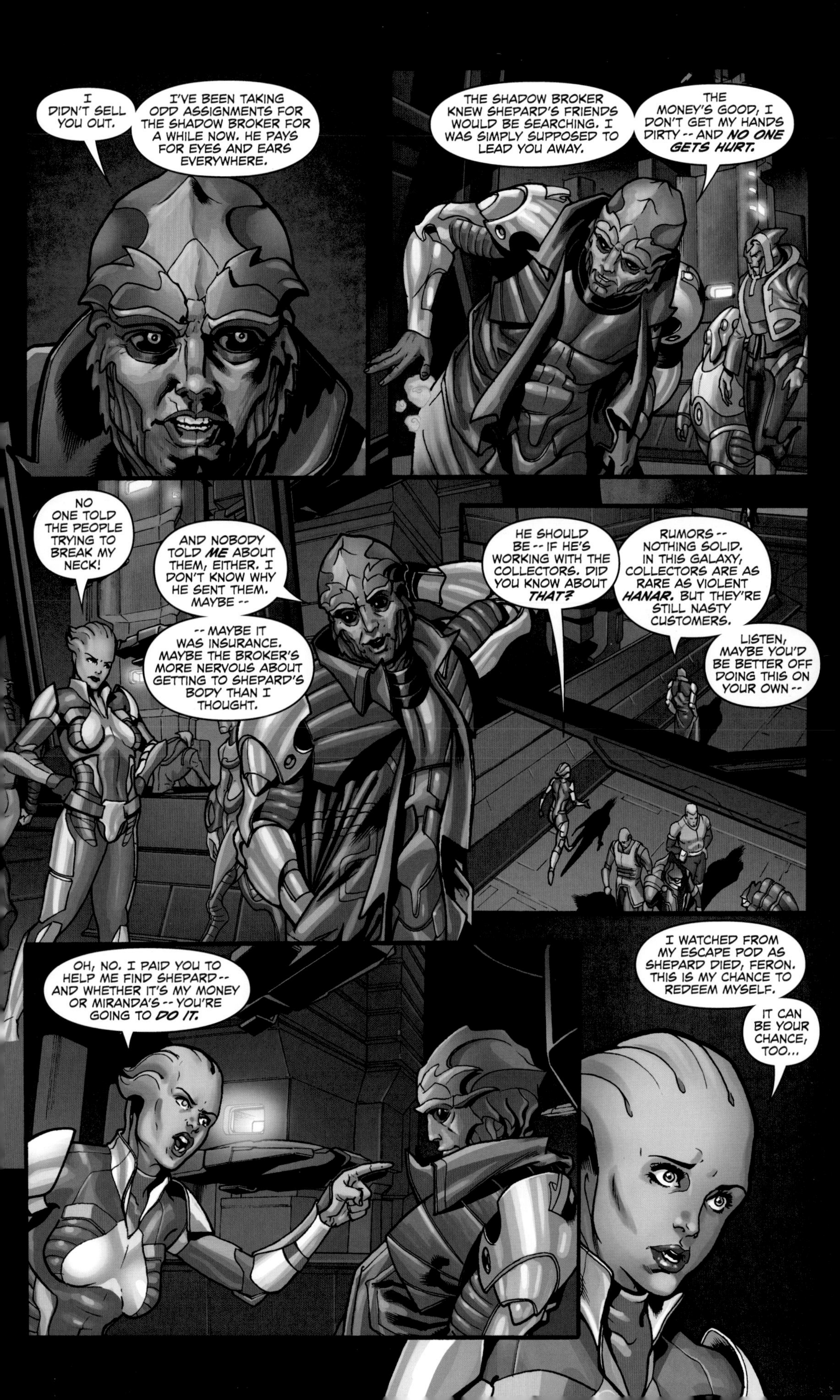
I DIDN'T SELL YOU OUT.
I'VE BEEN TAKING ODD ASSIGNMENTS FOR THE SHADOW BROKER FOR A WHILE NOW. HE PAYS FOR EYES AND EARS EVERYWHERE.
THE SHADOW BROKER KNEW SHEPARD'S FRIENDS WOULD BE SEARCHING. I WAS SIMPLY SUPPOSED TO LEAD YOU AWAY.
THE MONEY'S GOOD, I DON'T GET MY HANDS DIRTY -- AND ***NO ONE GETS HURT.***
NO ONE TOLD THE PEOPLE TRYING TO BREAK MY NECK!
AND NOBODY TOLD ***ME*** ABOUT THEM, EITHER. I DON'T KNOW WHY HE SENT THEM. MAYBE --
-- MAYBE IT WAS INSURANCE. MAYBE THE BROKER'S MORE NERVOUS ABOUT GETTING TO SHEPARD'S BODY THAN I THOUGHT.
HE SHOULD BE -- IF HE'S WORKING WITH THE COLLECTORS. DID YOU KNOW ABOUT ***THAT?***
RUMORS -- NOTHING SOLID. IN THIS GALAXY, COLLECTORS ARE AS RARE AS VIOLENT ***HANAR.*** BUT THEY'RE STILL NASTY CUSTOMERS.
LISTEN, MAYBE YOU'D BE BETTER OFF DOING THIS ON YOUR OWN --
OH, NO. I PAID YOU TO HELP ME FIND SHEPARD -- AND WHETHER IT'S MY MONEY OR MIRANDA'S -- YOU'RE GOING TO ***DO IT.***
I WATCHED FROM MY ESCAPE POD AS SHEPARD DIED, FERON. THIS IS MY CHANCE TO REDEEM MYSELF.
IT CAN BE YOUR CHANCE, TOO...

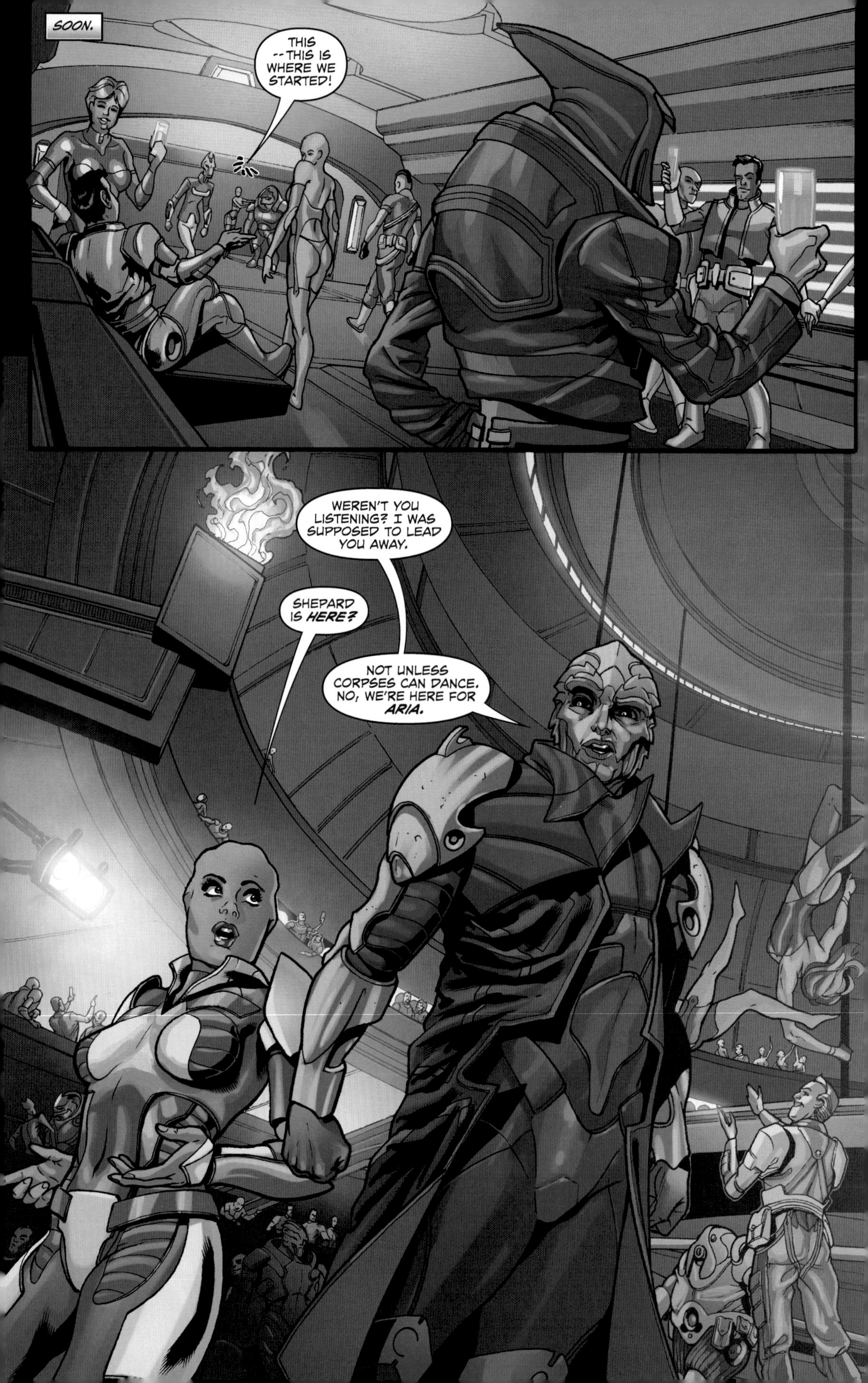
SOON.
THIS --THIS IS WHERE WE STARTED!
WEREN'T YOU LISTENING? I WAS SUPPOSED TO LEAD YOU AWAY.
SHEPARD IS *HERE?*
NOT UNLESS CORPSES CAN DANCE. NO, WE'RE HERE FOR *ARIA.*

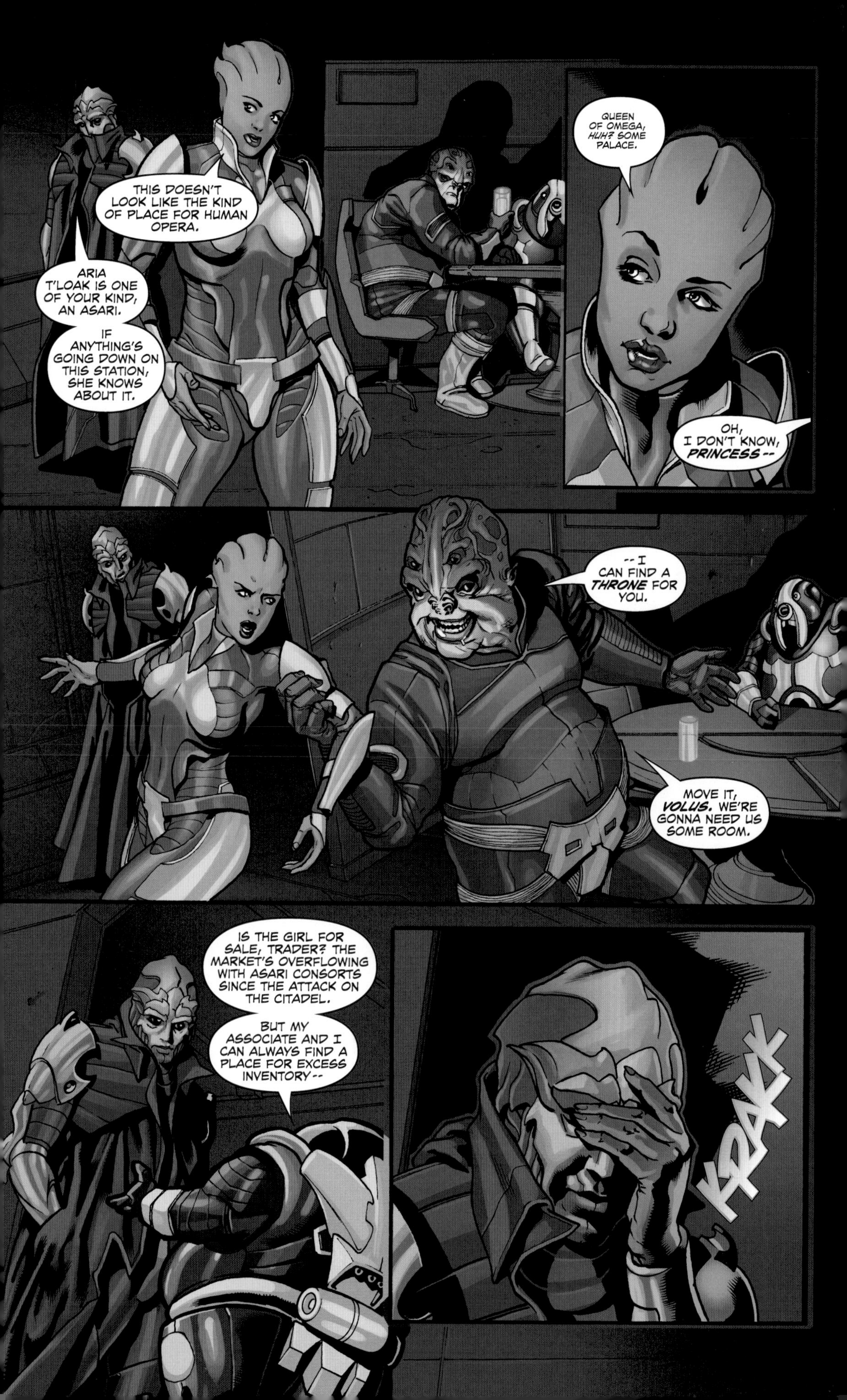
THIS DOESN'T LOOK LIKE THE KIND OF PLACE FOR HUMAN OPERA.
ARIA T'LOAK IS ONE OF YOUR KIND, AN ASARI.
IF ANYTHING'S GOING DOWN ON THIS STATION, SHE KNOWS ABOUT IT.
QUEEN OF OMEGA, *HUH?* SOME PALACE.
OH, I DON'T KNOW, ***PRINCESS***--
--I CAN FIND A ***THRONE*** FOR YOU.
MOVE IT, ***VOLUS.*** WE'RE GONNA NEED US SOME ROOM.
IS THE GIRL FOR SALE, TRADER? THE MARKET'S OVERFLOWING WITH ASARI CONSORTS SINCE THE ATTACK ON THE CITADEL.
BUT MY ASSOCIATE AND I CAN ALWAYS FIND A PLACE FOR EXCESS INVENTORY--
KRAKK

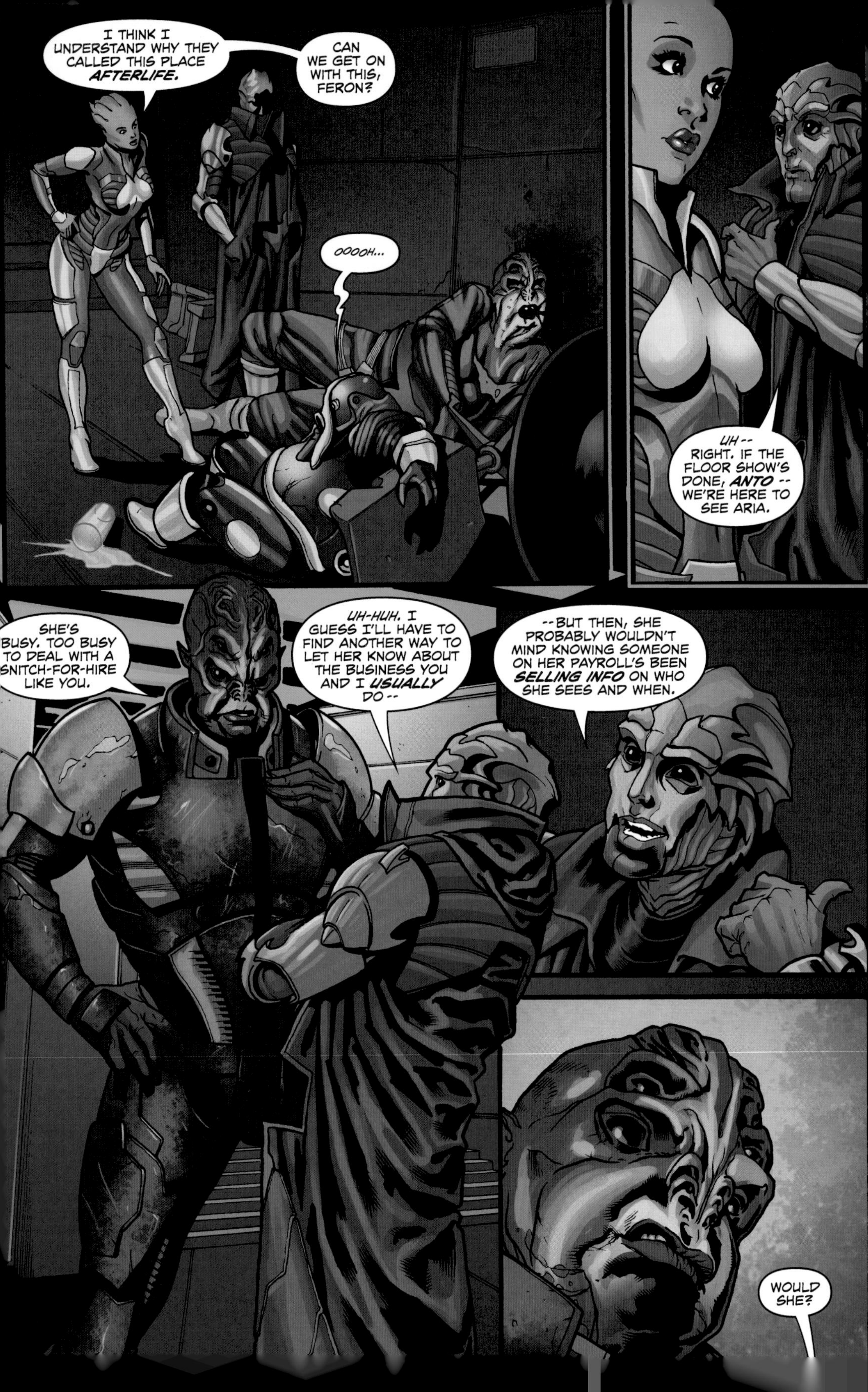
I THINK I UNDERSTAND WHY THEY CALLED THIS PLACE AFTERLIFE.
CAN WE GET ON WITH THIS, FERON?
OOOOH...
UH -- RIGHT. IF THE FLOOR SHOW'S DONE, ANTO -- WE'RE HERE TO SEE ARIA.
SHE'S BUSY. TOO BUSY TO DEAL WITH A SNITCH-FOR-HIRE LIKE YOU.
UH-HUH. I GUESS I'LL HAVE TO FIND ANOTHER WAY TO LET HER KNOW ABOUT THE BUSINESS YOU AND I USUALLY DO --
--BUT THEN, SHE PROBABLY WOULDN'T MIND KNOWING SOMEONE ON HER PAYROLL'S BEEN SELLING INFO ON WHO SHE SEES AND WHEN.
WOULD SHE?

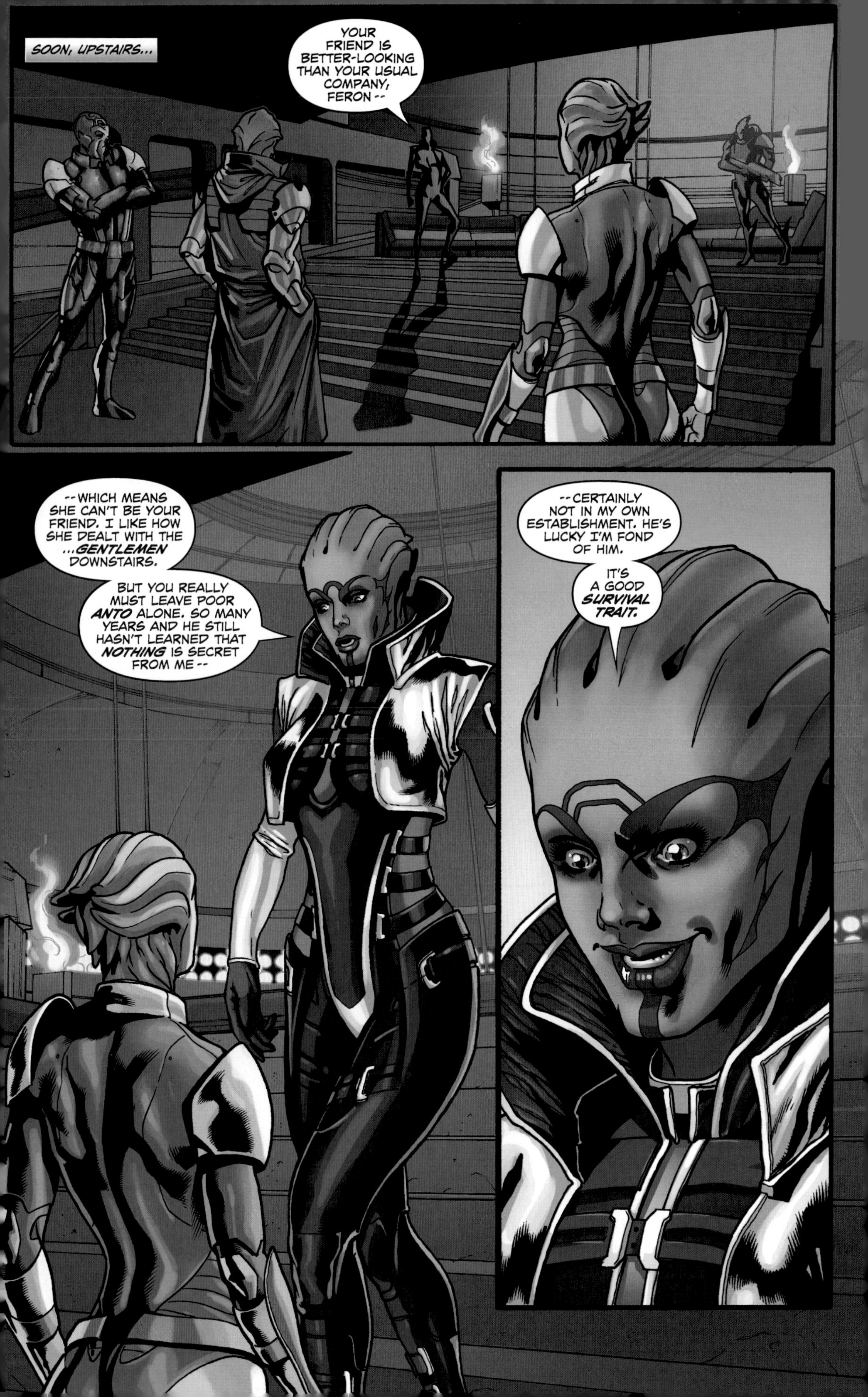
SOON, UPSTAIRS...
YOUR FRIEND IS BETTER-LOOKING THAN YOUR USUAL COMPANY, FERON --
--WHICH MEANS SHE CAN'T BE YOUR FRIEND. I LIKE HOW SHE DEALT WITH THE ...GENTLEMEN DOWNSTAIRS.
BUT YOU REALLY MUST LEAVE POOR ANTO ALONE. SO MANY YEARS AND HE STILL HASN'T LEARNED THAT NOTHING IS SECRET FROM ME --
--CERTAINLY NOT IN MY OWN ESTABLISHMENT. HE'S LUCKY I'M FOND OF HIM.
IT'S A GOOD SURVIVAL TRAIT.

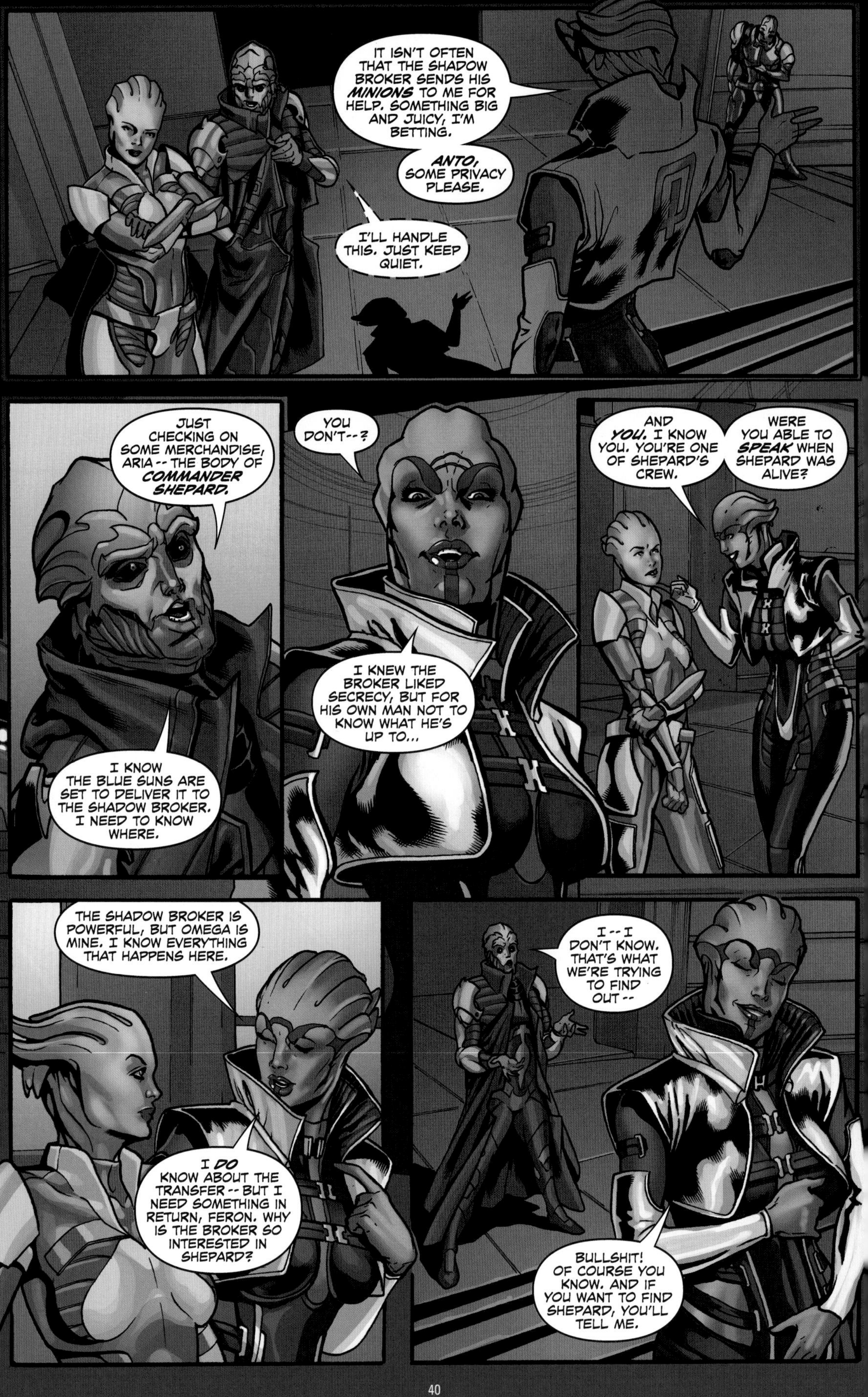

IT ISN'T OFTEN THAT THE SHADOW BROKER SENDS HIS MINIONS TO ME FOR HELP. SOMETHING BIG AND JUICY, I'M BETTING.
ANTO, SOME PRIVACY PLEASE.
I'LL HANDLE THIS. JUST KEEP QUIET.
JUST CHECKING ON SOME MERCHANDISE, ARIA -- THE BODY OF COMMANDER SHEPARD.
I KNOW THE BLUE SUNS ARE SET TO DELIVER IT TO THE SHADOW BROKER. I NEED TO KNOW WHERE.
YOU DON'T--?
I KNEW THE BROKER LIKED SECRECY, BUT FOR HIS OWN MAN NOT TO KNOW WHAT HE'S UP TO...
AND YOU. I KNOW YOU. YOU'RE ONE OF SHEPARD'S CREW.
WERE YOU ABLE TO SPEAK WHEN SHEPARD WAS ALIVE?
THE SHADOW BROKER IS POWERFUL, BUT OMEGA IS MINE. I KNOW EVERYTHING THAT HAPPENS HERE.
I DO KNOW ABOUT THE TRANSFER -- BUT I NEED SOMETHING IN RETURN, FERON. WHY IS THE BROKER SO INTERESTED IN SHEPARD?
I -- I DON'T KNOW. THAT'S WHAT WE'RE TRYING TO FIND OUT --
BULLSHIT! OF COURSE YOU KNOW. AND IF YOU WANT TO FIND SHEPARD, YOU'LL TELL ME.

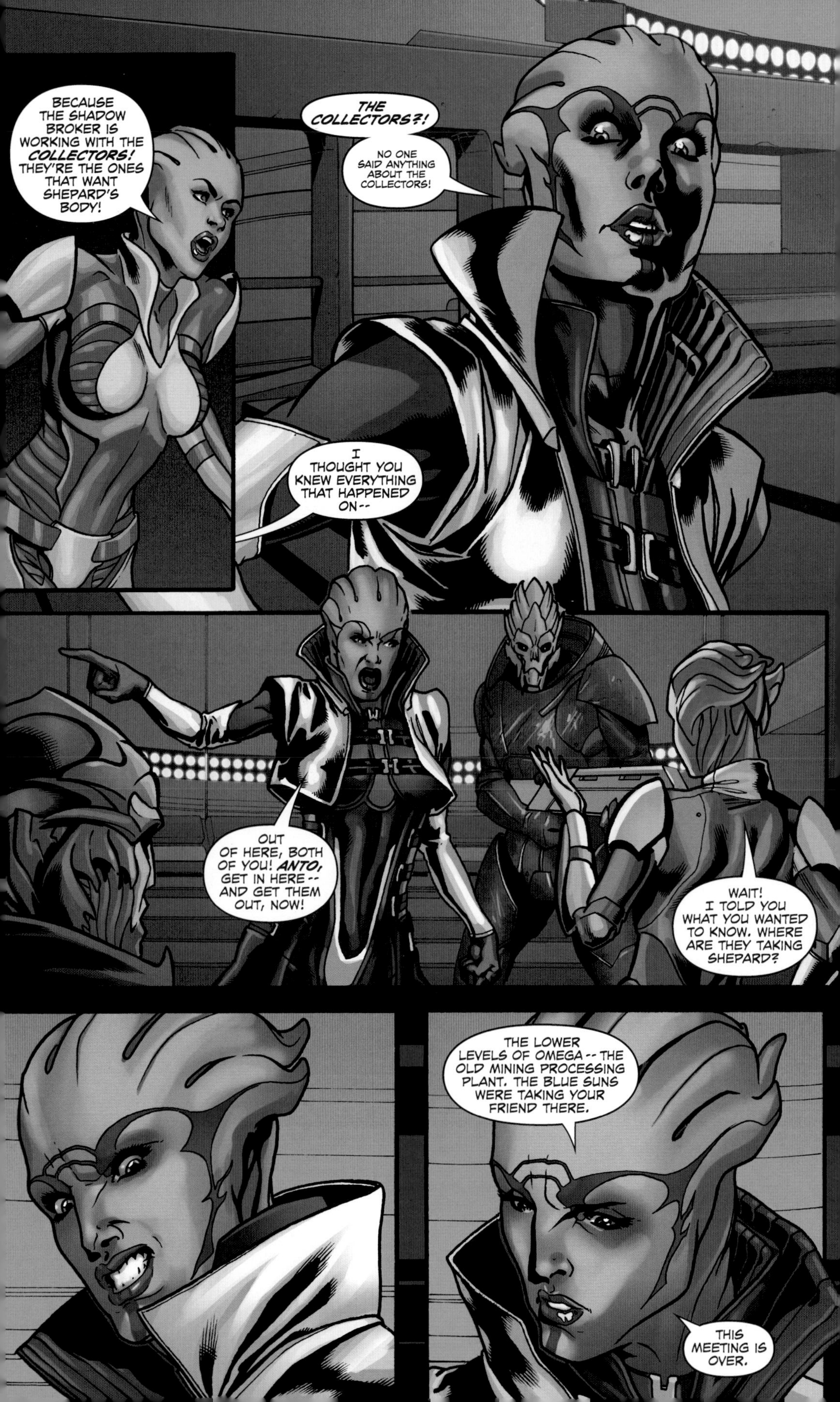
BECAUSE THE SHADOW BROKER IS WORKING WITH THE *COLLECTORS!* THEY'RE THE ONES THAT WANT SHEPARD'S BODY!
THE COLLECTORS?!
NO ONE SAID ANYTHING ABOUT THE COLLECTORS!
I THOUGHT YOU KNEW EVERYTHING THAT HAPPENED ON--
OUT OF HERE, BOTH OF YOU! *ANTO,* GET IN HERE-- AND GET THEM OUT, NOW!
WAIT! I TOLD YOU WHAT YOU WANTED TO KNOW. WHERE ARE THEY TAKING SHEPARD?
THE LOWER LEVELS OF OMEGA-- THE OLD MINING PROCESSING PLANT. THE BLUE SUNS WERE TAKING YOUR FRIEND THERE.
THIS MEETING IS OVER.

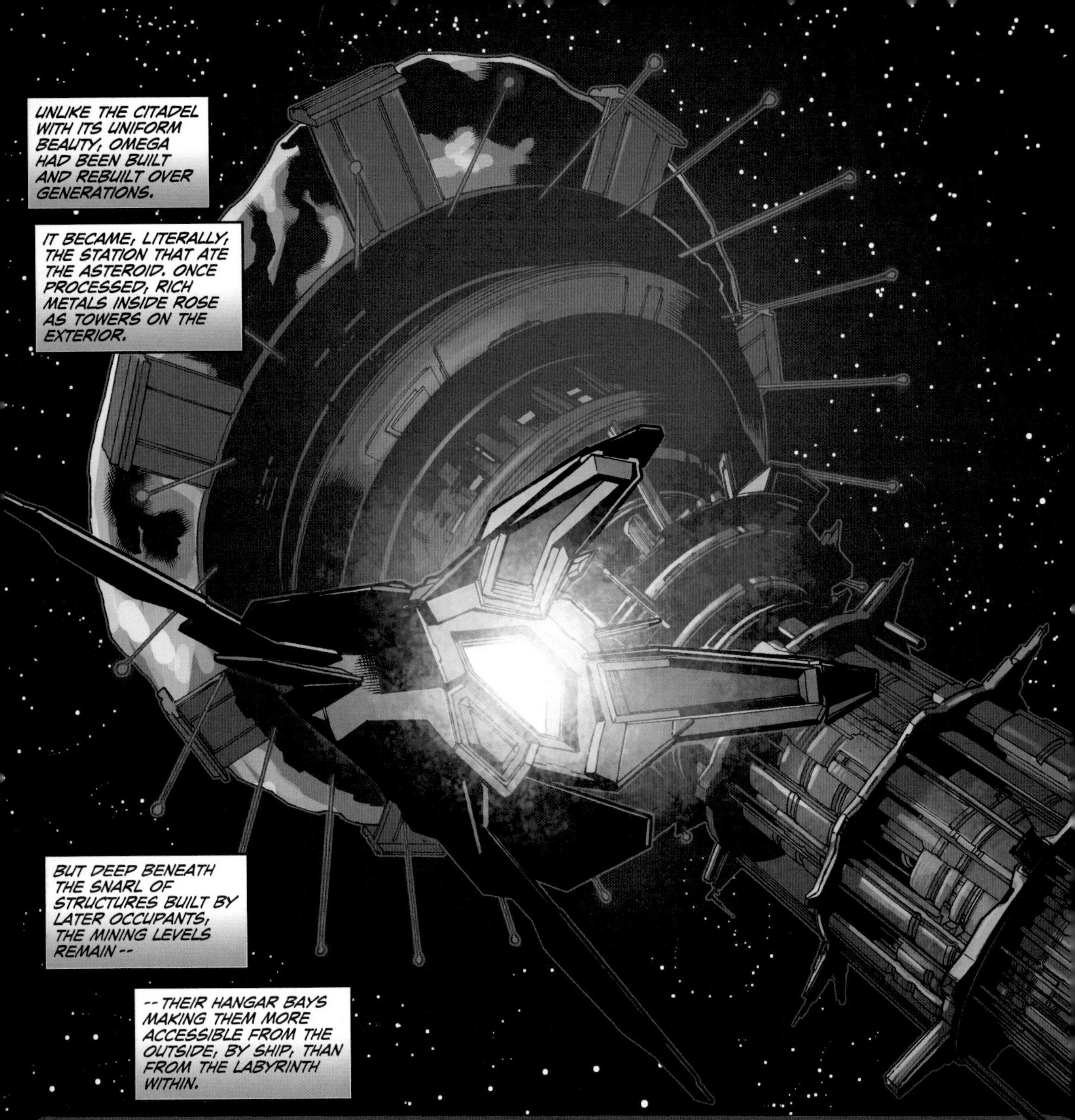
UNLIKE THE CITADEL WITH ITS UNIFORM BEAUTY, OMEGA HAD BEEN BUILT AND REBUILT OVER GENERATIONS.
IT BECAME, LITERALLY, THE STATION THAT ATE THE ASTEROID. ONCE PROCESSED, RICH METALS INSIDE ROSE AS TOWERS ON THE EXTERIOR.
BUT DEEP BENEATH THE SNARL OF STRUCTURES BUILT BY LATER OCCUPANTS, THE MINING LEVELS REMAIN --
-- THEIR HANGAR BAYS MAKING THEM MORE ACCESSIBLE FROM THE OUTSIDE, BY SHIP, THAN FROM THE LABYRINTH WITHIN.
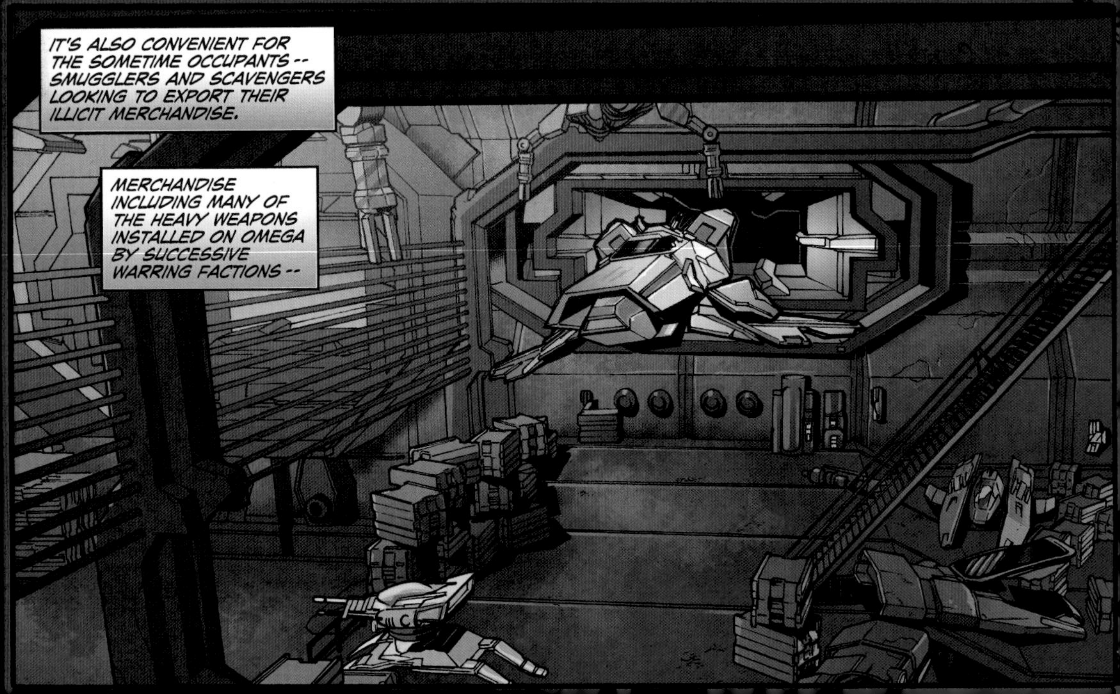
IT'S ALSO CONVENIENT FOR THE SOMETIME OCCUPANTS -- SMUGGLERS AND SCAVENGERS LOOKING TO EXPORT THEIR ILLICIT MERCHANDISE.
MERCHANDISE INCLUDING MANY OF THE HEAVY WEAPONS INSTALLED ON OMEGA BY SUCCESSIVE WARRING FACTIONS --

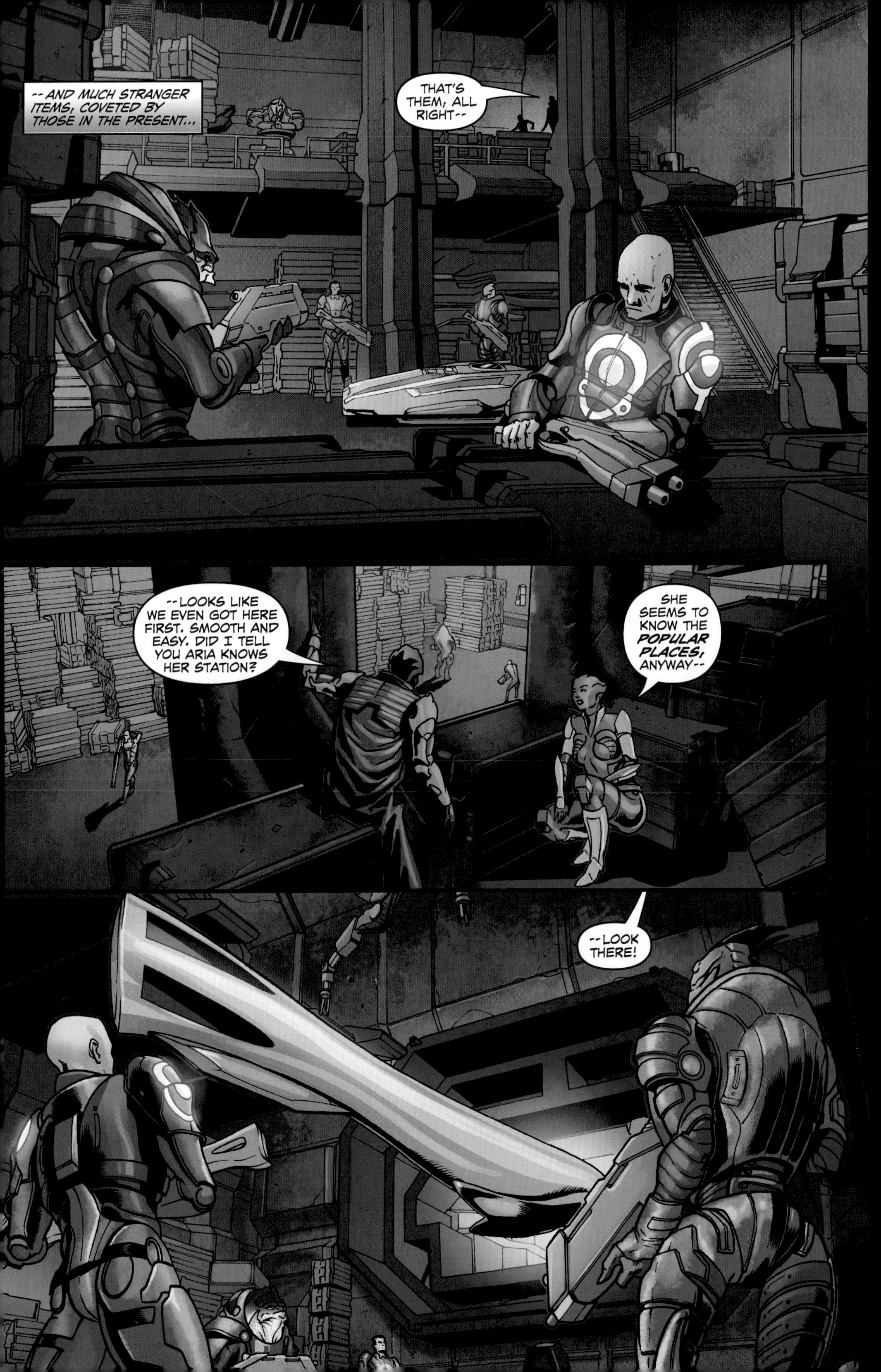
--AND MUCH STRANGER ITEMS, COVETED BY THOSE IN THE PRESENT...
THAT'S THEM, ALL RIGHT--
--LOOKS LIKE WE EVEN GOT HERE FIRST. SMOOTH AND EASY. DID I TELL YOU ARIA KNOWS HER STATION?
SHE SEEMS TO KNOW THE POPULAR PLACES, ANYWAY--
--LOOK THERE!

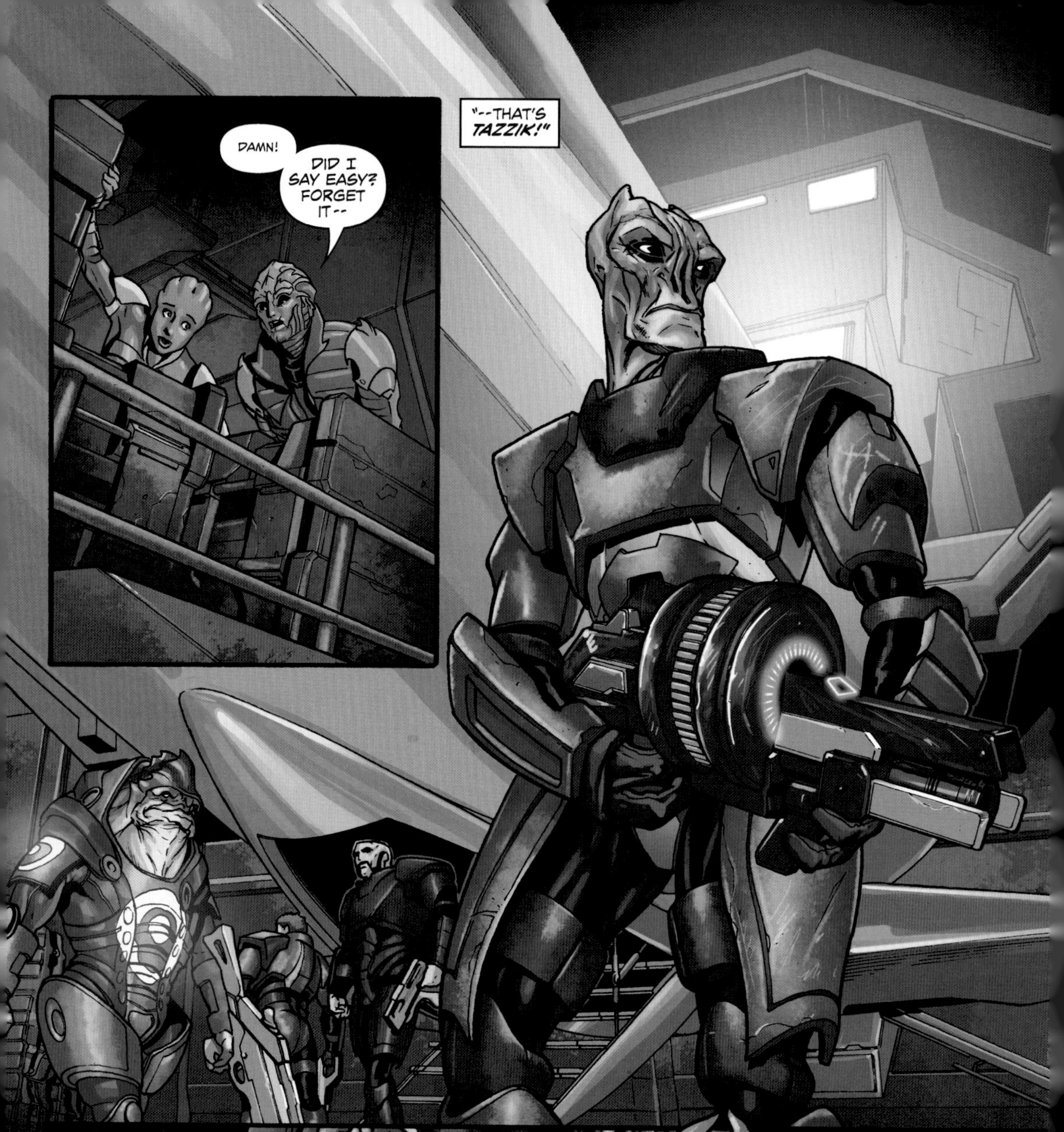
DAMN!
DID I SAY EASY? FORGET IT --
"--THAT'S *TAZZIK!*"
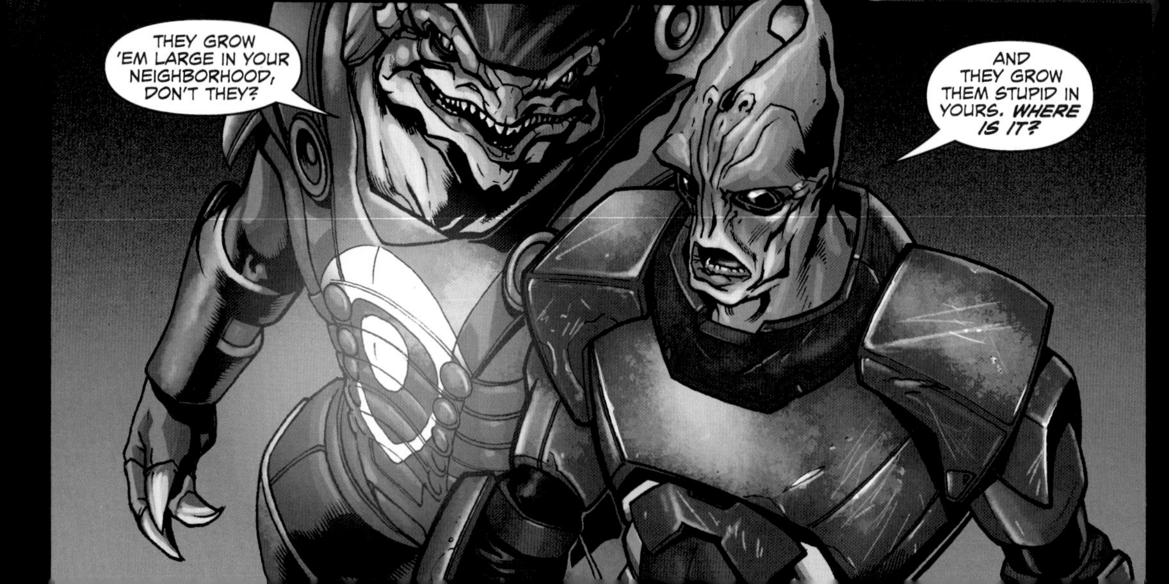
THEY GROW 'EM LARGE IN YOUR NEIGHBORHOOD, DON'T THEY?
AND THEY GROW THEM STUPID IN YOURS. ***WHERE IS IT?***

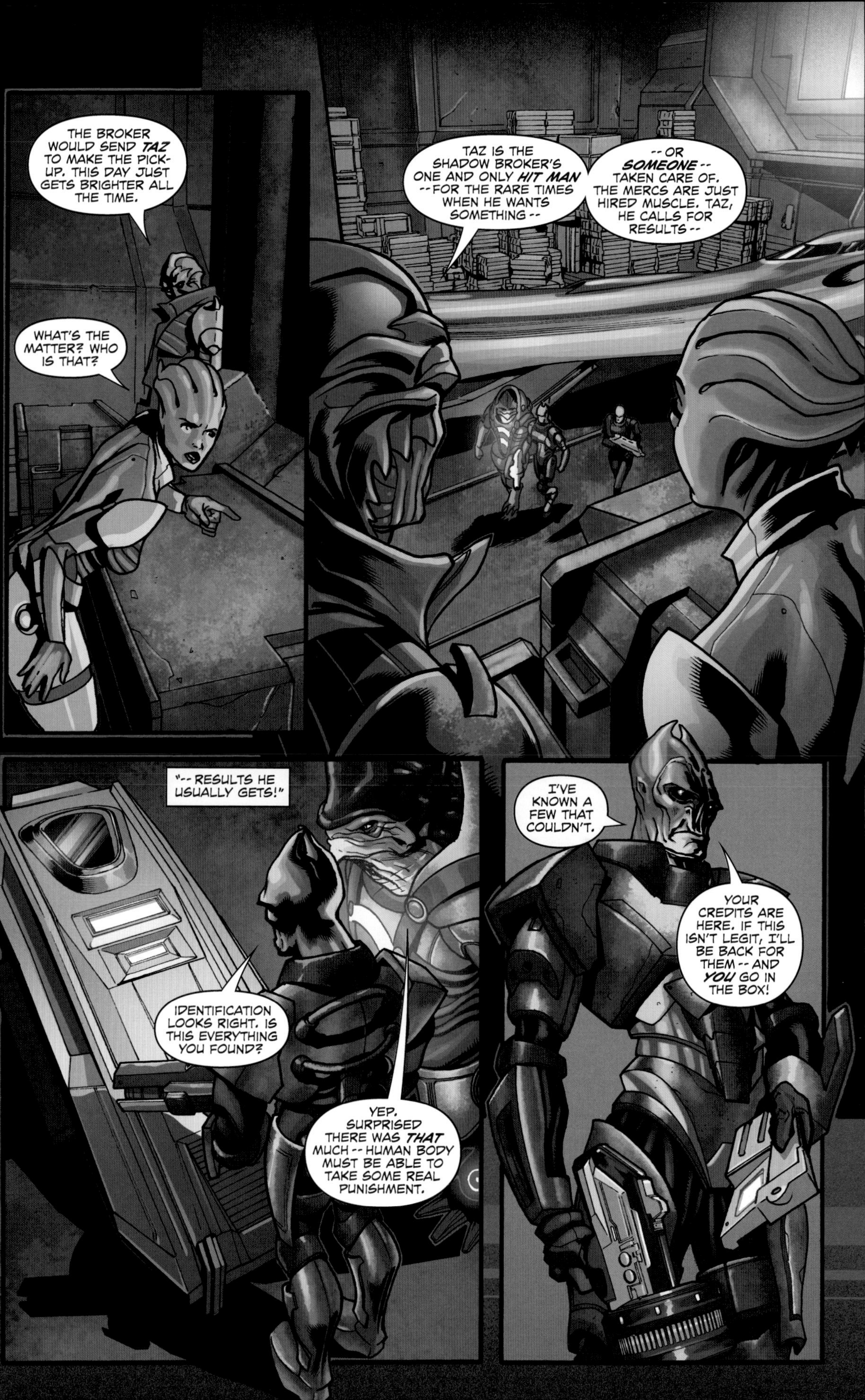
THE BROKER WOULD SEND TAZ TO MAKE THE PICK-UP. THIS DAY JUST GETS BRIGHTER ALL THE TIME.
WHAT'S THE MATTER? WHO IS THAT?
TAZ IS THE SHADOW BROKER'S ONE AND ONLY HIT MAN --FOR THE RARE TIMES WHEN HE WANTS SOMETHING --
--OR SOMEONE-- TAKEN CARE OF. THE MERCS ARE JUST HIRED MUSCLE. TAZ, HE CALLS FOR RESULTS --
"--RESULTS HE USUALLY GETS!"
IDENTIFICATION LOOKS RIGHT. IS THIS EVERYTHING YOU FOUND?
YEP. SURPRISED THERE WAS THAT MUCH--HUMAN BODY MUST BE ABLE TO TAKE SOME REAL PUNISHMENT.
I'VE KNOWN A FEW THAT COULDN'T.
YOUR CREDITS ARE HERE. IF THIS ISN'T LEGIT, I'LL BE BACK FOR THEM--AND YOU GO IN THE BOX!

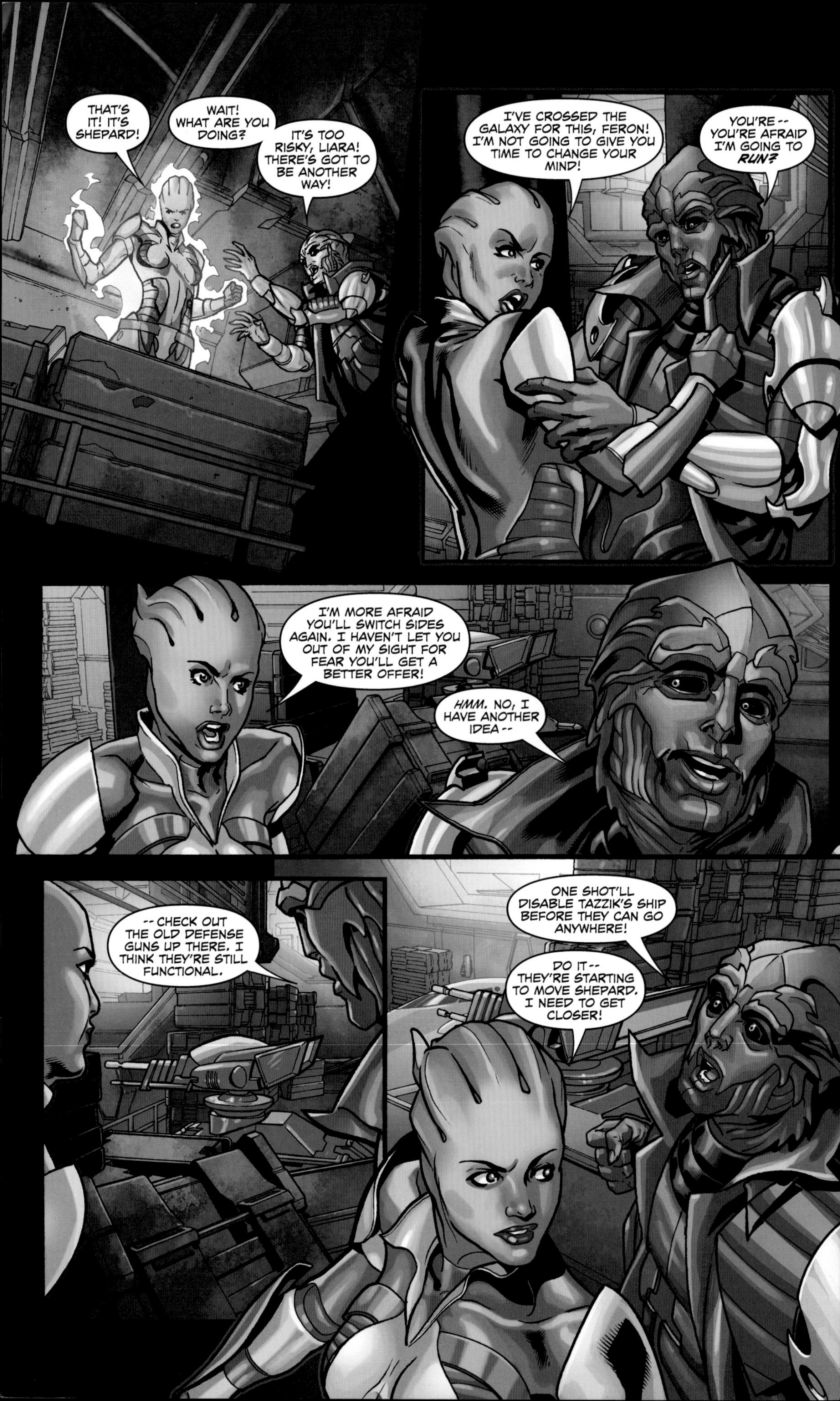
THAT'S IT! IT'S SHEPARD!
WAIT! WHAT ARE YOU DOING?
IT'S TOO RISKY, LIARA! THERE'S GOT TO BE ANOTHER WAY!
I'VE CROSSED THE GALAXY FOR THIS, FERON! I'M NOT GOING TO GIVE YOU TIME TO CHANGE YOUR MIND!
YOU'RE -- YOU'RE AFRAID I'M GOING TO *RUN?*
I'M MORE AFRAID YOU'LL SWITCH SIDES AGAIN. I HAVEN'T LET YOU OUT OF MY SIGHT FOR FEAR YOU'LL GET A BETTER OFFER!
HMM. NO, I HAVE ANOTHER IDEA --
-- CHECK OUT THE OLD DEFENSE GUNS UP THERE. I THINK THEY'RE STILL FUNCTIONAL.
ONE SHOT'LL DISABLE TAZZIK'S SHIP BEFORE THEY CAN GO ANYWHERE!
DO IT -- THEY'RE STARTING TO MOVE SHEPARD. I NEED TO GET CLOSER!

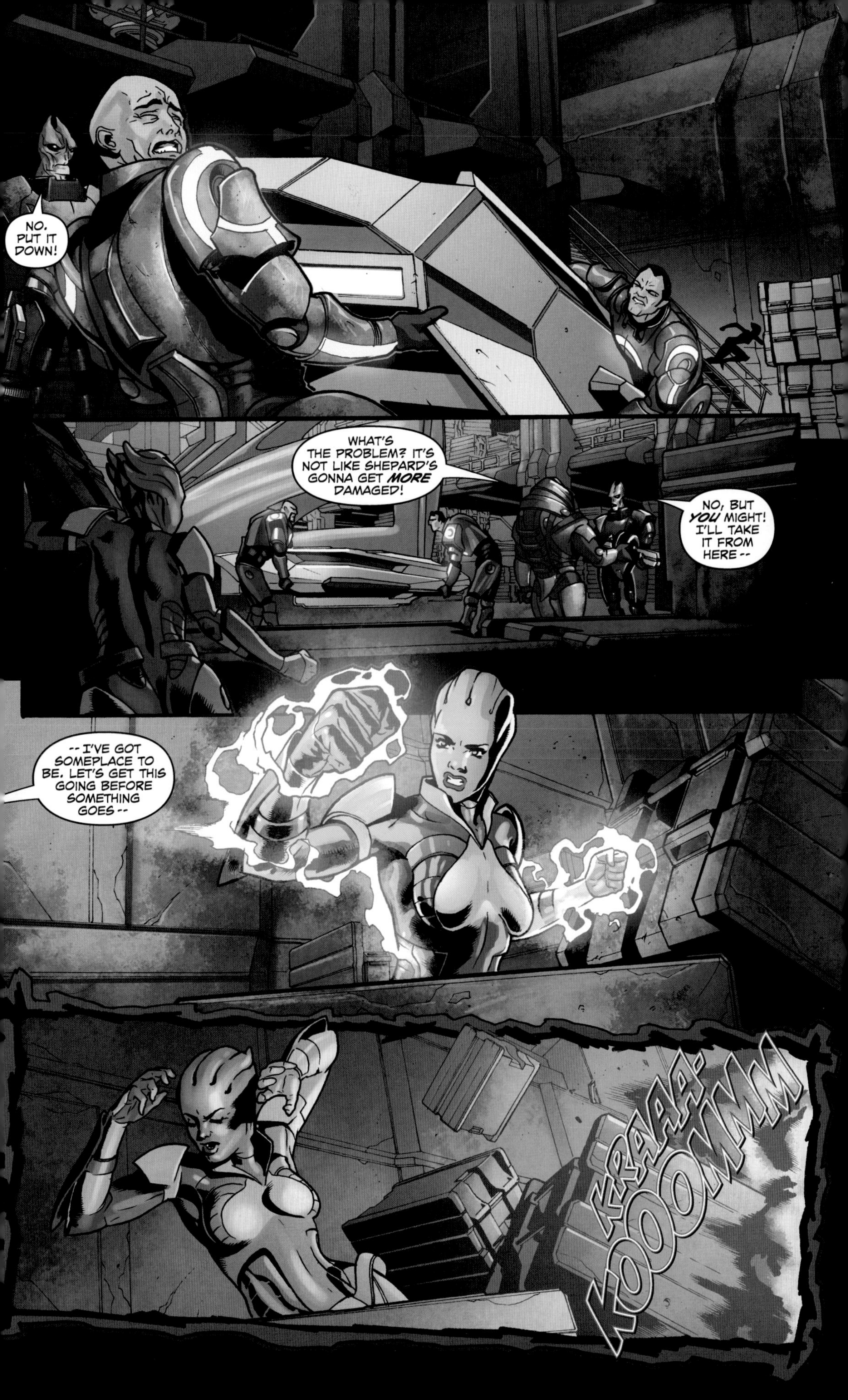
NO. PUT IT DOWN!
WHAT'S THE PROBLEM? IT'S NOT LIKE SHEPARD'S GONNA GET *MORE* DAMAGED!
NO, BUT *YOU* MIGHT! I'LL TAKE IT FROM HERE --
-- I'VE GOT SOMEPLACE TO BE. LET'S GET THIS GOING BEFORE SOMETHING GOES --
KRAAA-KOOOOMMM

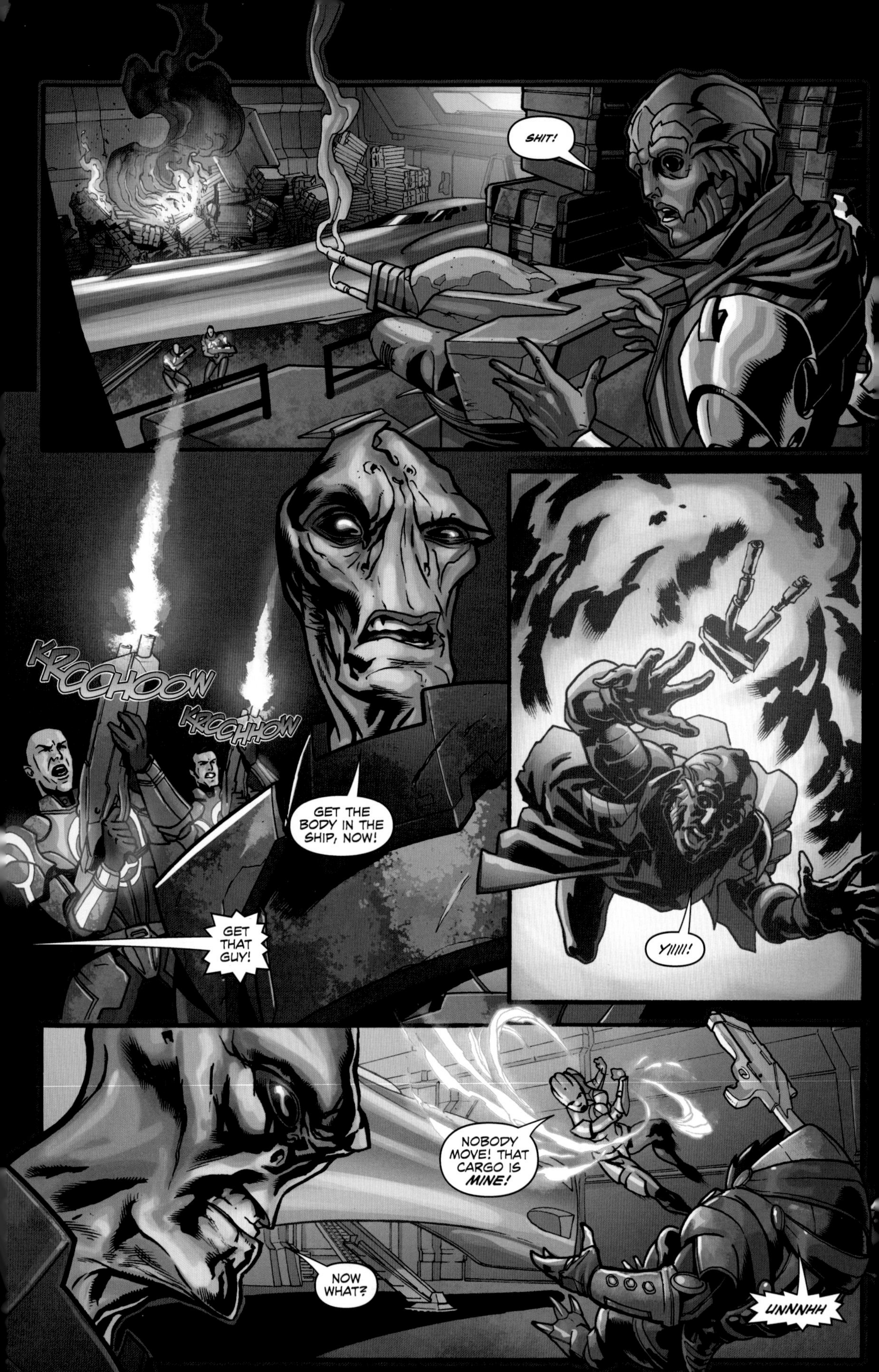
SHIT!
KROCHOOW
KROCHHOW
GET THE BODY IN THE SHIP, NOW!
GET THAT GUY!
YIIIII!
NOBODY MOVE! THAT CARGO IS ***MINE!***
NOW WHAT?
UNNNHH

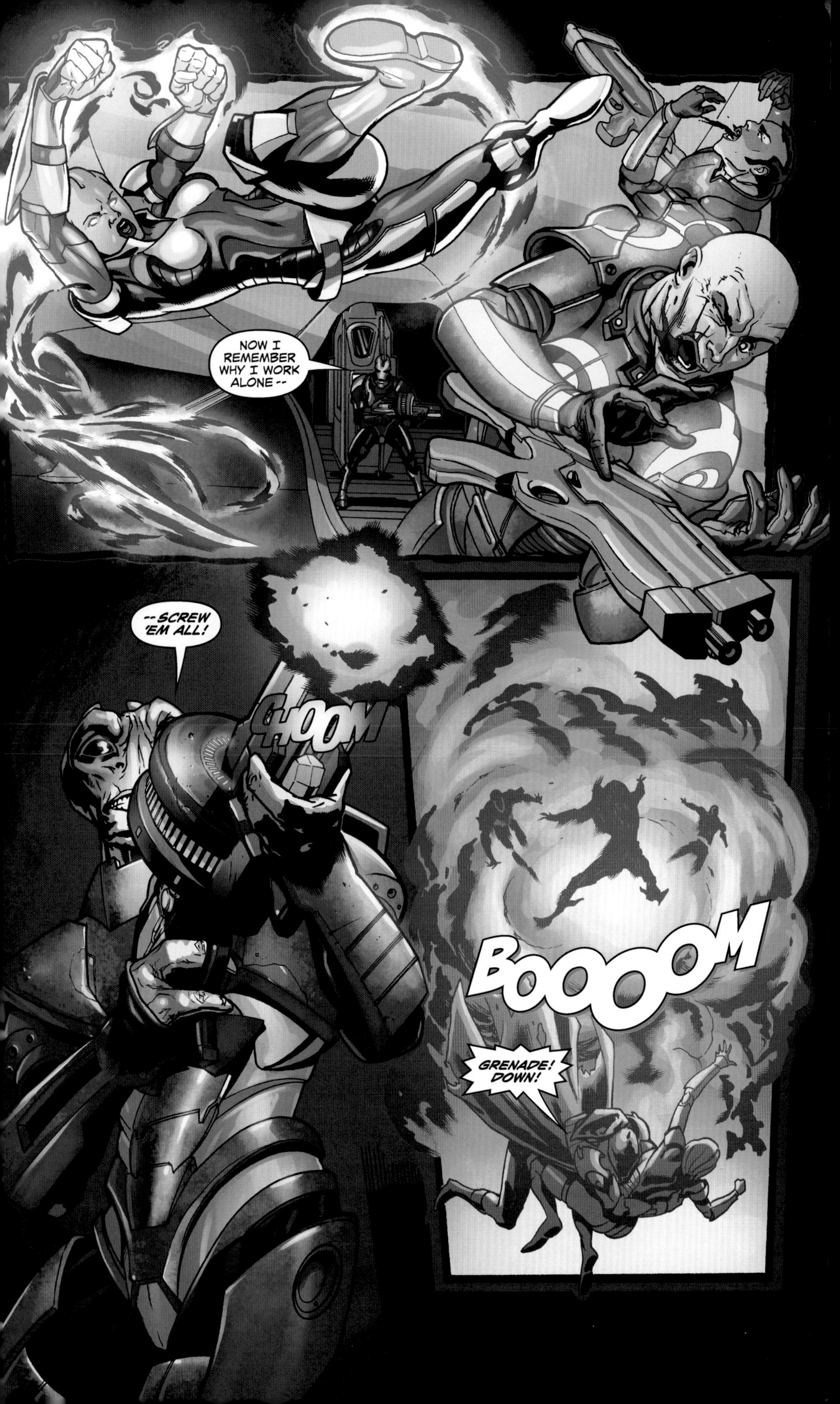
NOW I REMEMBER WHY I WORK ALONE --
--SCREW 'EM ALL!
CHOOM
BOOOOOM
GRENADE! DOWN!

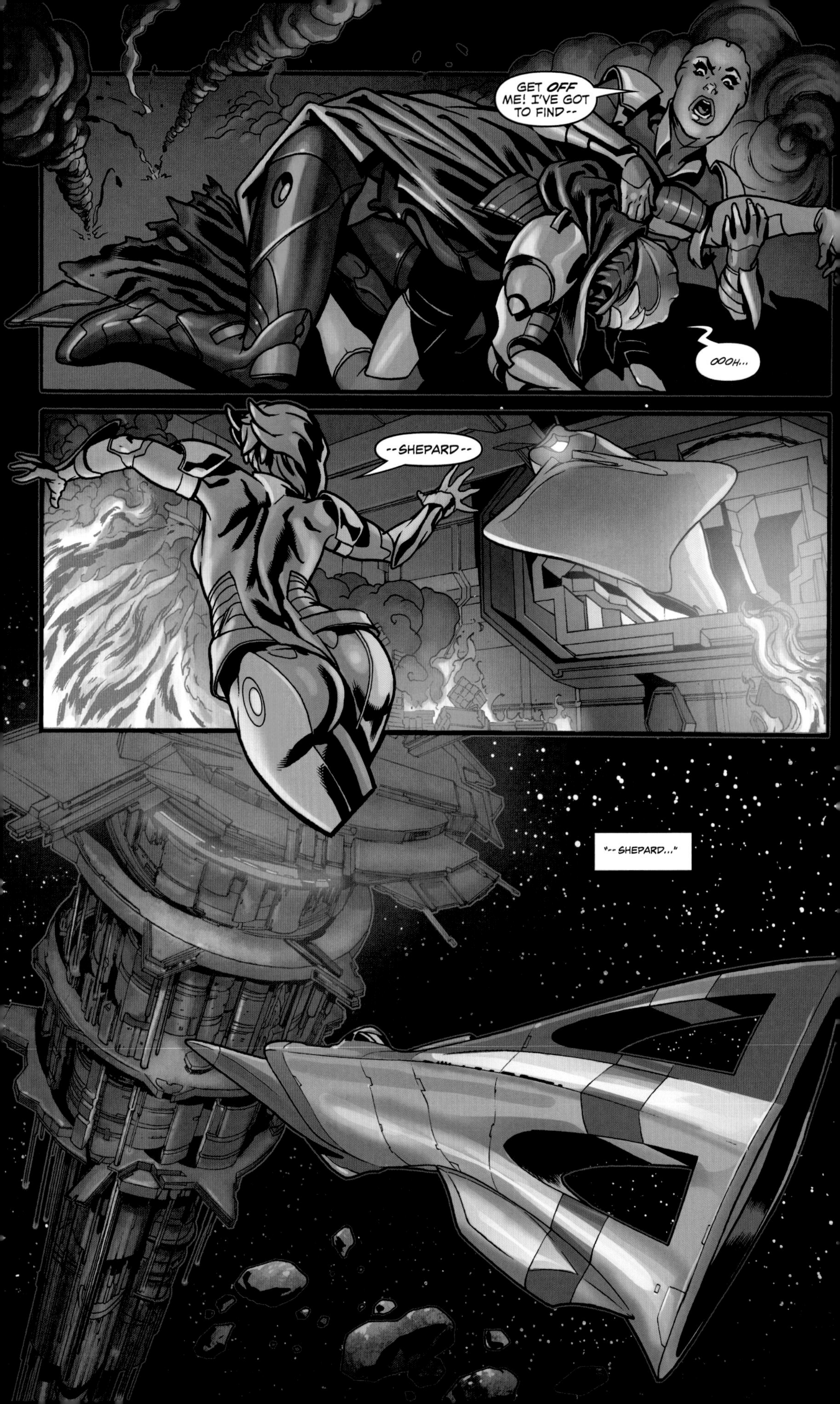
GET *OFF* ME! I'VE GOT TO FIND--
OOOH...
--SHEPARD--
"--SHEPARD..."

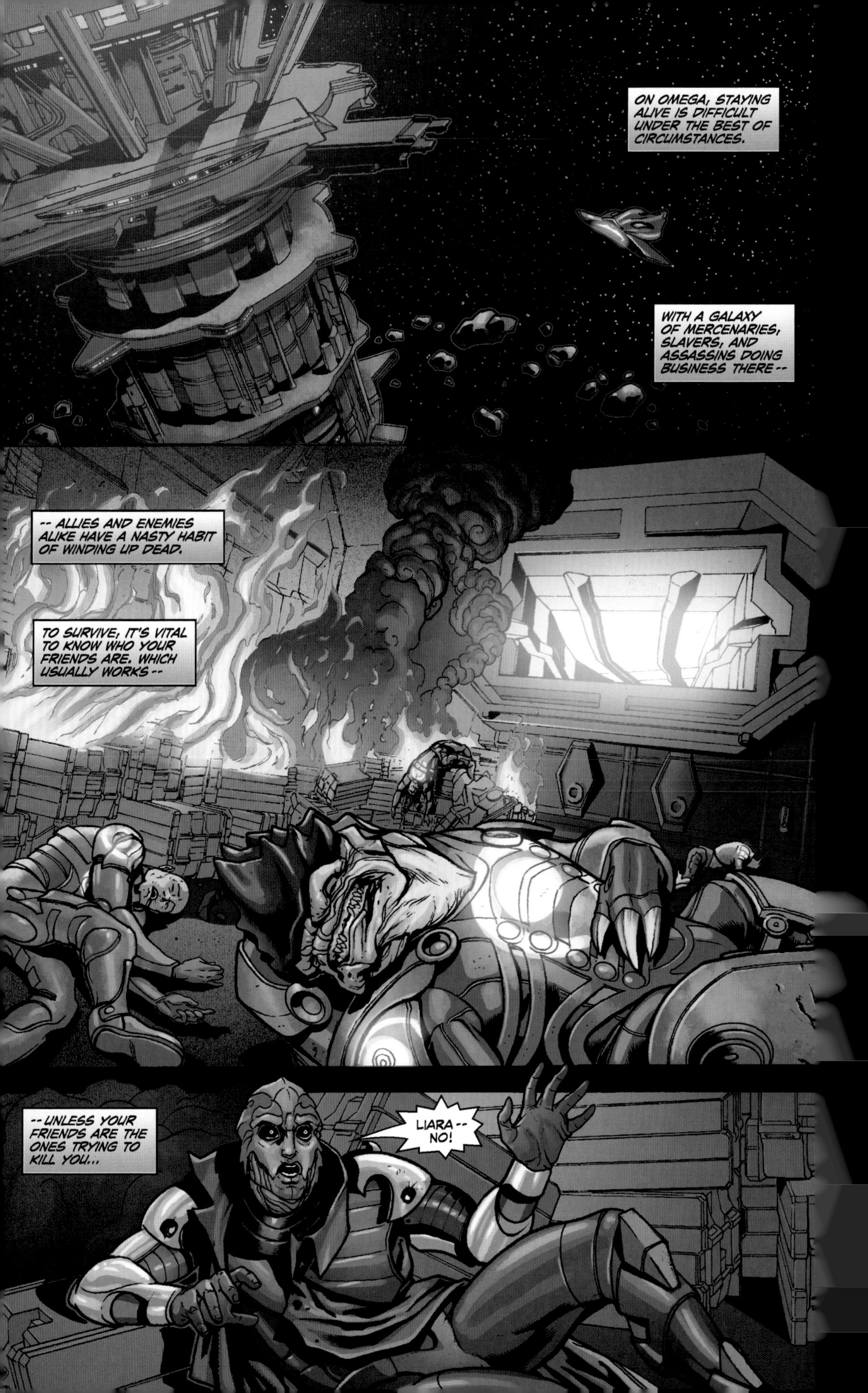
ON OMEGA, STAYING ALIVE IS DIFFICULT UNDER THE BEST OF CIRCUMSTANCES.
WITH A GALAXY OF MERCENARIES, SLAVERS, AND ASSASSINS DOING BUSINESS THERE--
-- ALLIES AND ENEMIES ALIKE HAVE A NASTY HABIT OF WINDING UP DEAD.
TO SURVIVE, IT'S VITAL TO KNOW WHO YOUR FRIENDS ARE. WHICH USUALLY WORKS--
--UNLESS YOUR FRIENDS ARE THE ONES TRYING TO KILL YOU...
LIARA-- NO!

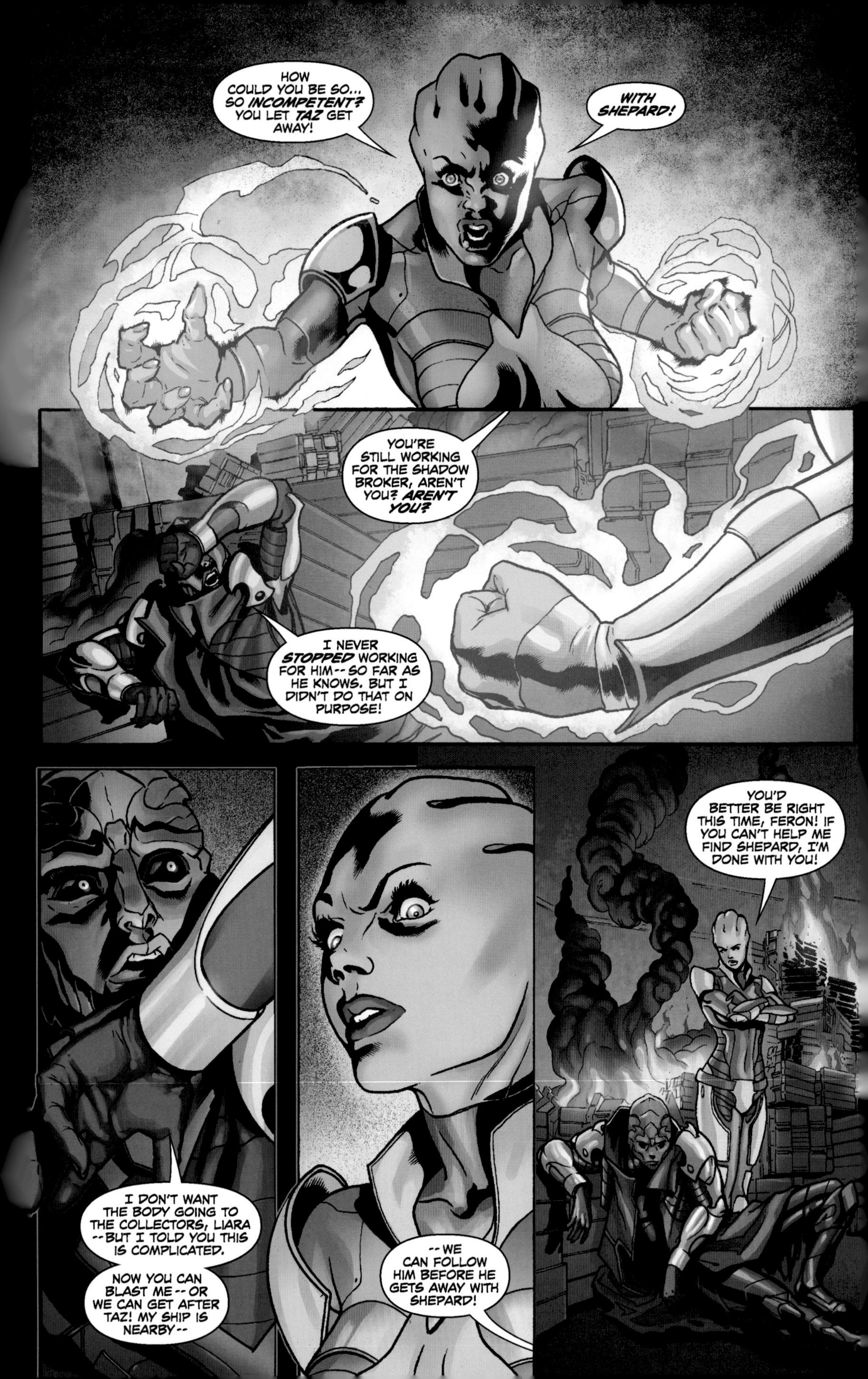
HOW COULD YOU BE SO... SO *INCOMPETENT?* YOU LET *TAZ* GET AWAY!
WITH SHEPARD!
YOU'RE STILL WORKING FOR THE SHADOW BROKER, AREN'T YOU? *AREN'T YOU?*
I NEVER *STOPPED* WORKING FOR HIM--SO FAR AS HE KNOWS. BUT I DIDN'T DO THAT ON PURPOSE!
I DON'T WANT THE BODY GOING TO THE COLLECTORS, LIARA--BUT I TOLD YOU THIS IS COMPLICATED.
NOW YOU CAN BLAST ME--OR WE CAN GET AFTER TAZ! MY SHIP IS NEARBY--
--WE CAN FOLLOW HIM BEFORE HE GETS AWAY WITH SHEPARD!
YOU'D BETTER BE RIGHT THIS TIME, FERON! IF YOU CAN'T HELP ME FIND SHEPARD, I'M DONE WITH YOU!

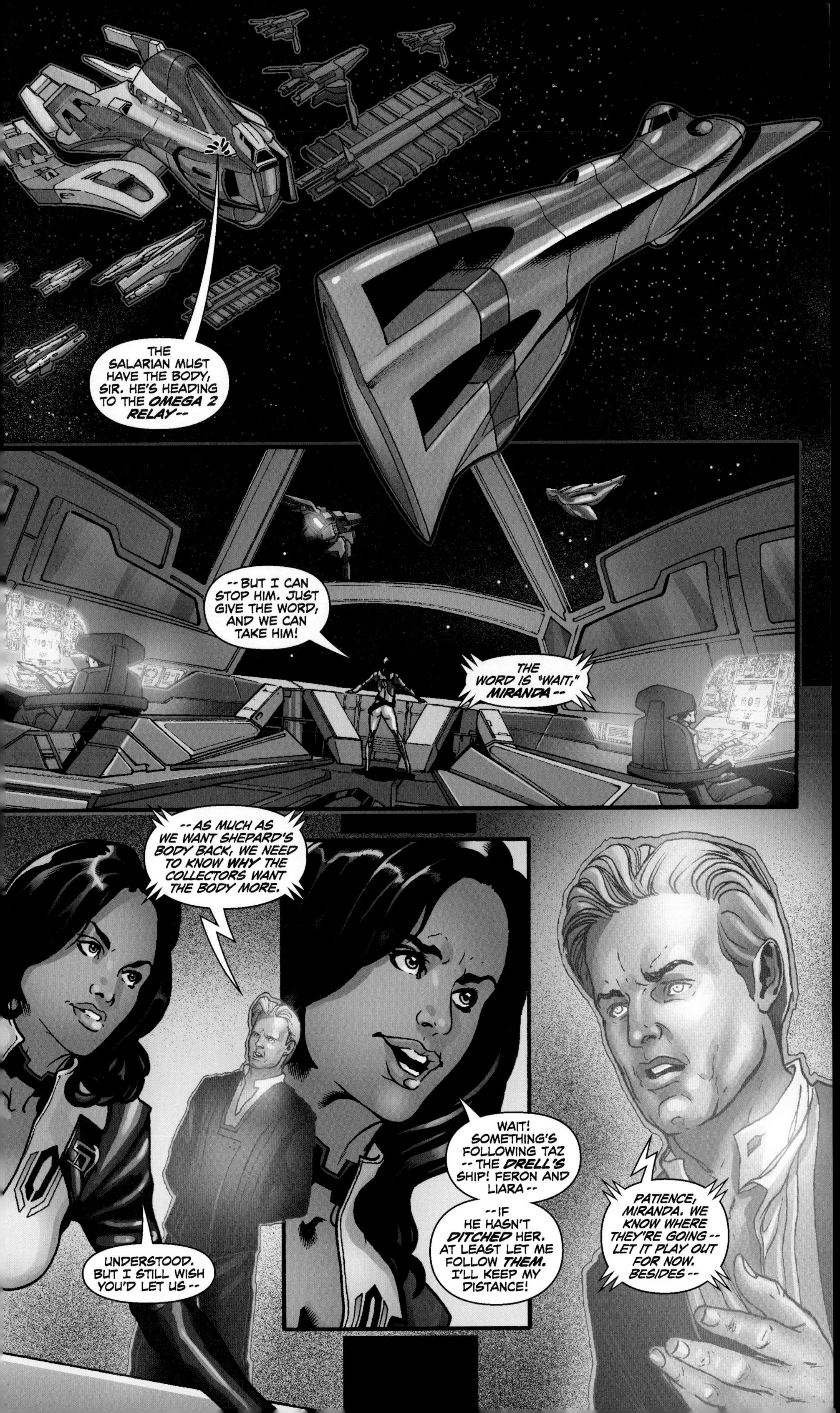
THE SALARIAN MUST HAVE THE BODY, SIR. HE'S HEADING TO THE *OMEGA 2 RELAY*--
--BUT I CAN STOP HIM. JUST GIVE THE WORD, AND WE CAN TAKE HIM!
THE WORD IS "WAIT," MIRANDA--
--AS MUCH AS WE WANT SHEPARD'S BODY BACK, WE NEED TO KNOW **WHY** THE COLLECTORS WANT THE BODY MORE.
UNDERSTOOD. BUT I STILL WISH YOU'D LET US--
WAIT! SOMETHING'S FOLLOWING TAZ --THE ***DRELL'S*** SHIP! FERON AND LIARA--
--IF HE HASN'T ***DITCHED*** HER. AT LEAST LET ME FOLLOW ***THEM.*** I'LL KEEP MY DISTANCE!
PATIENCE, MIRANDA. WE KNOW WHERE THEY'RE GOING--LET IT PLAY OUT FOR NOW. BESIDES--

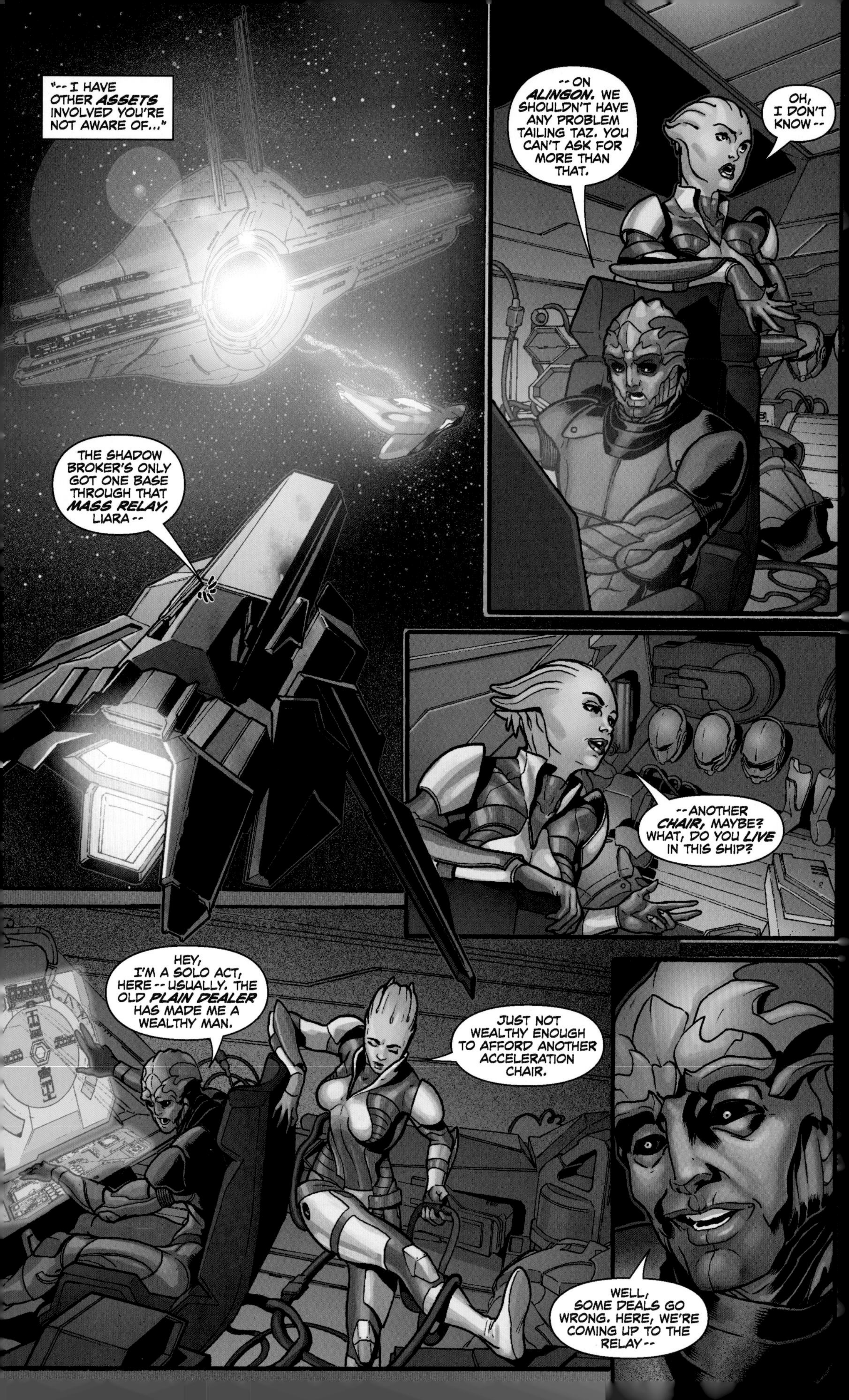
"-- I HAVE OTHER ASSETS INVOLVED YOU'RE NOT AWARE OF..."
THE SHADOW BROKER'S ONLY GOT ONE BASE THROUGH THAT MASS RELAY, LIARA --
-- ON ALINGON. WE SHOULDN'T HAVE ANY PROBLEM TAILING TAZ. YOU CAN'T ASK FOR MORE THAN THAT.
OH, I DON'T KNOW --
-- ANOTHER CHAIR, MAYBE? WHAT, DO YOU LIVE IN THIS SHIP?
HEY, I'M A SOLO ACT, HERE -- USUALLY. THE OLD PLAIN DEALER HAS MADE ME A WEALTHY MAN.
JUST NOT WEALTHY ENOUGH TO AFFORD ANOTHER ACCELERATION CHAIR.
WELL, SOME DEALS GO WRONG. HERE, WE'RE COMING UP TO THE RELAY --

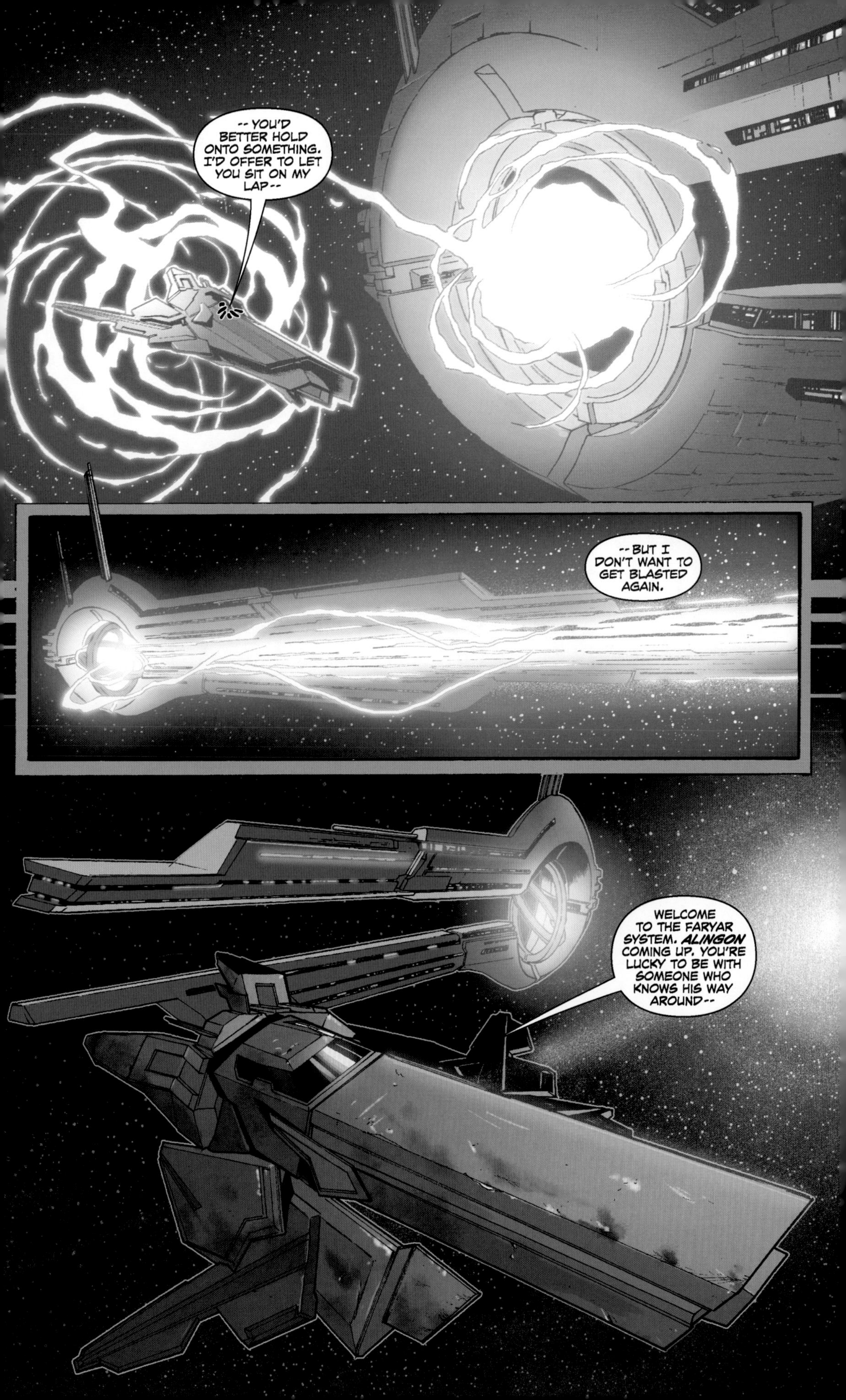
--YOU'D BETTER HOLD ONTO SOMETHING. I'D OFFER TO LET YOU SIT ON MY LAP--
--BUT I DON'T WANT TO GET BLASTED AGAIN.
WELCOME TO THE FARYAR SYSTEM. *ALINGON* COMING UP. YOU'RE LUCKY TO BE WITH SOMEONE WHO KNOWS HIS WAY AROUND--

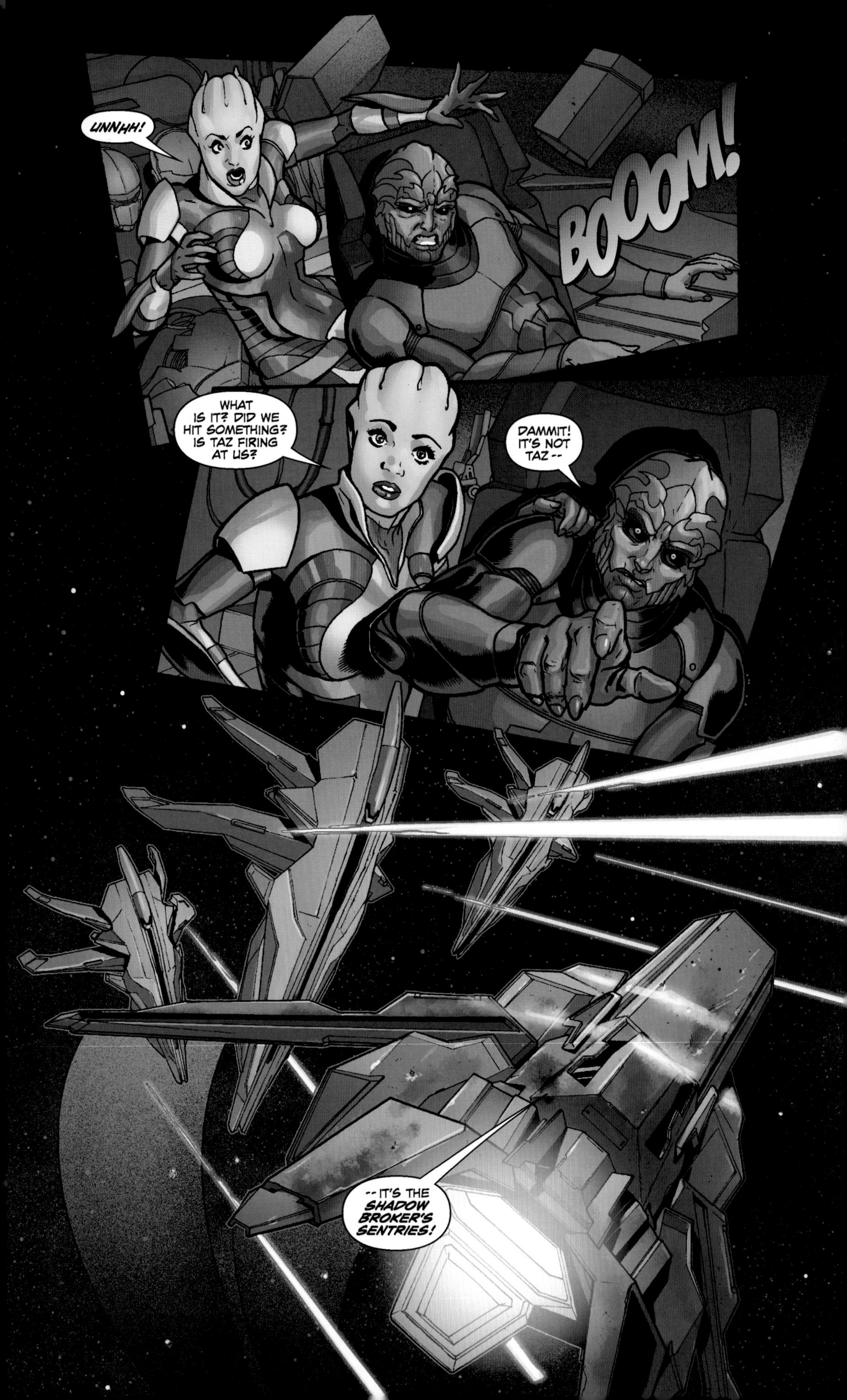
UNNHH!
BOOOM!
WHAT IS IT? DID WE HIT SOMETHING? IS TAZ FIRING AT US?
DAMMIT! IT'S NOT TAZ --
-- IT'S THE SHADOW BROKER'S SENTRIES!

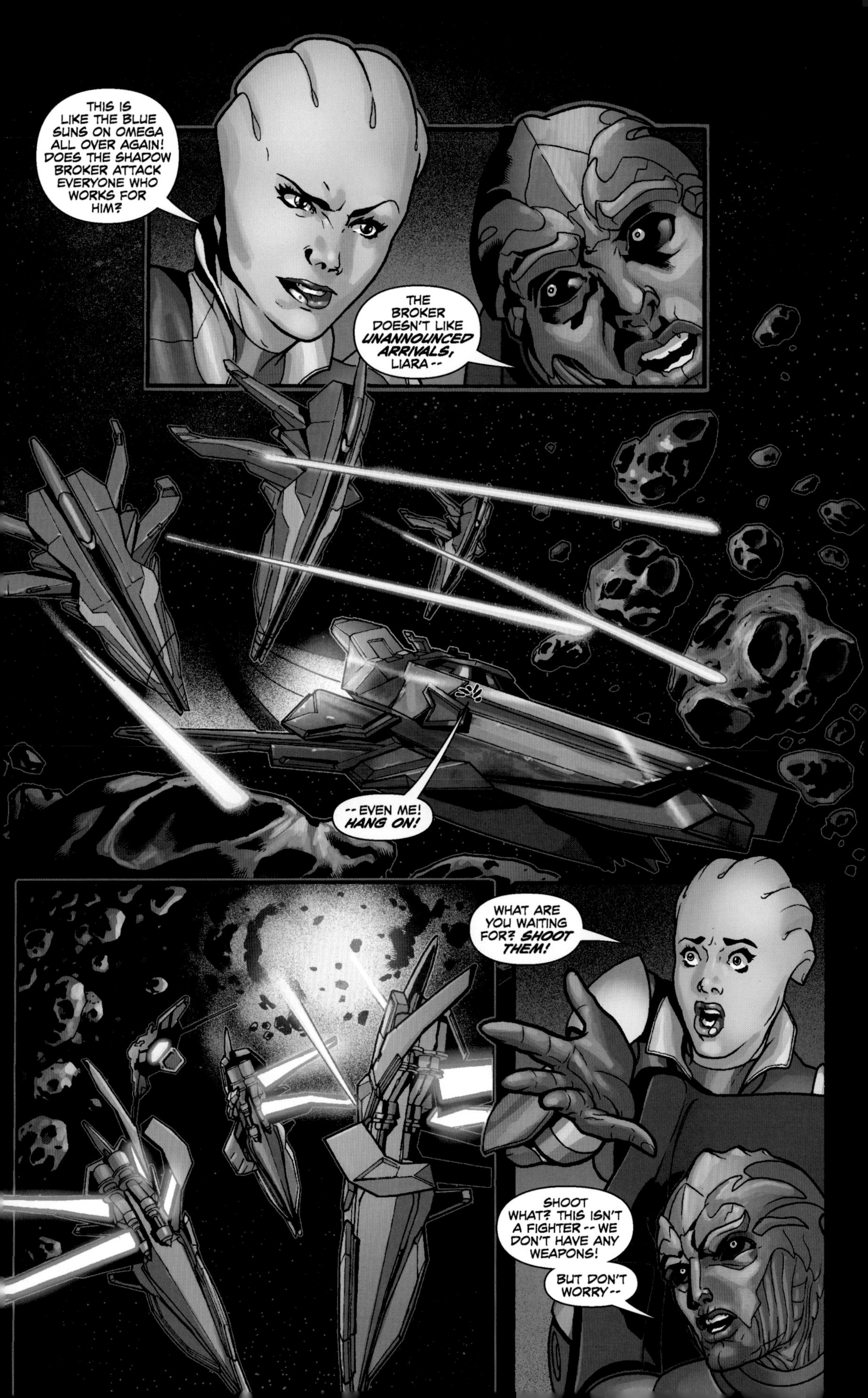
THIS IS LIKE THE BLUE SUNS ON OMEGA ALL OVER AGAIN! DOES THE SHADOW BROKER ATTACK EVERYONE WHO WORKS FOR HIM?
THE BROKER DOESN'T LIKE *UNANNOUNCED ARRIVALS,* LIARA --
-- EVEN ME! ***HANG ON!***
WHAT ARE YOU WAITING FOR? ***SHOOT THEM!***
SHOOT WHAT? THIS ISN'T A FIGHTER -- WE DON'T HAVE ANY WEAPONS!
BUT DON'T WORRY --

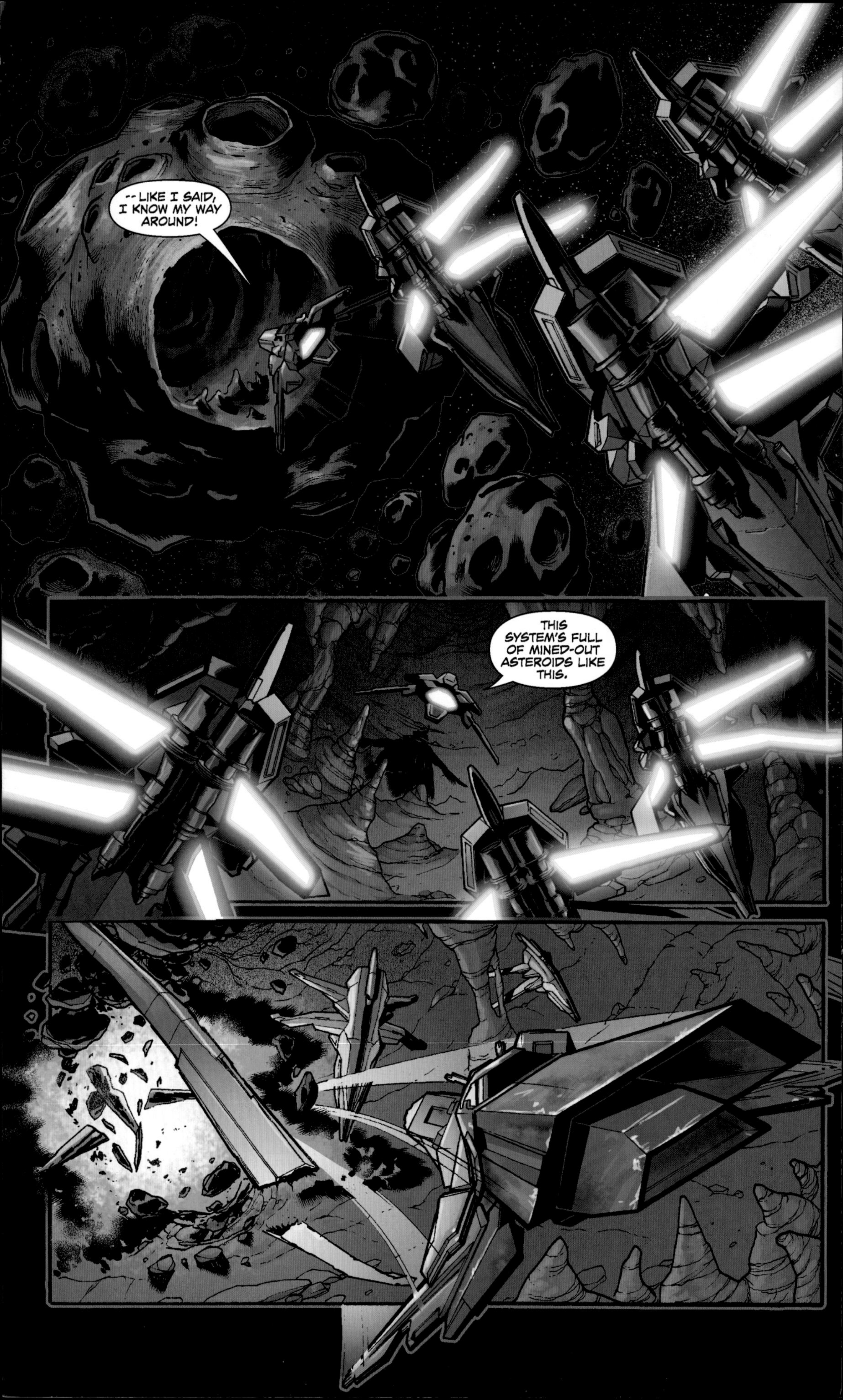
--LIKE I SAID, I KNOW MY WAY AROUND!
THIS SYSTEM'S FULL OF MINED-OUT ASTEROIDS LIKE THIS.

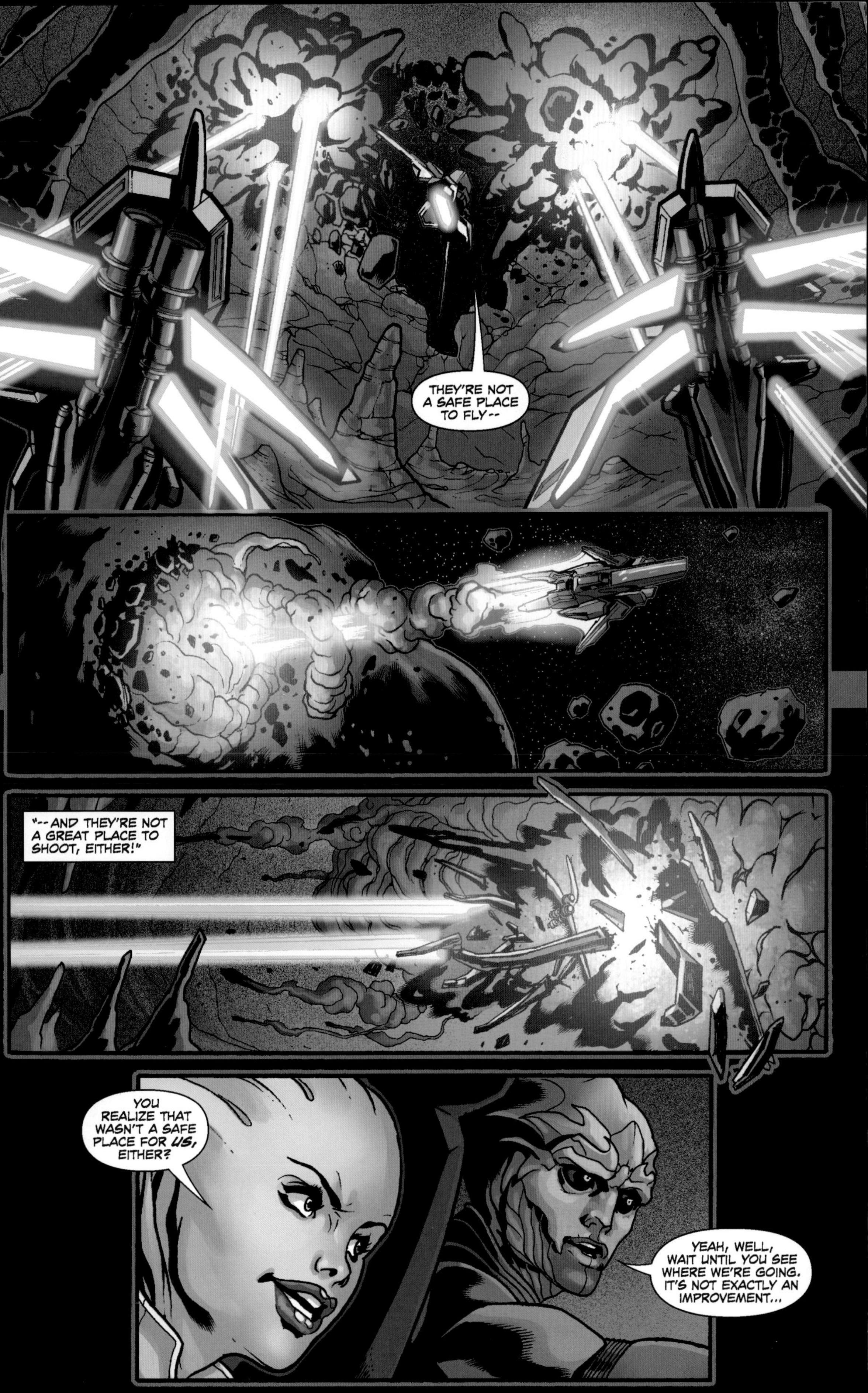
THEY'RE NOT A SAFE PLACE TO FLY--
"--AND THEY'RE NOT A GREAT PLACE TO SHOOT, EITHER!"
YOU REALIZE THAT WASN'T A SAFE PLACE FOR *US*, EITHER?
YEAH, WELL, WAIT UNTIL YOU SEE WHERE WE'RE GOING. IT'S NOT EXACTLY AN IMPROVEMENT...

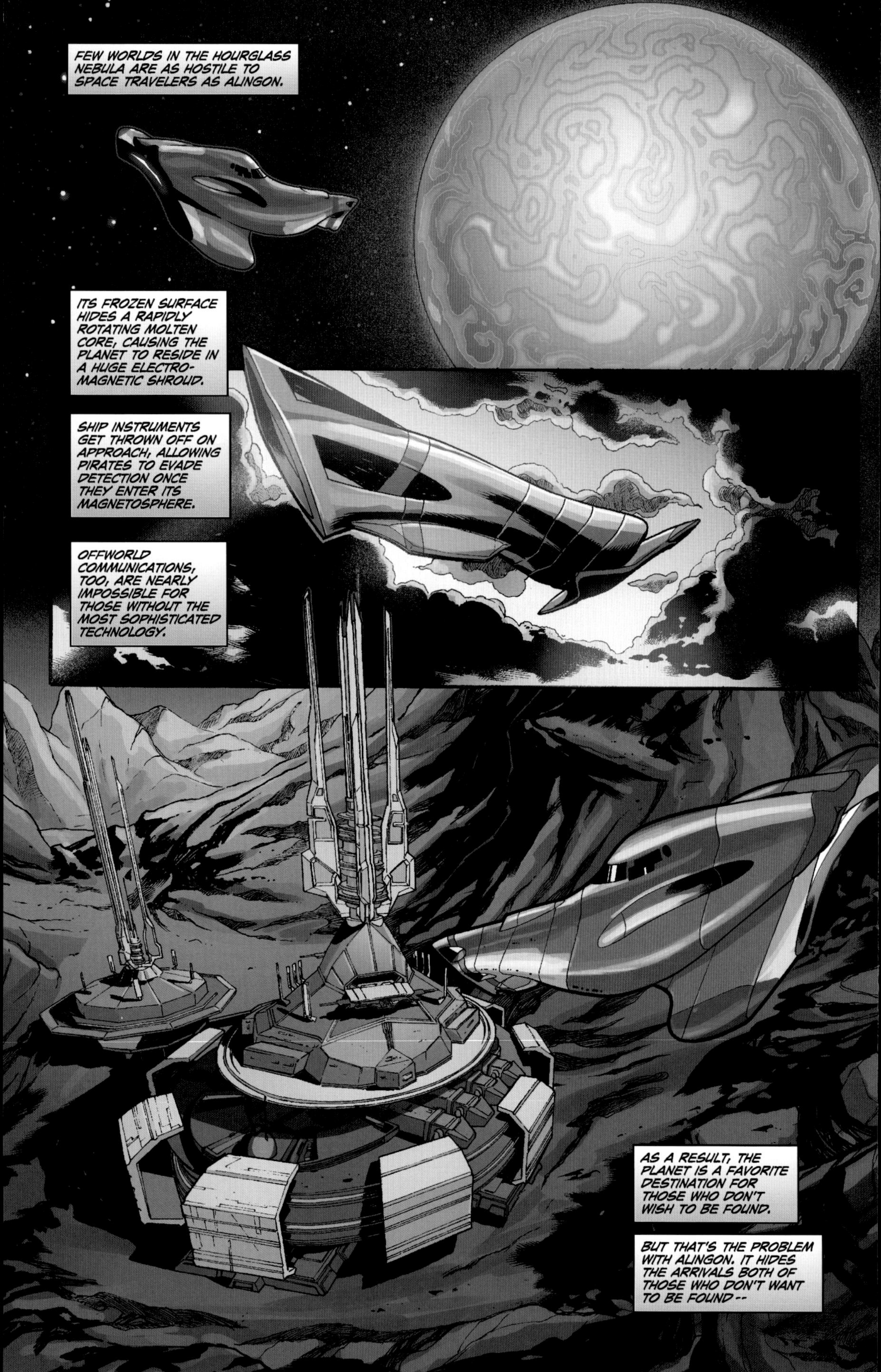
FEW WORLDS IN THE HOURGLASS NEBULA ARE AS HOSTILE TO SPACE TRAVELERS AS ALINGON.
ITS FROZEN SURFACE HIDES A RAPIDLY ROTATING MOLTEN CORE, CAUSING THE PLANET TO RESIDE IN A HUGE ELECTRO-MAGNETIC SHROUD.
SHIP INSTRUMENTS GET THROWN OFF ON APPROACH, ALLOWING PIRATES TO EVADE DETECTION ONCE THEY ENTER ITS MAGNETOSPHERE.
OFFWORLD COMMUNICATIONS, TOO, ARE NEARLY IMPOSSIBLE FOR THOSE WITHOUT THE MOST SOPHISTICATED TECHNOLOGY.
AS A RESULT, THE PLANET IS A FAVORITE DESTINATION FOR THOSE WHO DON'T WISH TO BE FOUND.
BUT THAT'S THE PROBLEM WITH ALINGON. IT HIDES THE ARRIVALS BOTH OF THOSE WHO DON'T WANT TO BE FOUND --

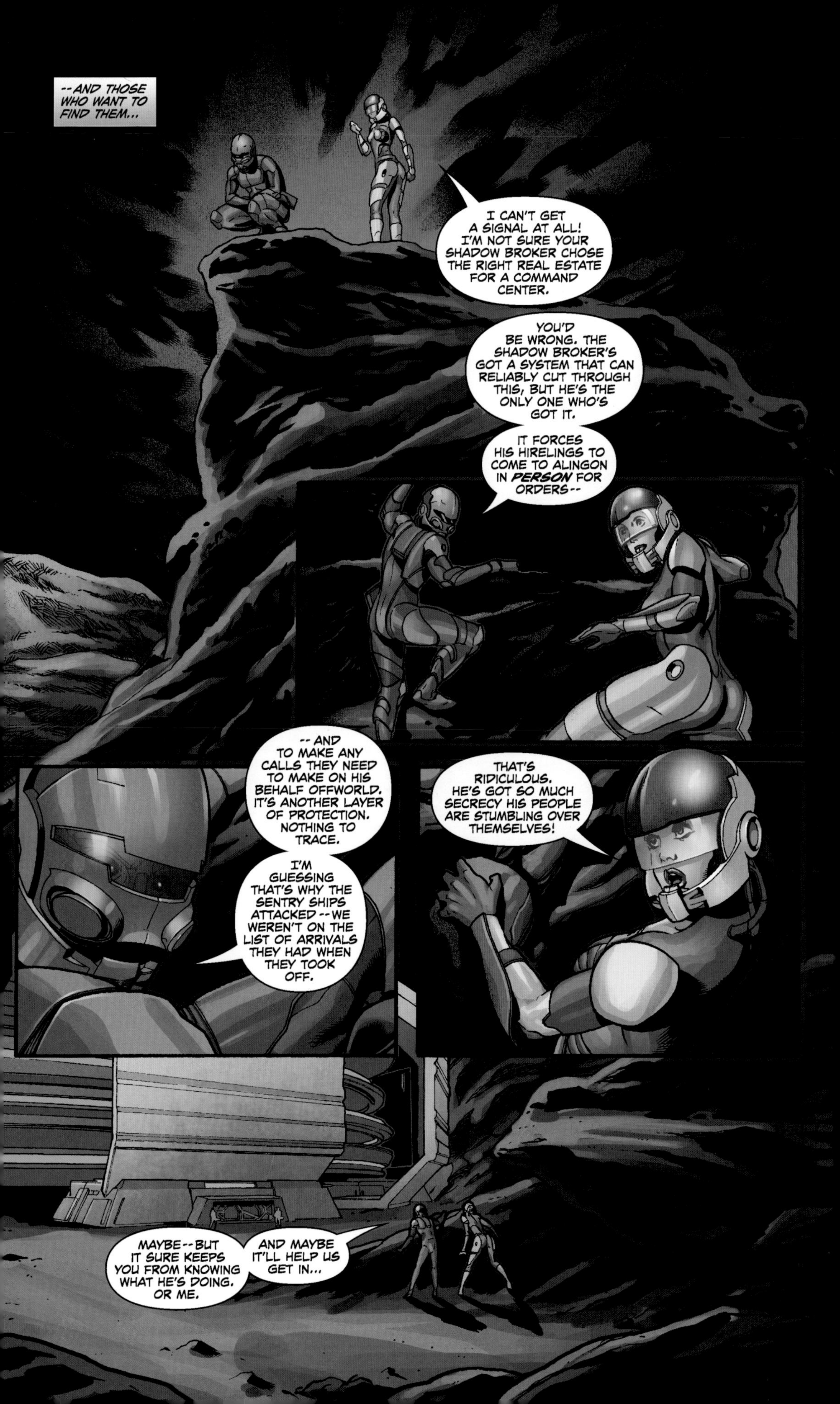
--AND THOSE WHO WANT TO FIND THEM...
I CAN'T GET A SIGNAL AT ALL! I'M NOT SURE YOUR SHADOW BROKER CHOSE THE RIGHT REAL ESTATE FOR A COMMAND CENTER.
YOU'D BE WRONG. THE SHADOW BROKER'S GOT A SYSTEM THAT CAN RELIABLY CUT THROUGH THIS, BUT HE'S THE ONLY ONE WHO'S GOT IT.
IT FORCES HIS HIRELINGS TO COME TO ALINGON IN *PERSON* FOR ORDERS--
--AND TO MAKE ANY CALLS THEY NEED TO MAKE ON HIS BEHALF OFFWORLD. IT'S ANOTHER LAYER OF PROTECTION. NOTHING TO TRACE.
I'M GUESSING THAT'S WHY THE SENTRY SHIPS ATTACKED--WE WEREN'T ON THE LIST OF ARRIVALS THEY HAD WHEN THEY TOOK OFF.
THAT'S RIDICULOUS. HE'S GOT SO MUCH SECRECY HIS PEOPLE ARE STUMBLING OVER THEMSELVES!
MAYBE--BUT IT SURE KEEPS YOU FROM KNOWING WHAT HE'S DOING. OR ME.
AND MAYBE IT'LL HELP US GET IN...

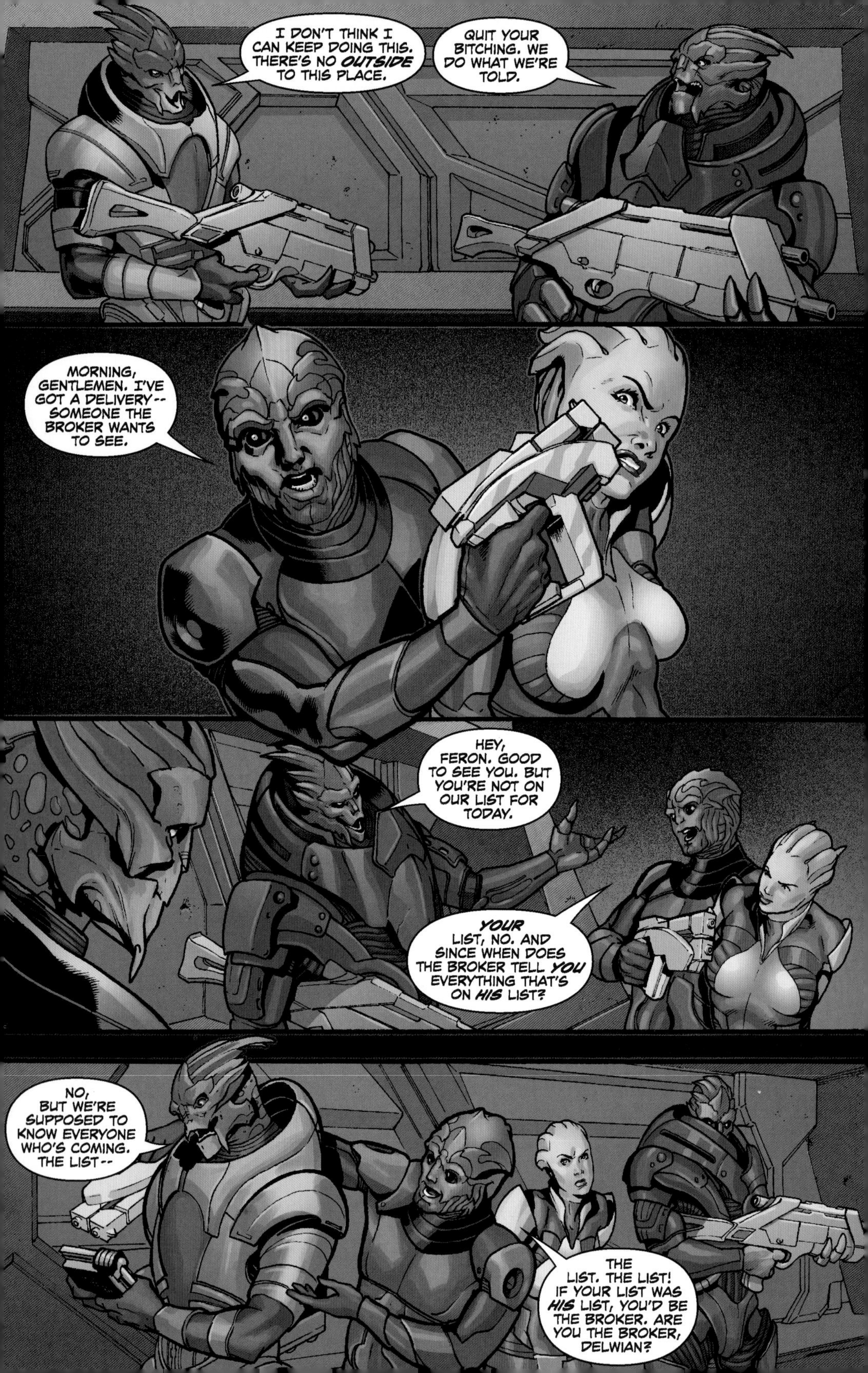
I DON'T THINK I CAN KEEP DOING THIS. THERE'S NO *OUTSIDE* TO THIS PLACE.
QUIT YOUR BITCHING. WE DO WHAT WE'RE TOLD.
MORNING, GENTLEMEN. I'VE GOT A DELIVERY-- SOMEONE THE BROKER WANTS TO SEE.
HEY, FERON. GOOD TO SEE YOU. BUT YOU'RE NOT ON OUR LIST FOR TODAY.
YOUR LIST, NO. AND SINCE WHEN DOES THE BROKER TELL *YOU* EVERYTHING THAT'S ON *HIS* LIST?
NO, BUT WE'RE SUPPOSED TO KNOW EVERYONE WHO'S COMING. THE LIST--
THE LIST. THE LIST! IF YOUR LIST WAS *HIS* LIST, YOU'D BE THE BROKER. ARE YOU THE BROKER, DELWIAN?

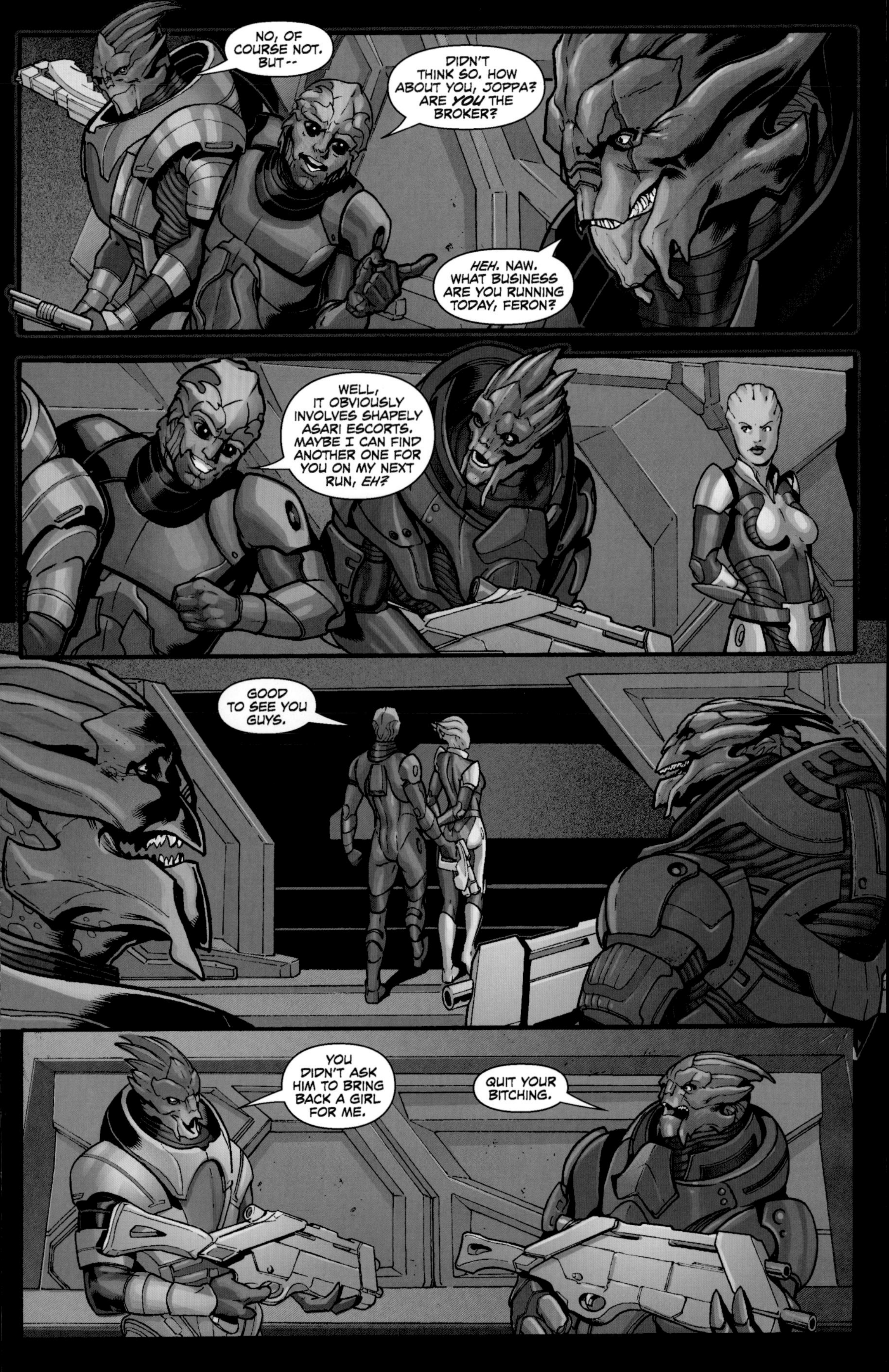
NO, OF COURSE NOT. BUT--
DIDN'T THINK SO. HOW ABOUT YOU, JOPPA? ARE *YOU* THE BROKER?
HEH. NAW. WHAT BUSINESS ARE YOU RUNNING TODAY, FERON?
WELL, IT OBVIOUSLY INVOLVES SHAPELY ASARI ESCORTS. MAYBE I CAN FIND ANOTHER ONE FOR YOU ON MY NEXT RUN, *EH?*
GOOD TO SEE YOU GUYS.
YOU DIDN'T ASK HIM TO BRING BACK A GIRL FOR ME.
QUIT YOUR BITCHING.

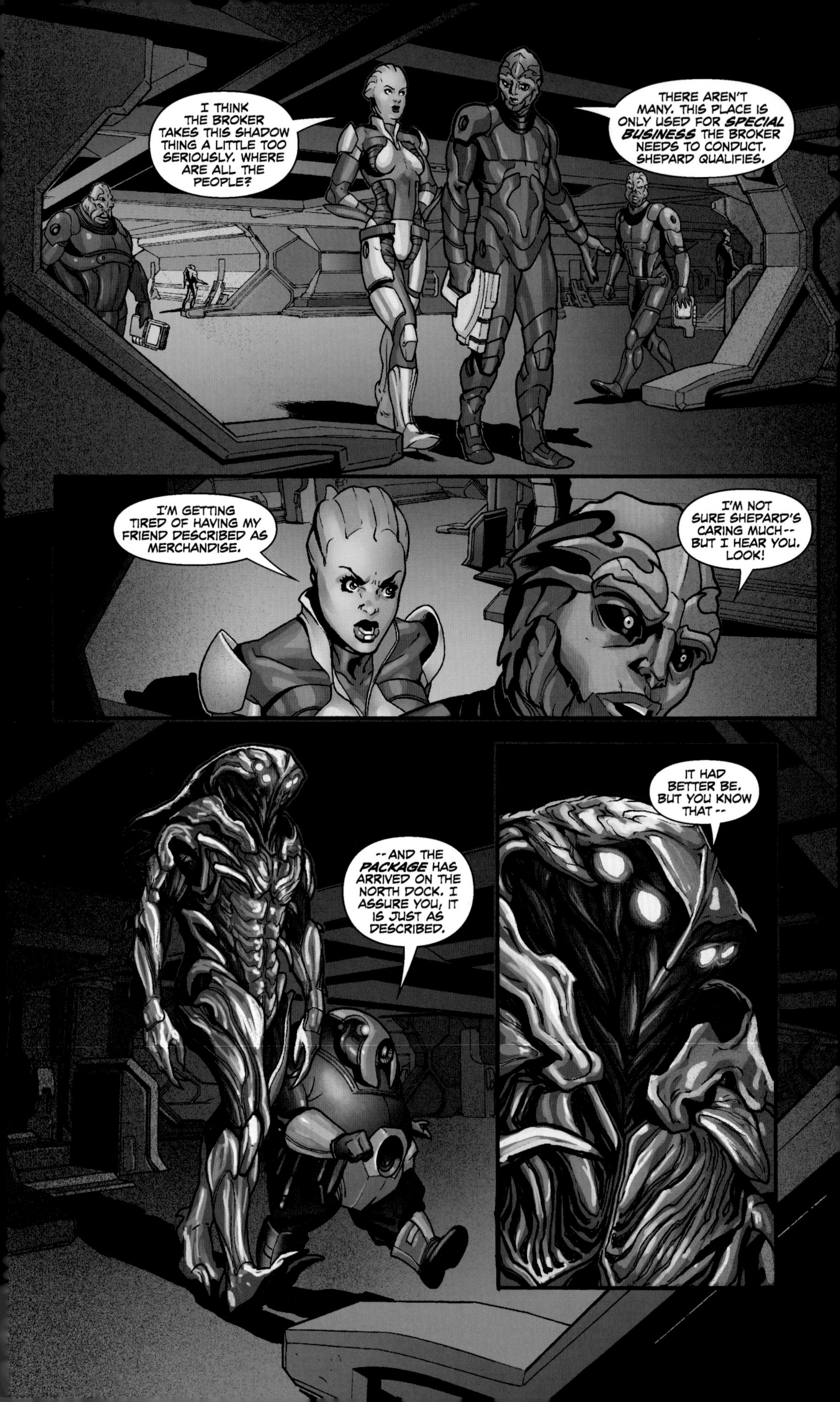
I THINK THE BROKER TAKES THIS SHADOW THING A LITTLE TOO SERIOUSLY. WHERE ARE ALL THE PEOPLE?
THERE AREN'T MANY. THIS PLACE IS ONLY USED FOR *SPECIAL BUSINESS* THE BROKER NEEDS TO CONDUCT. SHEPARD QUALIFIES.
I'M GETTING TIRED OF HAVING MY FRIEND DESCRIBED AS MERCHANDISE.
I'M NOT SURE SHEPARD'S CARING MUCH-- BUT I HEAR YOU. LOOK!
--AND THE *PACKAGE* HAS ARRIVED ON THE NORTH DOCK. I ASSURE YOU, IT IS JUST AS DESCRIBED.
IT HAD BETTER BE. BUT YOU KNOW THAT--

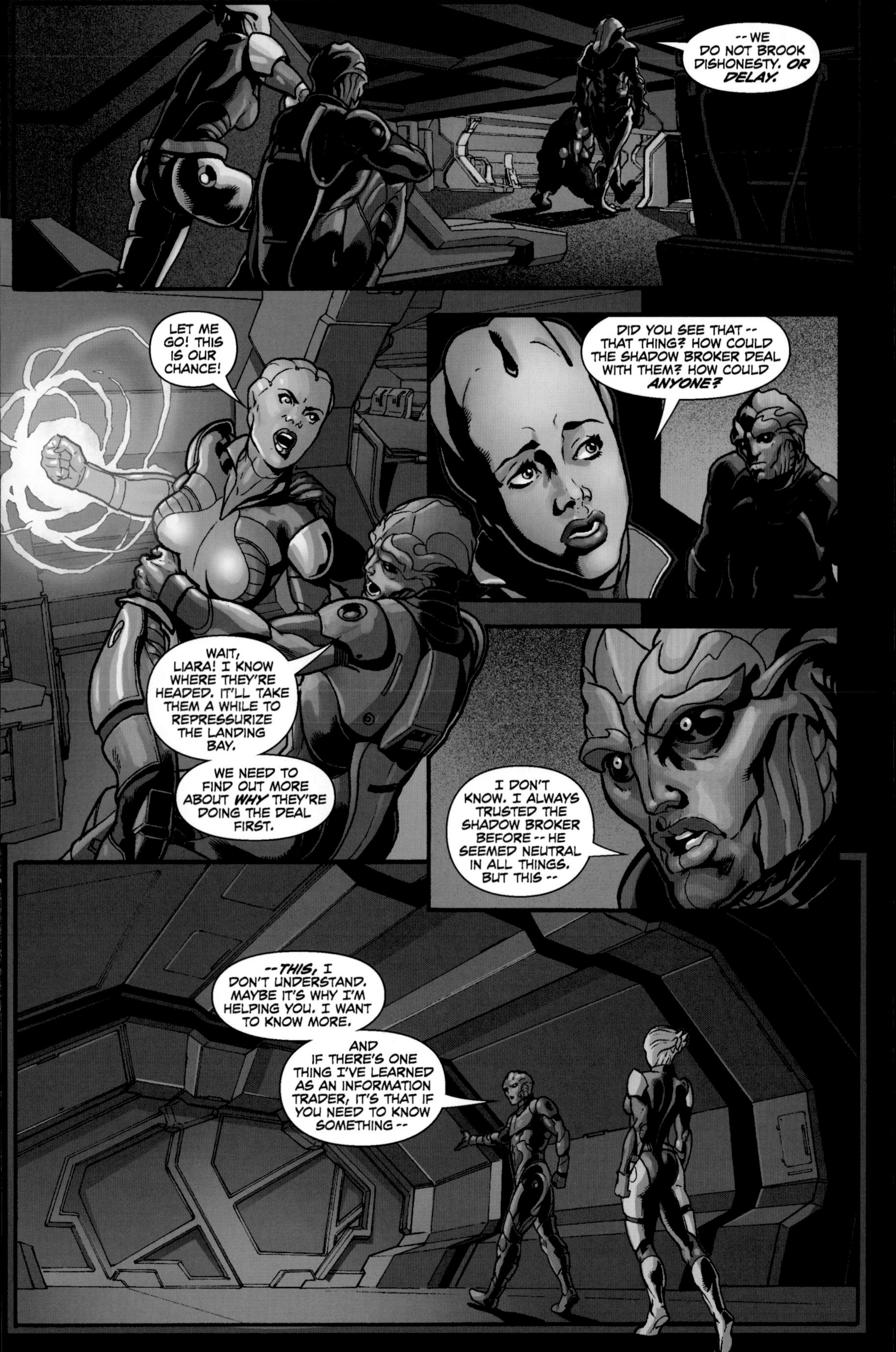
-- WE DO NOT BROOK DISHONESTY. *OR DELAY.*
LET ME GO! THIS IS OUR CHANCE!
WAIT, LIARA! I KNOW WHERE THEY'RE HEADED. IT'LL TAKE THEM A WHILE TO REPRESSURIZE THE LANDING BAY.
WE NEED TO FIND OUT MORE ABOUT *WHY* THEY'RE DOING THE DEAL FIRST.
DID YOU SEE THAT -- THAT THING? HOW COULD THE SHADOW BROKER DEAL WITH THEM? HOW COULD *ANYONE?*
I DON'T KNOW. I ALWAYS TRUSTED THE SHADOW BROKER BEFORE -- HE SEEMED NEUTRAL IN ALL THINGS. BUT THIS --
-- *THIS,* I DON'T UNDERSTAND. MAYBE IT'S WHY I'M HELPING YOU. I WANT TO KNOW MORE.
AND IF THERE'S ONE THING I'VE LEARNED AS AN INFORMATION TRADER, IT'S THAT IF YOU NEED TO KNOW SOMETHING --

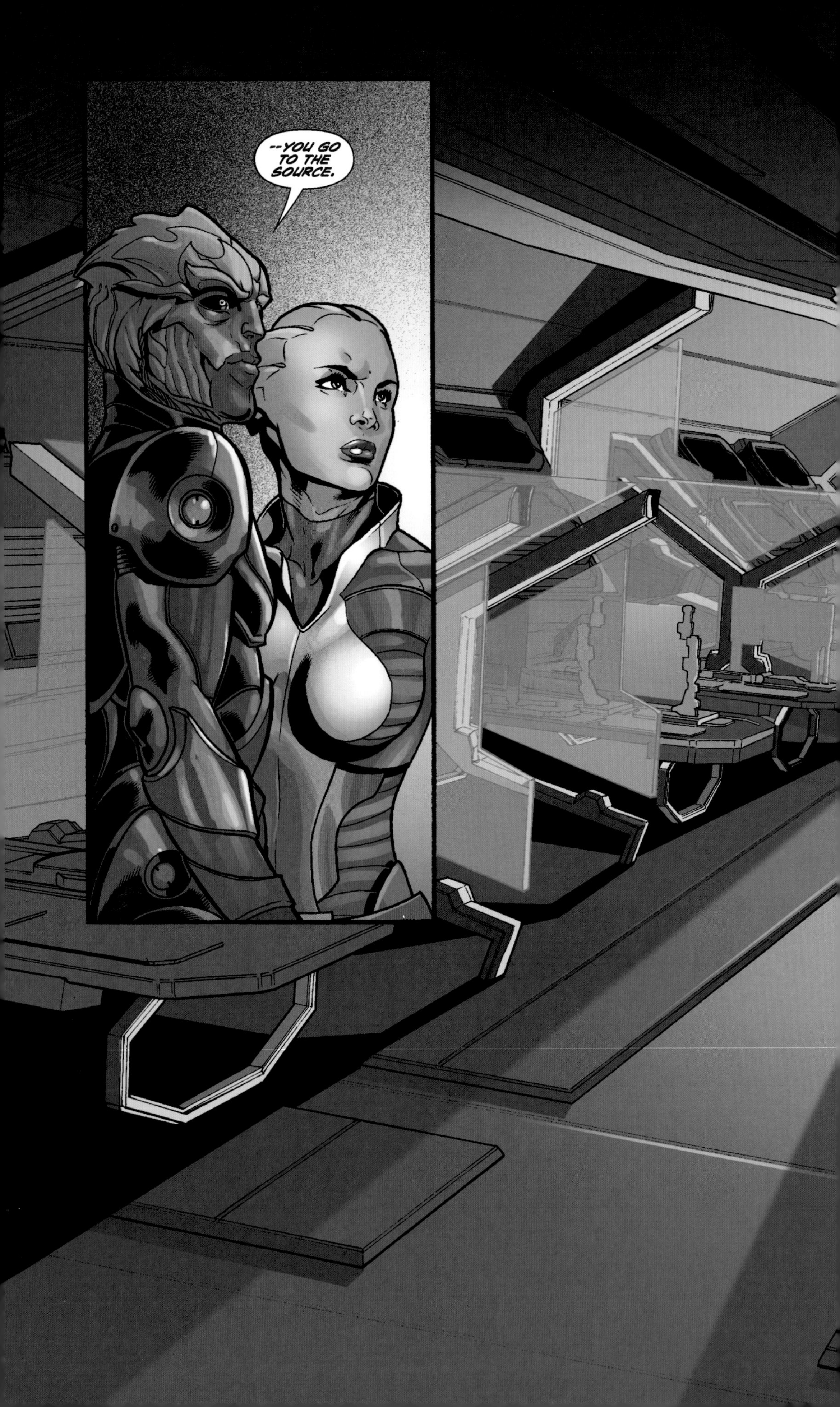
--YOU GO TO THE SOURCE.

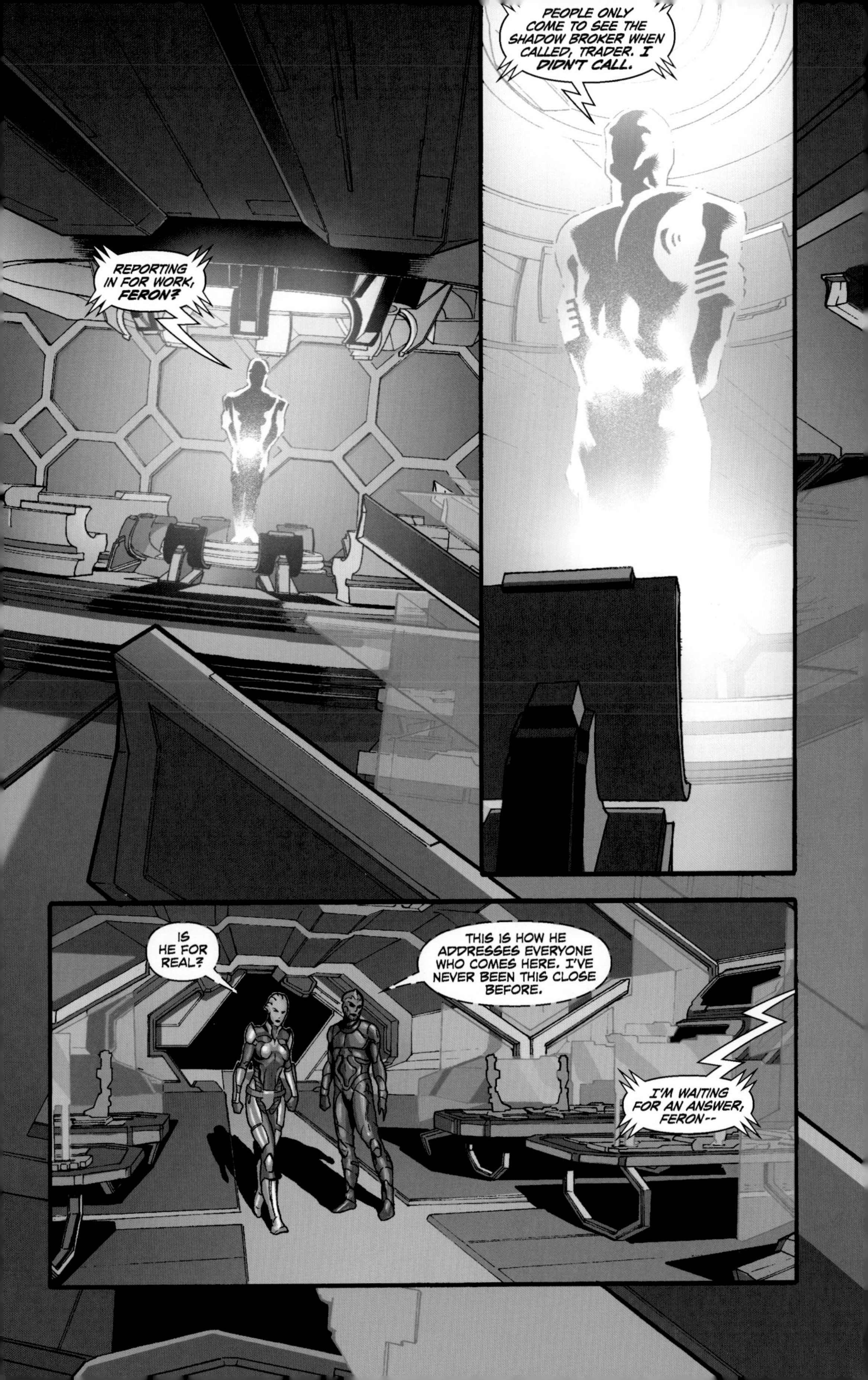
REPORTING IN FOR WORK, FERON?
PEOPLE ONLY COME TO SEE THE SHADOW BROKER WHEN CALLED, TRADER. I DIDN'T CALL.
IS HE FOR REAL?
THIS IS HOW HE ADDRESSES EVERYONE WHO COMES HERE. I'VE NEVER BEEN THIS CLOSE BEFORE.
I'M WAITING FOR AN ANSWER, FERON--

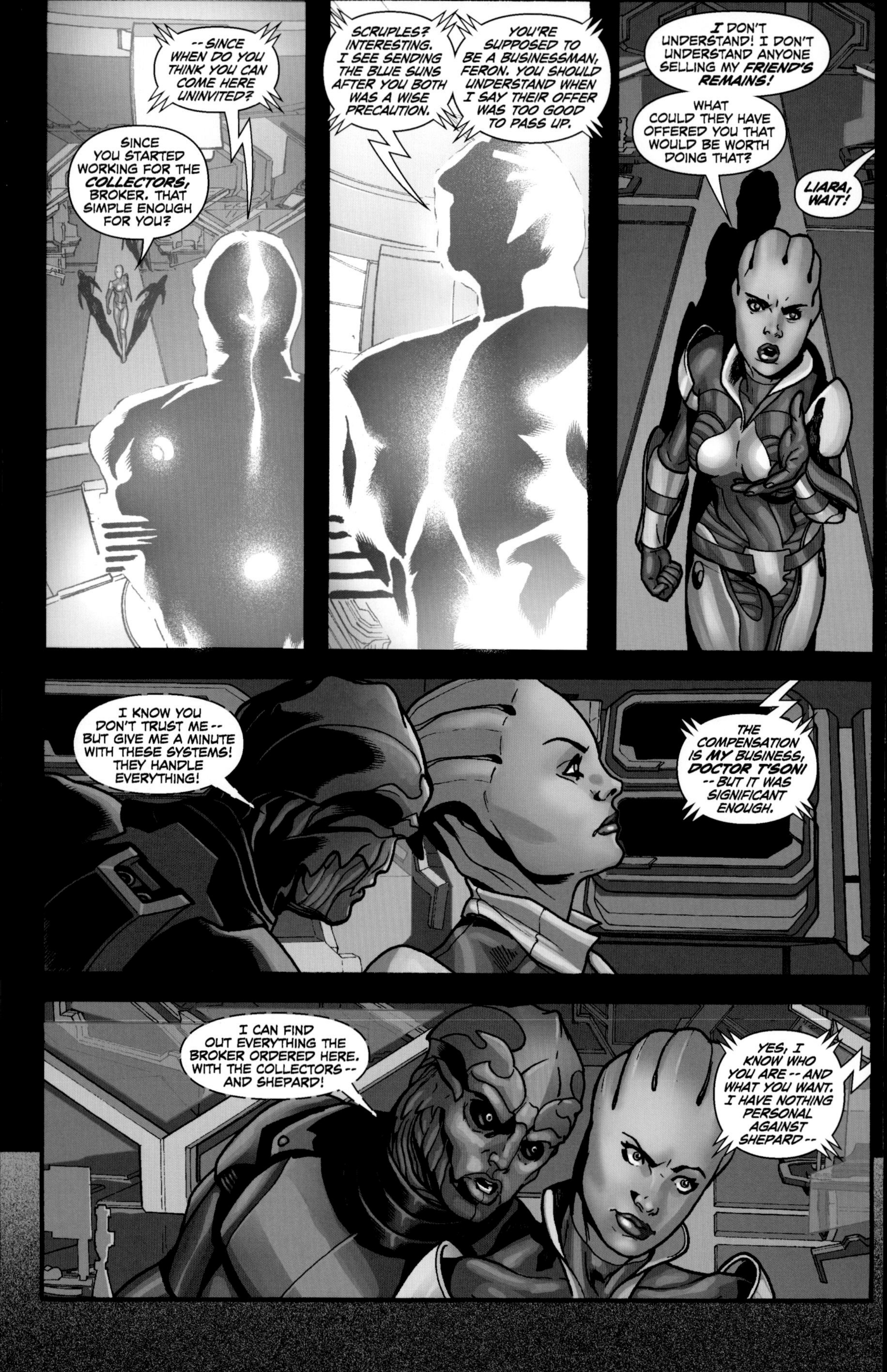

-- SINCE WHEN DO YOU THINK YOU CAN COME HERE UNINVITED?
SINCE YOU STARTED WORKING FOR THE COLLECTORS, BROKER. THAT SIMPLE ENOUGH FOR YOU?
SCRUPLES? INTERESTING. I SEE SENDING THE BLUE SUNS AFTER YOU BOTH WAS A WISE PRECAUTION.
YOU'RE SUPPOSED TO BE A BUSINESSMAN, FERON. YOU SHOULD UNDERSTAND WHEN I SAY THEIR OFFER WAS TOO GOOD TO PASS UP.
I DON'T UNDERSTAND! I DON'T UNDERSTAND ANYONE SELLING MY FRIEND'S REMAINS!
WHAT COULD THEY HAVE OFFERED YOU THAT WOULD BE WORTH DOING THAT?
LIARA, WAIT!
I KNOW YOU DON'T TRUST ME -- BUT GIVE ME A MINUTE WITH THESE SYSTEMS! THEY HANDLE EVERYTHING!
THE COMPENSATION IS MY BUSINESS, DOCTOR T'SONI -- BUT IT WAS SIGNIFICANT ENOUGH.
I CAN FIND OUT EVERYTHING THE BROKER ORDERED HERE. WITH THE COLLECTORS -- AND SHEPARD!
YES, I KNOW WHO YOU ARE -- AND WHAT YOU WANT. I HAVE NOTHING PERSONAL AGAINST SHEPARD --

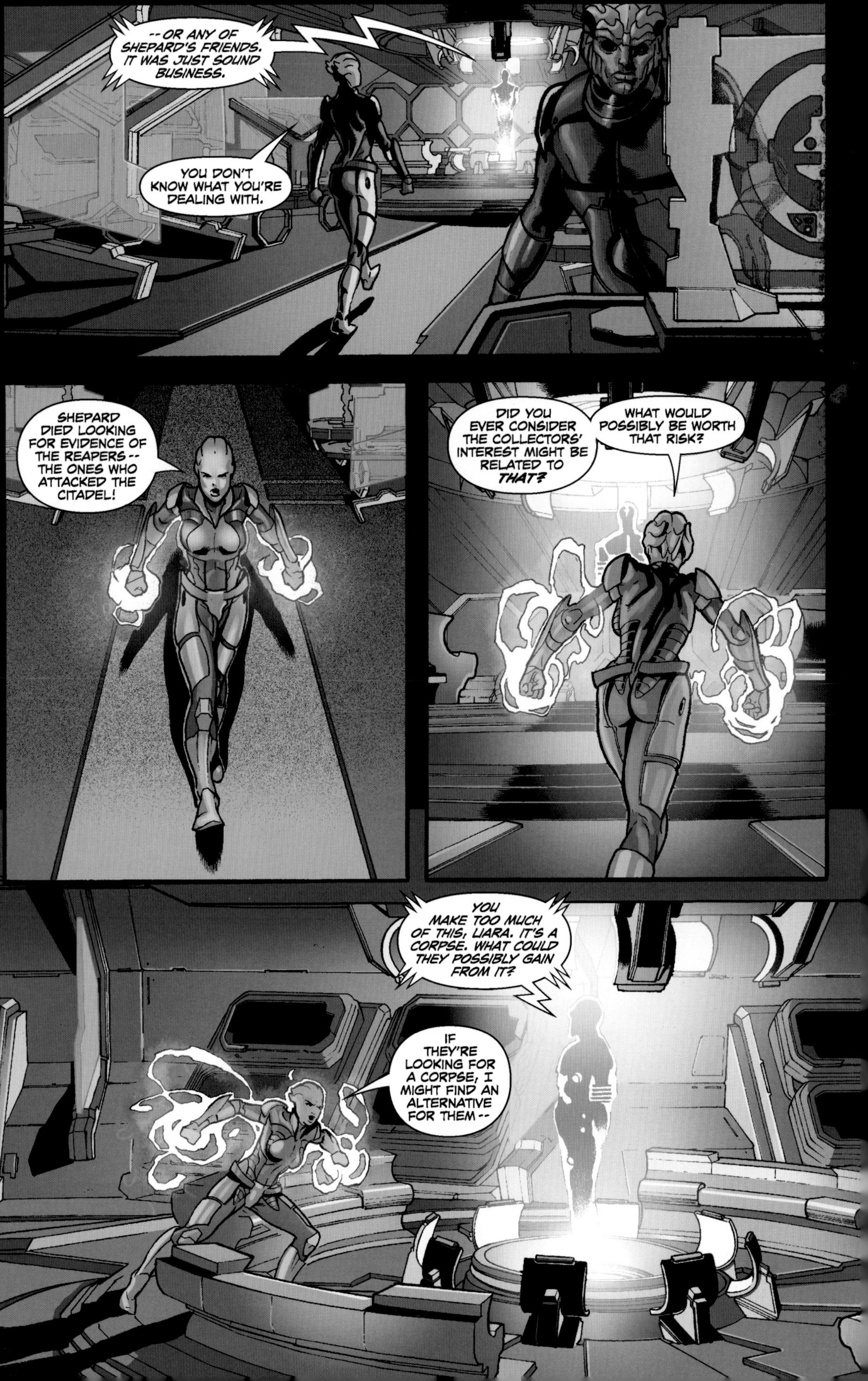
--OR ANY OF SHEPARD'S FRIENDS. IT WAS JUST SOUND BUSINESS.
YOU DON'T KNOW WHAT YOU'RE DEALING WITH.
SHEPARD DIED LOOKING FOR EVIDENCE OF THE REAPERS-- THE ONES WHO ATTACKED THE CITADEL!
DID YOU EVER CONSIDER THE COLLECTORS' INTEREST MIGHT BE RELATED TO *THAT?*
WHAT WOULD POSSIBLY BE WORTH THAT RISK?
YOU MAKE TOO MUCH OF THIS, LIARA. IT'S A CORPSE. WHAT COULD THEY POSSIBLY GAIN FROM IT?
IF THEY'RE LOOKING FOR A CORPSE, I MIGHT FIND AN ALTERNATIVE FOR THEM--

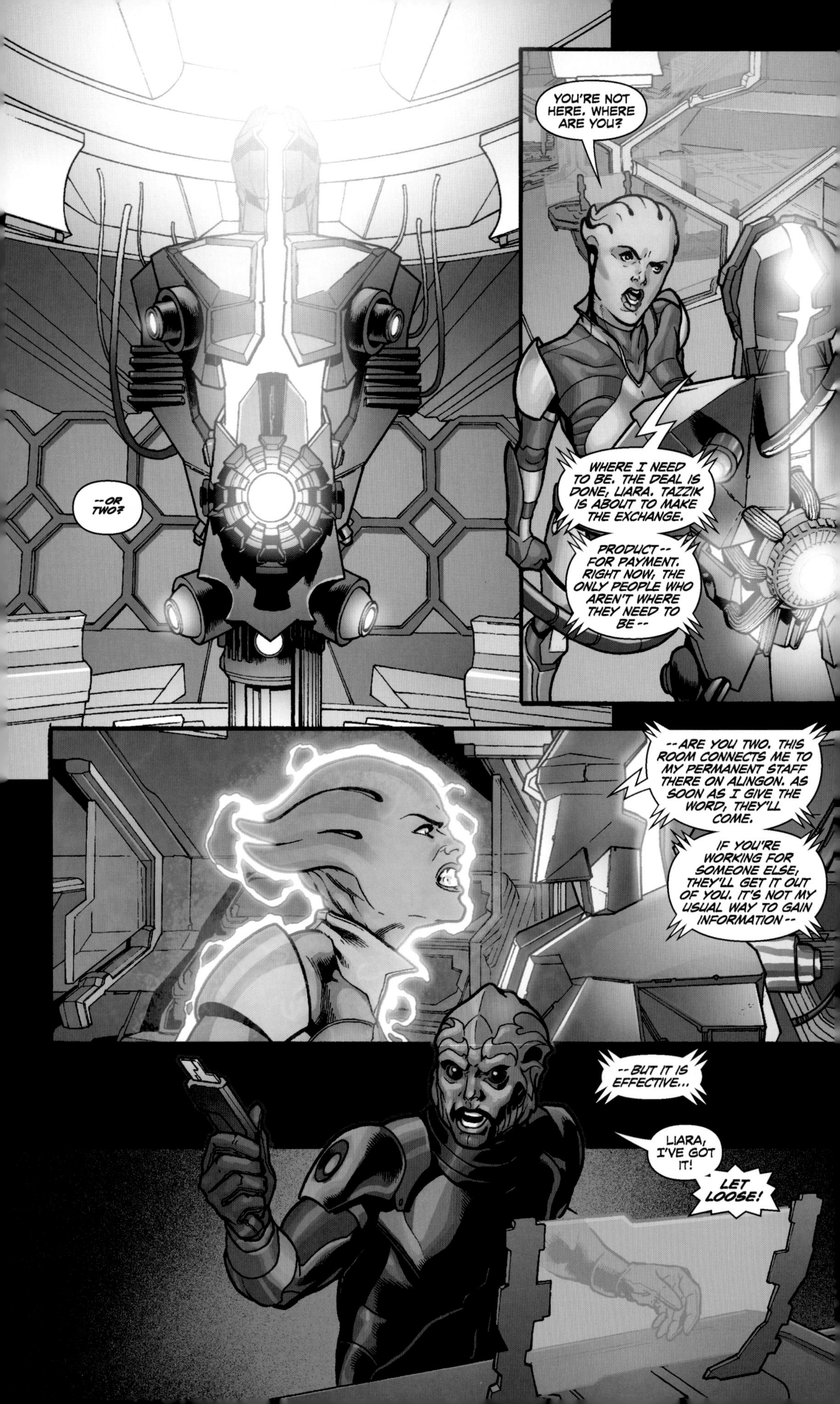
--OR TWO?
YOU'RE NOT HERE. WHERE ARE YOU?
WHERE I NEED TO BE. THE DEAL IS DONE, LIARA. TAZZIK IS ABOUT TO MAKE THE EXCHANGE.
PRODUCT-- FOR PAYMENT. RIGHT NOW, THE ONLY PEOPLE WHO AREN'T WHERE THEY NEED TO BE--
--ARE YOU TWO. THIS ROOM CONNECTS ME TO MY PERMANENT STAFF THERE ON ALINGON. AS SOON AS I GIVE THE WORD, THEY'LL COME.
IF YOU'RE WORKING FOR SOMEONE ELSE, THEY'LL GET IT OUT OF YOU. IT'S NOT MY USUAL WAY TO GAIN INFORMATION--
--BUT IT IS EFFECTIVE...
LIARA, I'VE GOT IT!
LET LOOSE!

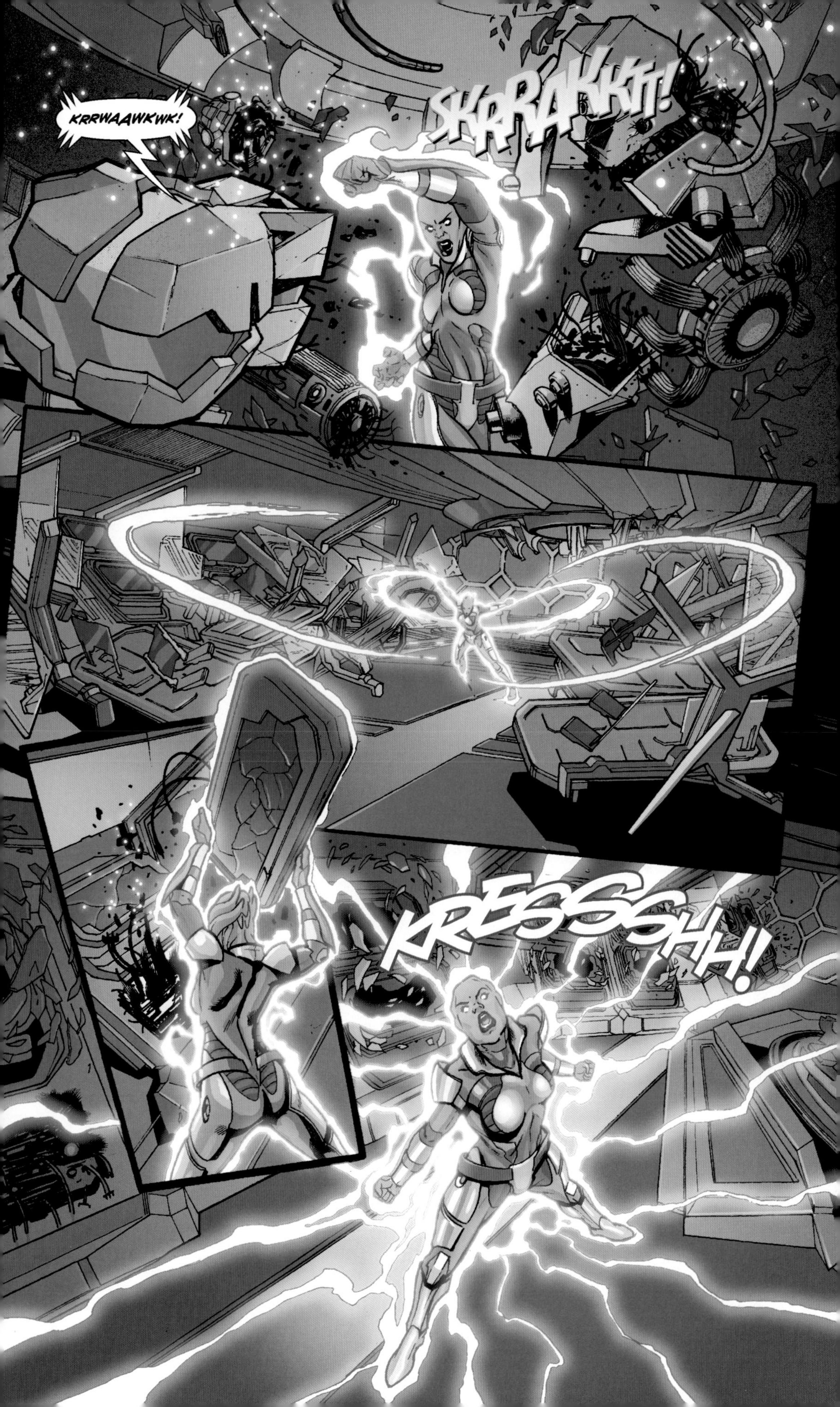
KRRWAAWKWK!
SKRRAKKKT!
KRESSSHH!

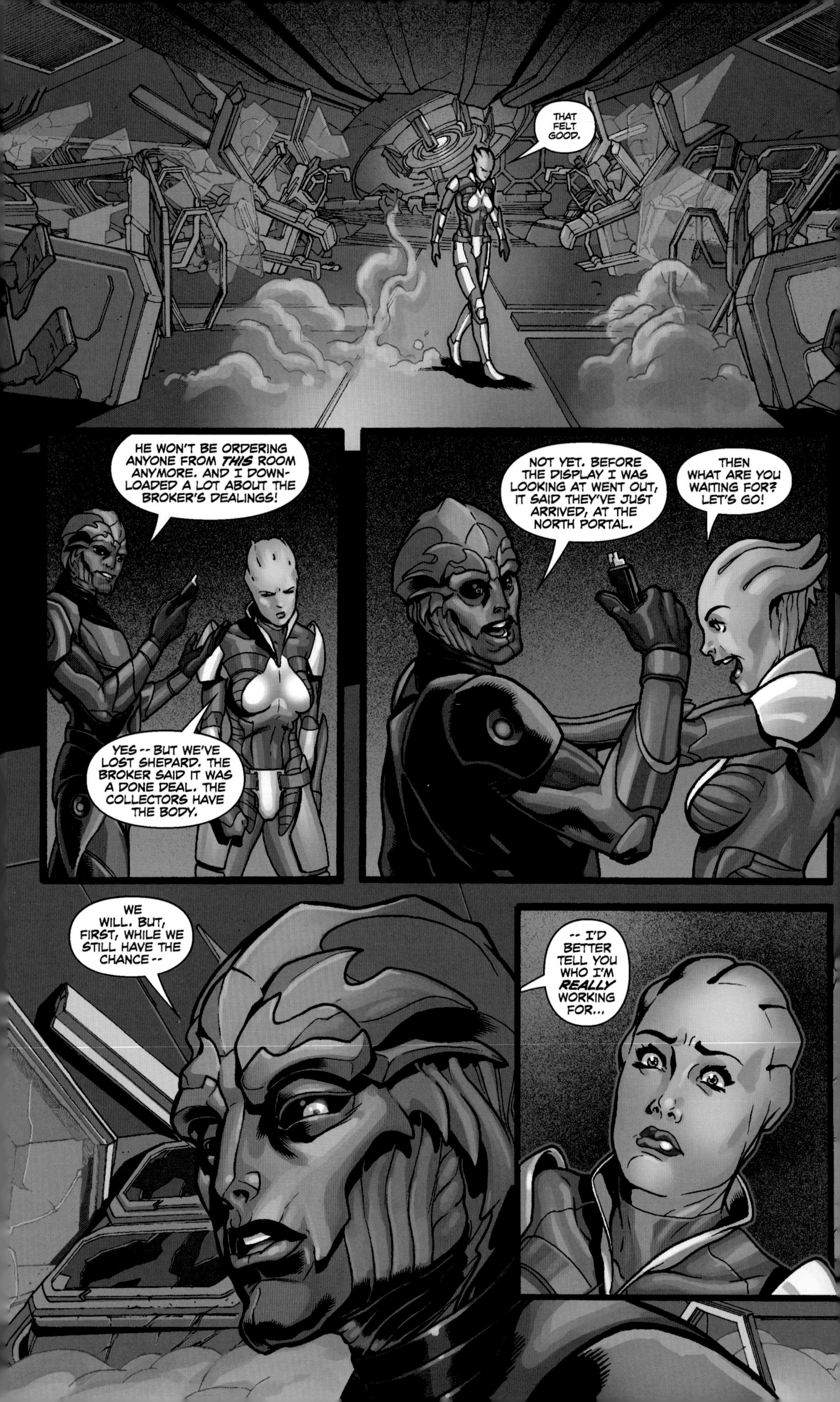

THAT FELT GOOD.
HE WON'T BE ORDERING ANYONE FROM THIS ROOM ANYMORE. AND I DOWN-LOADED A LOT ABOUT THE BROKER'S DEALINGS!
YES -- BUT WE'VE LOST SHEPARD. THE BROKER SAID IT WAS A DONE DEAL. THE COLLECTORS HAVE THE BODY.
NOT YET. BEFORE THE DISPLAY I WAS LOOKING AT WENT OUT, IT SAID THEY'VE JUST ARRIVED, AT THE NORTH PORTAL.
THEN WHAT ARE YOU WAITING FOR? LET'S GO!
WE WILL. BUT, FIRST, WHILE WE STILL HAVE THE CHANCE --
-- I'D BETTER TELL YOU WHO I'M REALLY WORKING FOR...

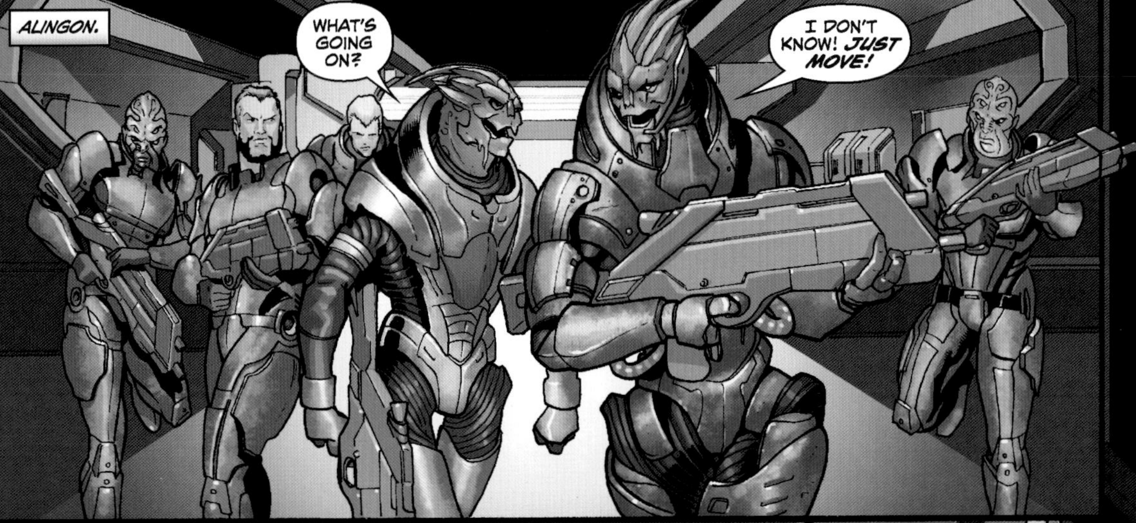
ALINGON.
WHAT'S GOING ON?
I DON'T KNOW! JUST MOVE!

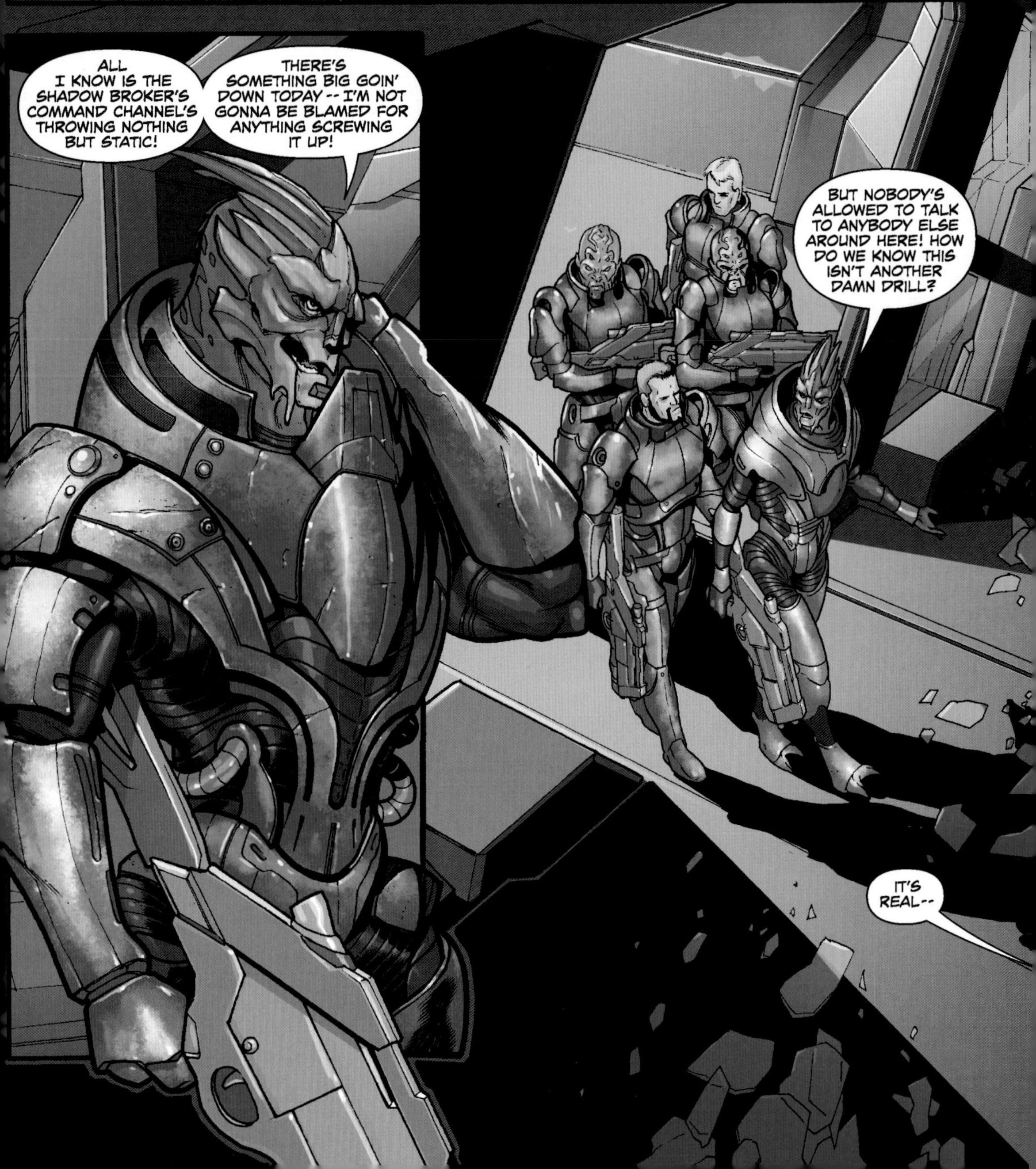
ALL I KNOW IS THE SHADOW BROKER'S COMMAND CHANNEL'S THROWING NOTHING BUT STATIC!
THERE'S SOMETHING BIG GOIN' DOWN TODAY -- I'M NOT GONNA BE BLAMED FOR ANYTHING SCREWING IT UP!
BUT NOBODY'S ALLOWED TO TALK TO ANYBODY ELSE AROUND HERE! HOW DO WE KNOW THIS ISN'T ANOTHER DAMN DRILL?
IT'S REAL--

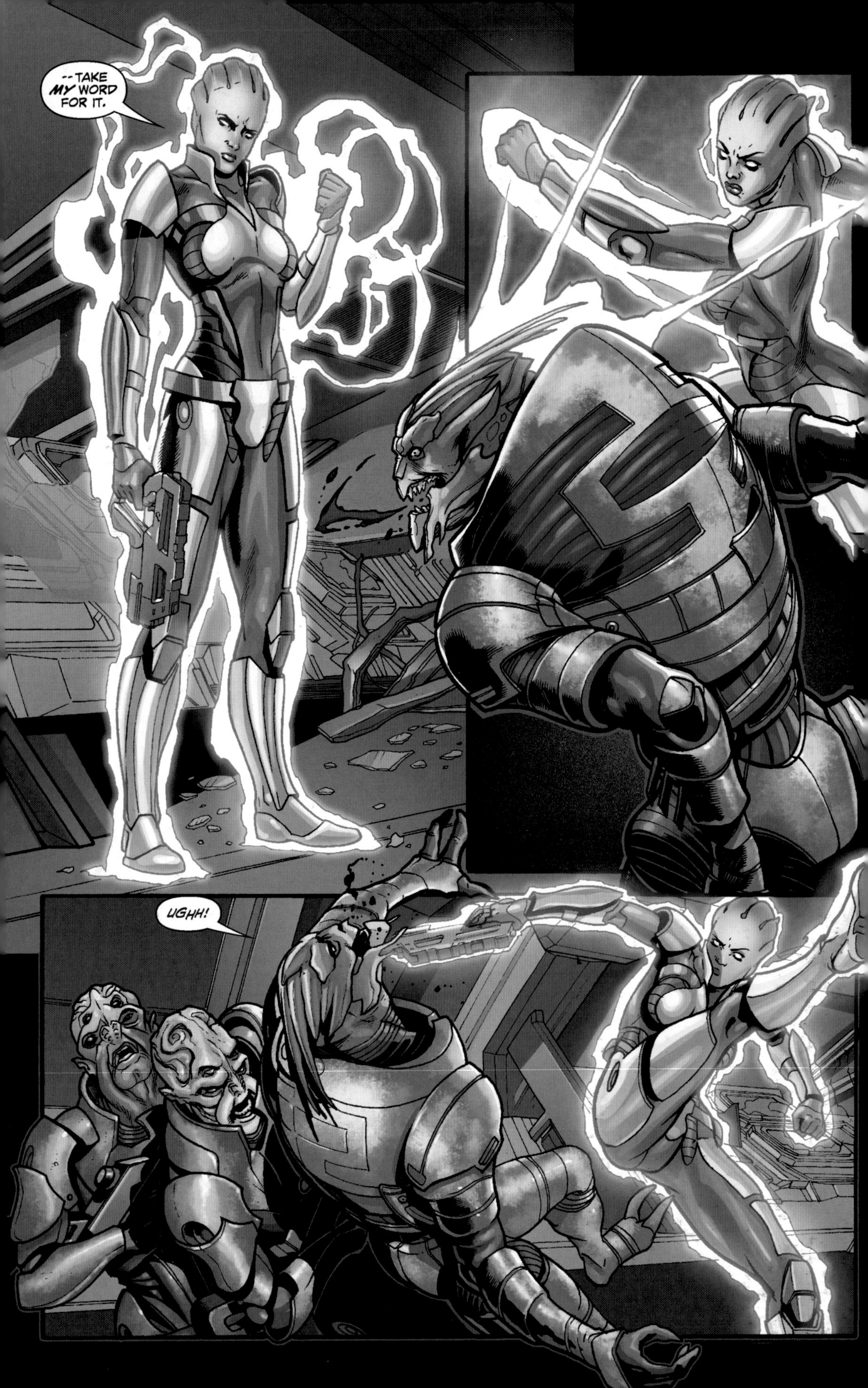
--TAKE *MY* WORD FOR IT.
UGHH!

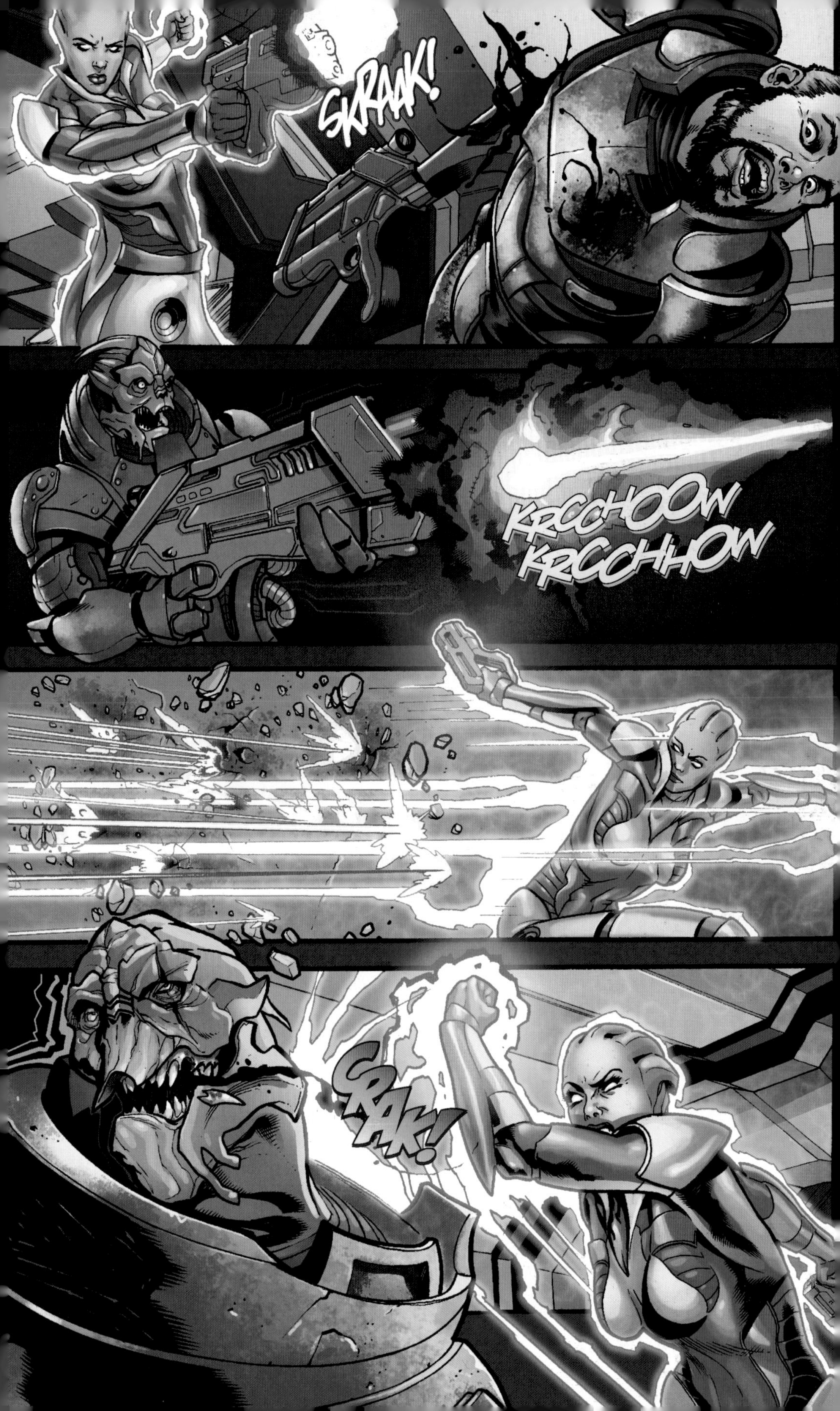
SKRAAK!
KRCCHOOOW
KRCCHHOW
CRAAK!

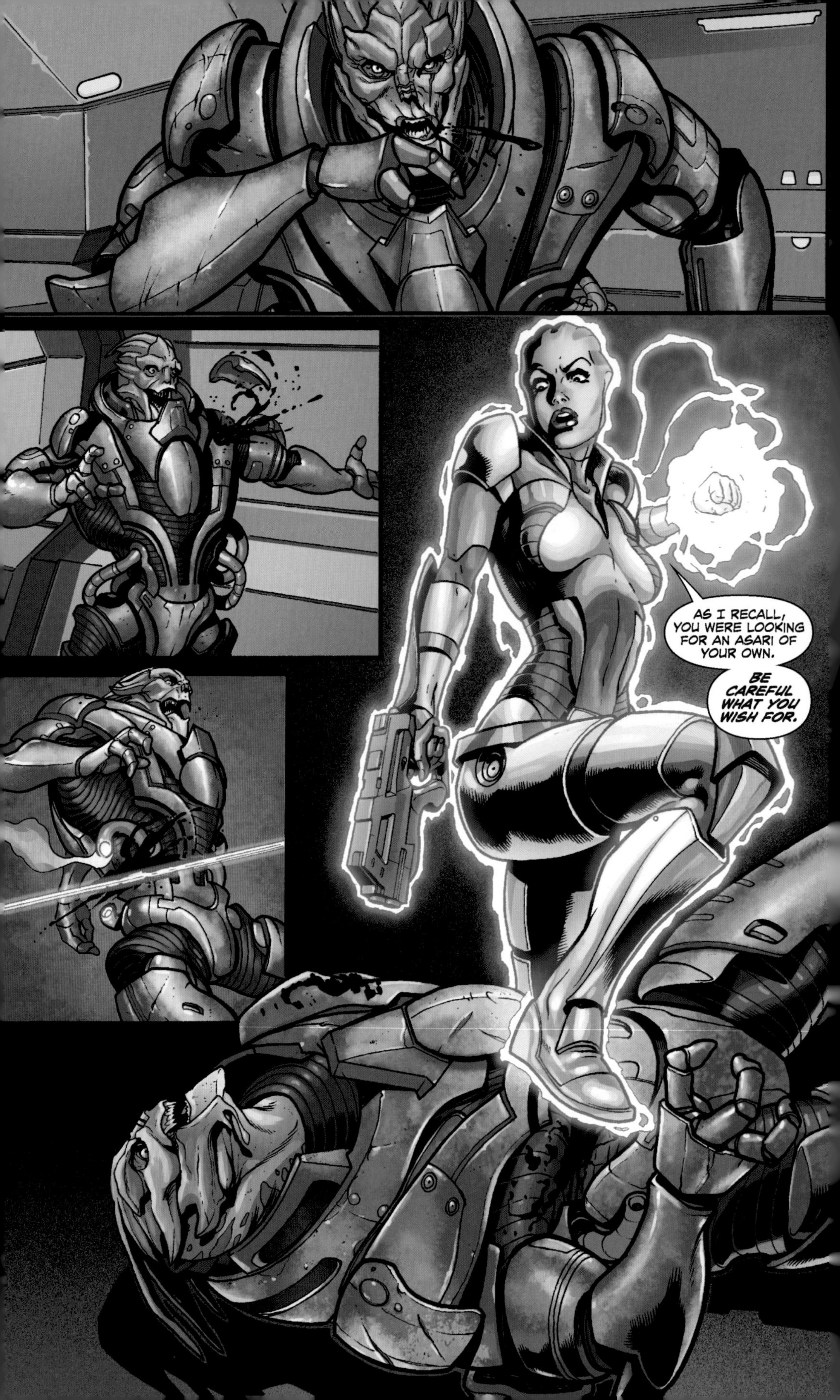
AS I RECALL, YOU WERE LOOKING FOR AN ASARI OF YOUR OWN.
BE CAREFUL WHAT YOU WISH FOR.

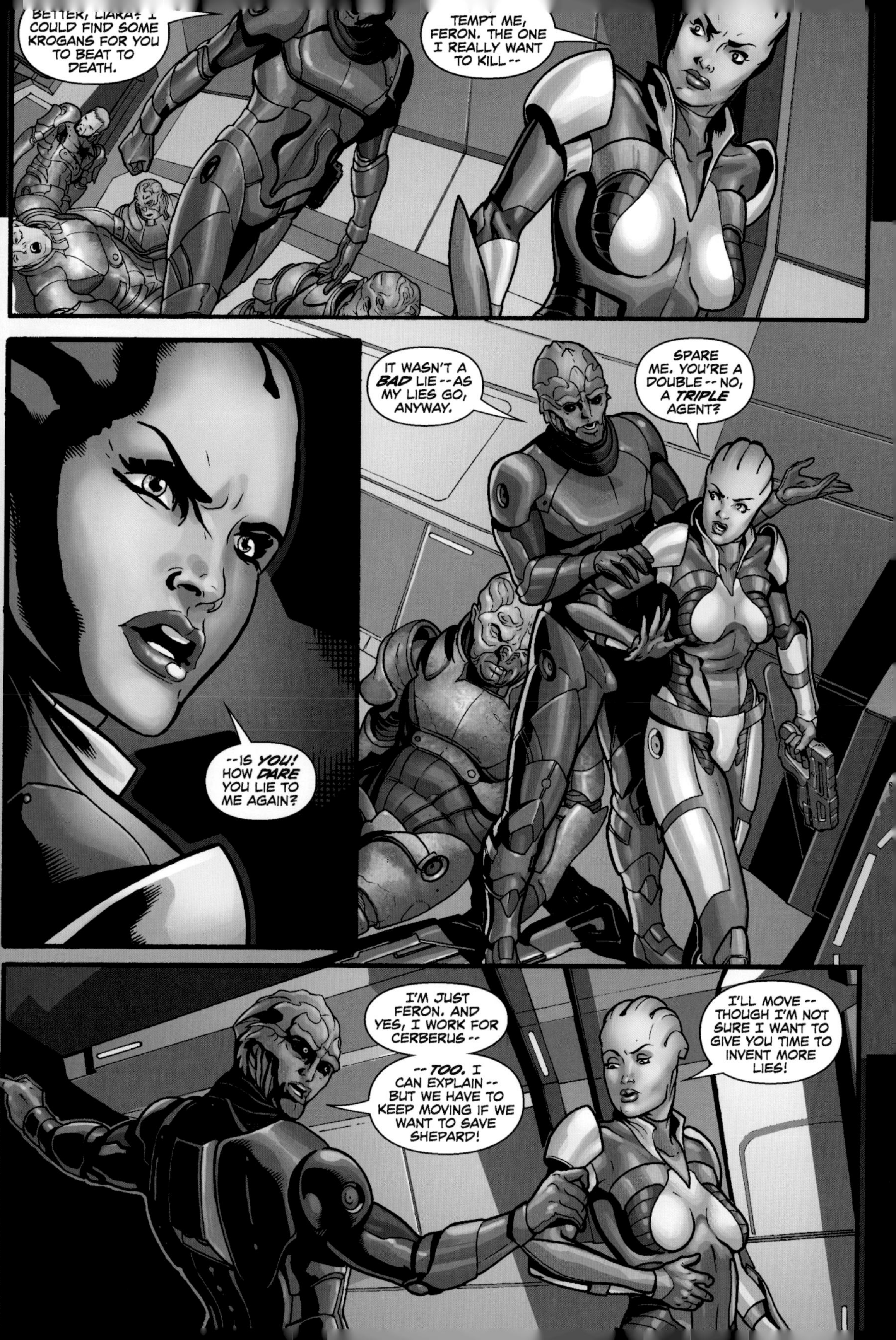

BETTER, LIARA? I COULD FIND SOME KROGANS FOR YOU TO BEAT TO DEATH.
TEMPT ME, FERON. THE ONE I REALLY WANT TO KILL --
--IS YOU! HOW DARE YOU LIE TO ME AGAIN?
IT WASN'T A BAD LIE -- AS MY LIES GO, ANYWAY.
SPARE ME. YOU'RE A DOUBLE -- NO, A TRIPLE AGENT?
I'M JUST FERON. AND YES, I WORK FOR CERBERUS --
-- TOO. I CAN EXPLAIN -- BUT WE HAVE TO KEEP MOVING IF WE WANT TO SAVE SHEPARD!
I'LL MOVE -- THOUGH I'M NOT SURE I WANT TO GIVE YOU TIME TO INVENT MORE LIES!

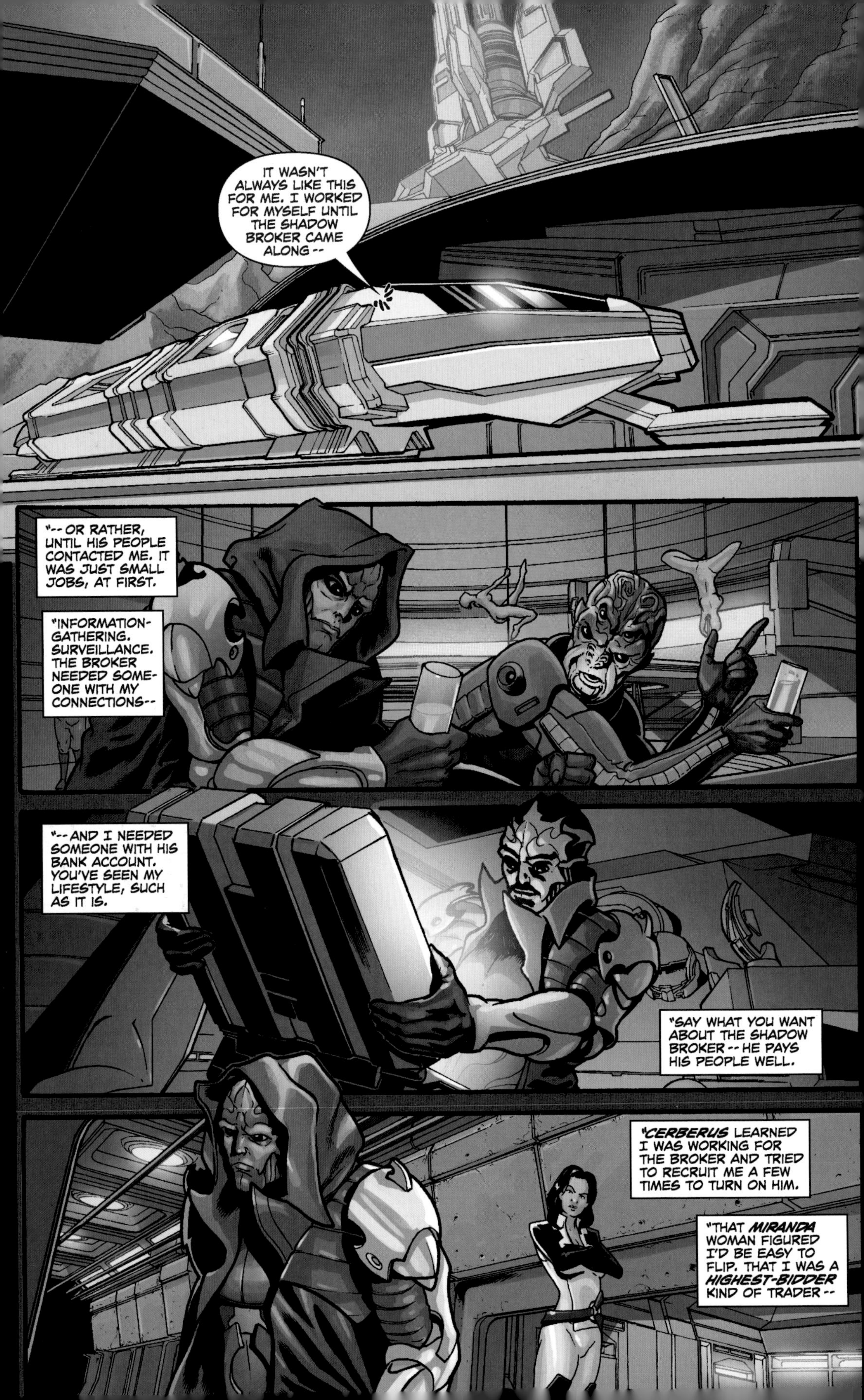
IT WASN'T ALWAYS LIKE THIS FOR ME. I WORKED FOR MYSELF UNTIL THE SHADOW BROKER CAME ALONG --
"-- OR RATHER, UNTIL HIS PEOPLE CONTACTED ME. IT WAS JUST SMALL JOBS, AT FIRST.
"INFORMATION-GATHERING. SURVEILLANCE. THE BROKER NEEDED SOME-ONE WITH MY CONNECTIONS--
"--AND I NEEDED SOMEONE WITH HIS BANK ACCOUNT. YOU'VE SEEN MY LIFESTYLE, SUCH AS IT IS.
"SAY WHAT YOU WANT ABOUT THE SHADOW BROKER -- HE PAYS HIS PEOPLE WELL.
"*CERBERUS* LEARNED I WAS WORKING FOR THE BROKER AND TRIED TO RECRUIT ME A FEW TIMES TO TURN ON HIM.
"THAT *MIRANDA* WOMAN FIGURED I'D BE EASY TO FLIP. THAT I WAS A *HIGHEST-BIDDER* KIND OF TRADER --

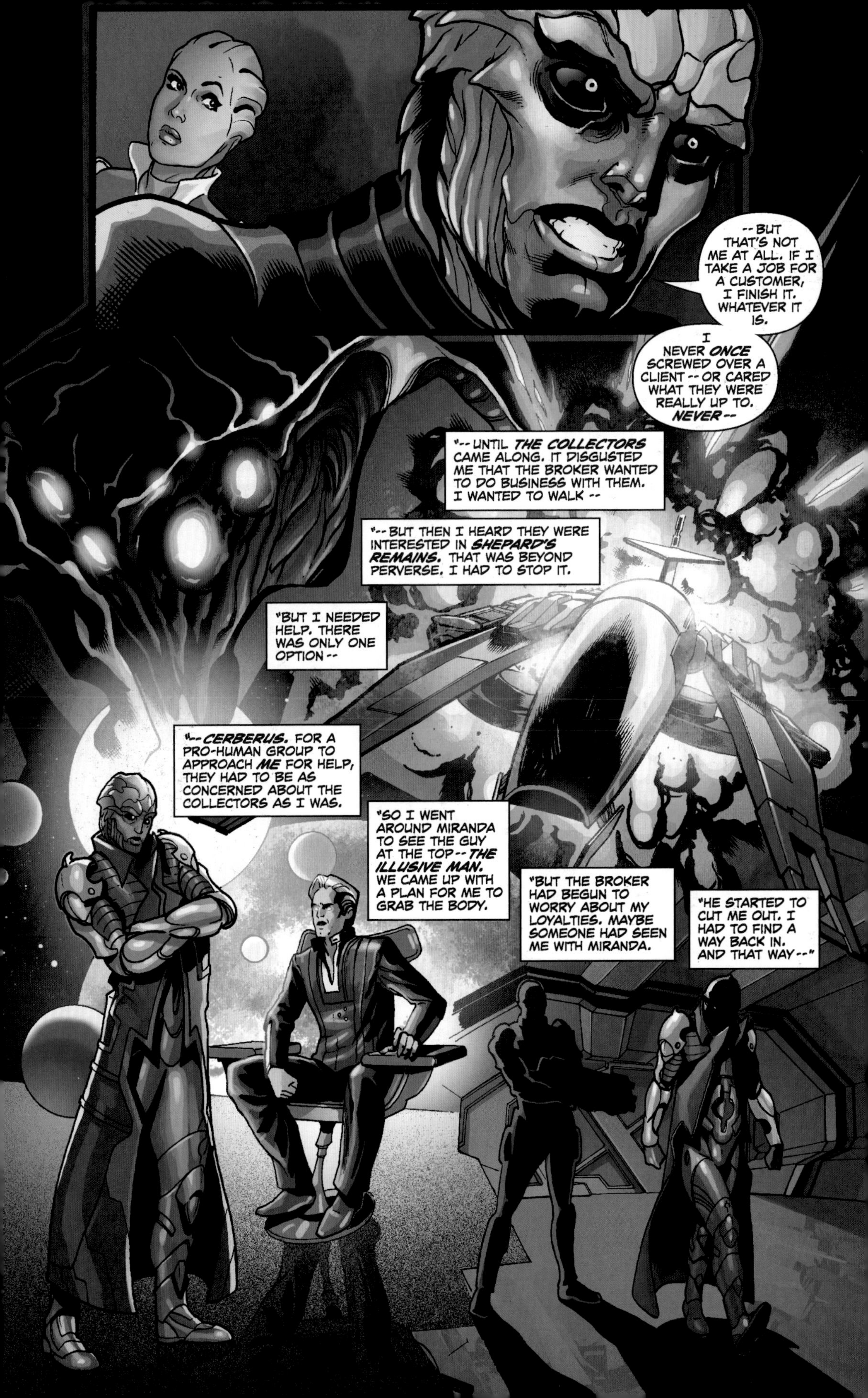

-- BUT THAT'S NOT ME AT ALL. IF I TAKE A JOB FOR A CUSTOMER, I FINISH IT. WHATEVER IT IS.
I NEVER *ONCE* SCREWED OVER A CLIENT -- OR CARED WHAT THEY WERE REALLY UP TO. *NEVER* --
"-- UNTIL *THE COLLECTORS* CAME ALONG. IT DISGUSTED ME THAT THE BROKER WANTED TO DO BUSINESS WITH THEM. I WANTED TO WALK --
"-- BUT THEN I HEARD THEY WERE INTERESTED IN *SHEPARD'S REMAINS.* THAT WAS BEYOND PERVERSE. I HAD TO STOP IT.
"BUT I NEEDED HELP. THERE WAS ONLY ONE OPTION --
"-- *CERBERUS.* FOR A PRO-HUMAN GROUP TO APPROACH *ME* FOR HELP, THEY HAD TO BE AS CONCERNED ABOUT THE COLLECTORS AS I WAS.
"SO I WENT AROUND MIRANDA TO SEE THE GUY AT THE TOP -- *THE ILLUSIVE MAN.* WE CAME UP WITH A PLAN FOR ME TO GRAB THE BODY.
"BUT THE BROKER HAD BEGUN TO WORRY ABOUT MY LOYALTIES. MAYBE SOMEONE HAD SEEN ME WITH MIRANDA.
"HE STARTED TO CUT ME OUT. I HAD TO FIND A WAY BACK IN. AND THAT WAY --"

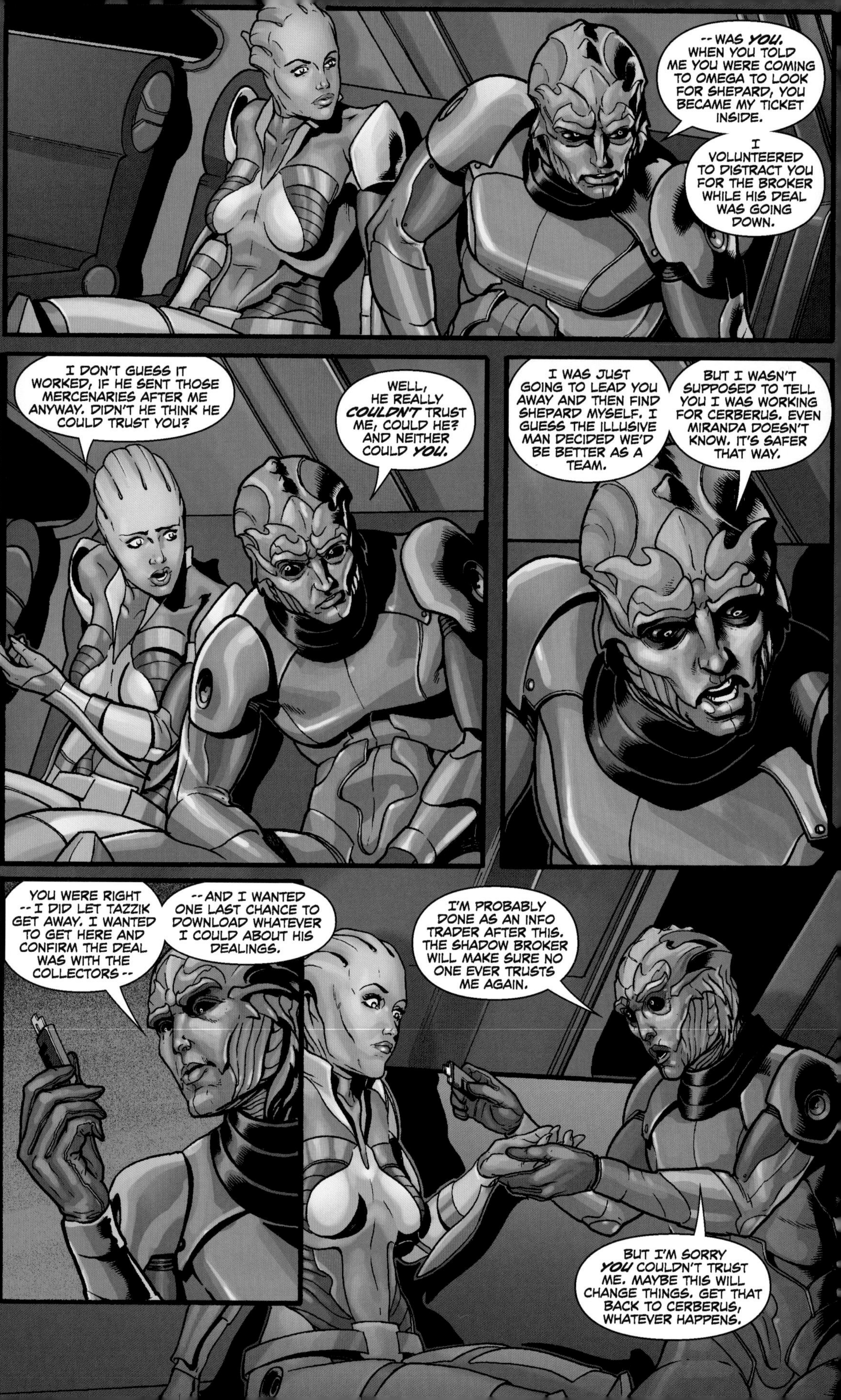
--WAS YOU. WHEN YOU TOLD ME YOU WERE COMING TO OMEGA TO LOOK FOR SHEPARD, YOU BECAME MY TICKET INSIDE.
I VOLUNTEERED TO DISTRACT YOU FOR THE BROKER WHILE HIS DEAL WAS GOING DOWN.
I DON'T GUESS IT WORKED, IF HE SENT THOSE MERCENARIES AFTER ME ANYWAY. DIDN'T HE THINK HE COULD TRUST YOU?
WELL, HE REALLY COULDN'T TRUST ME, COULD HE? AND NEITHER COULD YOU.
I WAS JUST GOING TO LEAD YOU AWAY AND THEN FIND SHEPARD MYSELF. I GUESS THE ILLUSIVE MAN DECIDED WE'D BE BETTER AS A TEAM.
BUT I WASN'T SUPPOSED TO TELL YOU I WAS WORKING FOR CERBERUS. EVEN MIRANDA DOESN'T KNOW. IT'S SAFER THAT WAY.
YOU WERE RIGHT --I DID LET TAZZIK GET AWAY. I WANTED TO GET HERE AND CONFIRM THE DEAL WAS WITH THE COLLECTORS--
--AND I WANTED ONE LAST CHANCE TO DOWNLOAD WHATEVER I COULD ABOUT HIS DEALINGS.
I'M PROBABLY DONE AS AN INFO TRADER AFTER THIS. THE SHADOW BROKER WILL MAKE SURE NO ONE EVER TRUSTS ME AGAIN.
BUT I'M SORRY YOU COULDN'T TRUST ME. MAYBE THIS WILL CHANGE THINGS. GET THAT BACK TO CERBERUS, WHATEVER HAPPENS.

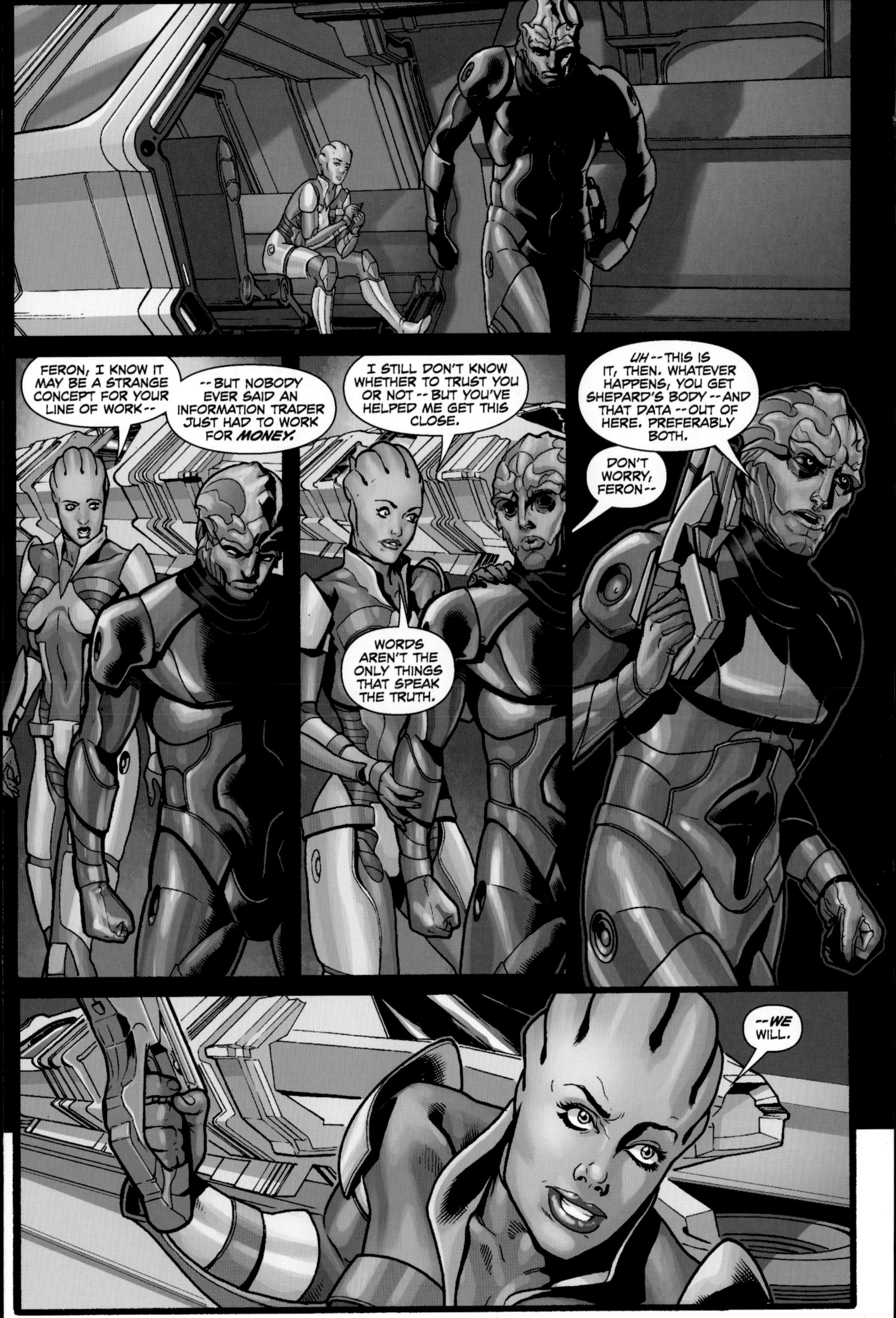
FERON, I KNOW IT MAY BE A STRANGE CONCEPT FOR YOUR LINE OF WORK--
--BUT NOBODY EVER SAID AN INFORMATION TRADER JUST HAD TO WORK FOR **MONEY.**
I STILL DON'T KNOW WHETHER TO TRUST YOU OR NOT--BUT YOU'VE HELPED ME GET THIS CLOSE.
WORDS AREN'T THE ONLY THINGS THAT SPEAK THE TRUTH.
UH--THIS IS IT, THEN. WHATEVER HAPPENS, YOU GET SHEPARD'S BODY--AND THAT DATA--OUT OF HERE. PREFERABLY BOTH.
DON'T WORRY, FERON--
--**WE** WILL.

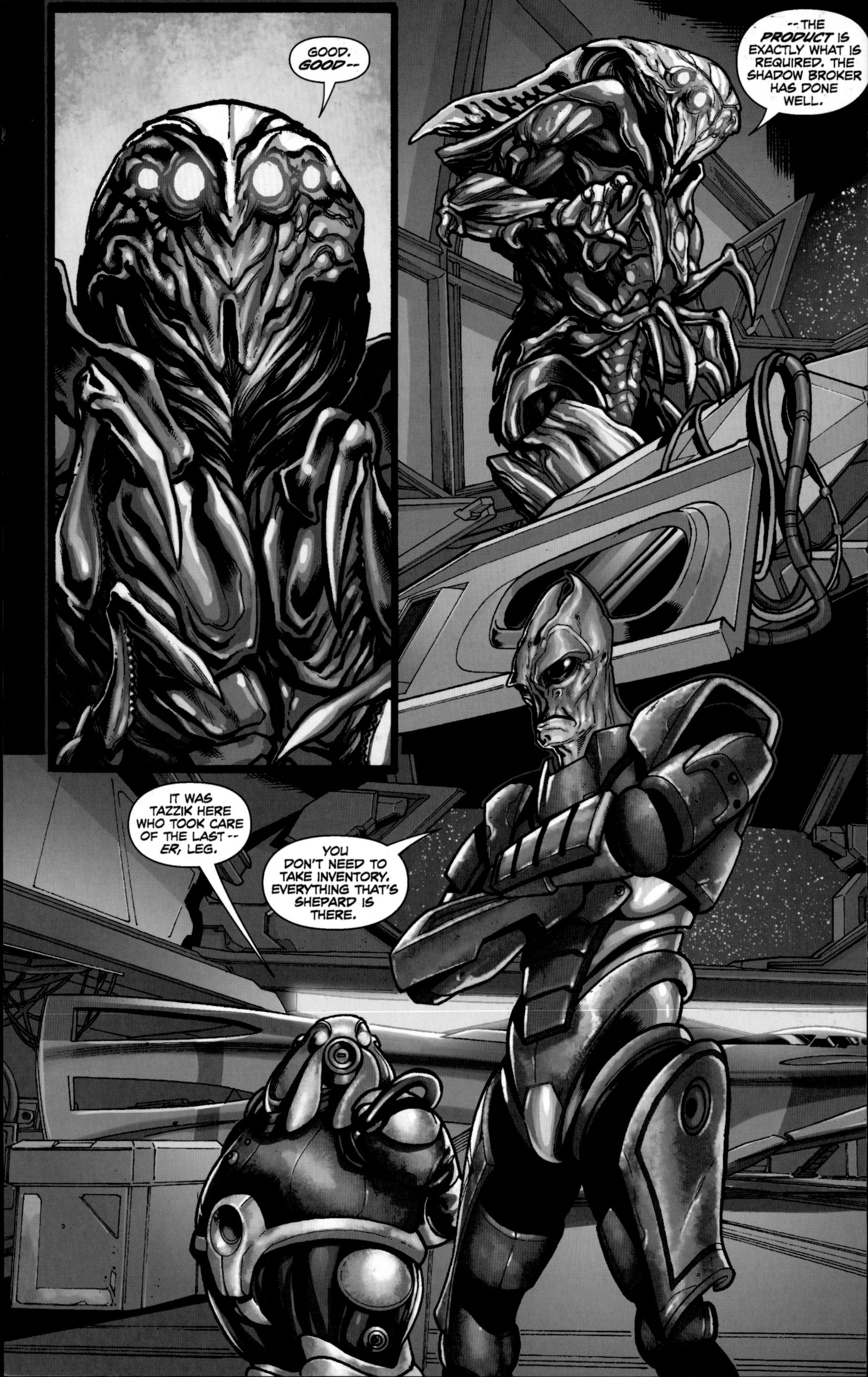
GOOD. *GOOD*--
--THE *PRODUCT* IS EXACTLY WHAT IS REQUIRED. THE SHADOW BROKER HAS DONE WELL.
IT WAS TAZZIK HERE WHO TOOK CARE OF THE LAST-- *ER*, LEG.
YOU DON'T NEED TO TAKE INVENTORY. EVERYTHING THAT'S SHEPARD IS THERE.

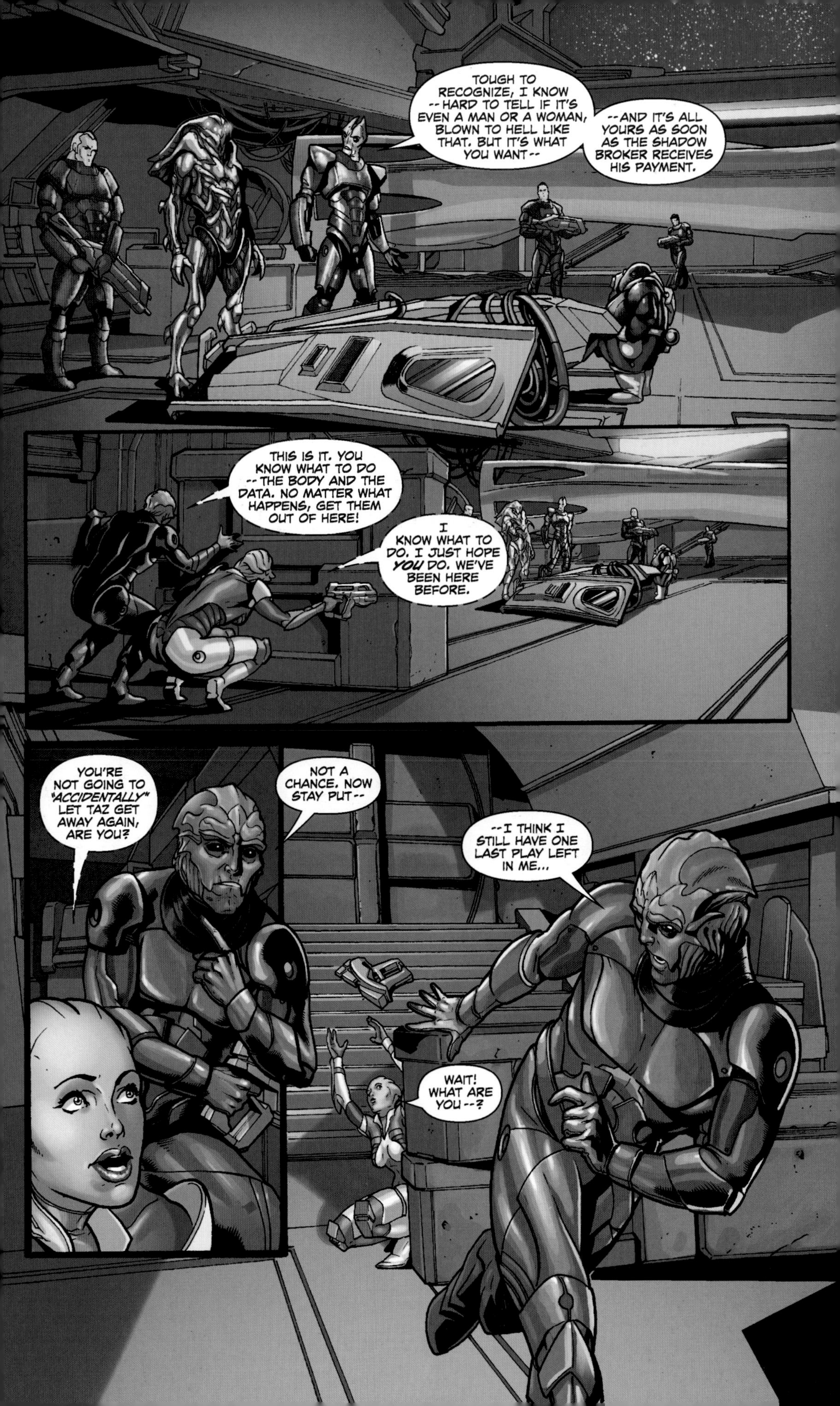
TOUGH TO RECOGNIZE, I KNOW --HARD TO TELL IF IT'S EVEN A MAN OR A WOMAN, BLOWN TO HELL LIKE THAT. BUT IT'S WHAT YOU WANT--
--AND IT'S ALL YOURS AS SOON AS THE SHADOW BROKER RECEIVES HIS PAYMENT.
THIS IS IT. YOU KNOW WHAT TO DO --THE BODY AND THE DATA. NO MATTER WHAT HAPPENS, GET THEM OUT OF HERE!
I KNOW WHAT TO DO. I JUST HOPE *YOU* DO. WE'VE BEEN HERE BEFORE.
YOU'RE NOT GOING TO *"ACCIDENTALLY"* LET TAZ GET AWAY AGAIN, ARE YOU?
NOT A CHANCE. NOW STAY PUT--
--I THINK I STILL HAVE ONE LAST PLAY LEFT IN ME...
WAIT! WHAT ARE YOU--?

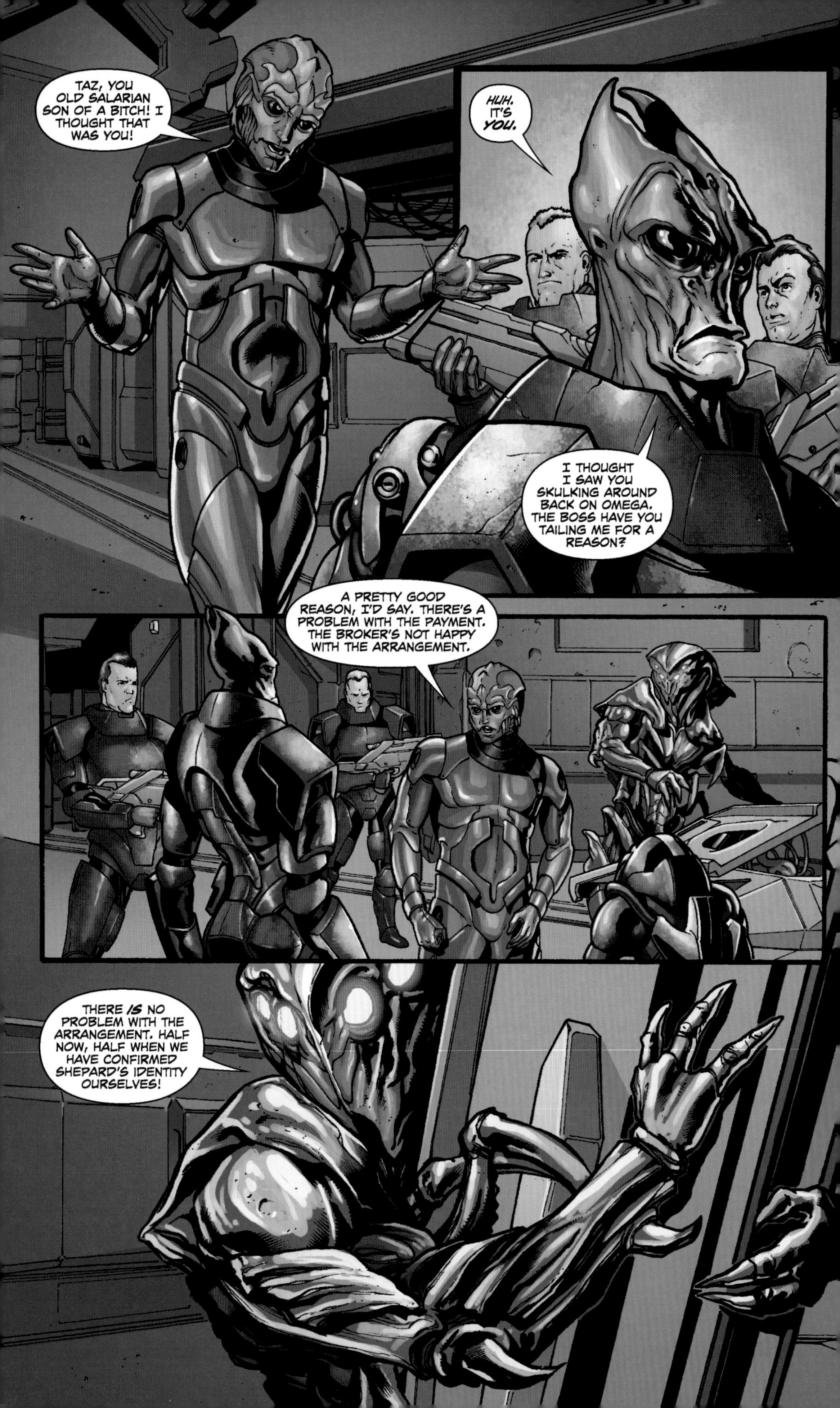
TAZ, YOU OLD SALARIAN SON OF A BITCH! I THOUGHT THAT WAS YOU!
HUH. IT'S *YOU.*
I THOUGHT I SAW YOU SKULKING AROUND BACK ON OMEGA. THE BOSS HAVE YOU TAILING ME FOR A REASON?
A PRETTY GOOD REASON, I'D SAY. THERE'S A PROBLEM WITH THE PAYMENT. THE BROKER'S NOT HAPPY WITH THE ARRANGEMENT.
THERE *IS* NO PROBLEM WITH THE ARRANGEMENT. HALF NOW, HALF WHEN WE HAVE CONFIRMED SHEPARD'S IDENTITY OURSELVES!

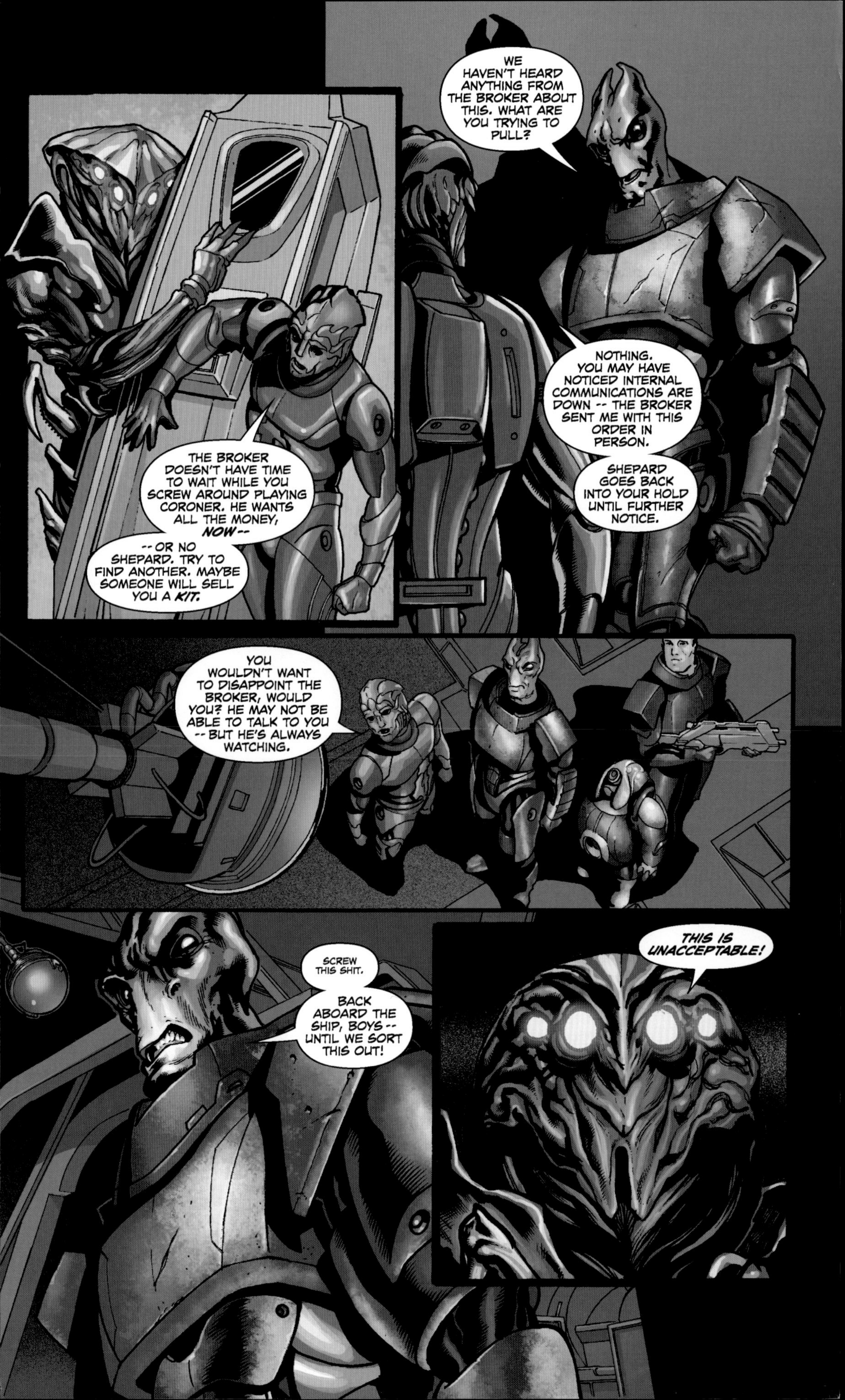
THE BROKER DOESN'T HAVE TIME TO WAIT WHILE YOU SCREW AROUND PLAYING CORONER. HE WANTS ALL THE MONEY, *NOW*--
--OR NO SHEPARD. TRY TO FIND ANOTHER. MAYBE SOMEONE WILL SELL YOU A *KIT*.
WE HAVEN'T HEARD ANYTHING FROM THE BROKER ABOUT THIS. WHAT ARE YOU TRYING TO PULL?
NOTHING. YOU MAY HAVE NOTICED INTERNAL COMMUNICATIONS ARE DOWN -- THE BROKER SENT ME WITH THIS ORDER IN PERSON.
SHEPARD GOES BACK INTO YOUR HOLD UNTIL FURTHER NOTICE.
YOU WOULDN'T WANT TO DISAPPOINT THE BROKER, WOULD YOU? HE MAY NOT BE ABLE TO TALK TO YOU -- BUT HE'S ALWAYS WATCHING.
SCREW THIS SHIT.
BACK ABOARD THE SHIP, BOYS -- UNTIL WE SORT THIS OUT!
THIS IS UNACCEPTABLE!

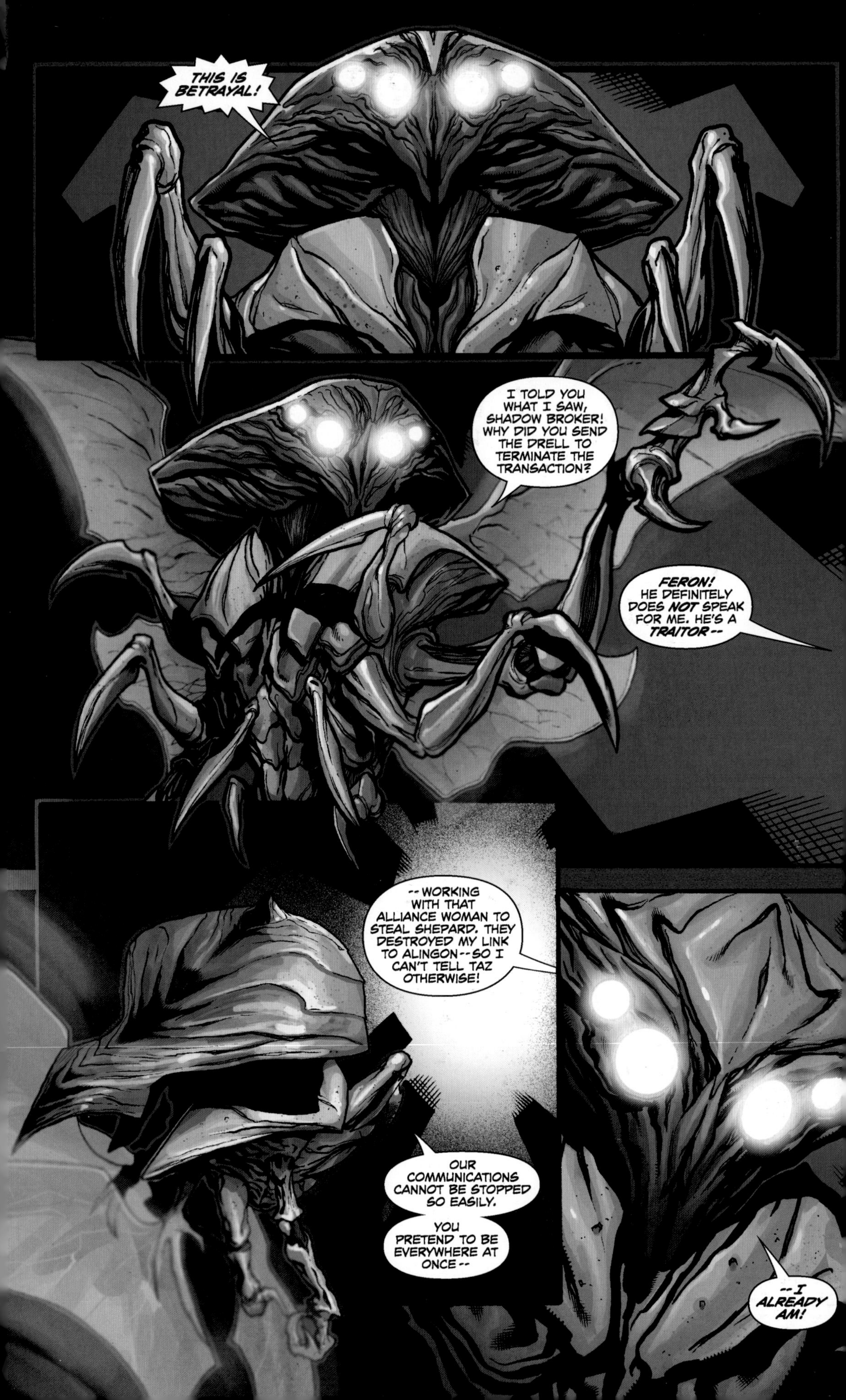
THIS IS BETRAYAL!
I TOLD YOU WHAT I SAW, SHADOW BROKER! WHY DID YOU SEND THE DRELL TO TERMINATE THE TRANSACTION?
FERON! HE DEFINITELY DOES NOT SPEAK FOR ME. HE'S A TRAITOR--
--WORKING WITH THAT ALLIANCE WOMAN TO STEAL SHEPARD. THEY DESTROYED MY LINK TO ALINGON--SO I CAN'T TELL TAZ OTHERWISE!
OUR COMMUNICATIONS CANNOT BE STOPPED SO EASILY.
YOU PRETEND TO BE EVERYWHERE AT ONCE--
--I ALREADY AM!

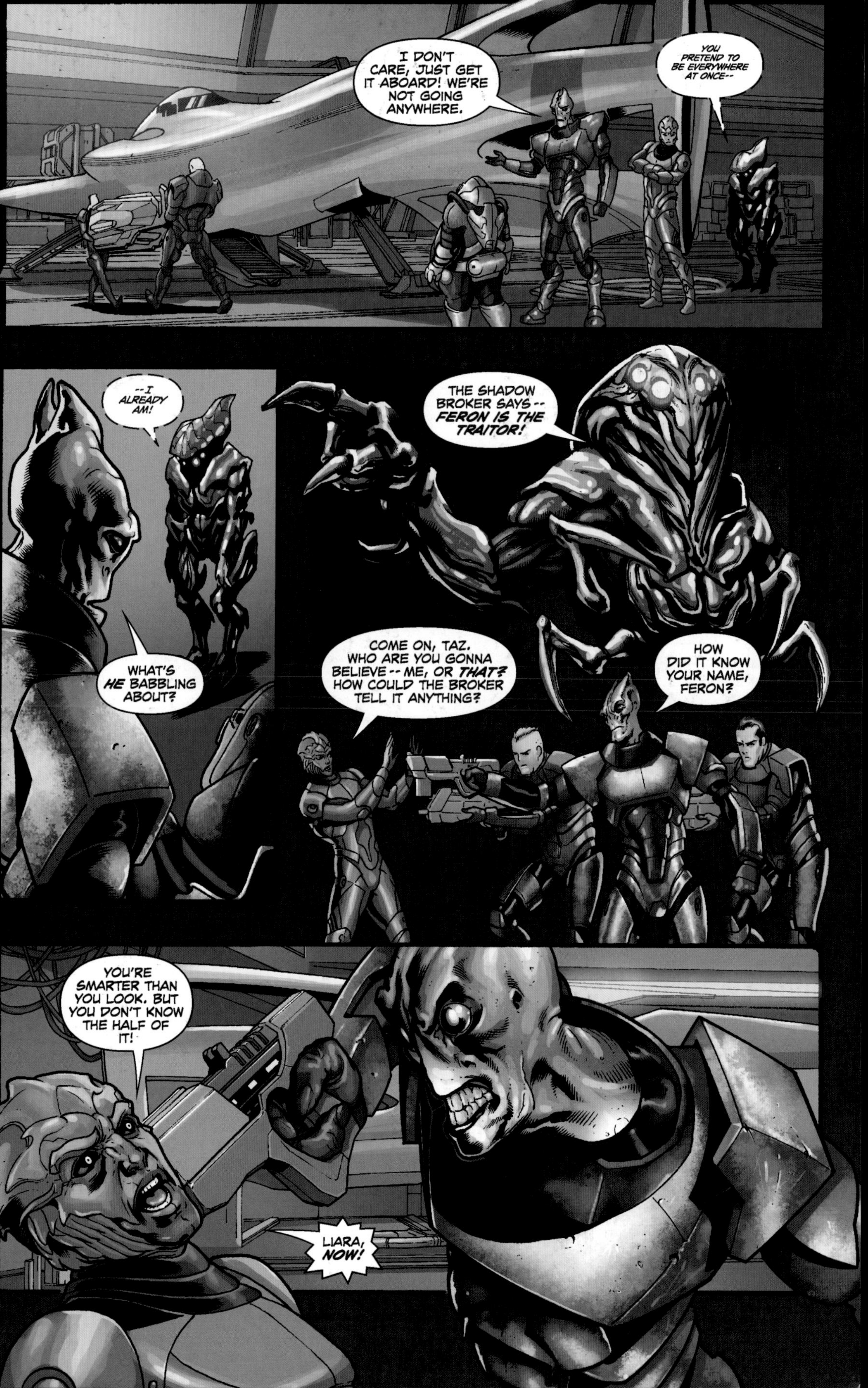
I DON'T CARE, JUST GET IT ABOARD! WE'RE NOT GOING ANYWHERE.
YOU PRETEND TO BE EVERYWHERE AT ONCE--
--I ALREADY AM!
WHAT'S *HE* BABBLING ABOUT?
THE SHADOW BROKER SAYS-- ***FERON IS THE TRAITOR!***
COME ON, TAZ. WHO ARE YOU GONNA BELIEVE--ME, OR *THAT*? HOW COULD THE BROKER TELL IT ANYTHING?
HOW DID IT KNOW YOUR NAME, FERON?
YOU'RE SMARTER THAN YOU LOOK. BUT YOU DON'T KNOW THE HALF OF IT!
LIARA, ***NOW!***

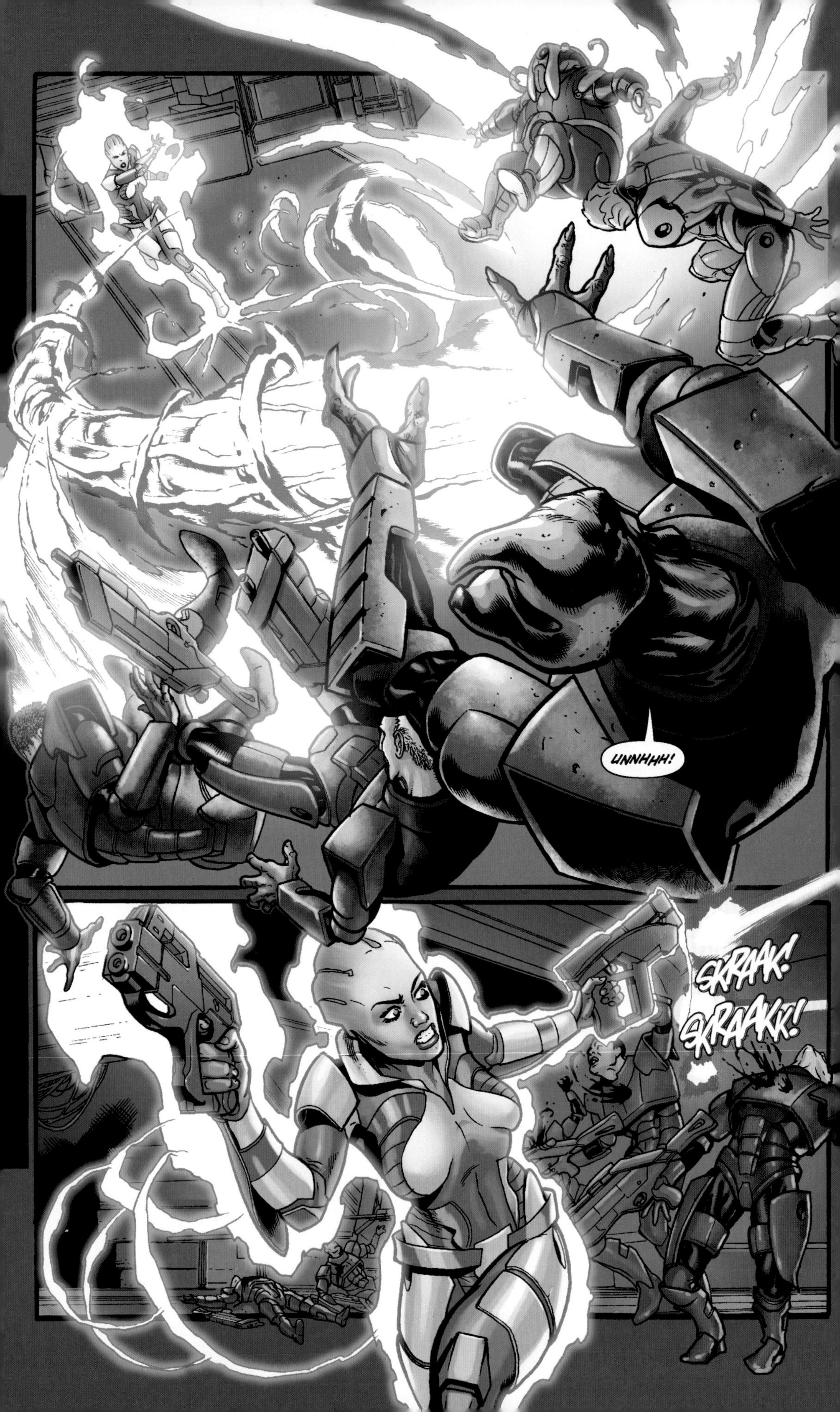
UNNHHH!
SKRAAK!
SKRAAKK!

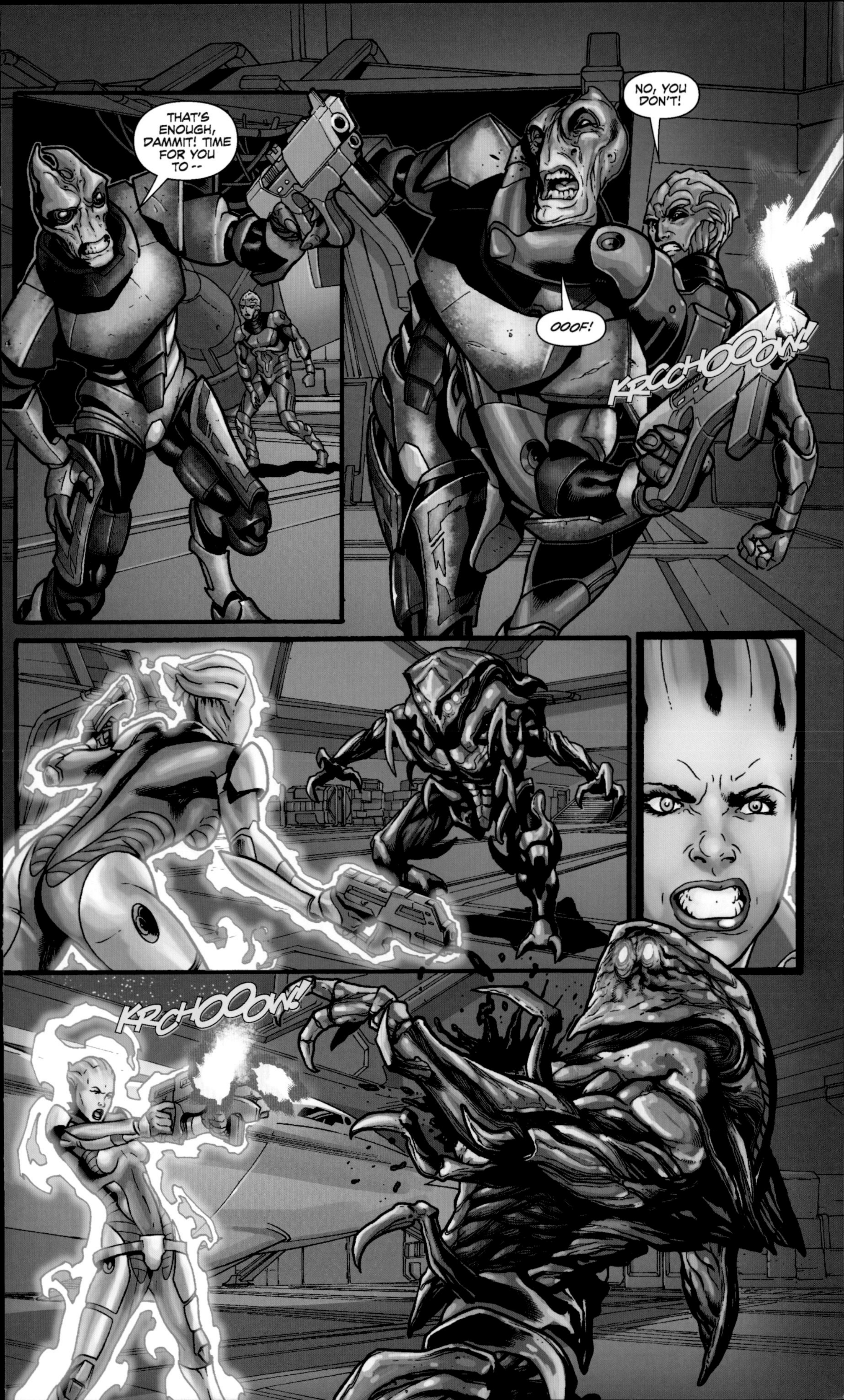
THAT'S ENOUGH, DAMMIT! TIME FOR YOU TO --
NO, YOU DON'T!
OOOF!
KRCCHOOOOW!
KRCHOOOW!

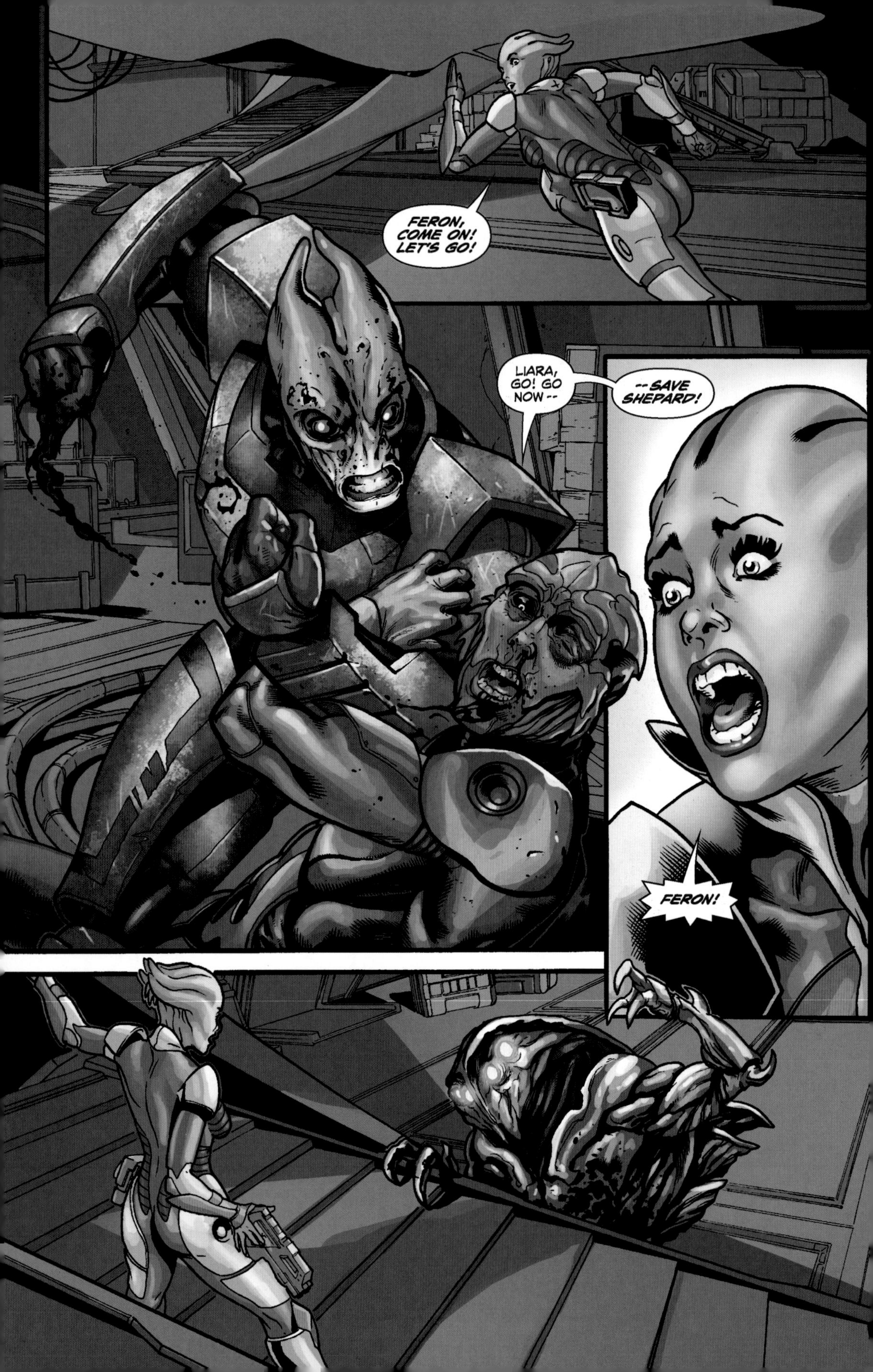
FERON, COME ON! LET'S GO!
LIARA, GO! GO NOW --
-- SAVE SHEPARD!
FERON!

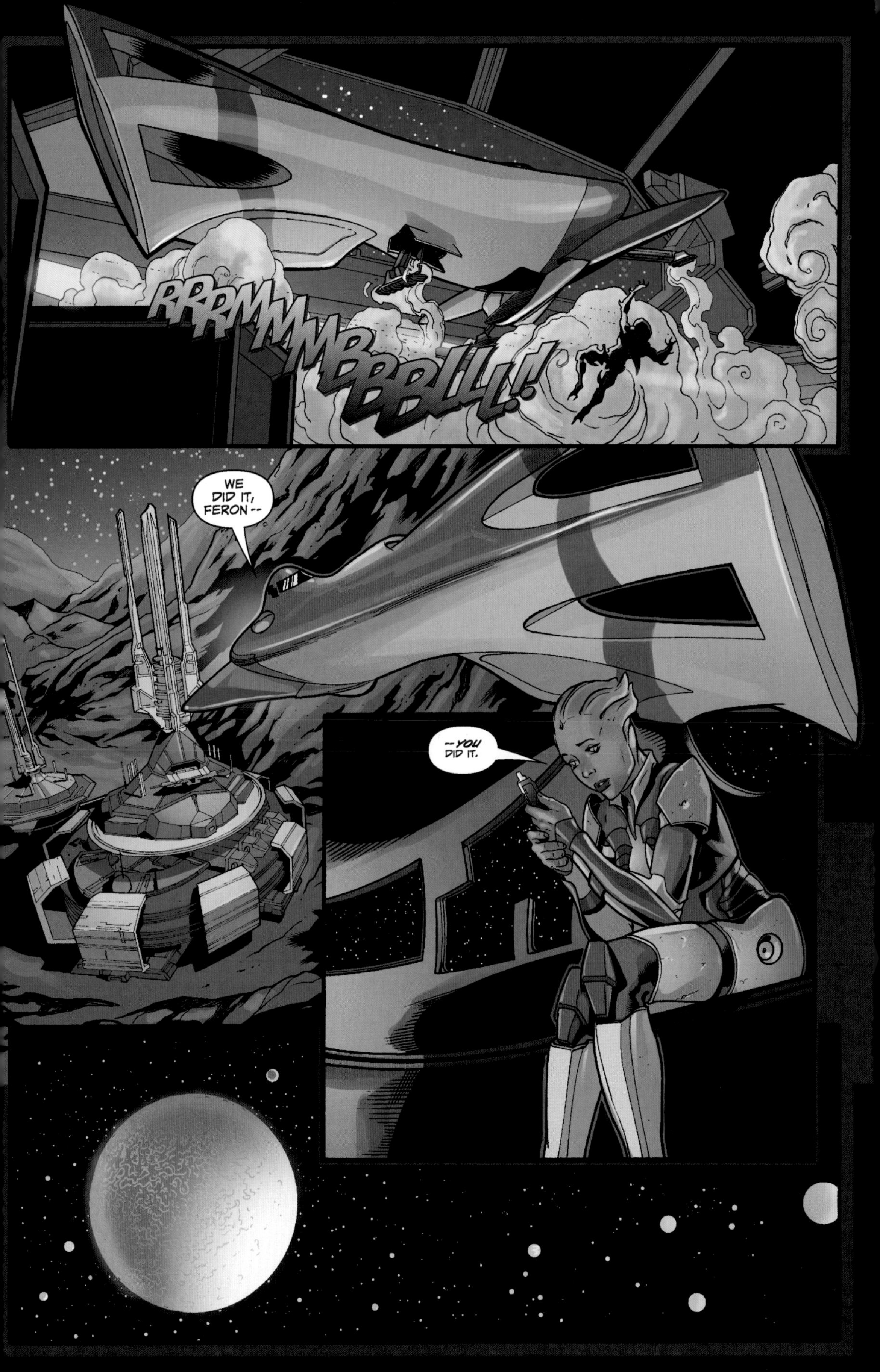
RRRMMMBBBLLL!!
WE DID IT, FERON --
-- YOU DID IT.

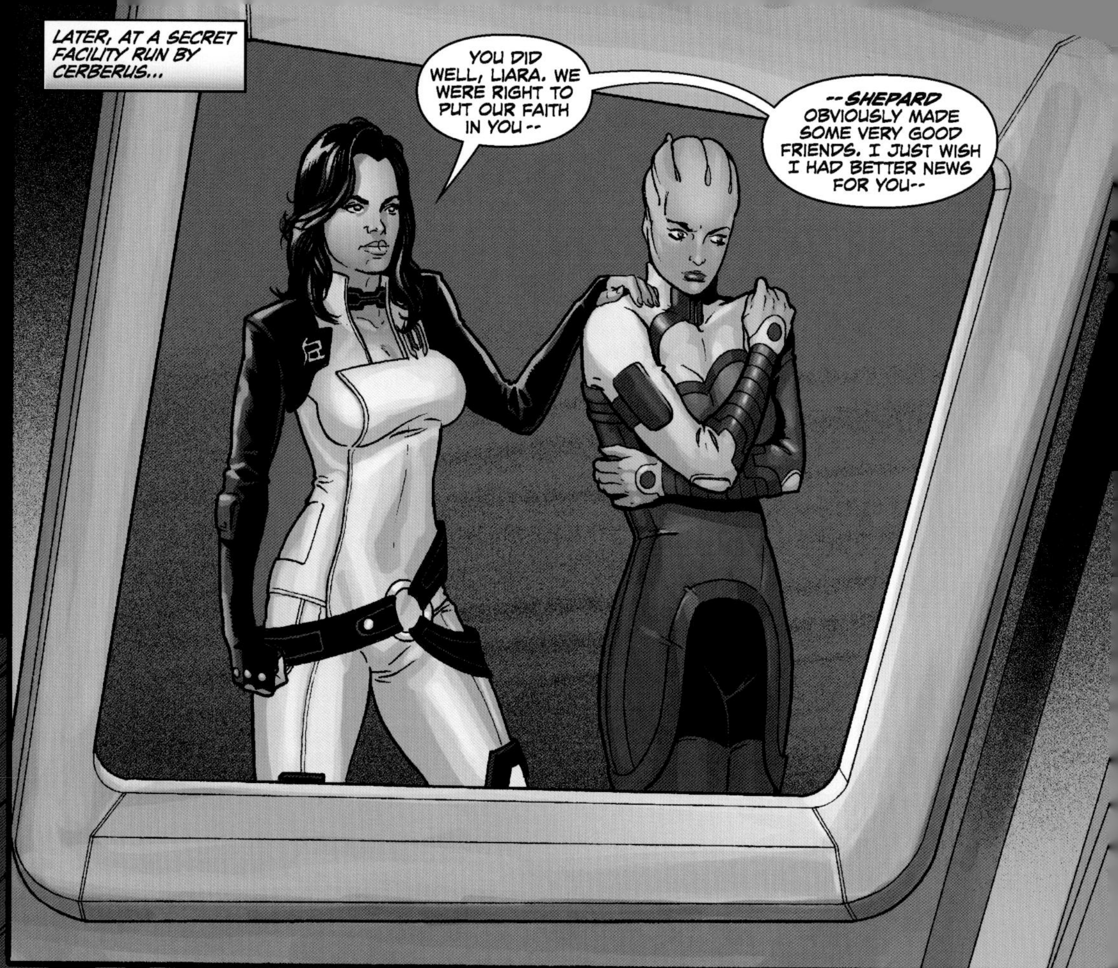
LATER, AT A SECRET FACILITY RUN BY CERBERUS...
YOU DID WELL, LIARA. WE WERE RIGHT TO PUT OUR FAITH IN YOU --
--SHEPARD OBVIOUSLY MADE SOME VERY GOOD FRIENDS. I JUST WISH I HAD BETTER NEWS FOR YOU--
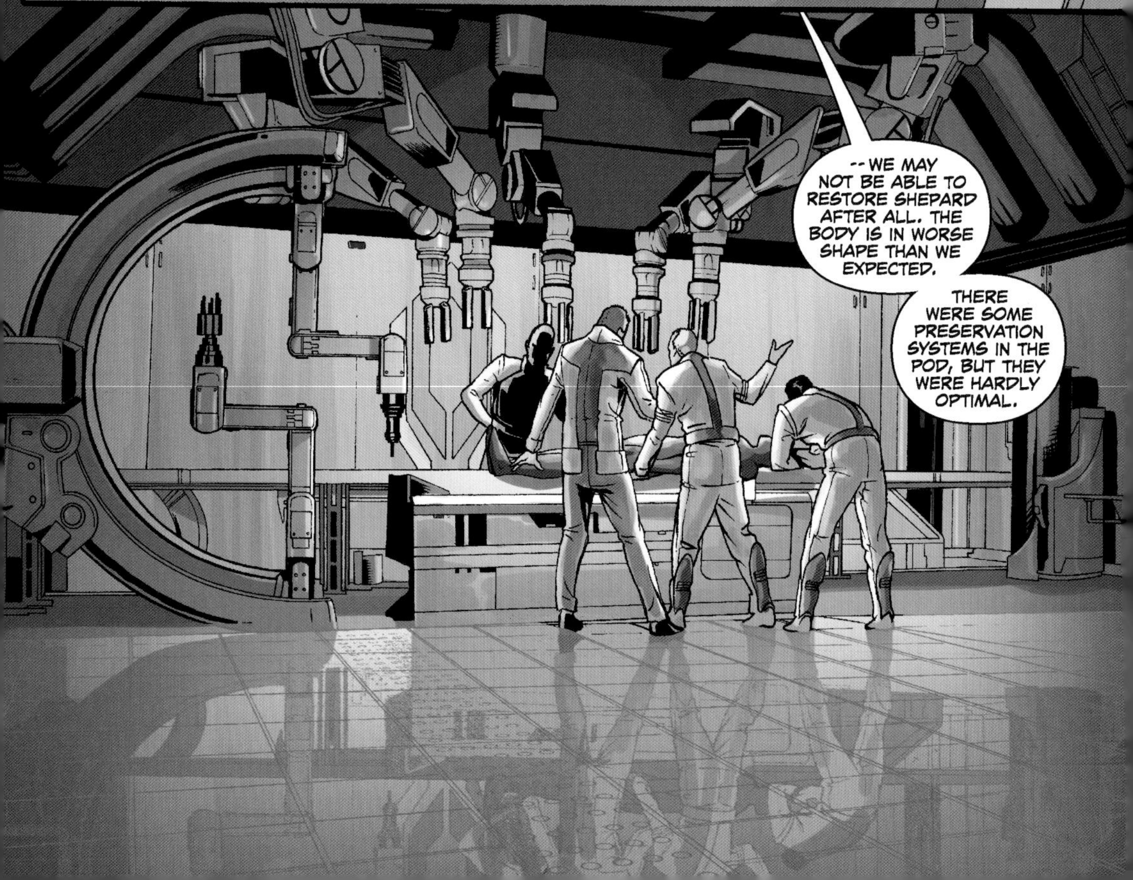
--WE MAY NOT BE ABLE TO RESTORE SHEPARD AFTER ALL. THE BODY IS IN WORSE SHAPE THAN WE EXPECTED.
THERE WERE SOME PRESERVATION SYSTEMS IN THE POD, BUT THEY WERE HARDLY OPTIMAL.

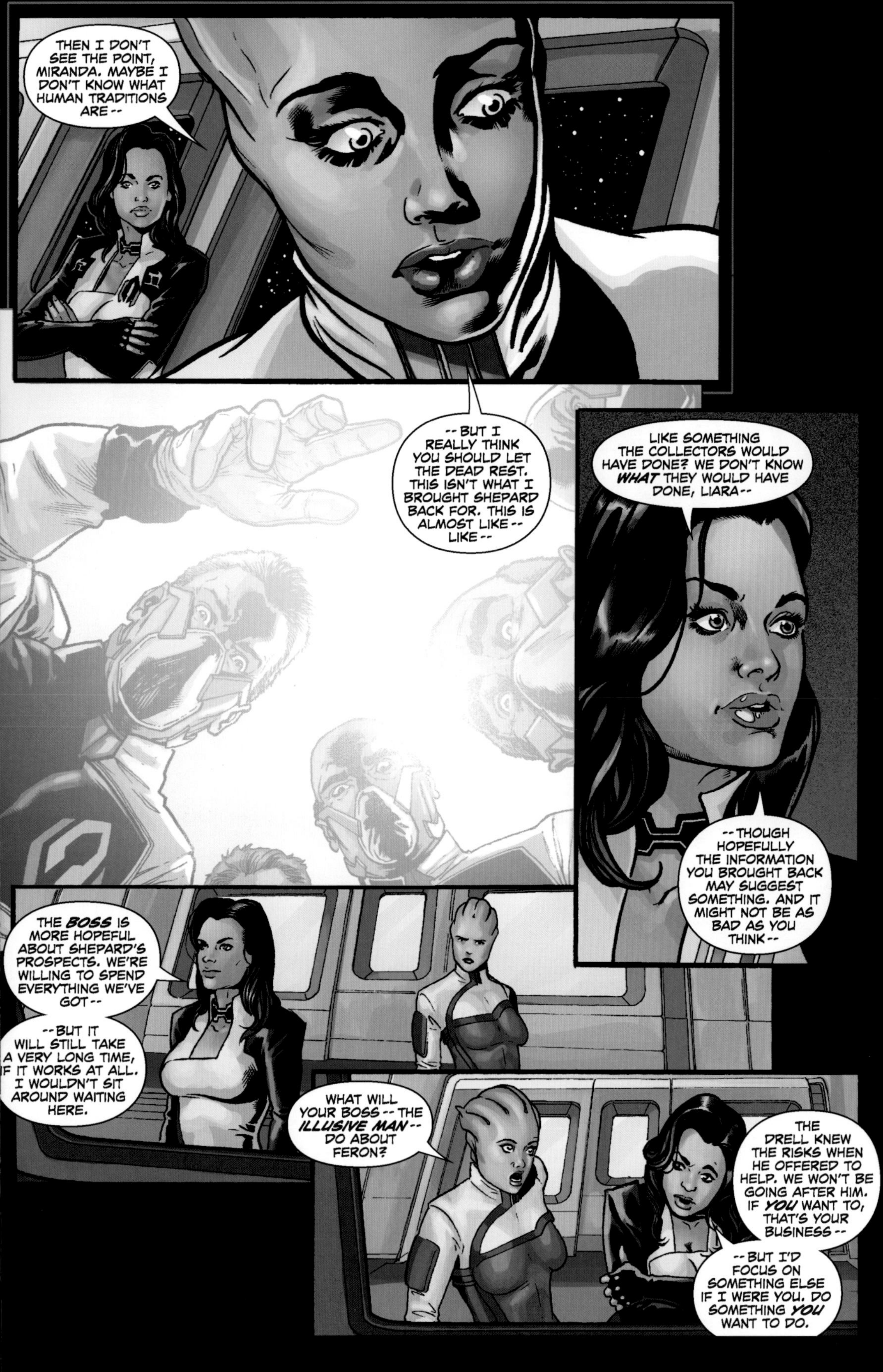
THEN I DON'T SEE THE POINT, MIRANDA. MAYBE I DON'T KNOW WHAT HUMAN TRADITIONS ARE --
-- BUT I REALLY THINK YOU SHOULD LET THE DEAD REST. THIS ISN'T WHAT I BROUGHT SHEPARD BACK FOR. THIS IS ALMOST LIKE -- LIKE --
LIKE SOMETHING THE COLLECTORS WOULD HAVE DONE? WE DON'T KNOW *WHAT* THEY WOULD HAVE DONE, LIARA --
-- THOUGH HOPEFULLY THE INFORMATION YOU BROUGHT BACK MAY SUGGEST SOMETHING. AND IT MIGHT NOT BE AS BAD AS YOU THINK --
THE *BOSS* IS MORE HOPEFUL ABOUT SHEPARD'S PROSPECTS. WE'RE WILLING TO SPEND EVERYTHING WE'VE GOT --
-- BUT IT WILL STILL TAKE A VERY LONG TIME, IF IT WORKS AT ALL. I WOULDN'T SIT AROUND WAITING HERE.
WHAT WILL YOUR BOSS -- THE *ILLUSIVE MAN* -- DO ABOUT FERON?
THE DRELL KNEW THE RISKS WHEN HE OFFERED TO HELP. WE WON'T BE GOING AFTER HIM. IF *YOU* WANT TO, THAT'S YOUR BUSINESS --
-- BUT I'D FOCUS ON SOMETHING ELSE IF I WERE YOU. DO SOMETHING *YOU* WANT TO DO.

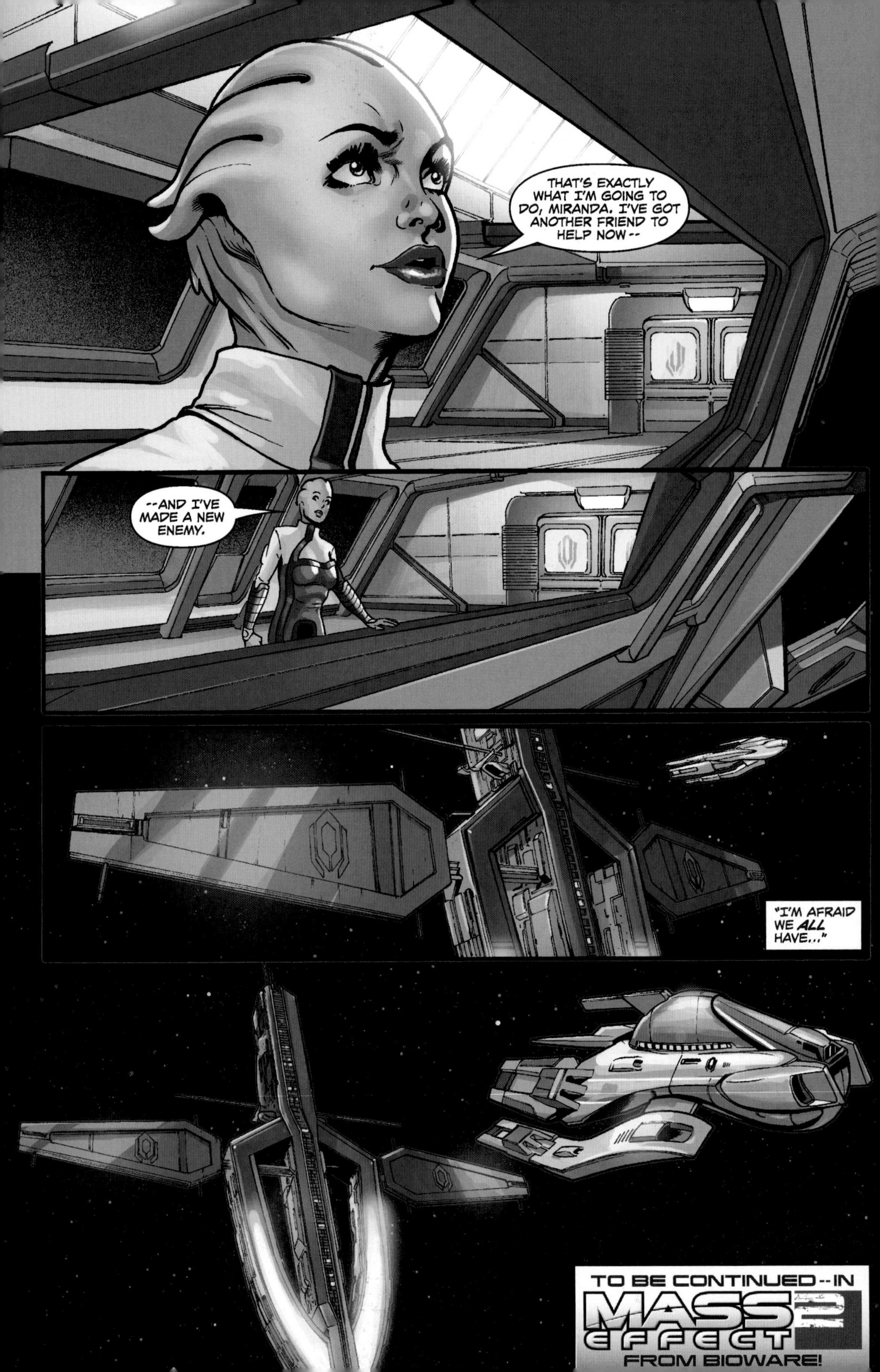

THAT'S EXACTLY WHAT I'M GOING TO DO, MIRANDA. I'VE GOT ANOTHER FRIEND TO HELP NOW--
--AND I'VE MADE A NEW ENEMY.
"I'M AFRAID WE ALL HAVE..."
TO BE CONTINUED--IN MASS EFFECT 2 FROM BIOWARE!

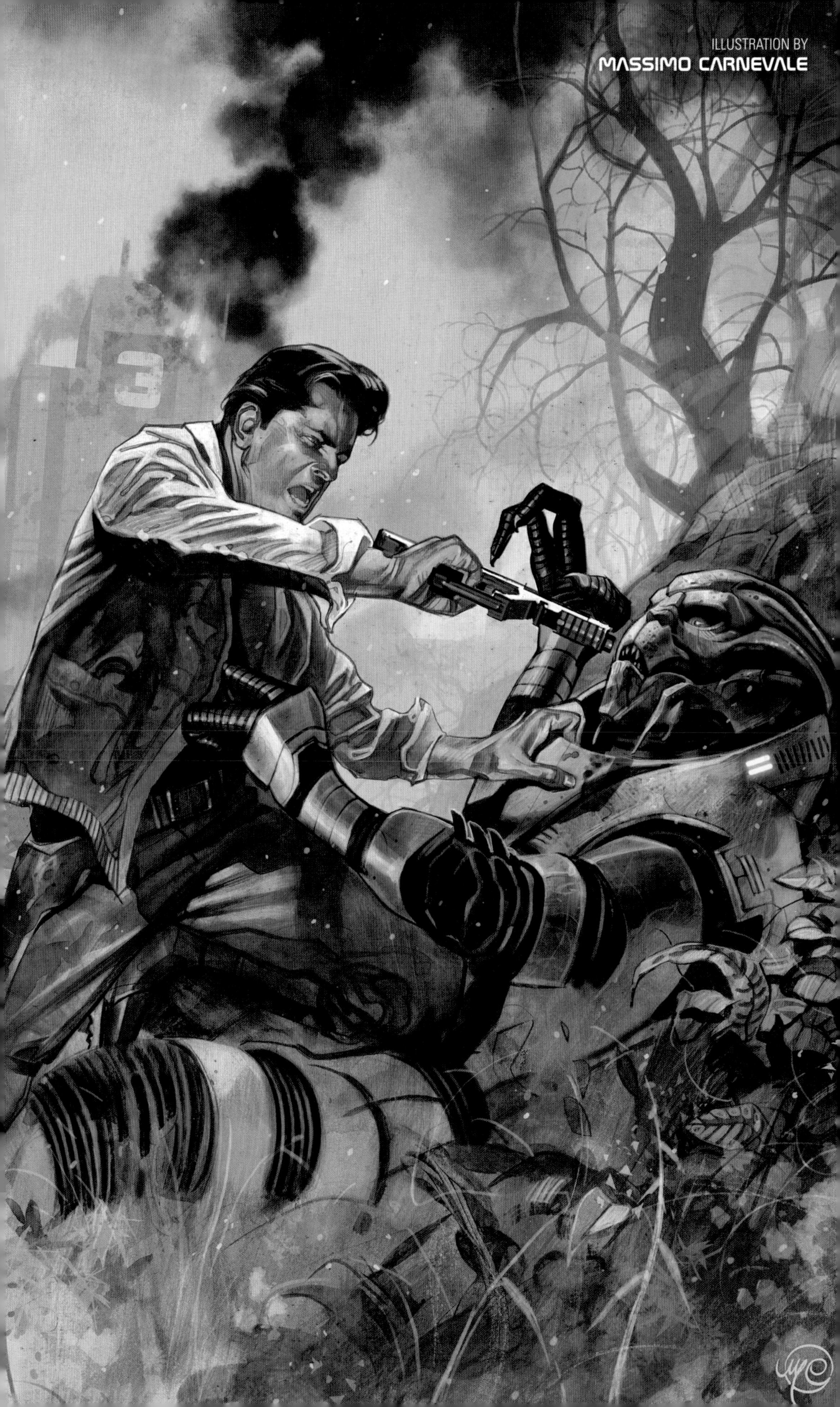

ILLUSTRATION BY
MASSIMO CARNEVALE

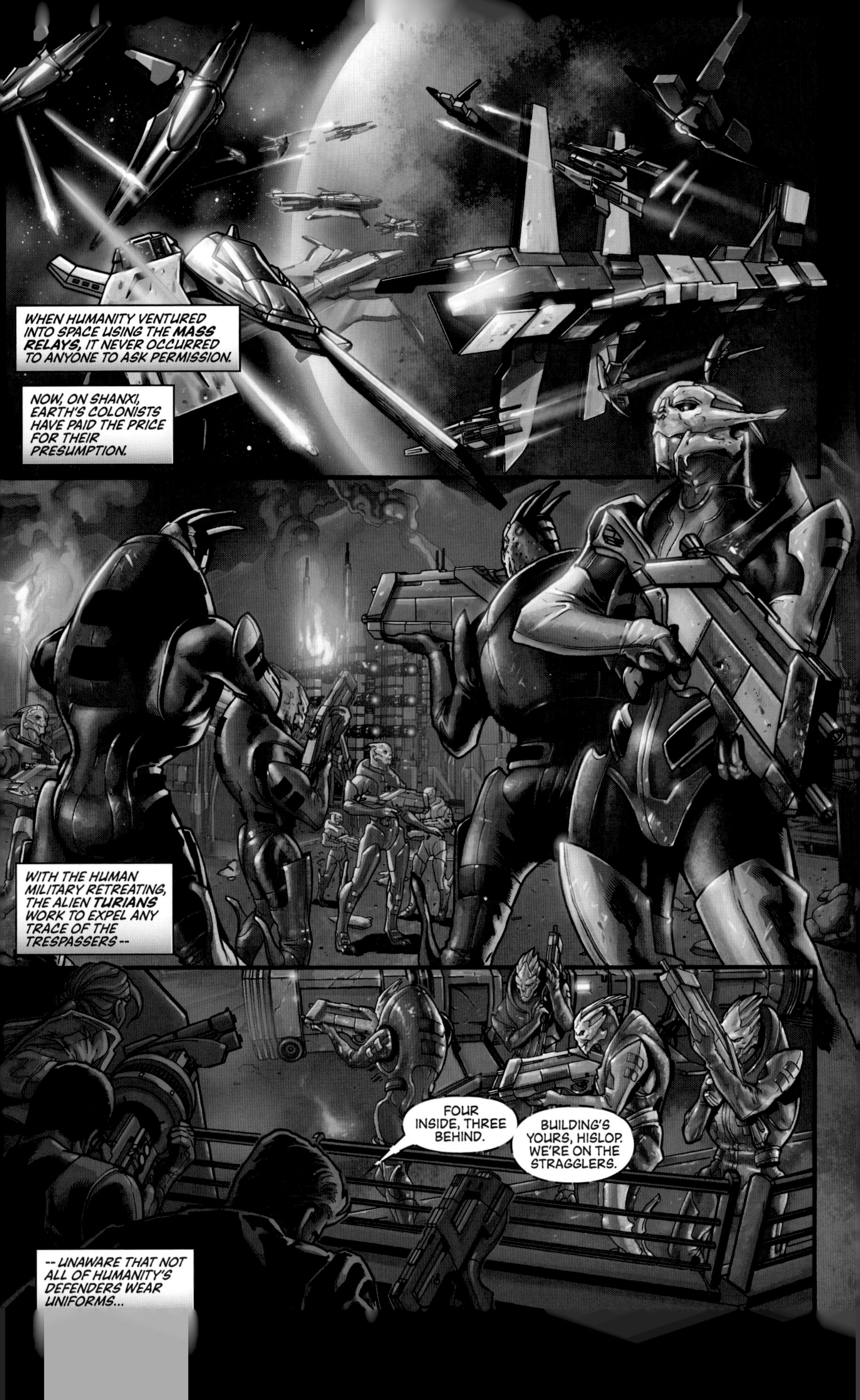
WHEN HUMANITY VENTURED INTO SPACE USING THE MASS RELAYS, IT NEVER OCCURRED TO ANYONE TO ASK PERMISSION.
NOW, ON SHANXI, EARTH'S COLONISTS HAVE PAID THE PRICE FOR THEIR PRESUMPTION.
WITH THE HUMAN MILITARY RETREATING, THE ALIEN TURIANS WORK TO EXPEL ANY TRACE OF THE TRESPASSERS --
FOUR INSIDE, THREE BEHIND.
BUILDING'S YOURS, HISLOP. WE'RE ON THE STRAGGLERS.
-- UNAWARE THAT NOT ALL OF HUMANITY'S DEFENDERS WEAR UNIFORMS...

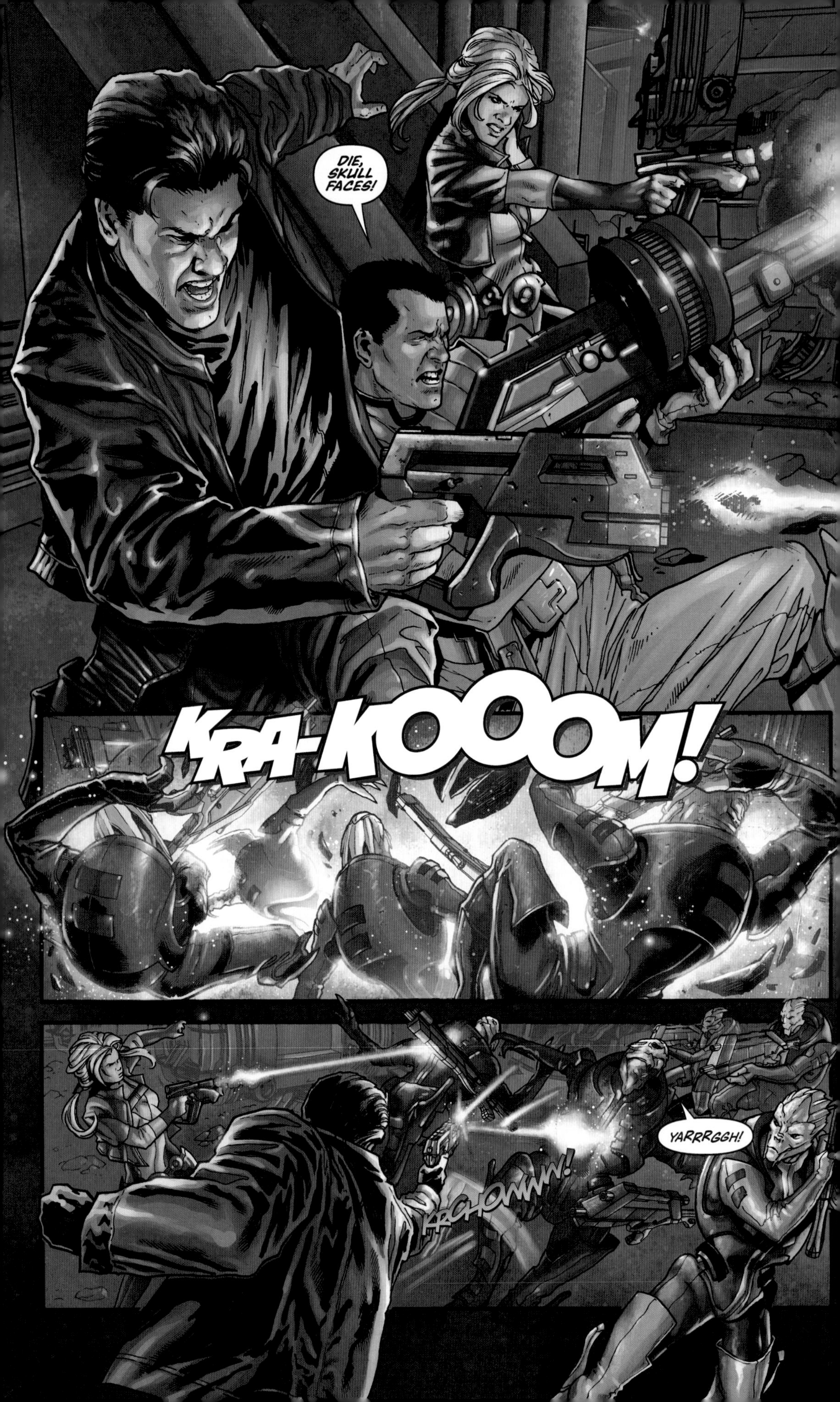
DIE, SKULL FACES!
KRA-KOOOOM!
KRCHOWWW!
YARRRGGH!

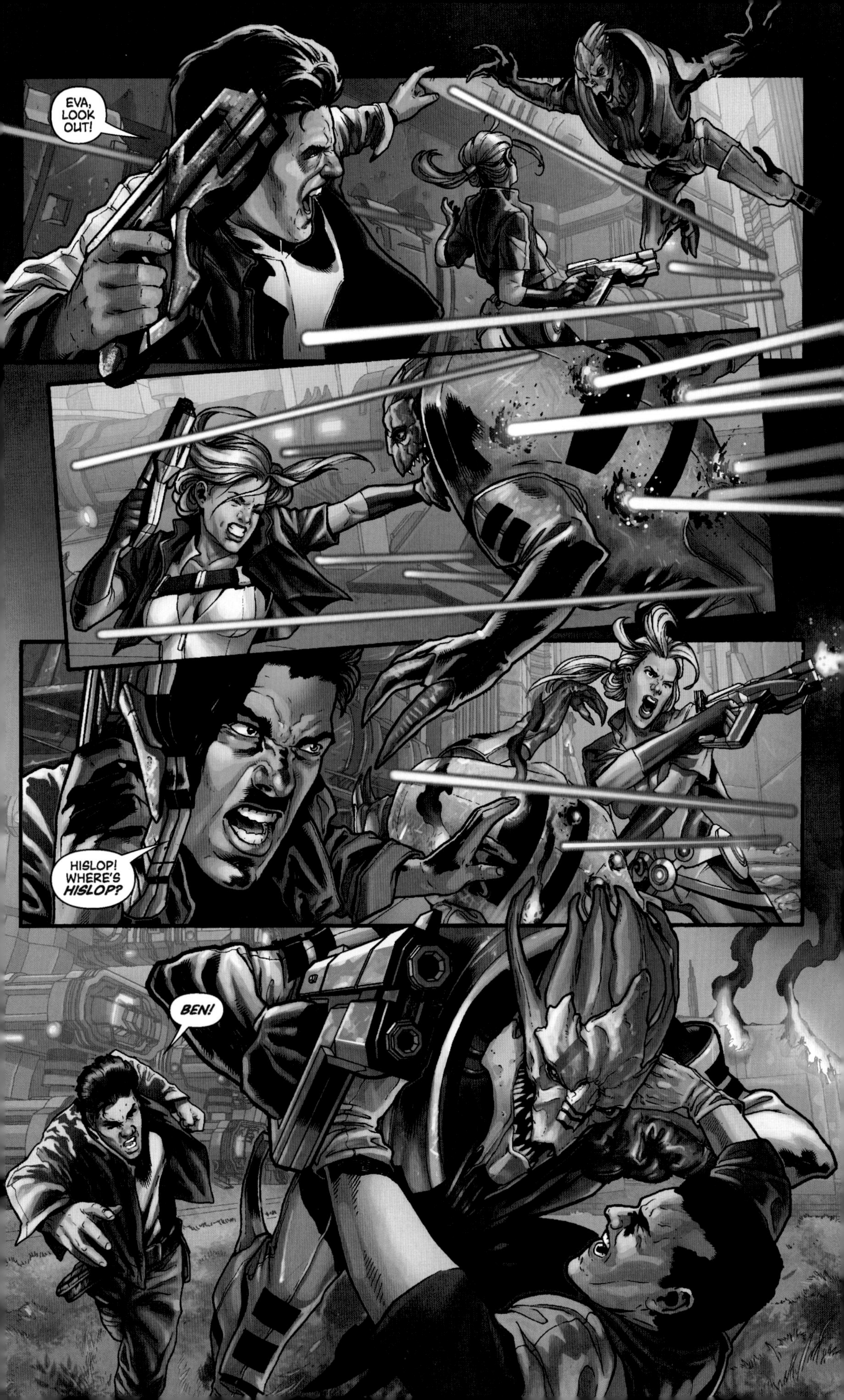
EVA, LOOK OUT!
HISLOP! WHERE'S *HISLOP?*
BEN!

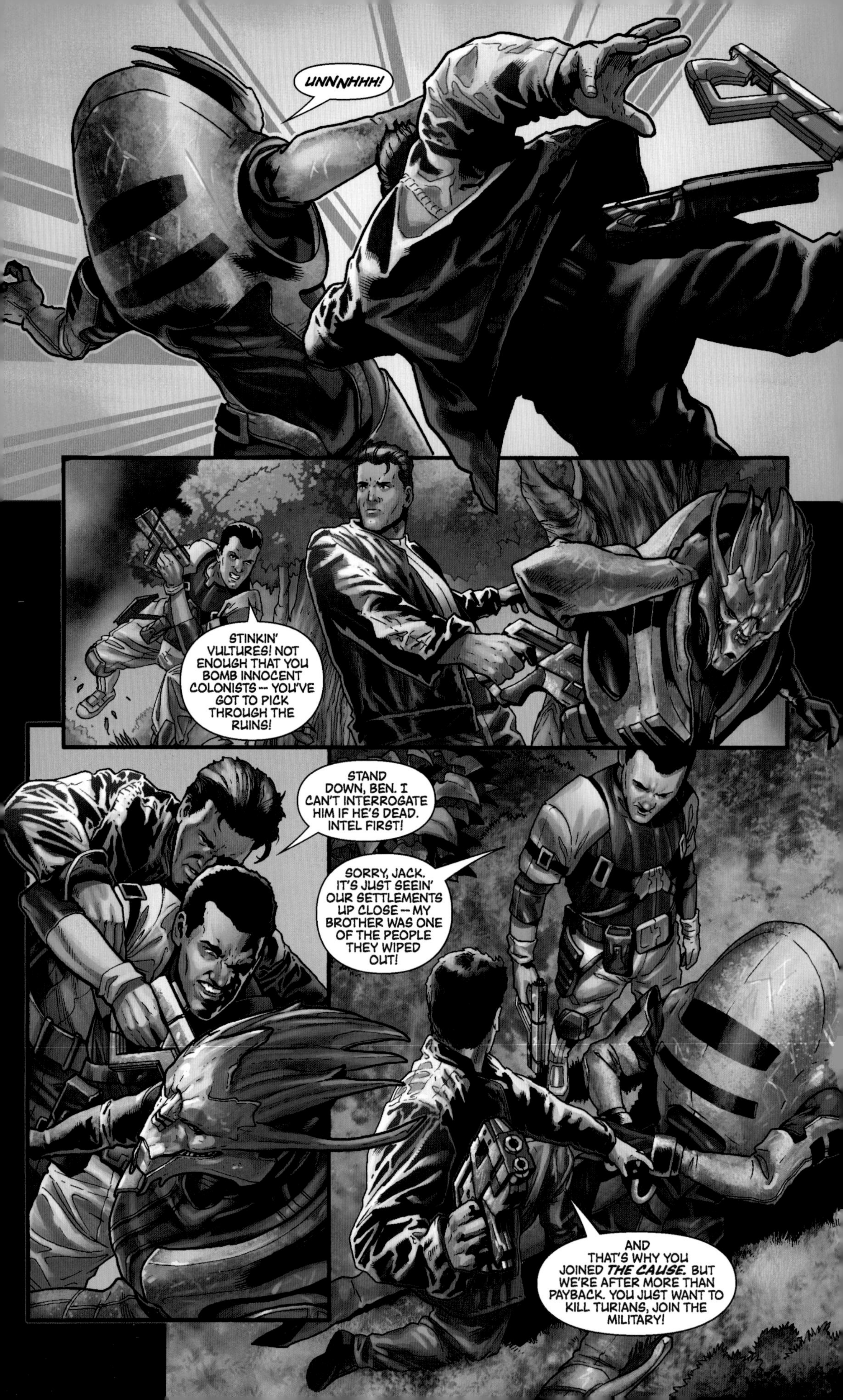
UNNNHHH!
STINKIN' VULTURES! NOT ENOUGH THAT YOU BOMB INNOCENT COLONISTS -- YOU'VE GOT TO PICK THROUGH THE RUINS!
STAND DOWN, BEN. I CAN'T INTERROGATE HIM IF HE'S DEAD. INTEL FIRST!
SORRY, JACK. IT'S JUST SEEIN' OUR SETTLEMENTS UP CLOSE -- MY BROTHER WAS ONE OF THE PEOPLE THEY WIPED OUT!
AND THAT'S WHY YOU JOINED THE CAUSE. BUT WE'RE AFTER MORE THAN PAYBACK. YOU JUST WANT TO KILL TURIANS, JOIN THE MILITARY!

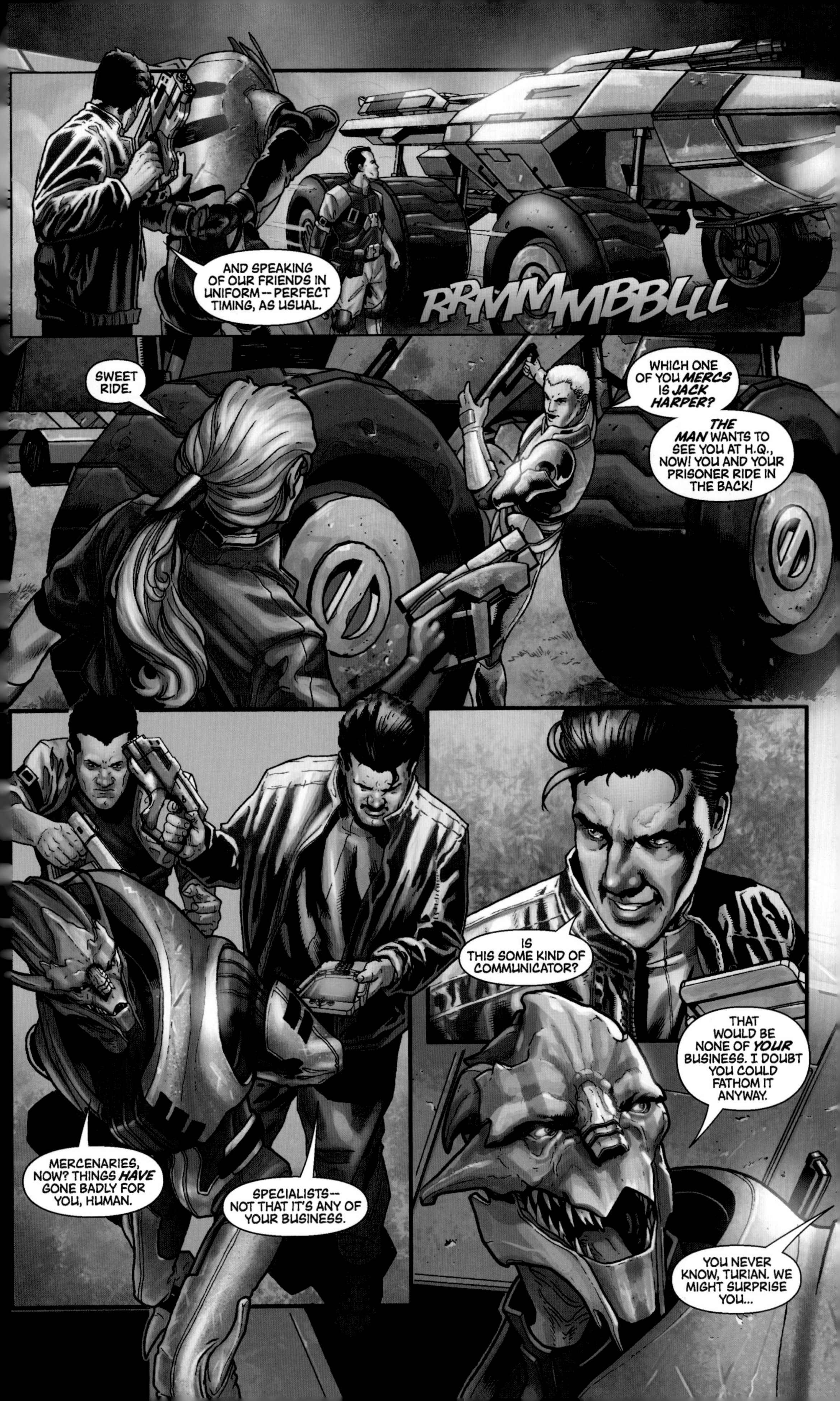
AND SPEAKING OF OUR FRIENDS IN UNIFORM -- PERFECT TIMING, AS USUAL.
RRMMMMBBLLL
SWEET RIDE.
WHICH ONE OF YOU *MERCS* IS *JACK HARPER?*
THE MAN WANTS TO SEE YOU AT H.Q., NOW! YOU AND YOUR PRISONER RIDE IN THE BACK!
MERCENARIES, NOW? THINGS ***HAVE*** GONE BADLY FOR YOU, HUMAN.
SPECIALISTS-- NOT THAT IT'S ANY OF YOUR BUSINESS.
IS THIS SOME KIND OF COMMUNICATOR?
THAT WOULD BE NONE OF ***YOUR*** BUSINESS. I DOUBT YOU COULD FATHOM IT ANYWAY.
YOU NEVER KNOW, TURIAN. WE MIGHT SURPRISE YOU...

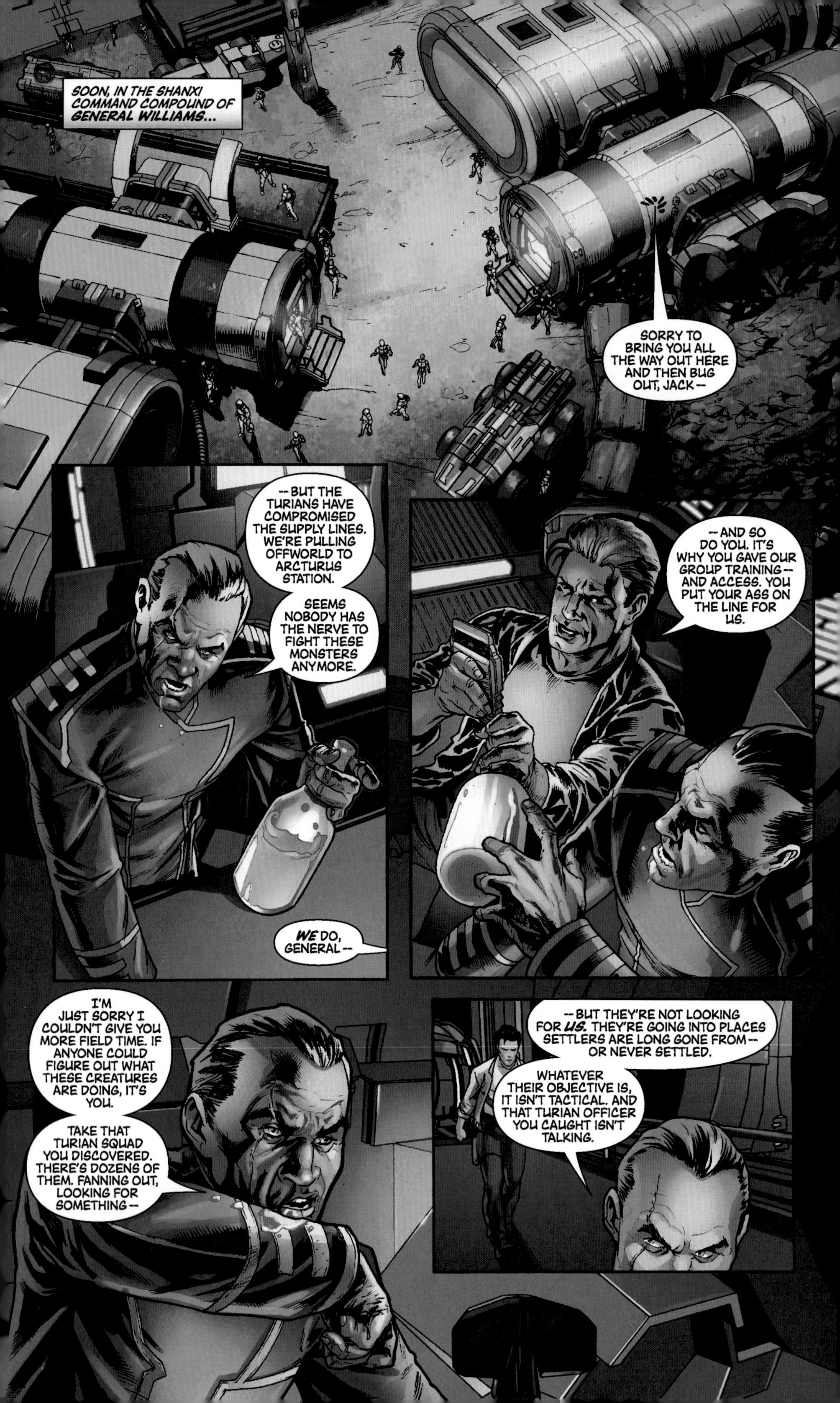
SOON, IN THE SHANXI COMMAND COMPOUND OF GENERAL WILLIAMS...
SORRY TO BRING YOU ALL THE WAY OUT HERE AND THEN BUG OUT, JACK --
-- BUT THE TURIANS HAVE COMPROMISED THE SUPPLY LINES. WE'RE PULLING OFFWORLD TO ARCTURUS STATION.
SEEMS NOBODY HAS THE NERVE TO FIGHT THESE MONSTERS ANYMORE.
WE DO, GENERAL --
-- AND SO DO YOU. IT'S WHY YOU GAVE OUR GROUP TRAINING -- AND ACCESS. YOU PUT YOUR ASS ON THE LINE FOR US.
I'M JUST SORRY I COULDN'T GIVE YOU MORE FIELD TIME. IF ANYONE COULD FIGURE OUT WHAT THESE CREATURES ARE DOING, IT'S YOU.
TAKE THAT TURIAN SQUAD YOU DISCOVERED. THERE'S DOZENS OF THEM. FANNING OUT, LOOKING FOR SOMETHING --
-- BUT THEY'RE NOT LOOKING FOR US. THEY'RE GOING INTO PLACES SETTLERS ARE LONG GONE FROM -- OR NEVER SETTLED.
WHATEVER THEIR OBJECTIVE IS, IT ISN'T TACTICAL. AND THAT TURIAN OFFICER YOU CAUGHT ISN'T TALKING.

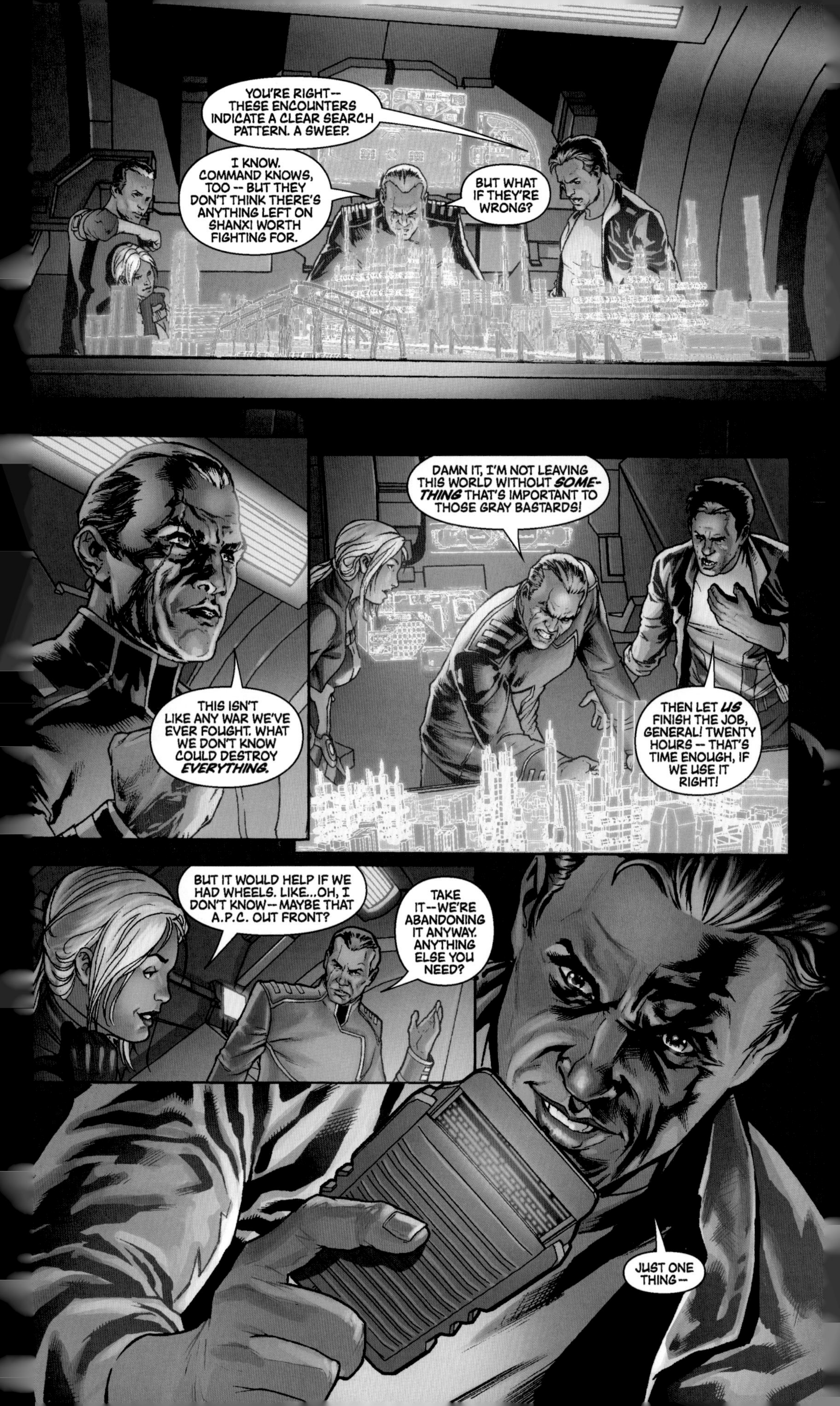
YOU'RE RIGHT-- THESE ENCOUNTERS INDICATE A CLEAR SEARCH PATTERN. A SWEEP.
I KNOW. COMMAND KNOWS, TOO -- BUT THEY DON'T THINK THERE'S ANYTHING LEFT ON SHANXI WORTH FIGHTING FOR.
BUT WHAT IF THEY'RE WRONG?
THIS ISN'T LIKE ANY WAR WE'VE EVER FOUGHT. WHAT WE DON'T KNOW COULD DESTROY EVERYTHING.
DAMN IT, I'M NOT LEAVING THIS WORLD WITHOUT SOMETHING THAT'S IMPORTANT TO THOSE GRAY BASTARDS!
THEN LET US FINISH THE JOB, GENERAL! TWENTY HOURS -- THAT'S TIME ENOUGH, IF WE USE IT RIGHT!
BUT IT WOULD HELP IF WE HAD WHEELS. LIKE...OH, I DON'T KNOW--MAYBE THAT A.P.C. OUT FRONT?
TAKE IT--WE'RE ABANDONING IT ANYWAY. ANYTHING ELSE YOU NEED?
JUST ONE THING--

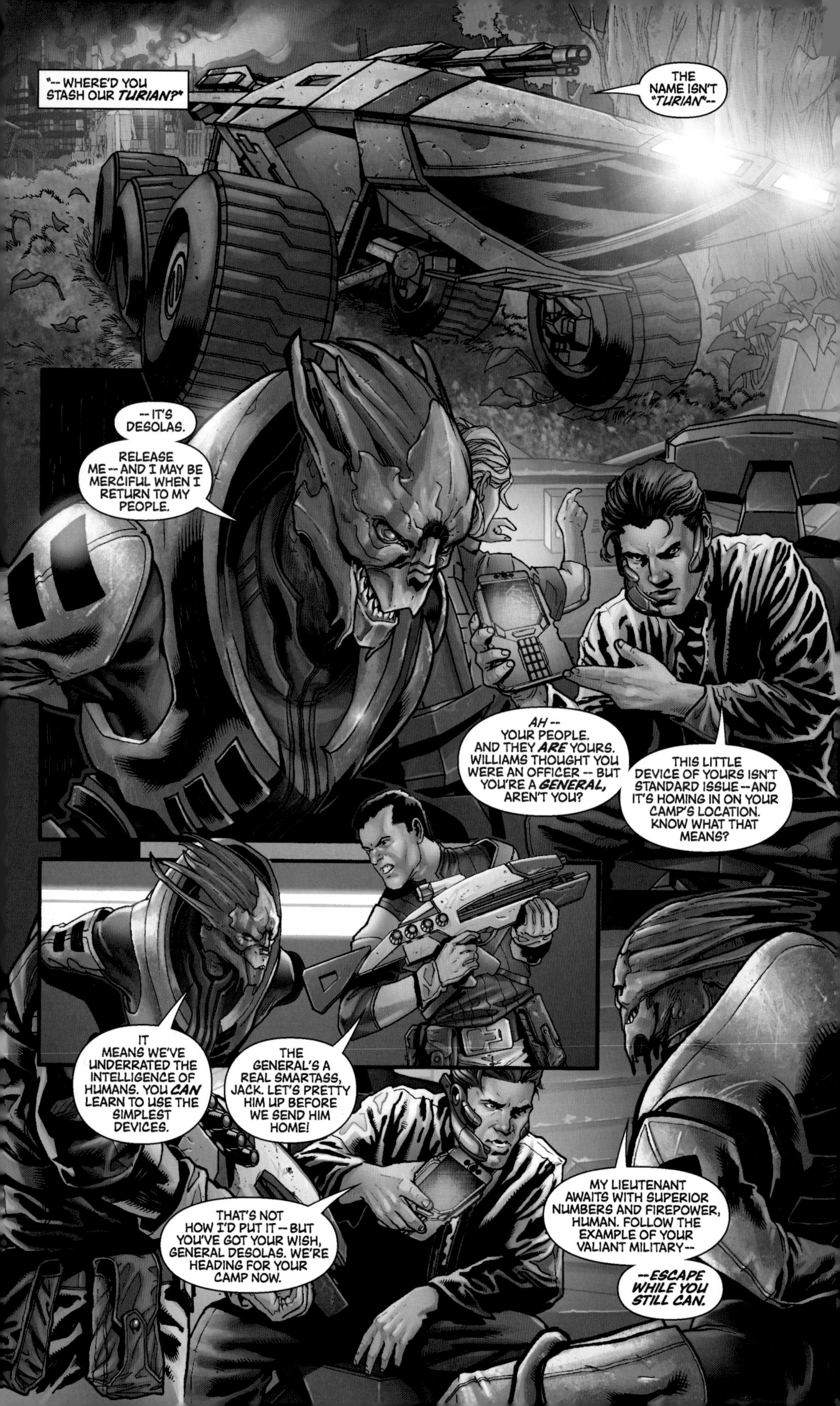
"-- WHERE'D YOU STASH OUR *TURIAN?*"
THE NAME ISN'T *"TURIAN"*--
-- IT'S DESOLAS.
RELEASE ME -- AND I MAY BE MERCIFUL WHEN I RETURN TO MY PEOPLE.
AH -- YOUR PEOPLE. AND THEY *ARE* YOURS. WILLIAMS THOUGHT YOU WERE AN OFFICER -- BUT YOU'RE A *GENERAL,* AREN'T YOU?
THIS LITTLE DEVICE OF YOURS ISN'T STANDARD ISSUE -- AND IT'S HOMING IN ON YOUR CAMP'S LOCATION. KNOW WHAT THAT MEANS?
IT MEANS WE'VE UNDERRATED THE INTELLIGENCE OF HUMANS. YOU *CAN* LEARN TO USE THE SIMPLEST DEVICES.
THE GENERAL'S A REAL SMARTASS, JACK. LET'S PRETTY HIM UP BEFORE WE SEND HIM HOME!
THAT'S NOT HOW I'D PUT IT -- BUT YOU'VE GOT YOUR WISH, GENERAL DESOLAS. WE'RE HEADING FOR YOUR CAMP NOW.
MY LIEUTENANT AWAITS WITH SUPERIOR NUMBERS AND FIREPOWER, HUMAN. FOLLOW THE EXAMPLE OF YOUR VALIANT MILITARY--
--ESCAPE WHILE YOU STILL CAN.

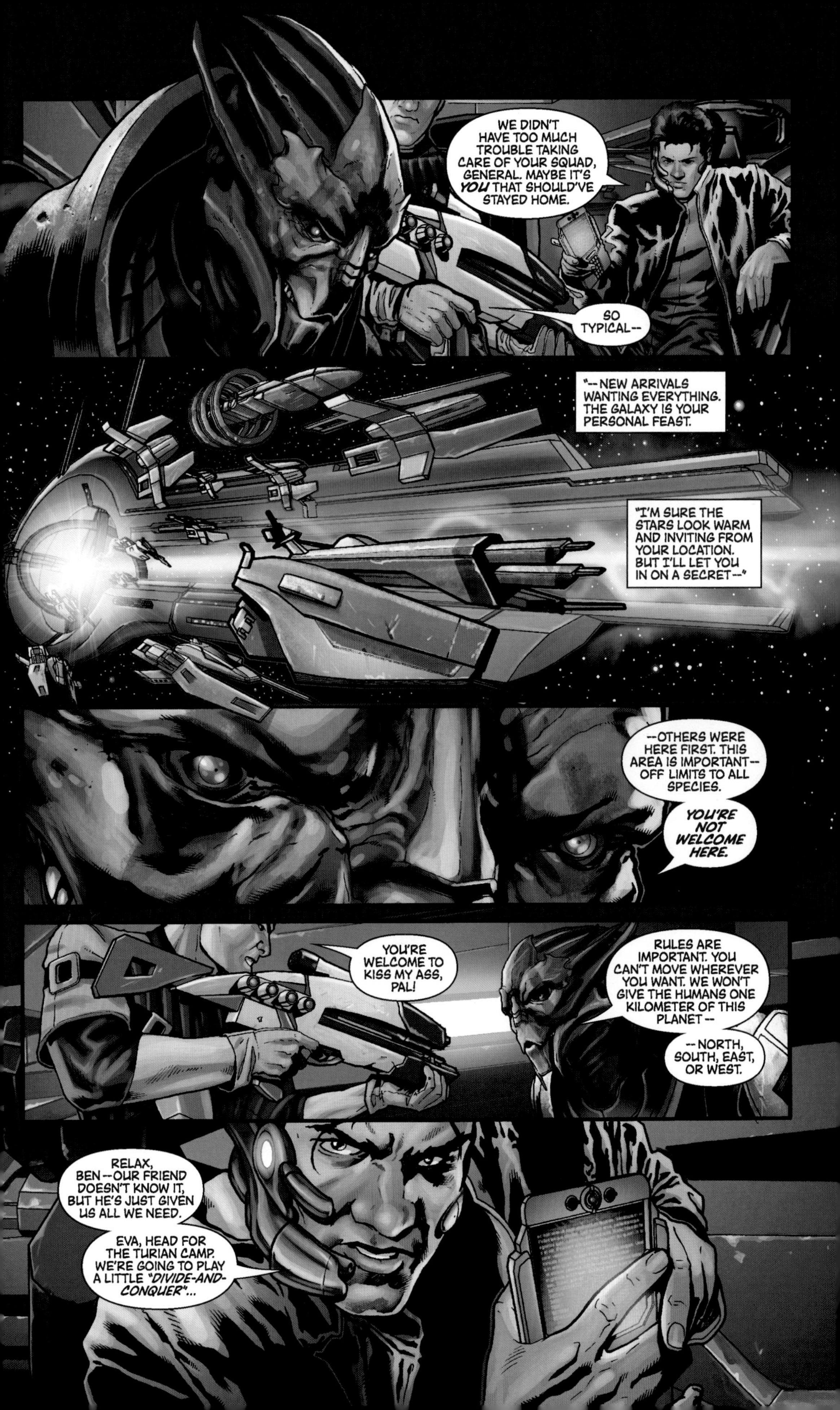
WE DIDN'T HAVE TOO MUCH TROUBLE TAKING CARE OF YOUR SQUAD, GENERAL. MAYBE IT'S *YOU* THAT SHOULD'VE STAYED HOME.
SO TYPICAL--
"--NEW ARRIVALS WANTING EVERYTHING. THE GALAXY IS YOUR PERSONAL FEAST.
"I'M SURE THE STARS LOOK WARM AND INVITING FROM YOUR LOCATION. BUT I'LL LET YOU IN ON A SECRET--"
--OTHERS WERE HERE FIRST. THIS AREA IS IMPORTANT--OFF LIMITS TO ALL SPECIES.
YOU'RE NOT WELCOME HERE.
YOU'RE WELCOME TO KISS MY ASS, PAL!
RULES ARE IMPORTANT. YOU CAN'T MOVE WHEREVER YOU WANT. WE WON'T GIVE THE HUMANS ONE KILOMETER OF THIS PLANET--
--NORTH, SOUTH, EAST, OR WEST.
RELAX, BEN--OUR FRIEND DOESN'T KNOW IT, BUT HE'S JUST GIVEN US ALL WE NEED.
EVA, HEAD FOR THE TURIAN CAMP. WE'RE GOING TO PLAY A LITTLE *"DIVIDE-AND-CONQUER"*...

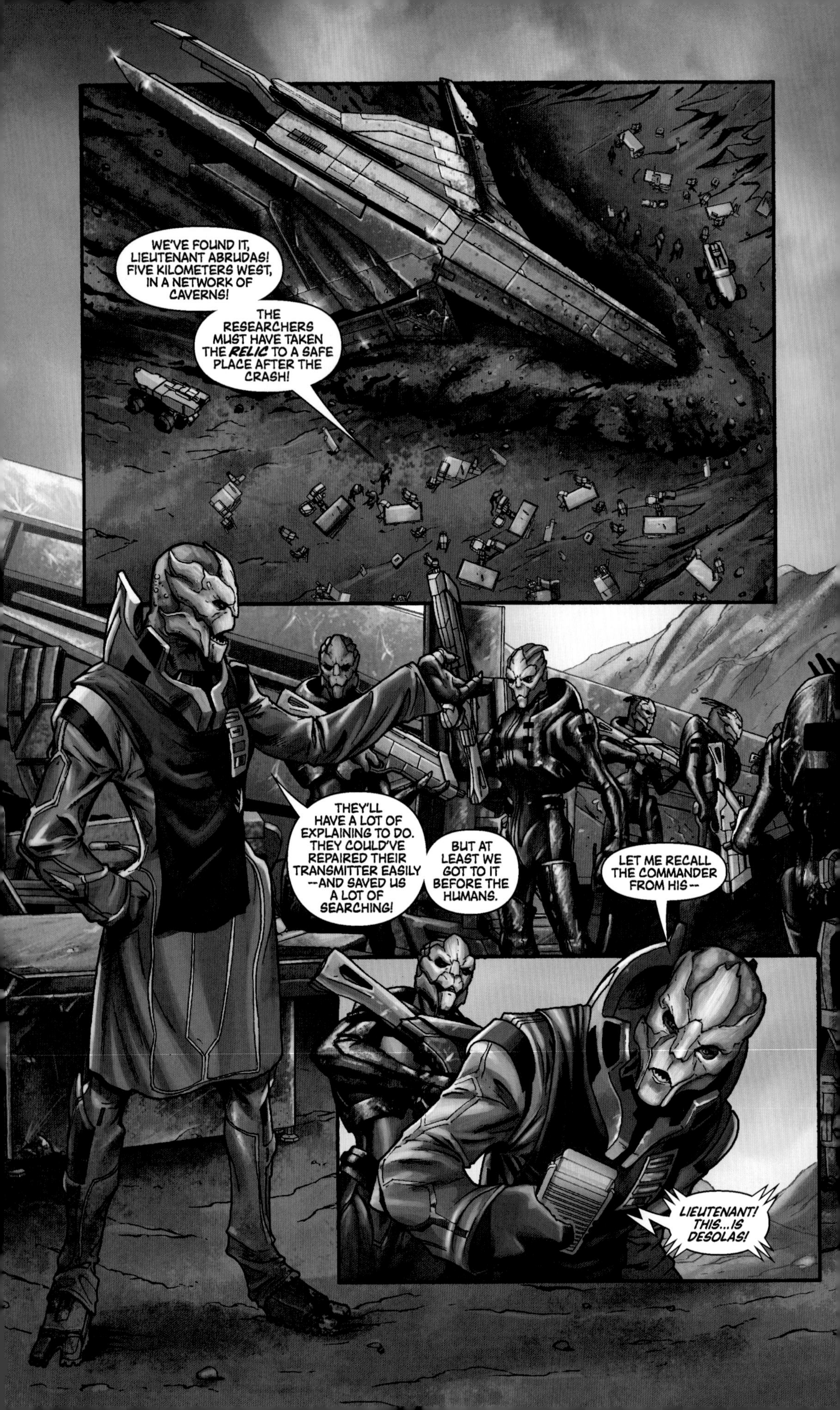
WE'VE FOUND IT, LIEUTENANT ABRUDAS! FIVE KILOMETERS WEST, IN A NETWORK OF CAVERNS!
THE RESEARCHERS MUST HAVE TAKEN THE *RELIC* TO A SAFE PLACE AFTER THE CRASH!
THEY'LL HAVE A LOT OF EXPLAINING TO DO. THEY COULD'VE REPAIRED THEIR TRANSMITTER EASILY --AND SAVED US A LOT OF SEARCHING!
BUT AT LEAST WE GOT TO IT BEFORE THE HUMANS.
LET ME RECALL THE COMMANDER FROM HIS--
LIEUTENANT! THIS...IS DESOLAS!

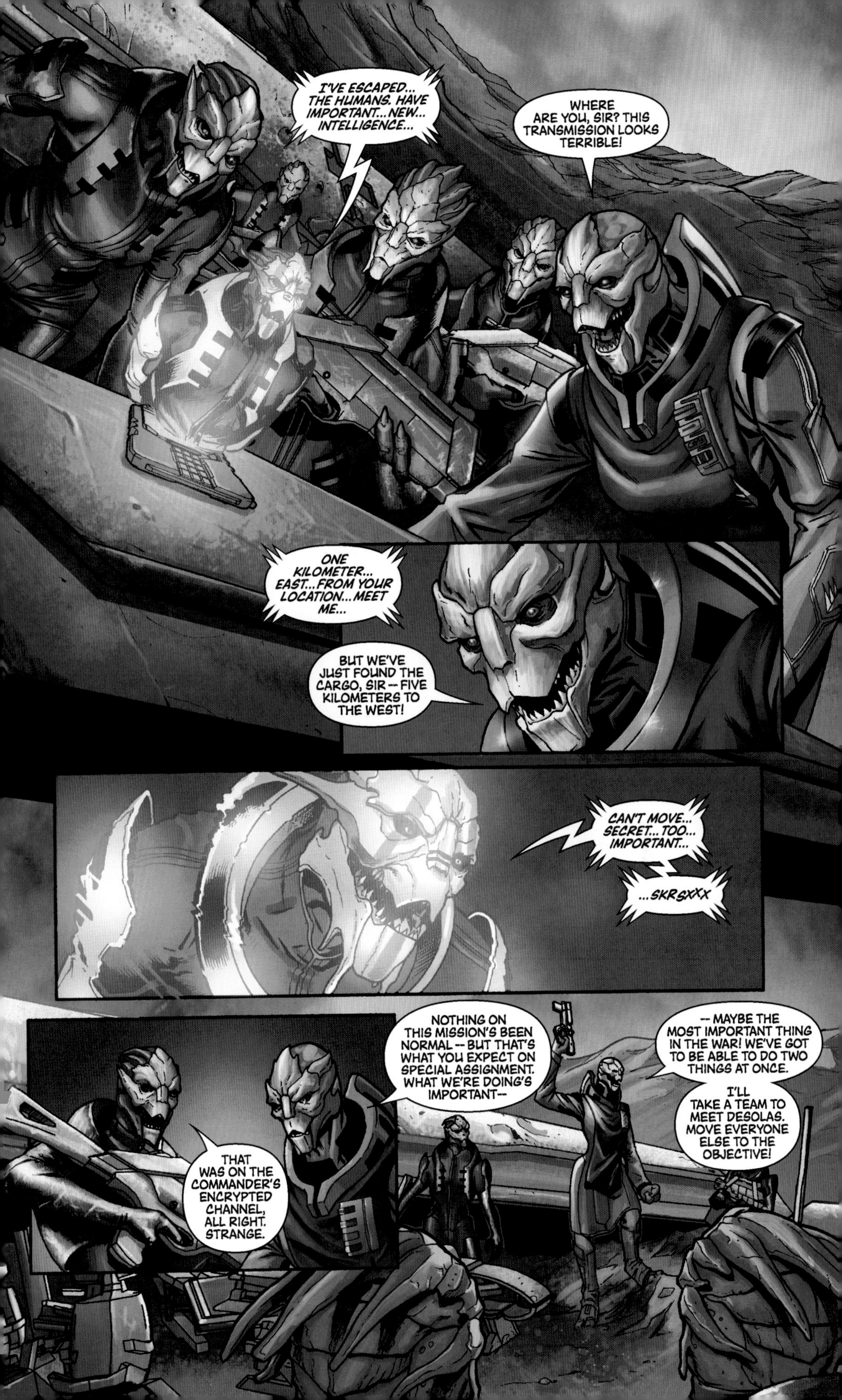
I'VE ESCAPED... THE HUMANS. HAVE IMPORTANT... NEW... INTELLIGENCE...
WHERE ARE YOU, SIR? THIS TRANSMISSION LOOKS TERRIBLE!
ONE KILOMETER... EAST... FROM YOUR LOCATION... MEET ME...
BUT WE'VE JUST FOUND THE CARGO, SIR -- FIVE KILOMETERS TO THE WEST!
CAN'T MOVE... SECRET... TOO... IMPORTANT...
...SKRSXXX
THAT WAS ON THE COMMANDER'S ENCRYPTED CHANNEL, ALL RIGHT. STRANGE.
NOTHING ON THIS MISSION'S BEEN NORMAL -- BUT THAT'S WHAT YOU EXPECT ON SPECIAL ASSIGNMENT. WHAT WE'RE DOING'S IMPORTANT--
-- MAYBE THE MOST IMPORTANT THING IN THE WAR! WE'VE GOT TO BE ABLE TO DO TWO THINGS AT ONCE.
I'LL TAKE A TEAM TO MEET DESOLAS. MOVE EVERYONE ELSE TO THE OBJECTIVE!

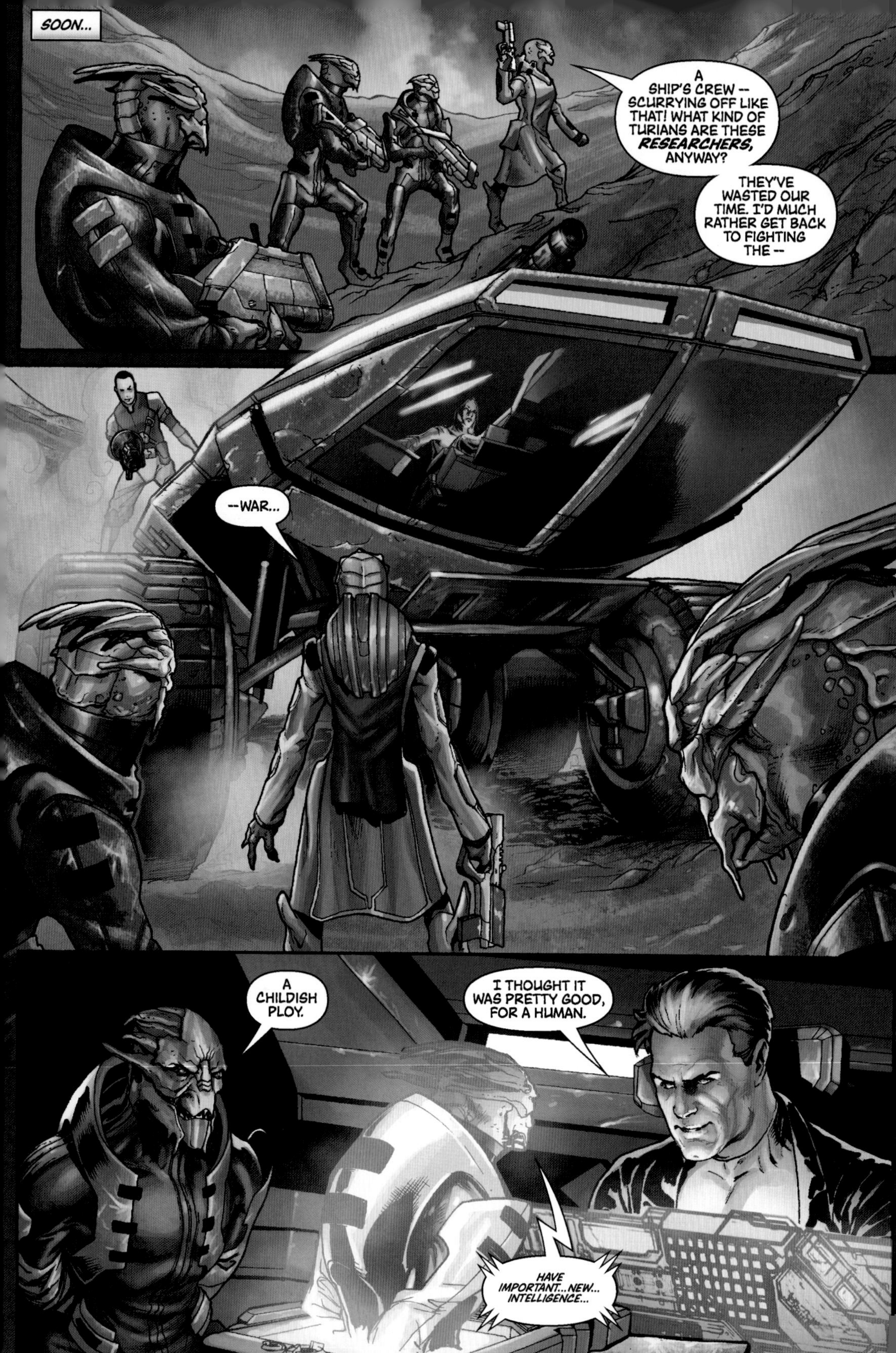
SOON...
A SHIP'S CREW -- SCURRYING OFF LIKE THAT! WHAT KIND OF TURIANS ARE THESE ***RESEARCHERS,*** ANYWAY?
THEY'VE WASTED OUR TIME. I'D MUCH RATHER GET BACK TO FIGHTING THE --
--WAR...
A CHILDISH PLOY.
I THOUGHT IT WAS PRETTY GOOD, FOR A HUMAN.
HAVE IMPORTANT...NEW... INTELLIGENCE...

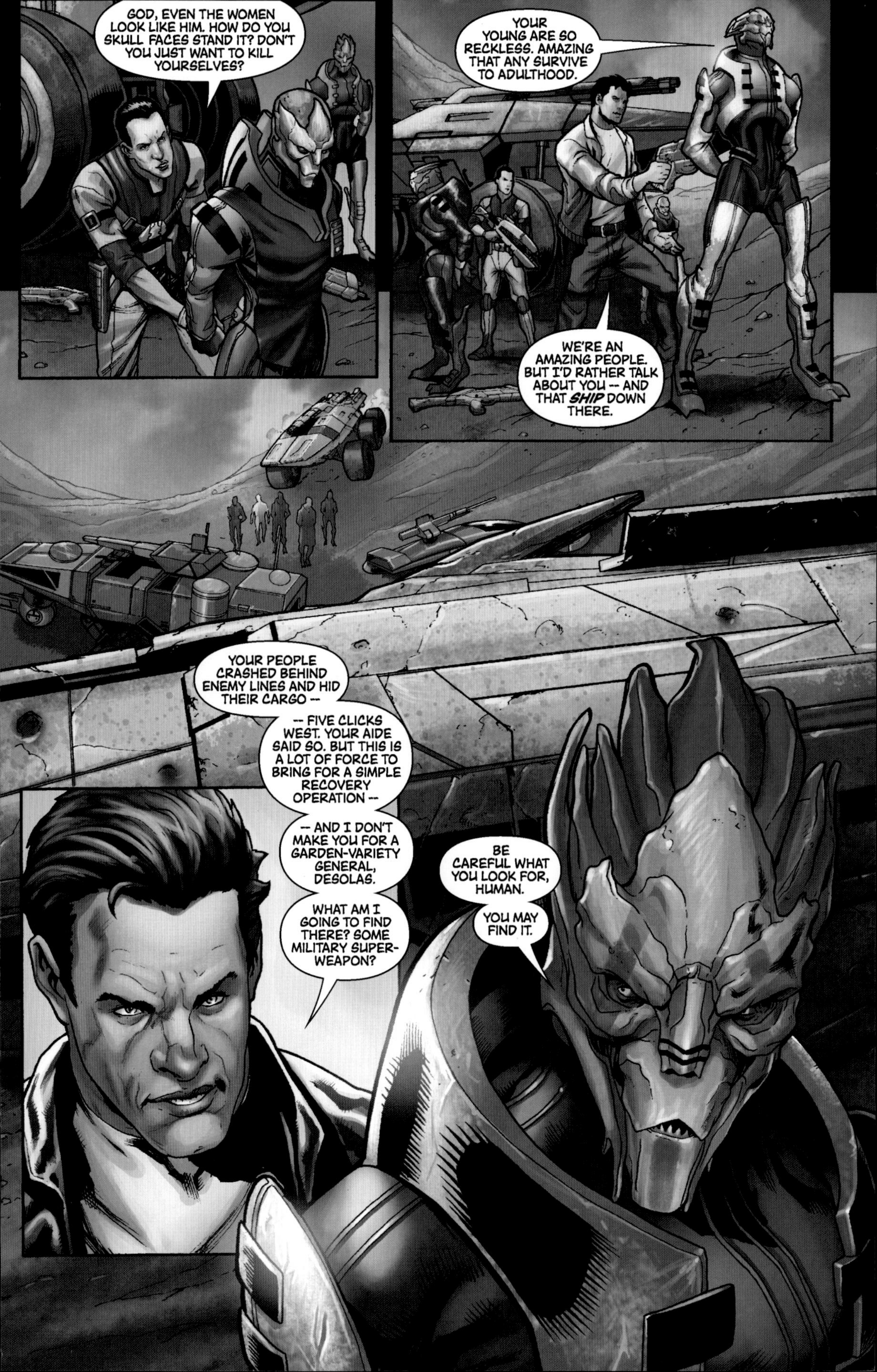
GOD, EVEN THE WOMEN LOOK LIKE HIM. HOW DO YOU SKULL FACES STAND IT? DON'T YOU JUST WANT TO KILL YOURSELVES?
YOUR YOUNG ARE SO RECKLESS. AMAZING THAT ANY SURVIVE TO ADULTHOOD.
WE'RE AN AMAZING PEOPLE. BUT I'D RATHER TALK ABOUT YOU -- AND THAT SHIP DOWN THERE.
YOUR PEOPLE CRASHED BEHIND ENEMY LINES AND HID THEIR CARGO --
-- FIVE CLICKS WEST. YOUR AIDE SAID SO. BUT THIS IS A LOT OF FORCE TO BRING FOR A SIMPLE RECOVERY OPERATION --
-- AND I DON'T MAKE YOU FOR A GARDEN-VARIETY GENERAL, DESOLAS.
WHAT AM I GOING TO FIND THERE? SOME MILITARY SUPER-WEAPON?
BE CAREFUL WHAT YOU LOOK FOR, HUMAN.
YOU MAY FIND IT.

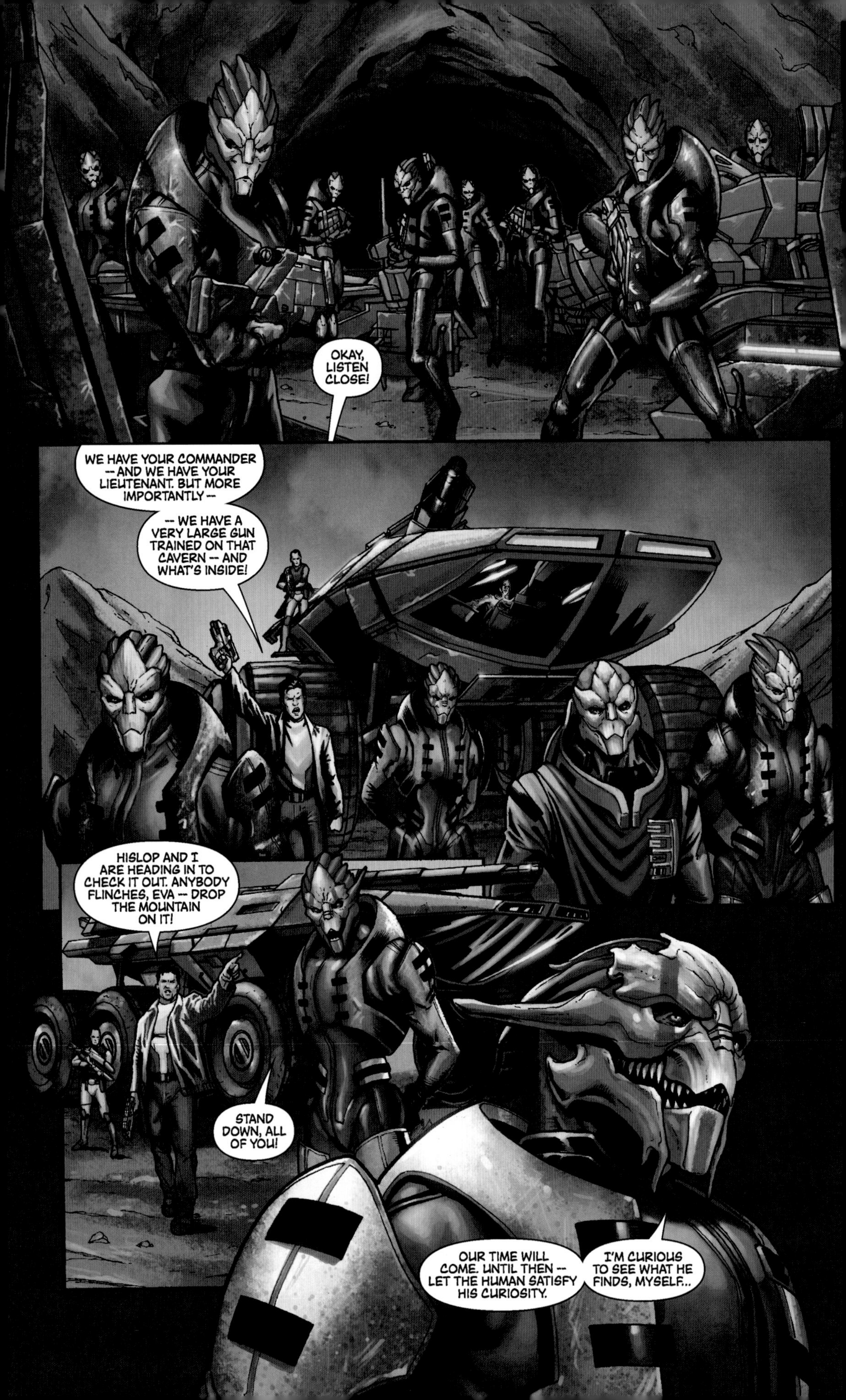
OKAY, LISTEN CLOSE!
WE HAVE YOUR COMMANDER -- AND WE HAVE YOUR LIEUTENANT. BUT MORE IMPORTANTLY --
-- WE HAVE A VERY LARGE GUN TRAINED ON THAT CAVERN -- AND WHAT'S INSIDE!
HISLOP AND I ARE HEADING IN TO CHECK IT OUT. ANYBODY FLINCHES, EVA -- DROP THE MOUNTAIN ON IT!
STAND DOWN, ALL OF YOU!
OUR TIME WILL COME. UNTIL THEN -- LET THE HUMAN SATISFY HIS CURIOSITY.
I'M CURIOUS TO SEE WHAT HE FINDS, MYSELF...

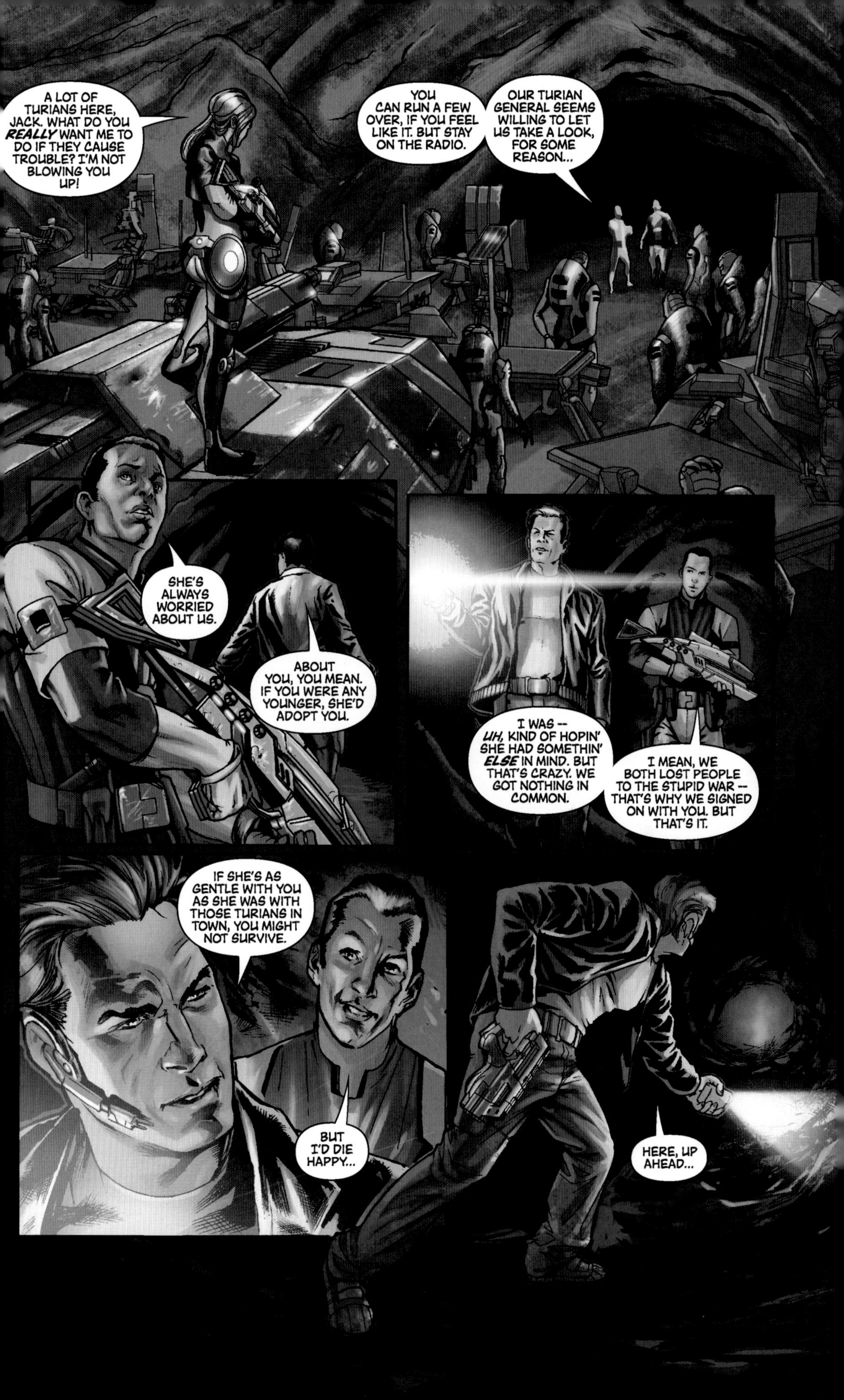
A LOT OF TURIANS HERE, JACK. WHAT DO YOU *REALLY* WANT ME TO DO IF THEY CAUSE TROUBLE? I'M NOT BLOWING YOU UP!
YOU CAN RUN A FEW OVER, IF YOU FEEL LIKE IT. BUT STAY ON THE RADIO.
OUR TURIAN GENERAL SEEMS WILLING TO LET US TAKE A LOOK, FOR SOME REASON...
SHE'S ALWAYS WORRIED ABOUT US.
ABOUT YOU, YOU MEAN. IF YOU WERE ANY YOUNGER, SHE'D ADOPT YOU.
I WAS -- *UH,* KIND OF HOPIN' SHE HAD SOMETHIN' *ELSE* IN MIND. BUT THAT'S CRAZY. WE GOT NOTHING IN COMMON.
I MEAN, WE BOTH LOST PEOPLE TO THE STUPID WAR -- THAT'S WHY WE SIGNED ON WITH YOU. BUT THAT'S IT.
IF SHE'S AS GENTLE WITH YOU AS SHE WAS WITH THOSE TURIANS IN TOWN, YOU MIGHT NOT SURVIVE.
BUT I'D DIE HAPPY...
HERE, UP AHEAD...

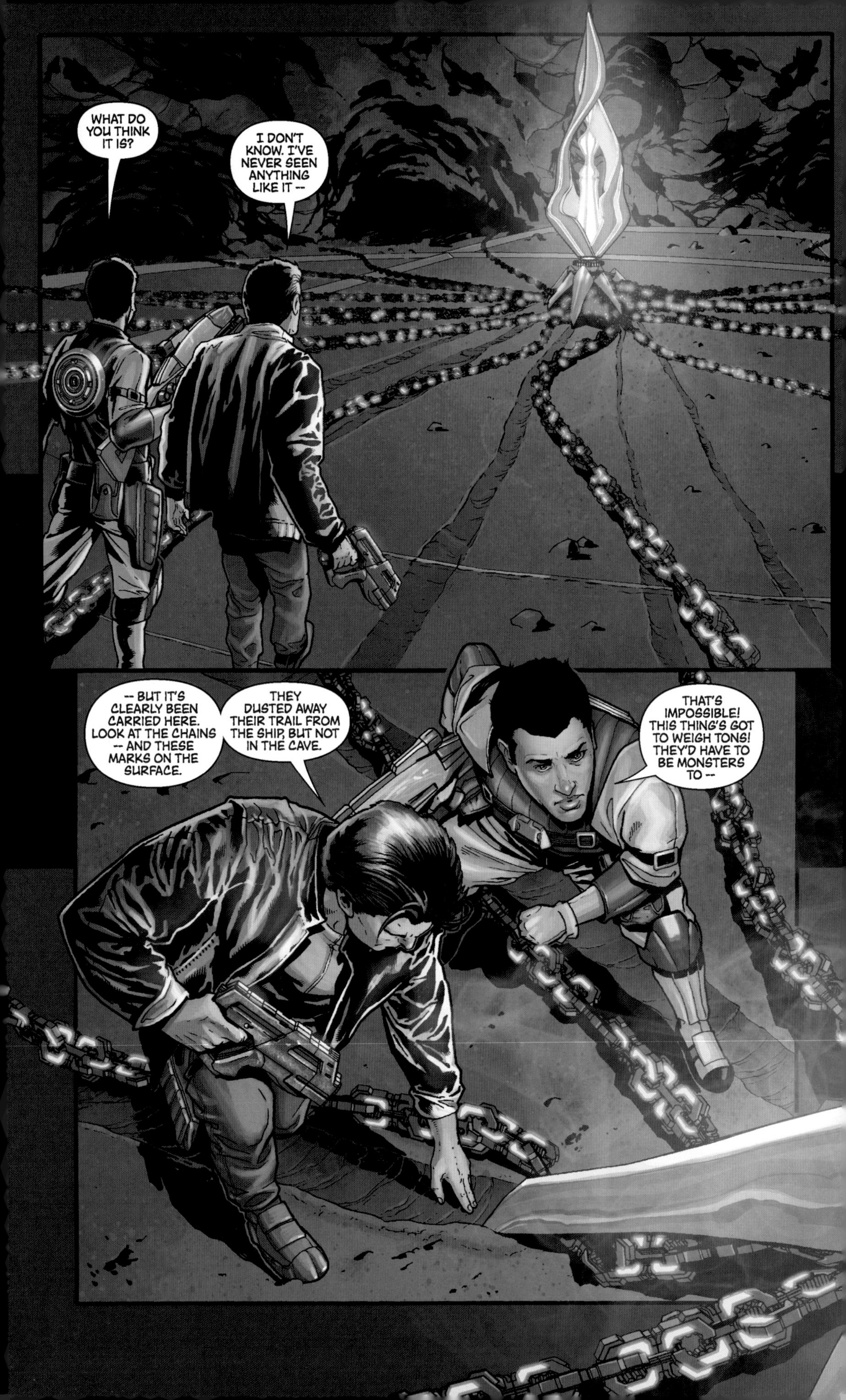
WHAT DO YOU THINK IT IS?
I DON'T KNOW. I'VE NEVER SEEN ANYTHING LIKE IT --
-- BUT IT'S CLEARLY BEEN CARRIED HERE. LOOK AT THE CHAINS -- AND THESE MARKS ON THE SURFACE.
THEY DUSTED AWAY THEIR TRAIL FROM THE SHIP, BUT NOT IN THE CAVE.
THAT'S IMPOSSIBLE! THIS THING'S GOT TO WEIGH TONS! THEY'D HAVE TO BE MONSTERS TO --

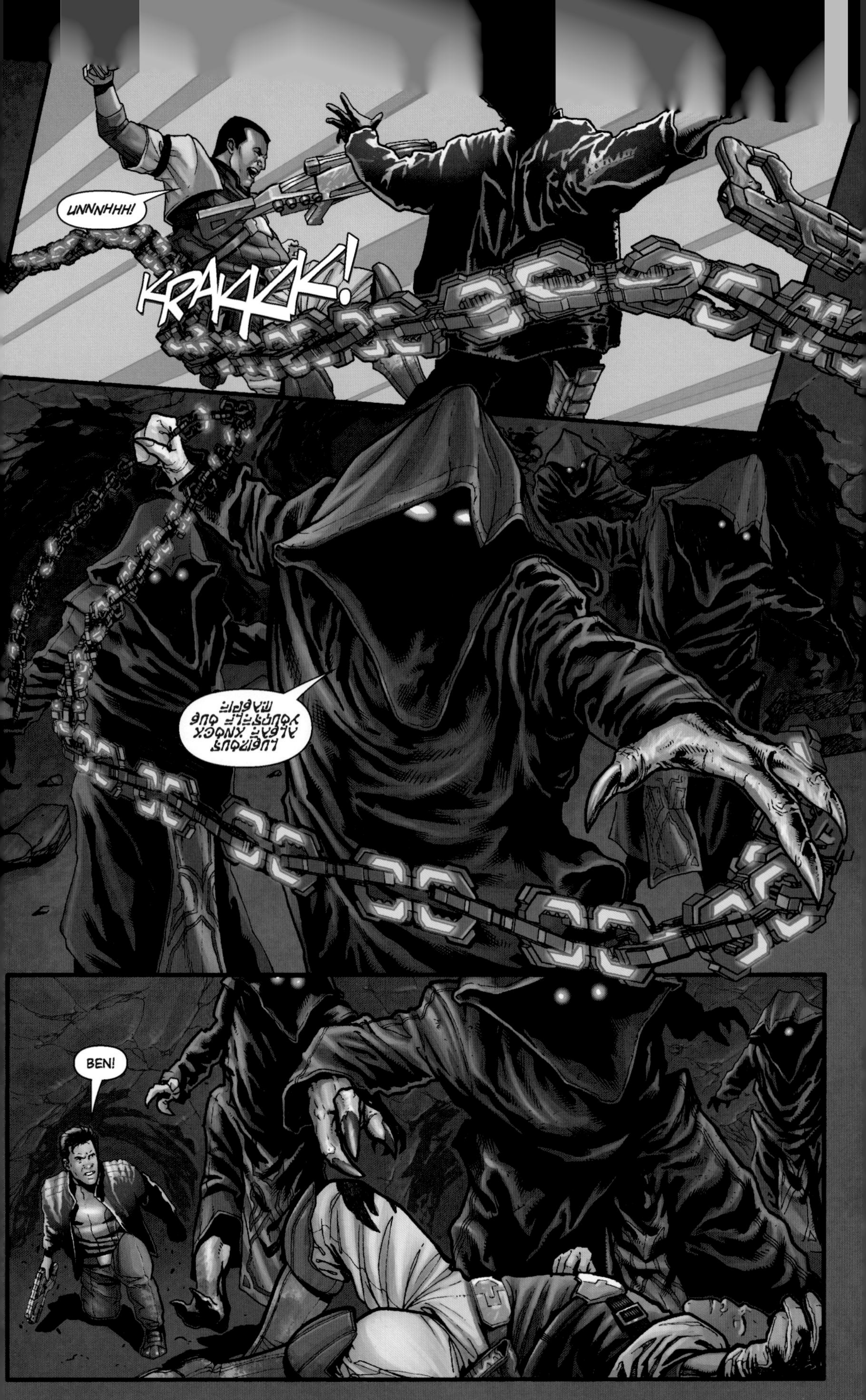
UNNNHHH!
KRAKKK!
BEN!

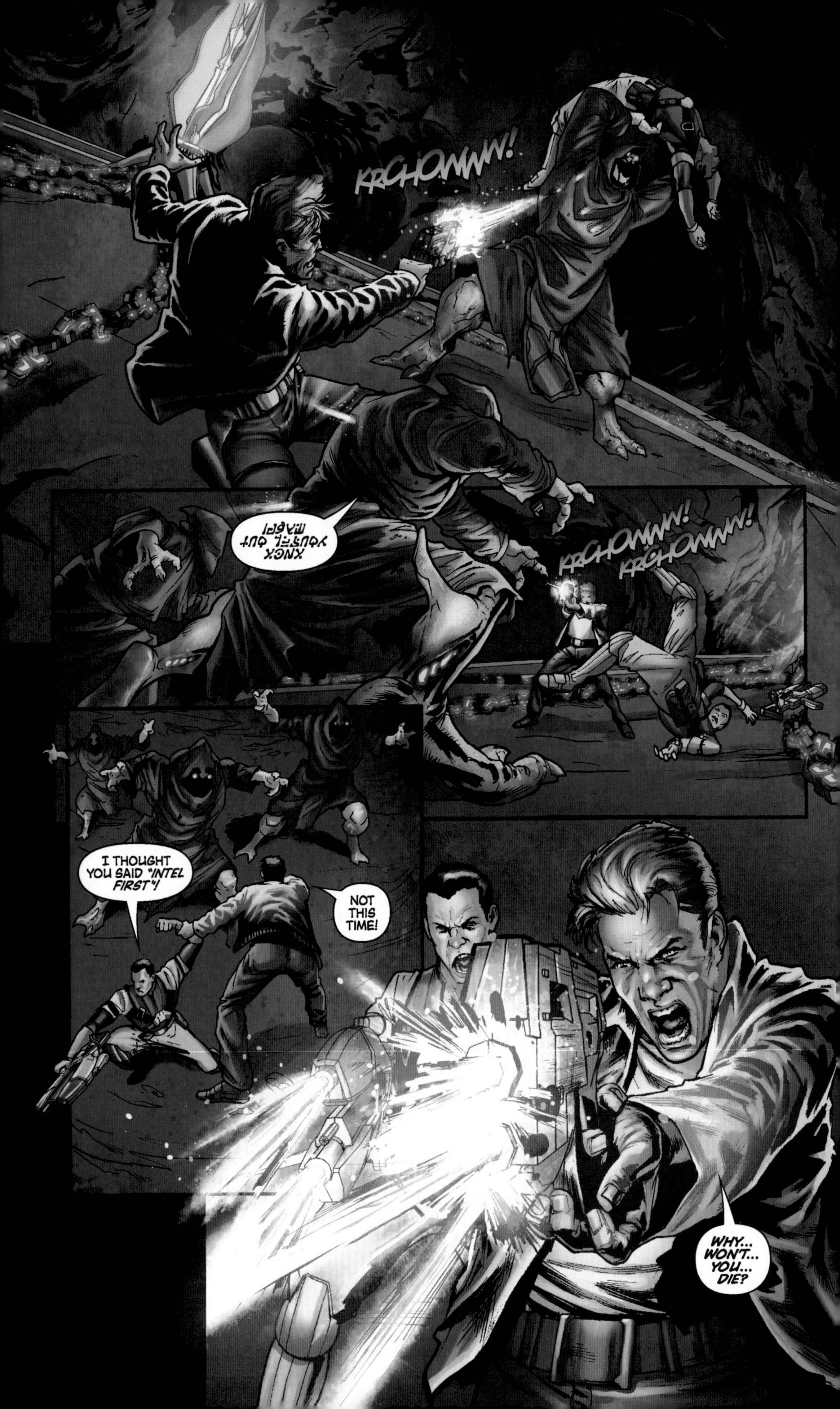
KRCHOWWW!
KRCHOWWW!
KRCHOWWW!
I THOUGHT YOU SAID "INTEL FIRST"!
NOT THIS TIME!
WHY... WON'T... YOU... DIE?

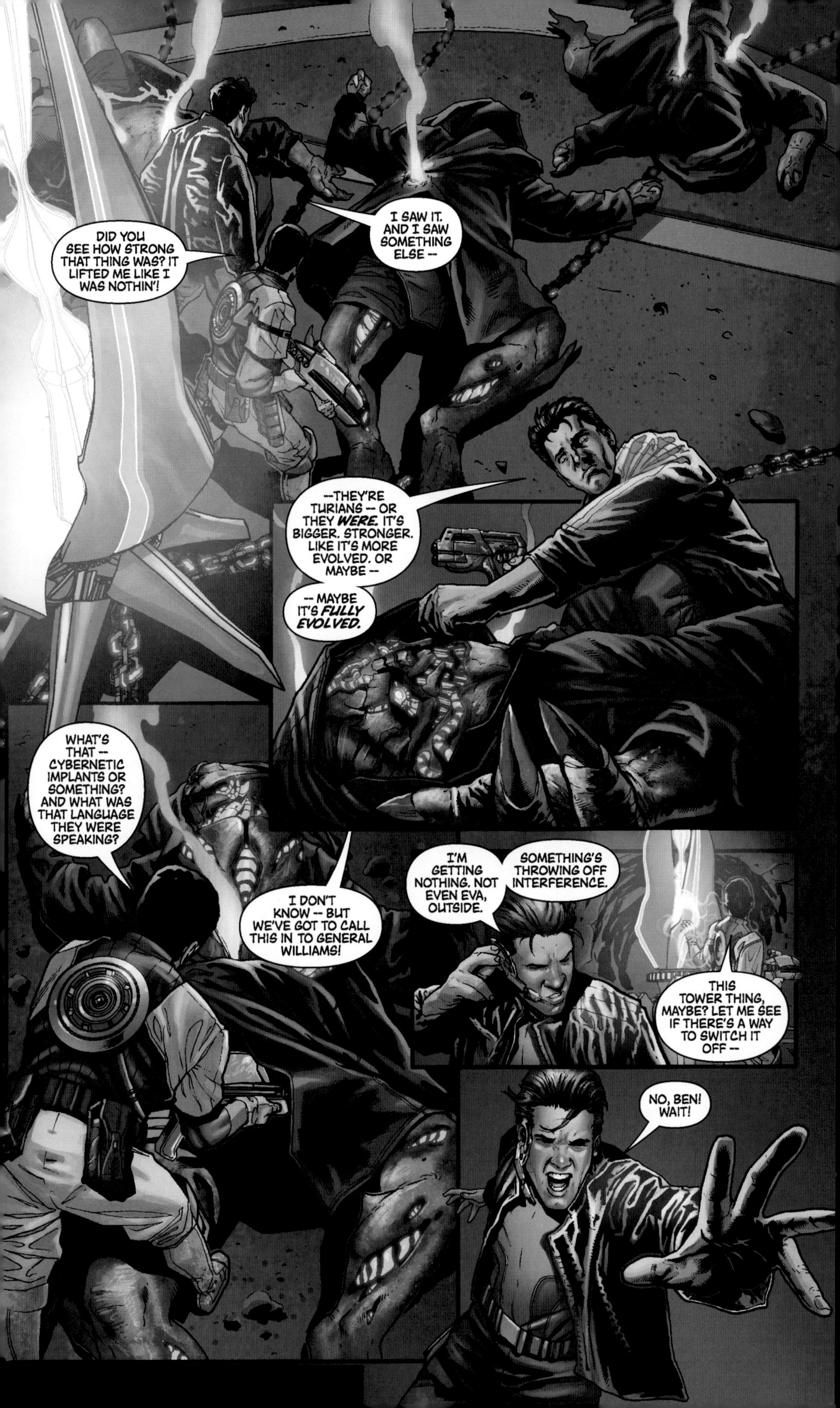
DID YOU SEE HOW STRONG THAT THING WAS? IT LIFTED ME LIKE I WAS NOTHIN'!
I SAW IT. AND I SAW SOMETHING ELSE --
--THEY'RE TURIANS -- OR THEY *WERE.* IT'S BIGGER. STRONGER. LIKE IT'S MORE EVOLVED. OR MAYBE --
-- MAYBE IT'S ***FULLY EVOLVED.***
WHAT'S THAT -- CYBERNETIC IMPLANTS OR SOMETHING? AND WHAT WAS THAT LANGUAGE THEY WERE SPEAKING?
I DON'T KNOW -- BUT WE'VE GOT TO CALL THIS IN TO GENERAL WILLIAMS!
I'M GETTING NOTHING. NOT EVEN EVA, OUTSIDE.
SOMETHING'S THROWING OFF INTERFERENCE.
THIS TOWER THING, MAYBE? LET ME SEE IF THERE'S A WAY TO SWITCH IT OFF --
NO, BEN! WAIT!

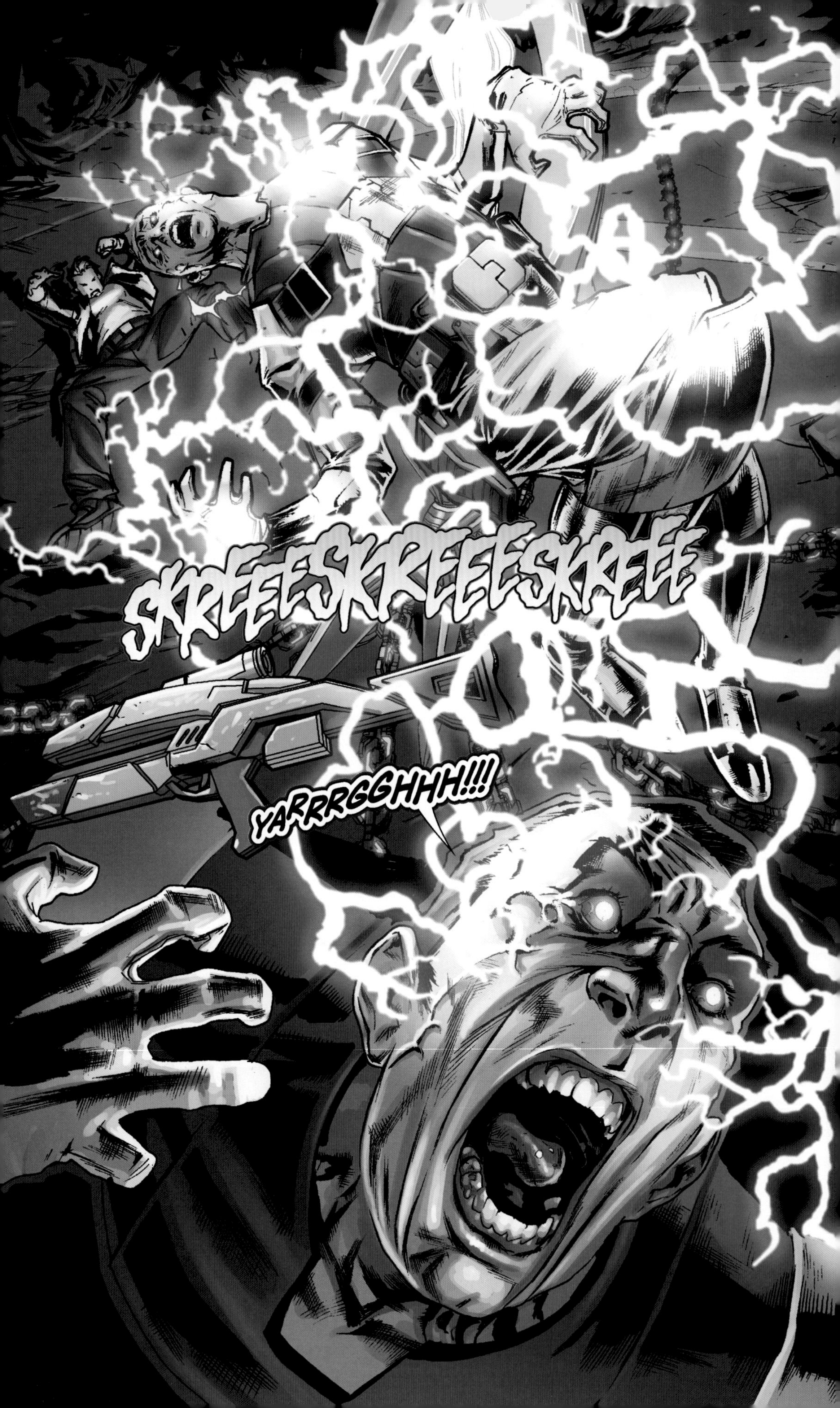
SKREEESKREEESKREEE
YARRRGGHHH!!!

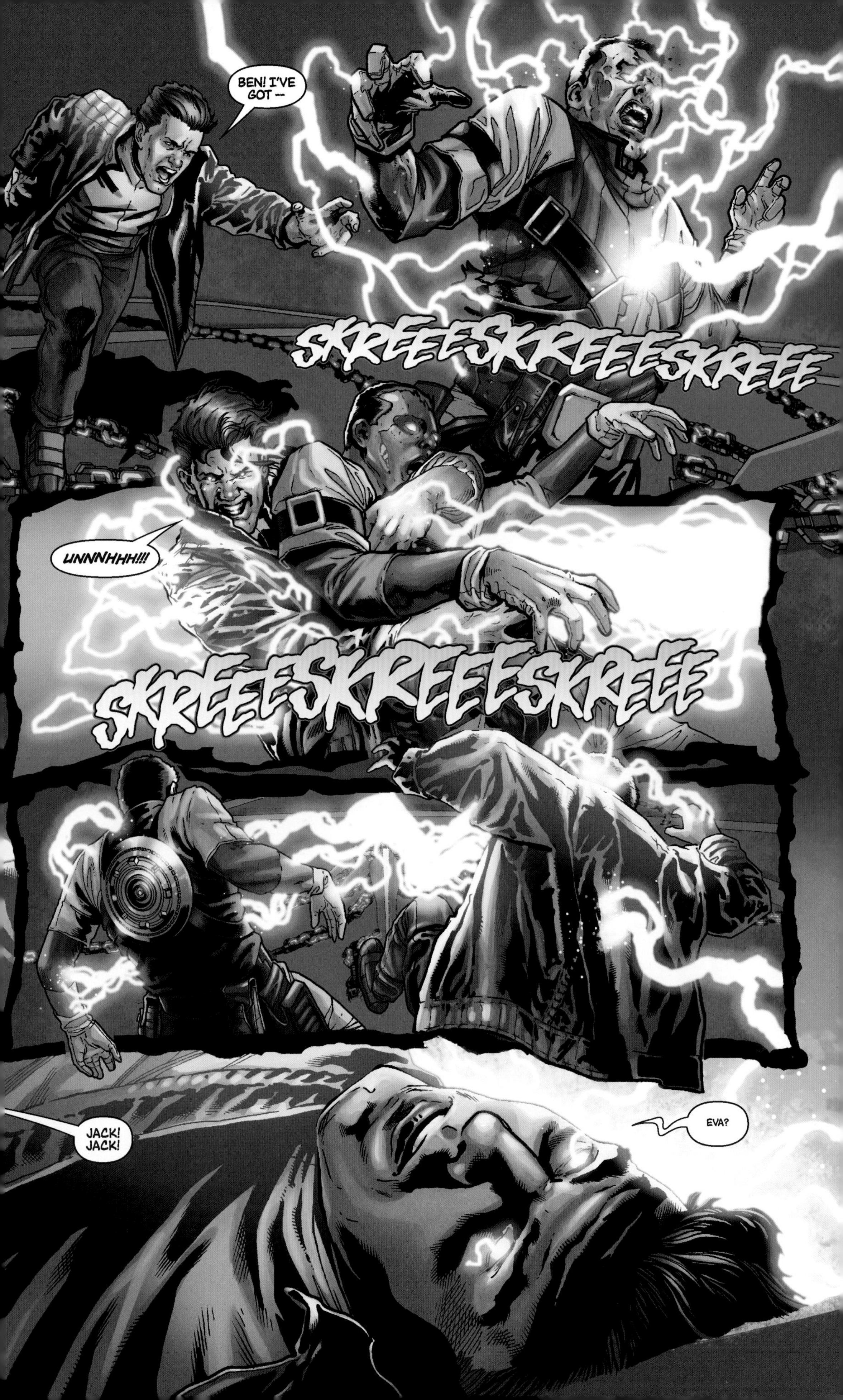
BEN! I'VE GOT --
SKREEESKREEESKREEE
UNNNHHH!!!
SKREEESKREEESKREEE
JACK! JACK!
EVA?

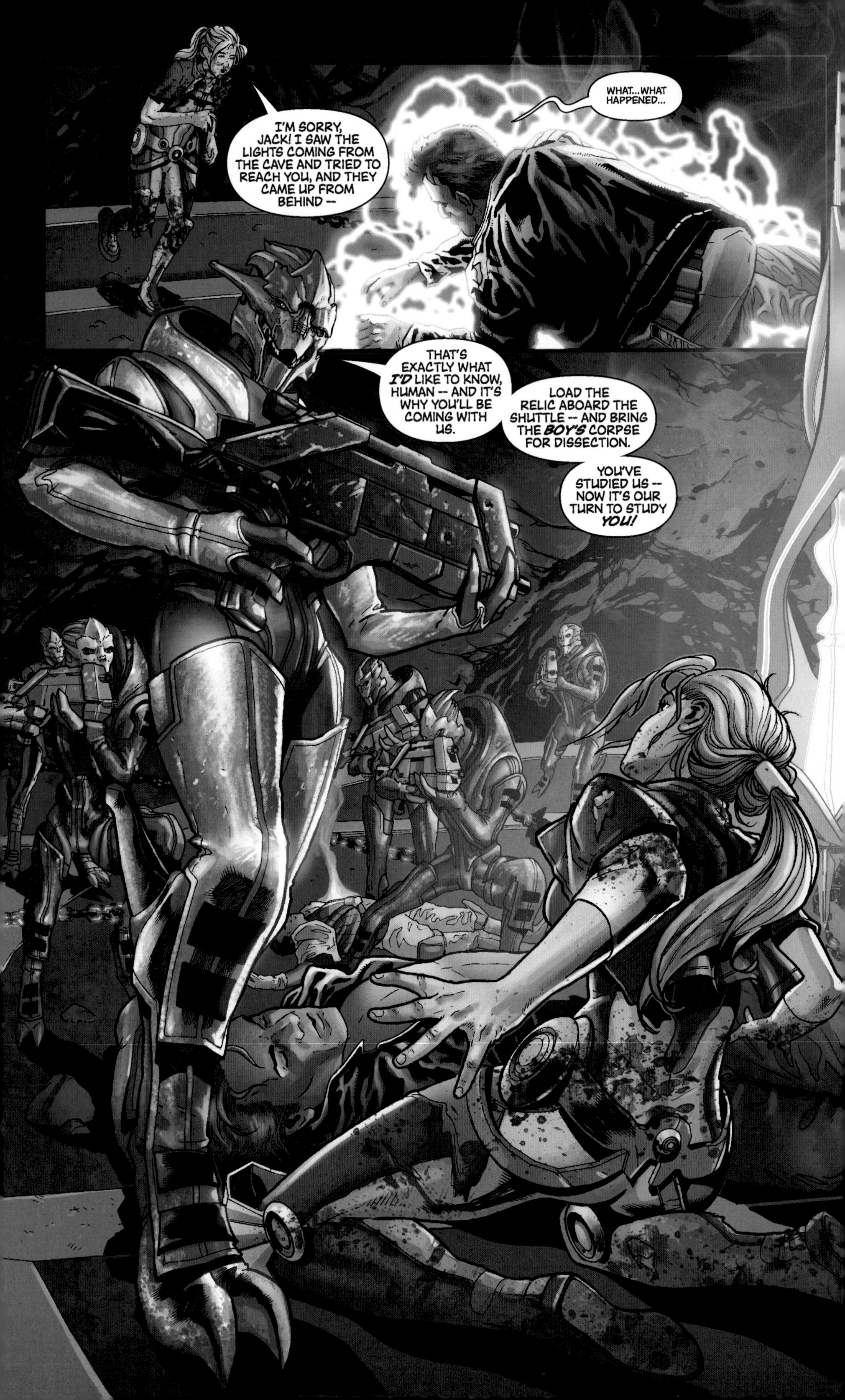
I'M SORRY, JACK! I SAW THE LIGHTS COMING FROM THE CAVE AND TRIED TO REACH YOU, AND THEY CAME UP FROM BEHIND --
WHAT...WHAT HAPPENED...
THAT'S EXACTLY WHAT *I'D* LIKE TO KNOW, HUMAN -- AND IT'S WHY YOU'LL BE COMING WITH US.
LOAD THE RELIC ABOARD THE SHUTTLE -- AND BRING THE *BOY'S* CORPSE FOR DISSECTION.
YOU'VE STUDIED US -- NOW IT'S OUR TURN TO STUDY *YOU!*

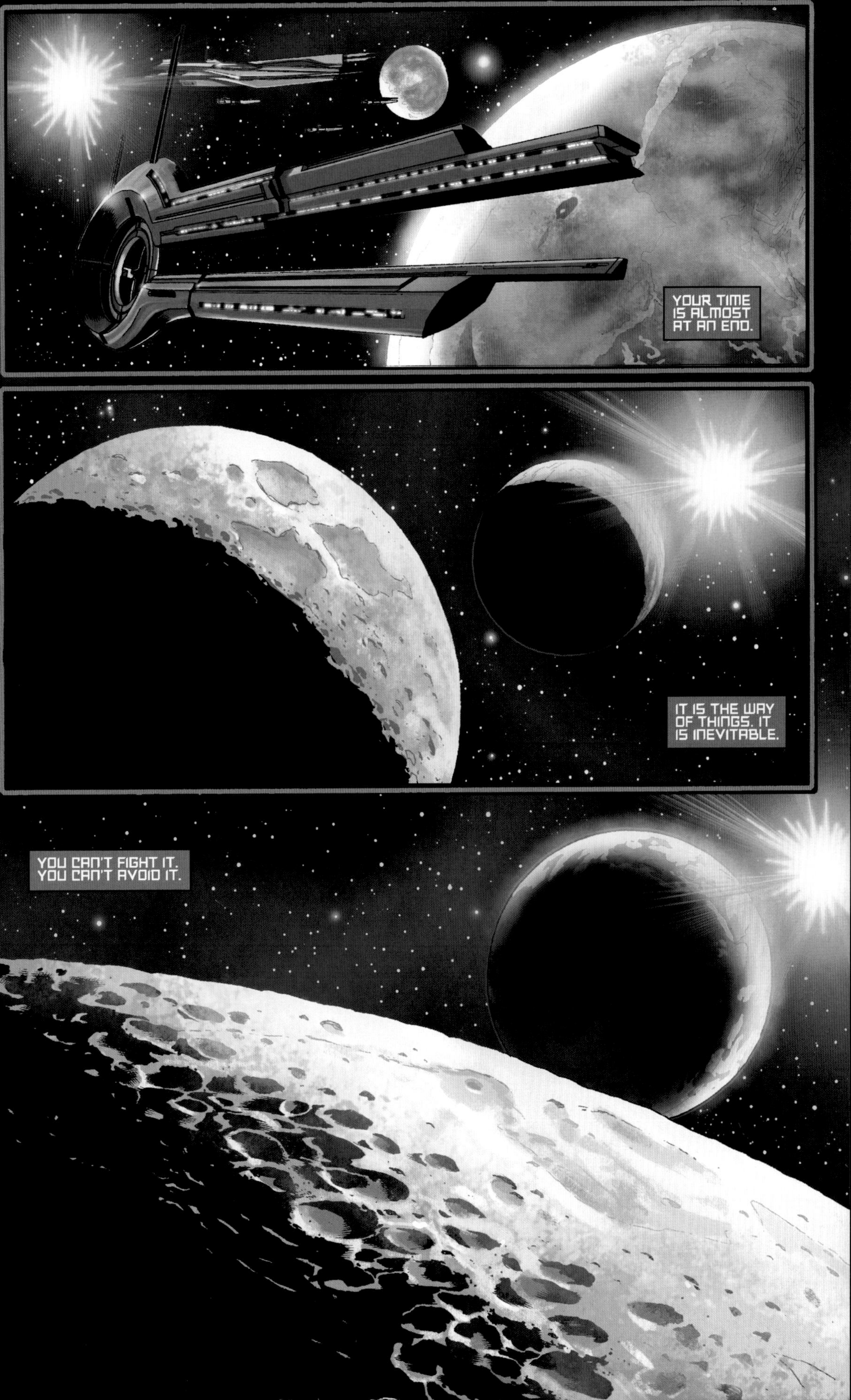
YOUR TIME IS ALMOST AT AN END.
IT IS THE WAY OF THINGS. IT IS INEVITABLE.
YOU CAN'T FIGHT IT. YOU CAN'T AVOID IT.

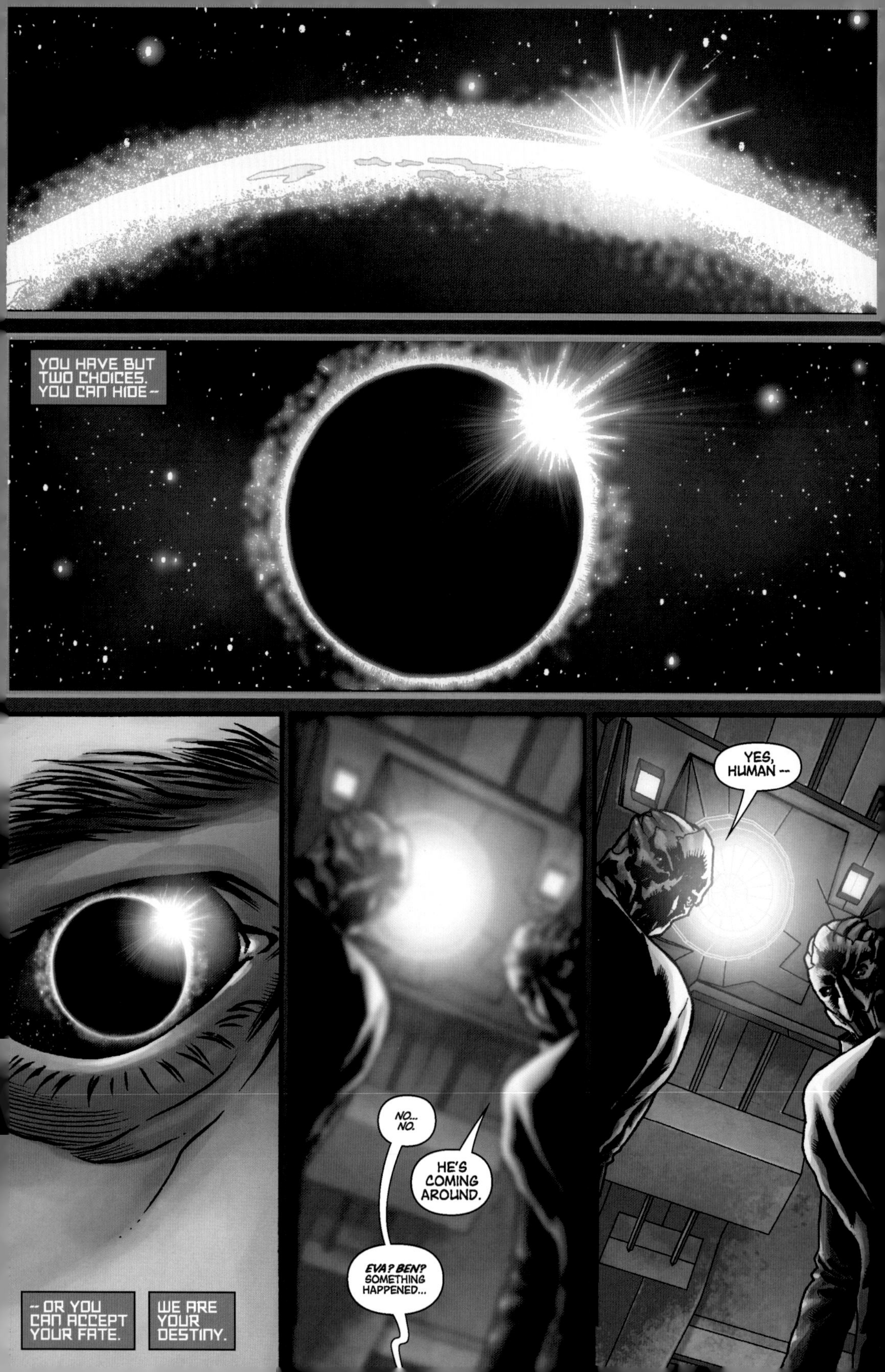
YOU HAVE BUT TWO CHOICES. YOU CAN HIDE--
--OR YOU CAN ACCEPT YOUR FATE.
WE ARE YOUR DESTINY.
NO... NO.
HE'S COMING AROUND.
EVA? BEN? SOMETHING HAPPENED...
YES, HUMAN --

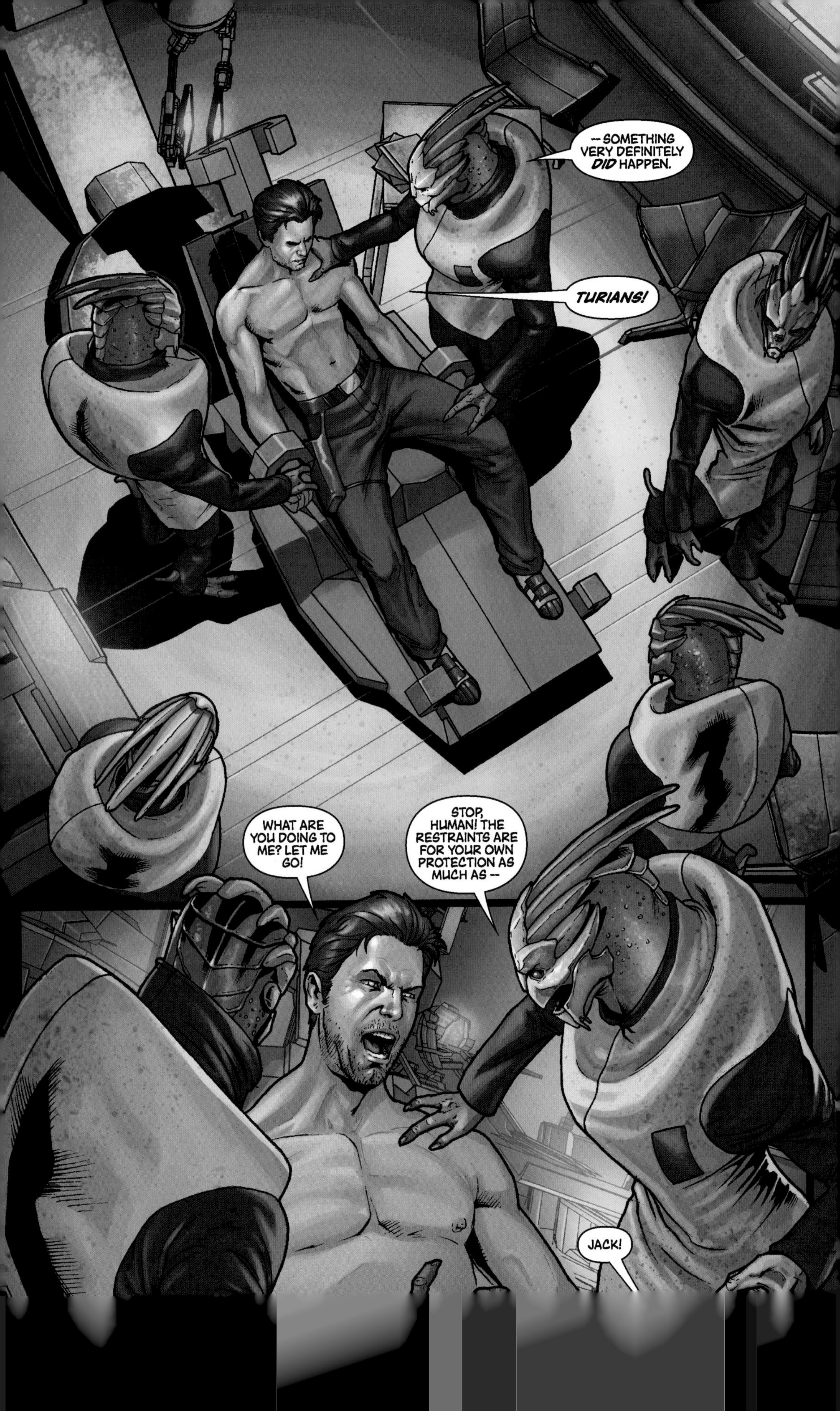
-- SOMETHING VERY DEFINITELY *DID* HAPPEN.
TURIANS!
WHAT ARE YOU DOING TO ME? LET ME GO!
STOP, HUMAN! THE RESTRAINTS ARE FOR YOUR OWN PROTECTION AS MUCH AS --
JACK!

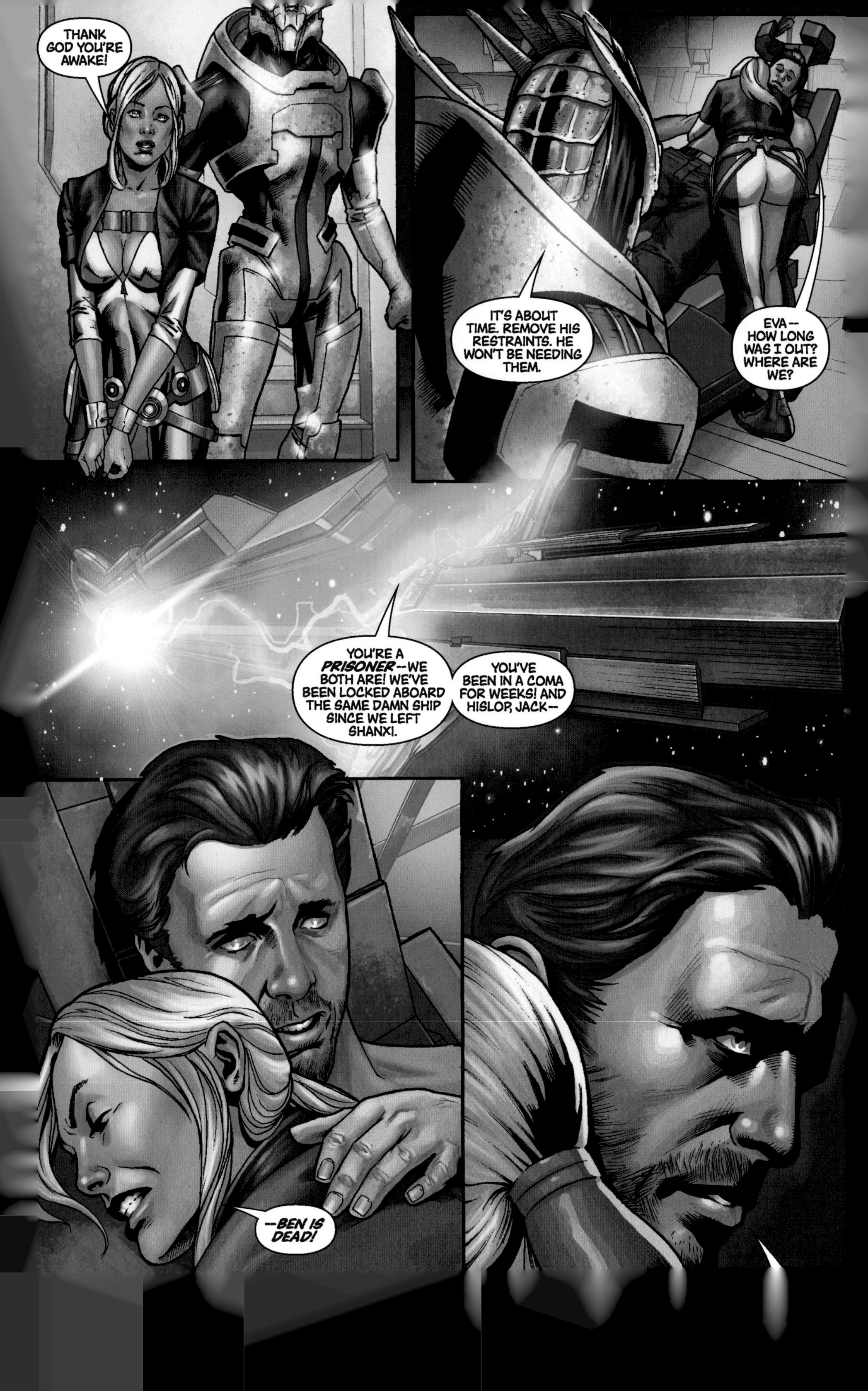
THANK GOD YOU'RE AWAKE!
IT'S ABOUT TIME. REMOVE HIS RESTRAINTS. HE WON'T BE NEEDING THEM.
EVA-- HOW LONG WAS I OUT? WHERE ARE WE?
YOU'RE A *PRISONER*--WE BOTH ARE! WE'VE BEEN LOCKED ABOARD THE SAME DAMN SHIP SINCE WE LEFT SHANXI.
YOU'VE BEEN IN A COMA FOR WEEKS! AND HISLOP, JACK--
--BEN IS DEAD!

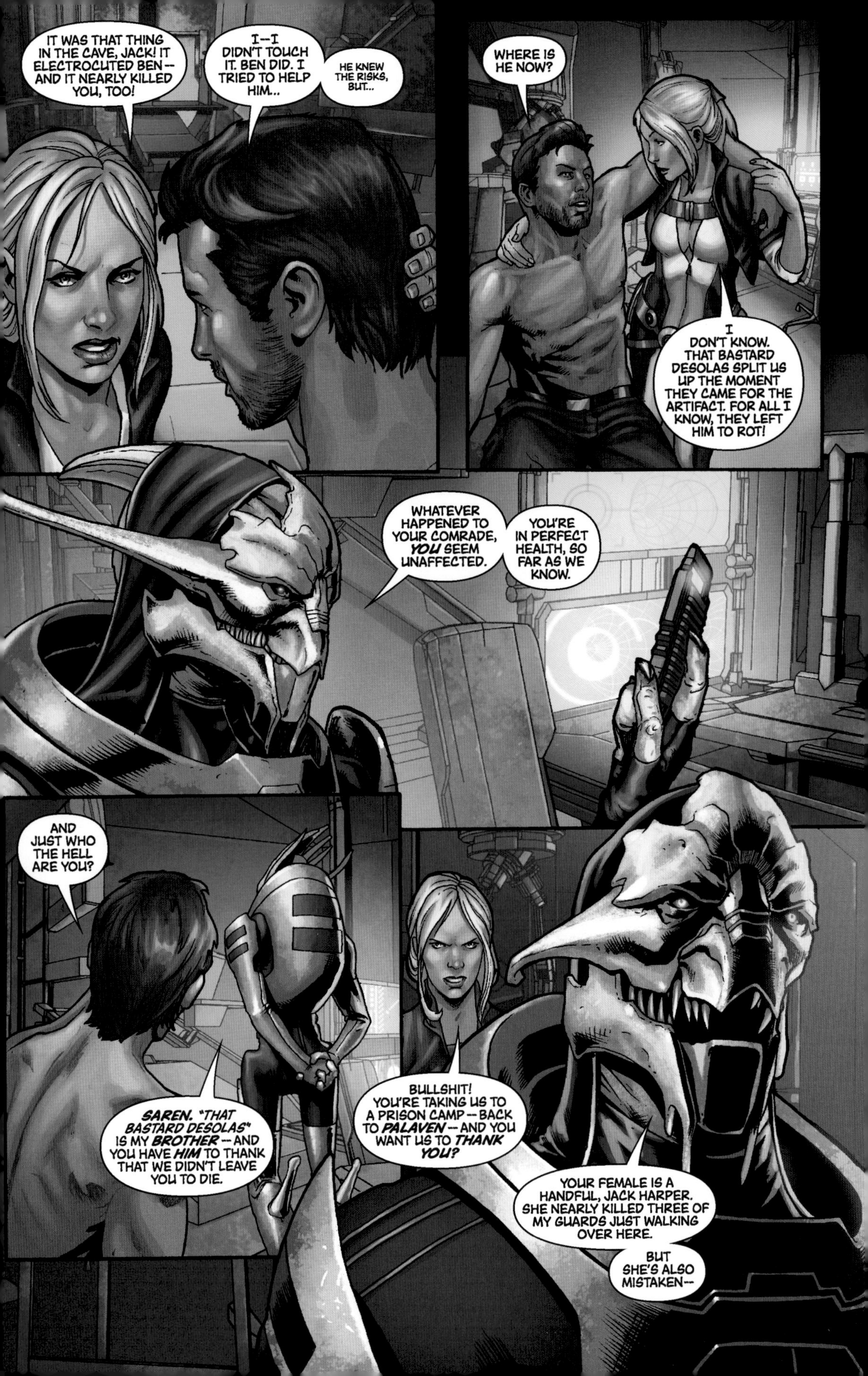
IT WAS THAT THING IN THE CAVE, JACK! IT ELECTROCUTED BEN -- AND IT NEARLY KILLED YOU, TOO!
I--I DIDN'T TOUCH IT. BEN DID. I TRIED TO HELP HIM...
HE KNEW THE RISKS, BUT...
WHERE IS HE NOW?
I DON'T KNOW. THAT BASTARD DESOLAS SPLIT US UP THE MOMENT THEY CAME FOR THE ARTIFACT. FOR ALL I KNOW, THEY LEFT HIM TO ROT!
WHATEVER HAPPENED TO YOUR COMRADE, YOU SEEM UNAFFECTED.
YOU'RE IN PERFECT HEALTH, SO FAR AS WE KNOW.
AND JUST WHO THE HELL ARE YOU?
SAREN. "THAT BASTARD DESOLAS" IS MY BROTHER -- AND YOU HAVE HIM TO THANK THAT WE DIDN'T LEAVE YOU TO DIE.
BULLSHIT! YOU'RE TAKING US TO A PRISON CAMP -- BACK TO PALAVEN -- AND YOU WANT US TO THANK YOU?
YOUR FEMALE IS A HANDFUL, JACK HARPER. SHE NEARLY KILLED THREE OF MY GUARDS JUST WALKING OVER HERE.
BUT SHE'S ALSO MISTAKEN--

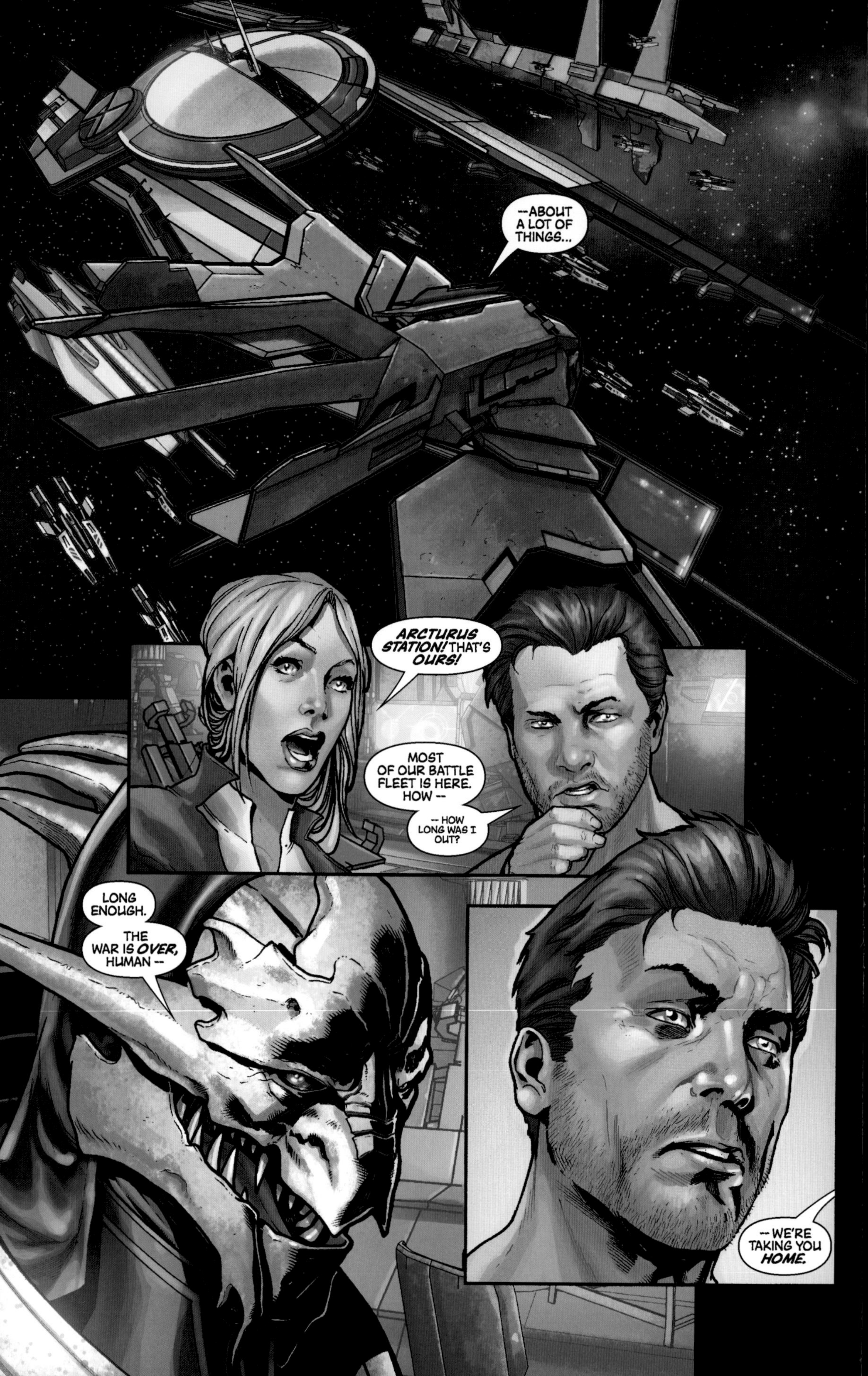
--ABOUT A LOT OF THINGS...
ARCTURUS STATION! THAT'S OURS!
MOST OF OUR BATTLE FLEET IS HERE. HOW --
-- HOW LONG WAS I OUT?
LONG ENOUGH.
THE WAR IS OVER, HUMAN --
-- WE'RE TAKING YOU HOME.

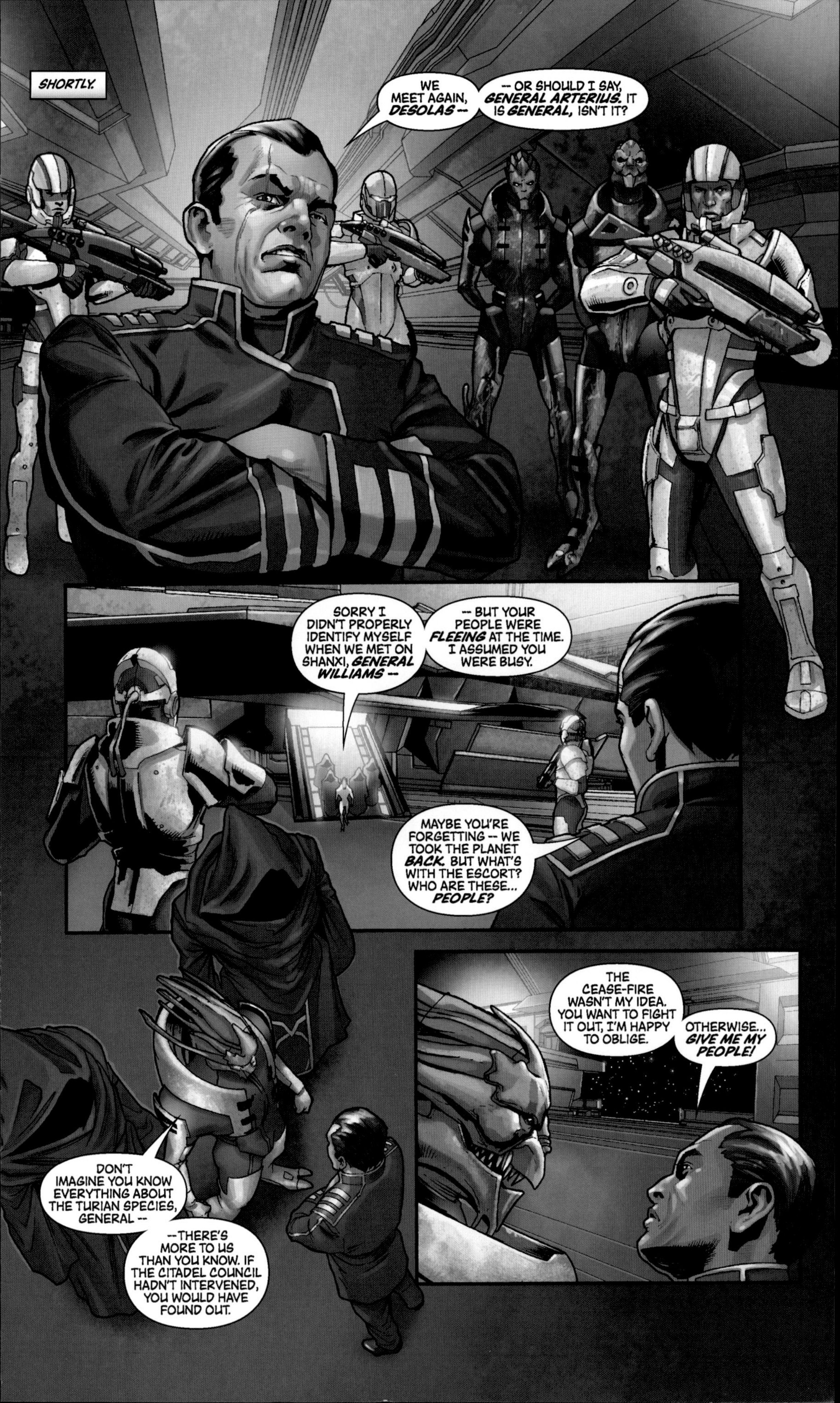
SHORTLY.
WE MEET AGAIN, DESOLAS --
-- OR SHOULD I SAY, GENERAL ARTERIUS. IT IS GENERAL, ISN'T IT?
SORRY I DIDN'T PROPERLY IDENTIFY MYSELF WHEN WE MET ON SHANXI, GENERAL WILLIAMS --
-- BUT YOUR PEOPLE WERE FLEEING AT THE TIME. I ASSUMED YOU WERE BUSY.
MAYBE YOU'RE FORGETTING -- WE TOOK THE PLANET BACK. BUT WHAT'S WITH THE ESCORT? WHO ARE THESE... PEOPLE?
DON'T IMAGINE YOU KNOW EVERYTHING ABOUT THE TURIAN SPECIES, GENERAL --
--THERE'S MORE TO US THAN YOU KNOW. IF THE CITADEL COUNCIL HADN'T INTERVENED, YOU WOULD HAVE FOUND OUT.
THE CEASE-FIRE WASN'T MY IDEA. YOU WANT TO FIGHT IT OUT, I'M HAPPY TO OBLIGE.
OTHERWISE... GIVE ME MY PEOPLE!

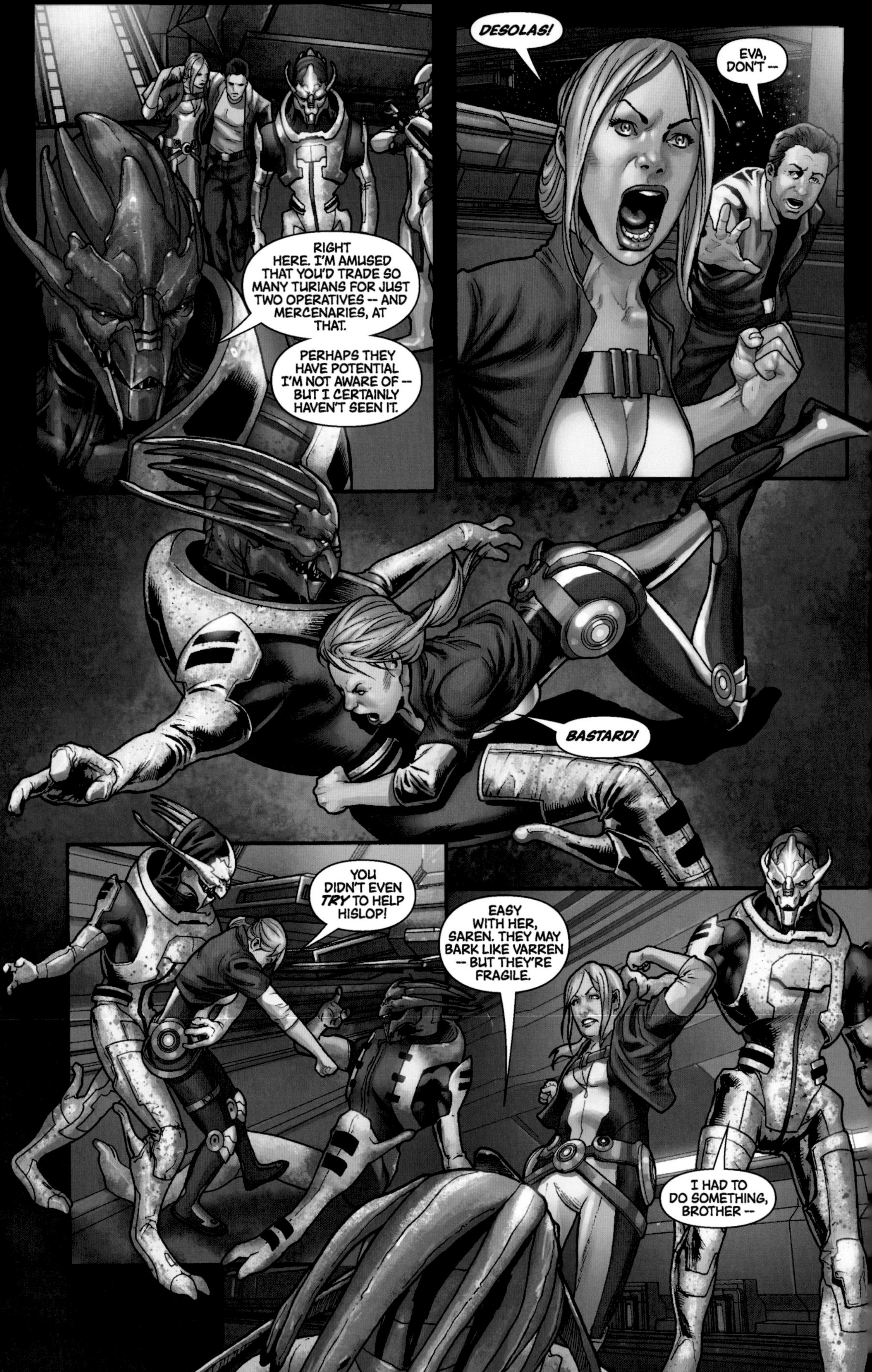
RIGHT HERE. I'M AMUSED THAT YOU'D TRADE SO MANY TURIANS FOR JUST TWO OPERATIVES -- AND MERCENARIES, AT THAT.
PERHAPS THEY HAVE POTENTIAL I'M NOT AWARE OF -- BUT I CERTAINLY HAVEN'T SEEN IT.
DESOLAS!
EVA, DON'T --
BASTARD!
YOU DIDN'T EVEN TRY TO HELP HISLOP!
EASY WITH HER, SAREN. THEY MAY BARK LIKE VARREN -- BUT THEY'RE FRAGILE.
I HAD TO DO SOMETHING, BROTHER --

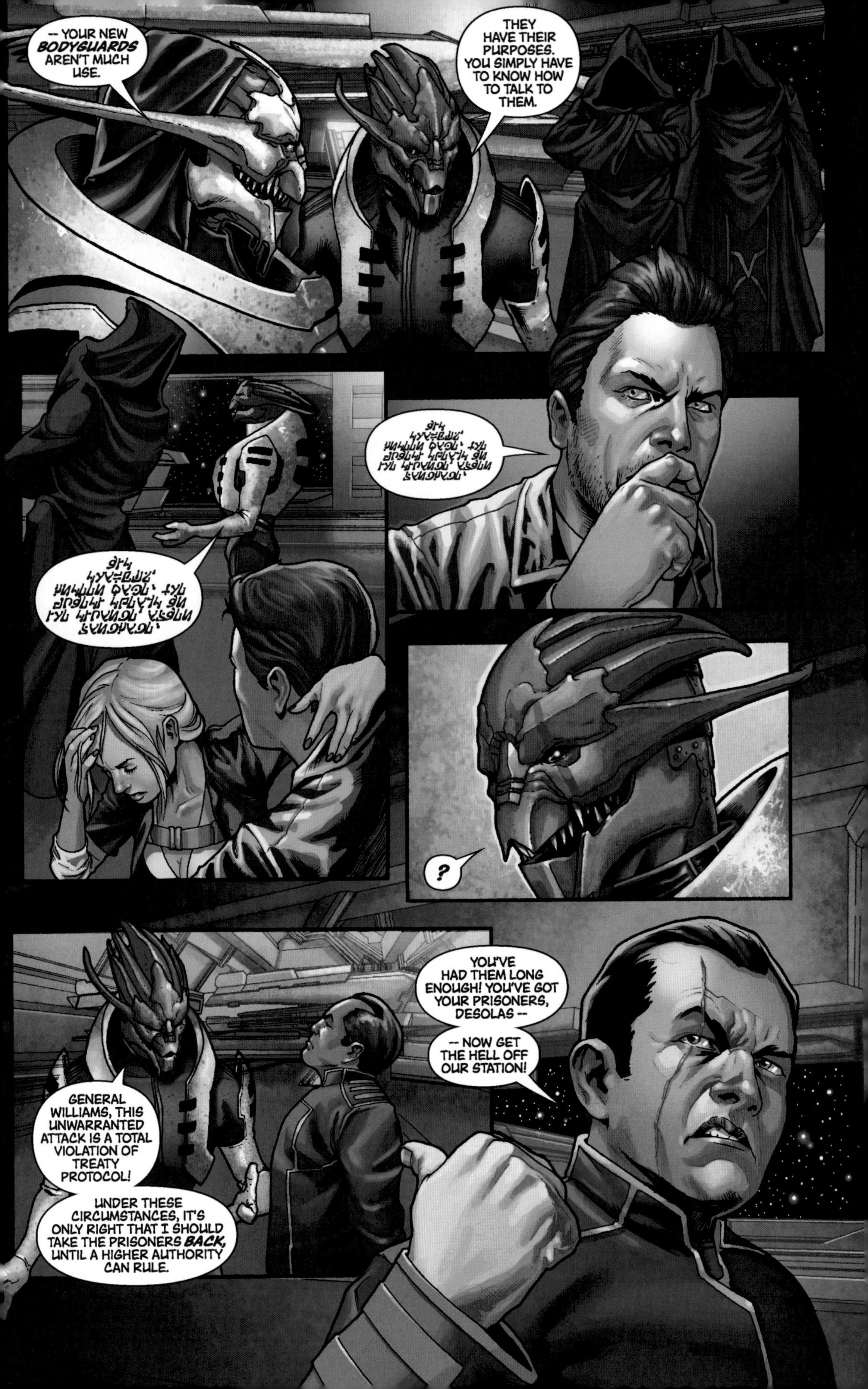
-- YOUR NEW *BODYGUARDS* AREN'T MUCH USE.
THEY HAVE THEIR PURPOSES. YOU SIMPLY HAVE TO KNOW HOW TO TALK TO THEM.
?
YOU'VE HAD THEM LONG ENOUGH! YOU'VE GOT YOUR PRISONERS, DESOLAS --
-- NOW GET THE HELL OFF OUR STATION!
GENERAL WILLIAMS, THIS UNWARRANTED ATTACK IS A TOTAL VIOLATION OF TREATY PROTOCOL!
UNDER THESE CIRCUMSTANCES, IT'S ONLY RIGHT THAT I SHOULD TAKE THE PRISONERS *BACK*, UNTIL A HIGHER AUTHORITY CAN RULE.

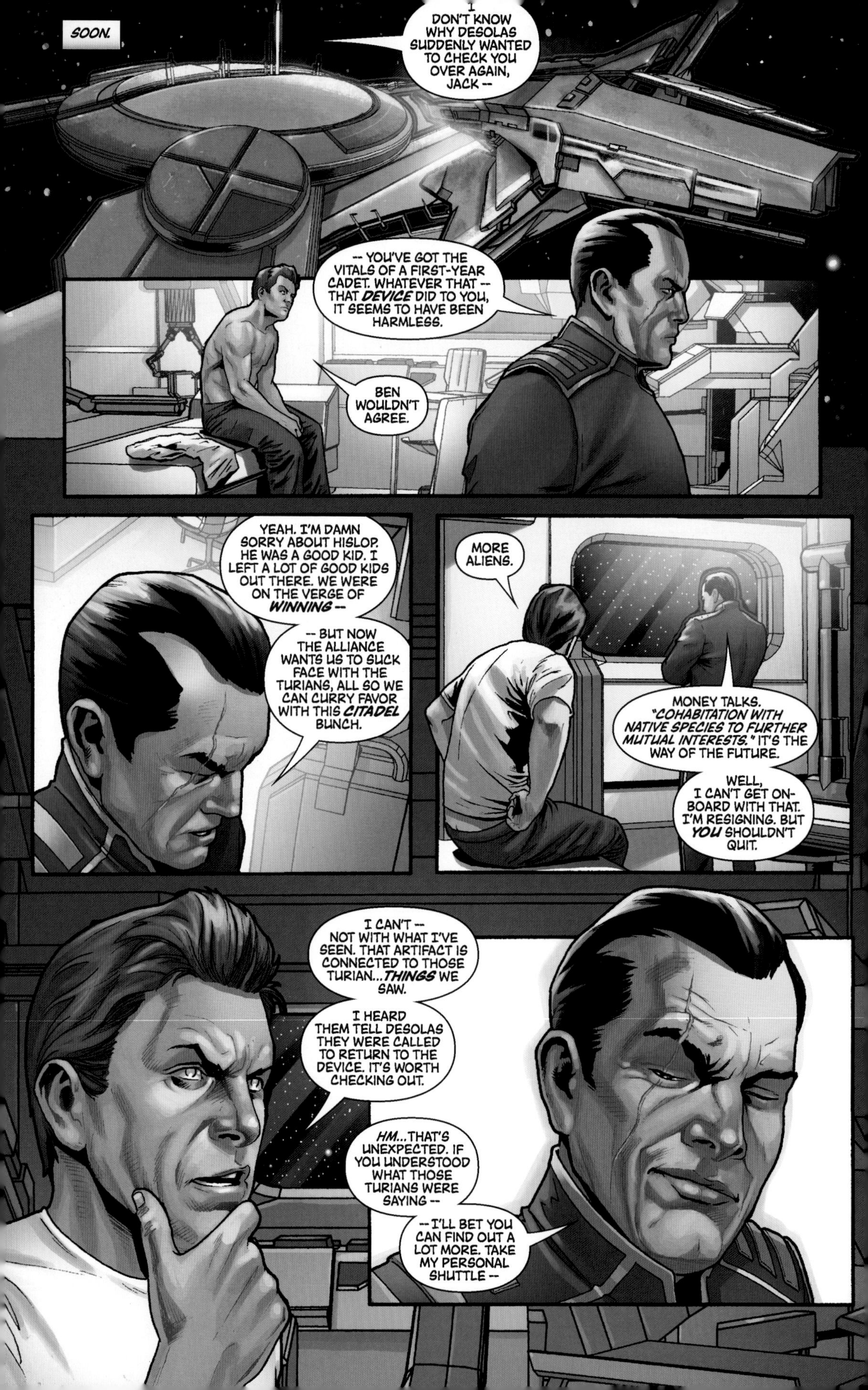
SOON.
I DON'T KNOW WHY DESOLAS SUDDENLY WANTED TO CHECK YOU OVER AGAIN, JACK --
-- YOU'VE GOT THE VITALS OF A FIRST-YEAR CADET. WHATEVER THAT -- THAT *DEVICE* DID TO YOU, IT SEEMS TO HAVE BEEN HARMLESS.
BEN WOULDN'T AGREE.
YEAH. I'M DAMN SORRY ABOUT HISLOP. HE WAS A GOOD KID. I LEFT A LOT OF GOOD KIDS OUT THERE. WE WERE ON THE VERGE OF *WINNING* --
-- BUT NOW THE ALLIANCE WANTS US TO SUCK FACE WITH THE TURIANS, ALL SO WE CAN CURRY FAVOR WITH THIS *CITADEL* BUNCH.
MORE ALIENS.
MONEY TALKS. *"COHABITATION WITH NATIVE SPECIES TO FURTHER MUTUAL INTERESTS."* IT'S THE WAY OF THE FUTURE.
WELL, I CAN'T GET ON-BOARD WITH THAT. I'M RESIGNING. BUT *YOU* SHOULDN'T QUIT.
I CAN'T -- NOT WITH WHAT I'VE SEEN. THAT ARTIFACT IS CONNECTED TO THOSE TURIAN...*THINGS* WE SAW.
I HEARD THEM TELL DESOLAS THEY WERE CALLED TO RETURN TO THE DEVICE. IT'S WORTH CHECKING OUT.
HM...THAT'S UNEXPECTED. IF YOU UNDERSTOOD WHAT THOSE TURIANS WERE SAYING --
-- I'LL BET YOU CAN FIND OUT A LOT MORE. TAKE MY PERSONAL SHUTTLE --

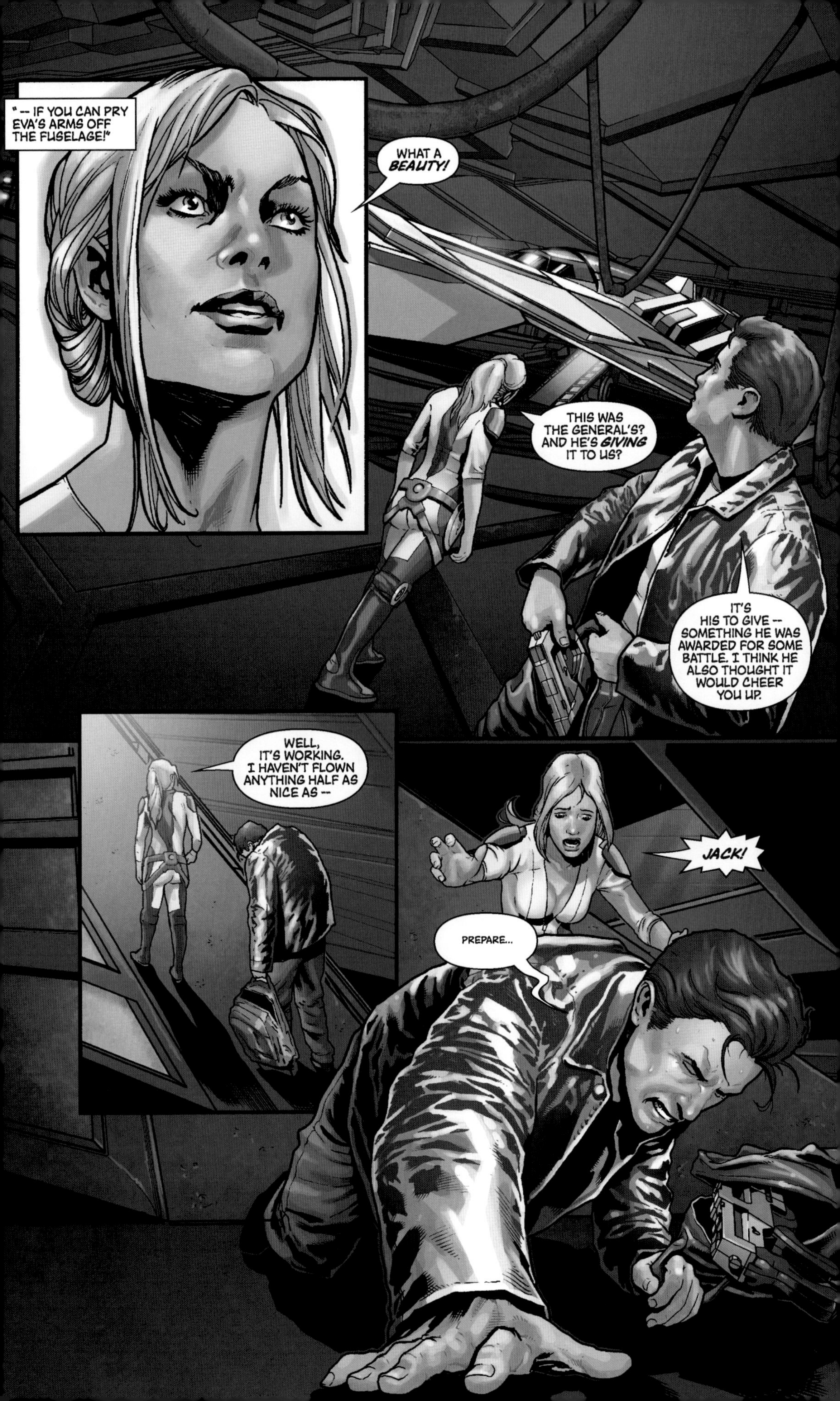

"-- IF YOU CAN PRY EVA'S ARMS OFF THE FUSELAGE!"
WHAT A *BEAUTY!*
THIS WAS THE GENERAL'S? AND HE'S *GIVING* IT TO US?
IT'S HIS TO GIVE -- SOMETHING HE WAS AWARDED FOR SOME BATTLE. I THINK HE ALSO THOUGHT IT WOULD CHEER YOU UP.
WELL, IT'S WORKING. I HAVEN'T FLOWN ANYTHING HALF AS NICE AS --
JACK!
PREPARE...

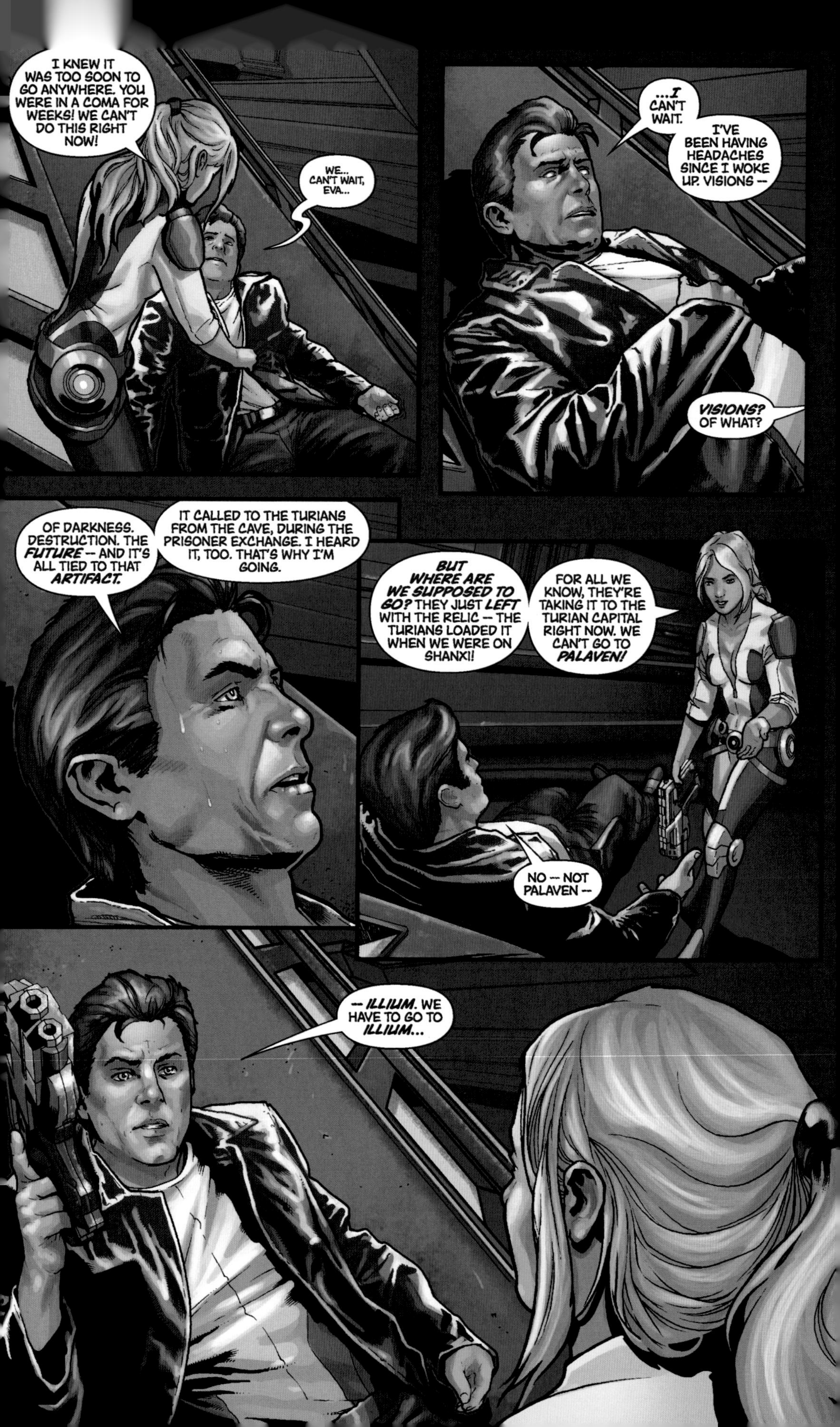
I KNEW IT WAS TOO SOON TO GO ANYWHERE. YOU WERE IN A COMA FOR WEEKS! WE CAN'T DO THIS RIGHT NOW!
WE... CAN'T WAIT, EVA...
...I CAN'T WAIT.
I'VE BEEN HAVING HEADACHES SINCE I WOKE UP. VISIONS --
VISIONS? OF WHAT?
OF DARKNESS. DESTRUCTION. THE FUTURE -- AND IT'S ALL TIED TO THAT ARTIFACT.
IT CALLED TO THE TURIANS FROM THE CAVE, DURING THE PRISONER EXCHANGE. I HEARD IT, TOO. THAT'S WHY I'M GOING.
BUT WHERE ARE WE SUPPOSED TO GO? THEY JUST LEFT WITH THE RELIC -- THE TURIANS LOADED IT WHEN WE WERE ON SHANXI!
FOR ALL WE KNOW, THEY'RE TAKING IT TO THE TURIAN CAPITAL RIGHT NOW. WE CAN'T GO TO PALAVEN!
NO -- NOT PALAVEN --
-- ILLIUM. WE HAVE TO GO TO ILLIUM...

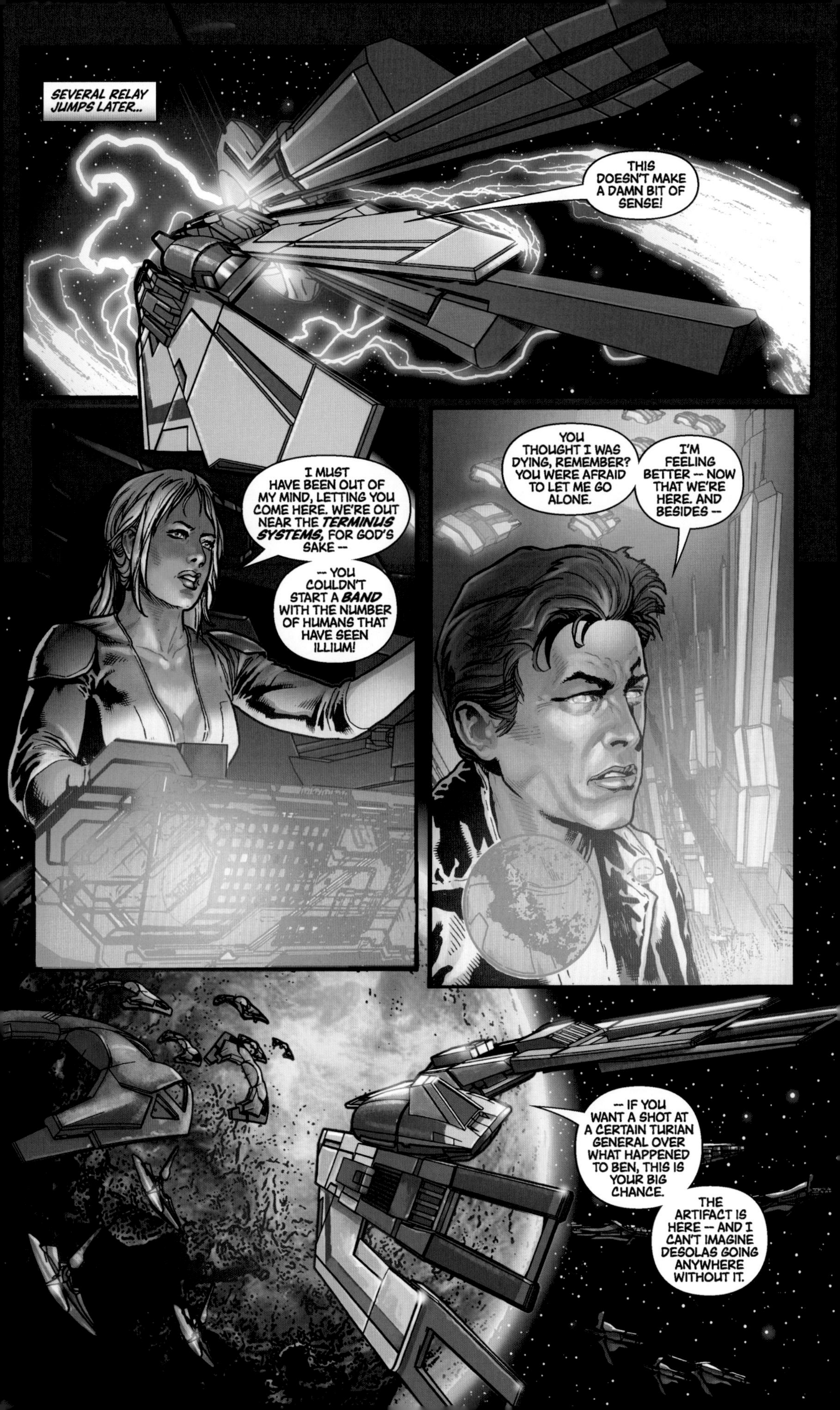

SEVERAL RELAY JUMPS LATER...
THIS DOESN'T MAKE A DAMN BIT OF SENSE!
I MUST HAVE BEEN OUT OF MY MIND, LETTING YOU COME HERE. WE'RE OUT NEAR THE TERMINUS SYSTEMS, FOR GOD'S SAKE --
-- YOU COULDN'T START A BAND WITH THE NUMBER OF HUMANS THAT HAVE SEEN ILLIUM!
YOU THOUGHT I WAS DYING, REMEMBER? YOU WERE AFRAID TO LET ME GO ALONE.
I'M FEELING BETTER -- NOW THAT WE'RE HERE. AND BESIDES --
-- IF YOU WANT A SHOT AT A CERTAIN TURIAN GENERAL OVER WHAT HAPPENED TO BEN, THIS IS YOUR BIG CHANCE.
THE ARTIFACT IS HERE -- AND I CAN'T IMAGINE DESOLAS GOING ANYWHERE WITHOUT IT.

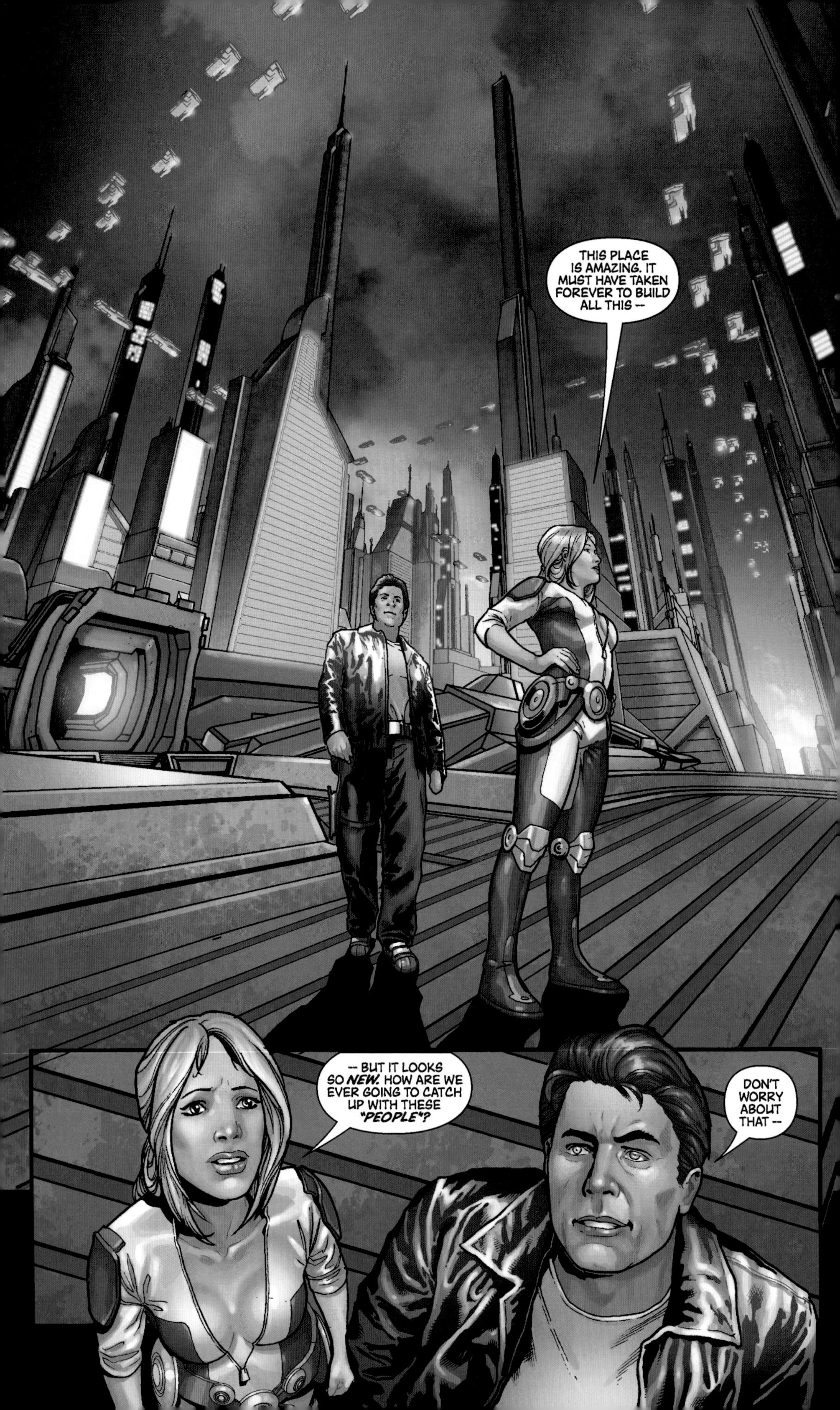
THIS PLACE IS AMAZING. IT MUST HAVE TAKEN FOREVER TO BUILD ALL THIS --
-- BUT IT LOOKS SO *NEW.* HOW ARE WE EVER GOING TO CATCH UP WITH THESE *"PEOPLE"*?
DON'T WORRY ABOUT THAT --

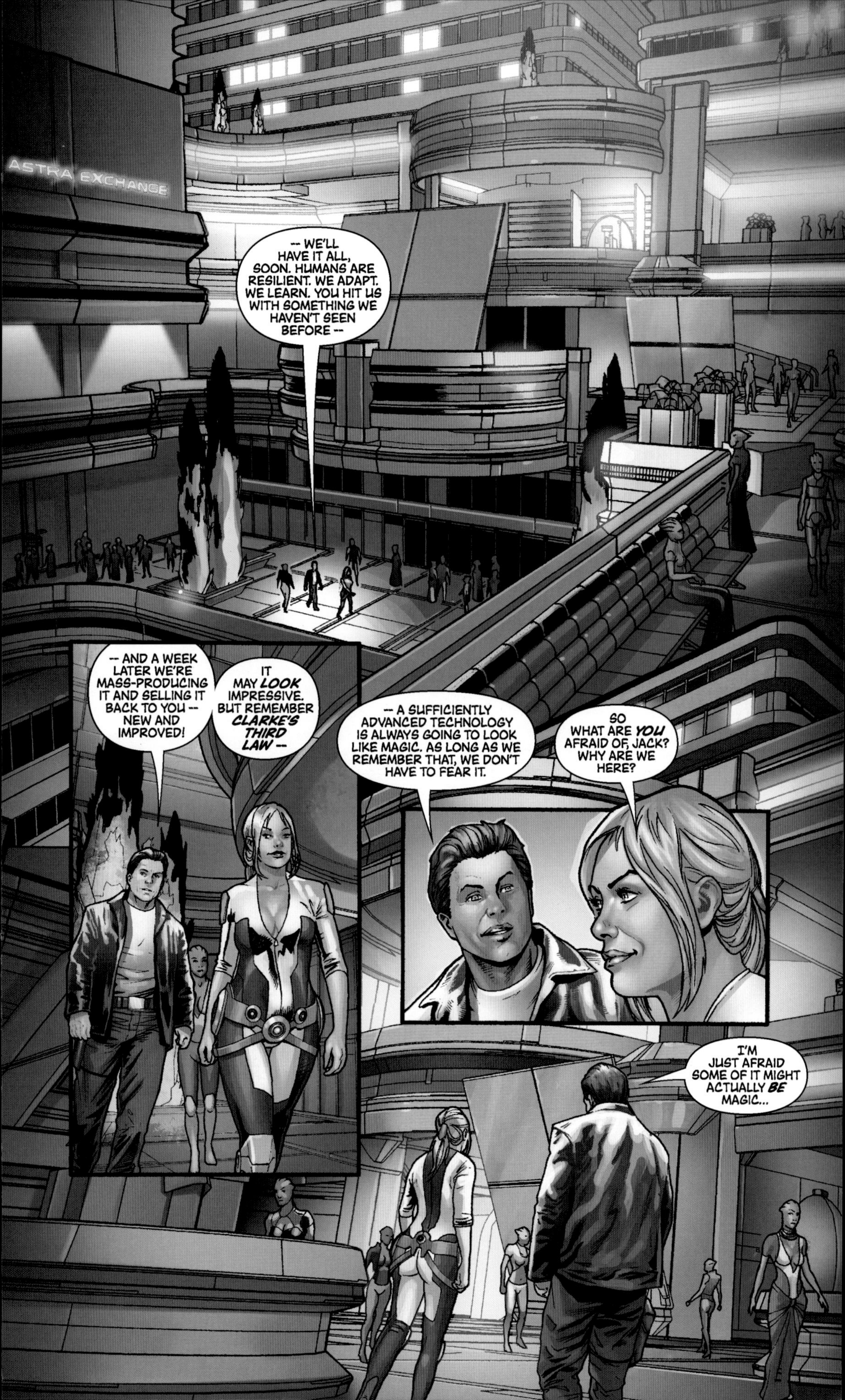
ASTRA EXCHANGE
-- WE'LL HAVE IT ALL, SOON. HUMANS ARE RESILIENT. WE ADAPT. WE LEARN. YOU HIT US WITH SOMETHING WE HAVEN'T SEEN BEFORE --
-- AND A WEEK LATER WE'RE MASS-PRODUCING IT AND SELLING IT BACK TO YOU -- NEW AND IMPROVED!
IT MAY *LOOK* IMPRESSIVE. BUT REMEMBER *CLARKE'S THIRD LAW* --
-- A SUFFICIENTLY ADVANCED TECHNOLOGY IS ALWAYS GOING TO LOOK LIKE MAGIC. AS LONG AS WE REMEMBER THAT, WE DON'T HAVE TO FEAR IT.
SO WHAT ARE *YOU* AFRAID OF, JACK? WHY ARE WE HERE?
I'M JUST AFRAID SOME OF IT MIGHT ACTUALLY *BE* MAGIC...

WERE YOU JUST SPEAKING IN ASARI WITH THOSE PEOPLE?

THEY'RE ASARI. I'M NOT SURE HOW ELSE I SHOULD SPEAK TO THEM.

HOW ABOUT USING A LANGUAGE YOU ACTUALLY *KNOW*?

HUH?

OH. YEAH, IT JUST CAME TO ME. STRANGE --

-- BUT I DON'T KNOW WHAT TO DO ABOUT IT.

HERE -- THESE CARS ARE FOR PUBLIC USE. BEEN ITCHING TO FLY A FOREIGN MODEL?

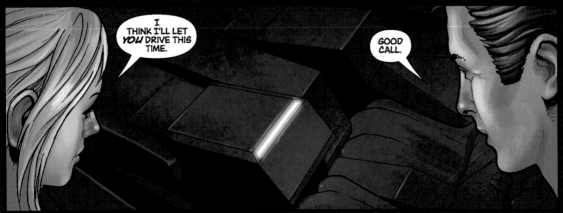

I THINK I'LL LET *YOU* DRIVE THIS TIME.

GOOD CALL.

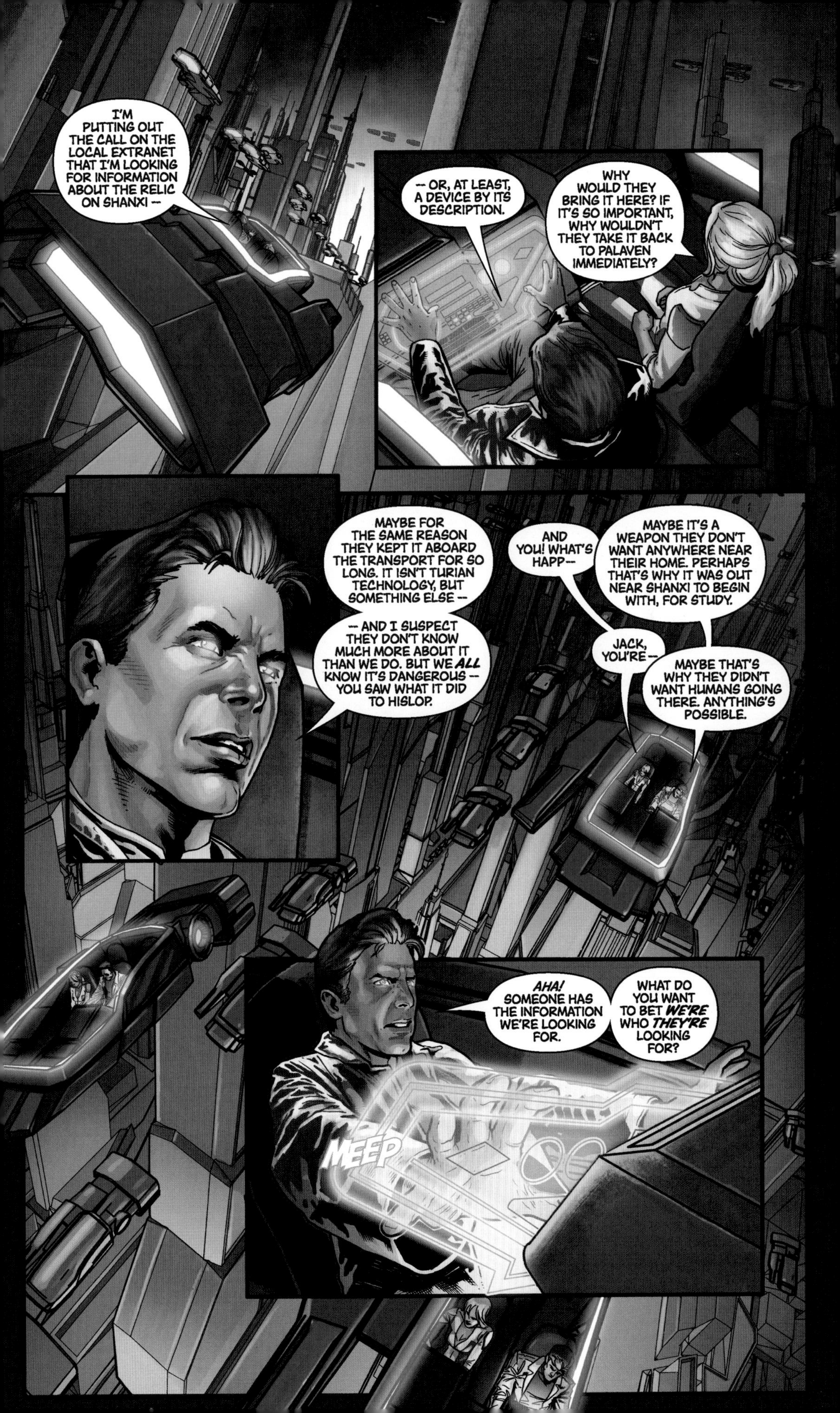
I'M PUTTING OUT THE CALL ON THE LOCAL EXTRANET THAT I'M LOOKING FOR INFORMATION ABOUT THE RELIC ON SHANXI --
-- OR, AT LEAST, A DEVICE BY ITS DESCRIPTION.
WHY WOULD THEY BRING IT HERE? IF IT'S SO IMPORTANT, WHY WOULDN'T THEY TAKE IT BACK TO PALAVEN IMMEDIATELY?
MAYBE FOR THE SAME REASON THEY KEPT IT ABOARD THE TRANSPORT FOR SO LONG. IT ISN'T TURIAN TECHNOLOGY, BUT SOMETHING ELSE --
-- AND I SUSPECT THEY DON'T KNOW MUCH MORE ABOUT IT THAN WE DO. BUT WE ALL KNOW IT'S DANGEROUS -- YOU SAW WHAT IT DID TO HISLOP.
AND YOU! WHAT'S HAPP--
MAYBE IT'S A WEAPON THEY DON'T WANT ANYWHERE NEAR THEIR HOME. PERHAPS THAT'S WHY IT WAS OUT NEAR SHANXI TO BEGIN WITH, FOR STUDY.
JACK, YOU'RE --
MAYBE THAT'S WHY THEY DIDN'T WANT HUMANS GOING THERE. ANYTHING'S POSSIBLE.
AHA! SOMEONE HAS THE INFORMATION WE'RE LOOKING FOR.
WHAT DO YOU WANT TO BET WE'RE WHO THEY'RE LOOKING FOR?
MEEP

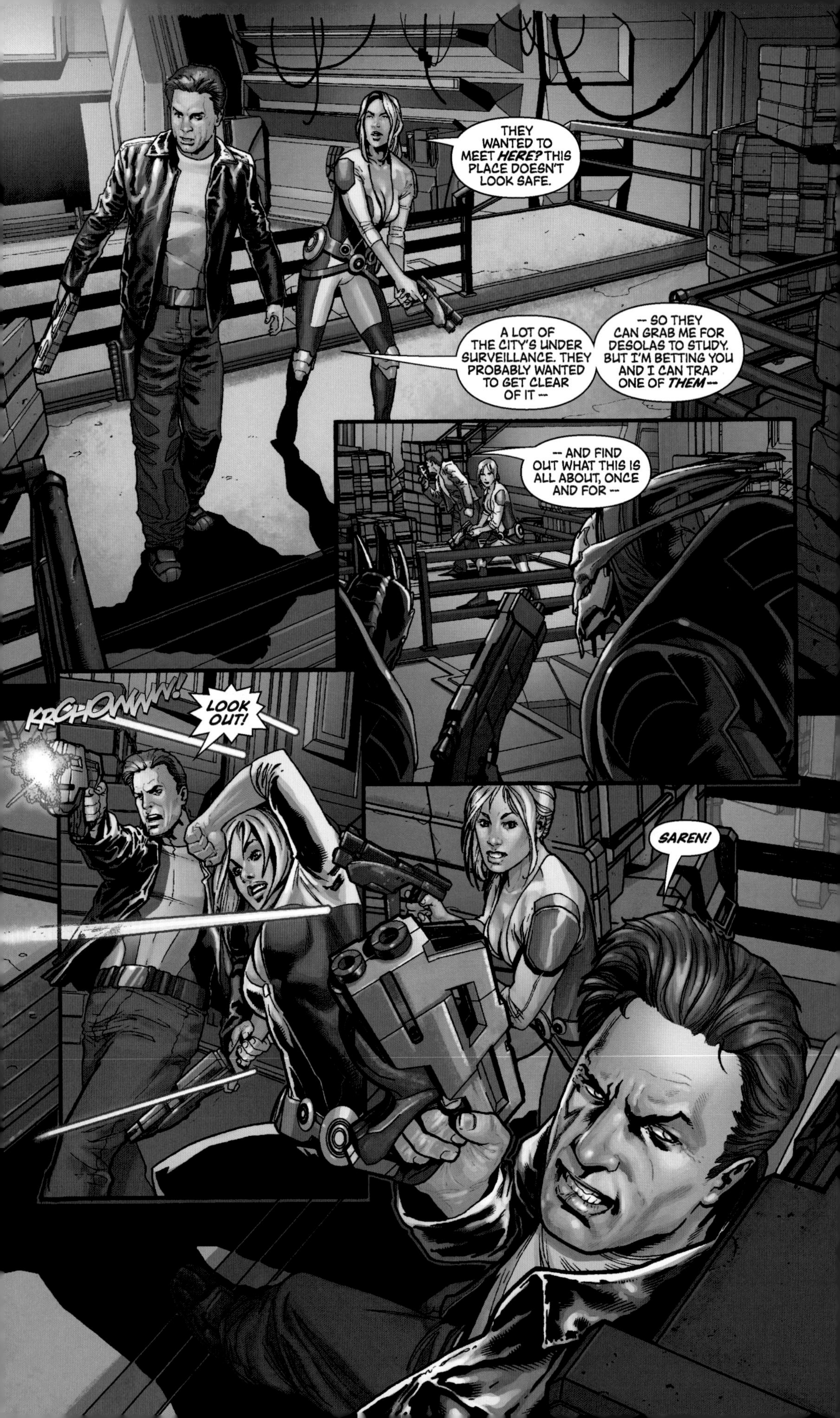
THEY WANTED TO MEET *HERE?* THIS PLACE DOESN'T LOOK SAFE.
A LOT OF THE CITY'S UNDER SURVEILLANCE. THEY PROBABLY WANTED TO GET CLEAR OF IT --
-- SO THEY CAN GRAB ME FOR DESOLAS TO STUDY. BUT I'M BETTING YOU AND I CAN TRAP ONE OF *THEM* --
-- AND FIND OUT WHAT THIS IS ALL ABOUT, ONCE AND FOR --
KRCHOWWW!
LOOK OUT!
SAREN!

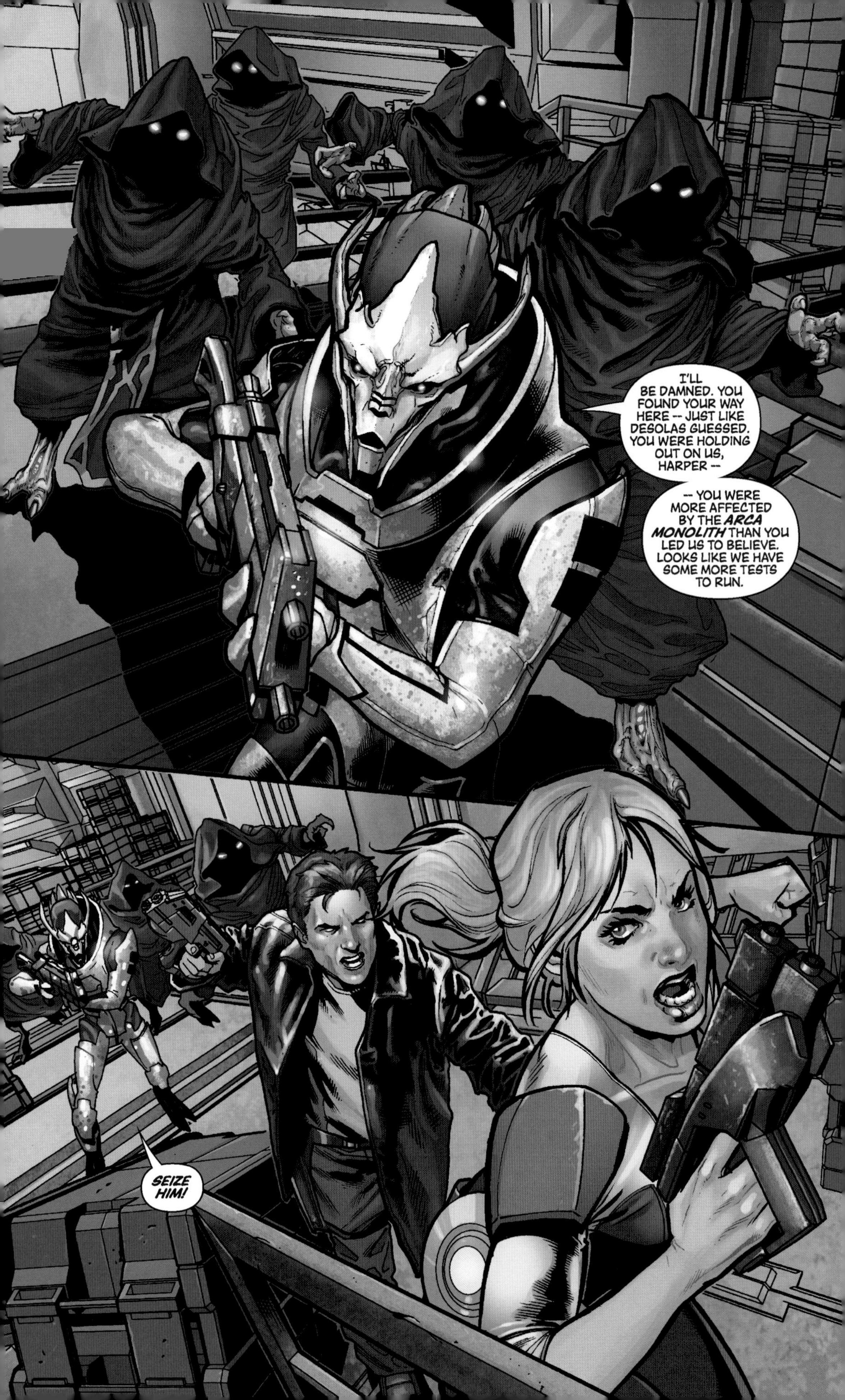
I'LL BE DAMNED. YOU FOUND YOUR WAY HERE -- JUST LIKE DESOLAS GUESSED. YOU WERE HOLDING OUT ON US, HARPER --
-- YOU WERE MORE AFFECTED BY THE ARCA MONOLITH THAN YOU LED US TO BELIEVE. LOOKS LIKE WE HAVE SOME MORE TESTS TO RUN.
SEIZE HIM!

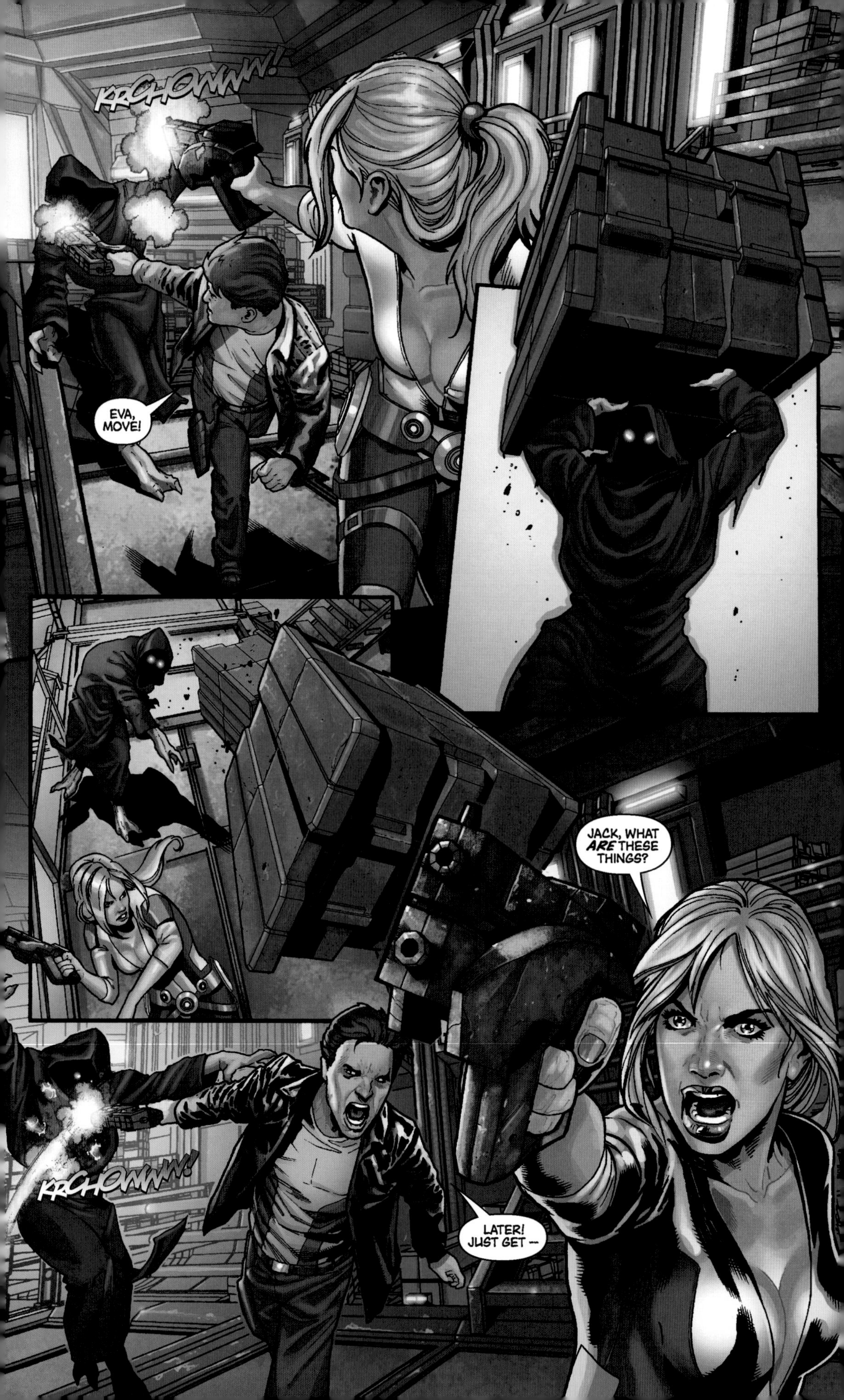
KRCHOWWW!
EVA, MOVE!
JACK, WHAT ARE THESE THINGS?
KRCHOWWW!
LATER! JUST GET --

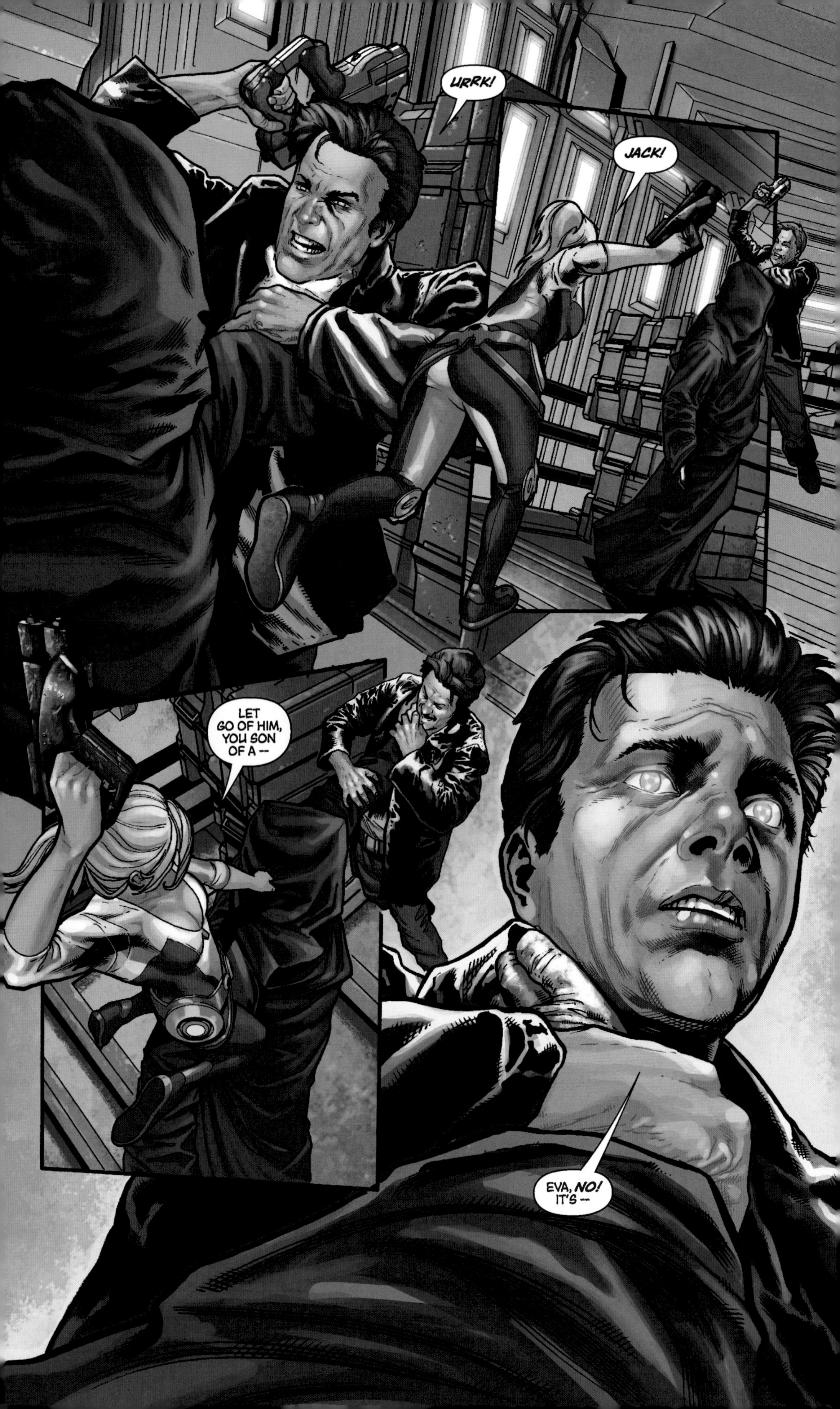
URRK!
JACK!
LET GO OF HIM, YOU SON OF A --
EVA, NO! IT'S --

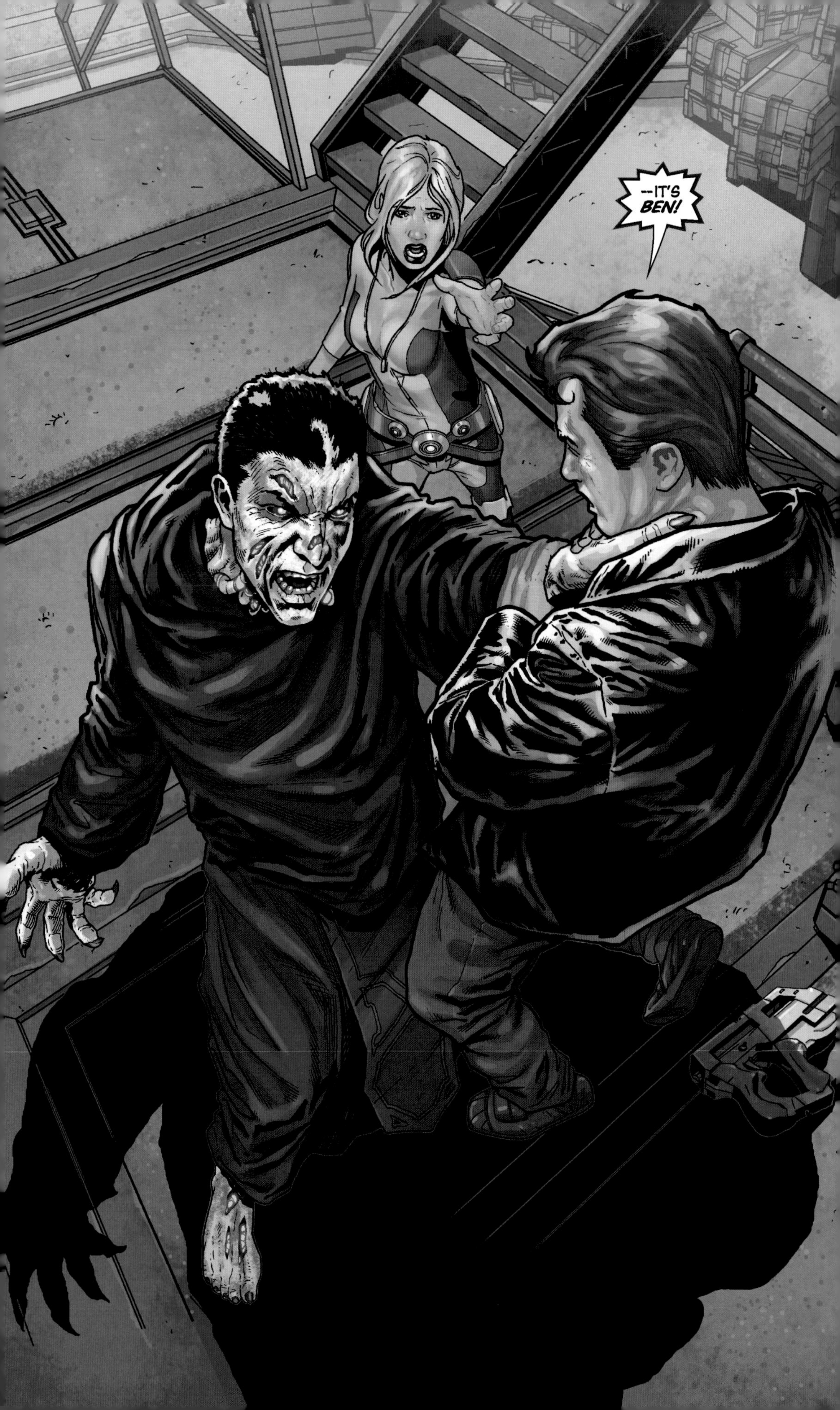
--IT'S BEN!

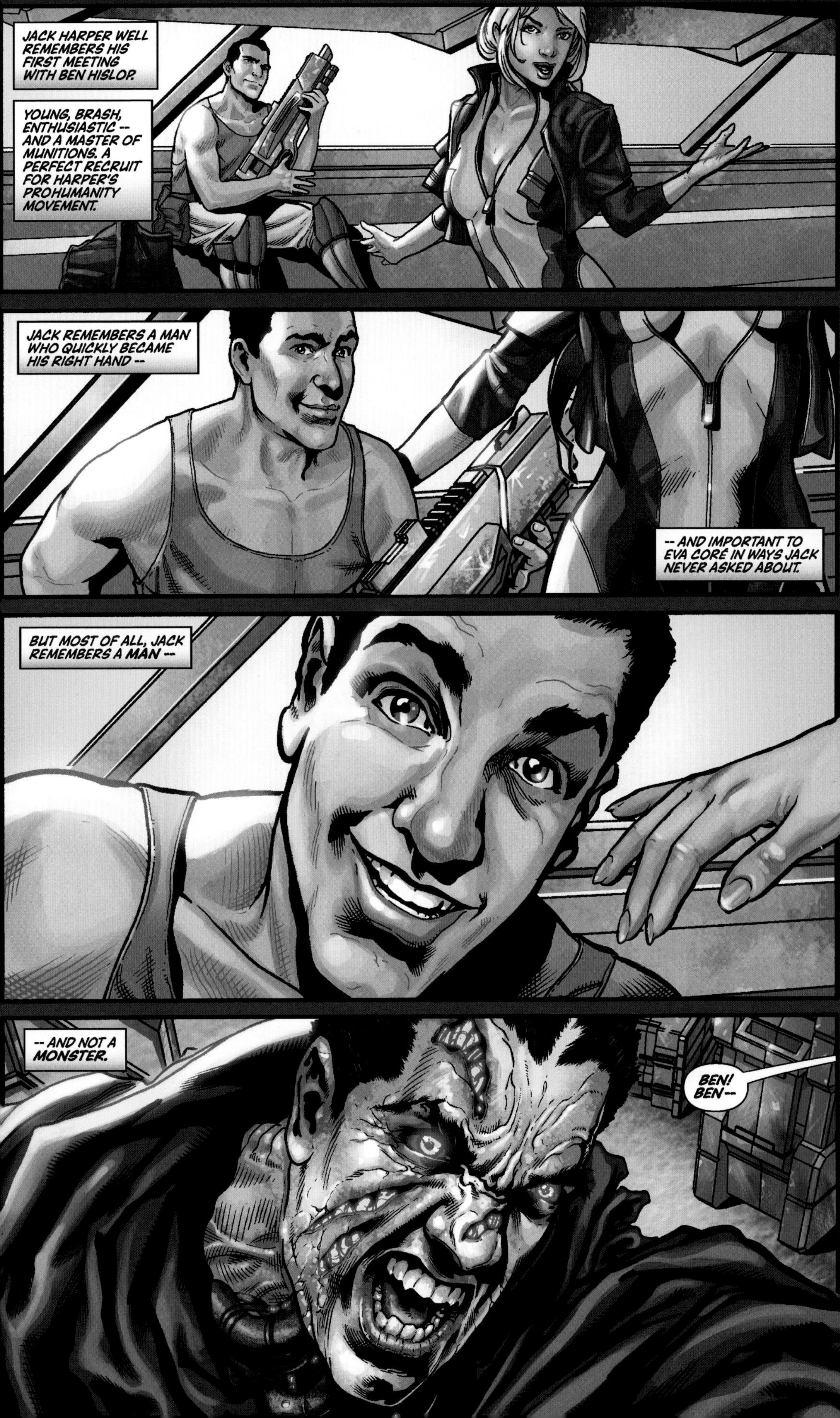
JACK HARPER WELL REMEMBERS HIS FIRST MEETING WITH BEN HISLOP.
YOUNG, BRASH, ENTHUSIASTIC -- AND A MASTER OF MUNITIONS. A PERFECT RECRUIT FOR HARPER'S PROHUMANITY MOVEMENT.
JACK REMEMBERS A MAN WHO QUICKLY BECAME HIS RIGHT HAND --
-- AND IMPORTANT TO EVA CORÉ IN WAYS JACK NEVER ASKED ABOUT.
BUT MOST OF ALL, JACK REMEMBERS A MAN --
-- AND NOT A MONSTER.
BEN! BEN--

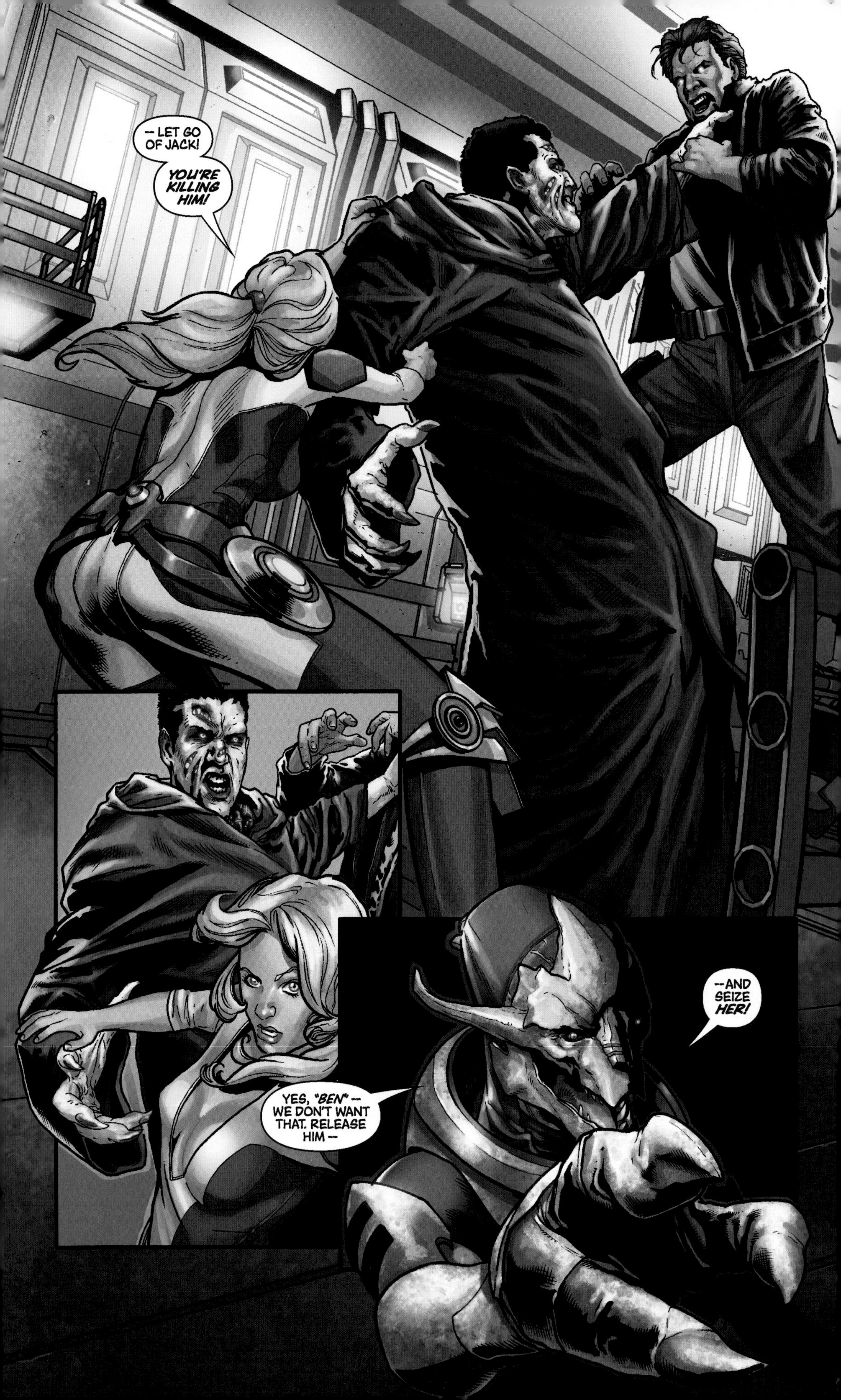

-- LET GO OF JACK! *YOU'RE KILLING HIM!*
YES, *"BEN"* -- WE DON'T WANT THAT. RELEASE HIM --
--AND SEIZE *HER!*

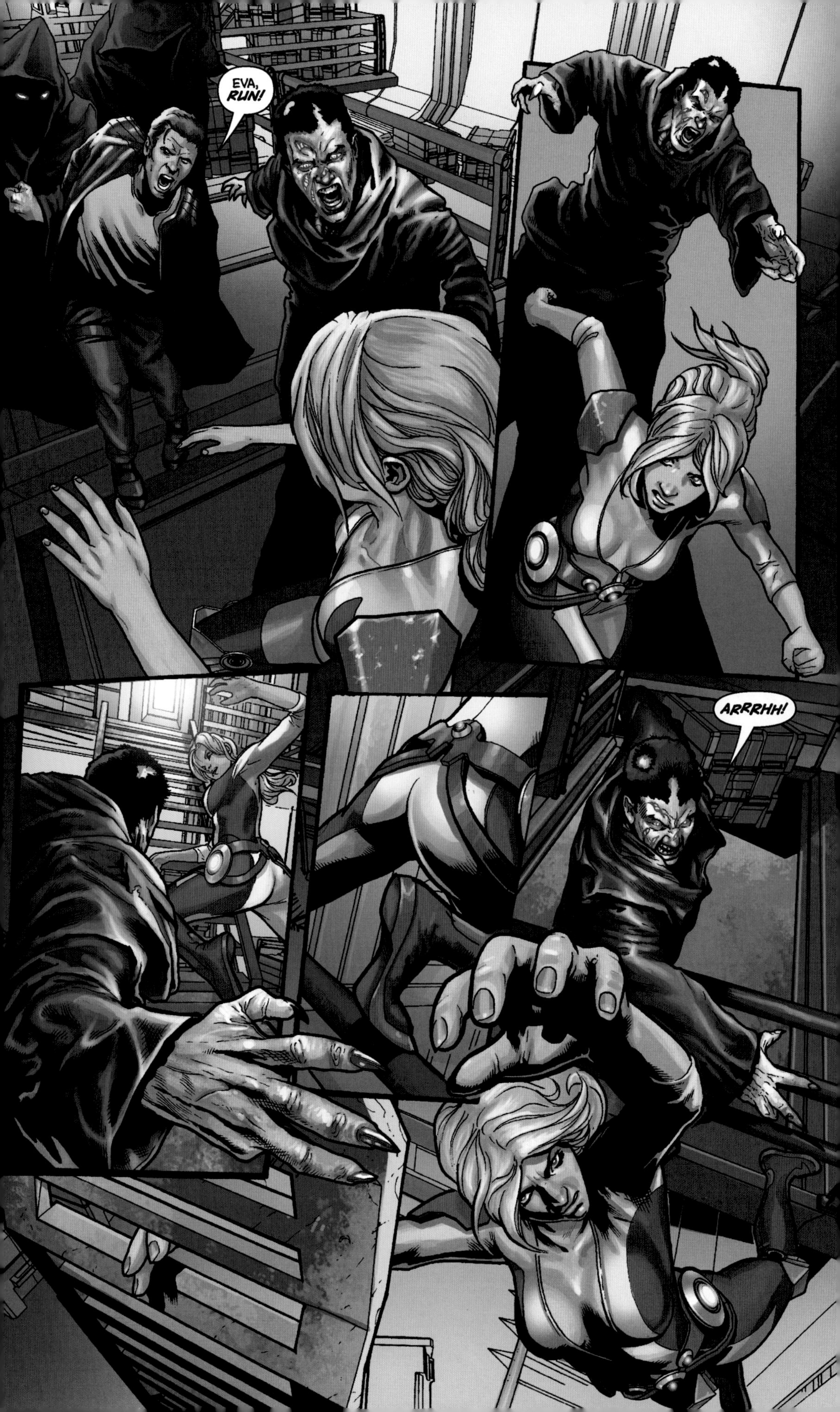
EVA, RUN!
ARRRHH!

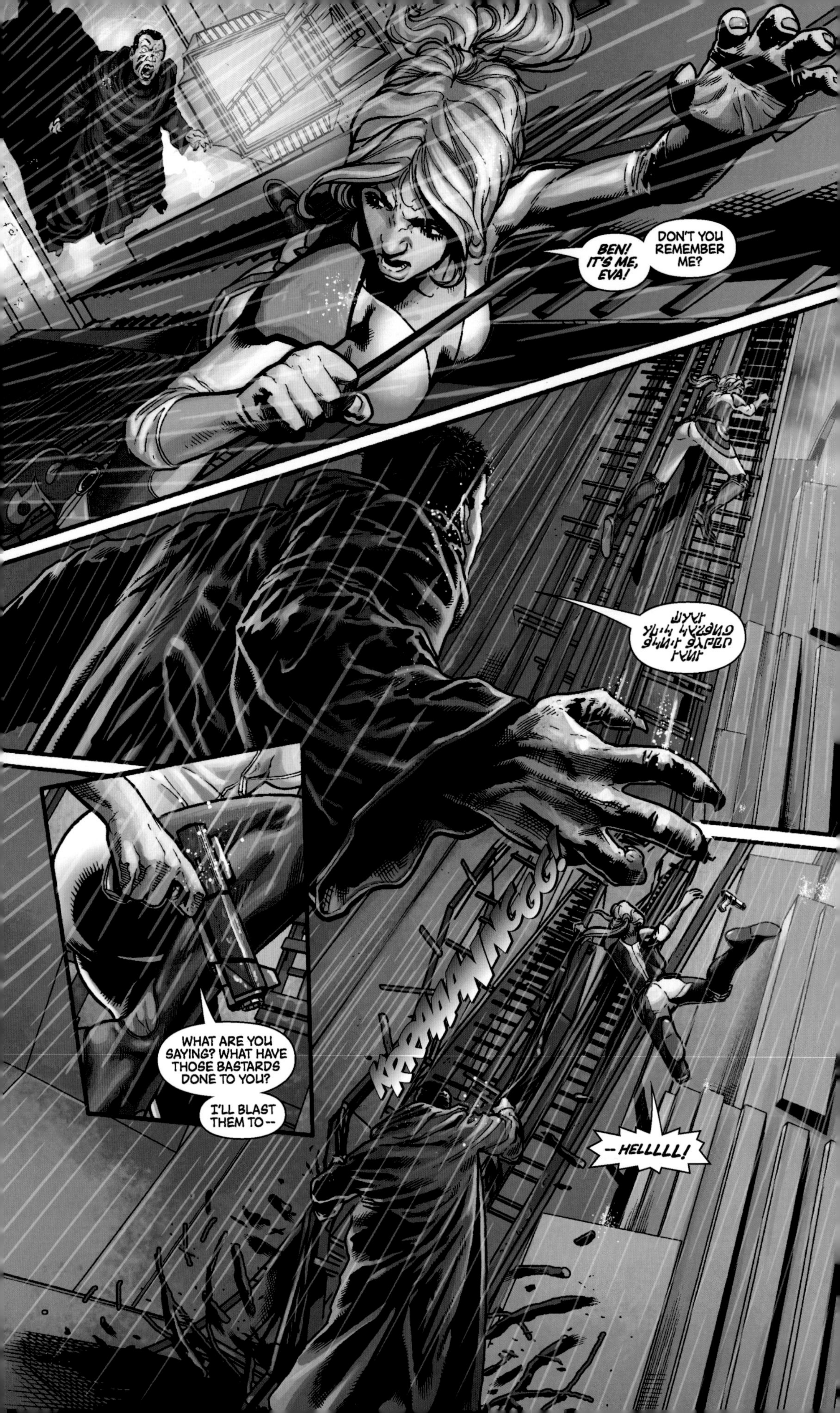
BEN! IT'S ME, EVA!
DON'T YOU REMEMBER ME?
WHAT ARE YOU SAYING? WHAT HAVE THOSE BASTARDS DONE TO YOU?
I'LL BLAST THEM TO--
KRAAAWNGGG!
--HELLLLL!

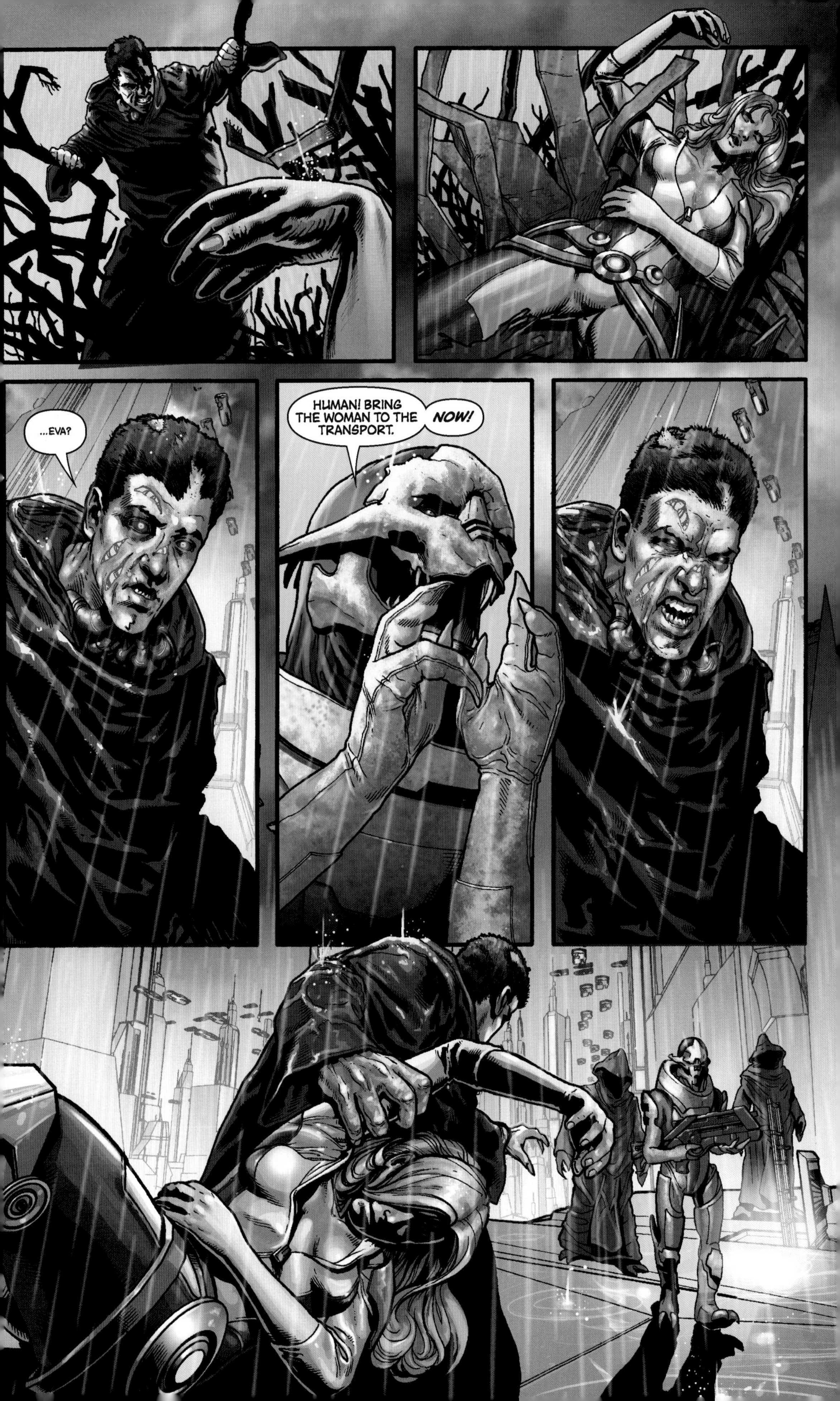
...EVA?
HUMAN! BRING THE WOMAN TO THE TRANSPORT.
NOW!

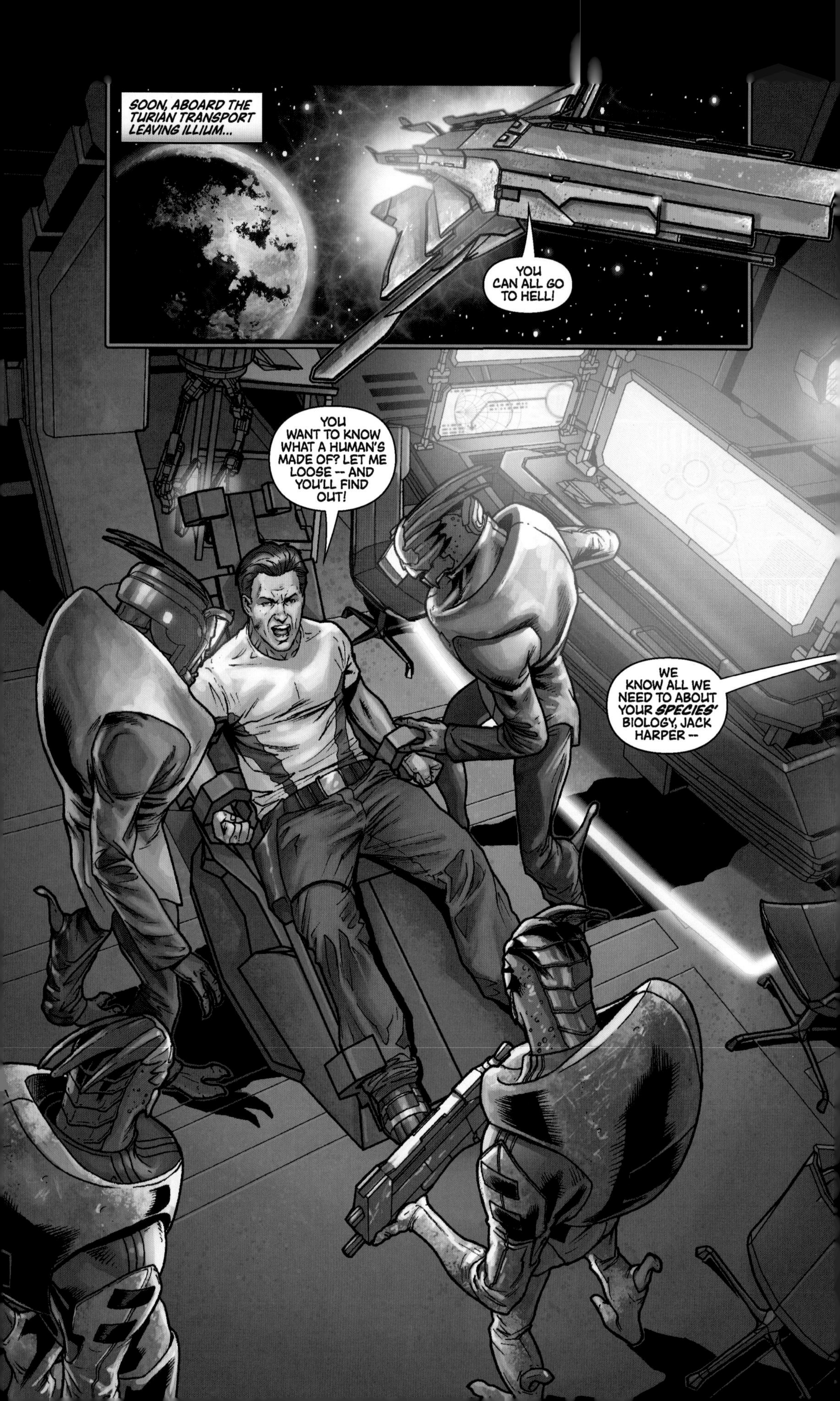
SOON, ABOARD THE TURIAN TRANSPORT LEAVING ILLIUM...
YOU CAN ALL GO TO HELL!
YOU WANT TO KNOW WHAT A HUMAN'S MADE OF? LET ME LOOSE -- AND YOU'LL FIND OUT!
WE KNOW ALL WE NEED TO ABOUT YOUR *SPECIES'* BIOLOGY, JACK HARPER --

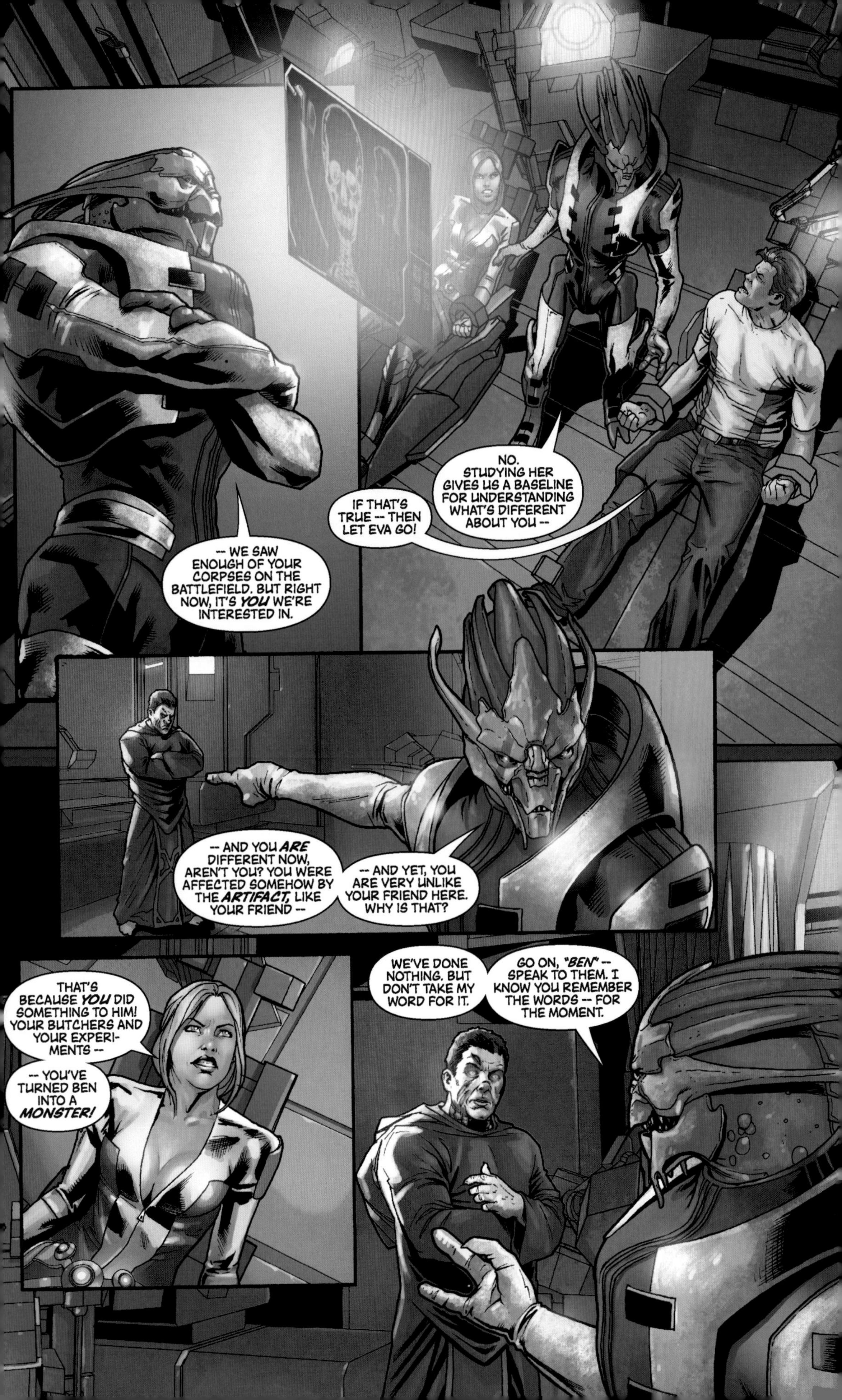
-- WE SAW ENOUGH OF YOUR CORPSES ON THE BATTLEFIELD. BUT RIGHT NOW, IT'S *YOU* WE'RE INTERESTED IN.
IF THAT'S TRUE -- THEN LET EVA GO!
NO. STUDYING HER GIVES US A BASELINE FOR UNDERSTANDING WHAT'S DIFFERENT ABOUT YOU --
-- AND YOU *ARE* DIFFERENT NOW, AREN'T YOU? YOU WERE AFFECTED SOMEHOW BY THE *ARTIFACT,* LIKE YOUR FRIEND --
-- AND YET, YOU ARE VERY UNLIKE YOUR FRIEND HERE. WHY IS THAT?
THAT'S BECAUSE *YOU* DID SOMETHING TO HIM! YOUR BUTCHERS AND YOUR EXPERI-MENTS --
-- YOU'VE TURNED BEN INTO A *MONSTER!*
WE'VE DONE NOTHING. BUT DON'T TAKE MY WORD FOR IT.
GO ON, *"BEN"* -- SPEAK TO THEM. I KNOW YOU REMEMBER THE WORDS -- FOR THE MOMENT.

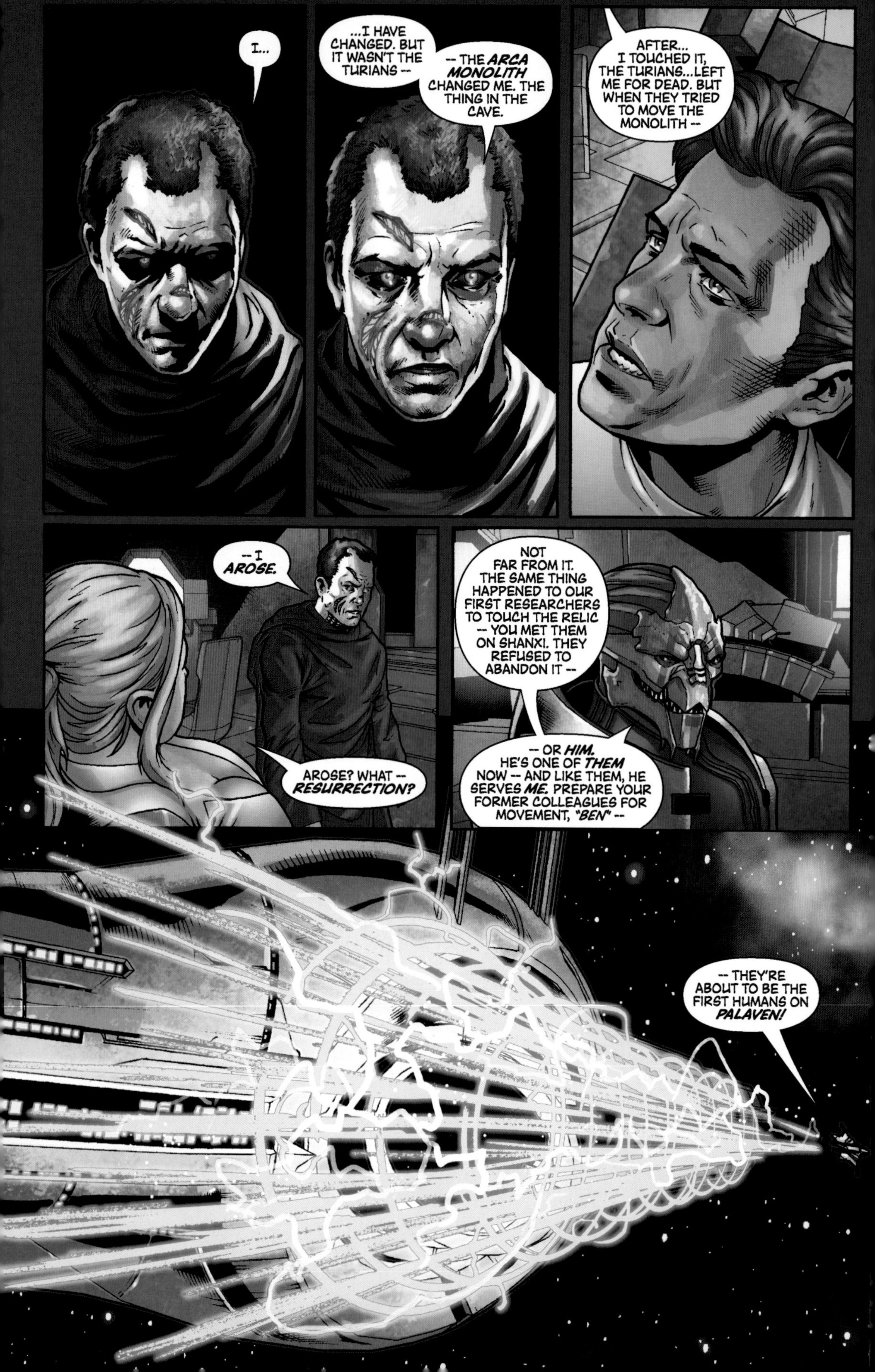
I...
...I HAVE CHANGED. BUT IT WASN'T THE TURIANS --
-- THE ARCA MONOLITH CHANGED ME. THE THING IN THE CAVE.
AFTER... I TOUCHED IT, THE TURIANS...LEFT ME FOR DEAD. BUT WHEN THEY TRIED TO MOVE THE MONOLITH --
-- I AROSE.
AROSE? WHAT -- RESURRECTION?
NOT FAR FROM IT. THE SAME THING HAPPENED TO OUR FIRST RESEARCHERS TO TOUCH THE RELIC -- YOU MET THEM ON SHANXI. THEY REFUSED TO ABANDON IT --
-- OR HIM. HE'S ONE OF THEM NOW -- AND LIKE THEM, HE SERVES ME. PREPARE YOUR FORMER COLLEAGUES FOR MOVEMENT, "BEN" --
-- THEY'RE ABOUT TO BE THE FIRST HUMANS ON PALAVEN!

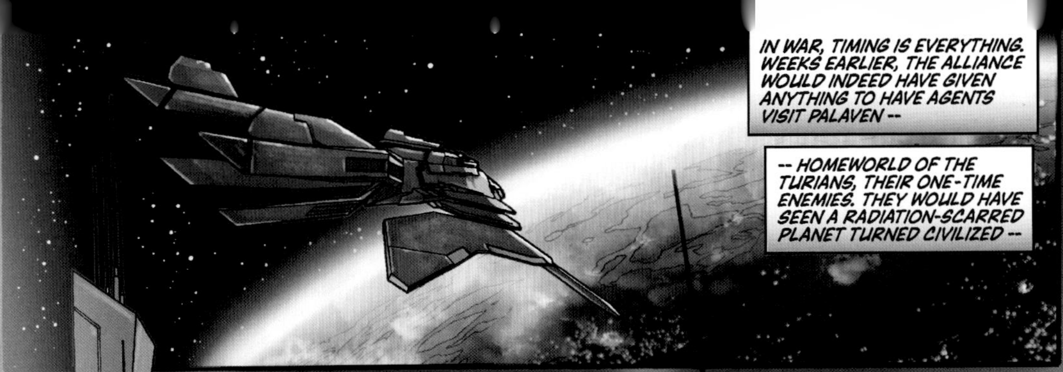
IN WAR, TIMING IS EVERYTHING. WEEKS EARLIER, THE ALLIANCE WOULD INDEED HAVE GIVEN ANYTHING TO HAVE AGENTS VISIT PALAVEN --
-- HOMEWORLD OF THE TURIANS, THEIR ONE-TIME ENEMIES. THEY WOULD HAVE SEEN A RADIATION-SCARRED PLANET TURNED CIVILIZED --
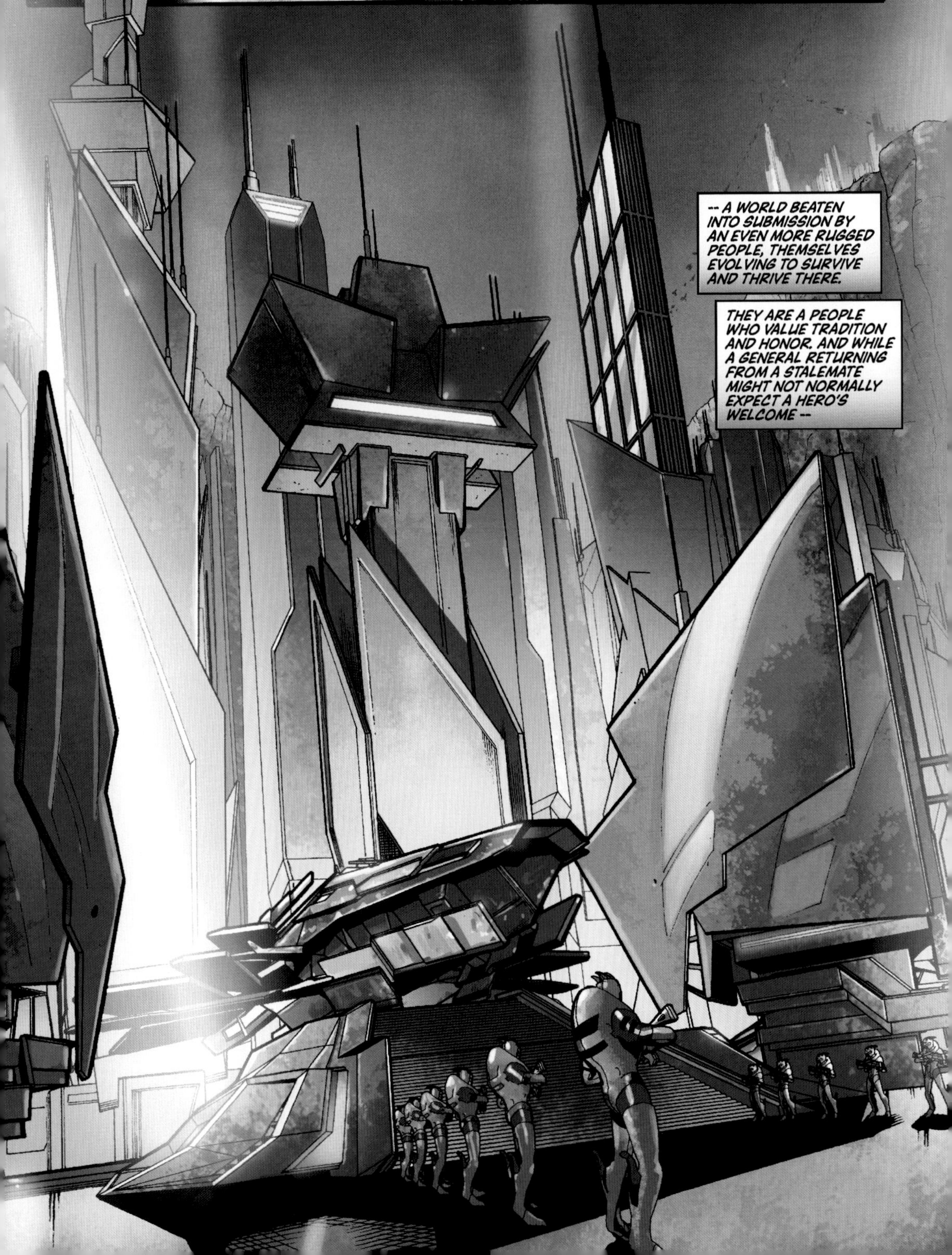
-- A WORLD BEATEN INTO SUBMISSION BY AN EVEN MORE RUGGED PEOPLE, THEMSELVES EVOLVING TO SURVIVE AND THRIVE THERE.
THEY ARE A PEOPLE WHO VALUE TRADITION AND HONOR. AND WHILE A GENERAL RETURNING FROM A STALEMATE MIGHT NOT NORMALLY EXPECT A HERO'S WELCOME --

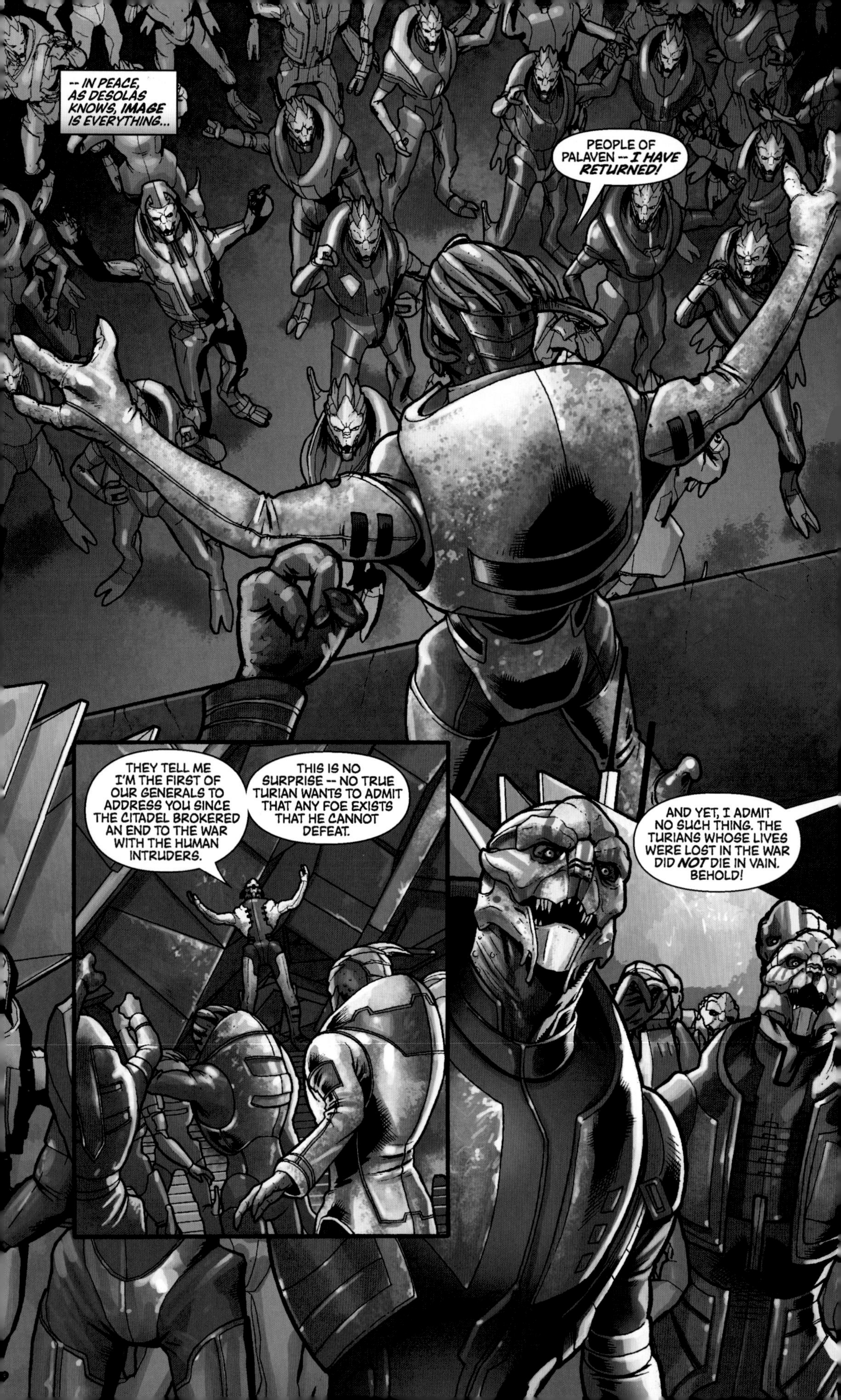
-- IN PEACE, AS DESOLAS KNOWS, IMAGE IS EVERYTHING...
PEOPLE OF PALAVEN -- I HAVE RETURNED!
THEY TELL ME I'M THE FIRST OF OUR GENERALS TO ADDRESS YOU SINCE THE CITADEL BROKERED AN END TO THE WAR WITH THE HUMAN INTRUDERS.
THIS IS NO SURPRISE -- NO TRUE TURIAN WANTS TO ADMIT THAT ANY FOE EXISTS THAT HE CANNOT DEFEAT.
AND YET, I ADMIT NO SUCH THING. THE TURIANS WHOSE LIVES WERE LOST IN THE WAR DID NOT DIE IN VAIN. BEHOLD!

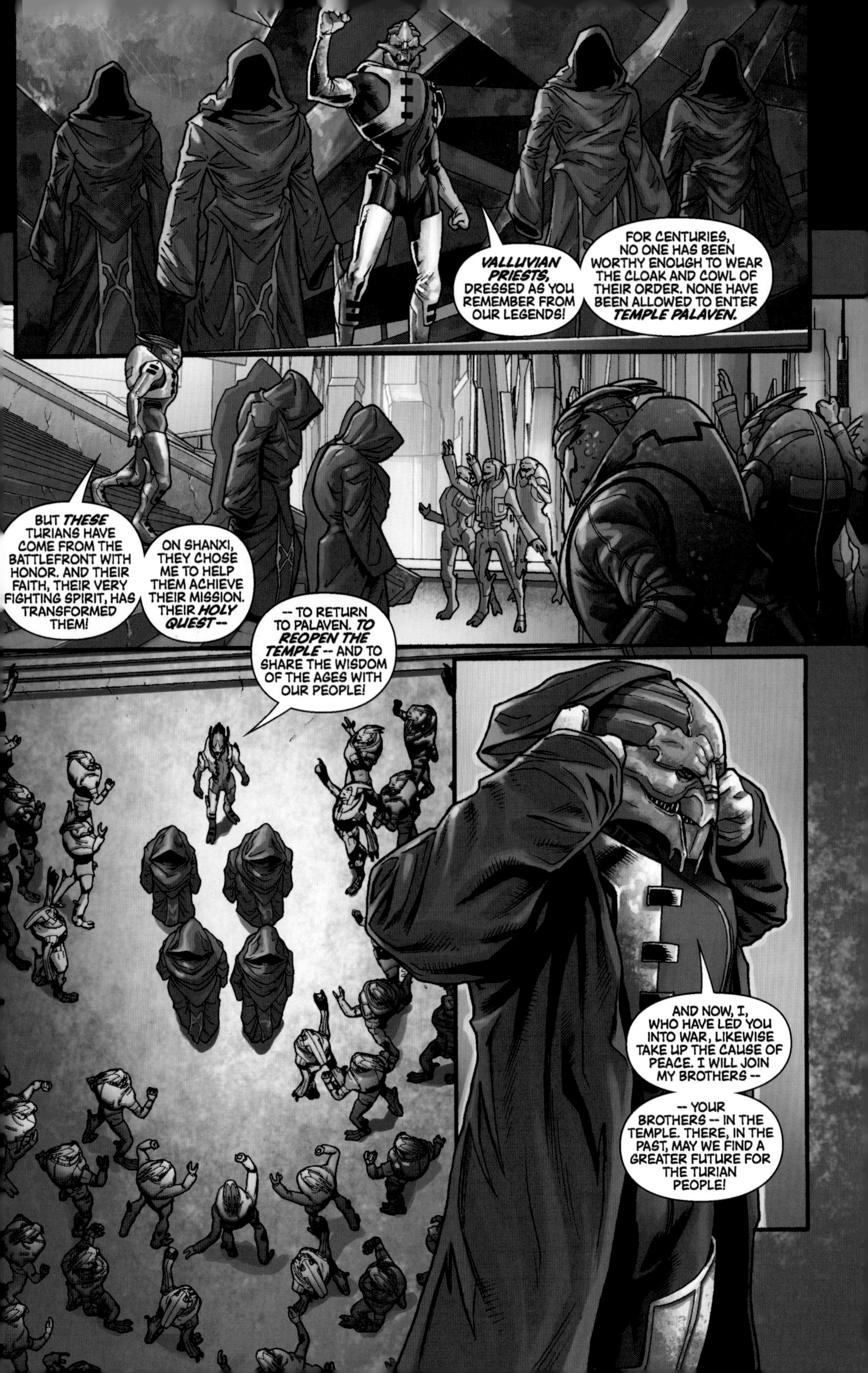
VALLUVIAN PRIESTS, DRESSED AS YOU REMEMBER FROM OUR LEGENDS!
FOR CENTURIES, NO ONE HAS BEEN WORTHY ENOUGH TO WEAR THE CLOAK AND COWL OF THEIR ORDER. NONE HAVE BEEN ALLOWED TO ENTER TEMPLE PALAVEN.
BUT THESE TURIANS HAVE COME FROM THE BATTLEFRONT WITH HONOR. AND THEIR FAITH, THEIR VERY FIGHTING SPIRIT, HAS TRANSFORMED THEM!
ON SHANXI, THEY CHOSE ME TO HELP THEM ACHIEVE THEIR MISSION. THEIR HOLY QUEST--
-- TO RETURN TO PALAVEN. TO REOPEN THE TEMPLE -- AND TO SHARE THE WISDOM OF THE AGES WITH OUR PEOPLE!
AND NOW, I, WHO HAVE LED YOU INTO WAR, LIKEWISE TAKE UP THE CAUSE OF PEACE. I WILL JOIN MY BROTHERS --
-- YOUR BROTHERS -- IN THE TEMPLE. THERE, IN THE PAST, MAY WE FIND A GREATER FUTURE FOR THE TURIAN PEOPLE!

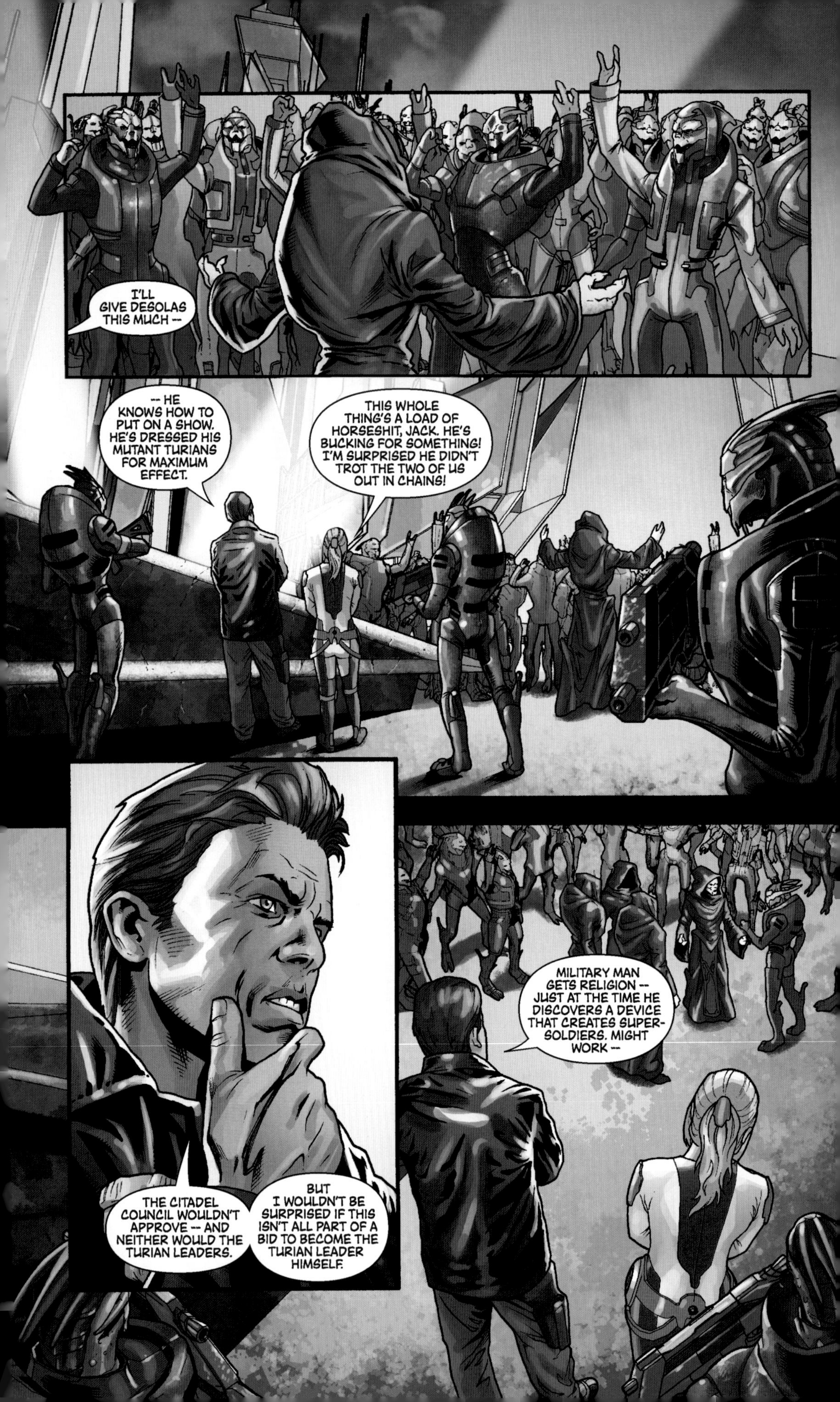
I'LL GIVE DESOLAS THIS MUCH --
-- HE KNOWS HOW TO PUT ON A SHOW. HE'S DRESSED HIS MUTANT TURIANS FOR MAXIMUM EFFECT.
THIS WHOLE THING'S A LOAD OF HORSESHIT, JACK. HE'S BUCKING FOR SOMETHING! I'M SURPRISED HE DIDN'T TROT THE TWO OF US OUT IN CHAINS!
THE CITADEL COUNCIL WOULDN'T APPROVE -- AND NEITHER WOULD THE TURIAN LEADERS.
BUT I WOULDN'T BE SURPRISED IF THIS ISN'T ALL PART OF A BID TO BECOME THE TURIAN LEADER HIMSELF.
MILITARY MAN GETS RELIGION -- JUST AT THE TIME HE DISCOVERS A DEVICE THAT CREATES SUPER-SOLDIERS. MIGHT WORK --

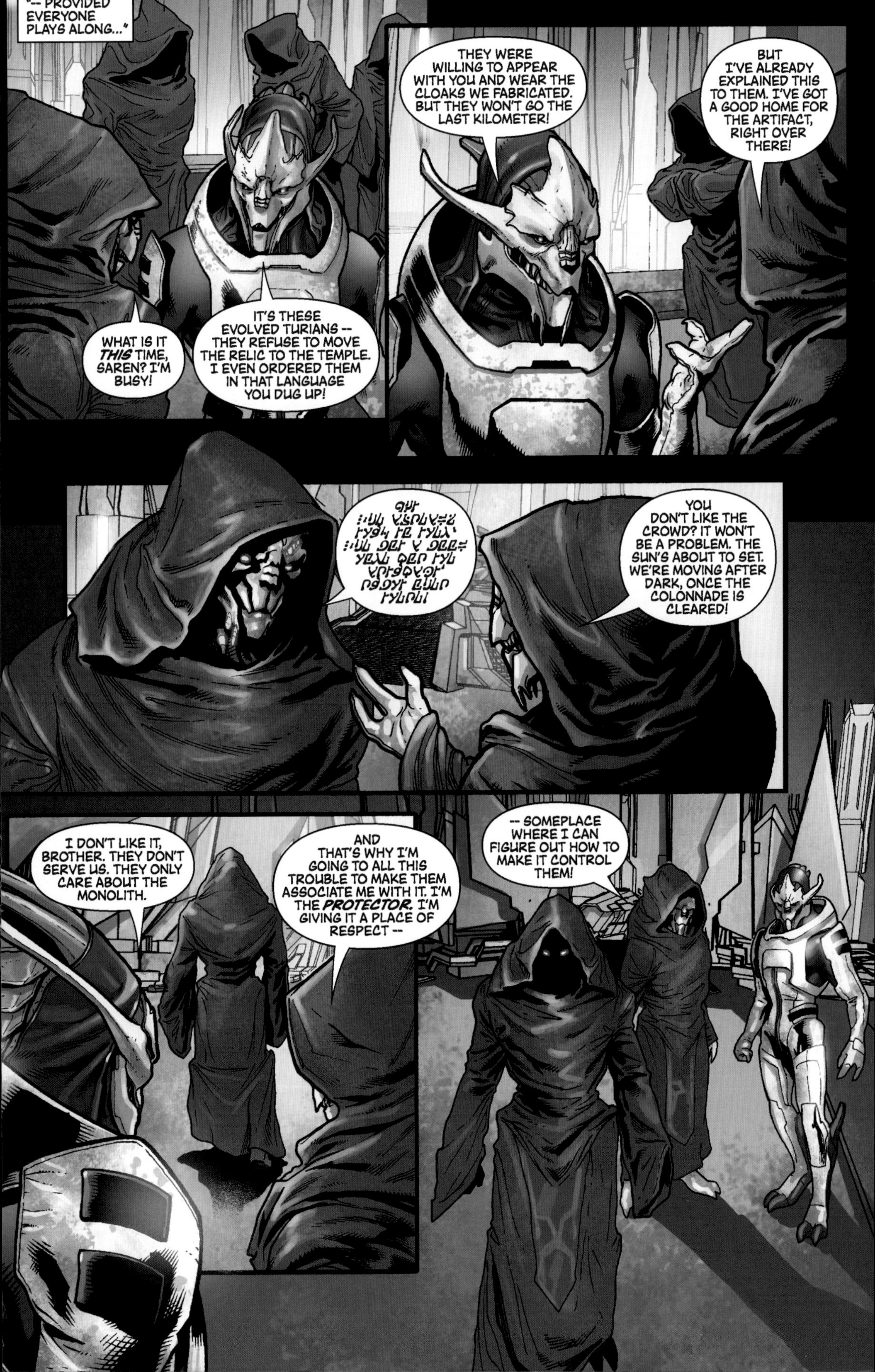
"-- PROVIDED EVERYONE PLAYS ALONG..."
WHAT IS IT *THIS* TIME, SAREN? I'M BUSY!
IT'S THESE EVOLVED TURIANS -- THEY REFUSE TO MOVE THE RELIC TO THE TEMPLE. I EVEN ORDERED THEM IN THAT LANGUAGE YOU DUG UP!
THEY WERE WILLING TO APPEAR WITH YOU AND WEAR THE CLOAKS WE FABRICATED. BUT THEY WON'T GO THE LAST KILOMETER!
BUT I'VE ALREADY EXPLAINED THIS TO THEM. I'VE GOT A GOOD HOME FOR THE ARTIFACT, RIGHT OVER THERE!
YOU DON'T LIKE THE CROWD? IT WON'T BE A PROBLEM. THE SUN'S ABOUT TO SET. WE'RE MOVING AFTER DARK, ONCE THE COLONNADE IS CLEARED!
I DON'T LIKE IT, BROTHER. THEY DON'T SERVE US. THEY ONLY CARE ABOUT THE MONOLITH.
AND THAT'S WHY I'M GOING TO ALL THIS TROUBLE TO MAKE THEM ASSOCIATE ME WITH IT. I'M THE ***PROTECTOR.*** I'M GIVING IT A PLACE OF RESPECT --
-- SOMEPLACE WHERE I CAN FIGURE OUT HOW TO MAKE IT CONTROL THEM!

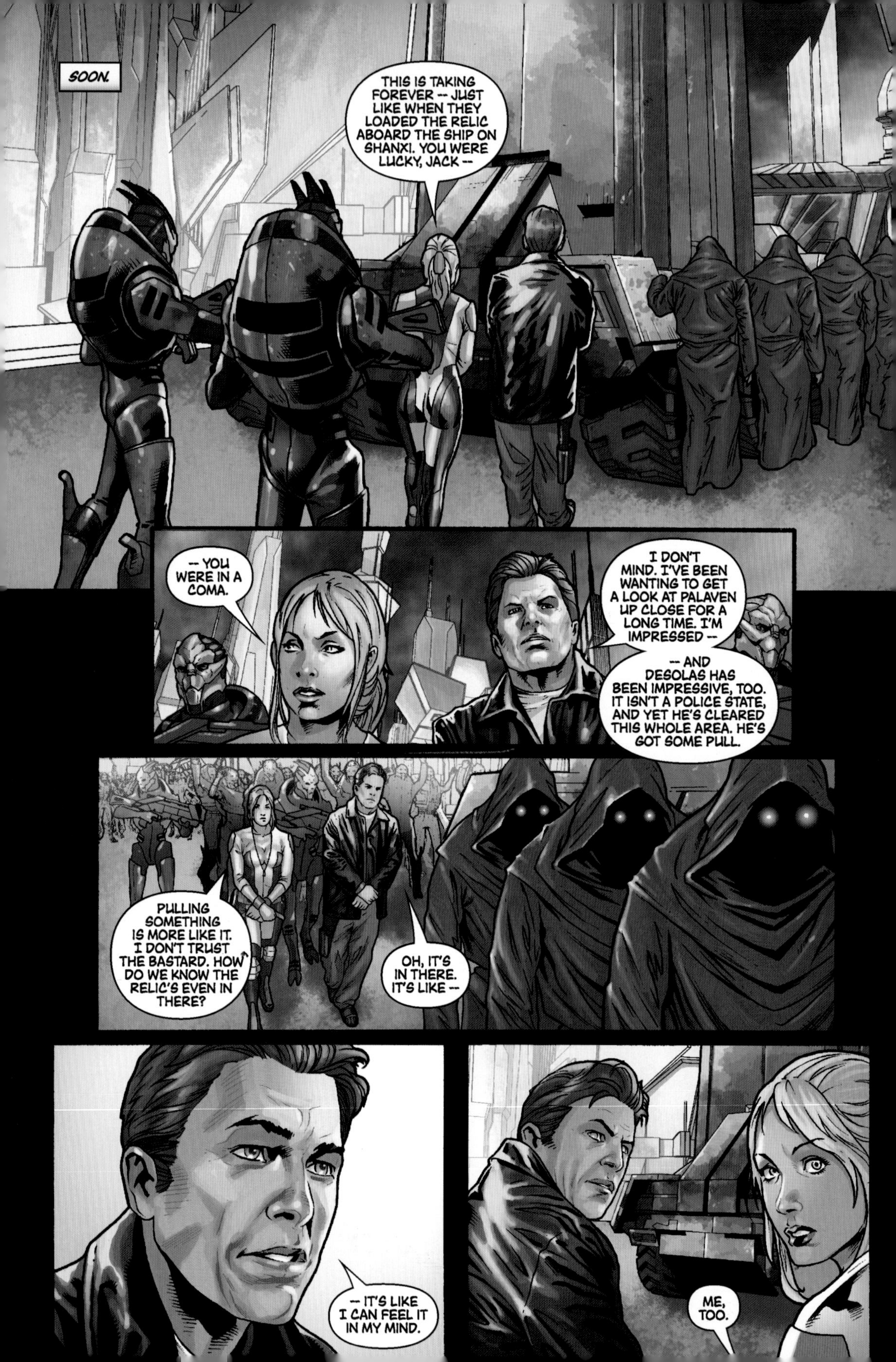
SOON.
THIS IS TAKING FOREVER -- JUST LIKE WHEN THEY LOADED THE RELIC ABOARD THE SHIP ON SHANXI. YOU WERE LUCKY, JACK --
-- YOU WERE IN A COMA.
I DON'T MIND. I'VE BEEN WANTING TO GET A LOOK AT PALAVEN UP CLOSE FOR A LONG TIME. I'M IMPRESSED --
-- AND DESOLAS HAS BEEN IMPRESSIVE, TOO. IT ISN'T A POLICE STATE, AND YET HE'S CLEARED THIS WHOLE AREA. HE'S GOT SOME PULL.
PULLING SOMETHING IS MORE LIKE IT. I DON'T TRUST THE BASTARD. HOW DO WE KNOW THE RELIC'S EVEN IN THERE?
OH, IT'S IN THERE. IT'S LIKE --
-- IT'S LIKE I CAN FEEL IT IN MY MIND.
ME, TOO.

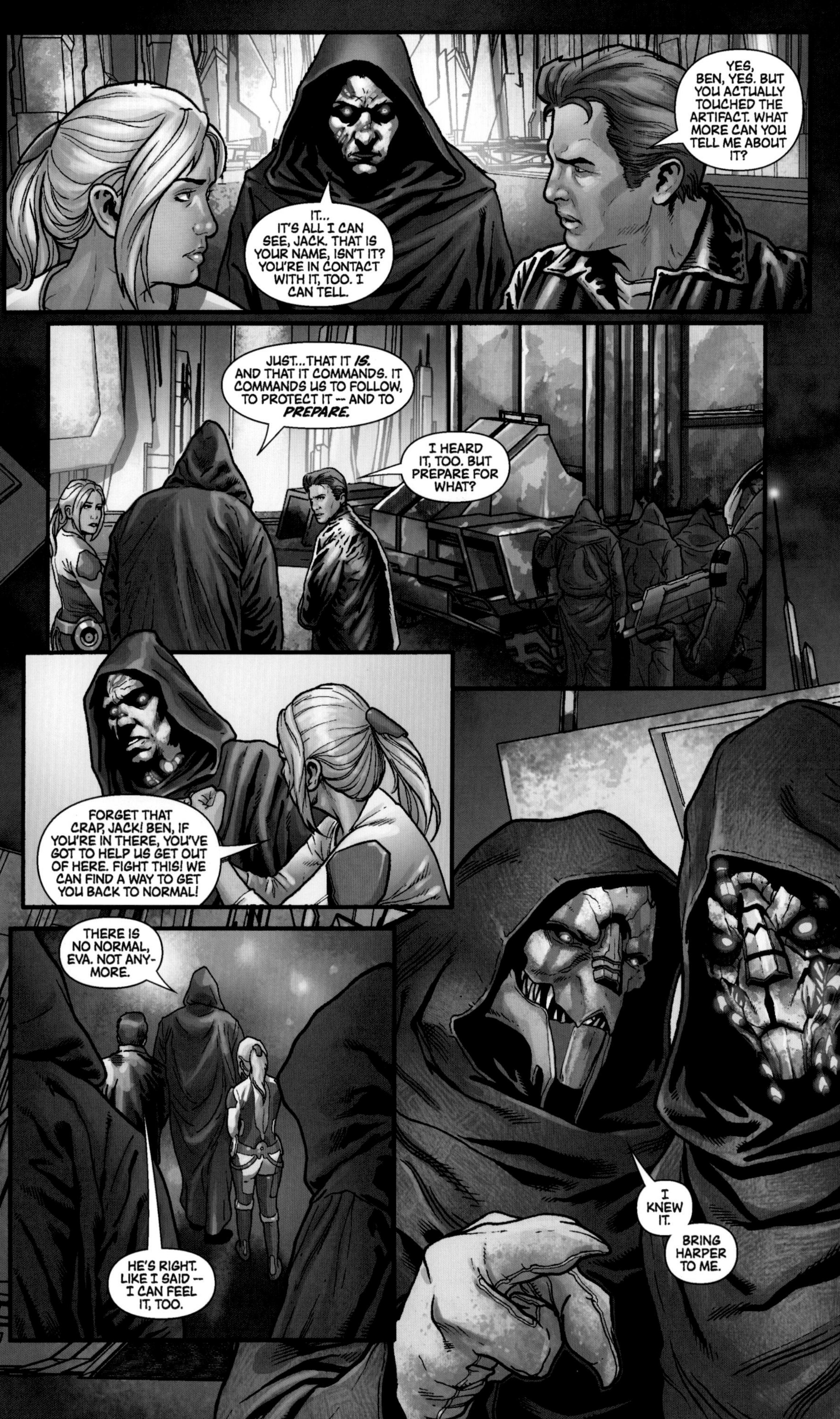
YES, BEN, YES. BUT YOU ACTUALLY TOUCHED THE ARTIFACT. WHAT MORE CAN YOU TELL ME ABOUT IT?
IT... IT'S ALL I CAN SEE, JACK. THAT IS YOUR NAME, ISN'T IT? YOU'RE IN CONTACT WITH IT, TOO. I CAN TELL.
JUST...THAT IT *IS.* AND THAT IT COMMANDS. IT COMMANDS US TO FOLLOW, TO PROTECT IT -- AND TO ***PREPARE.***
I HEARD IT, TOO. BUT PREPARE FOR WHAT?
FORGET THAT CRAP, JACK! BEN, IF YOU'RE IN THERE, YOU'VE GOT TO HELP US GET OUT OF HERE. FIGHT THIS! WE CAN FIND A WAY TO GET YOU BACK TO NORMAL!
THERE IS NO NORMAL, EVA. NOT ANY-MORE.
HE'S RIGHT. LIKE I SAID -- I CAN FEEL IT, TOO.
I KNEW IT.
BRING HARPER TO ME.

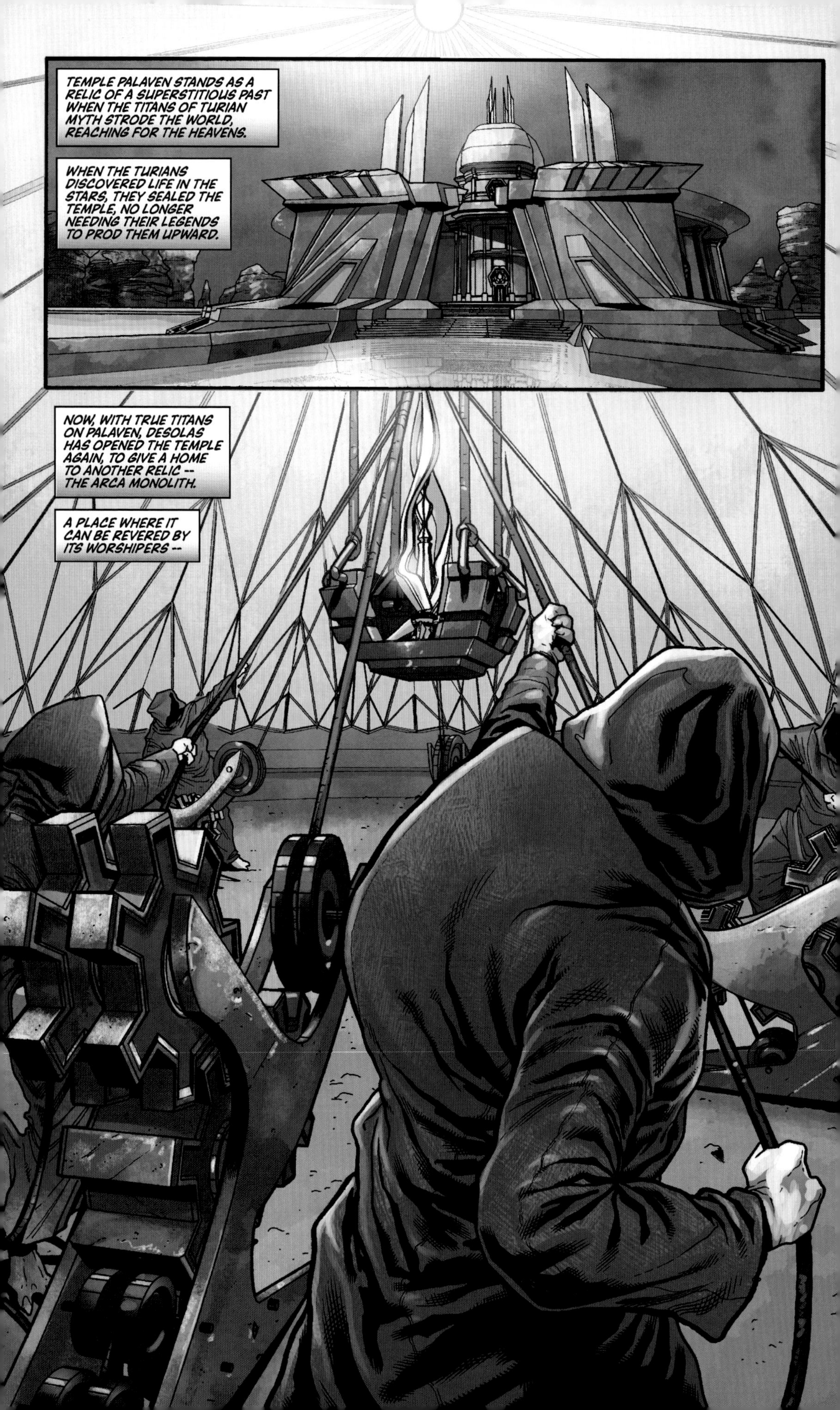
TEMPLE PALAVEN STANDS AS A RELIC OF A SUPERSTITIOUS PAST WHEN THE TITANS OF TURIAN MYTH STRODE THE WORLD, REACHING FOR THE HEAVENS.
WHEN THE TURIANS DISCOVERED LIFE IN THE STARS, THEY SEALED THE TEMPLE, NO LONGER NEEDING THEIR LEGENDS TO PROD THEM UPWARD.
NOW, WITH TRUE TITANS ON PALAVEN, DESOLAS HAS OPENED THE TEMPLE AGAIN, TO GIVE A HOME TO ANOTHER RELIC -- THE ARCA MONOLITH.
A PLACE WHERE IT CAN BE REVERED BY ITS WORSHIPERS --

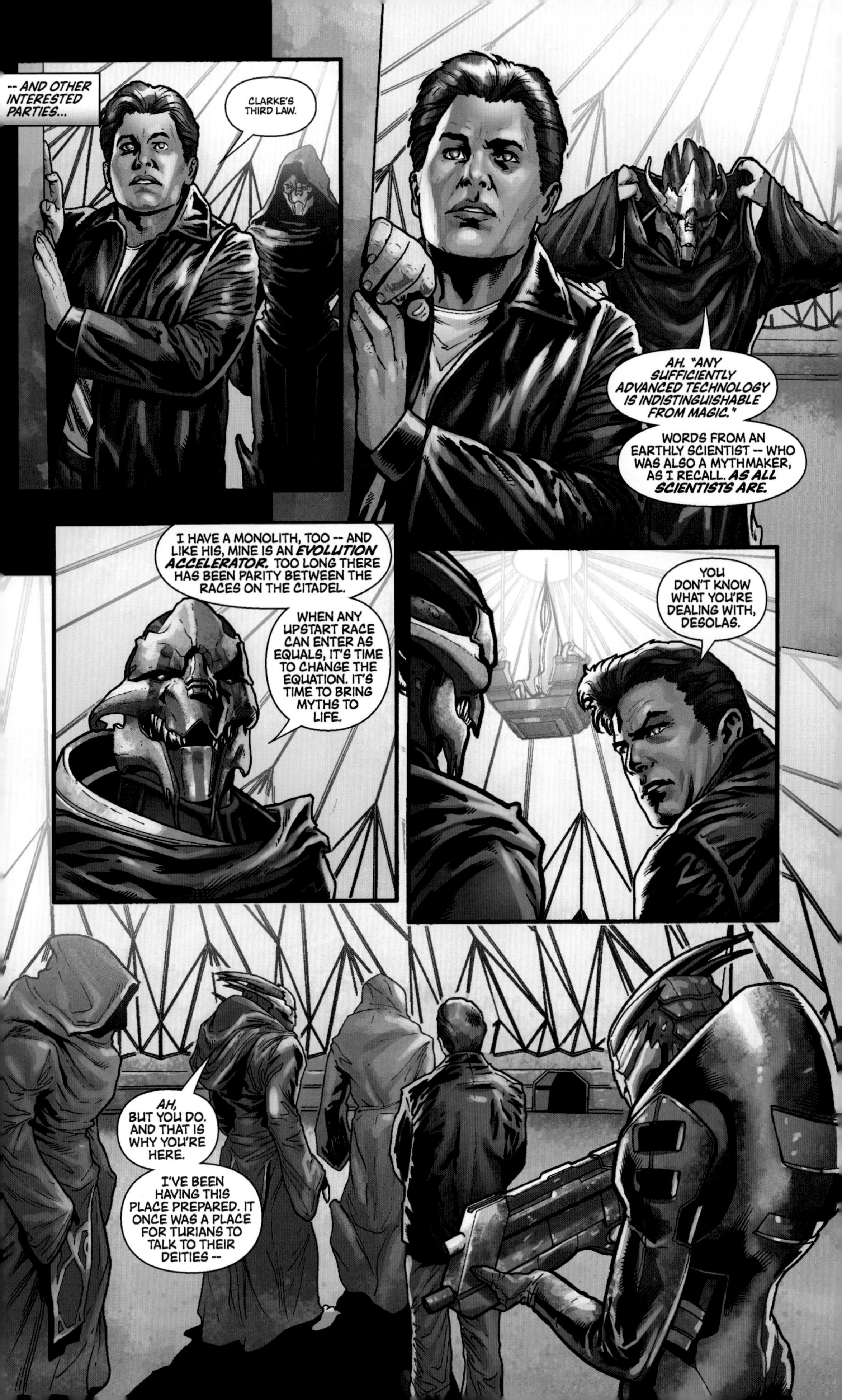
-- AND OTHER INTERESTED PARTIES...
CLARKE'S THIRD LAW.
AH. "ANY SUFFICIENTLY ADVANCED TECHNOLOGY IS INDISTINGUISHABLE FROM MAGIC."
WORDS FROM AN EARTHLY SCIENTIST -- WHO WAS ALSO A MYTHMAKER, AS I RECALL. AS ALL SCIENTISTS ARE.
I HAVE A MONOLITH, TOO -- AND LIKE HIS, MINE IS AN EVOLUTION ACCELERATOR. TOO LONG THERE HAS BEEN PARITY BETWEEN THE RACES ON THE CITADEL.
WHEN ANY UPSTART RACE CAN ENTER AS EQUALS, IT'S TIME TO CHANGE THE EQUATION. IT'S TIME TO BRING MYTHS TO LIFE.
YOU DON'T KNOW WHAT YOU'RE DEALING WITH, DESOLAS.
AH, BUT YOU DO. AND THAT IS WHY YOU'RE HERE.
I'VE BEEN HAVING THIS PLACE PREPARED. IT ONCE WAS A PLACE FOR TURIANS TO TALK TO THEIR DEITIES --

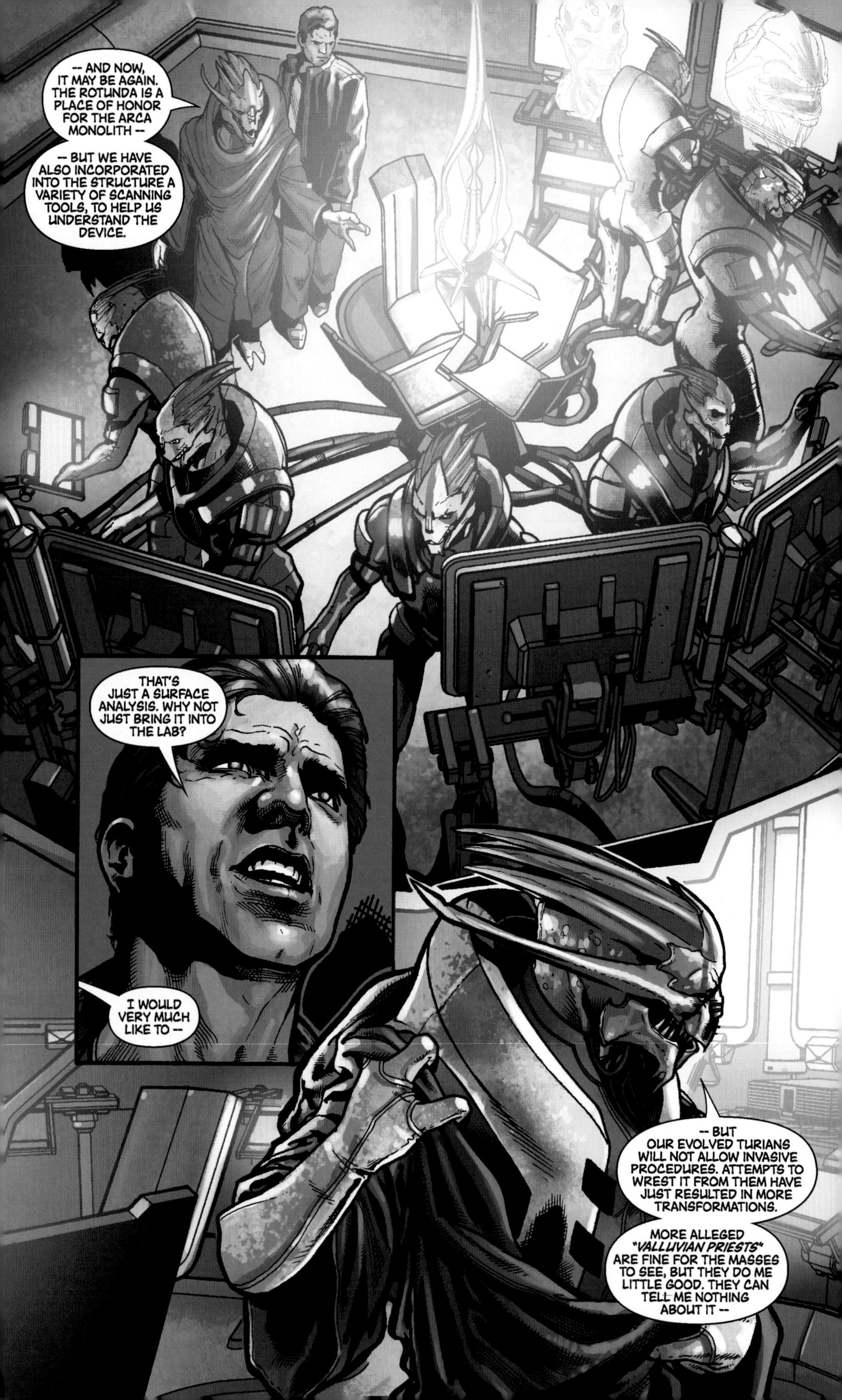
-- AND NOW, IT MAY BE AGAIN. THE ROTUNDA IS A PLACE OF HONOR FOR THE ARCA MONOLITH --
-- BUT WE HAVE ALSO INCORPORATED INTO THE STRUCTURE A VARIETY OF SCANNING TOOLS, TO HELP US UNDERSTAND THE DEVICE.
THAT'S JUST A SURFACE ANALYSIS. WHY NOT JUST BRING IT INTO THE LAB?
I WOULD VERY MUCH LIKE TO --
-- BUT OUR EVOLVED TURIANS WILL NOT ALLOW INVASIVE PROCEDURES. ATTEMPTS TO WREST IT FROM THEM HAVE JUST RESULTED IN MORE TRANSFORMATIONS.
MORE ALLEGED *"VALLUVIAN PRIESTS"* ARE FINE FOR THE MASSES TO SEE, BUT THEY DO ME LITTLE GOOD. THEY CAN TELL ME NOTHING ABOUT IT --

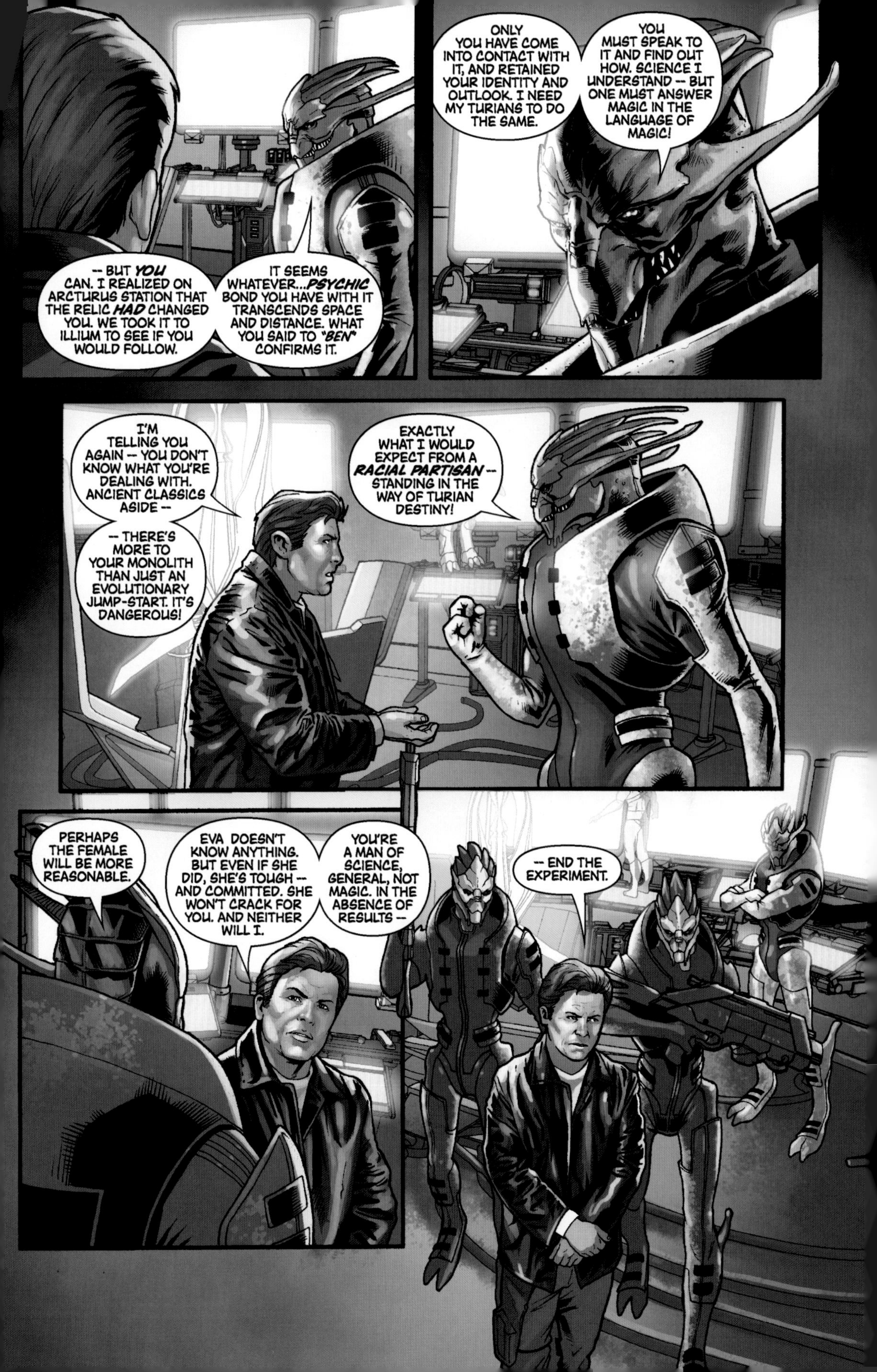
-- BUT YOU CAN. I REALIZED ON ARCTURUS STATION THAT THE RELIC HAD CHANGED YOU. WE TOOK IT TO ILLIUM TO SEE IF YOU WOULD FOLLOW.
IT SEEMS WHATEVER... PSYCHIC BOND YOU HAVE WITH IT TRANSCENDS SPACE AND DISTANCE. WHAT YOU SAID TO "BEN" CONFIRMS IT.
ONLY YOU HAVE COME INTO CONTACT WITH IT, AND RETAINED YOUR IDENTITY AND OUTLOOK. I NEED MY TURIANS TO DO THE SAME.
YOU MUST SPEAK TO IT AND FIND OUT HOW. SCIENCE I UNDERSTAND -- BUT ONE MUST ANSWER MAGIC IN THE LANGUAGE OF MAGIC!
I'M TELLING YOU AGAIN -- YOU DON'T KNOW WHAT YOU'RE DEALING WITH. ANCIENT CLASSICS ASIDE --
-- THERE'S MORE TO YOUR MONOLITH THAN JUST AN EVOLUTIONARY JUMP-START. IT'S DANGEROUS!
EXACTLY WHAT I WOULD EXPECT FROM A RACIAL PARTISAN -- STANDING IN THE WAY OF TURIAN DESTINY!
PERHAPS THE FEMALE WILL BE MORE REASONABLE.
EVA DOESN'T KNOW ANYTHING. BUT EVEN IF SHE DID, SHE'S TOUGH -- AND COMMITTED. SHE WON'T CRACK FOR YOU. AND NEITHER WILL I.
YOU'RE A MAN OF SCIENCE, GENERAL, NOT MAGIC. IN THE ABSENCE OF RESULTS --
-- END THE EXPERIMENT.

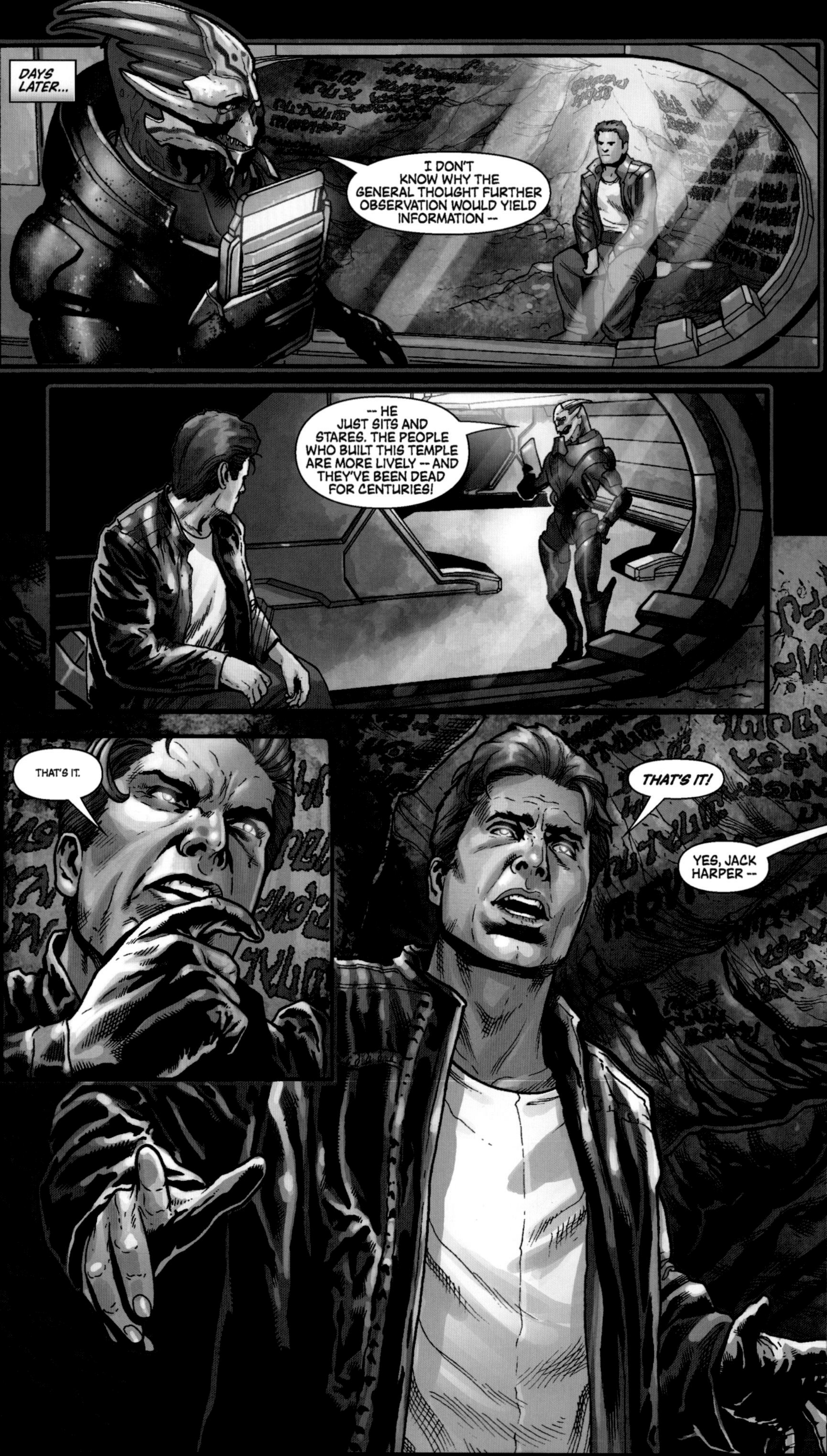
DAYS LATER...
I DON'T KNOW WHY THE GENERAL THOUGHT FURTHER OBSERVATION WOULD YIELD INFORMATION --
-- HE JUST SITS AND STARES. THE PEOPLE WHO BUILT THIS TEMPLE ARE MORE LIVELY -- AND THEY'VE BEEN DEAD FOR CENTURIES!
THAT'S IT.
THAT'S IT!
YES, JACK HARPER --

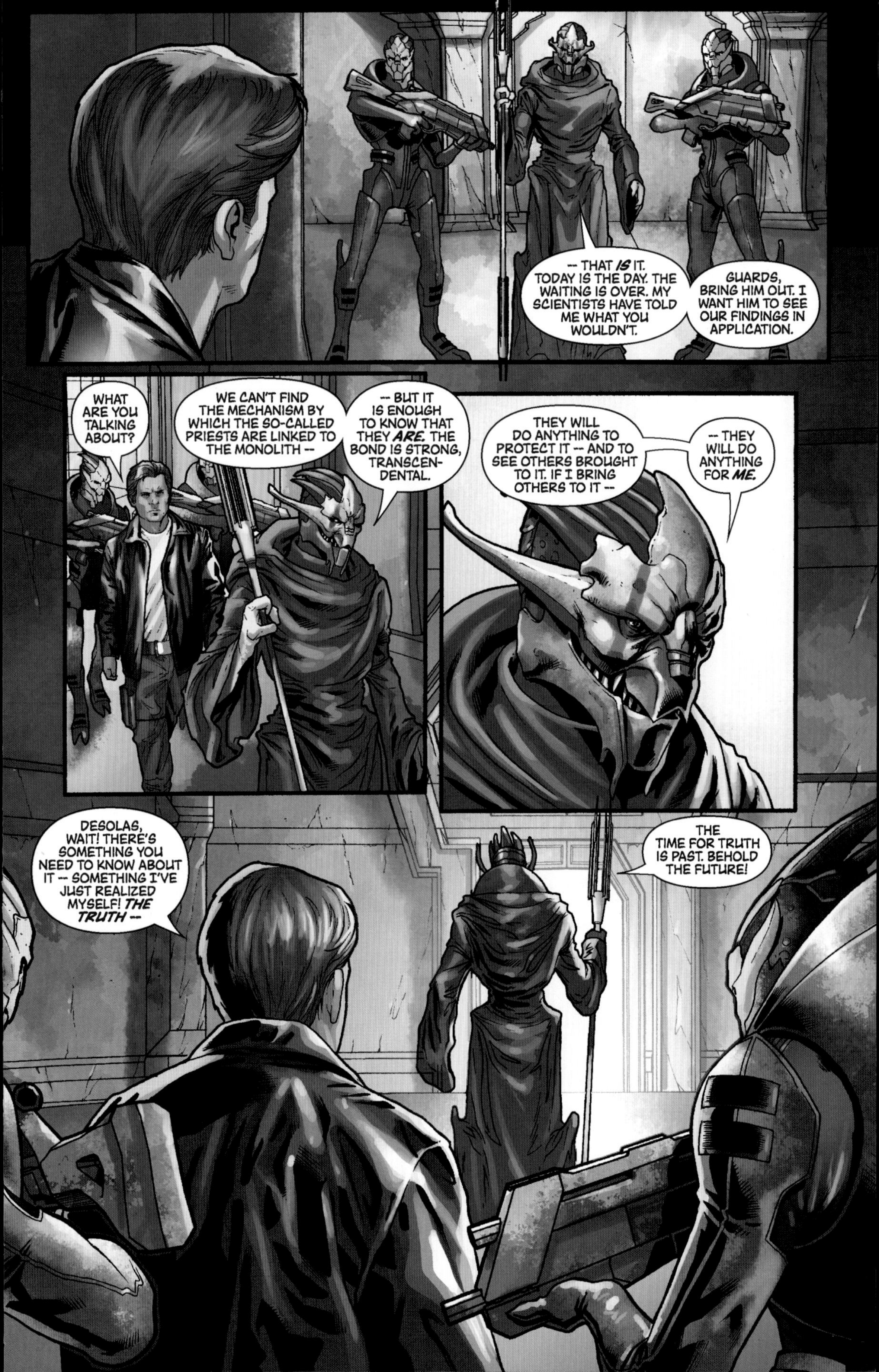
-- THAT *IS* IT. TODAY IS THE DAY. THE WAITING IS OVER. MY SCIENTISTS HAVE TOLD ME WHAT YOU WOULDN'T.
GUARDS, BRING HIM OUT. I WANT HIM TO SEE OUR FINDINGS IN APPLICATION.
WHAT ARE YOU TALKING ABOUT?
WE CAN'T FIND THE MECHANISM BY WHICH THE SO-CALLED PRIESTS ARE LINKED TO THE MONOLITH --
-- BUT IT IS ENOUGH TO KNOW THAT THEY *ARE*. THE BOND IS STRONG, TRANSCEN-DENTAL.
THEY WILL DO ANYTHING TO PROTECT IT -- AND TO SEE OTHERS BROUGHT TO IT. IF I BRING OTHERS TO IT --
-- THEY WILL DO ANYTHING FOR *ME.*
DESOLAS, WAIT! THERE'S SOMETHING YOU NEED TO KNOW ABOUT IT -- SOMETHING I'VE JUST REALIZED MYSELF! *THE TRUTH* --
THE TIME FOR TRUTH IS PAST. BEHOLD THE FUTURE!

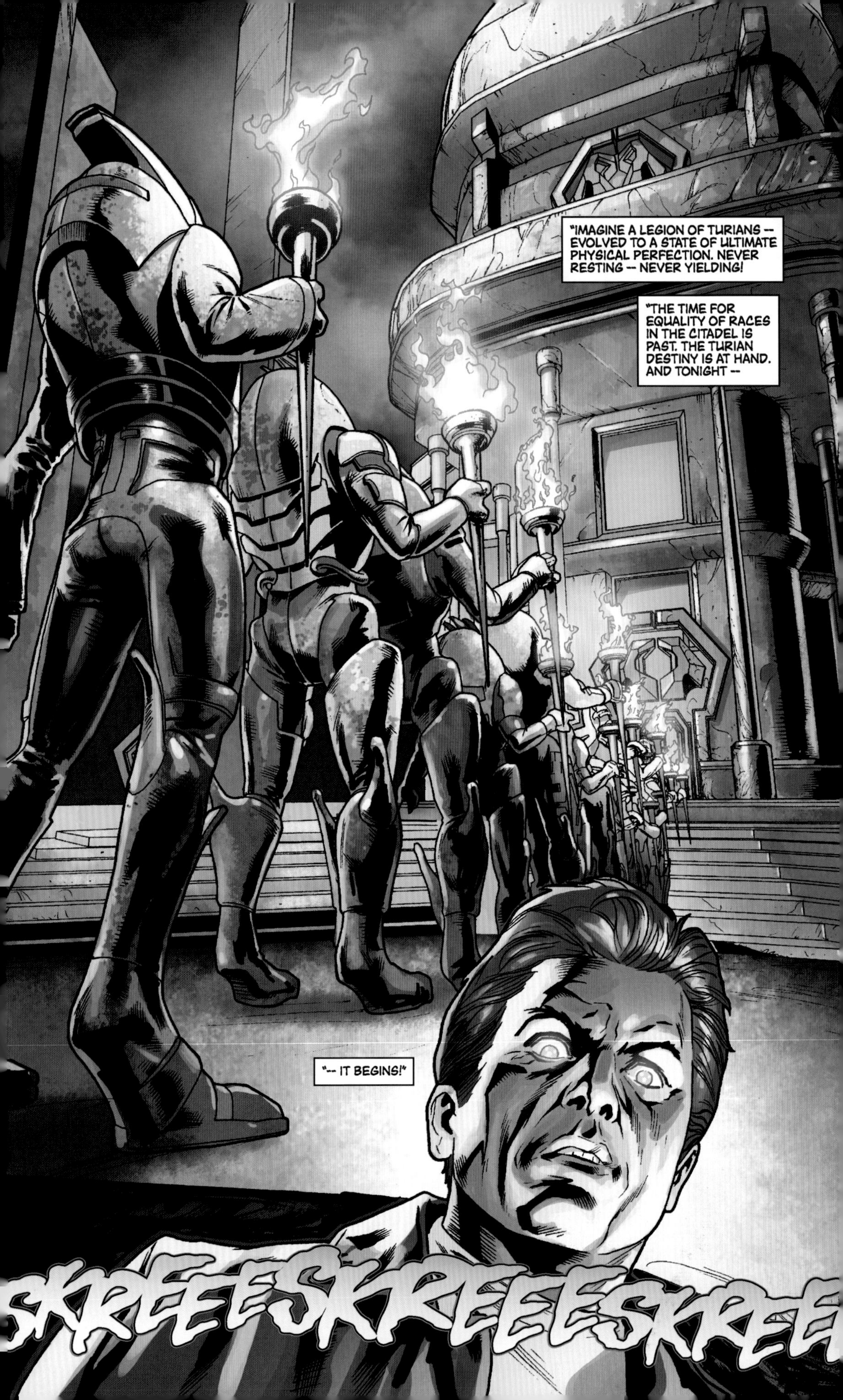
"IMAGINE A LEGION OF TURIANS -- EVOLVED TO A STATE OF ULTIMATE PHYSICAL PERFECTION. NEVER RESTING -- NEVER YIELDING!
"THE TIME FOR EQUALITY OF RACES IN THE CITADEL IS PAST. THE TURIAN DESTINY IS AT HAND. AND TONIGHT --
"-- IT BEGINS!"
SKREEESKREEESKREE

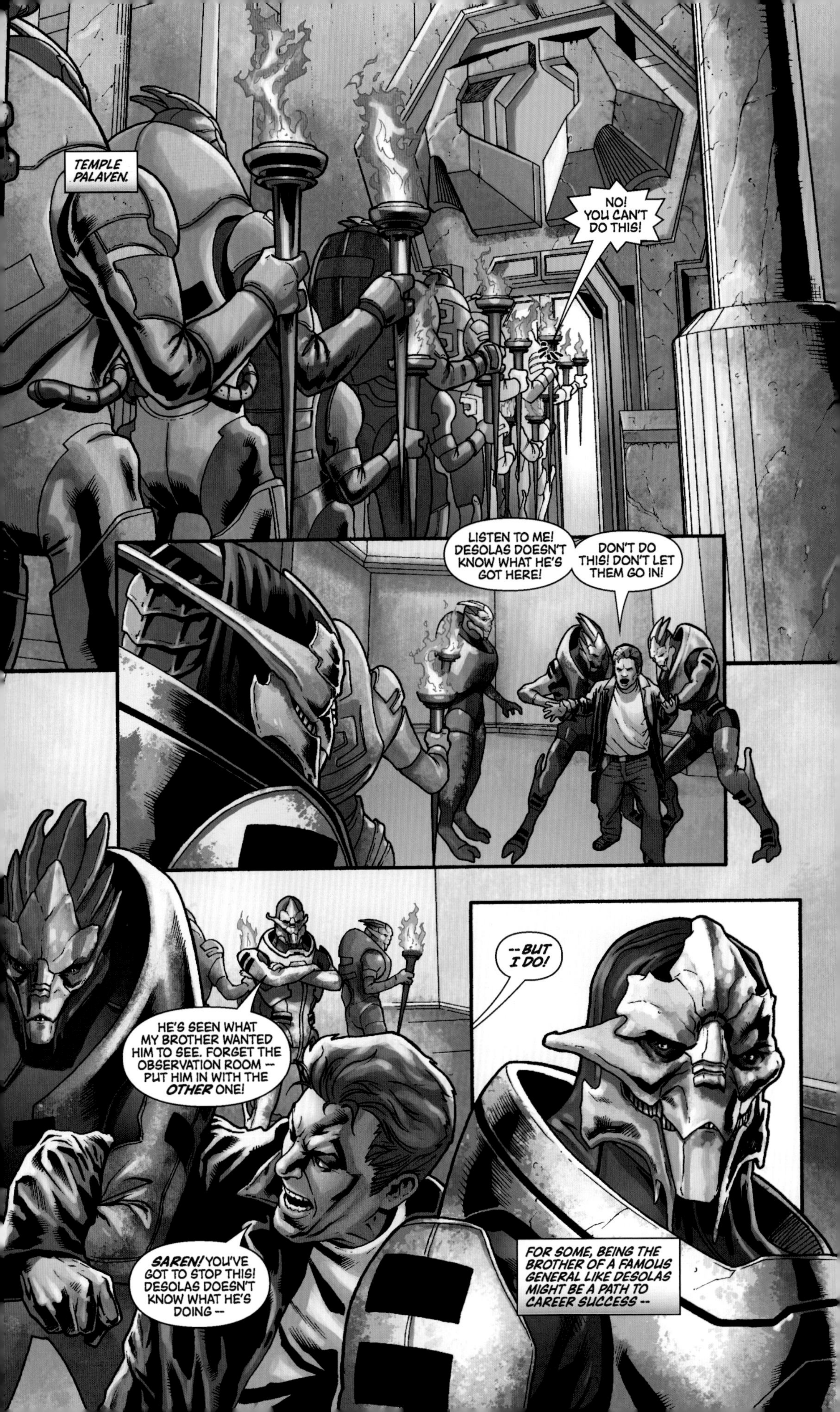
TEMPLE PALAVEN.
NO! YOU CAN'T DO THIS!
LISTEN TO ME! DESOLAS DOESN'T KNOW WHAT HE'S GOT HERE!
DON'T DO THIS! DON'T LET THEM GO IN!
HE'S SEEN WHAT MY BROTHER WANTED HIM TO SEE. FORGET THE OBSERVATION ROOM -- PUT HIM IN WITH THE OTHER ONE!
SAREN! YOU'VE GOT TO STOP THIS! DESOLAS DOESN'T KNOW WHAT HE'S DOING --
-- BUT I DO!
FOR SOME, BEING THE BROTHER OF A FAMOUS GENERAL LIKE DESOLAS MIGHT BE A PATH TO CAREER SUCCESS --

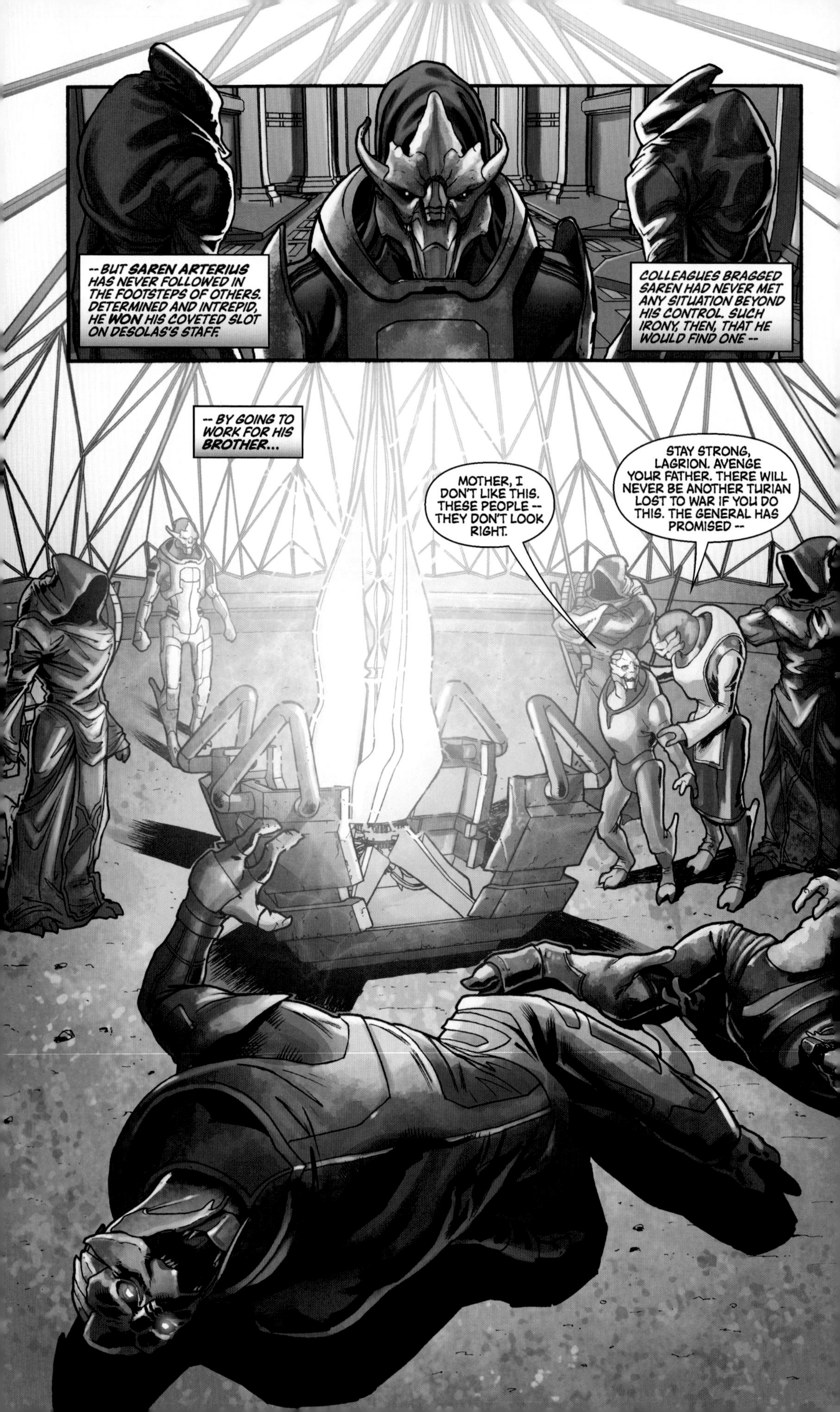
--BUT SAREN ARTERIUS HAS NEVER FOLLOWED IN THE FOOTSTEPS OF OTHERS. DETERMINED AND INTREPID, HE WON HIS COVETED SLOT ON DESOLAS'S STAFF.
COLLEAGUES BRAGGED SAREN HAD NEVER MET ANY SITUATION BEYOND HIS CONTROL. SUCH IRONY, THEN, THAT HE WOULD FIND ONE --
-- BY GOING TO WORK FOR HIS BROTHER...
MOTHER, I DON'T LIKE THIS. THESE PEOPLE -- THEY DON'T LOOK RIGHT.
STAY STRONG, LAGRION. AVENGE YOUR FATHER. THERE WILL NEVER BE ANOTHER TURIAN LOST TO WAR IF YOU DO THIS. THE GENERAL HAS PROMISED --

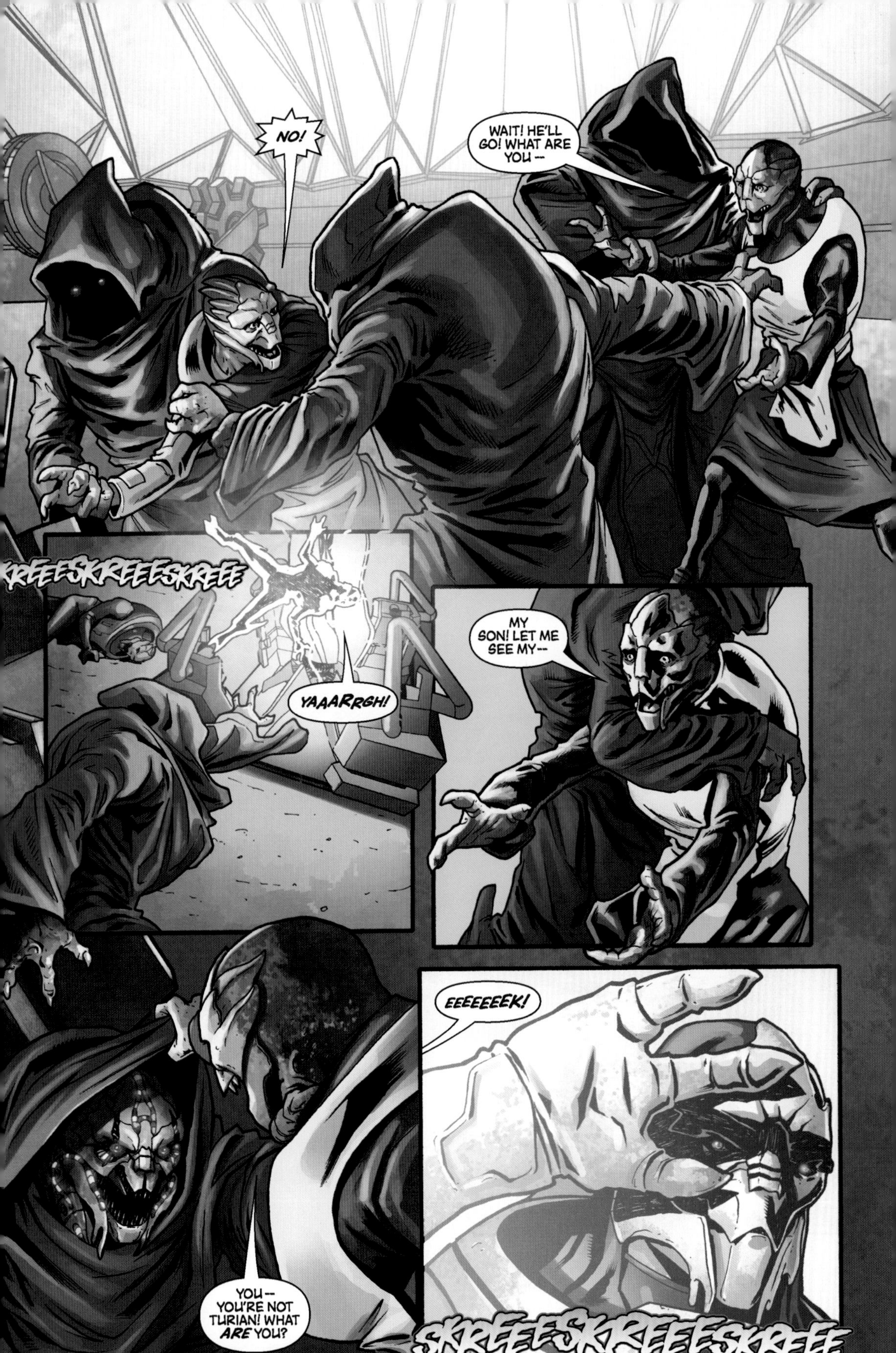
NO!
WAIT! HE'LL GO! WHAT ARE YOU --
KREEESKREEESKREEE
YAAARRGH!
MY SON! LET ME SEE MY--
YOU-- YOU'RE NOT TURIAN! WHAT *ARE* YOU?
EEEEEEEK!
SKREEESKREEESKREEE

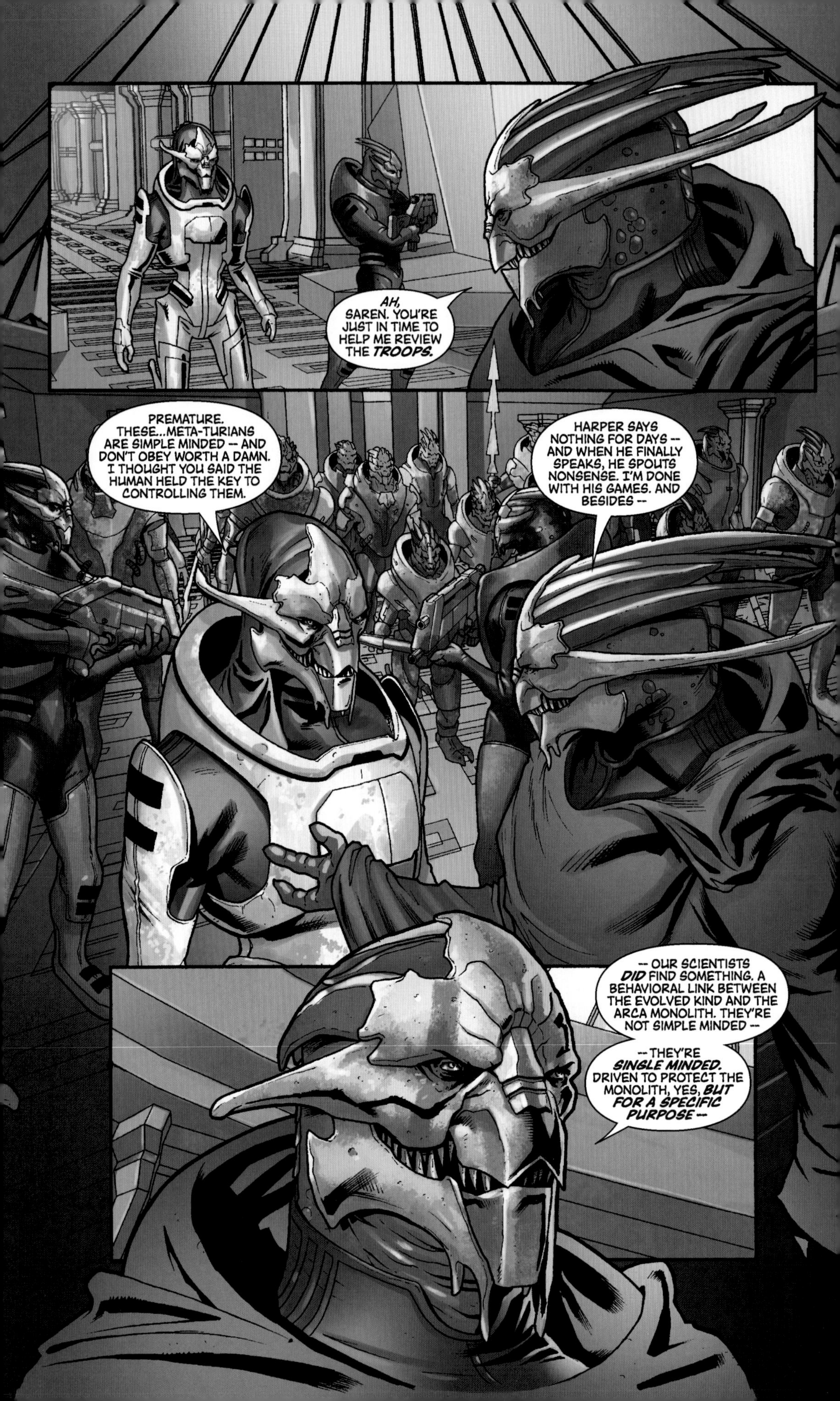
AH, SAREN. YOU'RE JUST IN TIME TO HELP ME REVIEW THE *TROOPS.*
PREMATURE. THESE...META-TURIANS ARE SIMPLE MINDED -- AND DON'T OBEY WORTH A DAMN. I THOUGHT YOU SAID THE HUMAN HELD THE KEY TO CONTROLLING THEM.
HARPER SAYS NOTHING FOR DAYS -- AND WHEN HE FINALLY SPEAKS, HE SPOUTS NONSENSE. I'M DONE WITH HIS GAMES. AND BESIDES --
-- OUR SCIENTISTS *DID* FIND SOMETHING. A BEHAVIORAL LINK BETWEEN THE EVOLVED KIND AND THE ARCA MONOLITH. THEY'RE NOT SIMPLE MINDED --
-- THEY'RE *SINGLE MINDED.* DRIVEN TO PROTECT THE MONOLITH, YES, *BUT FOR A SPECIFIC PURPOSE* --

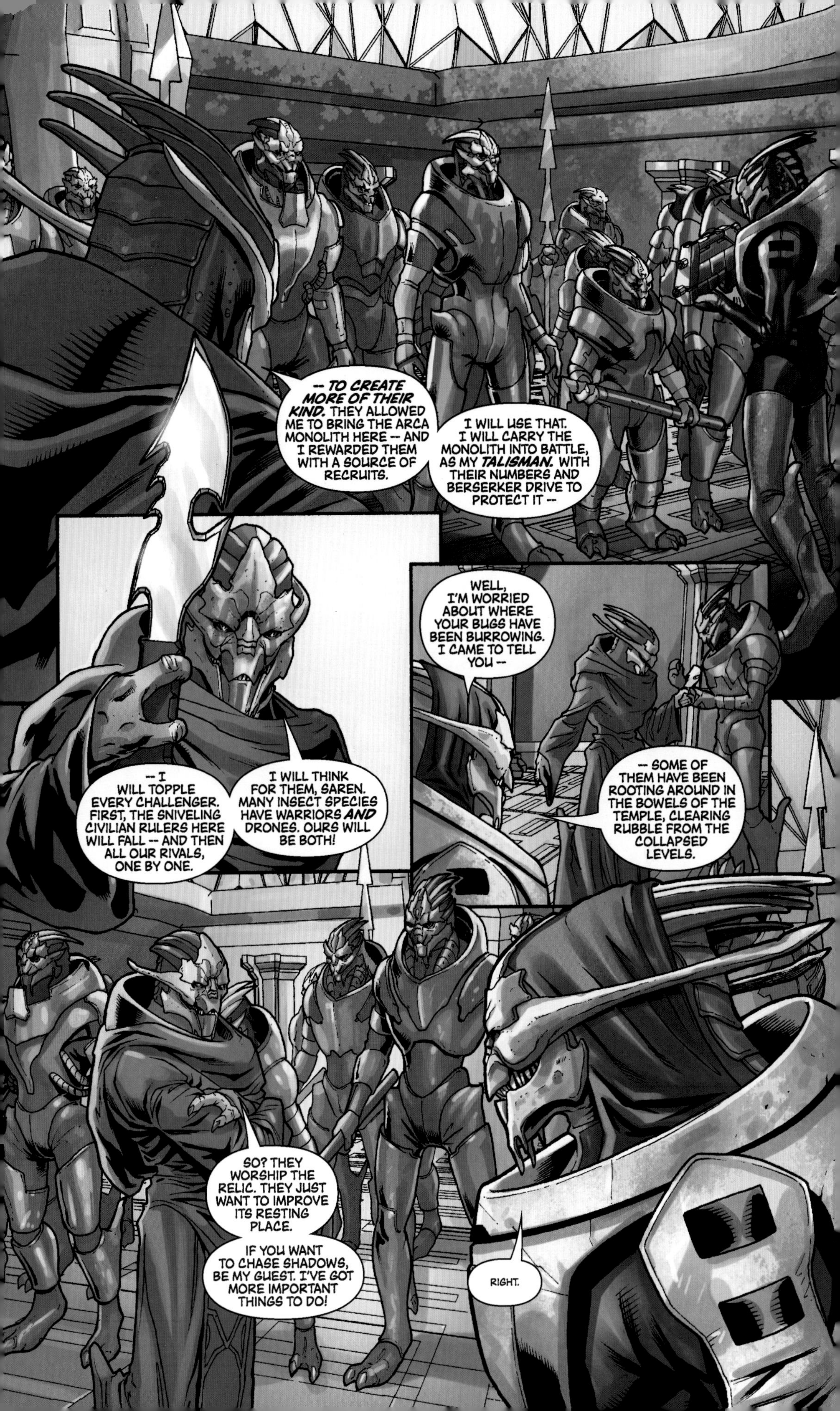
-- TO CREATE MORE OF THEIR KIND. THEY ALLOWED ME TO BRING THE ARCA MONOLITH HERE -- AND I REWARDED THEM WITH A SOURCE OF RECRUITS.
I WILL USE THAT. I WILL CARRY THE MONOLITH INTO BATTLE, AS MY TALISMAN. WITH THEIR NUMBERS AND BERSERKER DRIVE TO PROTECT IT --
-- I WILL TOPPLE EVERY CHALLENGER. FIRST, THE SNIVELING CIVILIAN RULERS HERE WILL FALL -- AND THEN ALL OUR RIVALS, ONE BY ONE.
I WILL THINK FOR THEM, SAREN. MANY INSECT SPECIES HAVE WARRIORS AND DRONES. OURS WILL BE BOTH!
WELL, I'M WORRIED ABOUT WHERE YOUR BUGS HAVE BEEN BURROWING. I CAME TO TELL YOU --
-- SOME OF THEM HAVE BEEN ROOTING AROUND IN THE BOWELS OF THE TEMPLE, CLEARING RUBBLE FROM THE COLLAPSED LEVELS.
SO? THEY WORSHIP THE RELIC. THEY JUST WANT TO IMPROVE ITS RESTING PLACE.
IF YOU WANT TO CHASE SHADOWS, BE MY GUEST. I'VE GOT MORE IMPORTANT THINGS TO DO!
RIGHT.

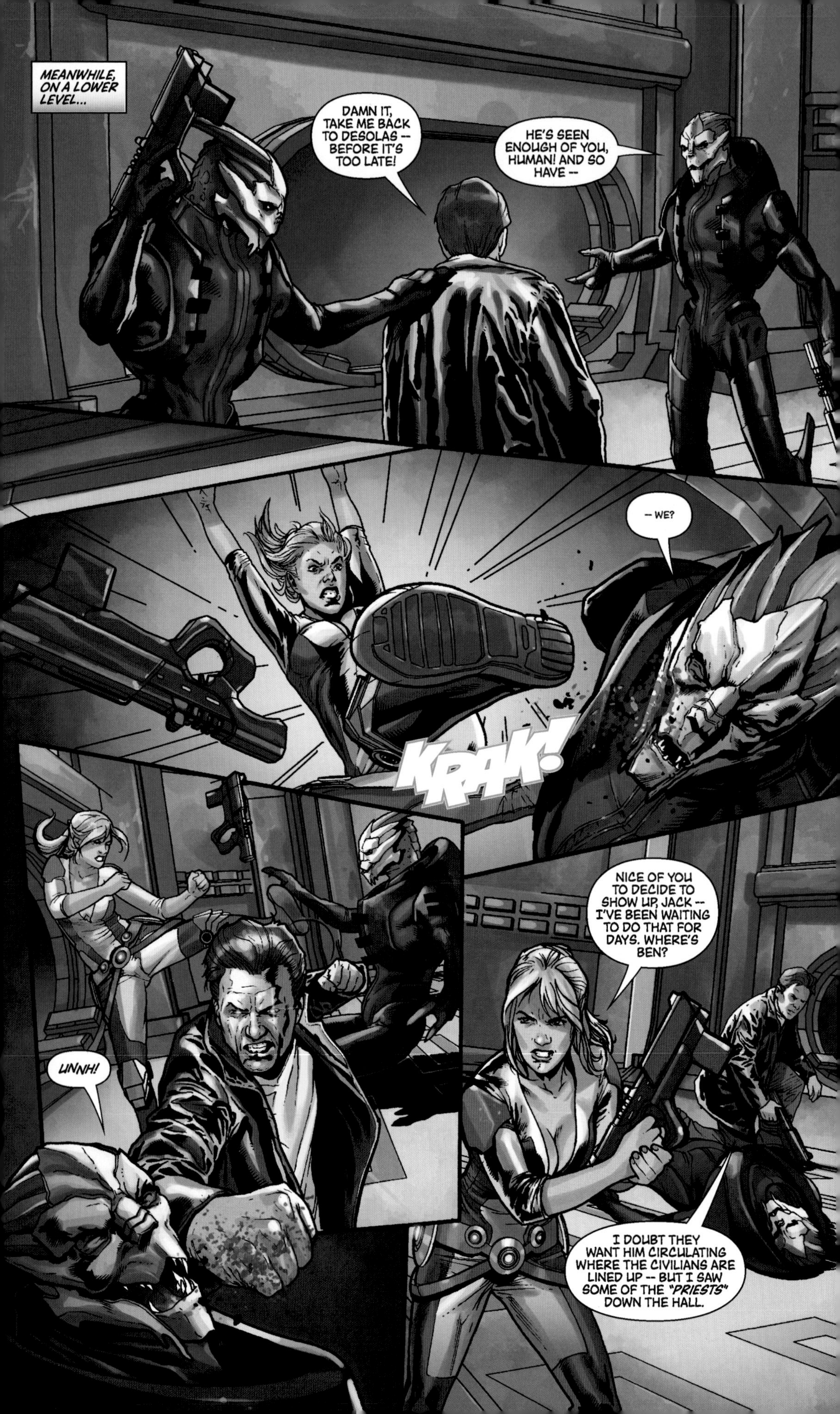
MEANWHILE, ON A LOWER LEVEL...
DAMN IT, TAKE ME BACK TO DESOLAS -- BEFORE IT'S TOO LATE!
HE'S SEEN ENOUGH OF YOU, HUMAN! AND SO HAVE --
-- WE?
KRAK!
UNNH!
NICE OF YOU TO DECIDE TO SHOW UP, JACK -- I'VE BEEN WAITING TO DO THAT FOR DAYS. WHERE'S BEN?
I DOUBT THEY WANT HIM CIRCULATING WHERE THE CIVILIANS ARE LINED UP -- BUT I SAW SOME OF THE "PRIESTS" DOWN THE HALL.

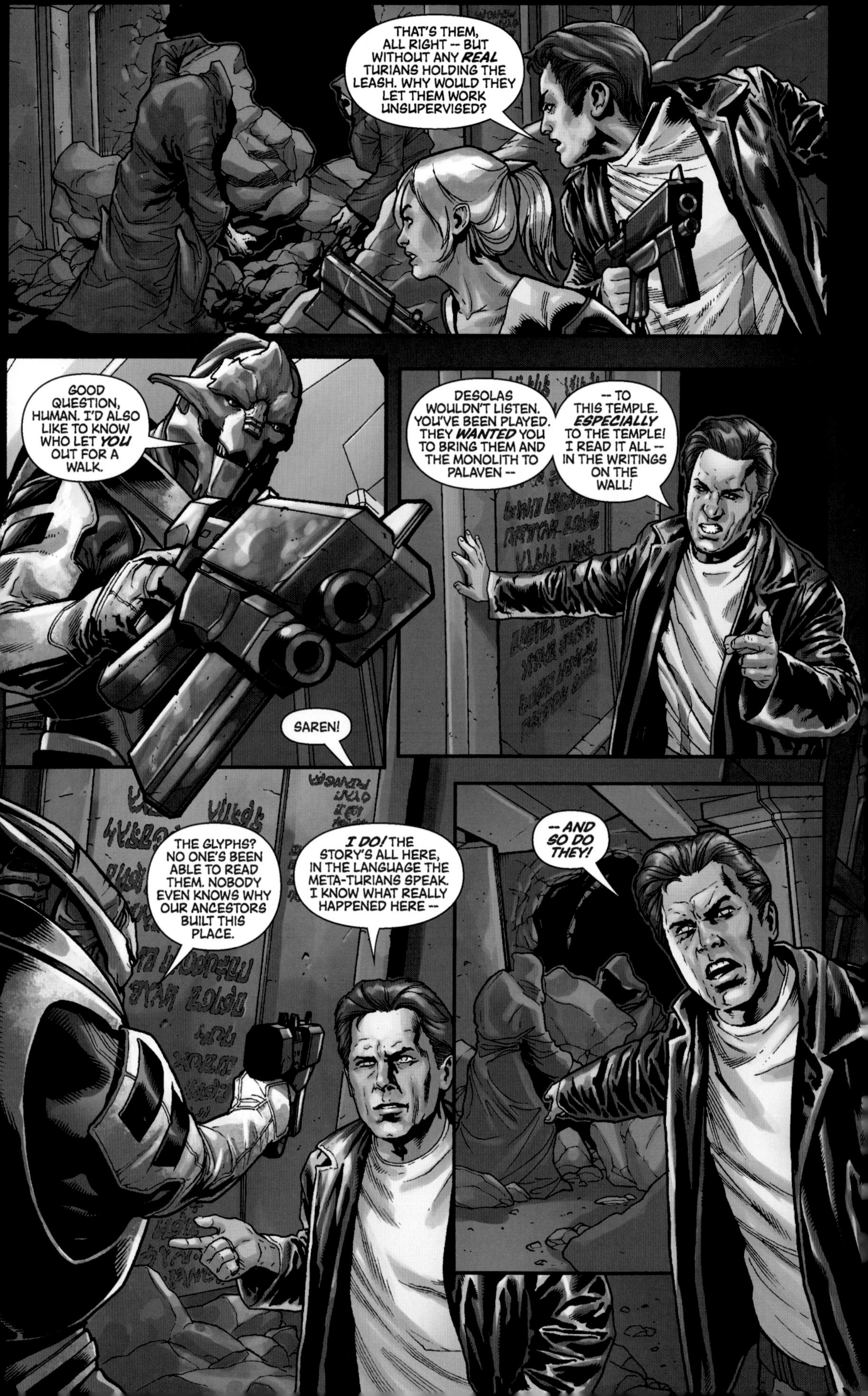
THAT'S THEM, ALL RIGHT -- BUT WITHOUT ANY *REAL* TURIANS HOLDING THE LEASH. WHY WOULD THEY LET THEM WORK UNSUPERVISED?
GOOD QUESTION, HUMAN. I'D ALSO LIKE TO KNOW WHO LET *YOU* OUT FOR A WALK.
SAREN!
DESOLAS WOULDN'T LISTEN. YOU'VE BEEN PLAYED. THEY *WANTED* YOU TO BRING THEM AND THE MONOLITH TO PALAVEN --
-- TO THIS TEMPLE. *ESPECIALLY* TO THE TEMPLE! I READ IT ALL -- IN THE WRITINGS ON THE WALL!
THE GLYPHS? NO ONE'S BEEN ABLE TO READ THEM. NOBODY EVEN KNOWS WHY OUR ANCESTORS BUILT THIS PLACE.
I DO! THE STORY'S ALL HERE, IN THE LANGUAGE THE META-TURIANS SPEAK. I KNOW WHAT REALLY HAPPENED HERE --
-- AND SO DO THEY!

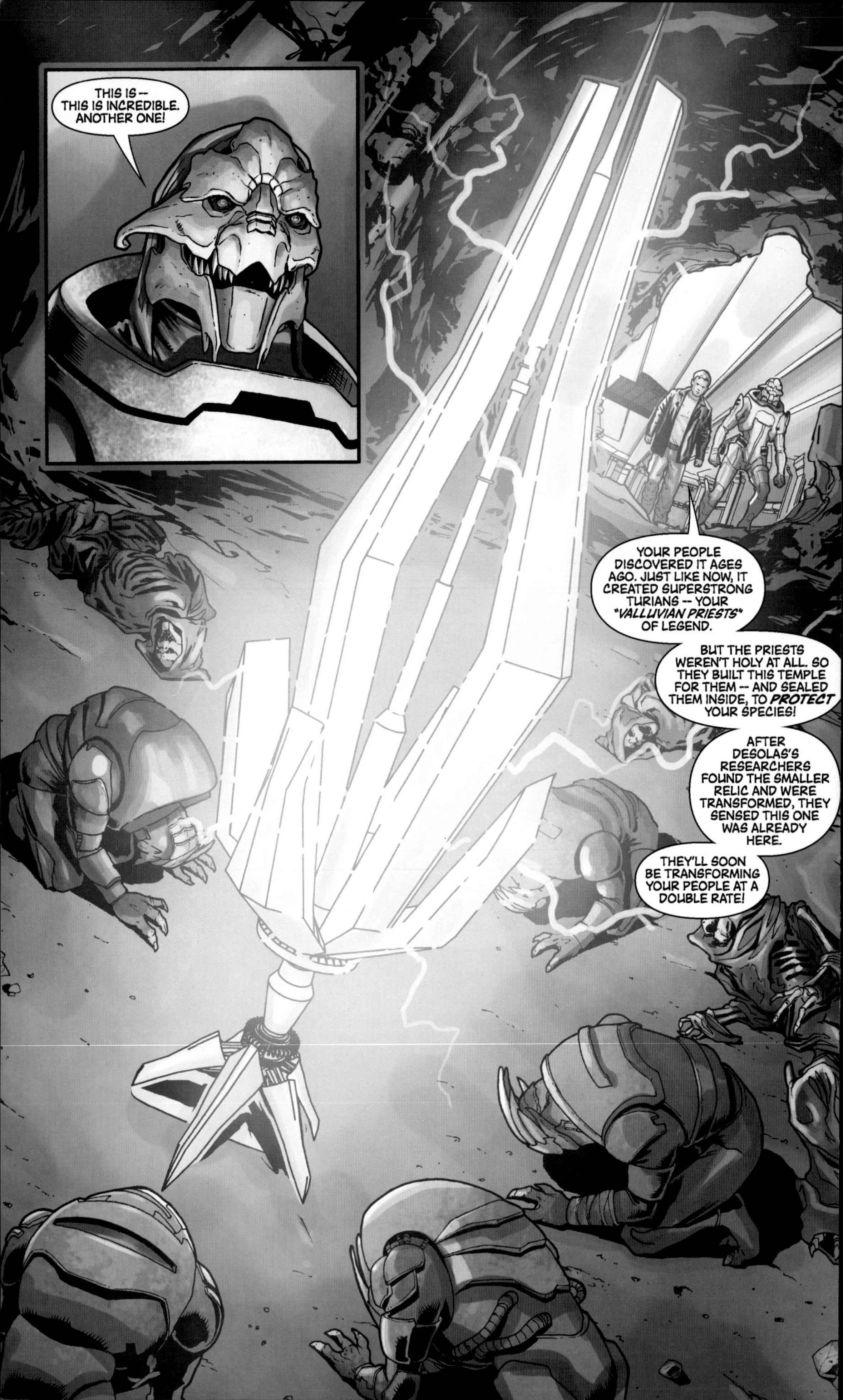
THIS IS -- THIS IS INCREDIBLE. ANOTHER ONE!
YOUR PEOPLE DISCOVERED IT AGES AGO. JUST LIKE NOW, IT CREATED SUPERSTRONG TURIANS -- YOUR "VALLUVIAN PRIESTS" OF LEGEND.
BUT THE PRIESTS WEREN'T HOLY AT ALL. SO THEY BUILT THIS TEMPLE FOR THEM -- AND SEALED THEM INSIDE, TO PROTECT YOUR SPECIES!
AFTER DESOLAS'S RESEARCHERS FOUND THE SMALLER RELIC AND WERE TRANSFORMED, THEY SENSED THIS ONE WAS ALREADY HERE.
THEY'LL SOON BE TRANSFORMING YOUR PEOPLE AT A DOUBLE RATE!

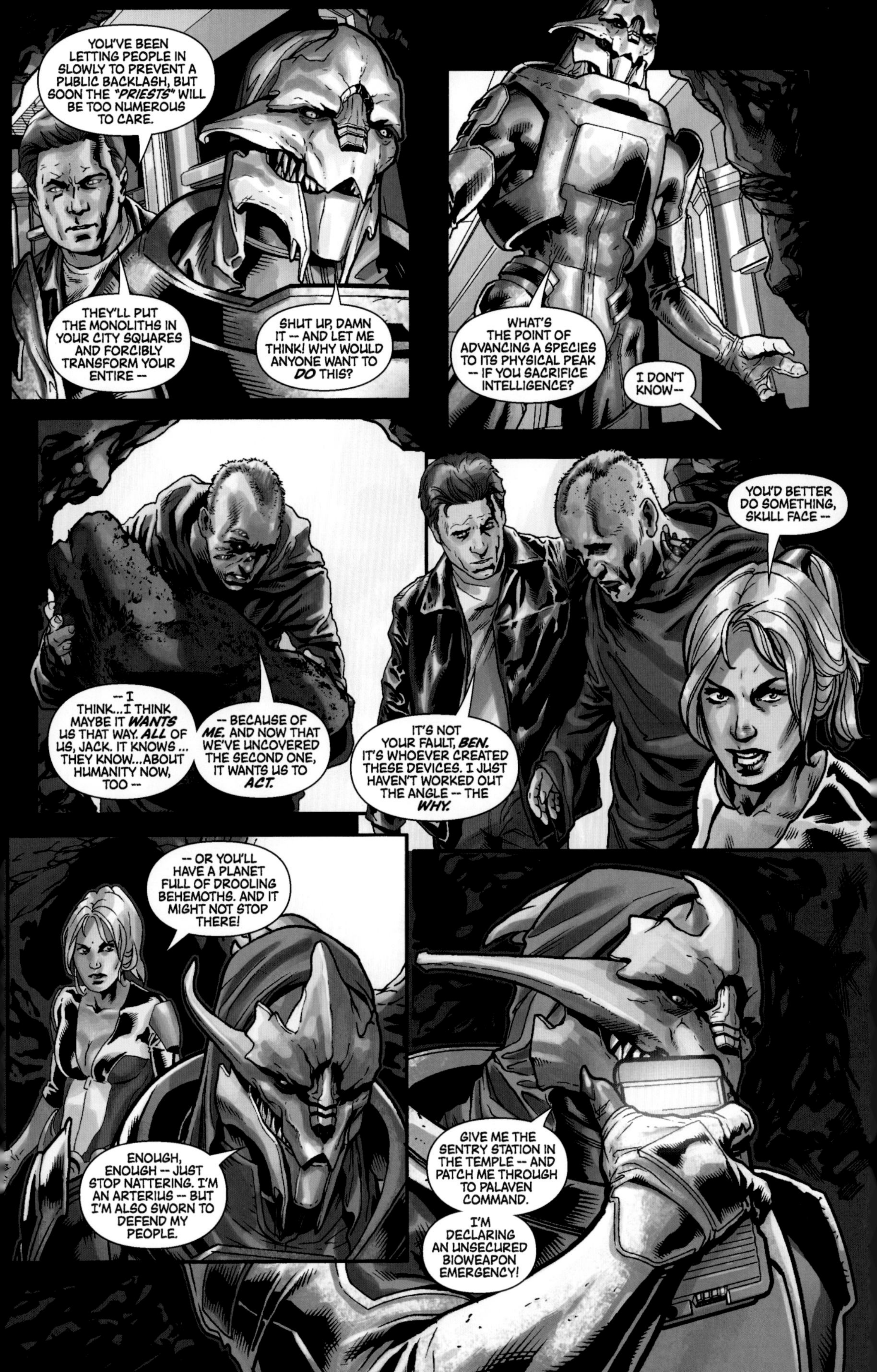

YOU'VE BEEN LETTING PEOPLE IN SLOWLY TO PREVENT A PUBLIC BACKLASH, BUT SOON THE "PRIESTS" WILL BE TOO NUMEROUS TO CARE.
THEY'LL PUT THE MONOLITHS IN YOUR CITY SQUARES AND FORCIBLY TRANSFORM YOUR ENTIRE --
SHUT UP, DAMN IT -- AND LET ME THINK! WHY WOULD ANYONE WANT TO *DO* THIS?
WHAT'S THE POINT OF ADVANCING A SPECIES TO ITS PHYSICAL PEAK -- IF YOU SACRIFICE INTELLIGENCE?
I DON'T KNOW--
-- I THINK...I THINK MAYBE IT *WANTS* US THAT WAY. *ALL* OF US, JACK. IT KNOWS ... THEY KNOW...ABOUT HUMANITY NOW, TOO --
-- BECAUSE OF *ME.* AND NOW THAT WE'VE UNCOVERED THE SECOND ONE, IT WANTS US TO *ACT.*
IT'S NOT YOUR FAULT, *BEN.* IT'S WHOEVER CREATED THESE DEVICES. I JUST HAVEN'T WORKED OUT THE ANGLE -- THE *WHY.*
YOU'D BETTER DO SOMETHING, SKULL FACE --
-- OR YOU'LL HAVE A PLANET FULL OF DROOLING BEHEMOTHS. AND IT MIGHT NOT STOP THERE!
ENOUGH, ENOUGH -- JUST STOP NATTERING. I'M AN ARTERIUS -- BUT I'M ALSO SWORN TO DEFEND MY PEOPLE.
GIVE ME THE SENTRY STATION IN THE TEMPLE -- AND PATCH ME THROUGH TO PALAVEN COMMAND.
I'M DECLARING AN UNSECURED BIOWEAPON EMERGENCY!

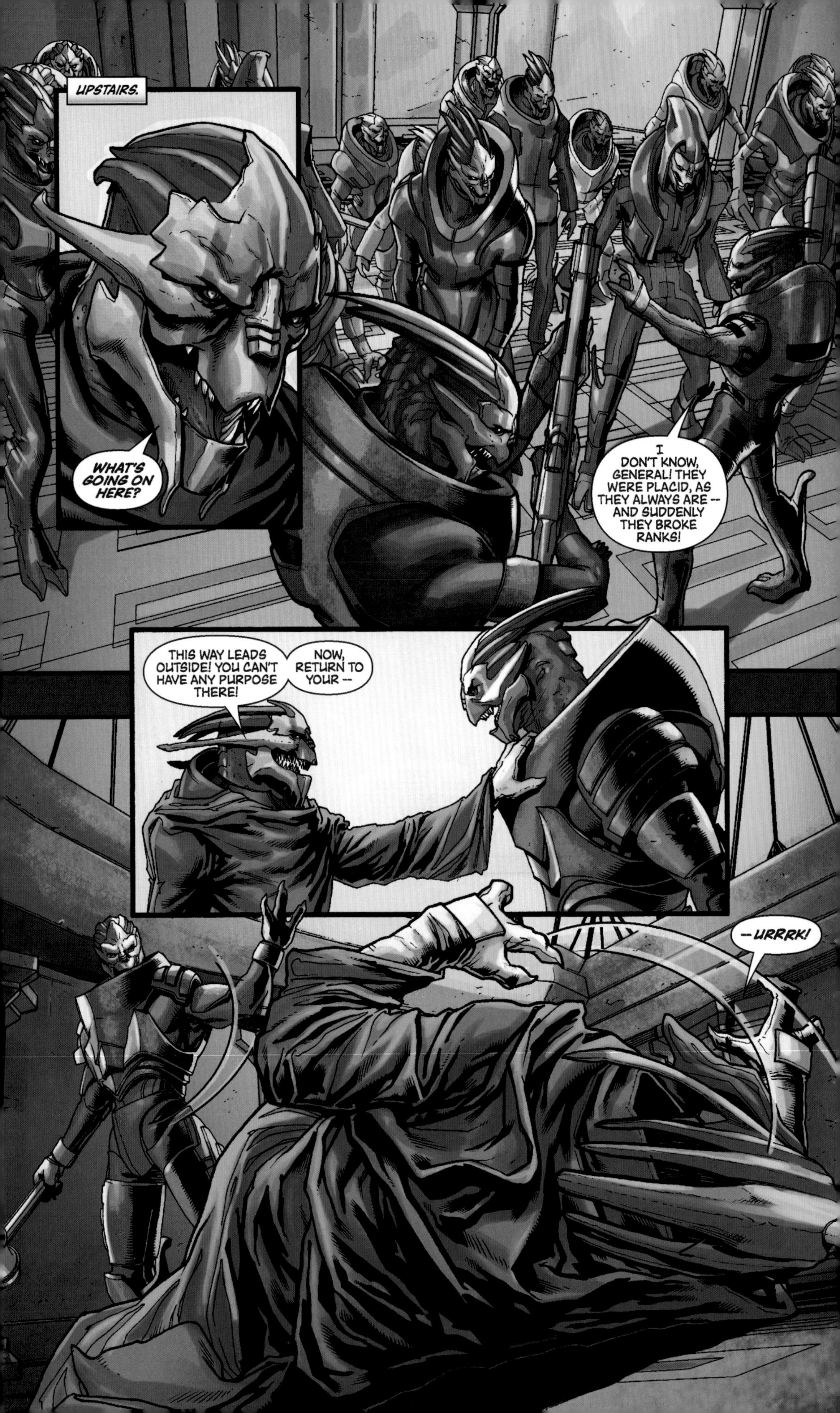
UPSTAIRS.
WHAT'S GOING ON HERE?
I DON'T KNOW, GENERAL! THEY WERE PLACID, AS THEY ALWAYS ARE -- AND SUDDENLY THEY BROKE RANKS!
THIS WAY LEADS OUTSIDE! YOU CAN'T HAVE ANY PURPOSE THERE!
NOW, RETURN TO YOUR --
--URRRK!

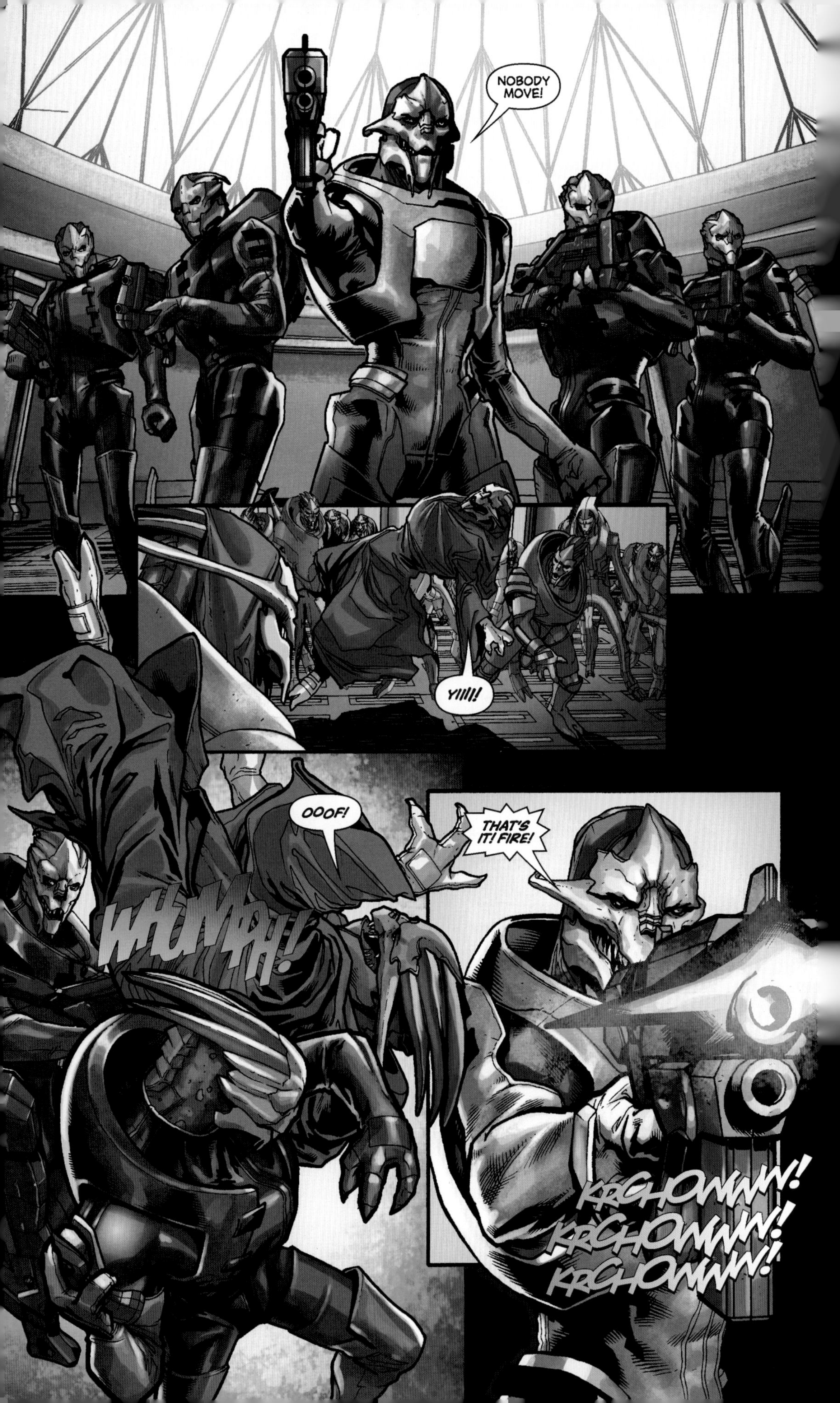
NOBODY MOVE!
YIIII!
OOOF!
WHUMPH!
THAT'S IT! FIRE!
KRCHOWWW!
KRCHOWWW!
KRCHOWWW!

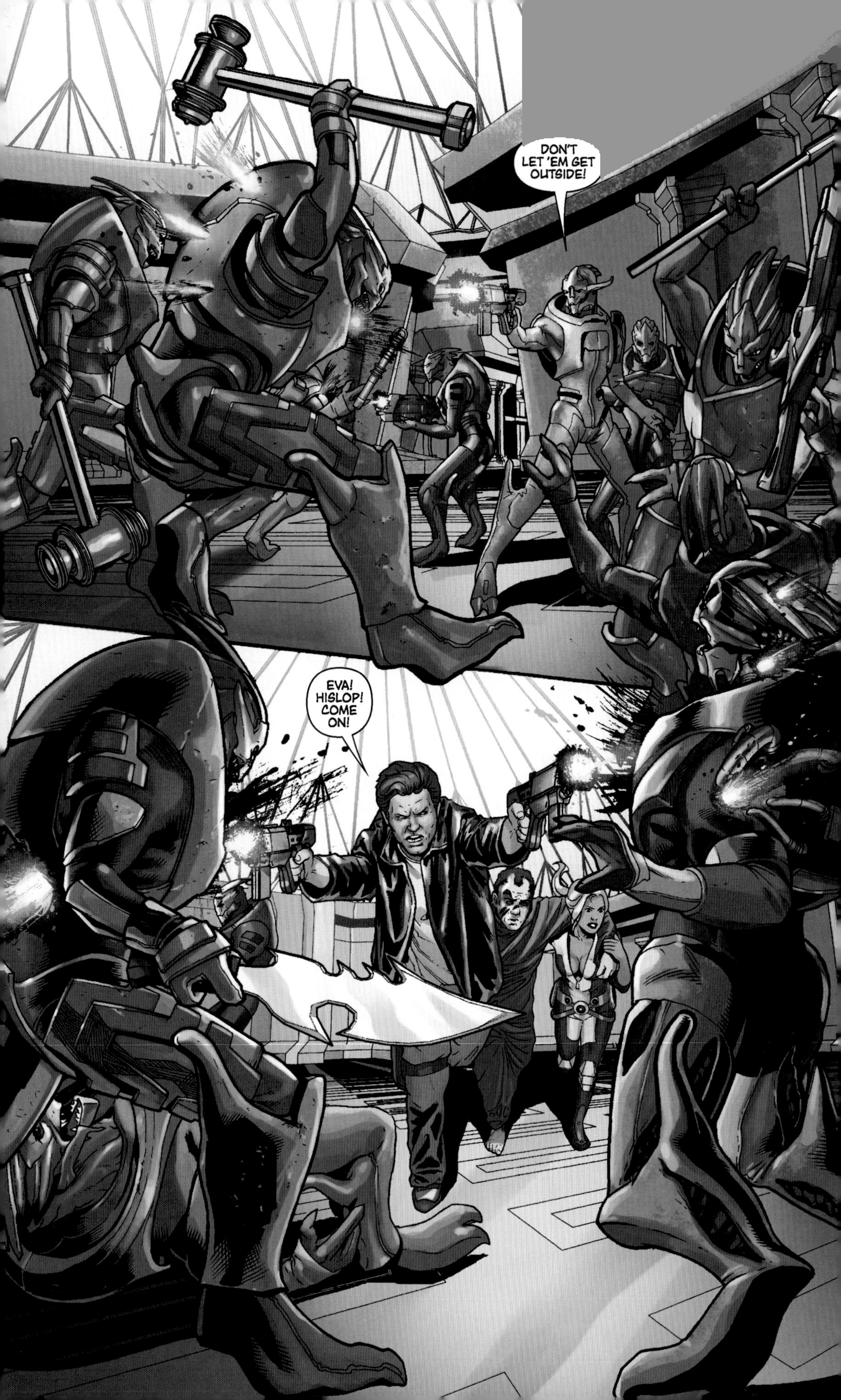
DON'T LET 'EM GET OUTSIDE!
EVA! HISLOP! COME ON!

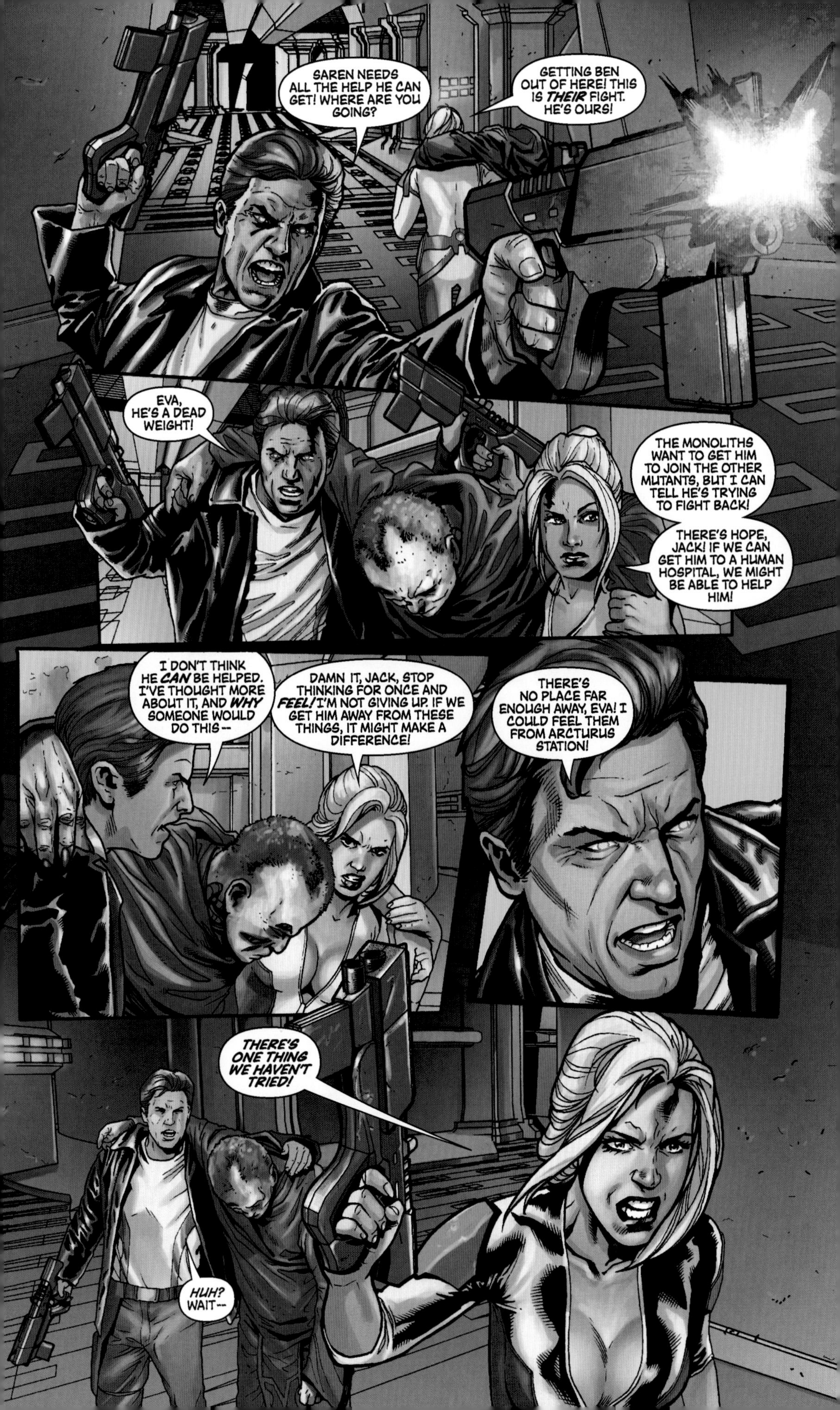
SAREN NEEDS ALL THE HELP HE CAN GET! WHERE ARE YOU GOING?
GETTING BEN OUT OF HERE! THIS IS *THEIR* FIGHT. HE'S OURS!
EVA, HE'S A DEAD WEIGHT!
THE MONOLITHS WANT TO GET HIM TO JOIN THE OTHER MUTANTS, BUT I CAN TELL HE'S TRYING TO FIGHT BACK!
THERE'S HOPE, JACK! IF WE CAN GET HIM TO A HUMAN HOSPITAL, WE MIGHT BE ABLE TO HELP HIM!
I DON'T THINK HE *CAN* BE HELPED. I'VE THOUGHT MORE ABOUT IT, AND *WHY* SOMEONE WOULD DO THIS--
DAMN IT, JACK, STOP THINKING FOR ONCE AND *FEEL!* I'M NOT GIVING UP. IF WE GET HIM AWAY FROM THESE THINGS, IT MIGHT MAKE A DIFFERENCE!
THERE'S NO PLACE FAR ENOUGH AWAY, EVA! I COULD FEEL THEM FROM ARCTURUS STATION!
THERE'S ONE THING WE HAVEN'T TRIED!
HUH? WAIT--

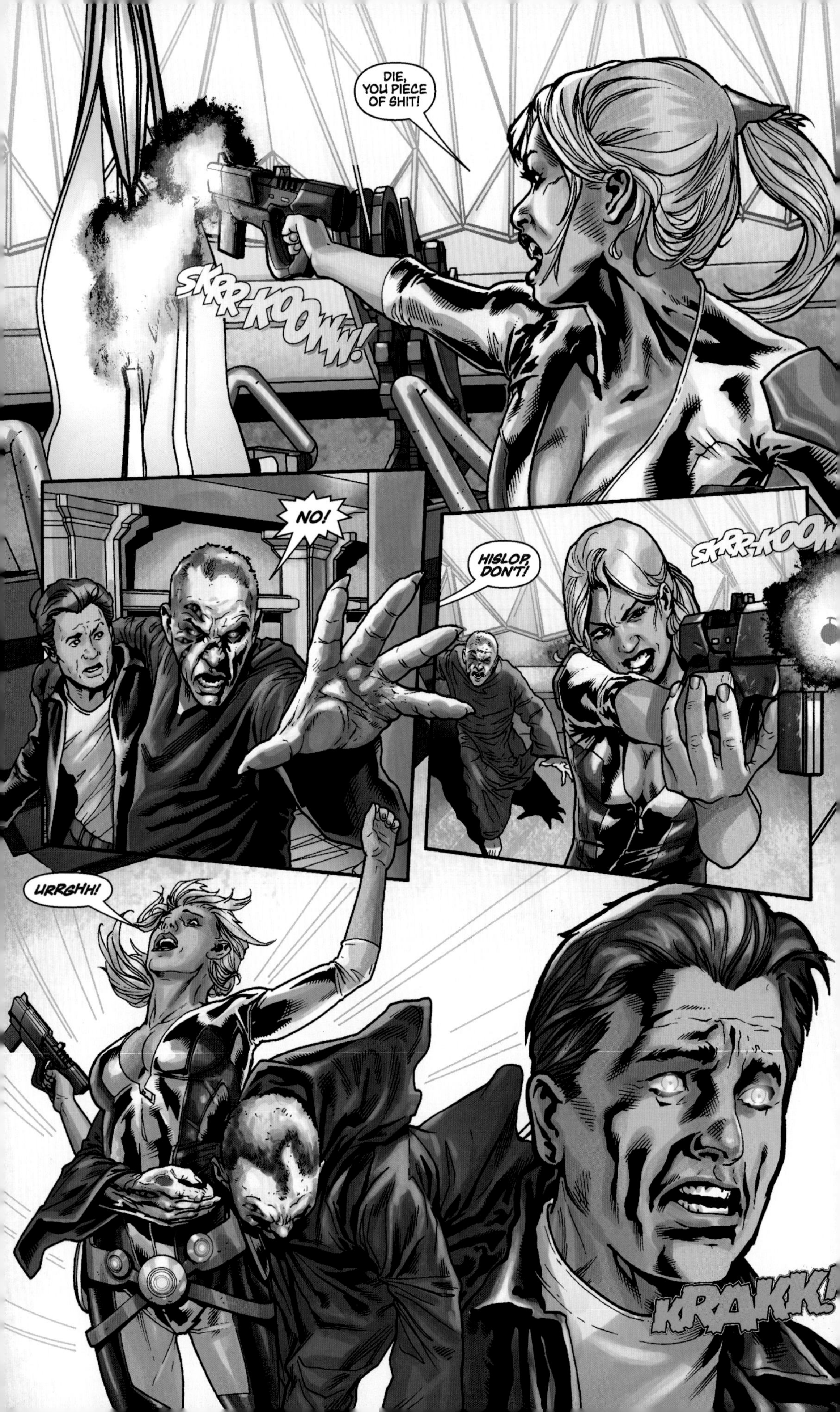
DIE, YOU PIECE OF SHIT!
SKRR-KOOWW!
NO!
HISLOP, DON'T!
SKRR-KOOW
URRGHH!
KRAKK!

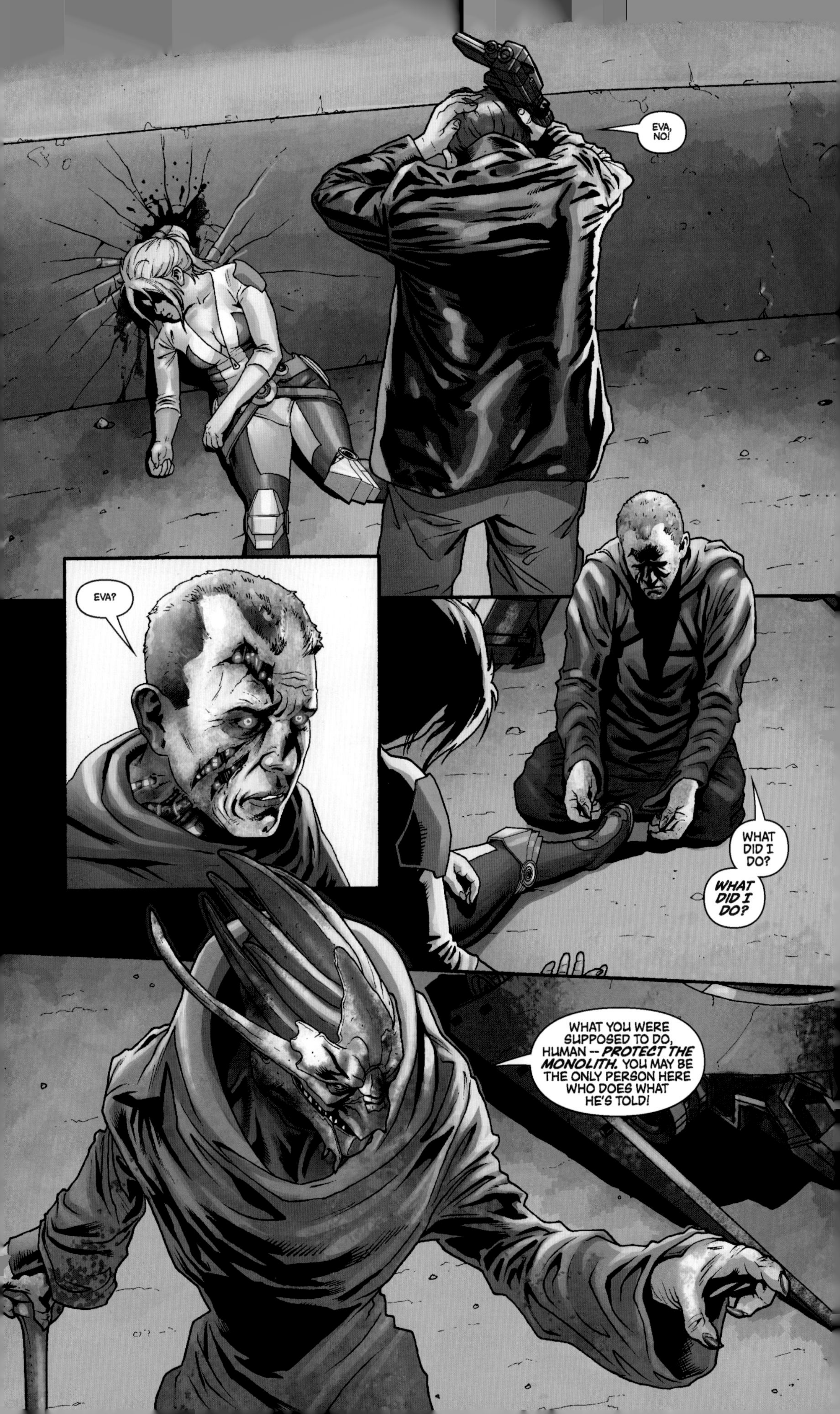
EVA, NO!
EVA?
WHAT DID I DO?
WHAT DID I DO?
WHAT YOU WERE SUPPOSED TO DO, HUMAN -- ***PROTECT THE MONOLITH.*** YOU MAY BE THE ONLY PERSON HERE WHO DOES WHAT HE'S TOLD!

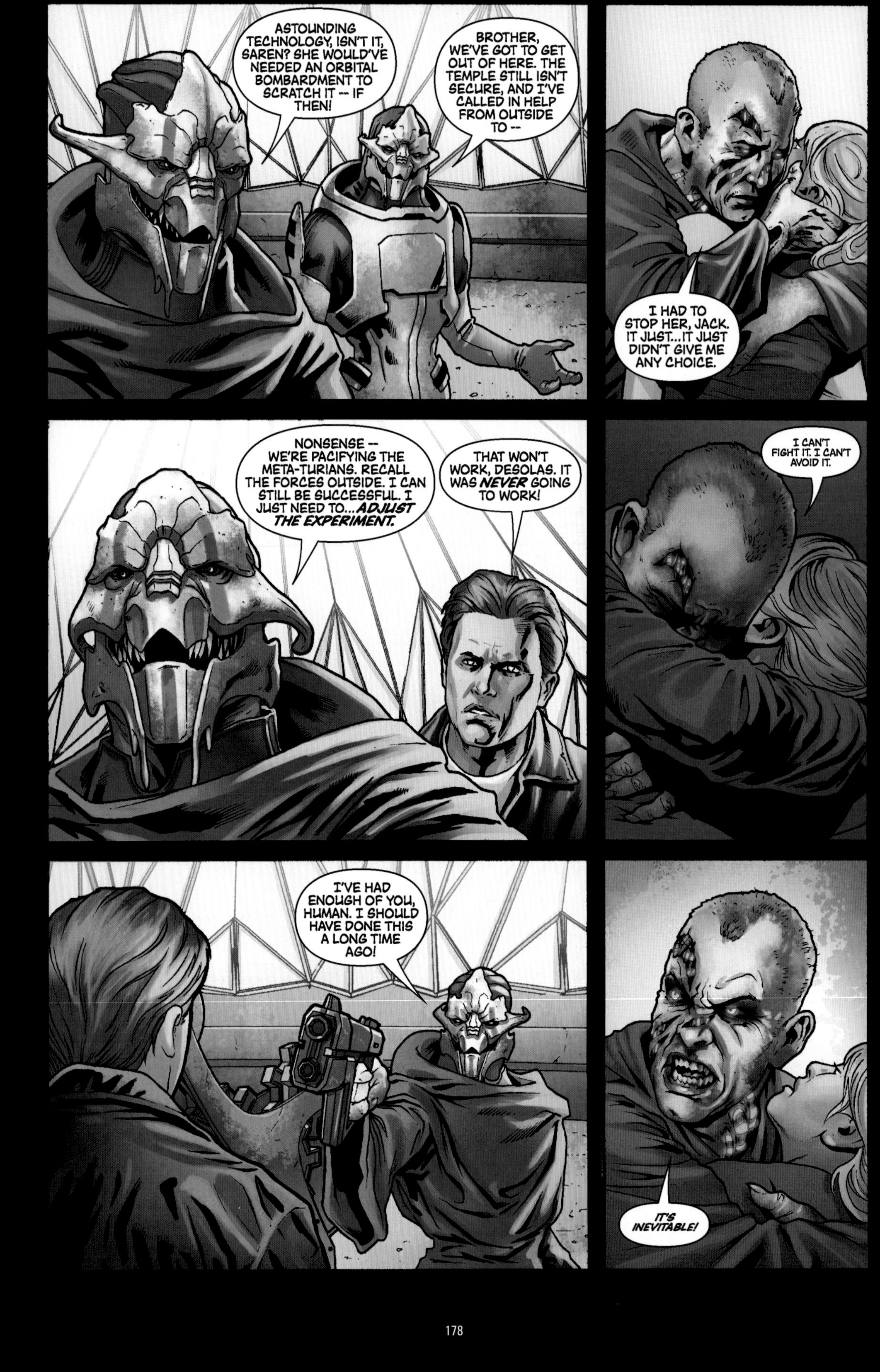
ASTOUNDING TECHNOLOGY, ISN'T IT, SAREN? SHE WOULD'VE NEEDED AN ORBITAL BOMBARDMENT TO SCRATCH IT -- IF THEN!
BROTHER, WE'VE GOT TO GET OUT OF HERE. THE TEMPLE STILL ISN'T SECURE, AND I'VE CALLED IN HELP FROM OUTSIDE TO --
I HAD TO STOP HER, JACK. IT JUST...IT JUST DIDN'T GIVE ME ANY CHOICE.
NONSENSE -- WE'RE PACIFYING THE META-TURIANS. RECALL THE FORCES OUTSIDE. I CAN STILL BE SUCCESSFUL. I JUST NEED TO...ADJUST THE EXPERIMENT.
THAT WON'T WORK, DESOLAS. IT WAS NEVER GOING TO WORK!
I CAN'T FIGHT IT. I CAN'T AVOID IT.
I'VE HAD ENOUGH OF YOU, HUMAN. I SHOULD HAVE DONE THIS A LONG TIME AGO!
IT'S INEVITABLE!

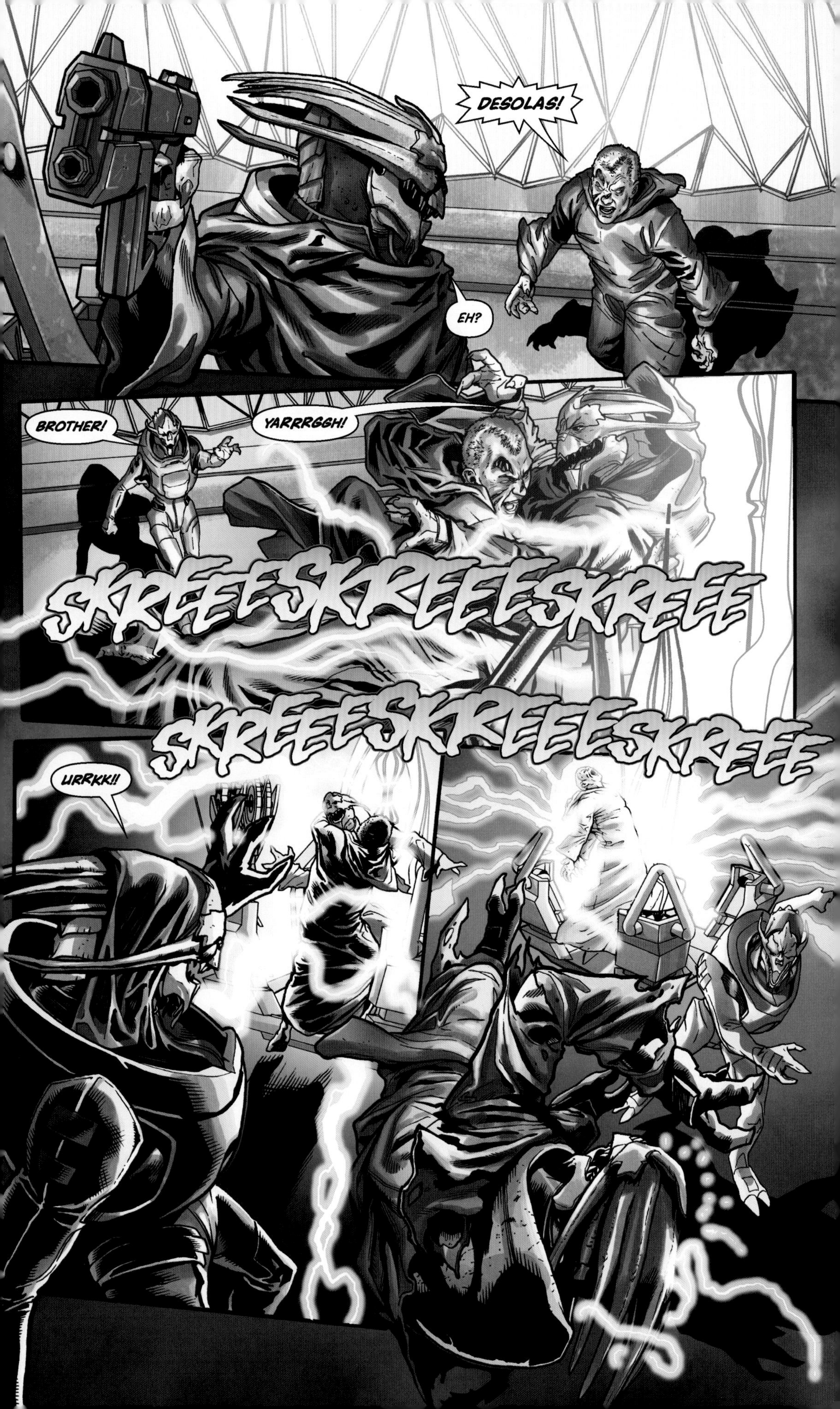
DESOLAS!
EH?
BROTHER!
YARRRGGH!
SKREEESKREEESKREEE
SKREEESKREEESKREEE
URRKK!!

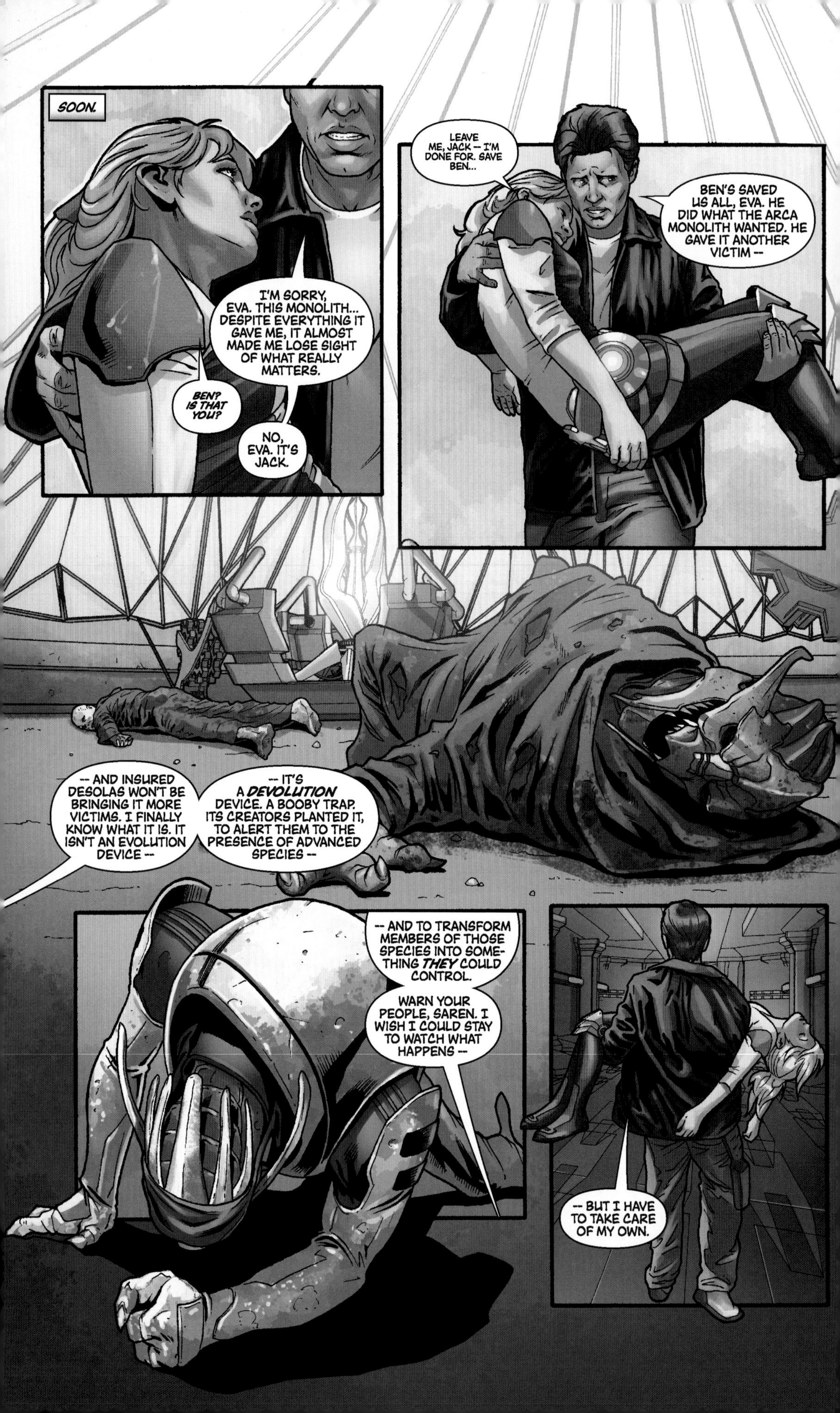
SOON.
BEN? IS THAT YOU?
I'M SORRY, EVA. THIS MONOLITH... DESPITE EVERYTHING IT GAVE ME, IT ALMOST MADE ME LOSE SIGHT OF WHAT REALLY MATTERS.
NO, EVA. IT'S JACK.
LEAVE ME, JACK -- I'M DONE FOR. SAVE BEN...
BEN'S SAVED US ALL, EVA. HE DID WHAT THE ARCA MONOLITH WANTED. HE GAVE IT ANOTHER VICTIM --
-- AND INSURED DESOLAS WON'T BE BRINGING IT MORE VICTIMS. I FINALLY KNOW WHAT IT IS. IT ISN'T AN EVOLUTION DEVICE --
-- IT'S A *DEVOLUTION* DEVICE. A BOOBY TRAP. ITS CREATORS PLANTED IT, TO ALERT THEM TO THE PRESENCE OF ADVANCED SPECIES --
-- AND TO TRANSFORM MEMBERS OF THOSE SPECIES INTO SOMETHING *THEY* COULD CONTROL.
WARN YOUR PEOPLE, SAREN. I WISH I COULD STAY TO WATCH WHAT HAPPENS --
-- BUT I HAVE TO TAKE CARE OF MY OWN.

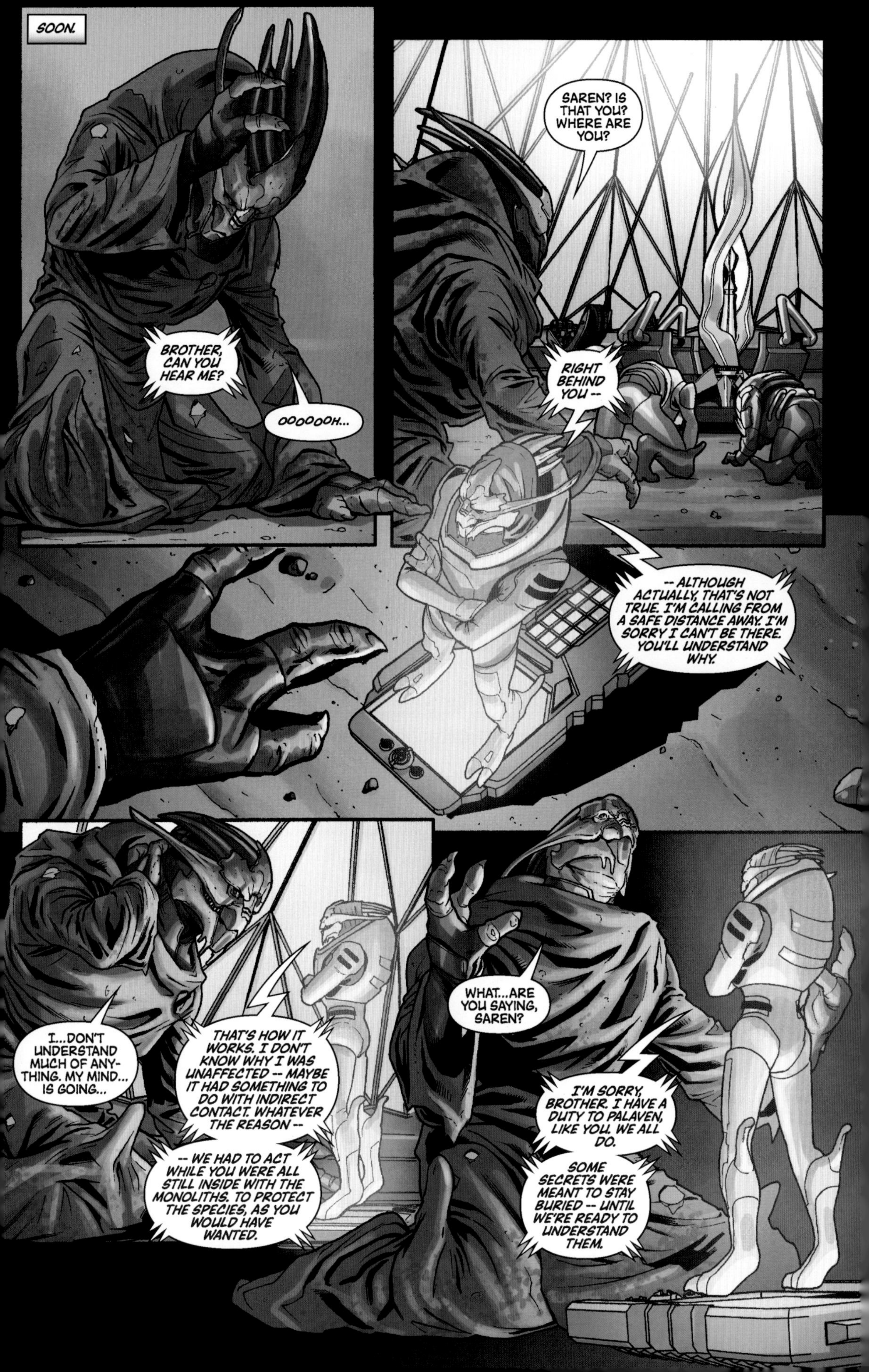
SOON.
BROTHER, CAN YOU HEAR ME?
OOOOOOH...
SAREN? IS THAT YOU? WHERE ARE YOU?
RIGHT BEHIND YOU --
-- ALTHOUGH ACTUALLY, THAT'S NOT TRUE. I'M CALLING FROM A SAFE DISTANCE AWAY. I'M SORRY I CAN'T BE THERE. YOU'LL UNDERSTAND WHY.
I...DON'T UNDERSTAND MUCH OF ANYTHING. MY MIND... IS GOING...
THAT'S HOW IT WORKS. I DON'T KNOW WHY I WAS UNAFFECTED -- MAYBE IT HAD SOMETHING TO DO WITH INDIRECT CONTACT. WHATEVER THE REASON --
-- WE HAD TO ACT WHILE YOU WERE ALL STILL INSIDE WITH THE MONOLITHS. TO PROTECT THE SPECIES, AS YOU WOULD HAVE WANTED.
WHAT...ARE YOU SAYING, SAREN?
I'M SORRY, BROTHER. I HAVE A DUTY TO PALAVEN, LIKE YOU. WE ALL DO.
SOME SECRETS WERE MEANT TO STAY BURIED -- UNTIL WE'RE READY TO UNDERSTAND THEM.

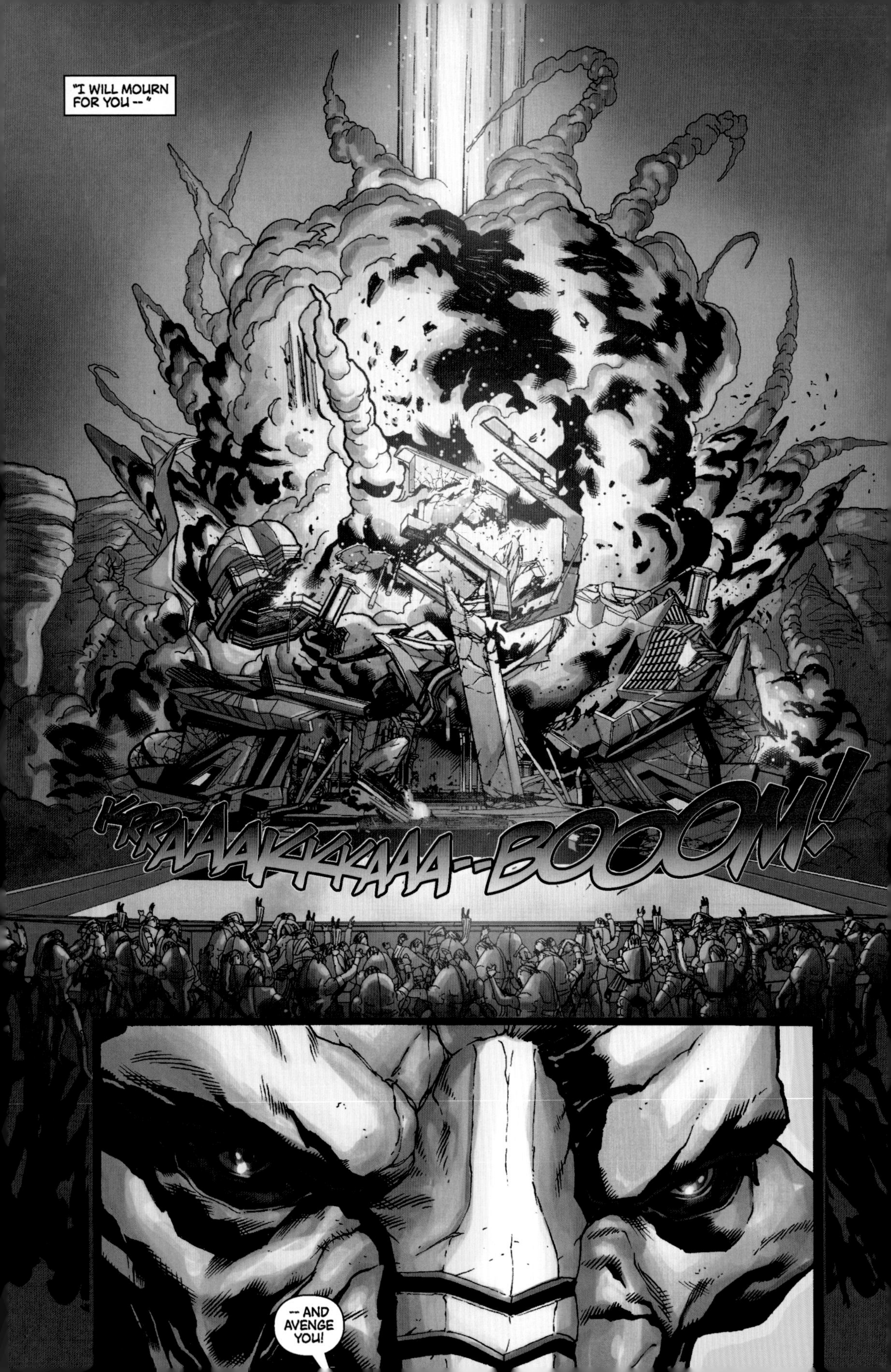
"I WILL MOURN FOR YOU --"
KRRAAAKKKAAA--BOOOM!
-- AND AVENGE YOU!

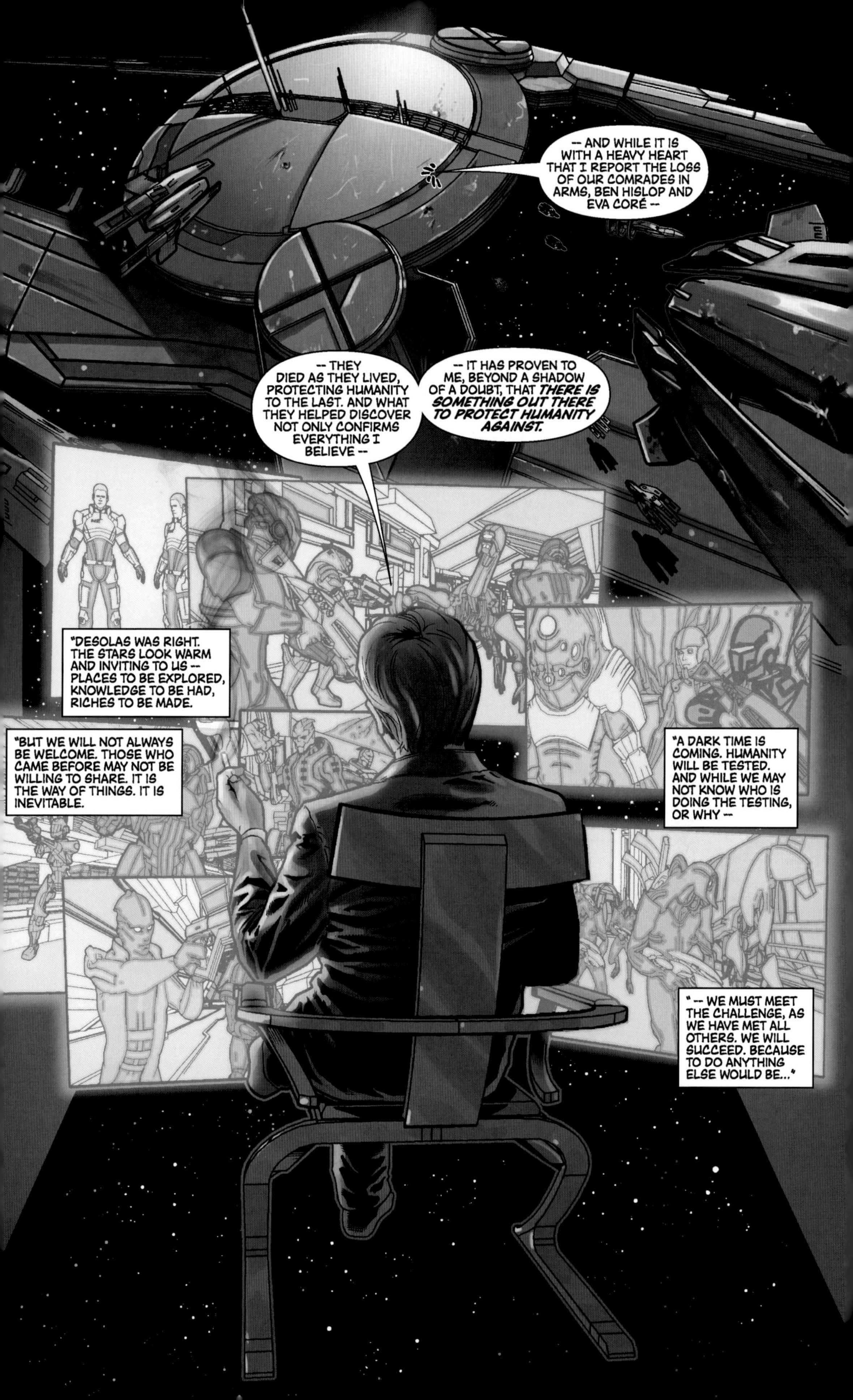
-- AND WHILE IT IS WITH A HEAVY HEART THAT I REPORT THE LOSS OF OUR COMRADES IN ARMS, BEN HISLOP AND EVA CORÉ --
-- THEY DIED AS THEY LIVED, PROTECTING HUMANITY TO THE LAST. AND WHAT THEY HELPED DISCOVER NOT ONLY CONFIRMS EVERYTHING I BELIEVE --
-- IT HAS PROVEN TO ME, BEYOND A SHADOW OF A DOUBT, THAT *THERE IS SOMETHING OUT THERE TO PROTECT HUMANITY AGAINST.*
"DESOLAS WAS RIGHT. THE STARS LOOK WARM AND INVITING TO US -- PLACES TO BE EXPLORED, KNOWLEDGE TO BE HAD, RICHES TO BE MADE.
"BUT WE WILL NOT ALWAYS BE WELCOME. THOSE WHO CAME BEFORE MAY NOT BE WILLING TO SHARE. IT IS THE WAY OF THINGS. IT IS INEVITABLE.
"A DARK TIME IS COMING. HUMANITY WILL BE TESTED. AND WHILE WE MAY NOT KNOW WHO IS DOING THE TESTING, OR WHY --
" -- WE MUST MEET THE CHALLENGE, AS WE HAVE MET ALL OTHERS. WE WILL SUCCEED. BECAUSE TO DO ANYTHING ELSE WOULD BE..."

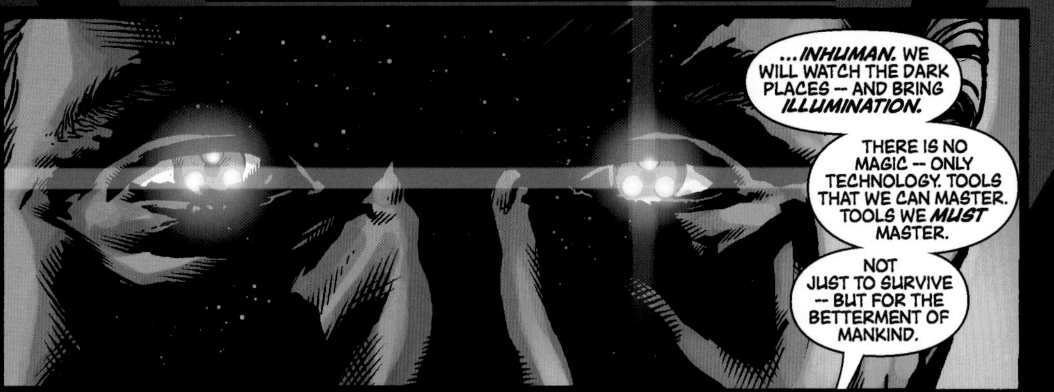
...INHUMAN. WE WILL WATCH THE DARK PLACES -- AND BRING ILLUMINATION.
THERE IS NO MAGIC -- ONLY TECHNOLOGY. TOOLS THAT WE CAN MASTER. TOOLS WE MUST MASTER.
NOT JUST TO SURVIVE -- BUT FOR THE BETTERMENT OF MANKIND.
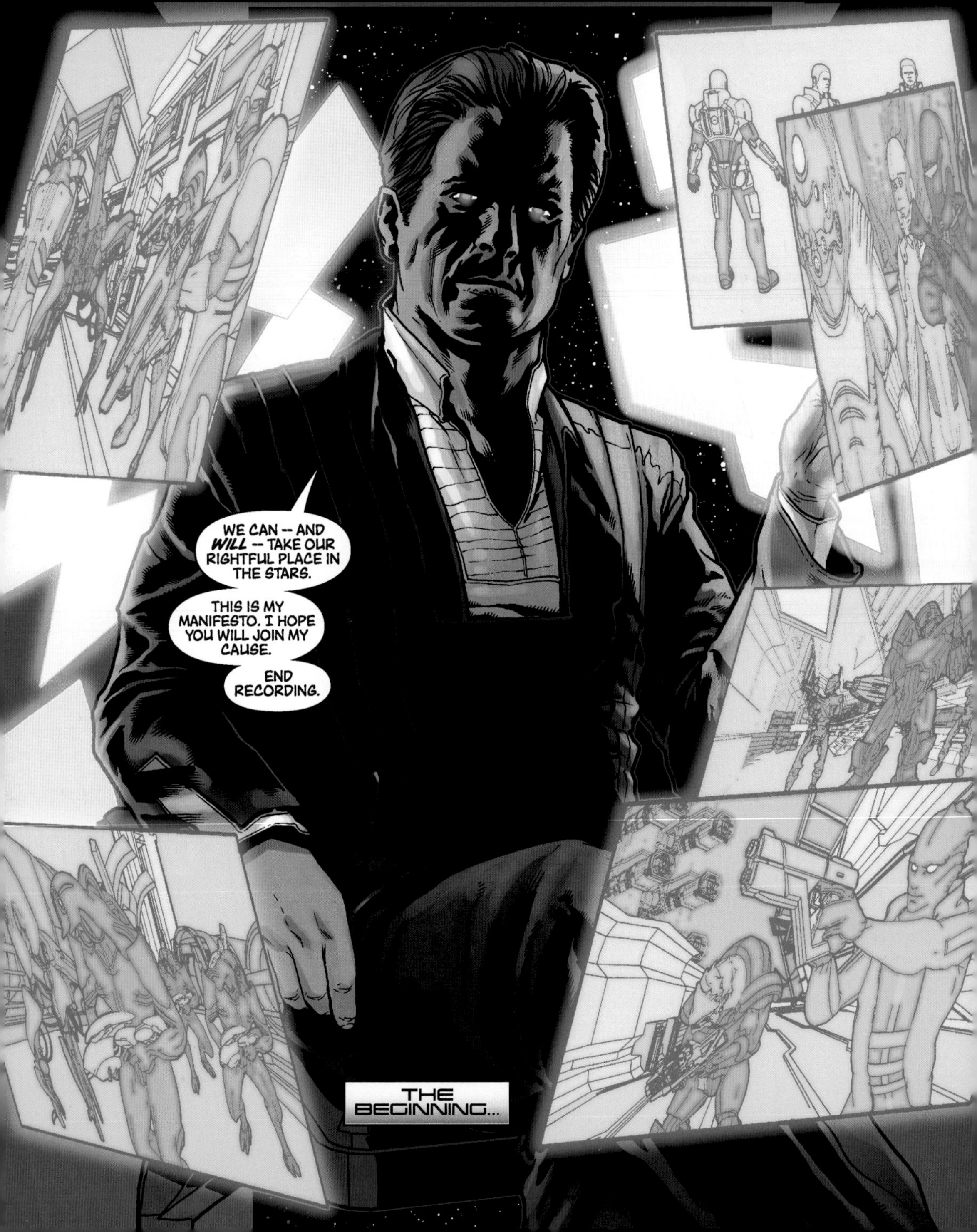
WE CAN -- AND WILL -- TAKE OUR RIGHTFUL PLACE IN THE STARS.
THIS IS MY MANIFESTO. I HOPE YOU WILL JOIN MY CAUSE.
END RECORDING.
THE BEGINNING...

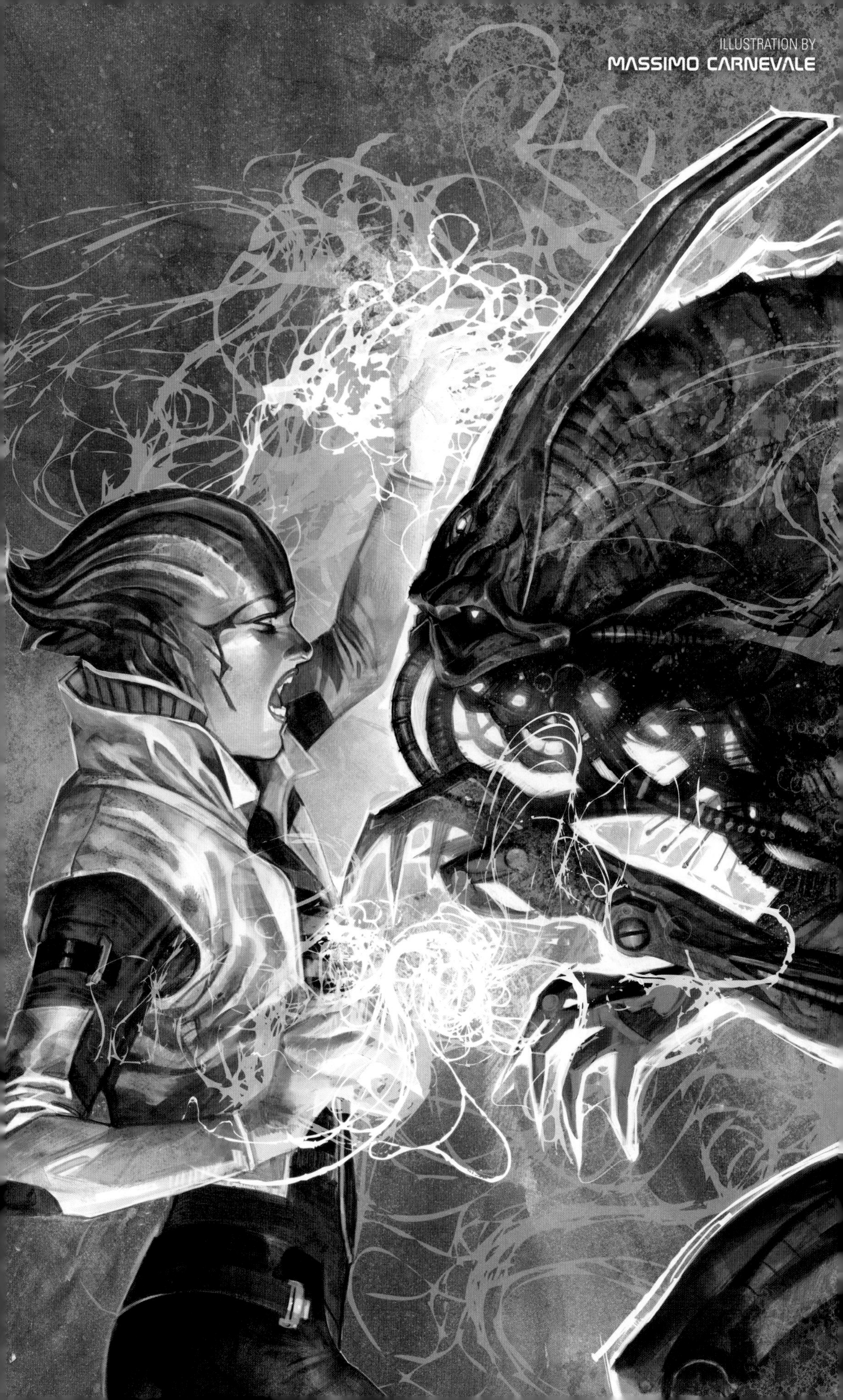
ILLUSTRATION BY
MASSIMO CARNEVALE

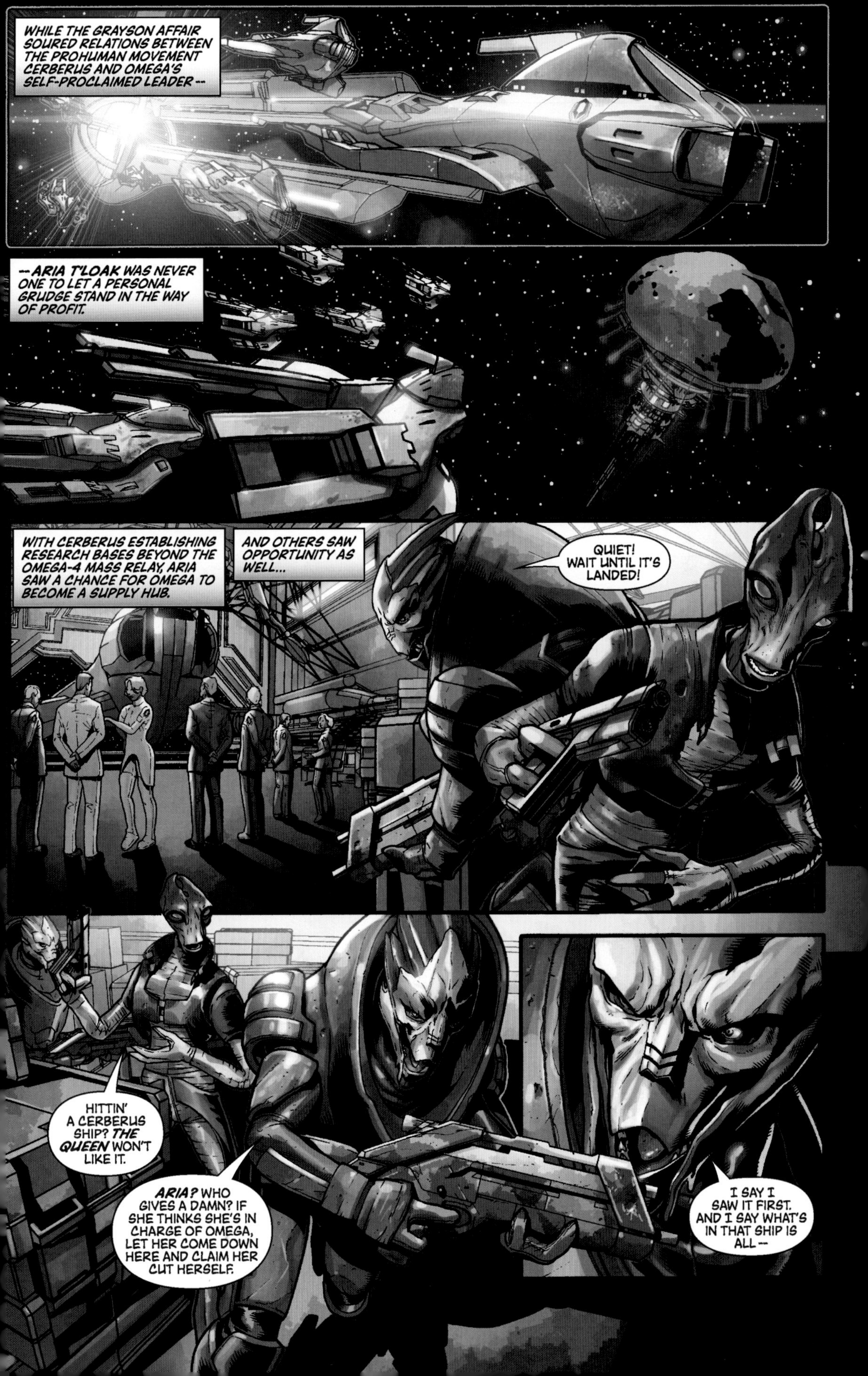
WHILE THE GRAYSON AFFAIR SOURED RELATIONS BETWEEN THE PROHUMAN MOVEMENT CERBERUS AND OMEGA'S SELF-PROCLAIMED LEADER --
--ARIA T'LOAK WAS NEVER ONE TO LET A PERSONAL GRUDGE STAND IN THE WAY OF PROFIT.
WITH CERBERUS ESTABLISHING RESEARCH BASES BEYOND THE OMEGA-4 MASS RELAY, ARIA SAW A CHANCE FOR OMEGA TO BECOME A SUPPLY HUB.
AND OTHERS SAW OPPORTUNITY AS WELL...
QUIET! WAIT UNTIL IT'S LANDED!
HITTIN' A CERBERUS SHIP? THE QUEEN WON'T LIKE IT.
ARIA? WHO GIVES A DAMN? IF SHE THINKS SHE'S IN CHARGE OF OMEGA, LET HER COME DOWN HERE AND CLAIM HER CUT HERSELF.
I SAY I SAW IT FIRST. AND I SAY WHAT'S IN THAT SHIP IS ALL --

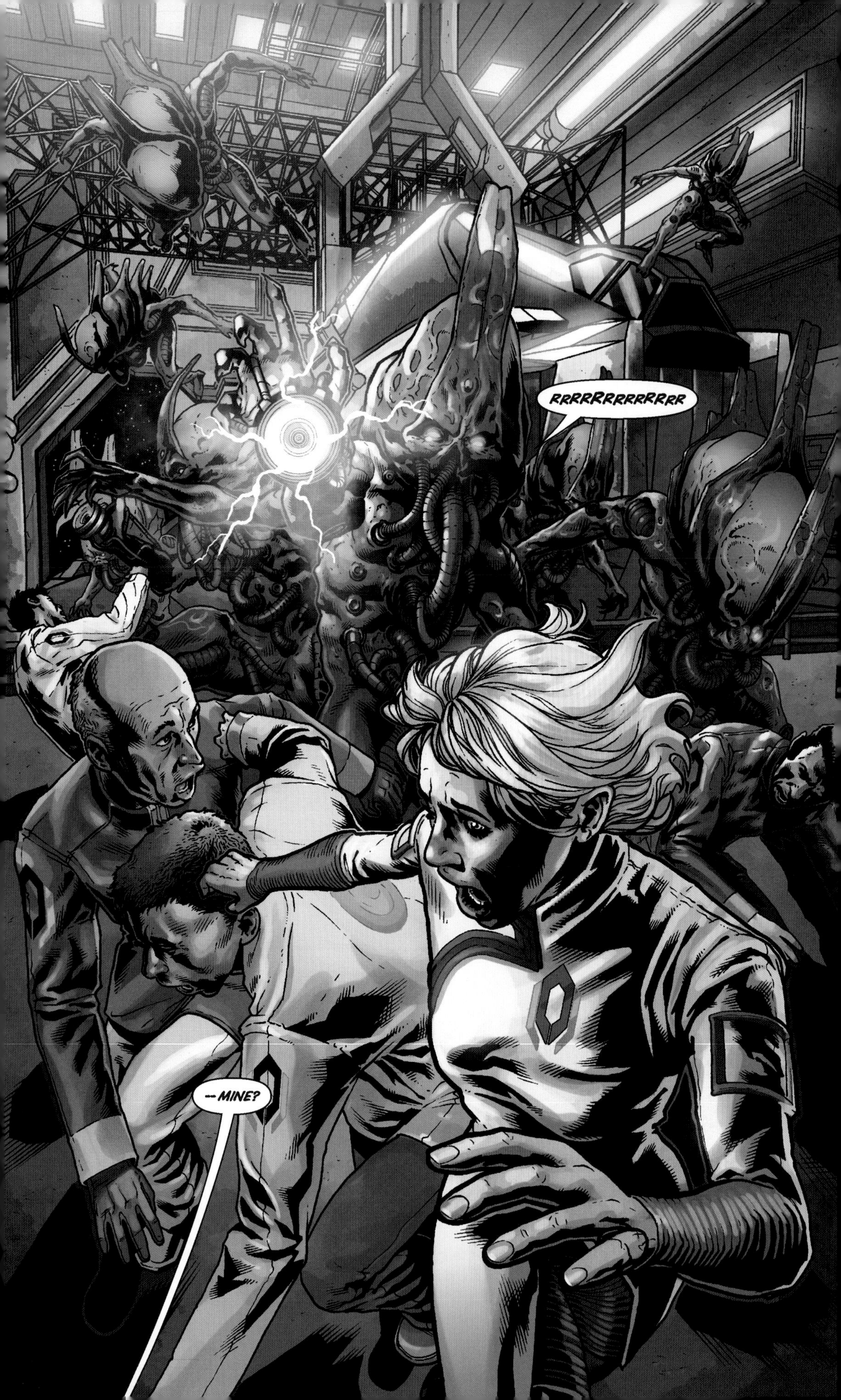
RRRRRRRRRRRRR
--MINE?

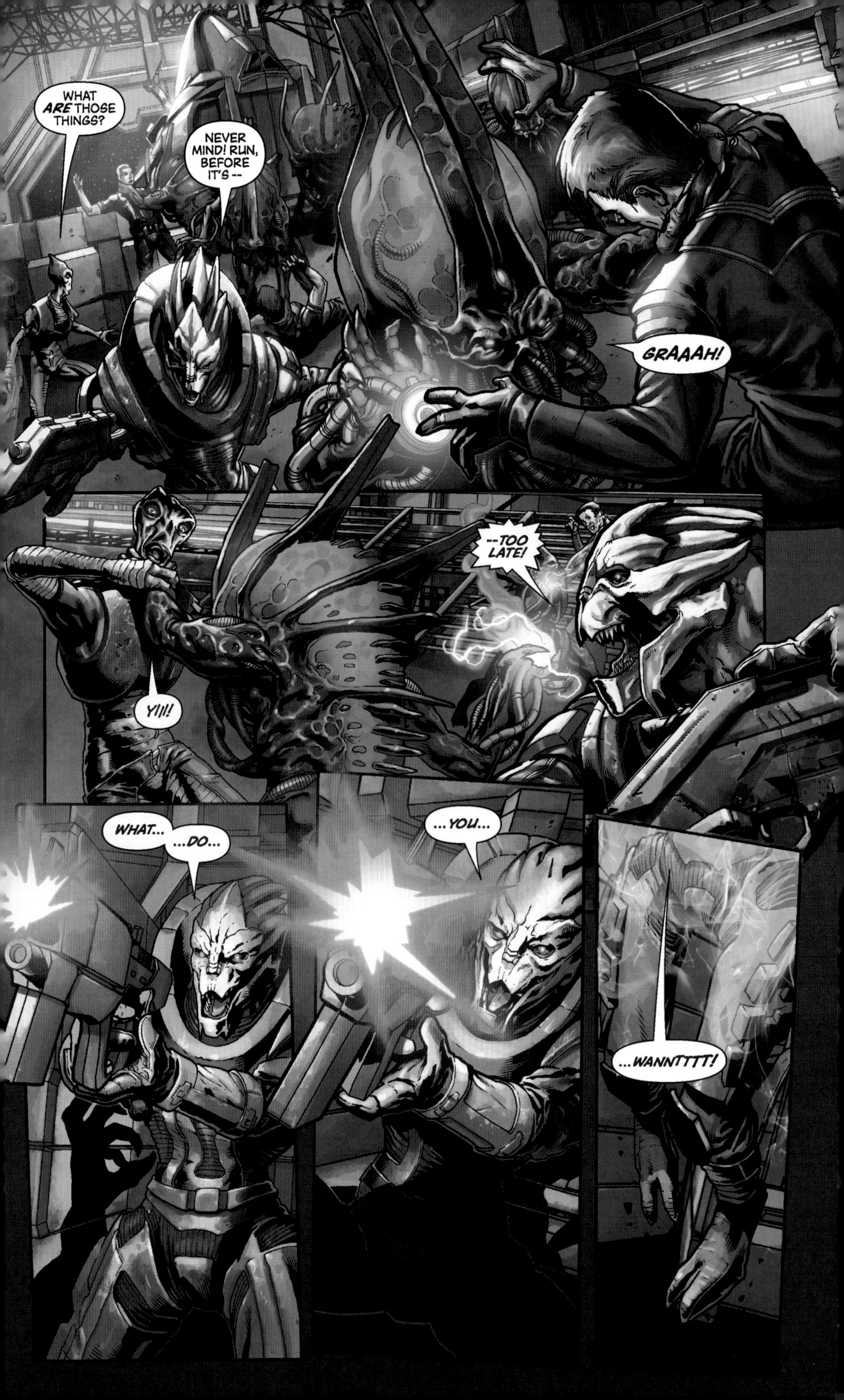
WHAT ARE THOSE THINGS?
NEVER MIND! RUN, BEFORE IT'S --
GRAAAH!
--TOO LATE!
YIII!
WHAT...
...DO...
...YOU...
...WANNTTTT!

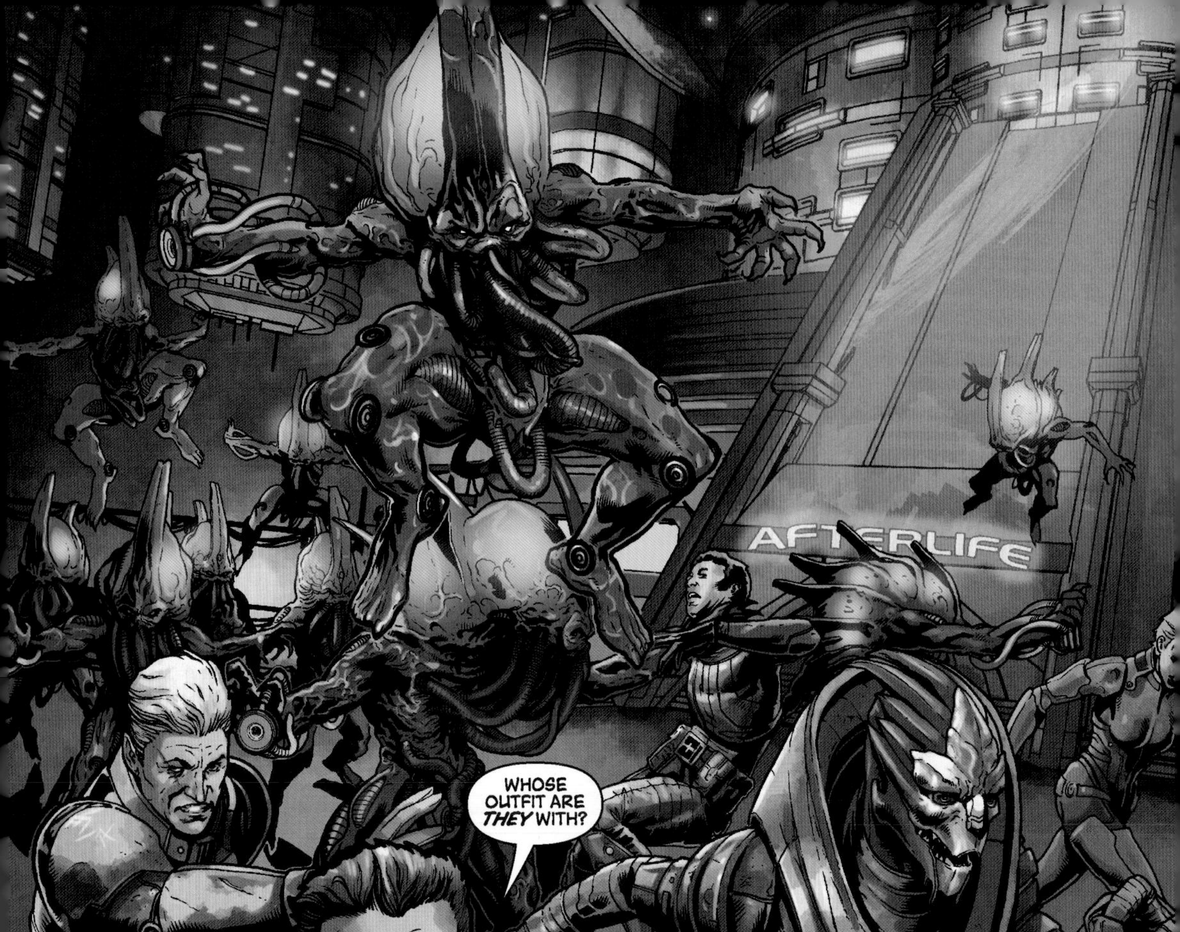
AFTERLIFE
WHOSE OUTFIT ARE *THEY* WITH?
I THINK-- *THEIR OWN!*
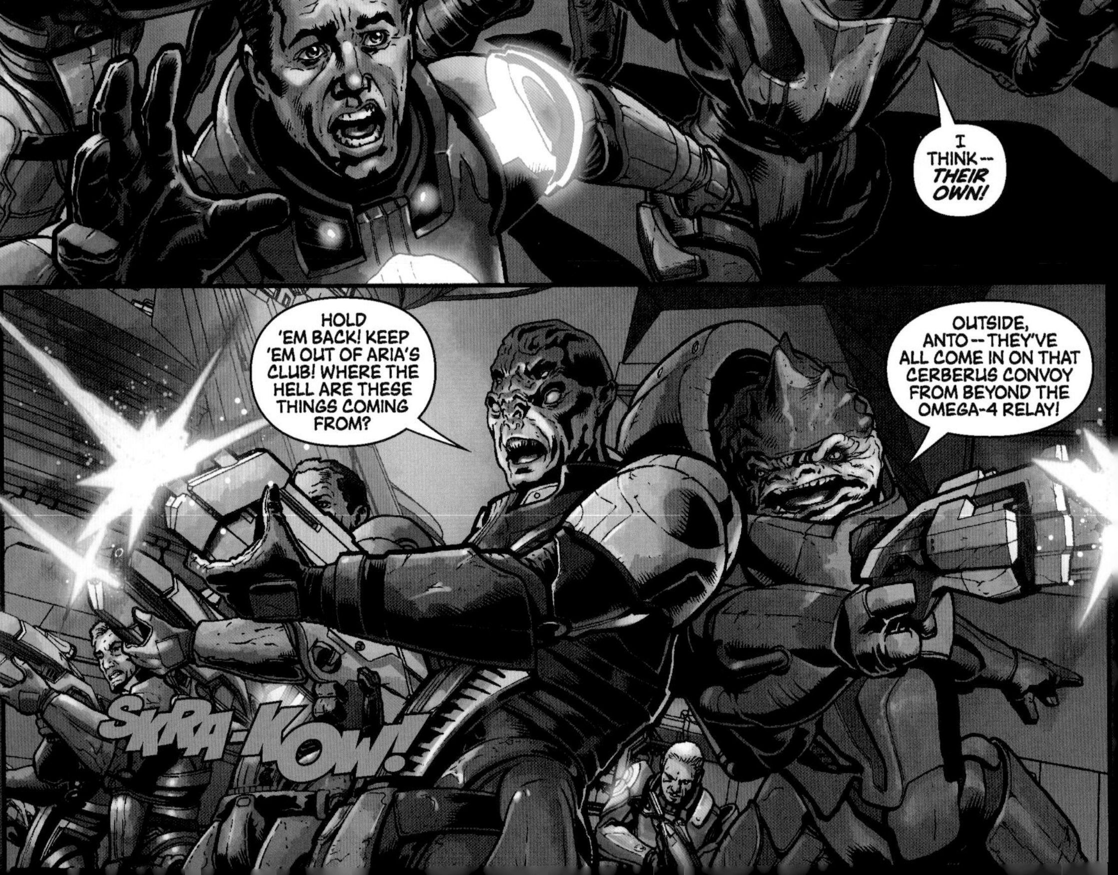
HOLD 'EM BACK! KEEP 'EM OUT OF ARIA'S CLUB! WHERE THE HELL ARE THESE THINGS COMING FROM?
OUTSIDE, ANTO-- THEY'VE ALL COME IN ON THAT CERBERUS CONVOY FROM BEYOND THE OMEGA-4 RELAY!
SKRA-KOW!

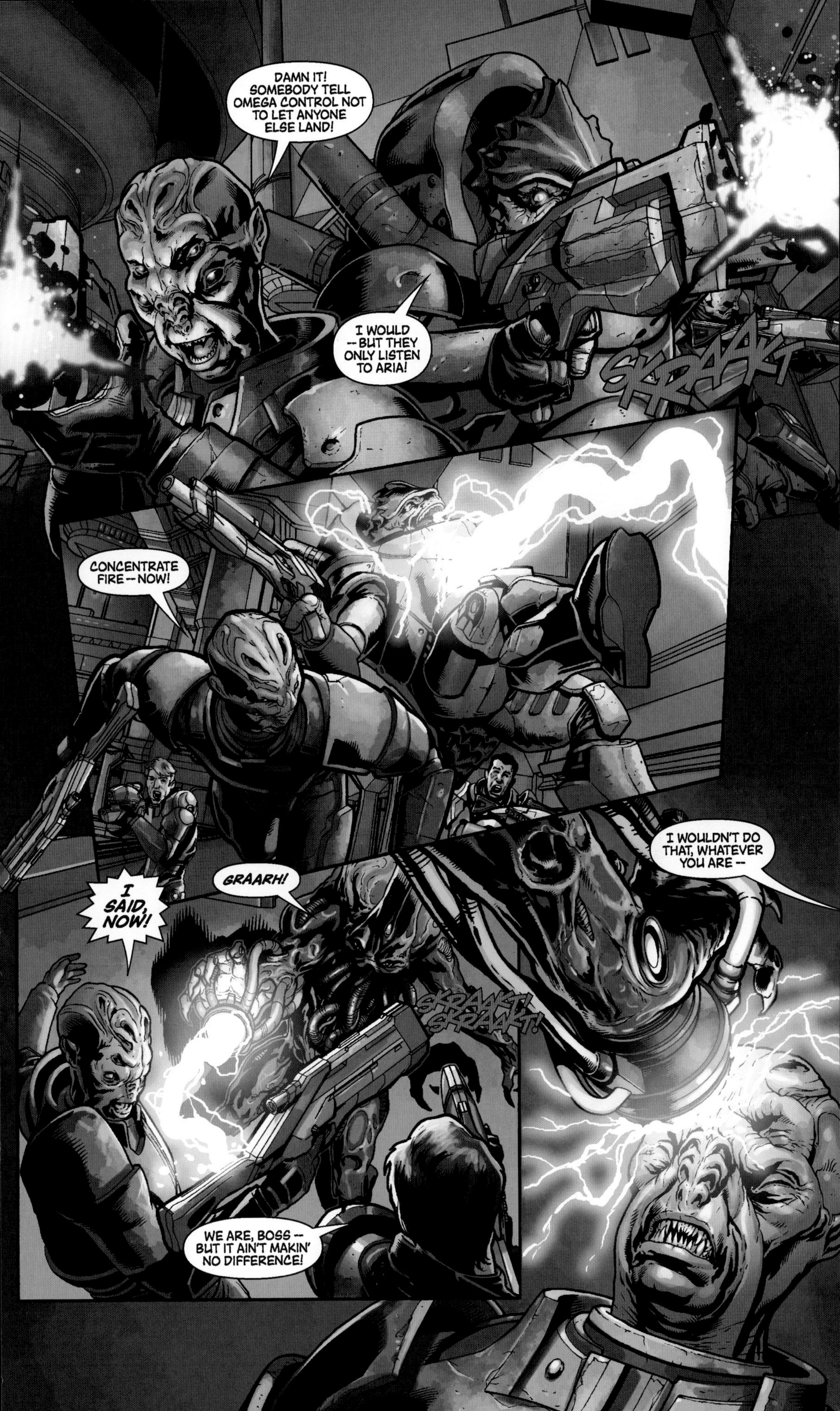
DAMN IT! SOMEBODY TELL OMEGA CONTROL NOT TO LET ANYONE ELSE LAND!
I WOULD --BUT THEY ONLY LISTEN TO ARIA!
SKRAAKT
CONCENTRATE FIRE--NOW!
I SAID, NOW!
GRAARH!
I WOULDN'T DO THAT, WHATEVER YOU ARE --
SKRAAKT! SKRAAKT!
WE ARE, BOSS -- BUT IT AIN'T MAKIN' NO DIFFERENCE!

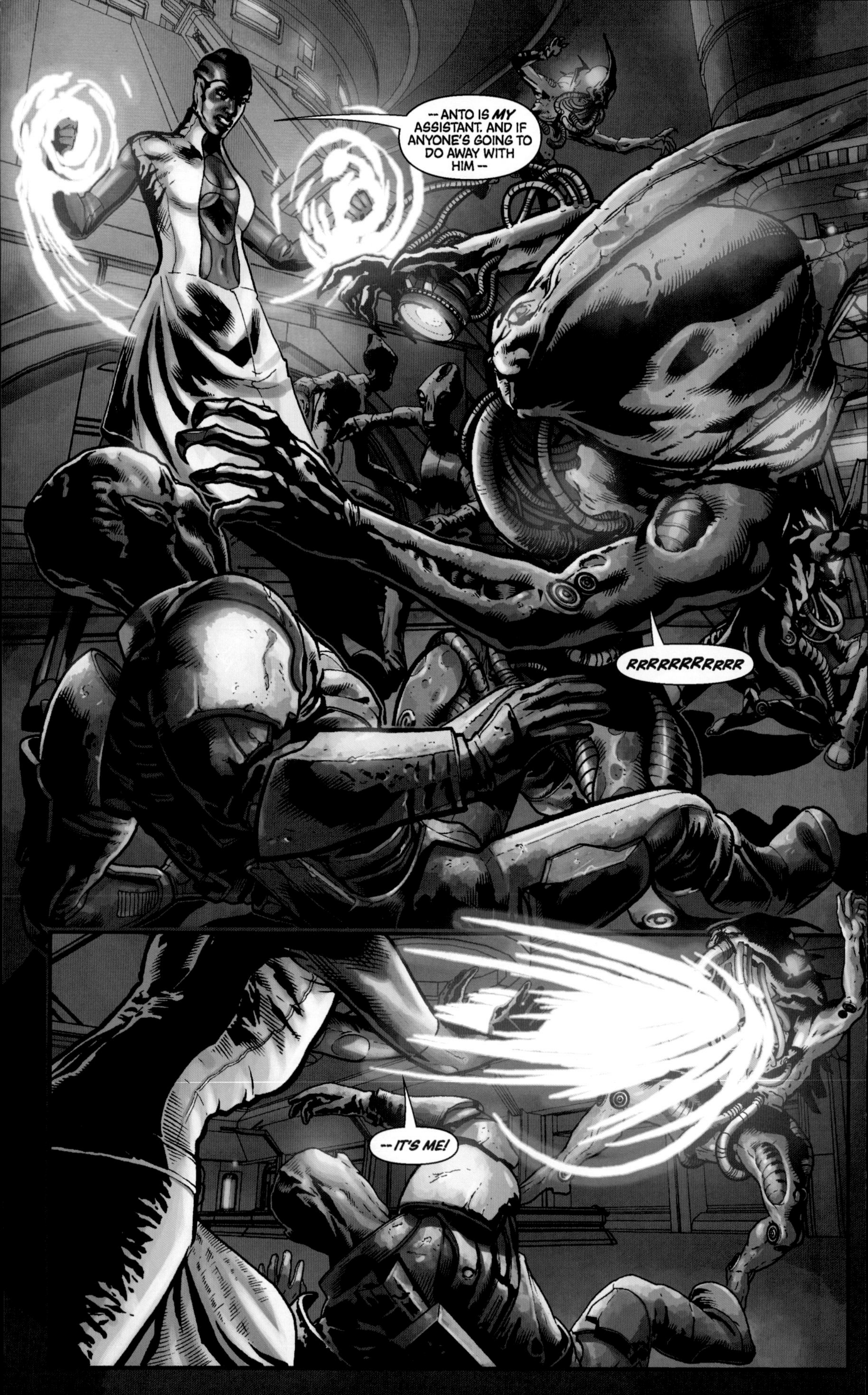
--ANTO IS *MY* ASSISTANT. AND IF ANYONE'S GOING TO DO AWAY WITH HIM --
RRRRRRRRRR
--*IT'S ME!*

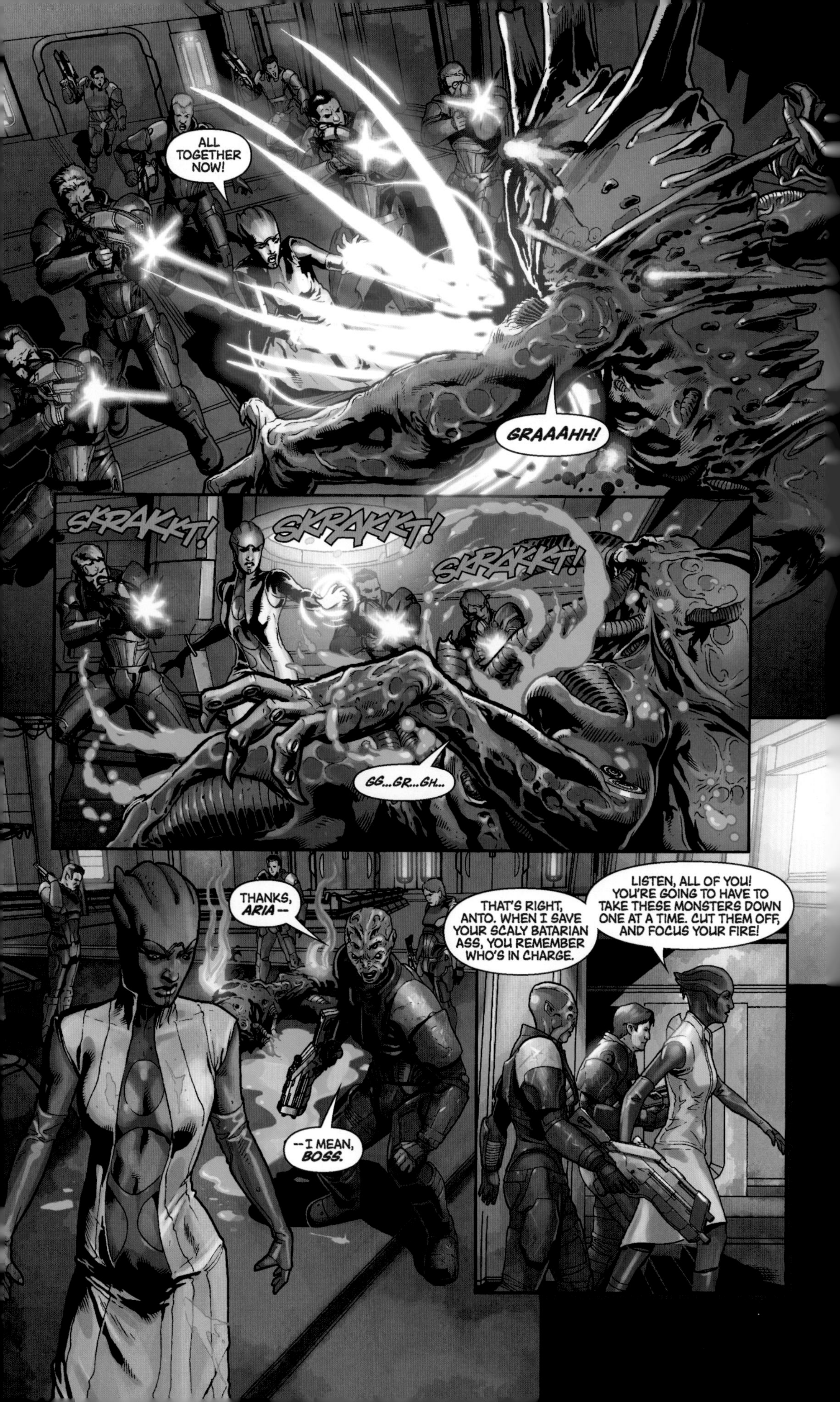
ALL TOGETHER NOW!
GRAAAHH!
SKRAKKT!
SKRAKKT!
SKRAKKT!
GG...GR...GH...
THANKS, ARIA --
--I MEAN, BOSS.
THAT'S RIGHT, ANTO. WHEN I SAVE YOUR SCALY BATARIAN ASS, YOU REMEMBER WHO'S IN CHARGE.
LISTEN, ALL OF YOU! YOU'RE GOING TO HAVE TO TAKE THESE MONSTERS DOWN ONE AT A TIME. CUT THEM OFF, AND FOCUS YOUR FIRE!

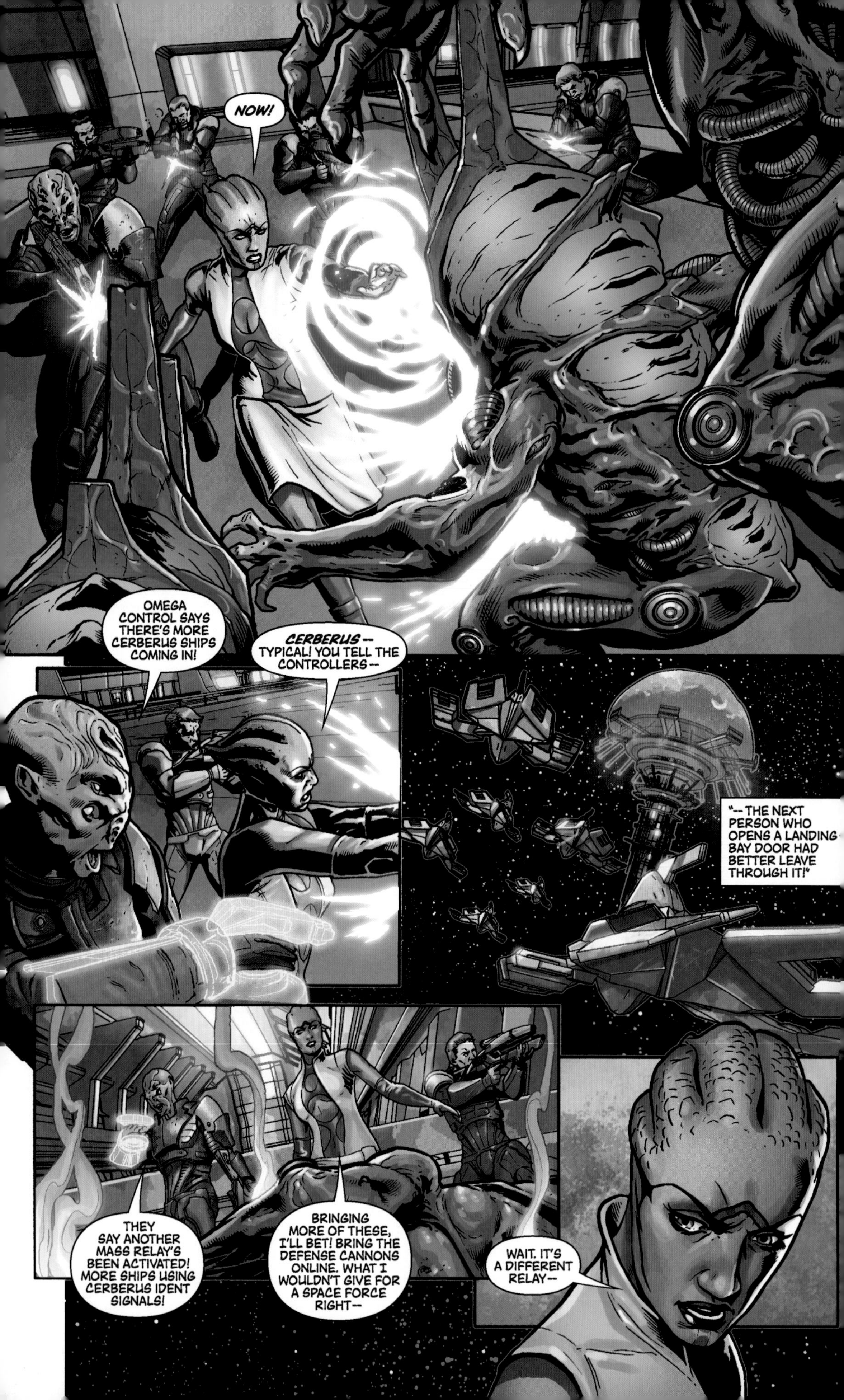
NOW!
OMEGA CONTROL SAYS THERE'S MORE CERBERUS SHIPS COMING IN!
CERBERUS -- TYPICAL! YOU TELL THE CONTROLLERS --
"-- THE NEXT PERSON WHO OPENS A LANDING BAY DOOR HAD BETTER LEAVE THROUGH IT!"
THEY SAY ANOTHER MASS RELAY'S BEEN ACTIVATED! MORE SHIPS USING CERBERUS IDENT SIGNALS!
BRINGING MORE OF THESE, I'LL BET! BRING THE DEFENSE CANNONS ONLINE. WHAT I WOULDN'T GIVE FOR A SPACE FORCE RIGHT--
WAIT. IT'S A DIFFERENT RELAY--

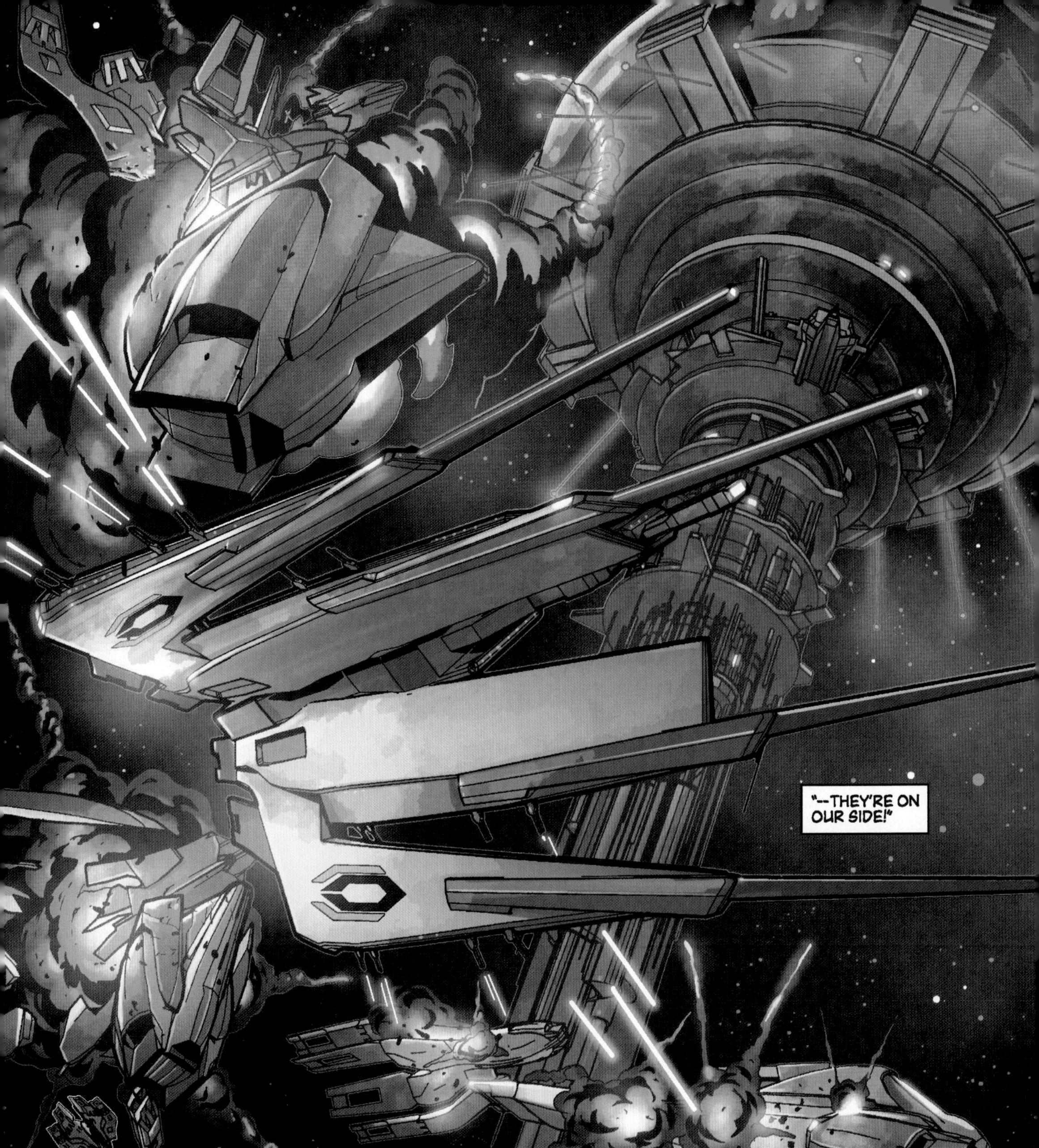
"--THEY'RE ON OUR SIDE!"

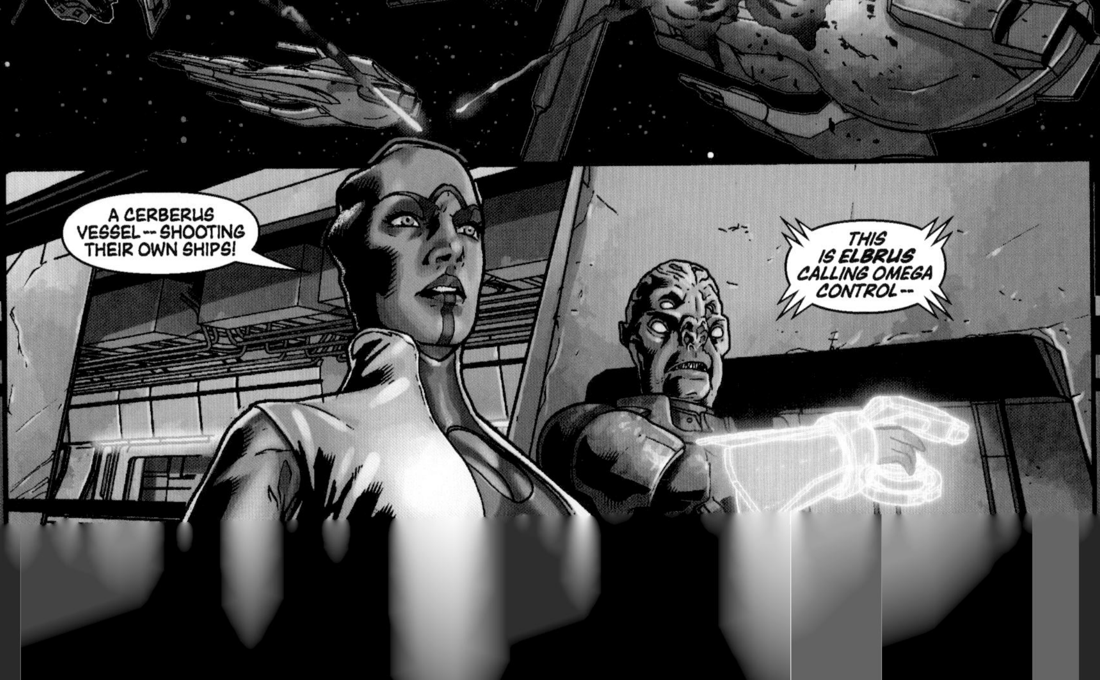
A CERBERUS VESSEL -- SHOOTING THEIR OWN SHIPS!
THIS IS ELBRUS CALLING OMEGA CONTROL --

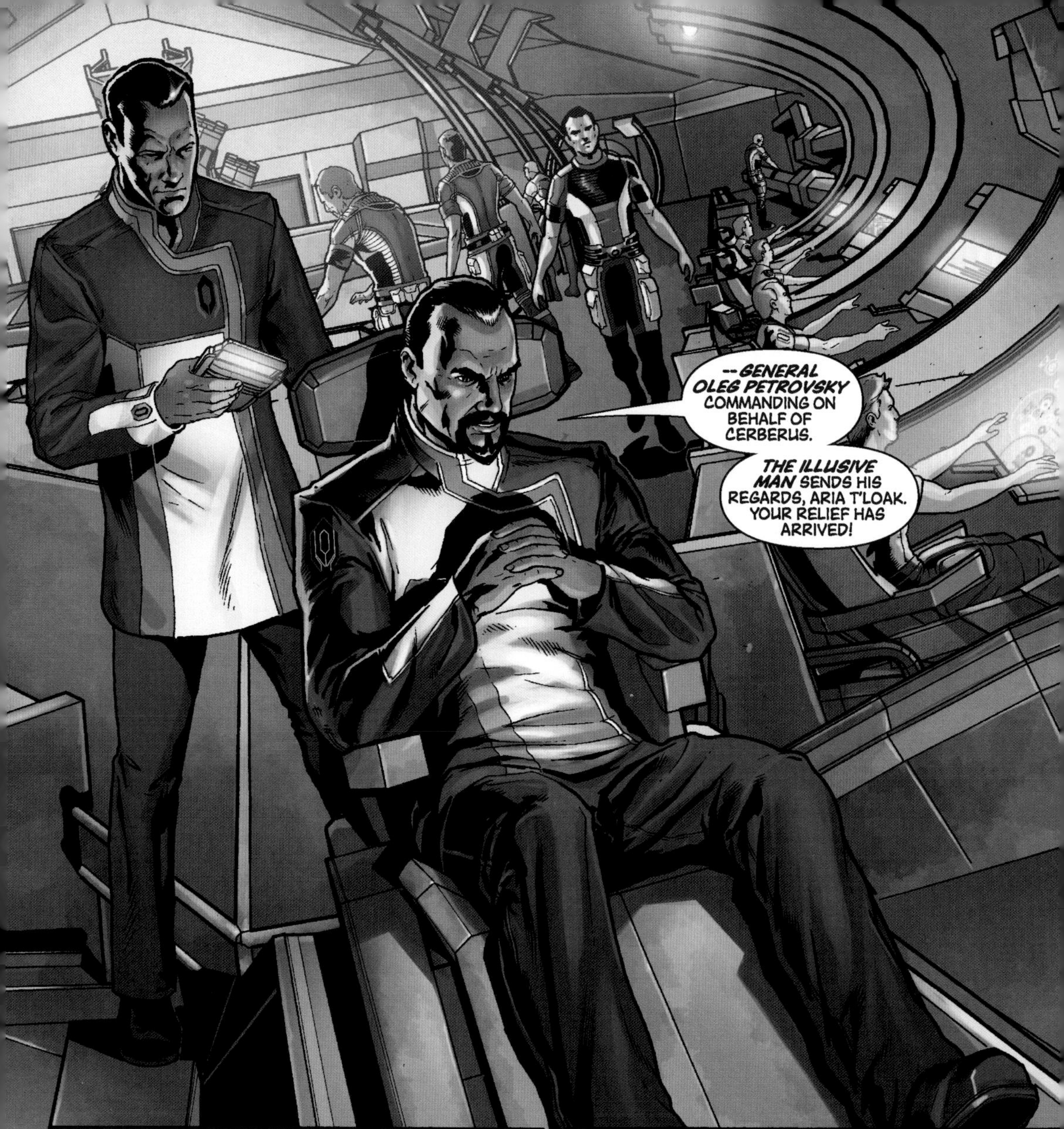
--GENERAL OLEG PETROVSKY COMMANDING ON BEHALF OF CERBERUS.
THE ILLUSIVE MAN SENDS HIS REGARDS, ARIA T'LOAK. YOUR RELIEF HAS ARRIVED!

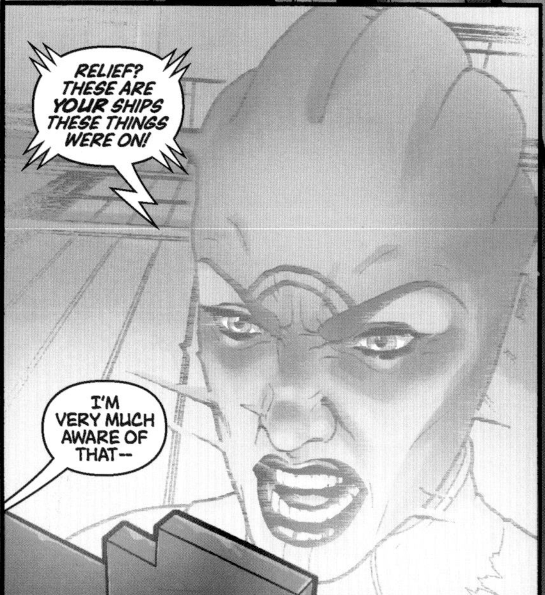
RELIEF? THESE ARE YOUR SHIPS THESE THINGS WERE ON!
I'M VERY MUCH AWARE OF THAT--

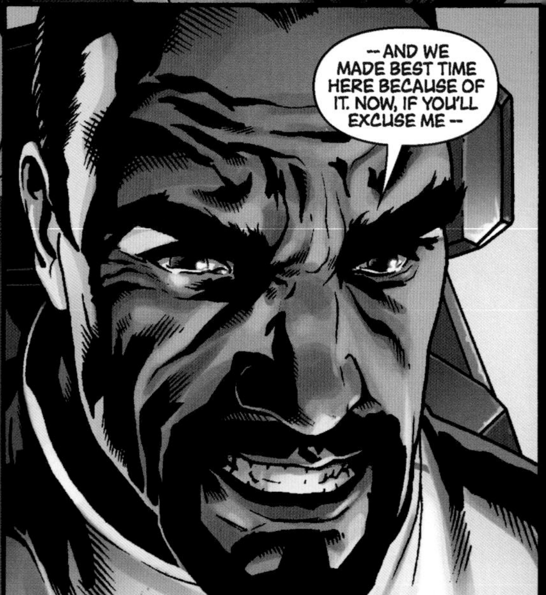
--AND WE MADE BEST TIME HERE BECAUSE OF IT. NOW, IF YOU'LL EXCUSE ME--

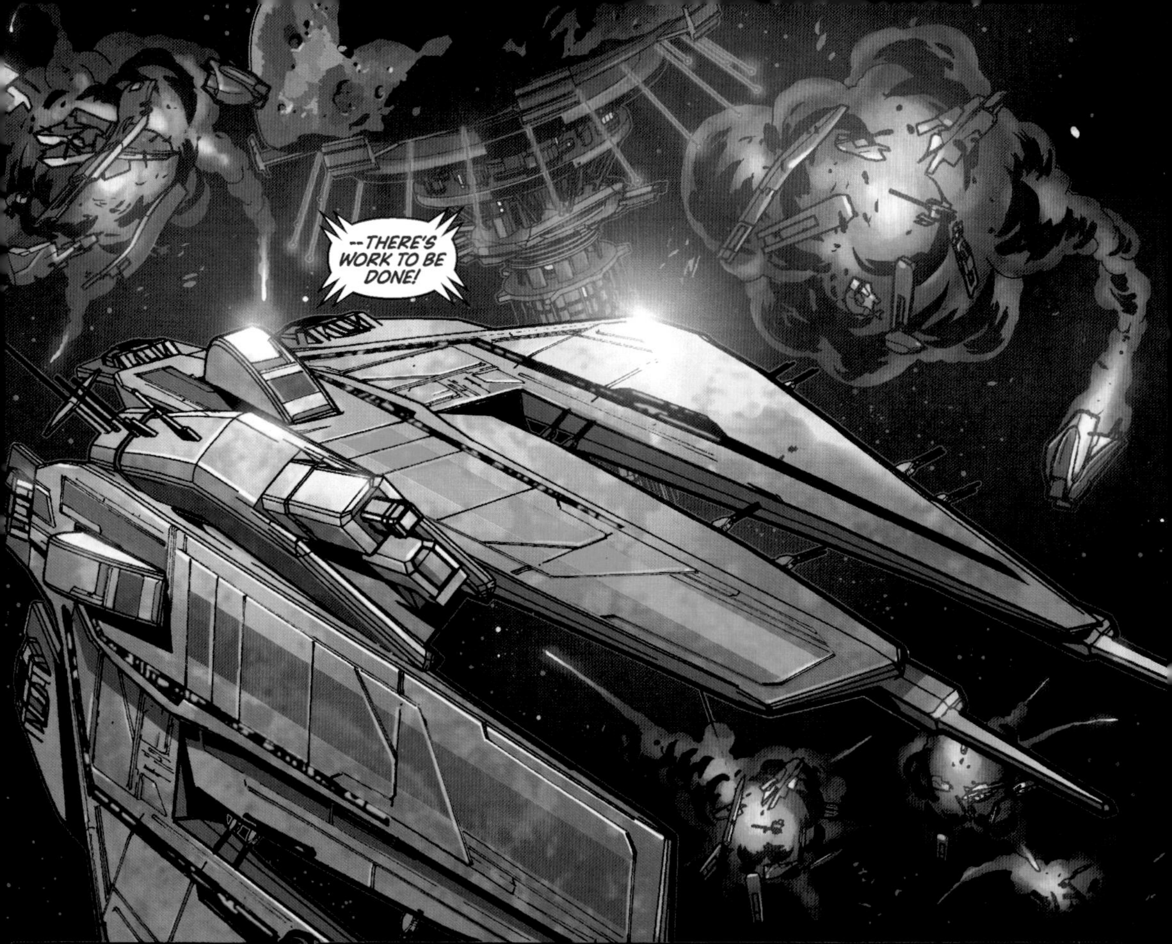
--THERE'S WORK TO BE DONE!

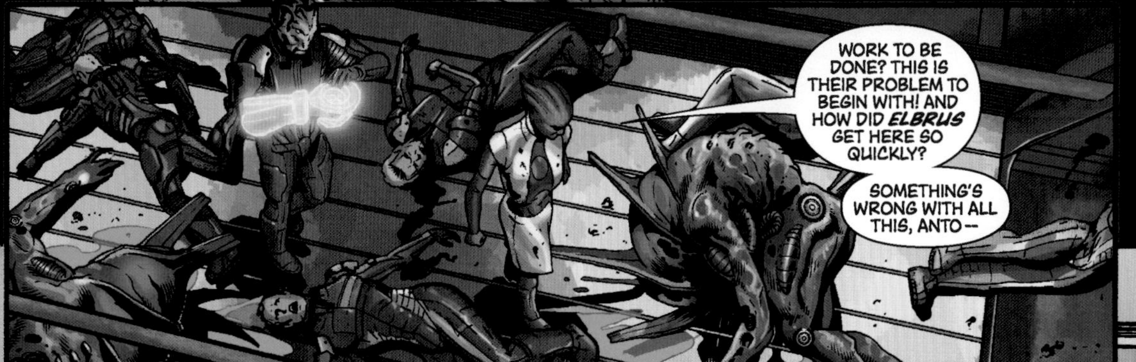
WORK TO BE DONE? THIS IS THEIR PROBLEM TO BEGIN WITH! AND HOW DID ELBRUS GET HERE SO QUICKLY?
SOMETHING'S WRONG WITH ALL THIS, ANTO--

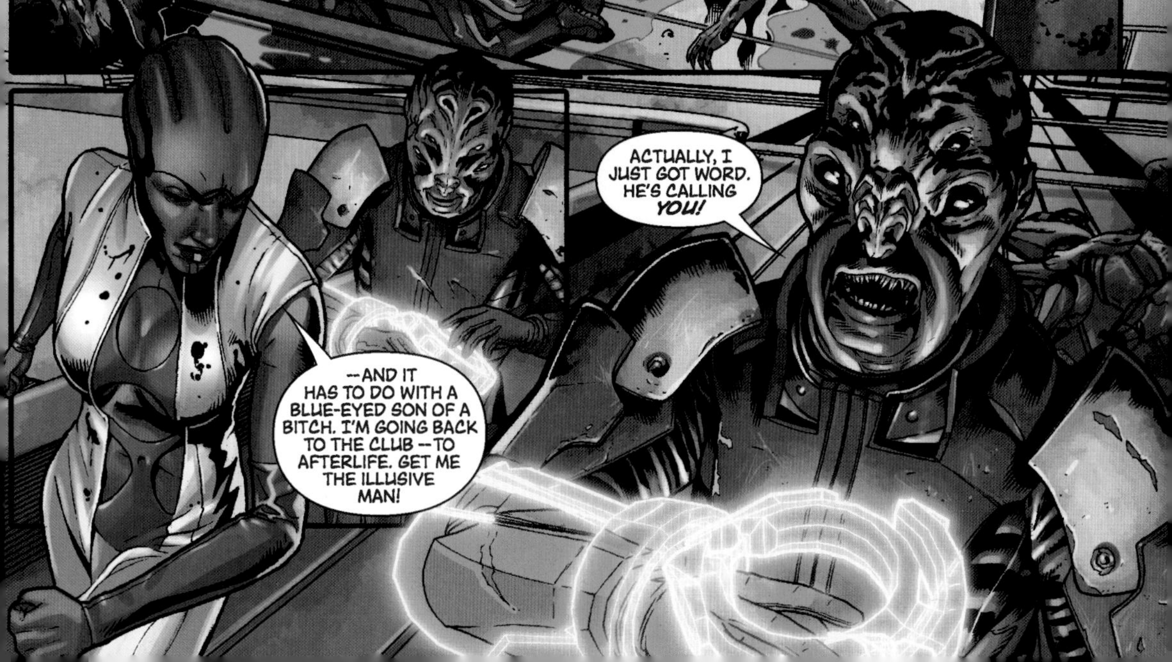
--AND IT HAS TO DO WITH A BLUE-EYED SON OF A BITCH. I'M GOING BACK TO THE CLUB --TO AFTERLIFE. GET ME THE ILLUSIVE MAN!
ACTUALLY, I JUST GOT WORD. HE'S CALLING YOU!

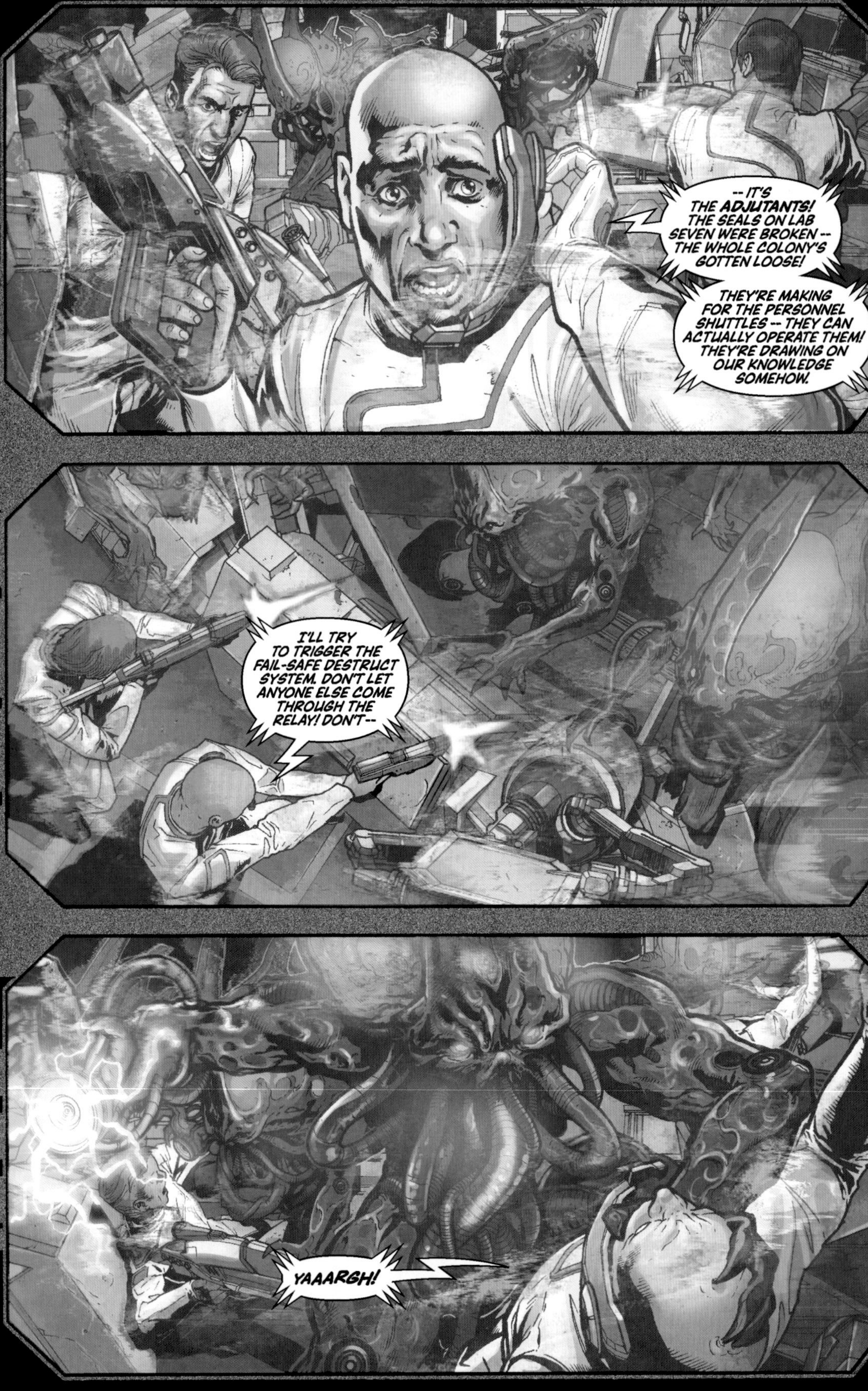
-- IT'S THE ADJUTANTS! THE SEALS ON LAB SEVEN WERE BROKEN -- THE WHOLE COLONY'S GOTTEN LOOSE!
THEY'RE MAKING FOR THE PERSONNEL SHUTTLES -- THEY CAN ACTUALLY OPERATE THEM! THEY'RE DRAWING ON OUR KNOWLEDGE SOMEHOW.
I'LL TRY TO TRIGGER THE FAIL-SAFE DESTRUCT SYSTEM. DON'T LET ANYONE ELSE COME THROUGH THE RELAY! DON'T--
YAAARGH!

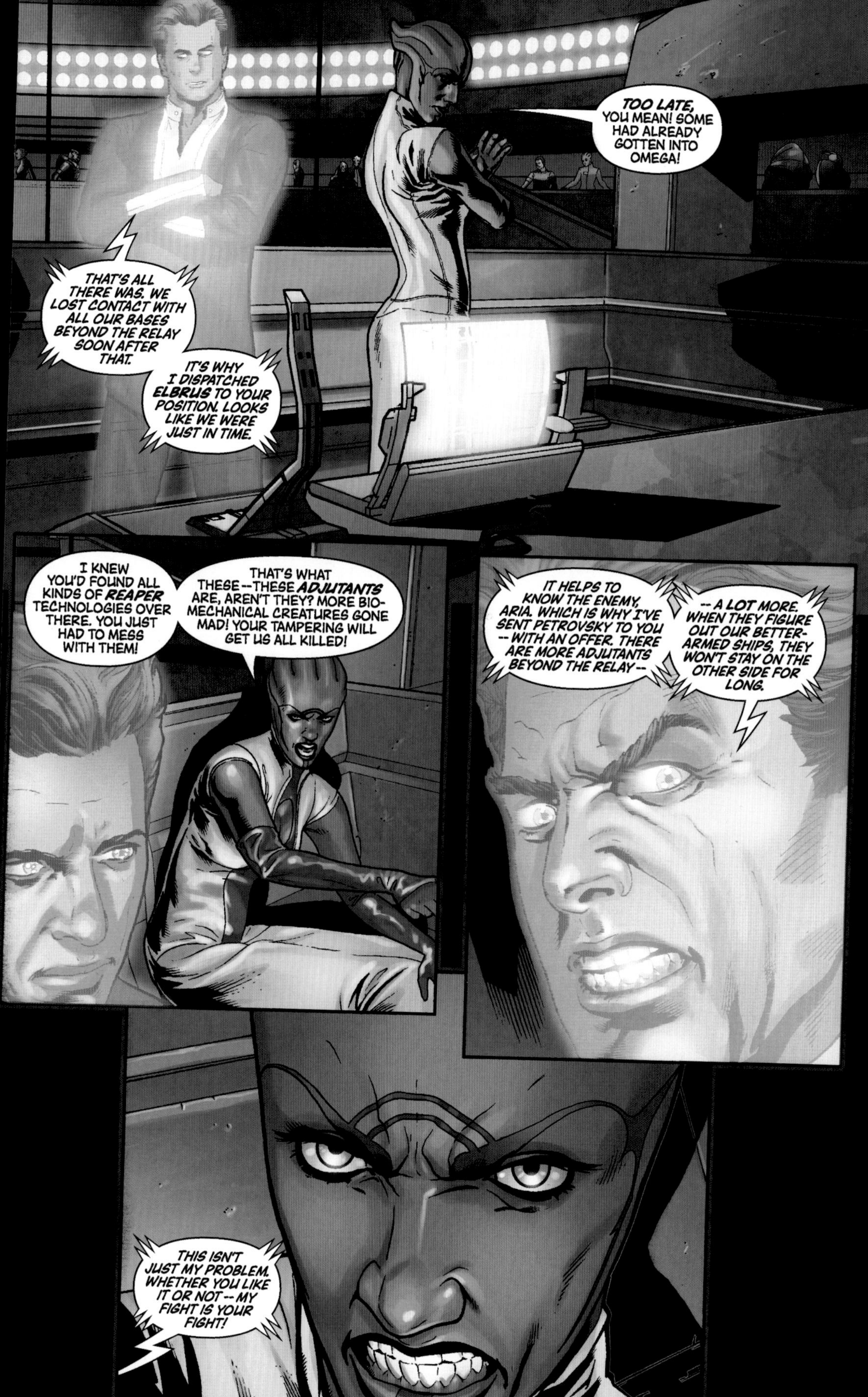
TOO LATE, YOU MEAN! SOME HAD ALREADY GOTTEN INTO OMEGA!
THAT'S ALL THERE WAS. WE LOST CONTACT WITH ALL OUR BASES BEYOND THE RELAY SOON AFTER THAT.
IT'S WHY I DISPATCHED ELBRUS TO YOUR POSITION. LOOKS LIKE WE WERE JUST IN TIME.
I KNEW YOU'D FOUND ALL KINDS OF REAPER TECHNOLOGIES OVER THERE. YOU JUST HAD TO MESS WITH THEM!
THAT'S WHAT THESE--THESE ADJUTANTS ARE, AREN'T THEY? MORE BIO-MECHANICAL CREATURES GONE MAD! YOUR TAMPERING WILL GET US ALL KILLED!
IT HELPS TO KNOW THE ENEMY, ARIA. WHICH IS WHY I'VE SENT PETROVSKY TO YOU --WITH AN OFFER. THERE ARE MORE ADJUTANTS BEYOND THE RELAY--
--A LOT MORE. WHEN THEY FIGURE OUT OUR BETTER-ARMED SHIPS, THEY WON'T STAY ON THE OTHER SIDE FOR LONG.
THIS ISN'T JUST MY PROBLEM. WHETHER YOU LIKE IT OR NOT--MY FIGHT IS YOUR FIGHT!

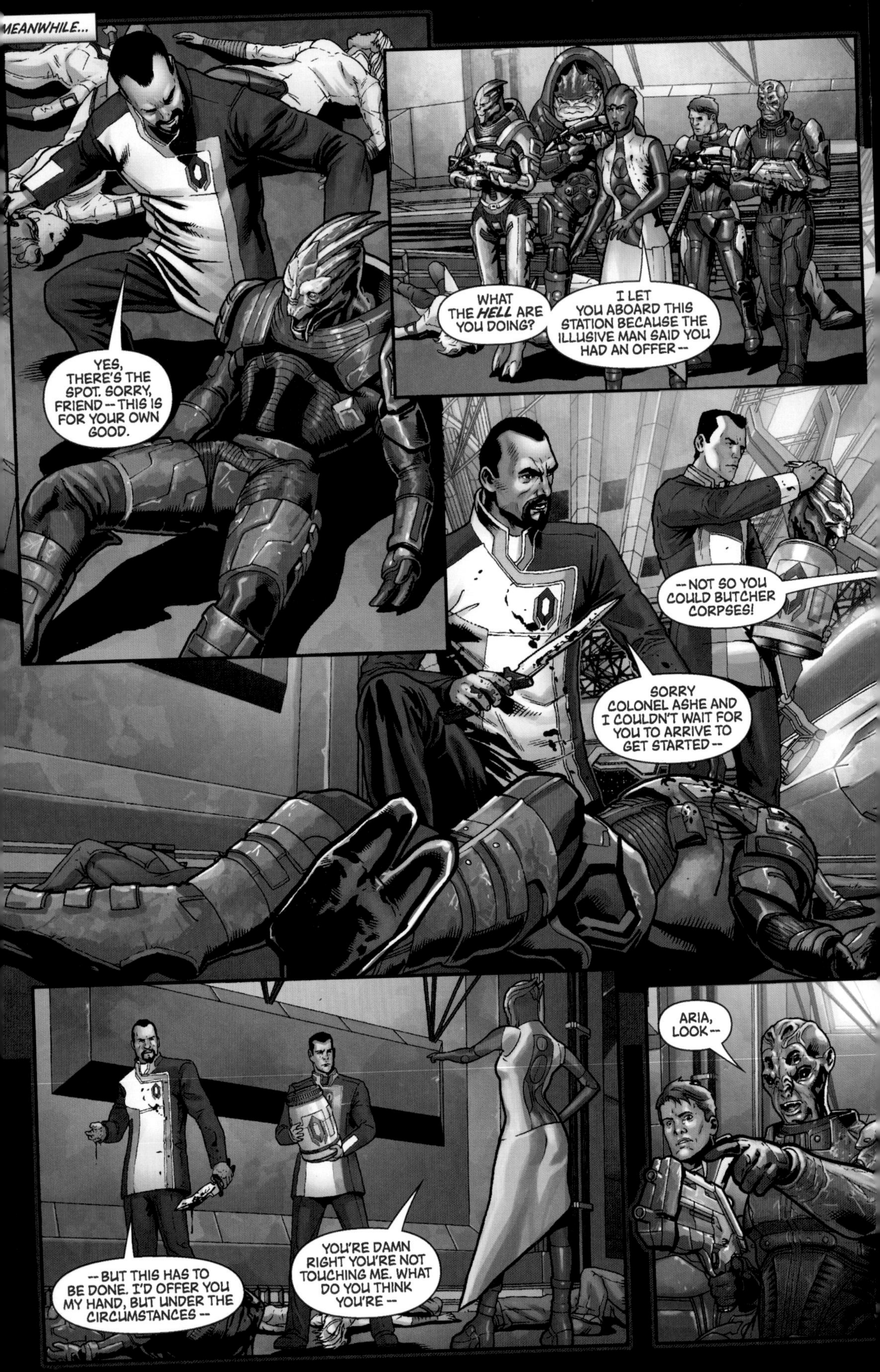
MEANWHILE...
YES, THERE'S THE SPOT. SORRY, FRIEND -- THIS IS FOR YOUR OWN GOOD.
WHAT THE HELL ARE YOU DOING?
I LET YOU ABOARD THIS STATION BECAUSE THE ILLUSIVE MAN SAID YOU HAD AN OFFER --
-- NOT SO YOU COULD BUTCHER CORPSES!
SORRY COLONEL ASHE AND I COULDN'T WAIT FOR YOU TO ARRIVE TO GET STARTED --
-- BUT THIS HAS TO BE DONE. I'D OFFER YOU MY HAND, BUT UNDER THE CIRCUMSTANCES --
YOU'RE DAMN RIGHT YOU'RE NOT TOUCHING ME. WHAT DO YOU THINK YOU'RE --
ARIA, LOOK --

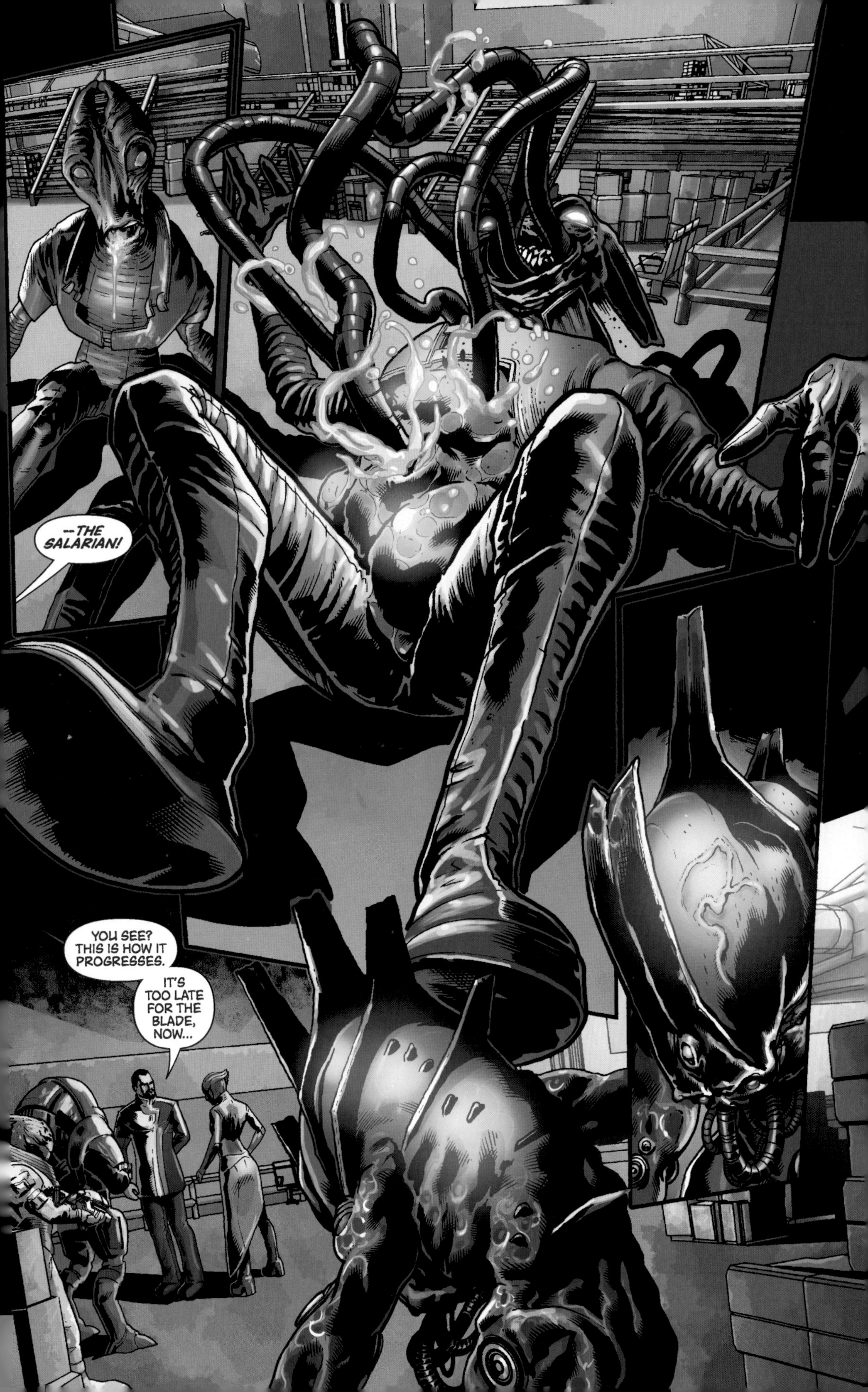
--THE SALARIAN!
YOU SEE? THIS IS HOW IT PROGRESSES.
IT'S TOO LATE FOR THE BLADE, NOW...

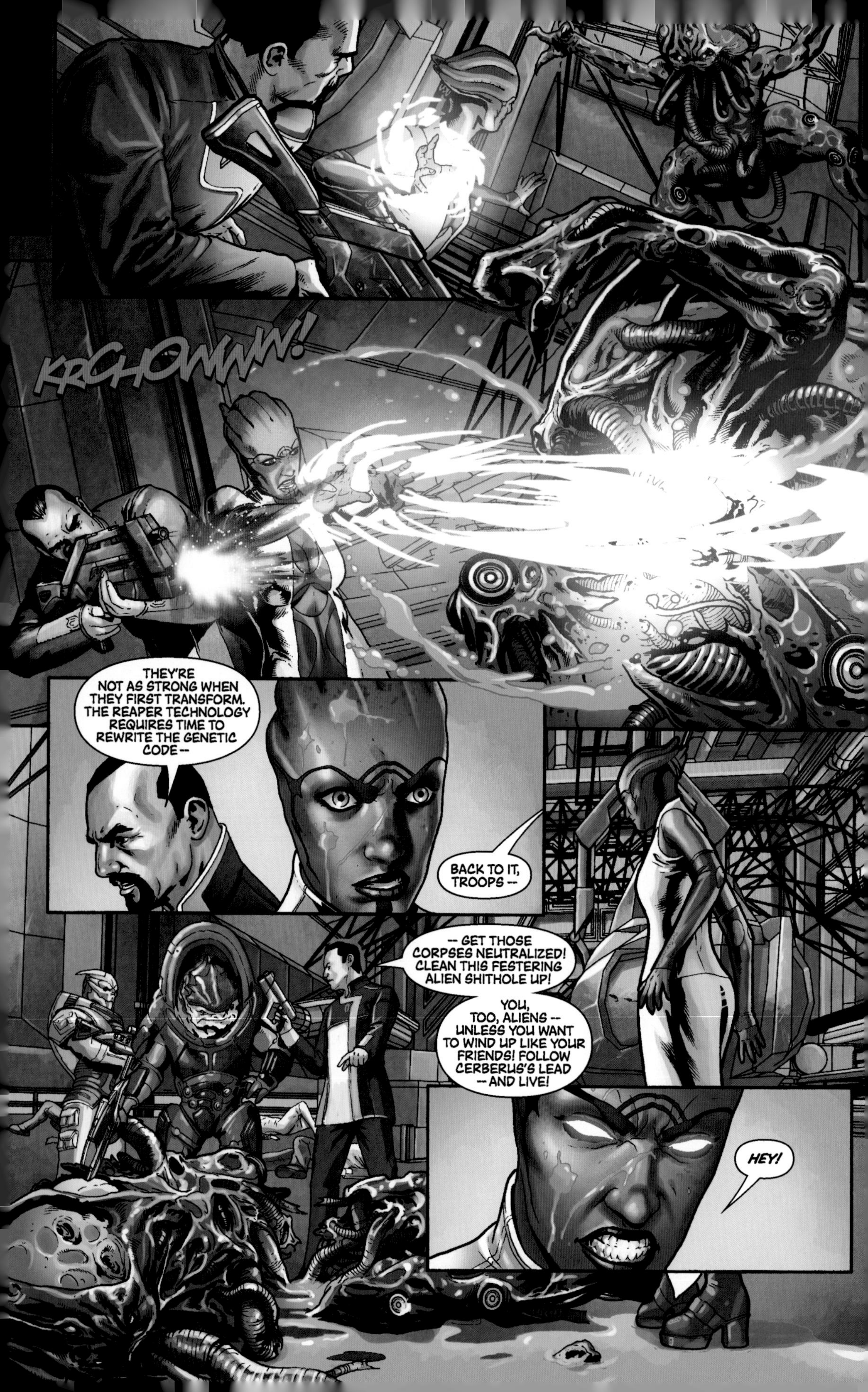
KRCHOWWW!
THEY'RE NOT AS STRONG WHEN THEY FIRST TRANSFORM. THE REAPER TECHNOLOGY REQUIRES TIME TO REWRITE THE GENETIC CODE --
BACK TO IT, TROOPS --
-- GET THOSE CORPSES NEUTRALIZED! CLEAN THIS FESTERING ALIEN SHITHOLE UP!
YOU, TOO, ALIENS -- UNLESS YOU WANT TO WIND UP LIKE YOUR FRIENDS! FOLLOW CERBERUS'S LEAD -- AND LIVE!
HEY!

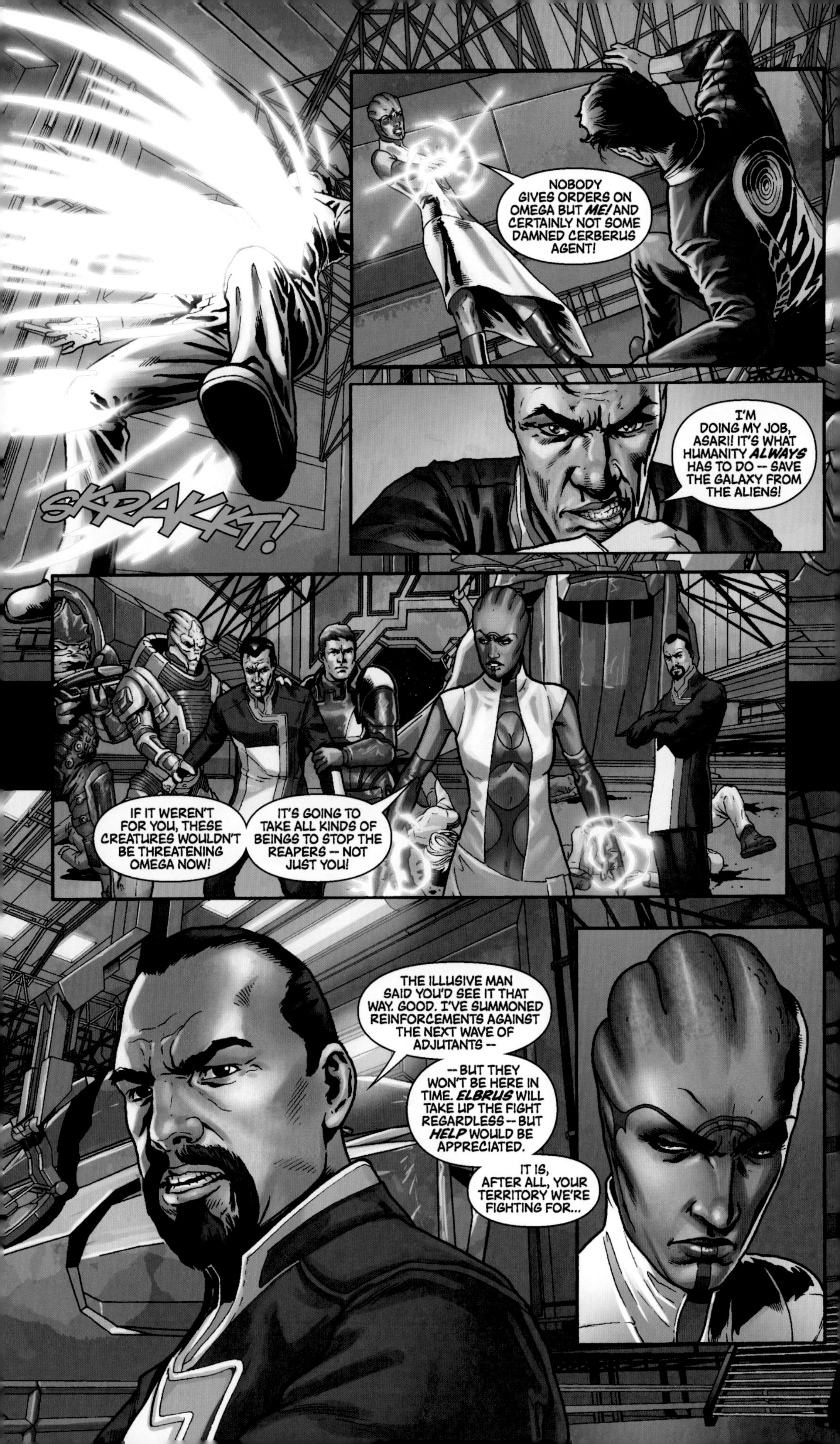

SKRAKKT!
NOBODY GIVES ORDERS ON OMEGA BUT ME! AND CERTAINLY NOT SOME DAMNED CERBERUS AGENT!
I'M DOING MY JOB, ASARI! IT'S WHAT HUMANITY ALWAYS HAS TO DO -- SAVE THE GALAXY FROM THE ALIENS!
IF IT WEREN'T FOR YOU, THESE CREATURES WOULDN'T BE THREATENING OMEGA NOW!
IT'S GOING TO TAKE ALL KINDS OF BEINGS TO STOP THE REAPERS -- NOT JUST YOU!
THE ILLUSIVE MAN SAID YOU'D SEE IT THAT WAY. GOOD. I'VE SUMMONED REINFORCEMENTS AGAINST THE NEXT WAVE OF ADJUTANTS --
-- BUT THEY WON'T BE HERE IN TIME. ELBRUS WILL TAKE UP THE FIGHT REGARDLESS -- BUT HELP WOULD BE APPRECIATED.
IT IS, AFTER ALL, YOUR TERRITORY WE'RE FIGHTING FOR...

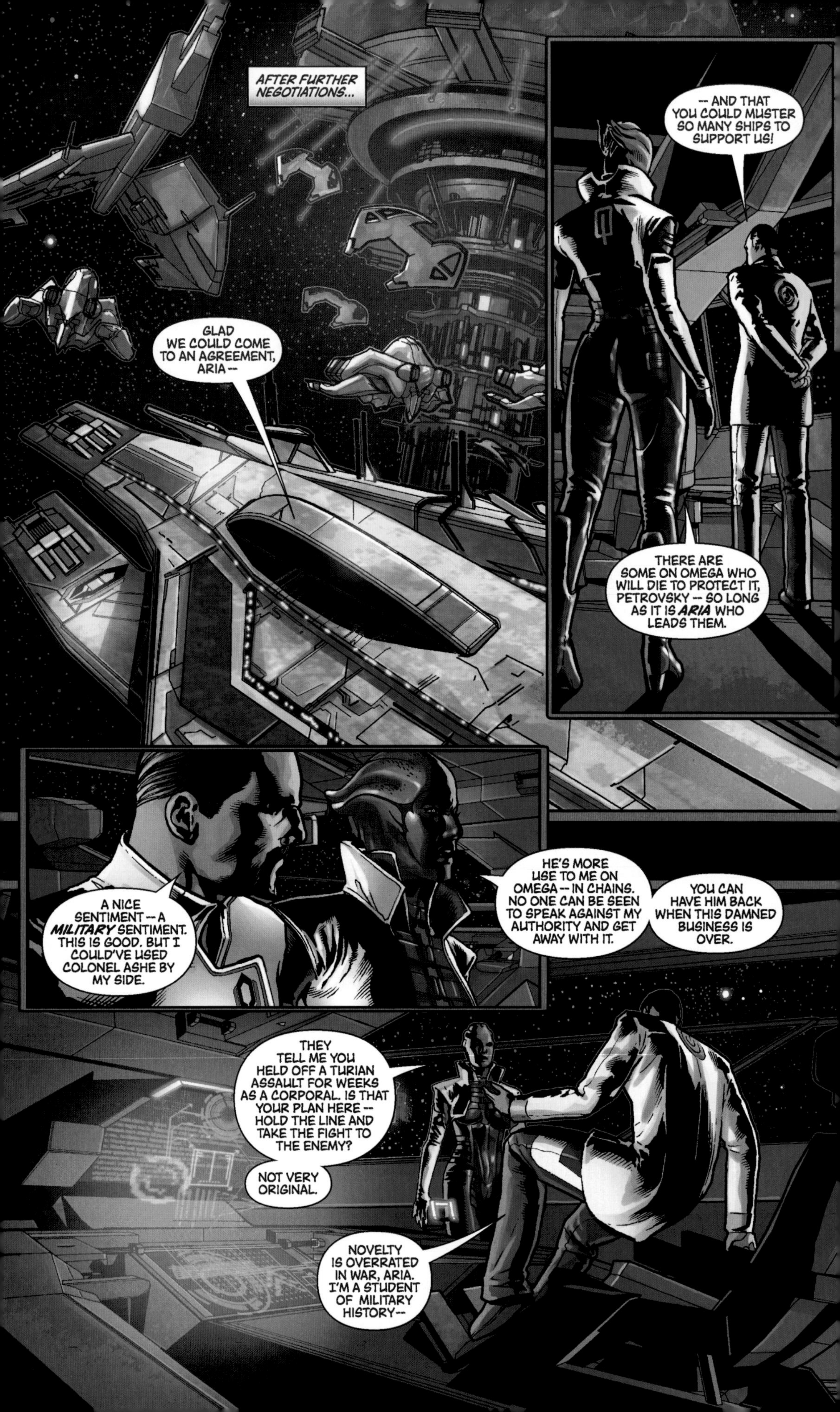
AFTER FURTHER NEGOTIATIONS...
GLAD WE COULD COME TO AN AGREEMENT, ARIA --
-- AND THAT YOU COULD MUSTER SO MANY SHIPS TO SUPPORT US!
THERE ARE SOME ON OMEGA WHO WILL DIE TO PROTECT IT, PETROVSKY -- SO LONG AS IT IS *ARIA* WHO LEADS THEM.
A NICE SENTIMENT -- A *MILITARY* SENTIMENT. THIS IS GOOD. BUT I COULD'VE USED COLONEL ASHE BY MY SIDE.
HE'S MORE USE TO ME ON OMEGA -- IN CHAINS. NO ONE CAN BE SEEN TO SPEAK AGAINST MY AUTHORITY AND GET AWAY WITH IT.
YOU CAN HAVE HIM BACK WHEN THIS DAMNED BUSINESS IS OVER.
THEY TELL ME YOU HELD OFF A TURIAN ASSAULT FOR WEEKS AS A CORPORAL. IS THAT YOUR PLAN HERE -- HOLD THE LINE AND TAKE THE FIGHT TO THE ENEMY?
NOT VERY ORIGINAL.
NOVELTY IS OVERRATED IN WAR, ARIA. I'M A STUDENT OF MILITARY HISTORY--

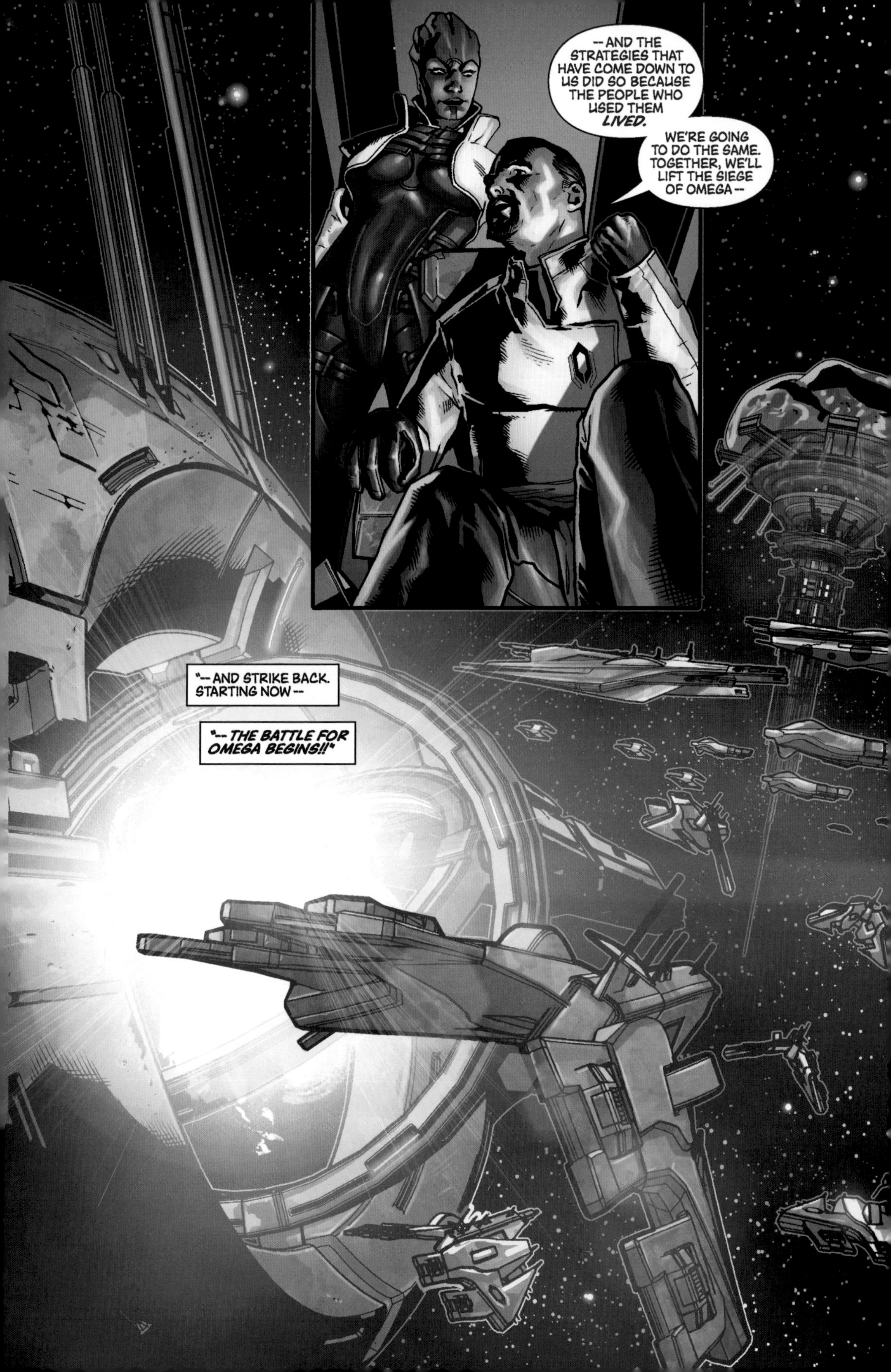
-- AND THE STRATEGIES THAT HAVE COME DOWN TO US DID SO BECAUSE THE PEOPLE WHO USED THEM *LIVED.*
WE'RE GOING TO DO THE SAME. TOGETHER, WE'LL LIFT THE SIEGE OF OMEGA --
"-- AND STRIKE BACK. STARTING NOW --
"-- *THE BATTLE FOR OMEGA BEGINS!!*"

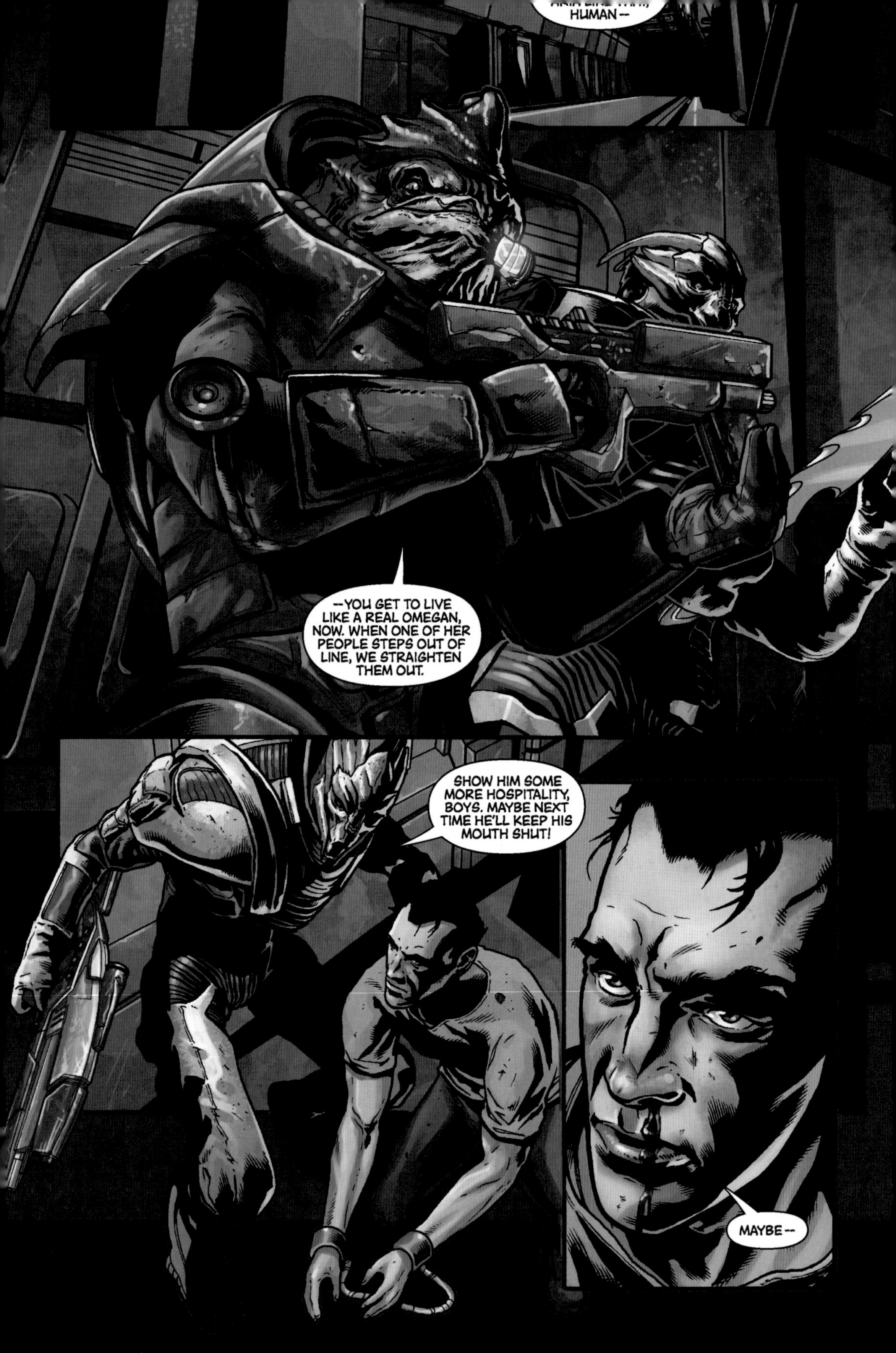
HUMAN --
--YOU GET TO LIVE LIKE A REAL OMEGAN, NOW. WHEN ONE OF HER PEOPLE STEPS OUT OF LINE, WE STRAIGHTEN THEM OUT.
SHOW HIM SOME MORE HOSPITALITY, BOYS. MAYBE NEXT TIME HE'LL KEEP HIS MOUTH SHUT!
MAYBE --

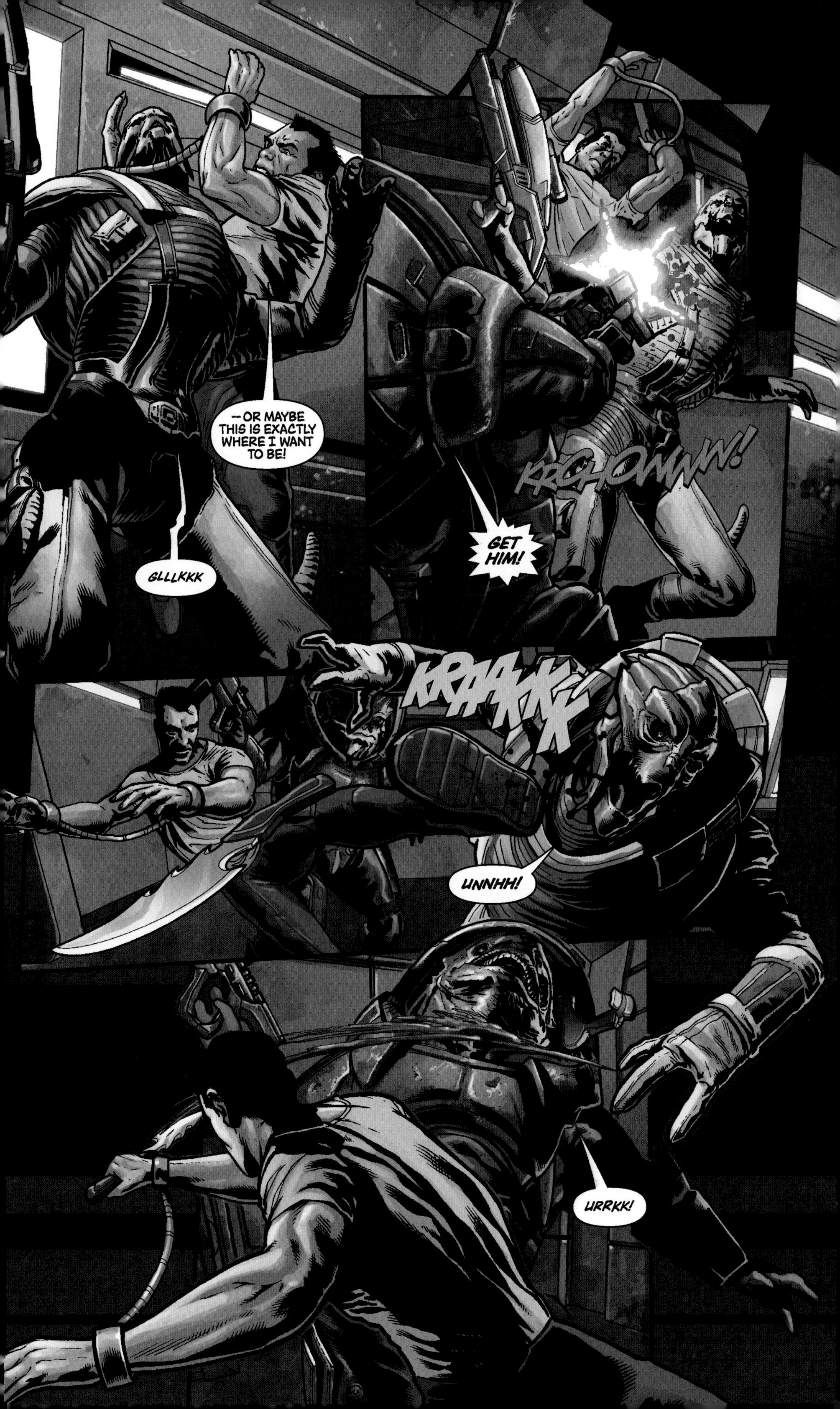
--OR MAYBE THIS IS EXACTLY WHERE I WANT TO BE!
GLLLKKK
KRCHOWWW!
GET HIM!
KRAAKKK
UNNHH!
URRKK!

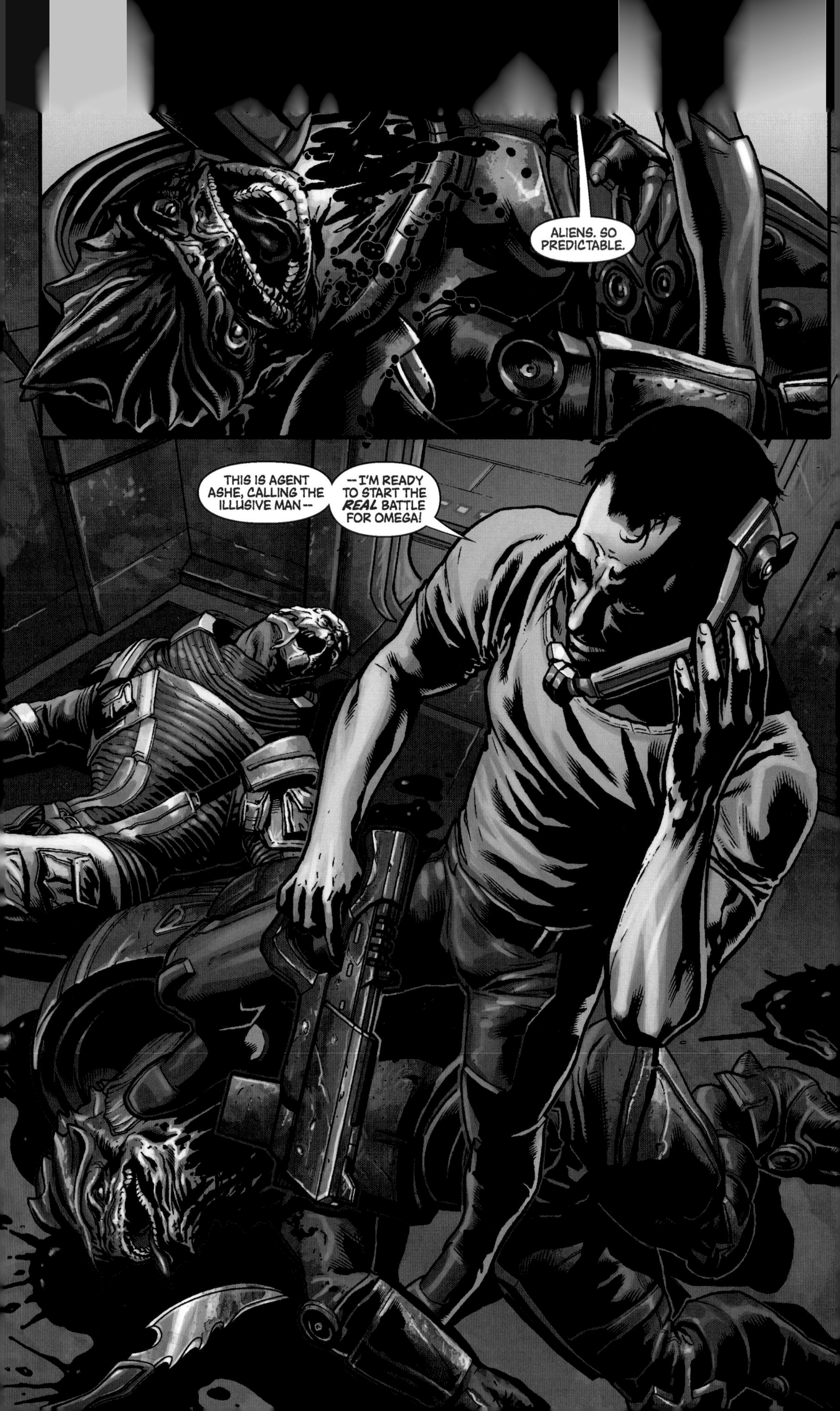
ALIENS. SO PREDICTABLE.
THIS IS AGENT ASHE, CALLING THE ILLUSIVE MAN --
-- I'M READY TO START THE *REAL* BATTLE FOR OMEGA!

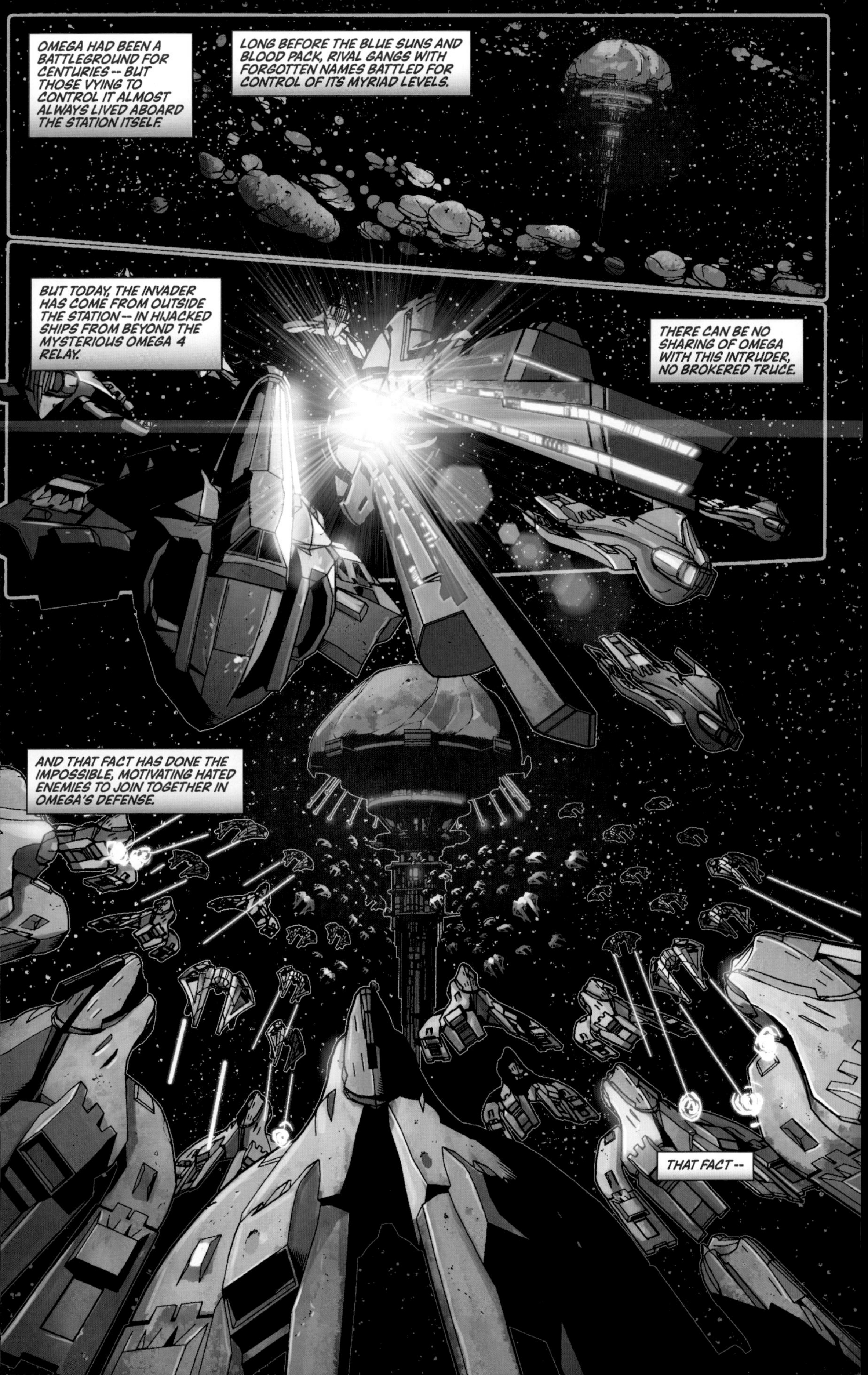
OMEGA HAD BEEN A BATTLEGROUND FOR CENTURIES -- BUT THOSE VYING TO CONTROL IT ALMOST ALWAYS LIVED ABOARD THE STATION ITSELF.
LONG BEFORE THE BLUE SUNS AND BLOOD PACK, RIVAL GANGS WITH FORGOTTEN NAMES BATTLED FOR CONTROL OF ITS MYRIAD LEVELS.
BUT TODAY, THE INVADER HAS COME FROM OUTSIDE THE STATION -- IN HIJACKED SHIPS FROM BEYOND THE MYSTERIOUS OMEGA 4 RELAY.
THERE CAN BE NO SHARING OF OMEGA WITH THIS INTRUDER, NO BROKERED TRUCE.
AND THAT FACT HAS DONE THE IMPOSSIBLE, MOTIVATING HATED ENEMIES TO JOIN TOGETHER IN OMEGA'S DEFENSE.
THAT FACT --

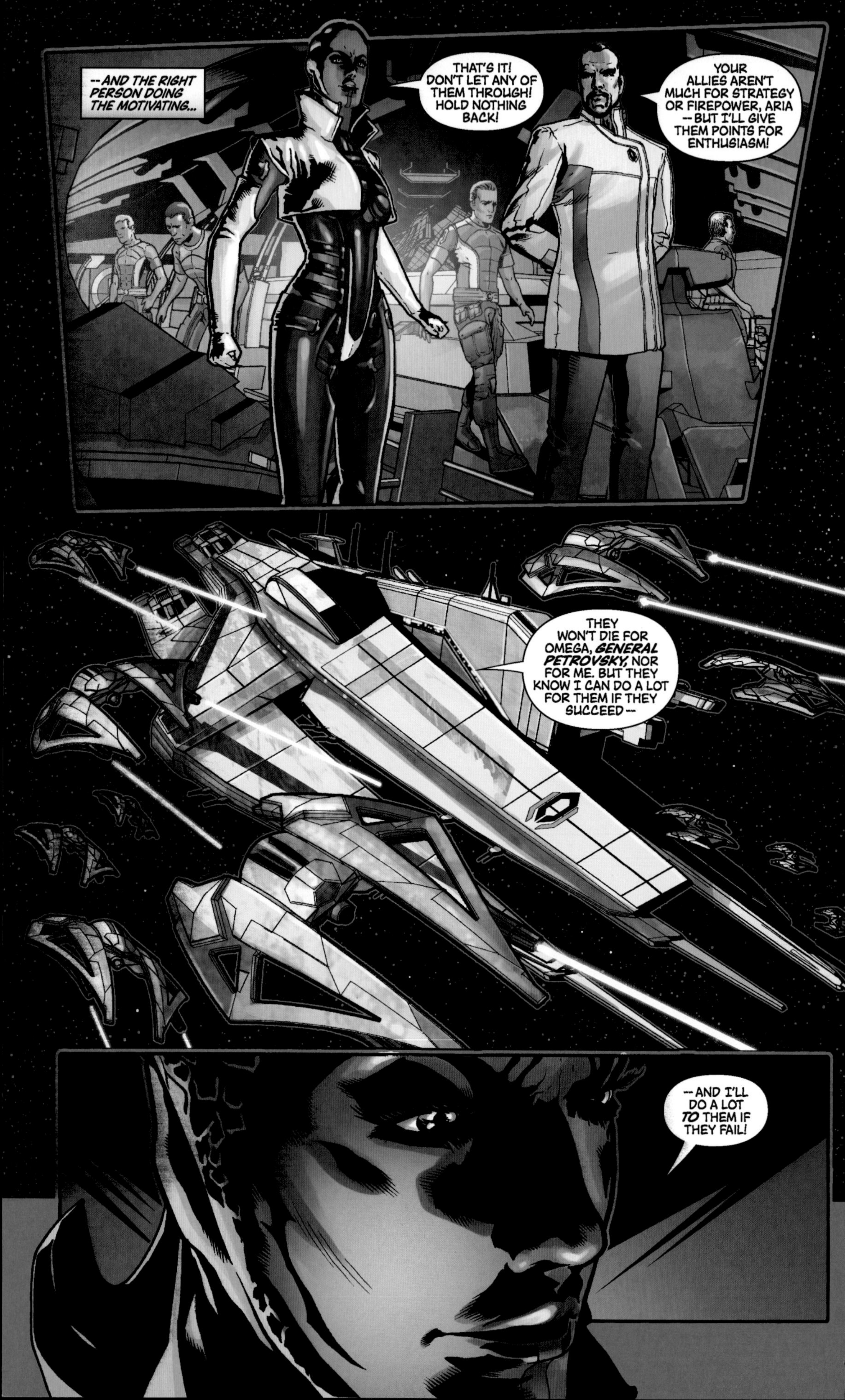
--AND THE RIGHT PERSON DOING THE MOTIVATING...
THAT'S IT! DON'T LET ANY OF THEM THROUGH! HOLD NOTHING BACK!
YOUR ALLIES AREN'T MUCH FOR STRATEGY OR FIREPOWER, ARIA --BUT I'LL GIVE THEM POINTS FOR ENTHUSIASM!
THEY WON'T DIE FOR OMEGA, GENERAL PETROVSKY, NOR FOR ME. BUT THEY KNOW I CAN DO A LOT FOR THEM IF THEY SUCCEED--
--AND I'LL DO A LOT TO THEM IF THEY FAIL!

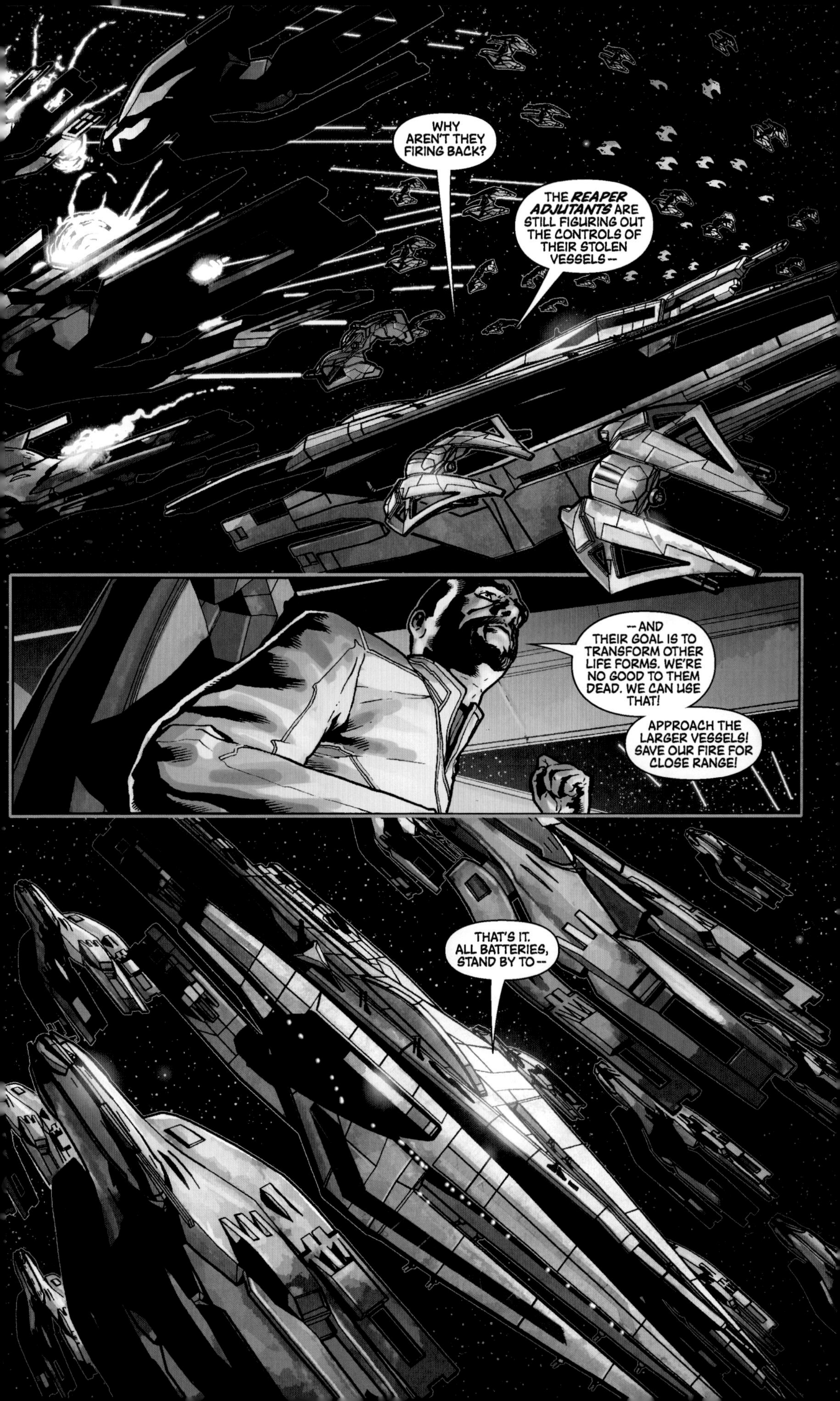
WHY AREN'T THEY FIRING BACK?
THE *REAPER ADJUTANTS* ARE STILL FIGURING OUT THE CONTROLS OF THEIR STOLEN VESSELS --
-- AND THEIR GOAL IS TO TRANSFORM OTHER LIFE FORMS. WE'RE NO GOOD TO THEM DEAD. WE CAN USE THAT!
APPROACH THE LARGER VESSELS! SAVE OUR FIRE FOR CLOSE RANGE!
THAT'S IT. ALL BATTERIES, STAND BY TO --

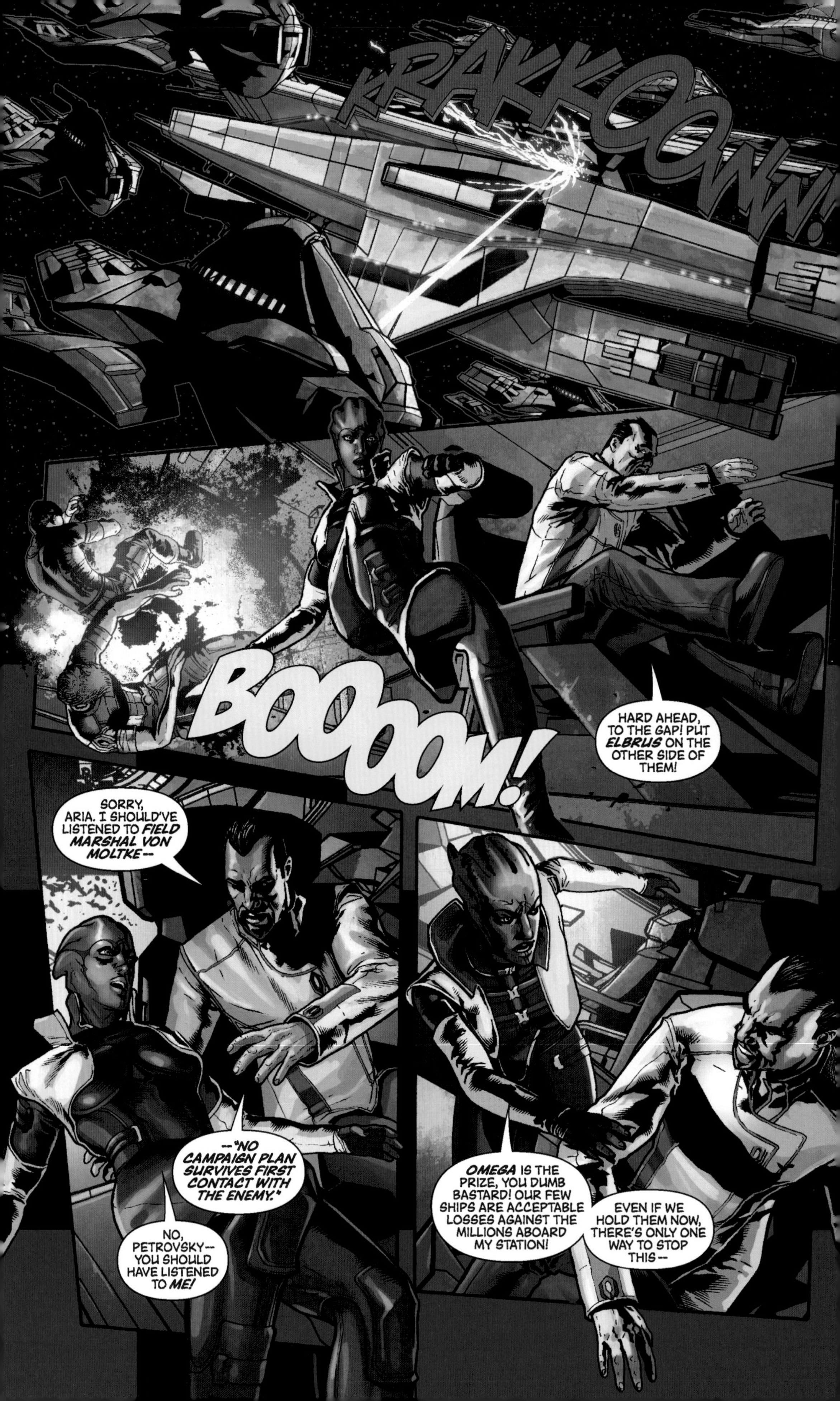
KRAKKOOWW!
BOOOOM!
HARD AHEAD, TO THE GAP! PUT *ELBRUS* ON THE OTHER SIDE OF THEM!
SORRY, ARIA. I SHOULD'VE LISTENED TO *FIELD MARSHAL VON MOLTKE*--
--*"NO CAMPAIGN PLAN SURVIVES FIRST CONTACT WITH THE ENEMY."*
NO, PETROVSKY-- YOU SHOULD HAVE LISTENED TO *ME!*
OMEGA IS THE PRIZE, YOU DUMB BASTARD! OUR FEW SHIPS ARE ACCEPTABLE LOSSES AGAINST THE MILLIONS ABOARD MY STATION!
EVEN IF WE HOLD THEM NOW, THERE'S ONLY ONE WAY TO STOP THIS--

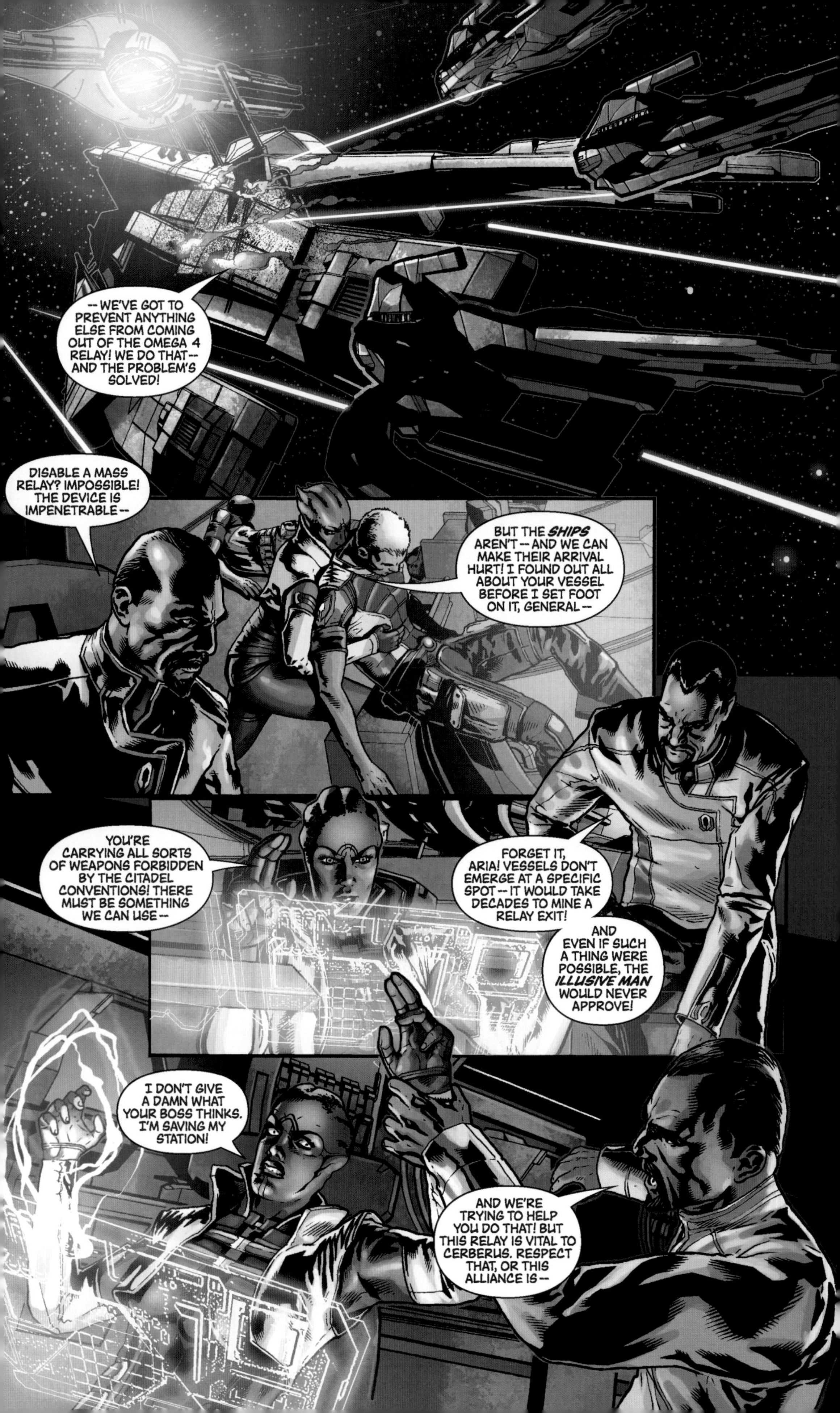
-- WE'VE GOT TO PREVENT ANYTHING ELSE FROM COMING OUT OF THE OMEGA 4 RELAY! WE DO THAT -- AND THE PROBLEM'S SOLVED!
DISABLE A MASS RELAY? IMPOSSIBLE! THE DEVICE IS IMPENETRABLE --
BUT THE *SHIPS* AREN'T -- AND WE CAN MAKE THEIR ARRIVAL HURT! I FOUND OUT ALL ABOUT YOUR VESSEL BEFORE I SET FOOT ON IT, GENERAL --
YOU'RE CARRYING ALL SORTS OF WEAPONS FORBIDDEN BY THE CITADEL CONVENTIONS! THERE MUST BE SOMETHING WE CAN USE --
FORGET IT, ARIA! VESSELS DON'T EMERGE AT A SPECIFIC SPOT -- IT WOULD TAKE DECADES TO MINE A RELAY EXIT!
AND EVEN IF SUCH A THING WERE POSSIBLE, THE *ILLUSIVE MAN* WOULD NEVER APPROVE!
I DON'T GIVE A DAMN WHAT YOUR BOSS THINKS. I'M SAVING MY STATION!
AND WE'RE TRYING TO HELP YOU DO THAT! BUT THIS RELAY IS VITAL TO CERBERUS. RESPECT THAT, OR THIS ALLIANCE IS --

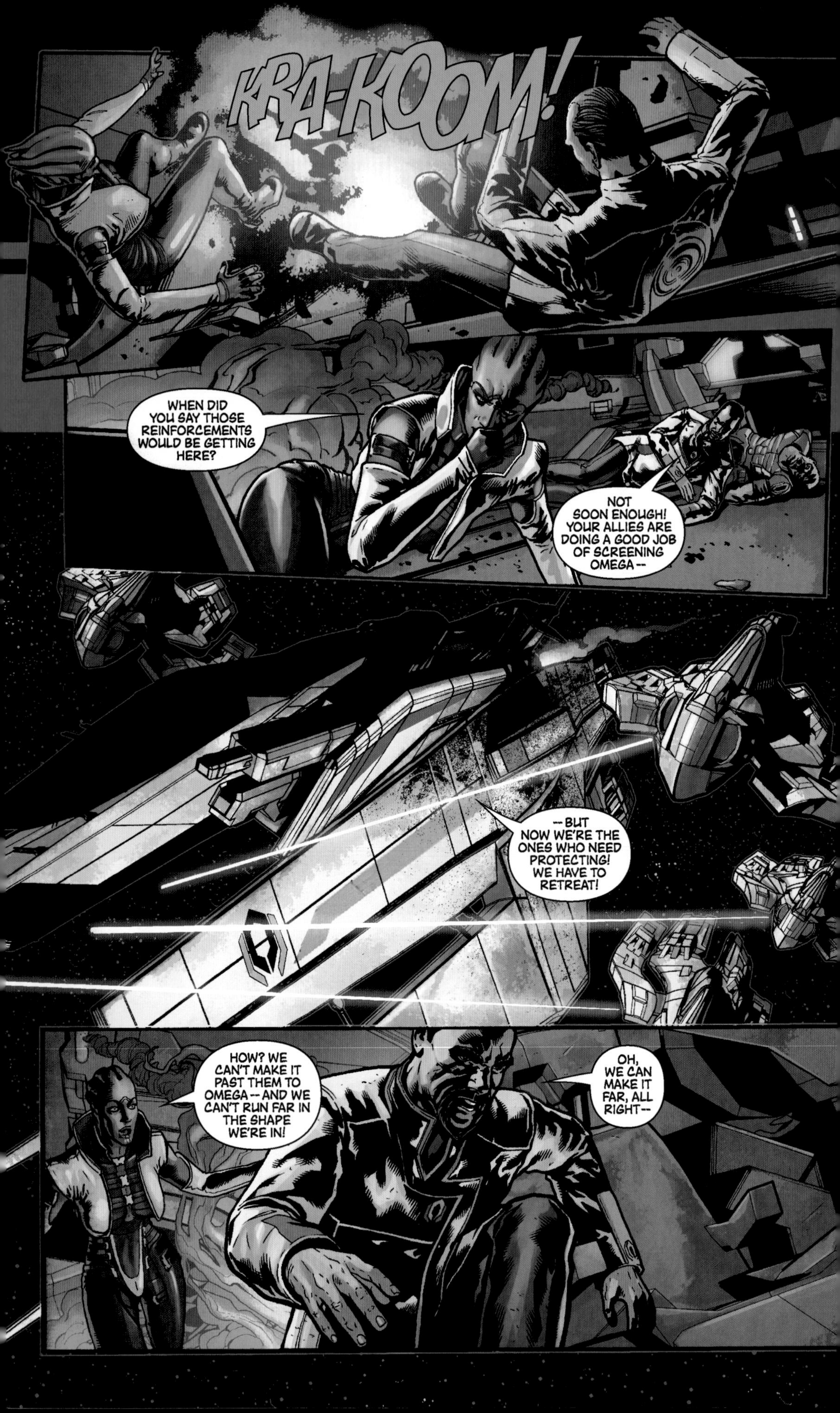
KRA-KOOM!
WHEN DID YOU SAY THOSE REINFORCEMENTS WOULD BE GETTING HERE?
NOT SOON ENOUGH! YOUR ALLIES ARE DOING A GOOD JOB OF SCREENING OMEGA --
-- BUT NOW WE'RE THE ONES WHO NEED PROTECTING! WE HAVE TO RETREAT!
HOW? WE CAN'T MAKE IT PAST THEM TO OMEGA -- AND WE CAN'T RUN FAR IN THE SHAPE WE'RE IN!
OH, WE CAN MAKE IT FAR, ALL RIGHT --

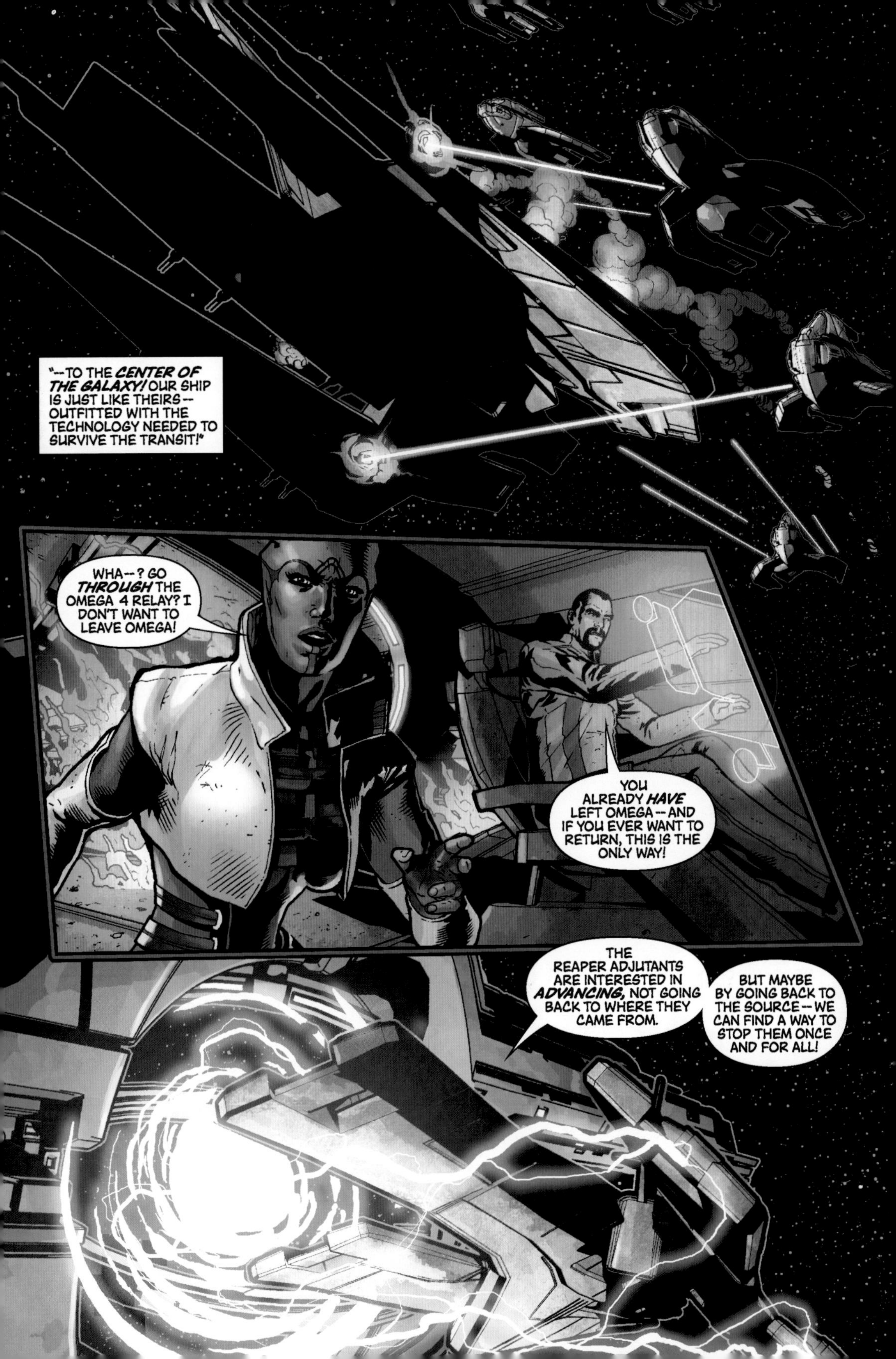
"--TO THE CENTER OF THE GALAXY! OUR SHIP IS JUST LIKE THEIRS-- OUTFITTED WITH THE TECHNOLOGY NEEDED TO SURVIVE THE TRANSIT!"
WHA--? GO THROUGH THE OMEGA 4 RELAY? I DON'T WANT TO LEAVE OMEGA!
YOU ALREADY HAVE LEFT OMEGA--AND IF YOU EVER WANT TO RETURN, THIS IS THE ONLY WAY!
THE REAPER ADJUTANTS ARE INTERESTED IN ADVANCING, NOT GOING BACK TO WHERE THEY CAME FROM.
BUT MAYBE BY GOING BACK TO THE SOURCE--WE CAN FIND A WAY TO STOP THEM ONCE AND FOR ALL!

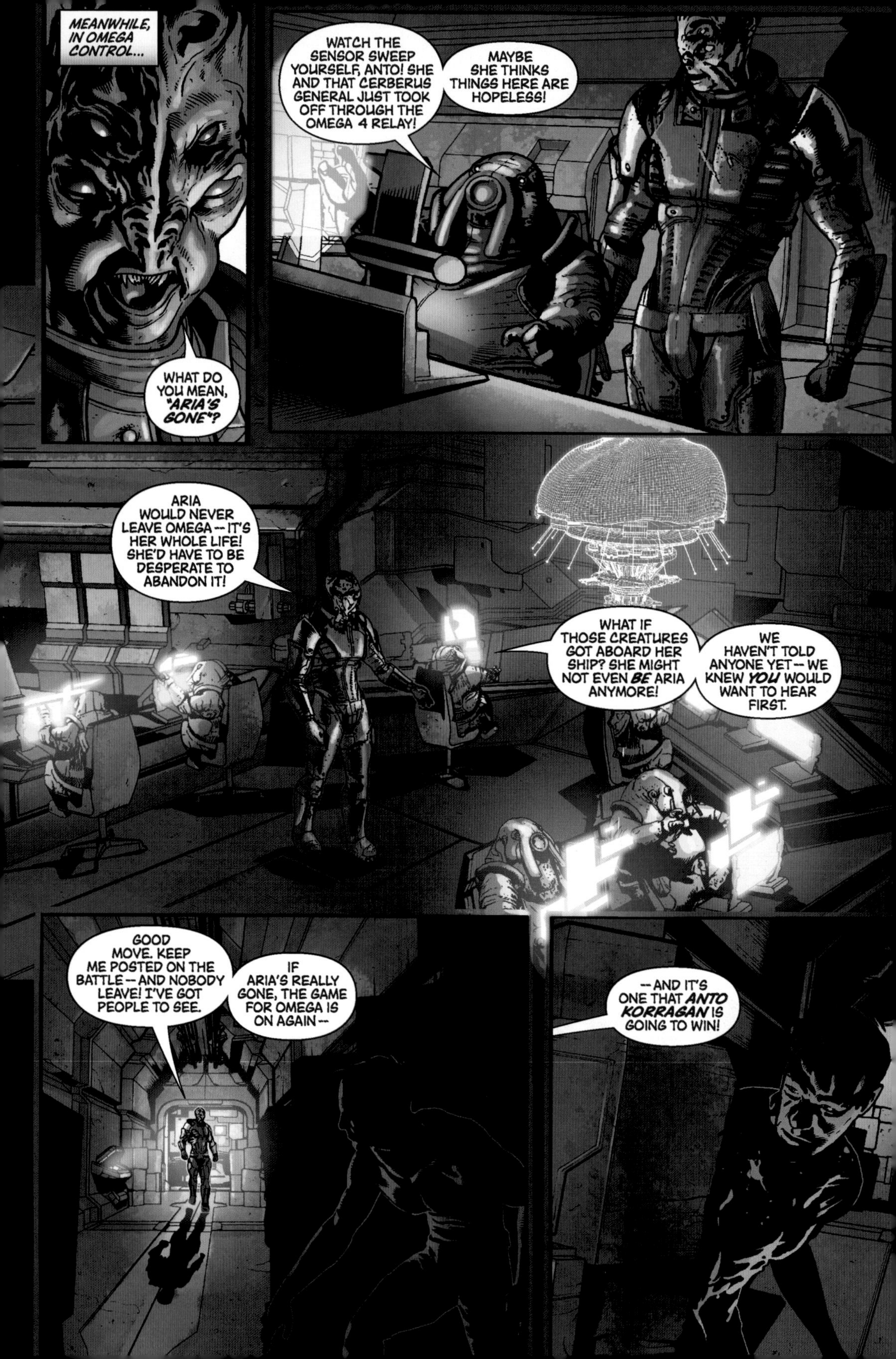

MEANWHILE, IN OMEGA CONTROL...
WHAT DO YOU MEAN, *"ARIA'S GONE"*?
WATCH THE SENSOR SWEEP YOURSELF, ANTO! SHE AND THAT CERBERUS GENERAL JUST TOOK OFF THROUGH THE OMEGA 4 RELAY!
MAYBE SHE THINKS THINGS HERE ARE HOPELESS!
ARIA WOULD NEVER LEAVE OMEGA -- IT'S HER WHOLE LIFE! SHE'D HAVE TO BE DESPERATE TO ABANDON IT!
WHAT IF THOSE CREATURES GOT ABOARD HER SHIP? SHE MIGHT NOT EVEN *BE* ARIA ANYMORE!
WE HAVEN'T TOLD ANYONE YET -- WE KNEW *YOU* WOULD WANT TO HEAR FIRST.
GOOD MOVE. KEEP ME POSTED ON THE BATTLE -- AND NOBODY LEAVE! I'VE GOT PEOPLE TO SEE.
IF ARIA'S REALLY GONE, THE GAME FOR OMEGA IS ON AGAIN --
-- AND IT'S ONE THAT *ANTO KORRAGAN* IS GOING TO WIN!

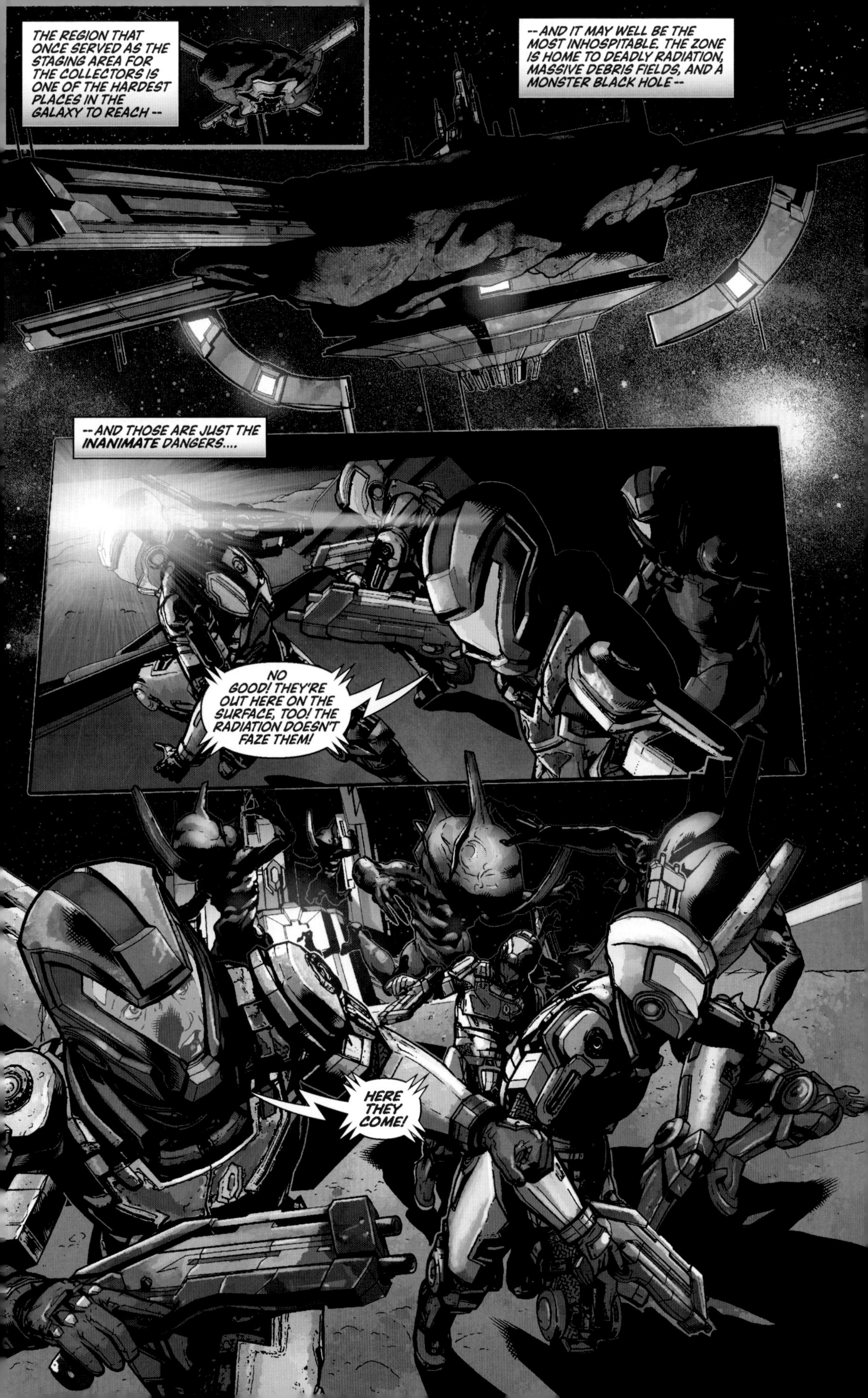
THE REGION THAT ONCE SERVED AS THE STAGING AREA FOR THE COLLECTORS IS ONE OF THE HARDEST PLACES IN THE GALAXY TO REACH --
-- AND IT MAY WELL BE THE MOST INHOSPITABLE. THE ZONE IS HOME TO DEADLY RADIATION, MASSIVE DEBRIS FIELDS, AND A MONSTER BLACK HOLE --
-- AND THOSE ARE JUST THE INANIMATE DANGERS....
NO GOOD! THEY'RE OUT HERE ON THE SURFACE, TOO! THE RADIATION DOESN'T FAZE THEM!
HERE THEY COME!

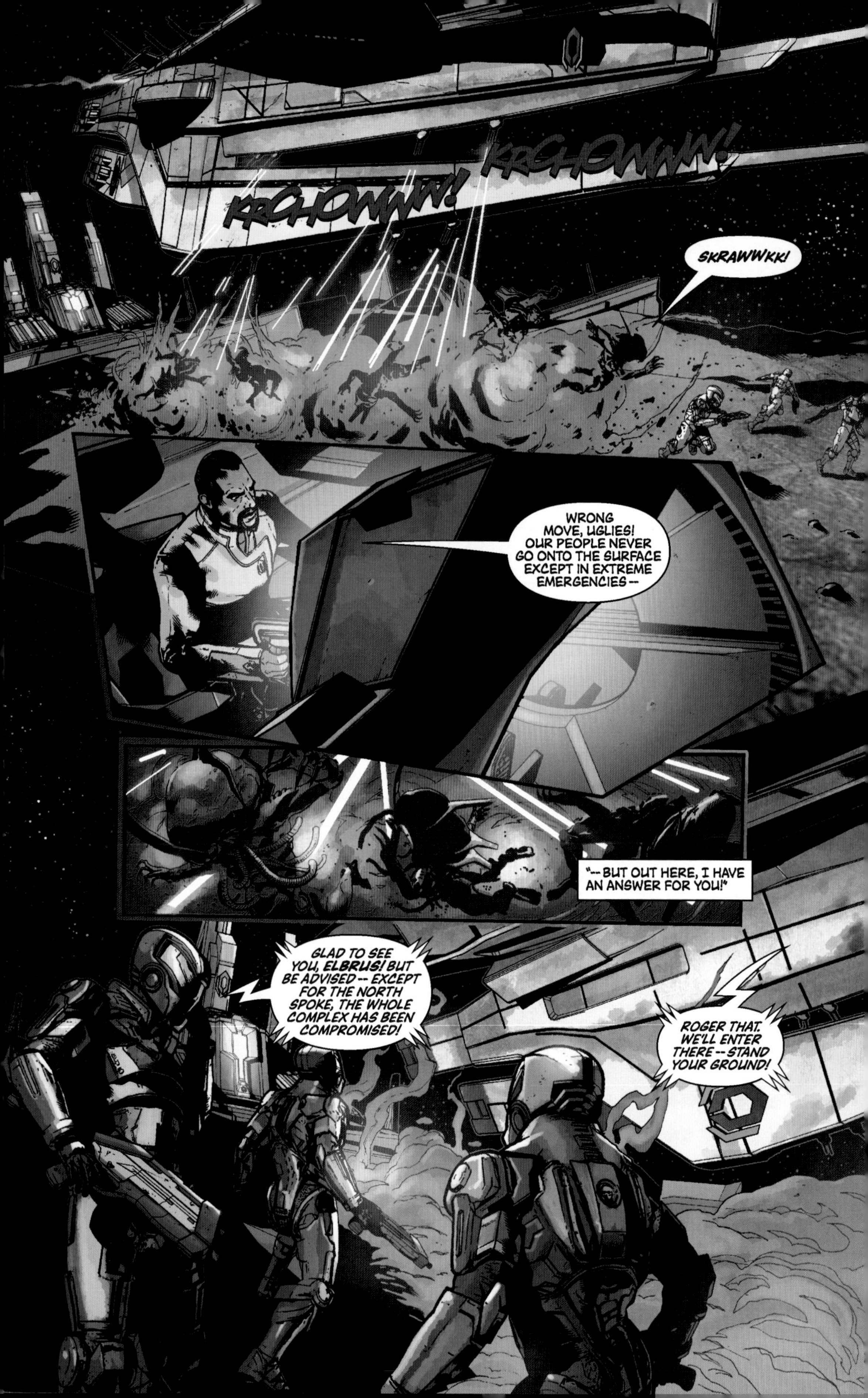
KRCHOWWW!
KRCHOWWW!
SKRAWWKK!
WRONG MOVE, UGLIES! OUR PEOPLE NEVER GO ONTO THE SURFACE EXCEPT IN EXTREME EMERGENCIES --
"-- BUT OUT HERE, I HAVE AN ANSWER FOR YOU!"
GLAD TO SEE YOU, ELBRUS! BUT BE ADVISED -- EXCEPT FOR THE NORTH SPOKE, THE WHOLE COMPLEX HAS BEEN COMPROMISED!
ROGER THAT. WE'LL ENTER THERE -- STAND YOUR GROUND!

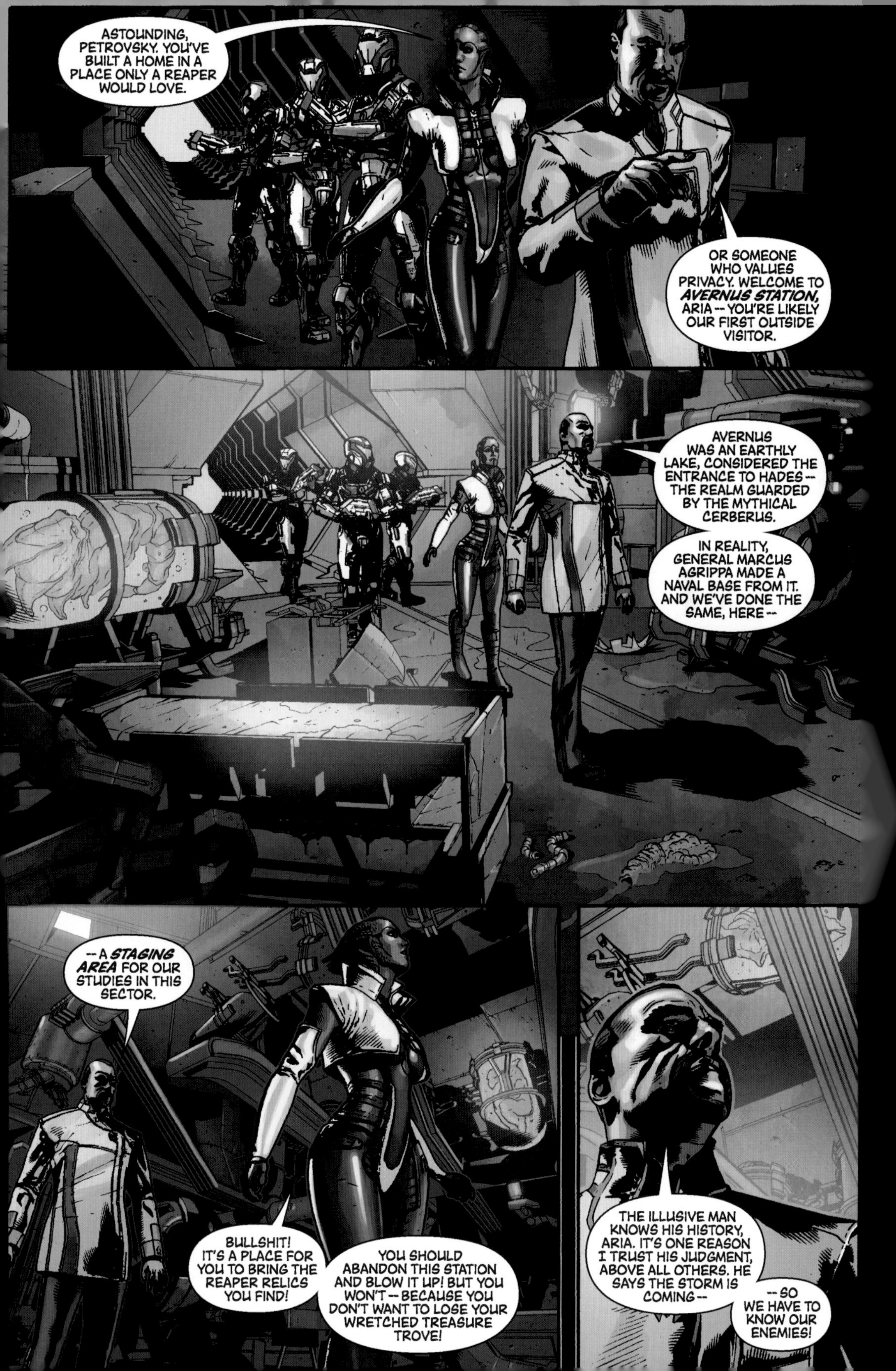
ASTOUNDING, PETROVSKY. YOU'VE BUILT A HOME IN A PLACE ONLY A REAPER WOULD LOVE.
OR SOMEONE WHO VALUES PRIVACY. WELCOME TO AVERNUS STATION, ARIA -- YOU'RE LIKELY OUR FIRST OUTSIDE VISITOR.
AVERNUS WAS AN EARTHLY LAKE, CONSIDERED THE ENTRANCE TO HADES -- THE REALM GUARDED BY THE MYTHICAL CERBERUS.
IN REALITY, GENERAL MARCUS AGRIPPA MADE A NAVAL BASE FROM IT. AND WE'VE DONE THE SAME, HERE --
-- A STAGING AREA FOR OUR STUDIES IN THIS SECTOR.
BULLSHIT! IT'S A PLACE FOR YOU TO BRING THE REAPER RELICS YOU FIND!
YOU SHOULD ABANDON THIS STATION AND BLOW IT UP! BUT YOU WON'T -- BECAUSE YOU DON'T WANT TO LOSE YOUR WRETCHED TREASURE TROVE!
THE ILLUSIVE MAN KNOWS HIS HISTORY, ARIA. IT'S ONE REASON I TRUST HIS JUDGMENT, ABOVE ALL OTHERS. HE SAYS THE STORM IS COMING --
-- SO WE HAVE TO KNOW OUR ENEMIES!

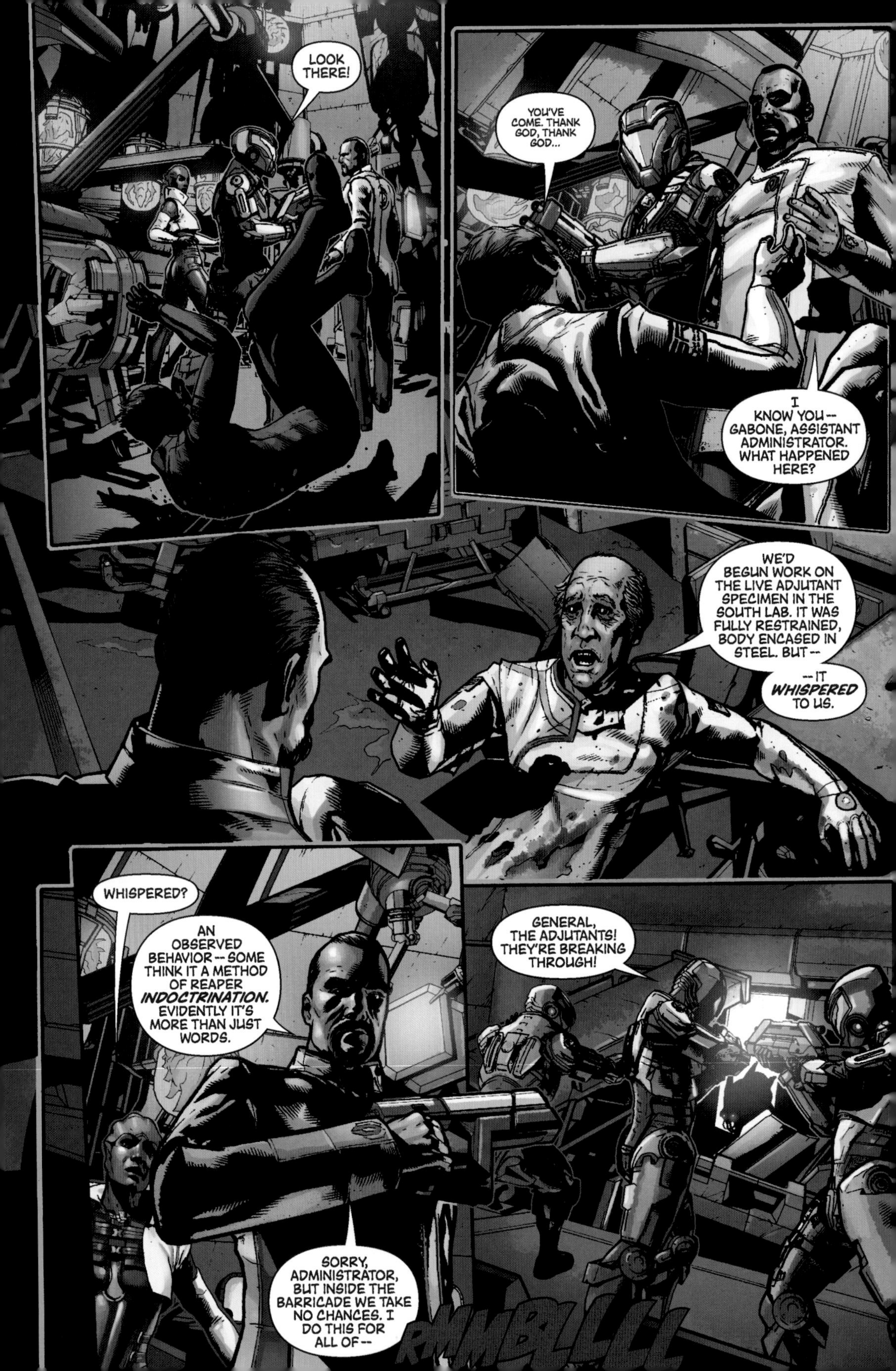
LOOK THERE!
YOU'VE COME. THANK GOD, THANK GOD...
I KNOW YOU -- GABONE, ASSISTANT ADMINISTRATOR. WHAT HAPPENED HERE?
WE'D BEGUN WORK ON THE LIVE ADJUTANT SPECIMEN IN THE SOUTH LAB. IT WAS FULLY RESTRAINED, BODY ENCASED IN STEEL. BUT --
-- IT *WHISPERED* TO US.
WHISPERED?
AN OBSERVED BEHAVIOR -- SOME THINK IT A METHOD OF REAPER *INDOCTRINATION.* EVIDENTLY IT'S MORE THAN JUST WORDS.
SORRY, ADMINISTRATOR, BUT INSIDE THE BARRICADE WE TAKE NO CHANCES. I DO THIS FOR ALL OF --
GENERAL, THE ADJUTANTS! THEY'RE BREAKING THROUGH!
RMMBLLL

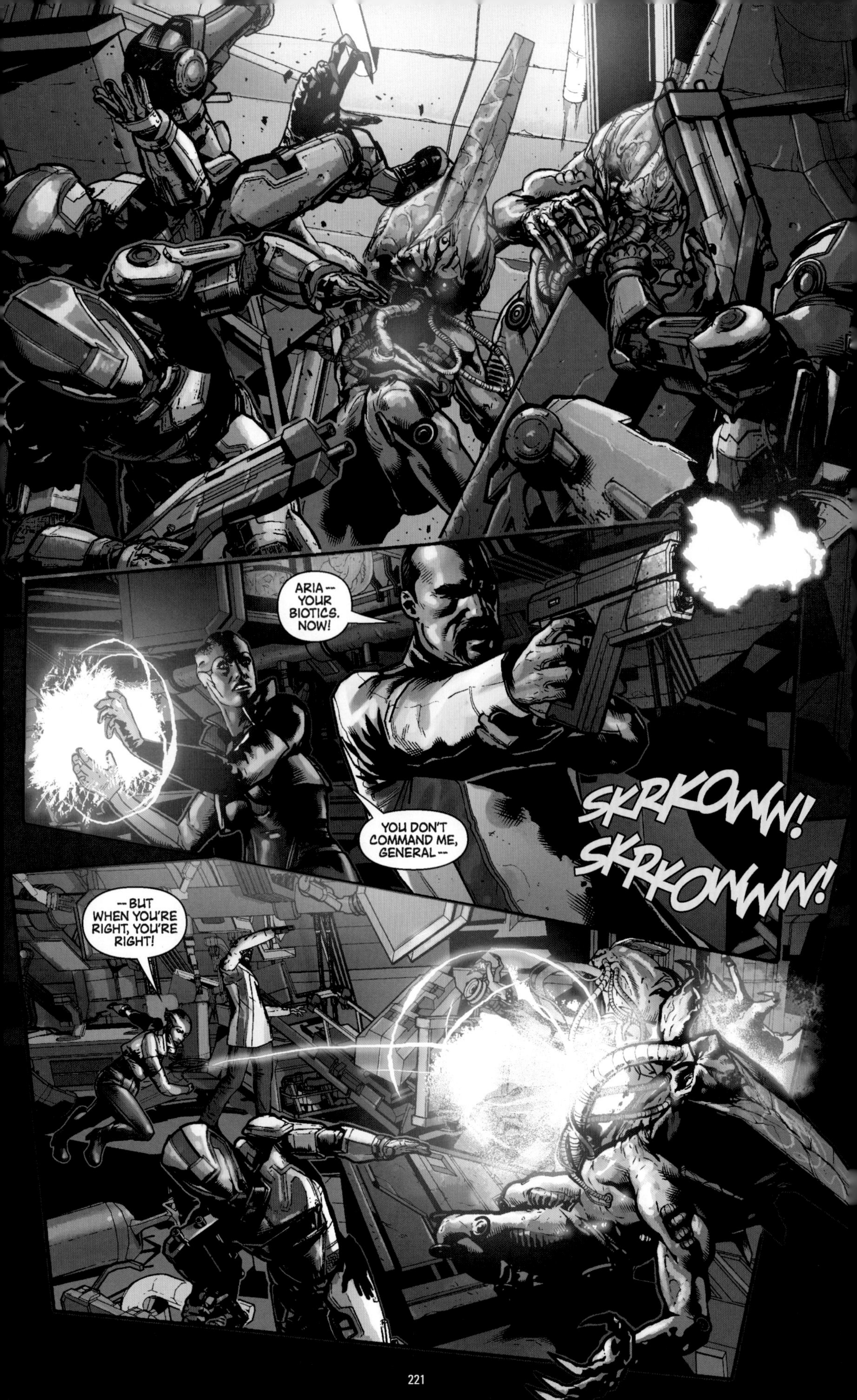
ARIA -- YOUR BIOTICS. NOW!
YOU DON'T COMMAND ME, GENERAL --
SKRKOWW! SKRKOWWW!
-- BUT WHEN YOU'RE RIGHT, YOU'RE RIGHT!

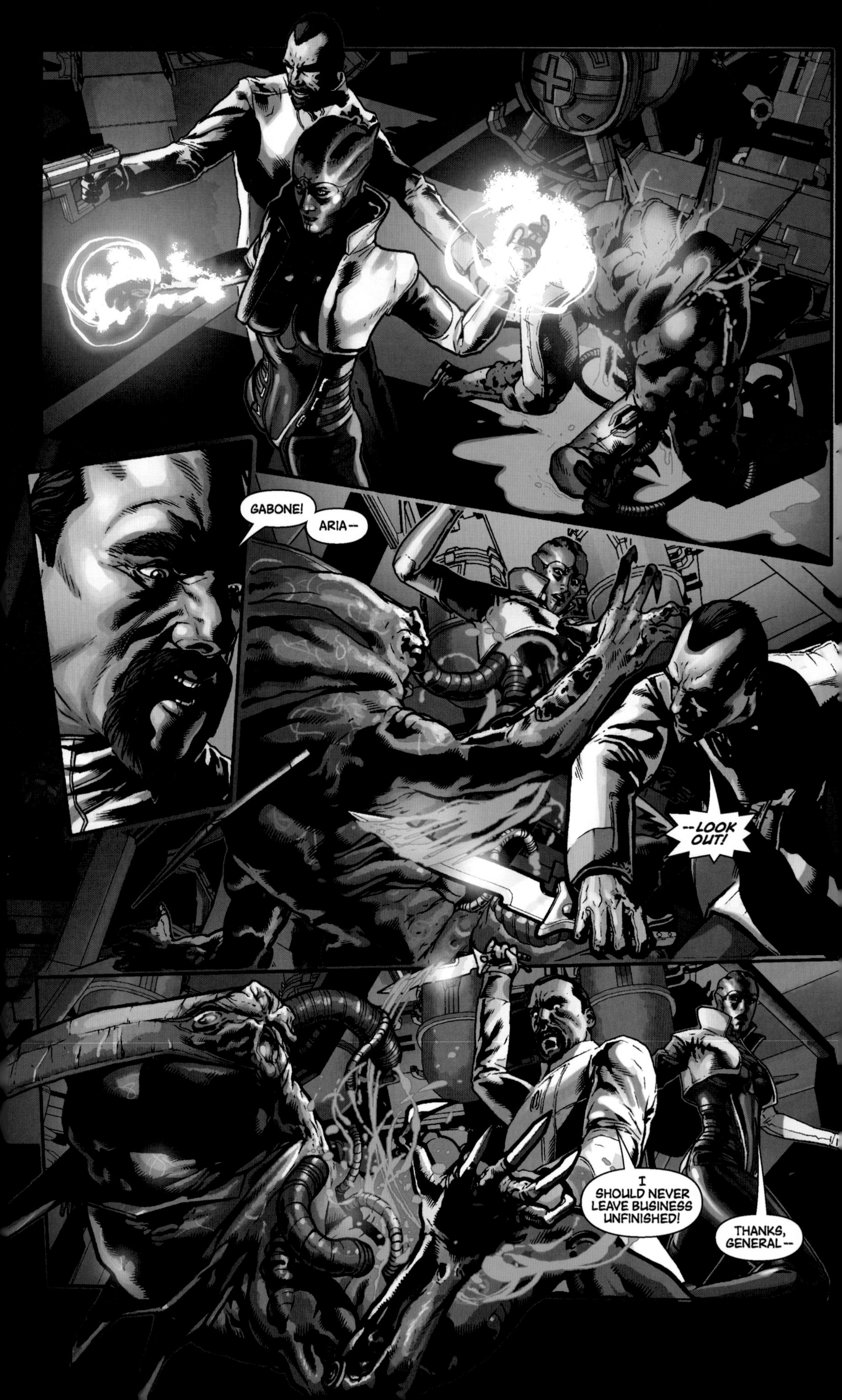
GABONE!
ARIA--
--LOOK OUT!
I SHOULD NEVER LEAVE BUSINESS UNFINISHED!
THANKS, GENERAL--

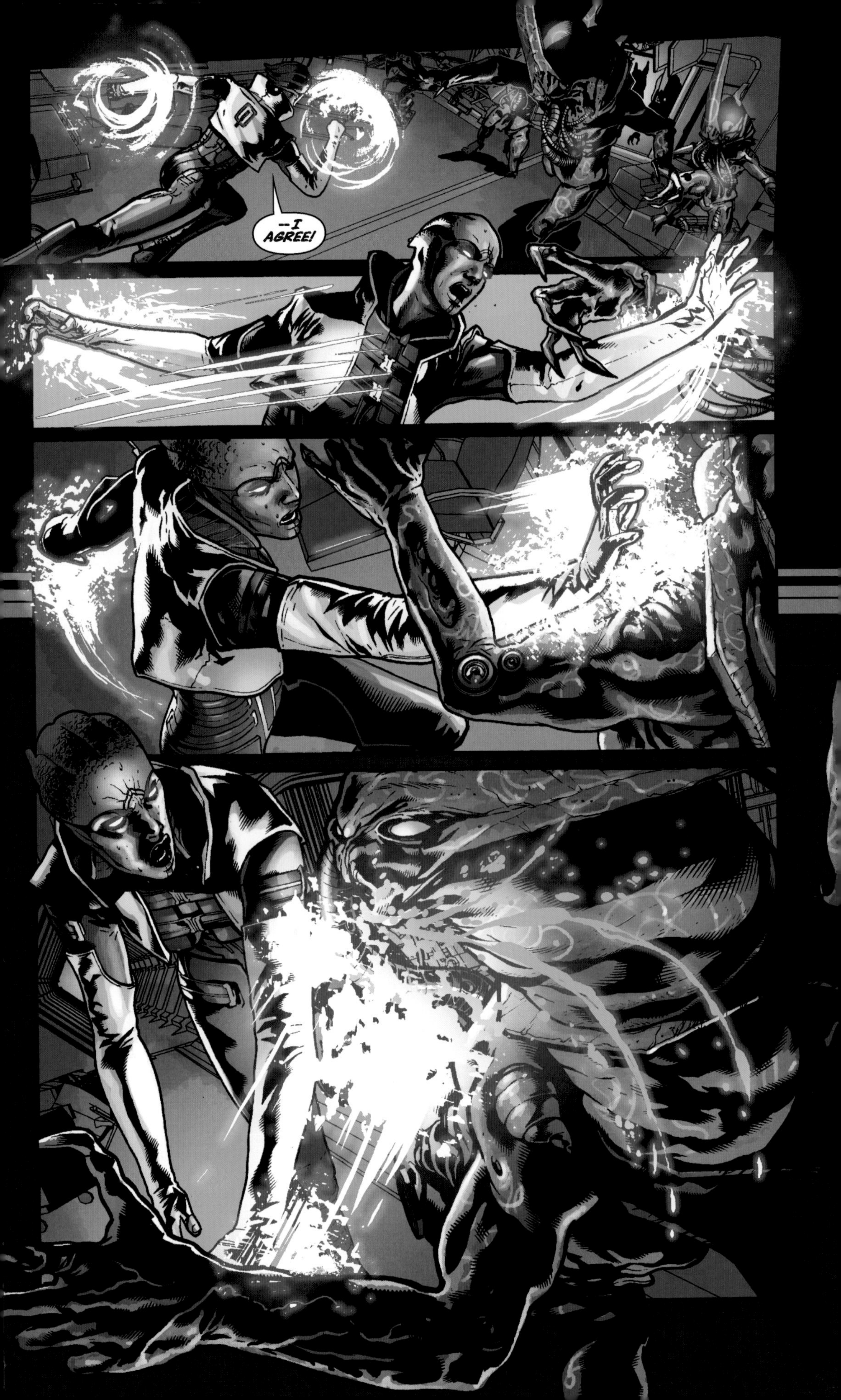
--I AGREE!

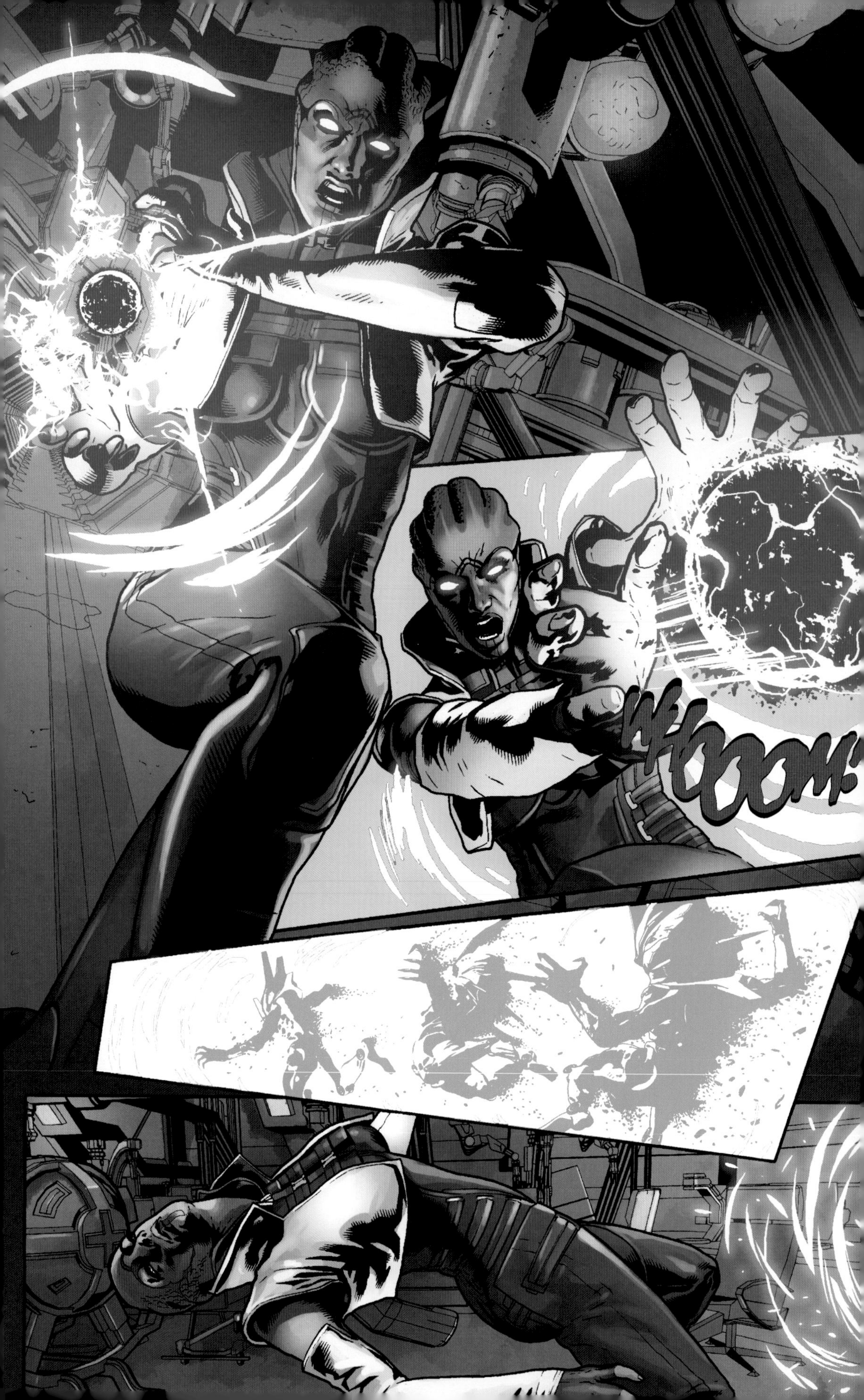
WHOOOM!

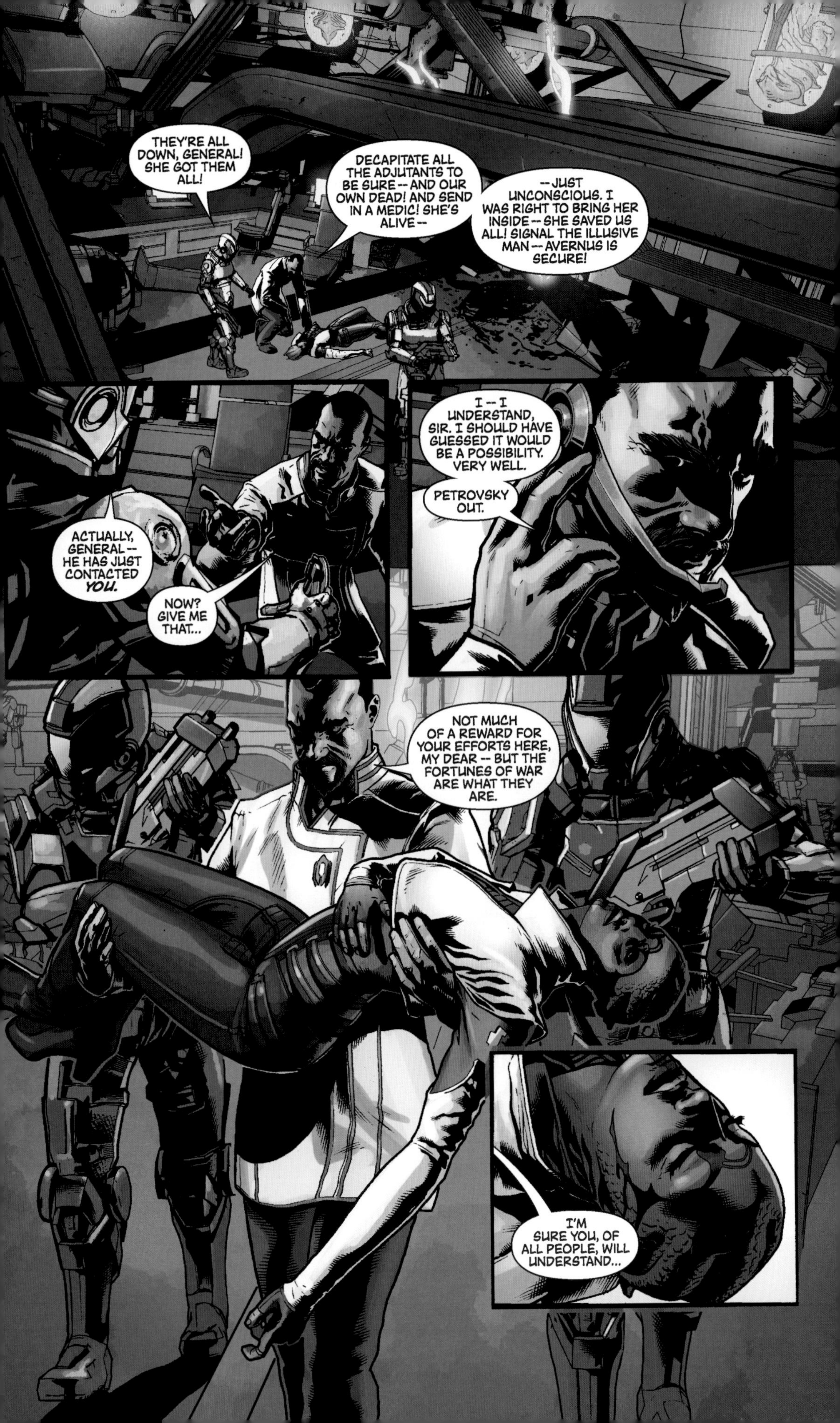
THEY'RE ALL DOWN, GENERAL! SHE GOT THEM ALL!
DECAPITATE ALL THE ADJUTANTS TO BE SURE -- AND OUR OWN DEAD! AND SEND IN A MEDIC! SHE'S ALIVE --
-- JUST UNCONSCIOUS. I WAS RIGHT TO BRING HER INSIDE -- SHE SAVED US ALL! SIGNAL THE ILLUSIVE MAN -- AVERNUS IS SECURE!
ACTUALLY, GENERAL -- HE HAS JUST CONTACTED *YOU.*
NOW? GIVE ME THAT...
I -- I UNDERSTAND, SIR. I SHOULD HAVE GUESSED IT WOULD BE A POSSIBILITY. VERY WELL.
PETROVSKY OUT.
NOT MUCH OF A REWARD FOR YOUR EFFORTS HERE, MY DEAR -- BUT THE FORTUNES OF WAR ARE WHAT THEY ARE.
I'M SURE YOU, OF ALL PEOPLE, WILL UNDERSTAND...

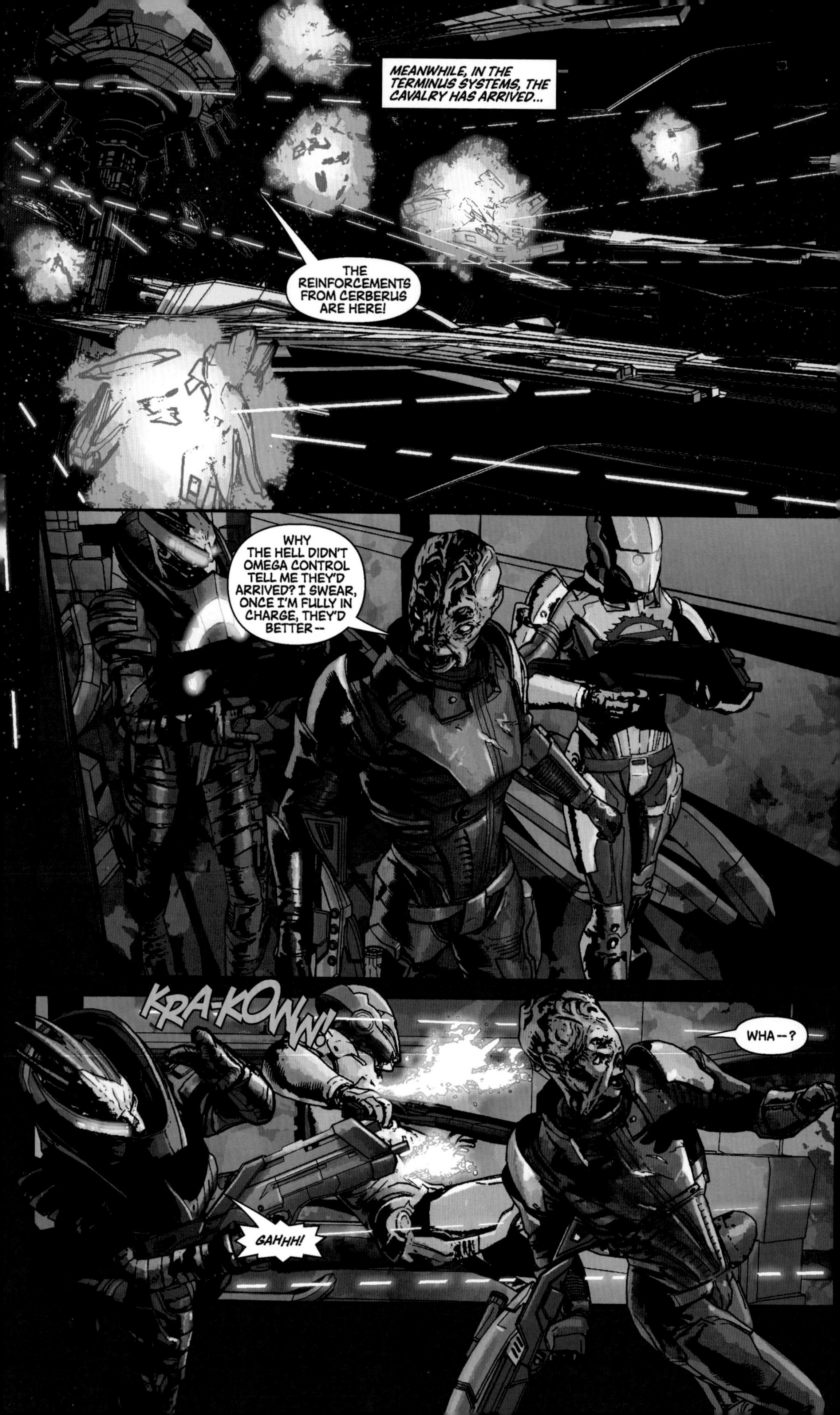
MEANWHILE, IN THE TERMINUS SYSTEMS, THE CAVALRY HAS ARRIVED...
THE REINFORCEMENTS FROM CERBERUS ARE HERE!
WHY THE HELL DIDN'T OMEGA CONTROL TELL ME THEY'D ARRIVED? I SWEAR, ONCE I'M FULLY IN CHARGE, THEY'D BETTER--
KRA-KOWW!
WHA--?
GAHHH!

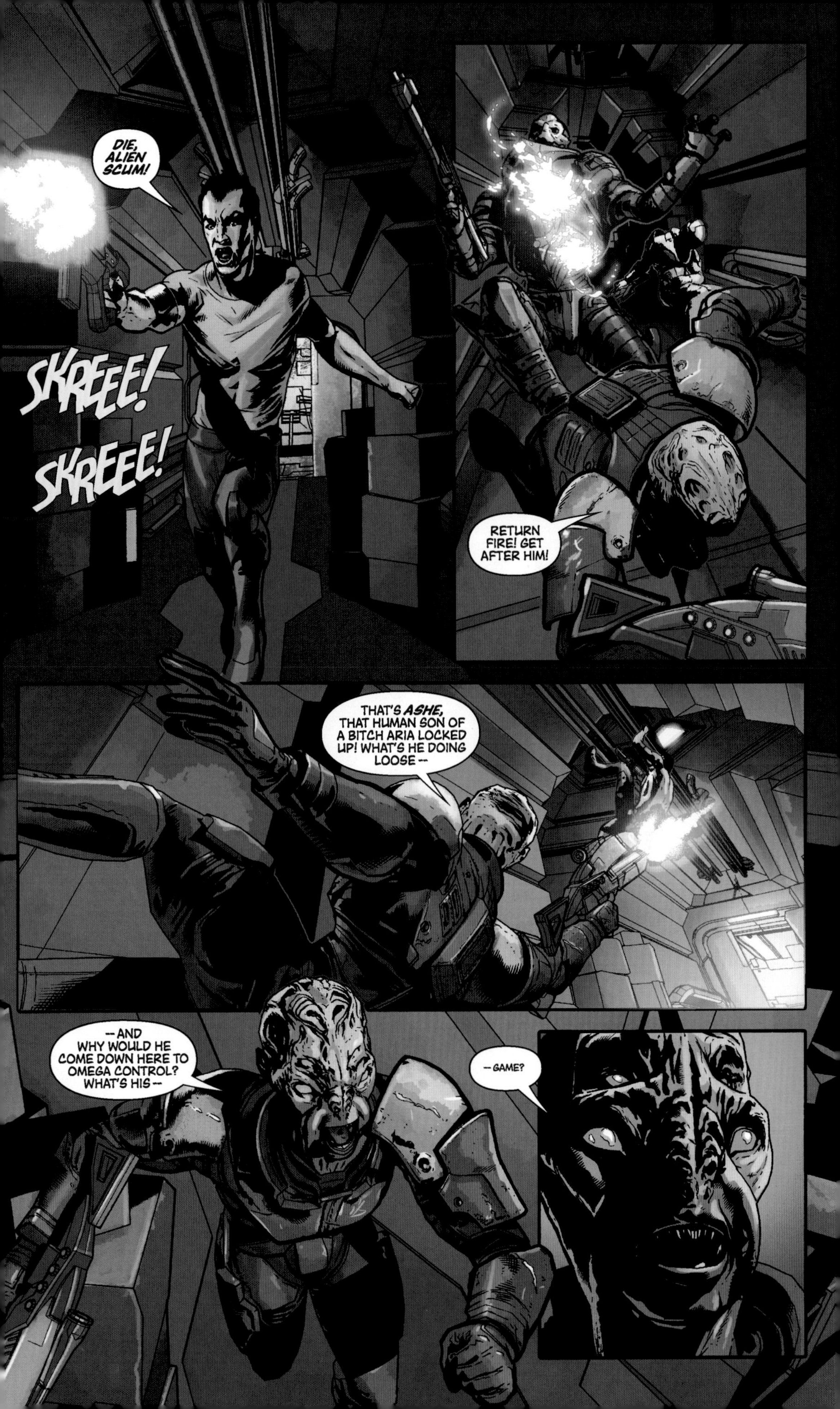
DIE, ALIEN SCUM!
SKREEE!
SKREEE!
RETURN FIRE! GET AFTER HIM!
THAT'S ASHE, THAT HUMAN SON OF A BITCH ARIA LOCKED UP! WHAT'S HE DOING LOOSE --
-- AND WHY WOULD HE COME DOWN HERE TO OMEGA CONTROL? WHAT'S HIS --
-- GAME?

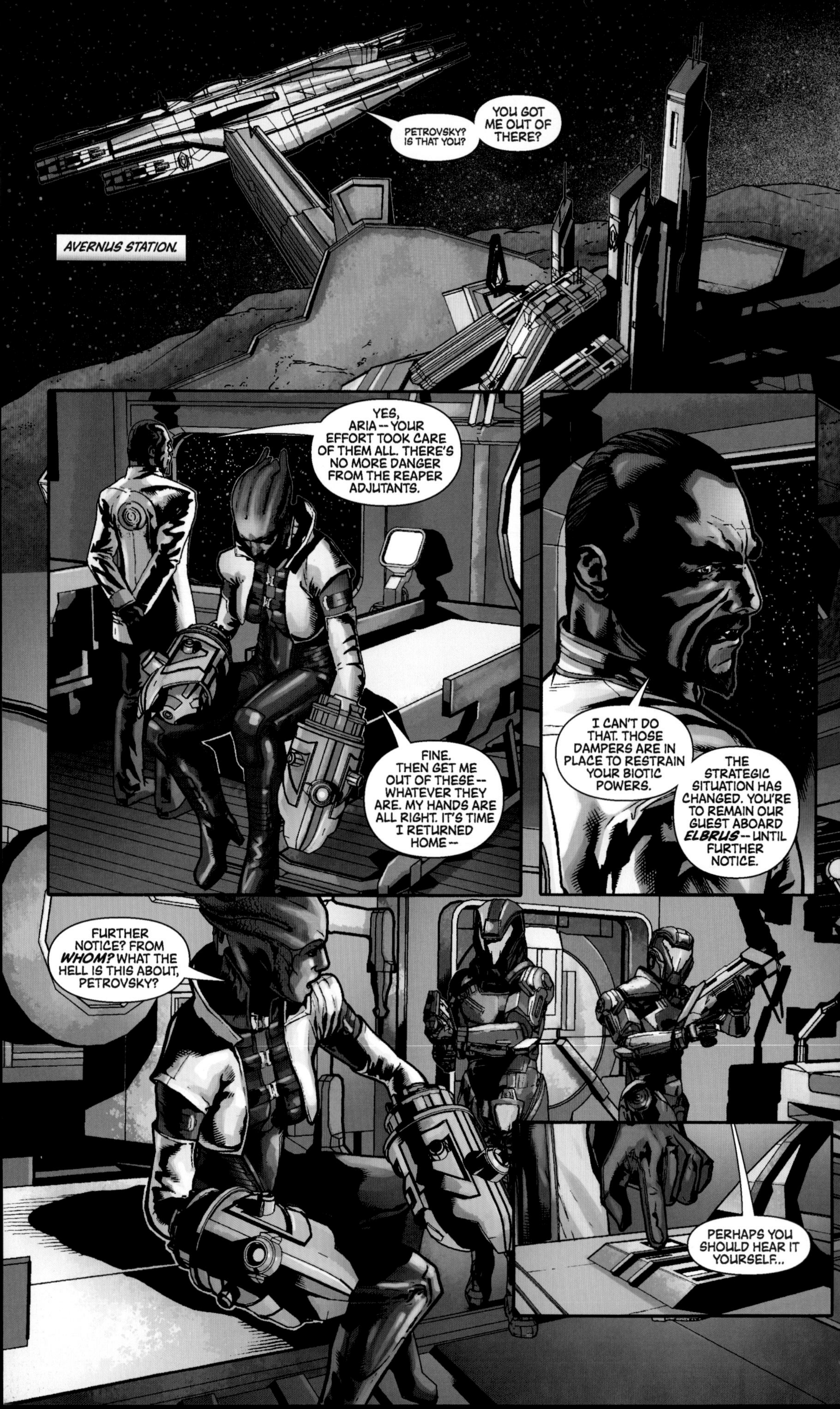
PETROVSKY? IS THAT YOU?
YOU GOT ME OUT OF THERE?
AVERNUS STATION.
YES, ARIA -- YOUR EFFORT TOOK CARE OF THEM ALL. THERE'S NO MORE DANGER FROM THE REAPER ADJUTANTS.
FINE. THEN GET ME OUT OF THESE -- WHATEVER THEY ARE. MY HANDS ARE ALL RIGHT. IT'S TIME I RETURNED HOME --
I CAN'T DO THAT. THOSE DAMPERS ARE IN PLACE TO RESTRAIN YOUR BIOTIC POWERS.
THE STRATEGIC SITUATION HAS CHANGED. YOU'RE TO REMAIN OUR GUEST ABOARD *ELBRUS* -- UNTIL FURTHER NOTICE.
FURTHER NOTICE? FROM *WHOM?* WHAT THE HELL IS THIS ABOUT, PETROVSKY?
PERHAPS YOU SHOULD HEAR IT YOURSELF...

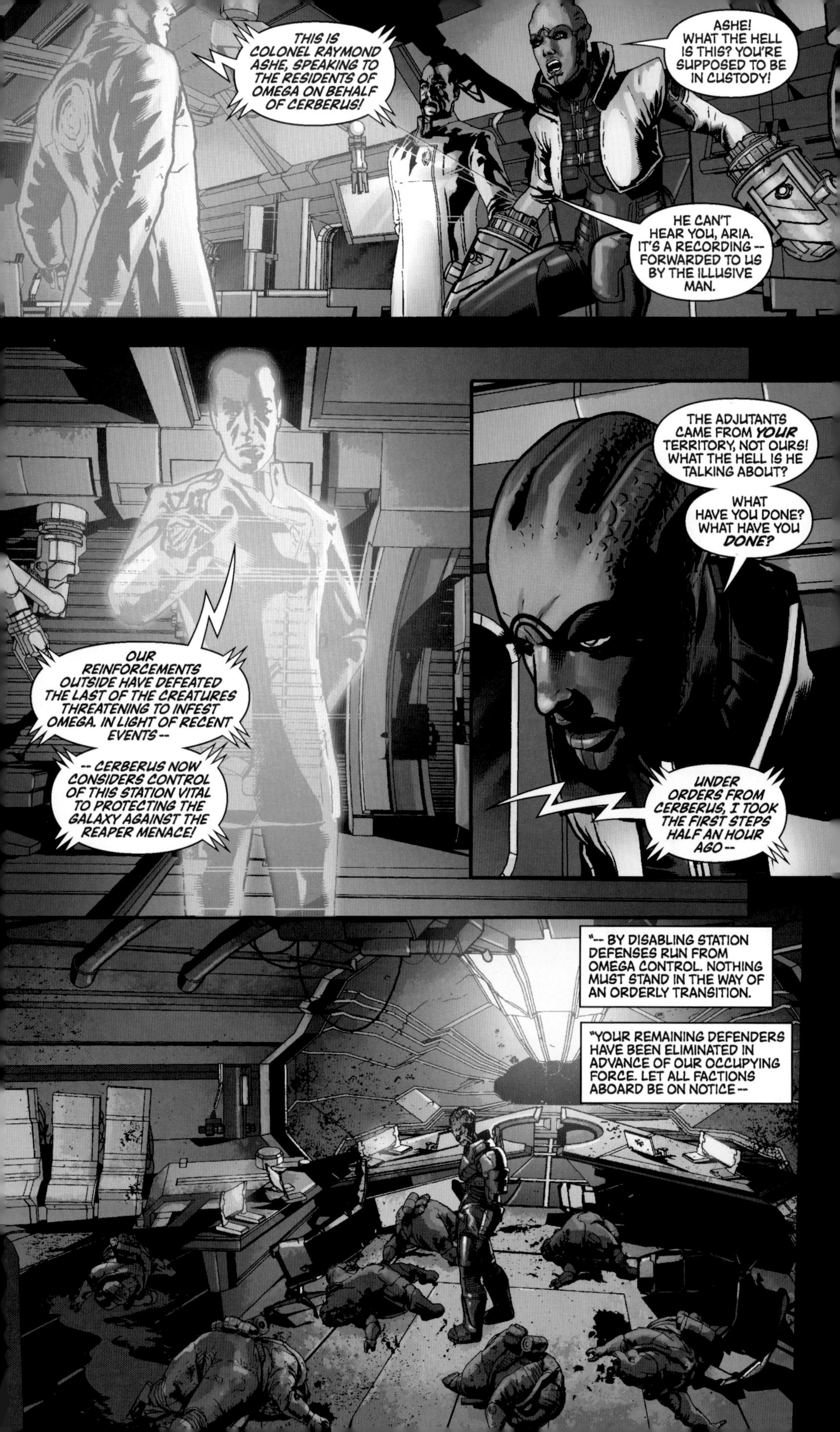
THIS IS COLONEL RAYMOND ASHE, SPEAKING TO THE RESIDENTS OF OMEGA ON BEHALF OF CERBERUS!
ASHE! WHAT THE HELL IS THIS? YOU'RE SUPPOSED TO BE IN CUSTODY!
HE CAN'T HEAR YOU, ARIA. IT'S A RECORDING -- FORWARDED TO US BY THE ILLUSIVE MAN.
OUR REINFORCEMENTS OUTSIDE HAVE DEFEATED THE LAST OF THE CREATURES THREATENING TO INFEST OMEGA. IN LIGHT OF RECENT EVENTS --
-- CERBERUS NOW CONSIDERS CONTROL OF THIS STATION VITAL TO PROTECTING THE GALAXY AGAINST THE REAPER MENACE!
THE ADJUTANTS CAME FROM *YOUR* TERRITORY, NOT OURS! WHAT THE HELL IS HE TALKING ABOUT?
WHAT HAVE YOU DONE? WHAT HAVE YOU *DONE?*
UNDER ORDERS FROM CERBERUS, I TOOK THE FIRST STEPS HALF AN HOUR AGO --
"-- BY DISABLING STATION DEFENSES RUN FROM OMEGA CONTROL. NOTHING MUST STAND IN THE WAY OF AN ORDERLY TRANSITION.
"YOUR REMAINING DEFENDERS HAVE BEEN ELIMINATED IN ADVANCE OF OUR OCCUPYING FORCE. LET ALL FACTIONS ABOARD BE ON NOTICE --

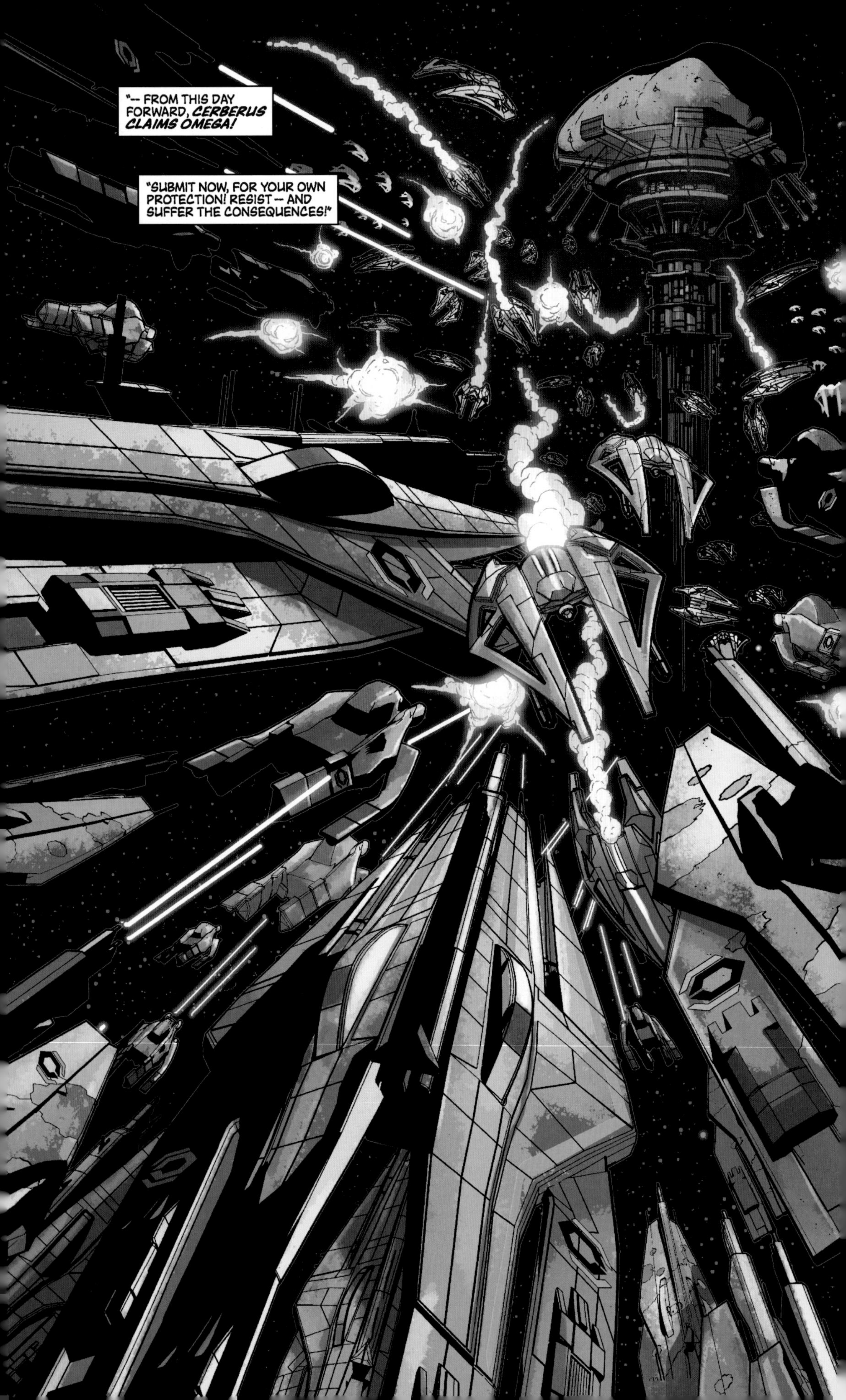
"-- FROM THIS DAY FORWARD, CERBERUS CLAIMS OMEGA!
"SUBMIT NOW, FOR YOUR OWN PROTECTION! RESIST -- AND SUFFER THE CONSEQUENCES!"

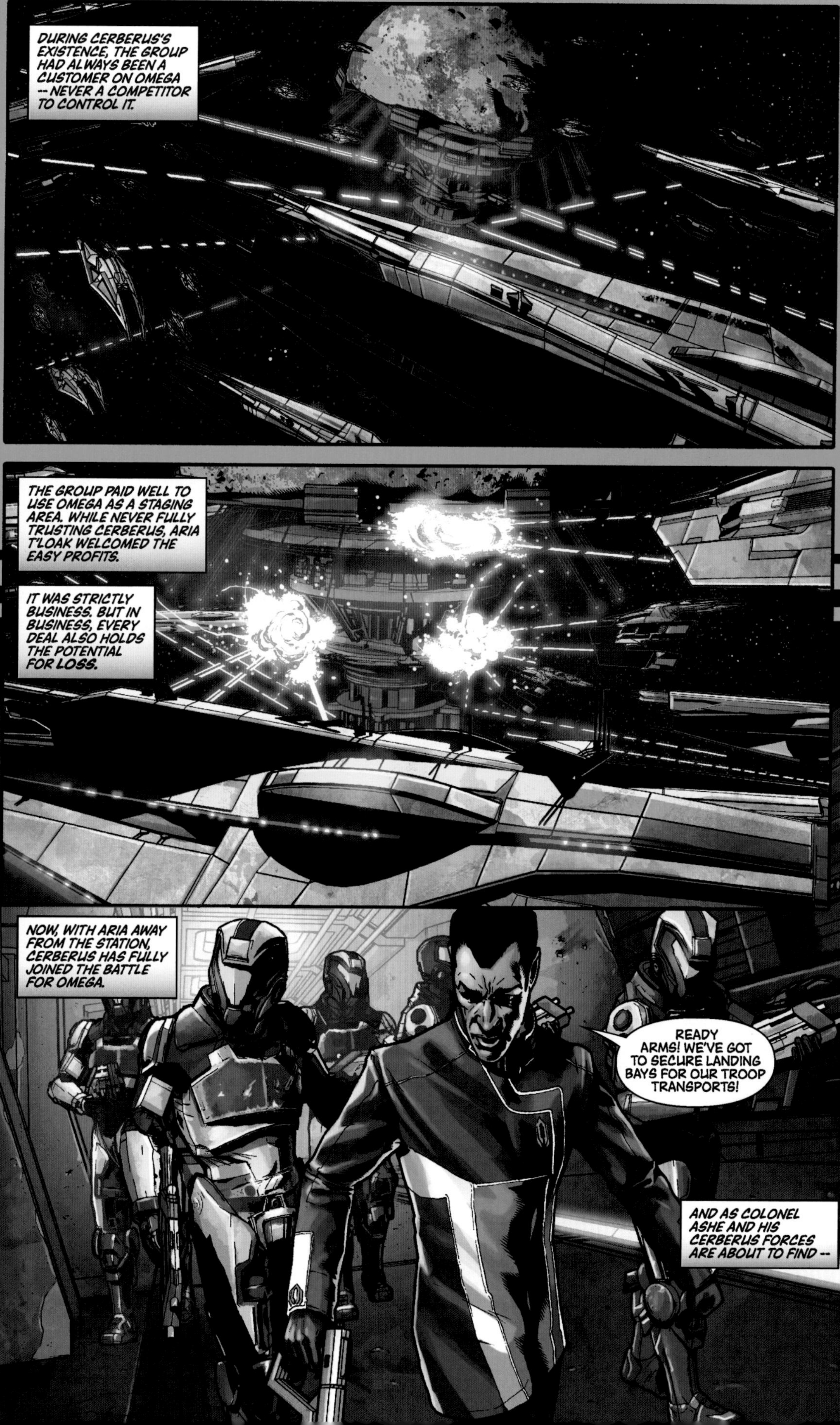
DURING CERBERUS'S EXISTENCE, THE GROUP HAD ALWAYS BEEN A CUSTOMER ON OMEGA -- NEVER A COMPETITOR TO CONTROL IT.
THE GROUP PAID WELL TO USE OMEGA AS A STAGING AREA. WHILE NEVER FULLY TRUSTING CERBERUS, ARIA T'LOAK WELCOMED THE EASY PROFITS.
IT WAS STRICTLY BUSINESS. BUT IN BUSINESS, EVERY DEAL ALSO HOLDS THE POTENTIAL FOR LOSS.
NOW, WITH ARIA AWAY FROM THE STATION, CERBERUS HAS FULLY JOINED THE BATTLE FOR OMEGA.
READY ARMS! WE'VE GOT TO SECURE LANDING BAYS FOR OUR TROOP TRANSPORTS!
AND AS COLONEL ASHE AND HIS CERBERUS FORCES ARE ABOUT TO FIND --

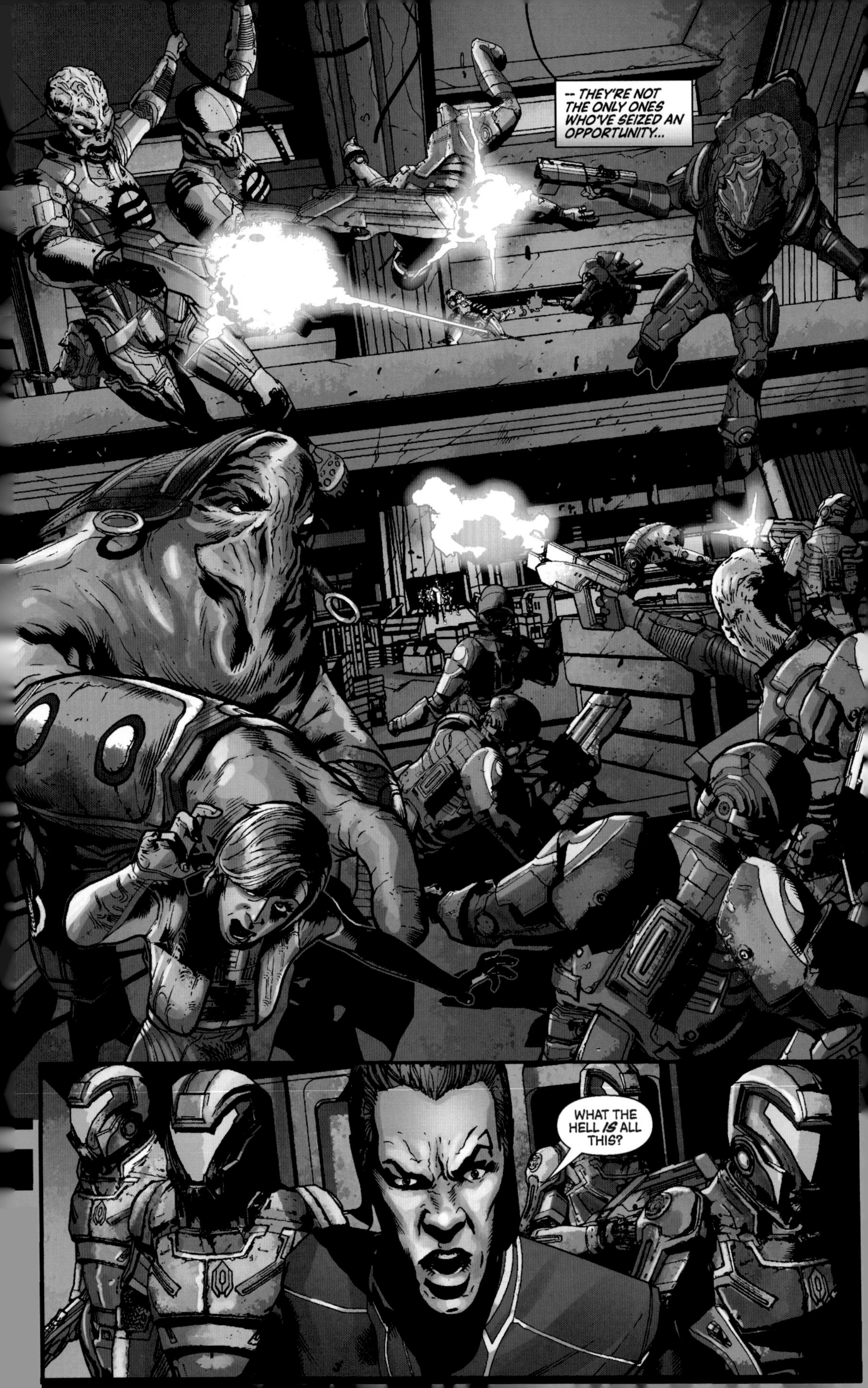
-- THEY'RE NOT THE ONLY ONES WHO'VE SEIZED AN OPPORTUNITY...
WHAT THE HELL *IS* ALL THIS?

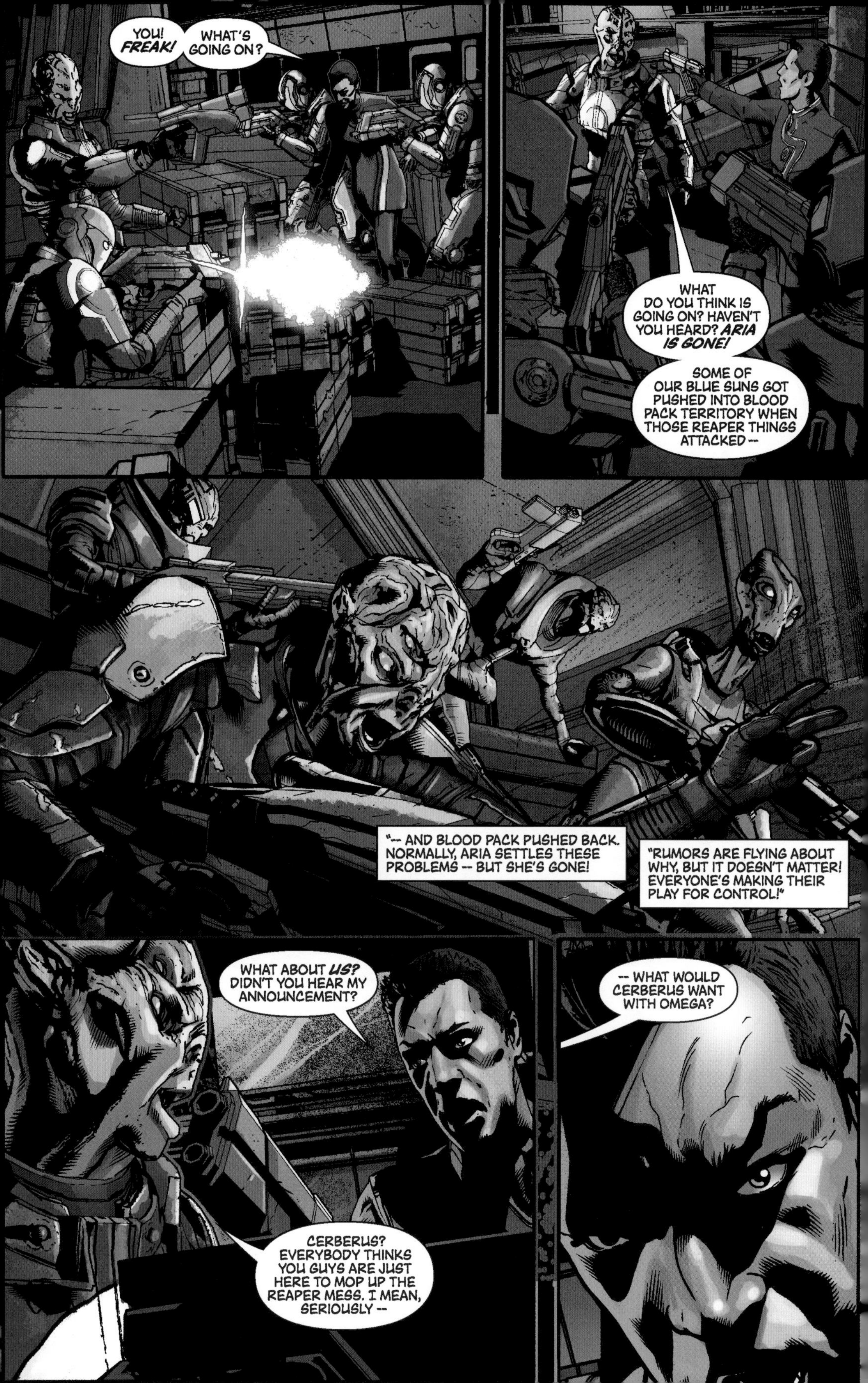
YOU! *FREAK!*
WHAT'S GOING ON?
WHAT DO YOU THINK IS GOING ON? HAVEN'T YOU HEARD? *ARIA IS GONE!*
SOME OF OUR BLUE SUNS GOT PUSHED INTO BLOOD PACK TERRITORY WHEN THOSE REAPER THINGS ATTACKED --
"-- AND BLOOD PACK PUSHED BACK. NORMALLY, ARIA SETTLES THESE PROBLEMS -- BUT SHE'S GONE!
"RUMORS ARE FLYING ABOUT WHY, BUT IT DOESN'T MATTER! EVERYONE'S MAKING THEIR PLAY FOR CONTROL!"
WHAT ABOUT *US?* DIDN'T YOU HEAR MY ANNOUNCEMENT?
CERBERUS? EVERYBODY THINKS YOU GUYS ARE JUST HERE TO MOP UP THE REAPER MESS. I MEAN, SERIOUSLY --
-- WHAT WOULD CERBERUS WANT WITH OMEGA?

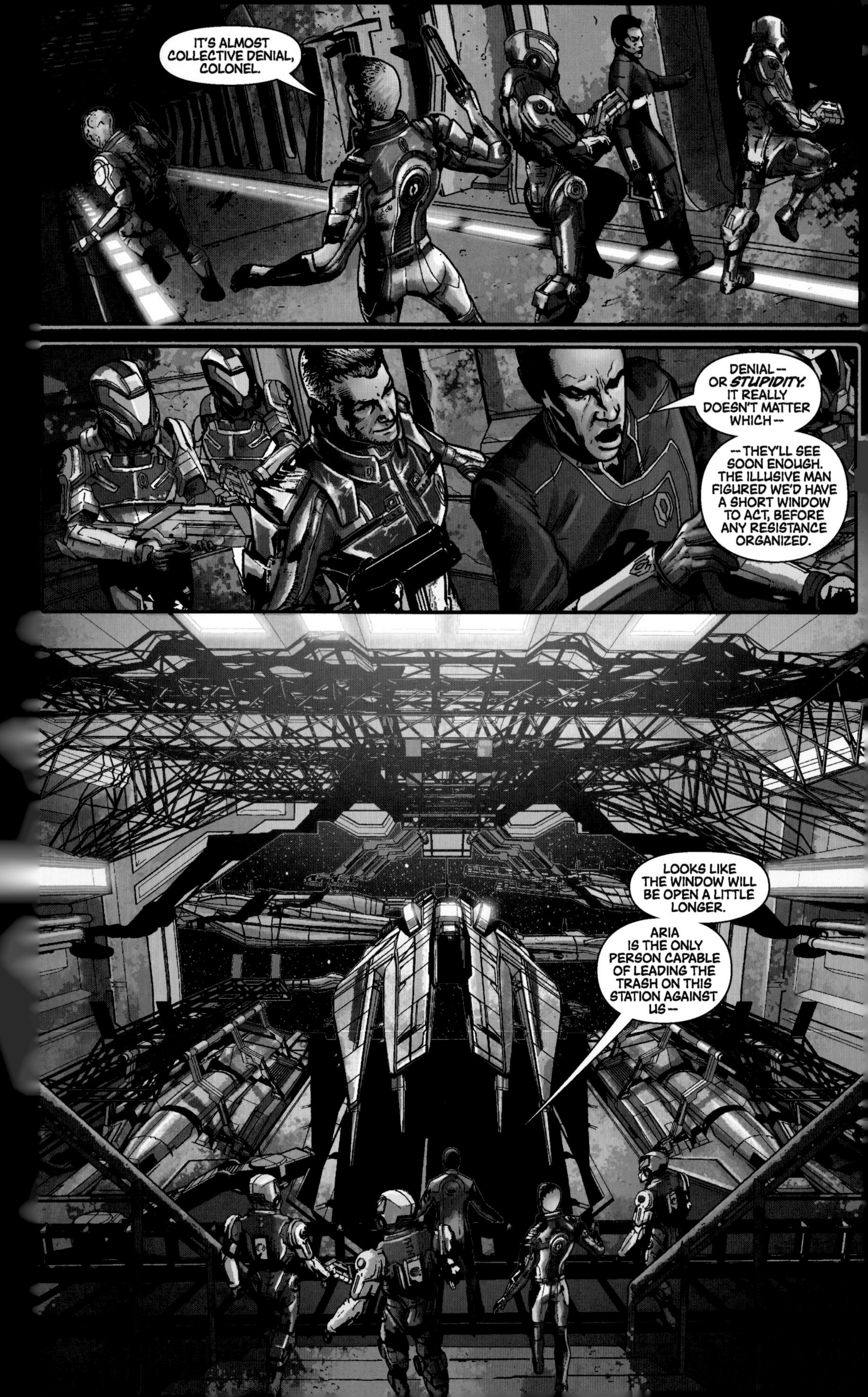
IT'S ALMOST COLLECTIVE DENIAL, COLONEL.
DENIAL -- OR STUPIDITY. IT REALLY DOESN'T MATTER WHICH --
-- THEY'LL SEE SOON ENOUGH. THE ILLUSIVE MAN FIGURED WE'D HAVE A SHORT WINDOW TO ACT, BEFORE ANY RESISTANCE ORGANIZED.
LOOKS LIKE THE WINDOW WILL BE OPEN A LITTLE LONGER.
ARIA IS THE ONLY PERSON CAPABLE OF LEADING THE TRASH ON THIS STATION AGAINST US --

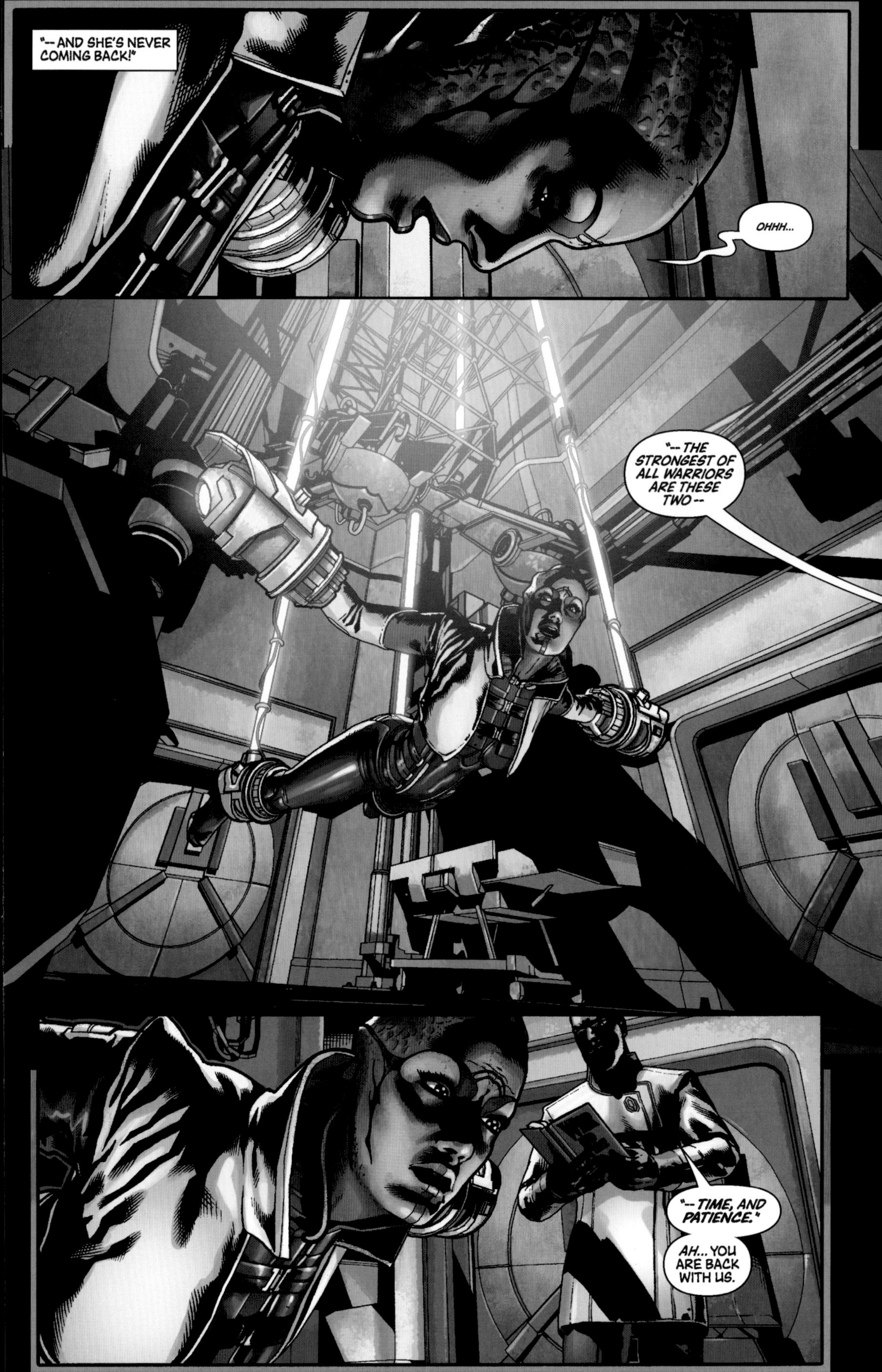
"-- AND SHE'S NEVER COMING BACK!"
OHHH...
"-- THE STRONGEST OF ALL WARRIORS ARE THESE TWO --
"-- TIME, AND PATIENCE."
AH... YOU ARE BACK WITH US.

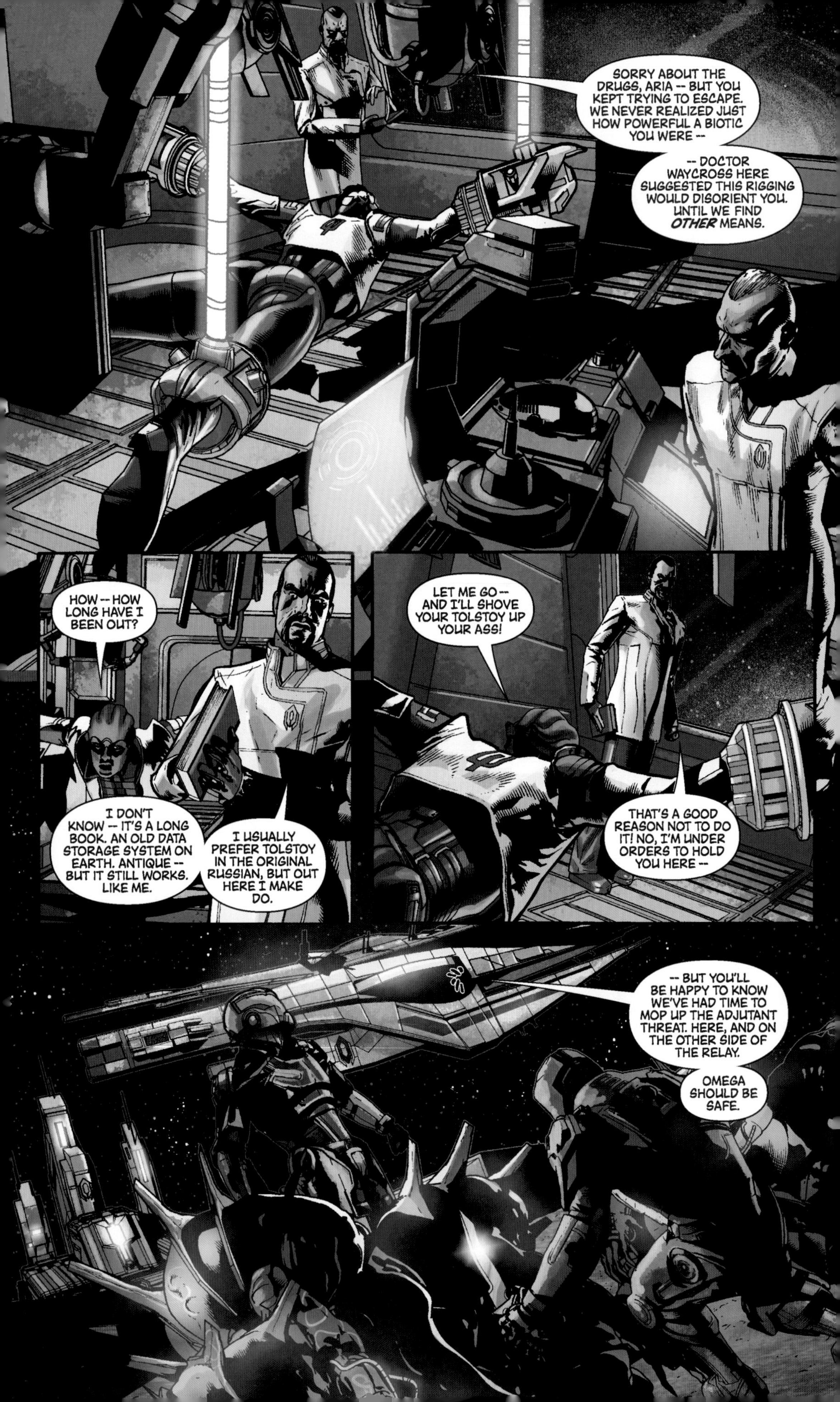

SORRY ABOUT THE DRUGS, ARIA -- BUT YOU KEPT TRYING TO ESCAPE. WE NEVER REALIZED JUST HOW POWERFUL A BIOTIC YOU WERE --
-- DOCTOR WAYCROSS HERE SUGGESTED THIS RIGGING WOULD DISORIENT YOU. UNTIL WE FIND *OTHER* MEANS.
HOW -- HOW LONG HAVE I BEEN OUT?
I DON'T KNOW -- IT'S A LONG BOOK. AN OLD DATA STORAGE SYSTEM ON EARTH. ANTIQUE -- BUT IT STILL WORKS. LIKE ME.
I USUALLY PREFER TOLSTOY IN THE ORIGINAL RUSSIAN, BUT OUT HERE I MAKE DO.
LET ME GO -- AND I'LL SHOVE YOUR TOLSTOY UP YOUR ASS!
THAT'S A GOOD REASON NOT TO DO IT! NO, I'M UNDER ORDERS TO HOLD YOU HERE --
-- BUT YOU'LL BE HAPPY TO KNOW WE'VE HAD TIME TO MOP UP THE ADJUTANT THREAT. HERE, AND ON THE OTHER SIDE OF THE RELAY.
OMEGA SHOULD BE SAFE.

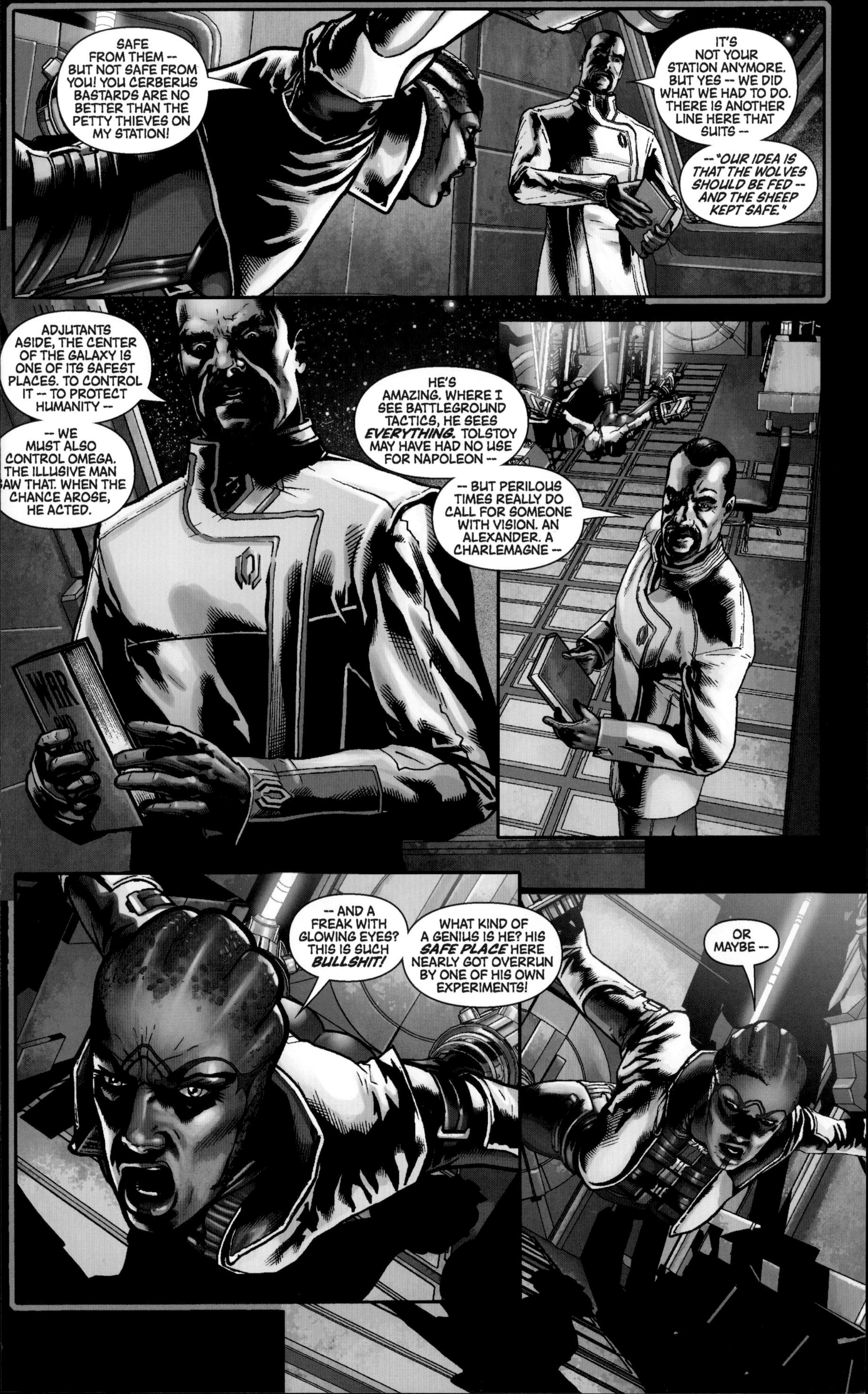
SAFE FROM THEM -- BUT NOT SAFE FROM YOU! YOU CERBERUS BASTARDS ARE NO BETTER THAN THE PETTY THIEVES ON MY STATION!
IT'S NOT YOUR STATION ANYMORE. BUT YES -- WE DID WHAT WE HAD TO DO. THERE IS ANOTHER LINE HERE THAT SUITS --
-- "OUR IDEA IS THAT THE WOLVES SHOULD BE FED -- AND THE SHEEP KEPT SAFE."
ADJUTANTS ASIDE, THE CENTER OF THE GALAXY IS ONE OF ITS SAFEST PLACES. TO CONTROL IT -- TO PROTECT HUMANITY --
-- WE MUST ALSO CONTROL OMEGA. THE ILLUSIVE MAN SAW THAT. WHEN THE CHANCE AROSE, HE ACTED.
HE'S AMAZING. WHERE I SEE BATTLEGROUND TACTICS, HE SEES *EVERYTHING.* TOLSTOY MAY HAVE HAD NO USE FOR NAPOLEON --
-- BUT PERILOUS TIMES REALLY DO CALL FOR SOMEONE WITH VISION. AN ALEXANDER. A CHARLEMAGNE --
-- AND A FREAK WITH GLOWING EYES? THIS IS SUCH *BULLSHIT!*
WHAT KIND OF A GENIUS IS HE? HIS *SAFE PLACE* HERE NEARLY GOT OVERRUN BY ONE OF HIS OWN EXPERIMENTS!
OR MAYBE --

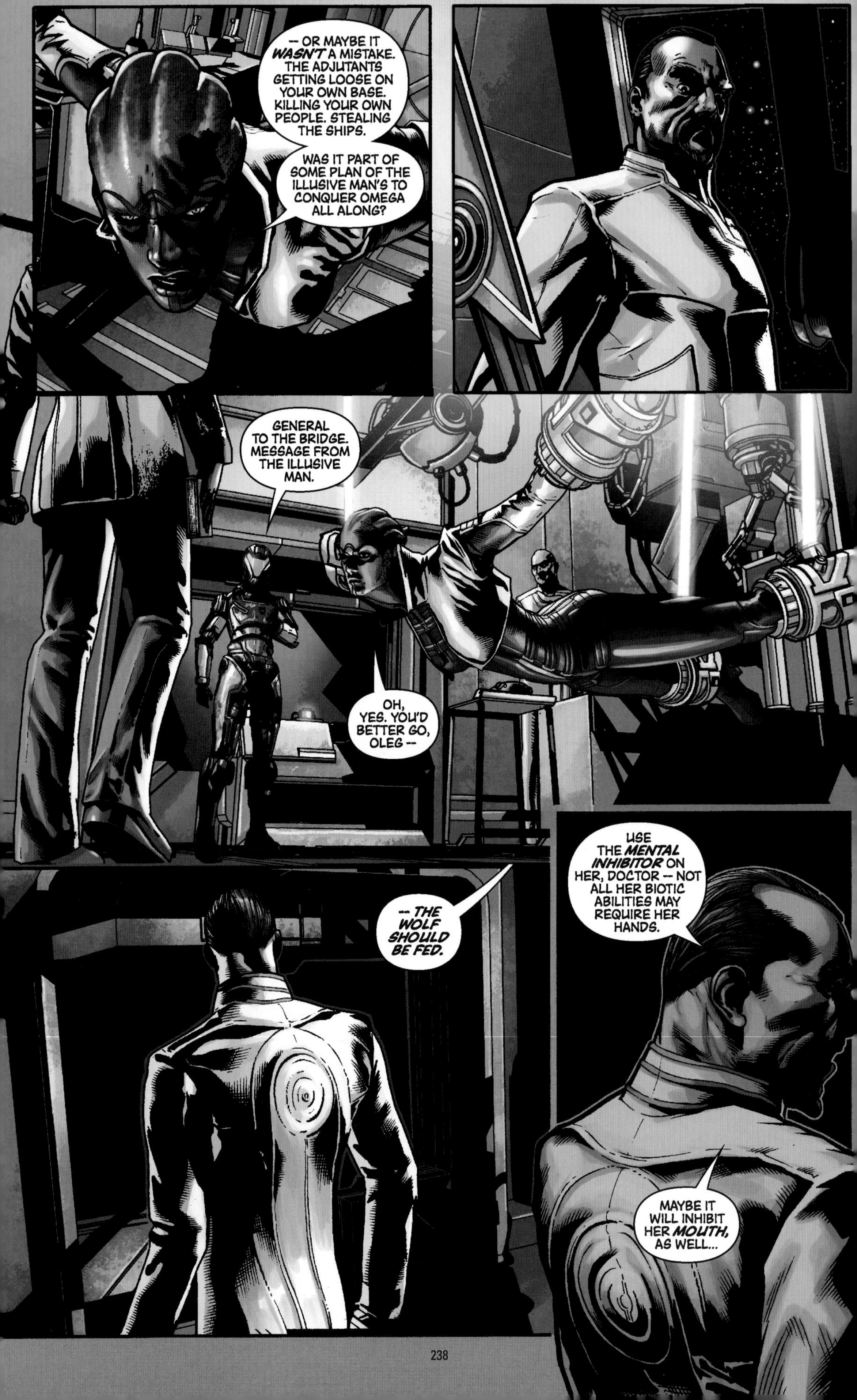
-- OR MAYBE IT WASN'T A MISTAKE. THE ADJUTANTS GETTING LOOSE ON YOUR OWN BASE. KILLING YOUR OWN PEOPLE. STEALING THE SHIPS.
WAS IT PART OF SOME PLAN OF THE ILLUSIVE MAN'S TO CONQUER OMEGA ALL ALONG?
GENERAL TO THE BRIDGE. MESSAGE FROM THE ILLUSIVE MAN.
OH, YES. YOU'D BETTER GO, OLEG --
-- THE WOLF SHOULD BE FED.
USE THE MENTAL INHIBITOR ON HER, DOCTOR -- NOT ALL HER BIOTIC ABILITIES MAY REQUIRE HER HANDS.
MAYBE IT WILL INHIBIT HER MOUTH, AS WELL...

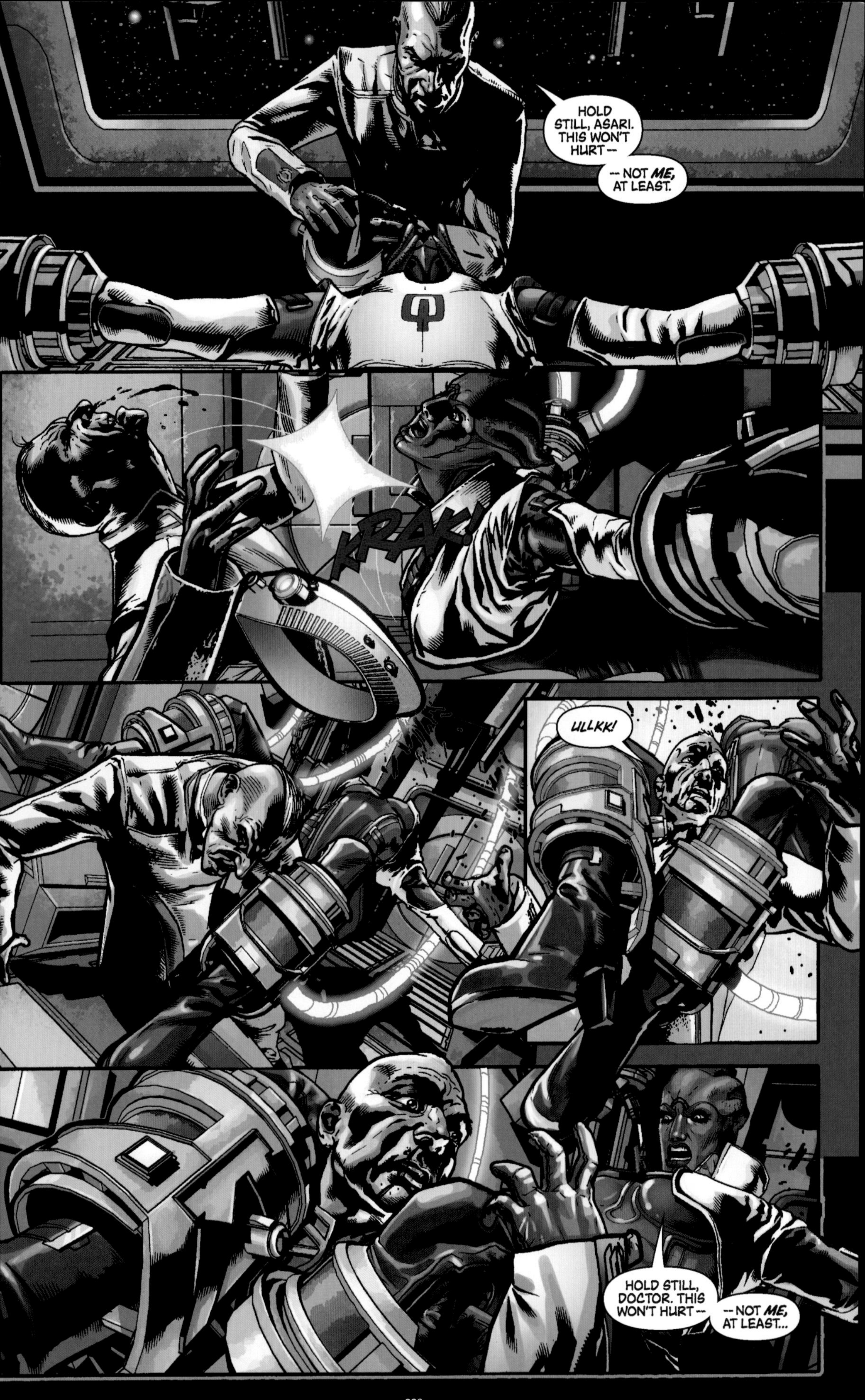
HOLD STILL, ASARI. THIS WON'T HURT --
-- NOT *ME*, AT LEAST.
KRAK!
ULLKK!
HOLD STILL, DOCTOR. THIS WON'T HURT --
-- NOT *ME*, AT LEAST...

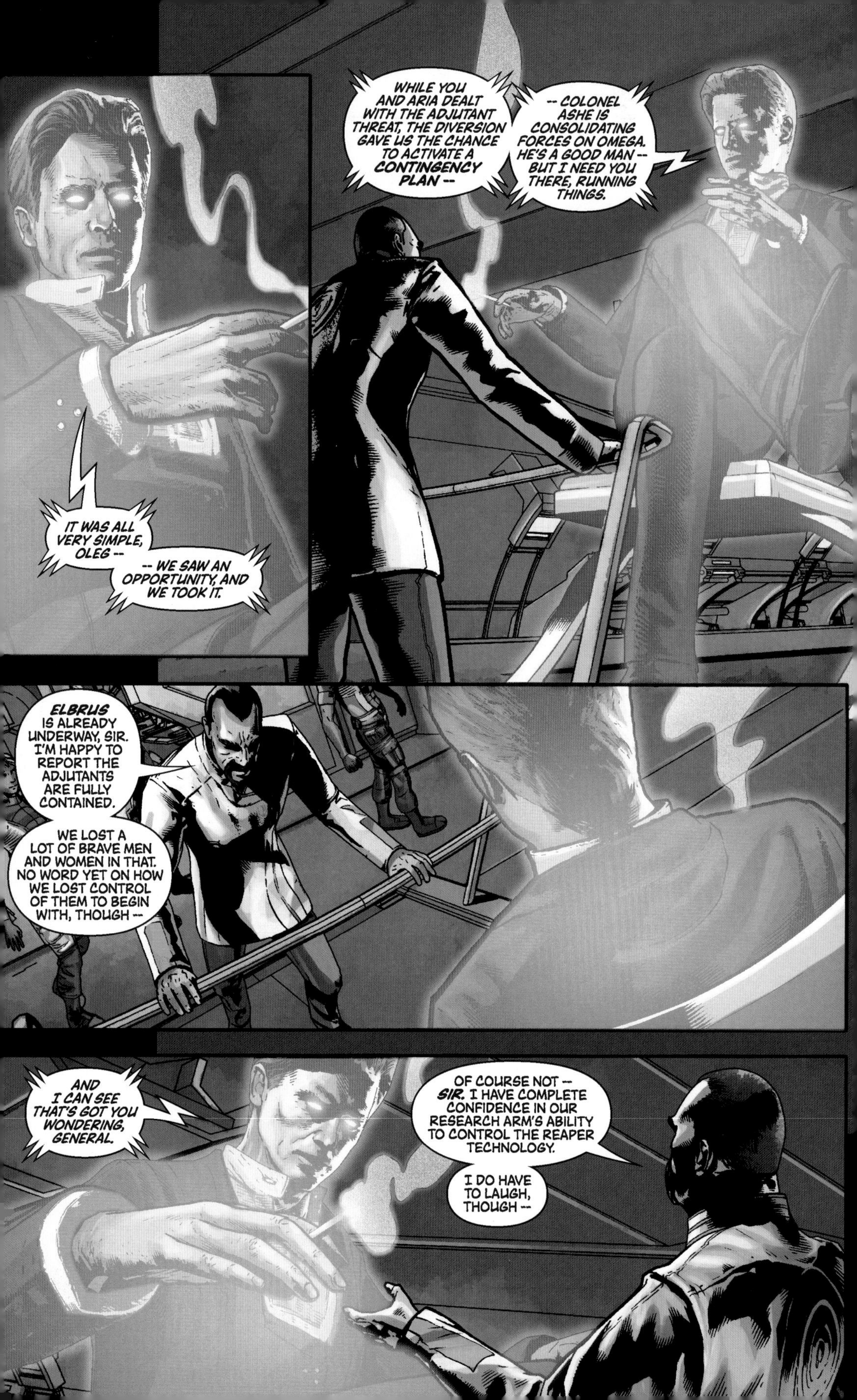
IT WAS ALL VERY SIMPLE, OLEG --
-- WE SAW AN OPPORTUNITY, AND WE TOOK IT.
WHILE YOU AND ARIA DEALT WITH THE ADJUTANT THREAT, THE DIVERSION GAVE US THE CHANCE TO ACTIVATE A CONTINGENCY PLAN --
-- COLONEL ASHE IS CONSOLIDATING FORCES ON OMEGA. HE'S A GOOD MAN -- BUT I NEED YOU THERE, RUNNING THINGS.
ELBRUS IS ALREADY UNDERWAY, SIR. I'M HAPPY TO REPORT THE ADJUTANTS ARE FULLY CONTAINED.
WE LOST A LOT OF BRAVE MEN AND WOMEN IN THAT. NO WORD YET ON HOW WE LOST CONTROL OF THEM TO BEGIN WITH, THOUGH --
AND I CAN SEE THAT'S GOT YOU WONDERING, GENERAL.
OF COURSE NOT -- SIR. I HAVE COMPLETE CONFIDENCE IN OUR RESEARCH ARM'S ABILITY TO CONTROL THE REAPER TECHNOLOGY.
I DO HAVE TO LAUGH, THOUGH --

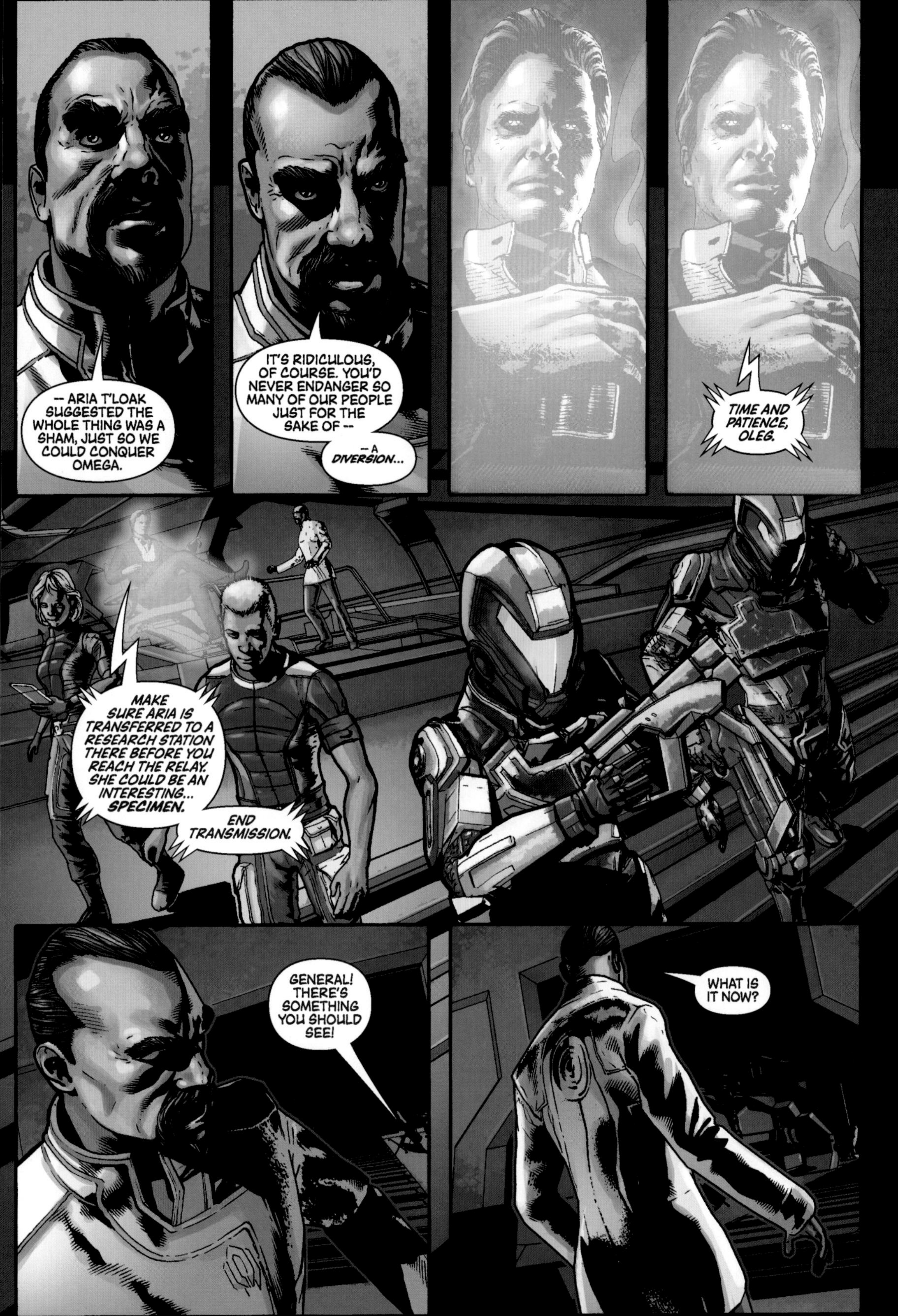
-- ARIA T'LOAK SUGGESTED THE WHOLE THING WAS A SHAM, JUST SO WE COULD CONQUER OMEGA.
IT'S RIDICULOUS, OF COURSE. YOU'D NEVER ENDANGER SO MANY OF OUR PEOPLE JUST FOR THE SAKE OF --
-- A *DIVERSION...*
TIME AND PATIENCE, OLEG.
MAKE SURE ARIA IS TRANSFERRED TO A RESEARCH STATION THERE BEFORE YOU REACH THE RELAY. SHE COULD BE AN INTERESTING... ***SPECIMEN.***
END TRANSMISSION.
GENERAL! THERE'S SOMETHING YOU SHOULD SEE!
WHAT IS IT NOW?

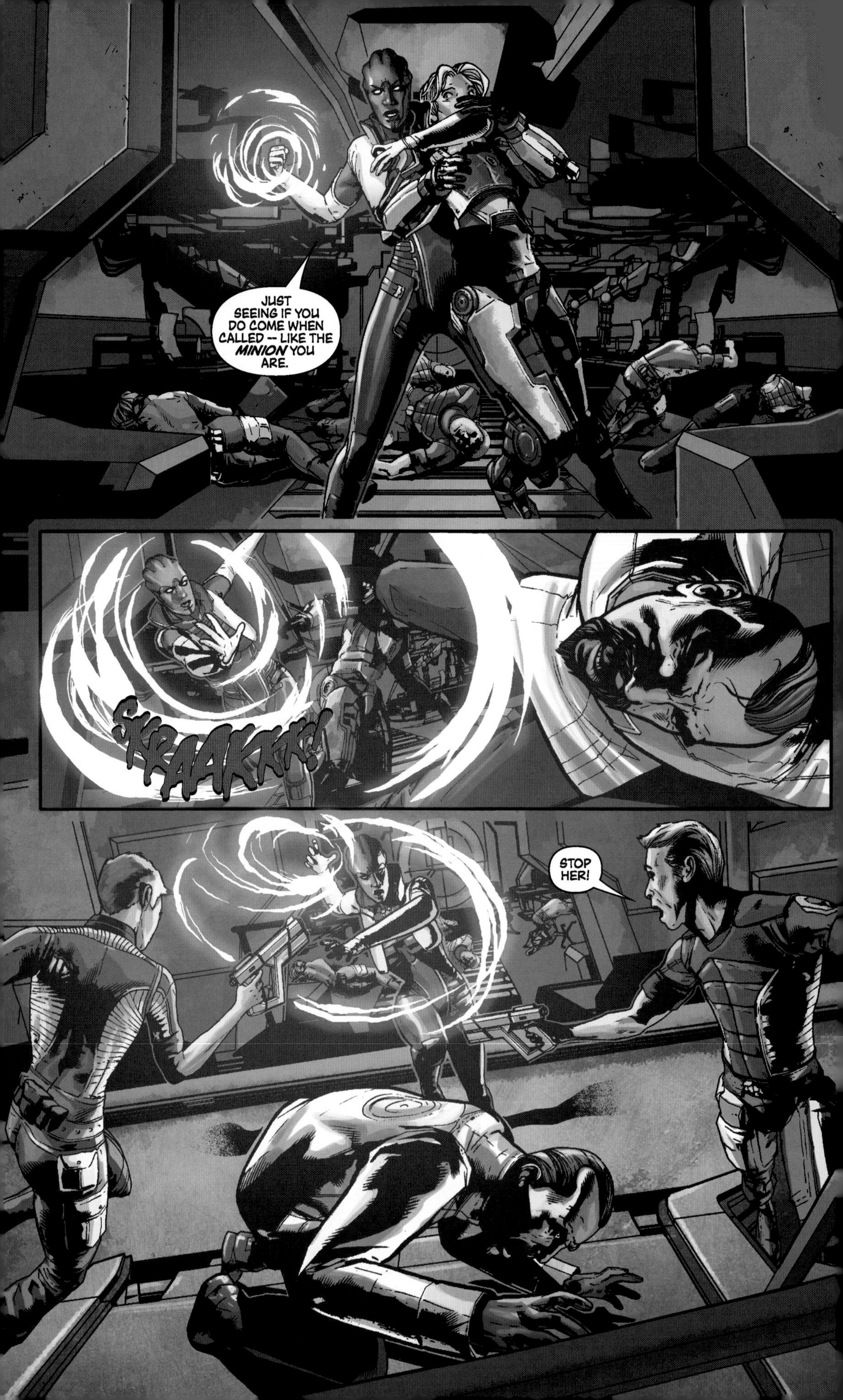
JUST SEEING IF YOU DO COME WHEN CALLED -- LIKE THE *MINION* YOU ARE.
SKRAAKKK!
STOP HER!

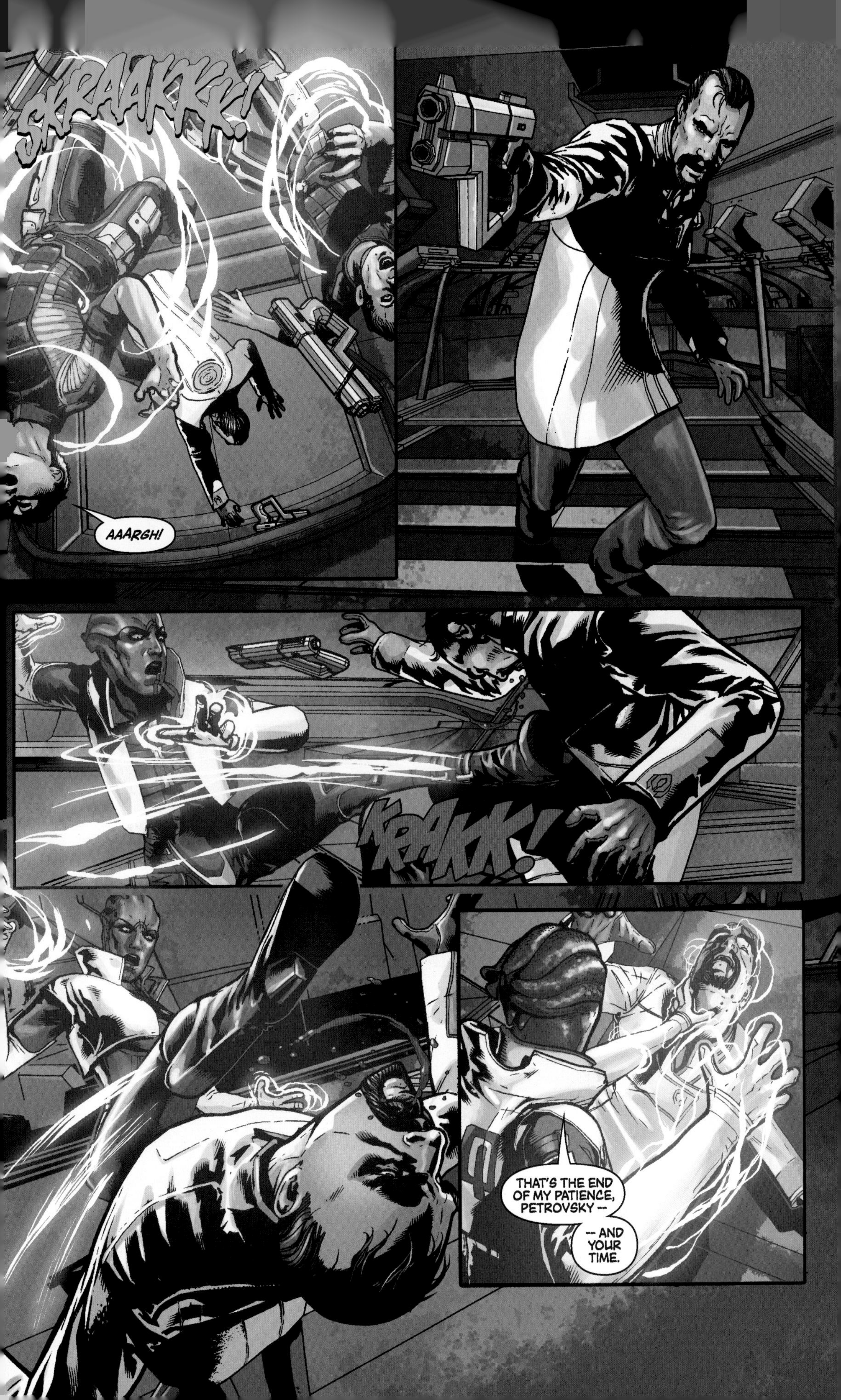
SKRAAKKK!
AAARGH!
KRAKK!
THAT'S THE END OF MY PATIENCE, PETROVSKY --
-- AND YOUR TIME.

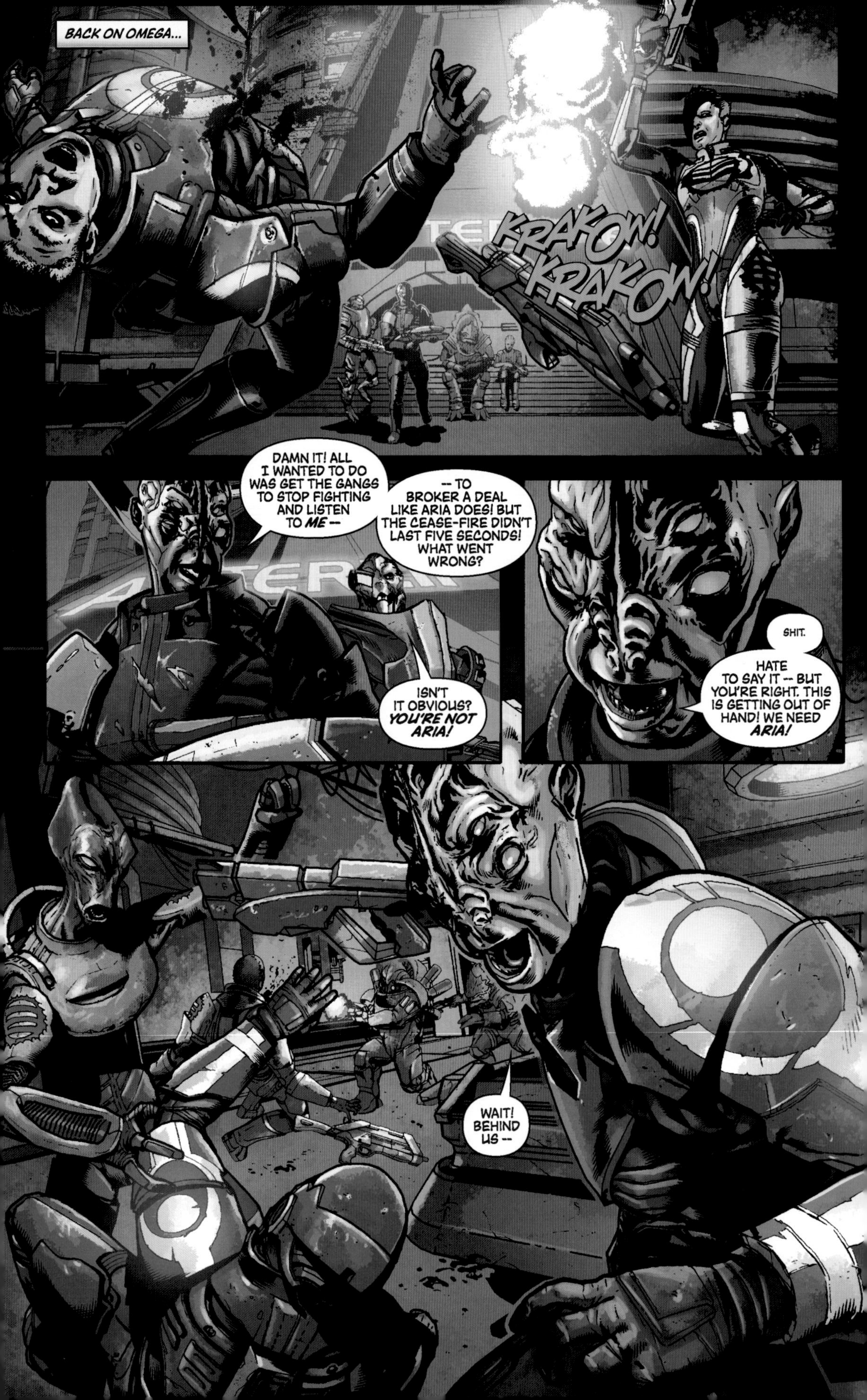
BACK ON OMEGA...
KRAKOW! KRAKOW!
DAMN IT! ALL I WANTED TO DO WAS GET THE GANGS TO STOP FIGHTING AND LISTEN TO ME --
-- TO BROKER A DEAL LIKE ARIA DOES! BUT THE CEASE-FIRE DIDN'T LAST FIVE SECONDS! WHAT WENT WRONG?
ISN'T IT OBVIOUS? YOU'RE NOT ARIA!
SHIT.
HATE TO SAY IT -- BUT YOU'RE RIGHT. THIS IS GETTING OUT OF HAND! WE NEED ARIA!
WAIT! BEHIND US --

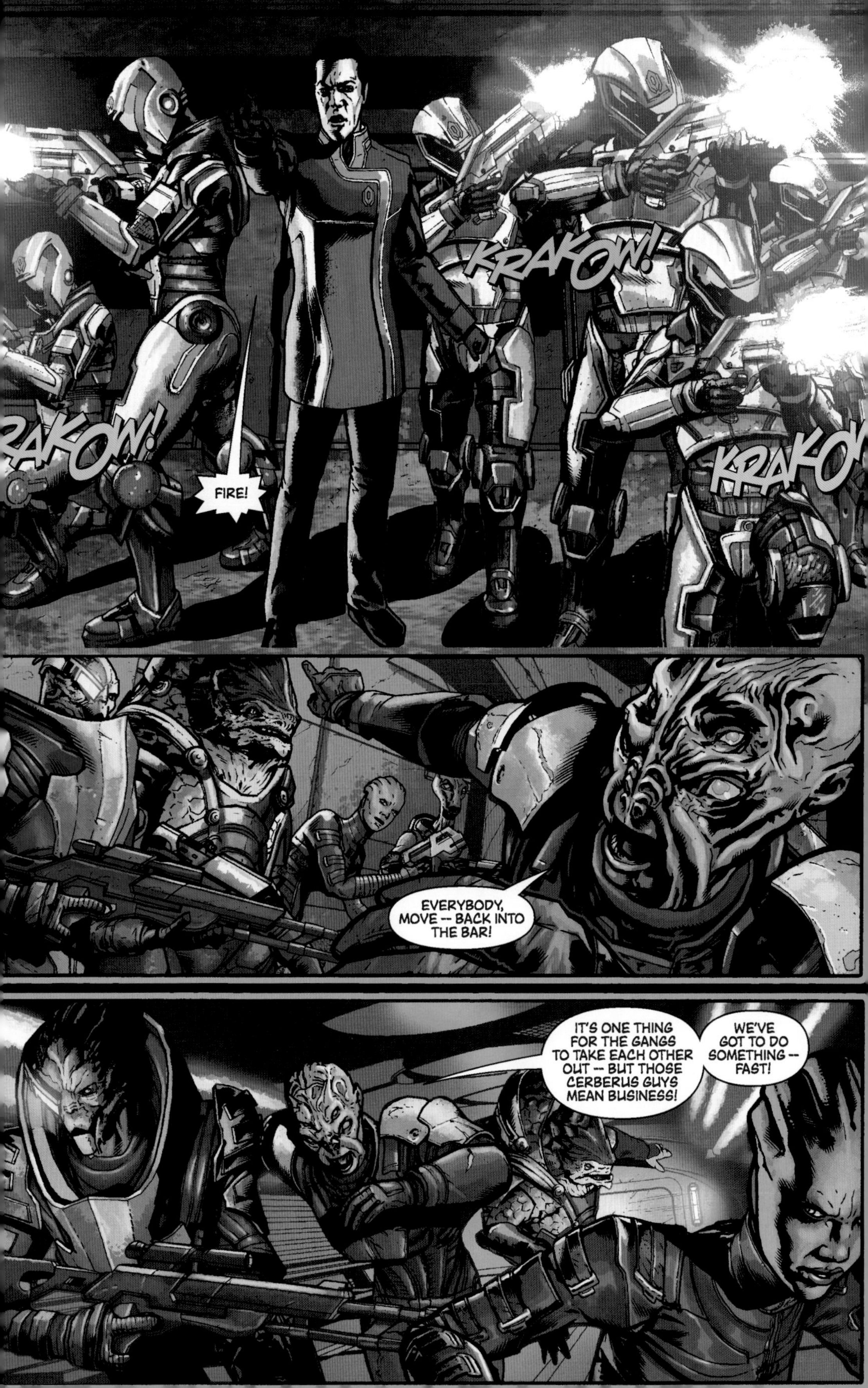
KRAKOW!
FIRE!
KRAKOW!
KRAKO
EVERYBODY, MOVE -- BACK INTO THE BAR!
IT'S ONE THING FOR THE GANGS TO TAKE EACH OTHER OUT -- BUT THOSE CERBERUS GUYS MEAN BUSINESS!
WE'VE GOT TO DO SOMETHING -- FAST!

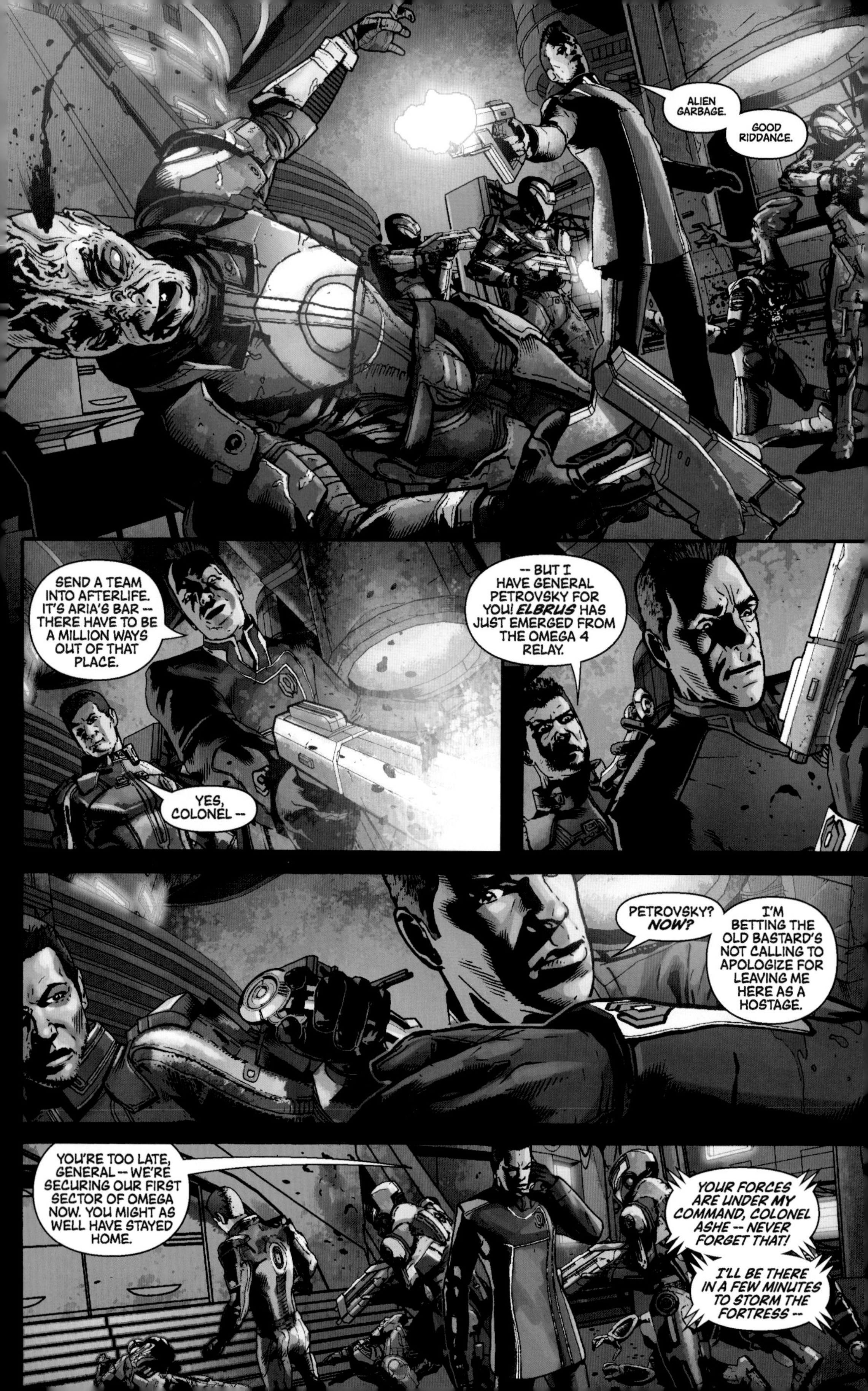
ALIEN GARBAGE.
GOOD RIDDANCE.
SEND A TEAM INTO AFTERLIFE. IT'S ARIA'S BAR -- THERE HAVE TO BE A MILLION WAYS OUT OF THAT PLACE.
YES, COLONEL --
-- BUT I HAVE GENERAL PETROVSKY FOR YOU! *ELBRUS* HAS JUST EMERGED FROM THE OMEGA 4 RELAY.
PETROVSKY? *NOW?*
I'M BETTING THE OLD BASTARD'S NOT CALLING TO APOLOGIZE FOR LEAVING ME HERE AS A HOSTAGE.
YOU'RE TOO LATE, GENERAL -- WE'RE SECURING OUR FIRST SECTOR OF OMEGA NOW. YOU MIGHT AS WELL HAVE STAYED HOME.
*YOUR FORCES ARE UNDER **MY** COMMAND, COLONEL ASHE -- NEVER FORGET THAT!*
I'LL BE THERE IN A FEW MINUTES TO STORM THE FORTRESS --

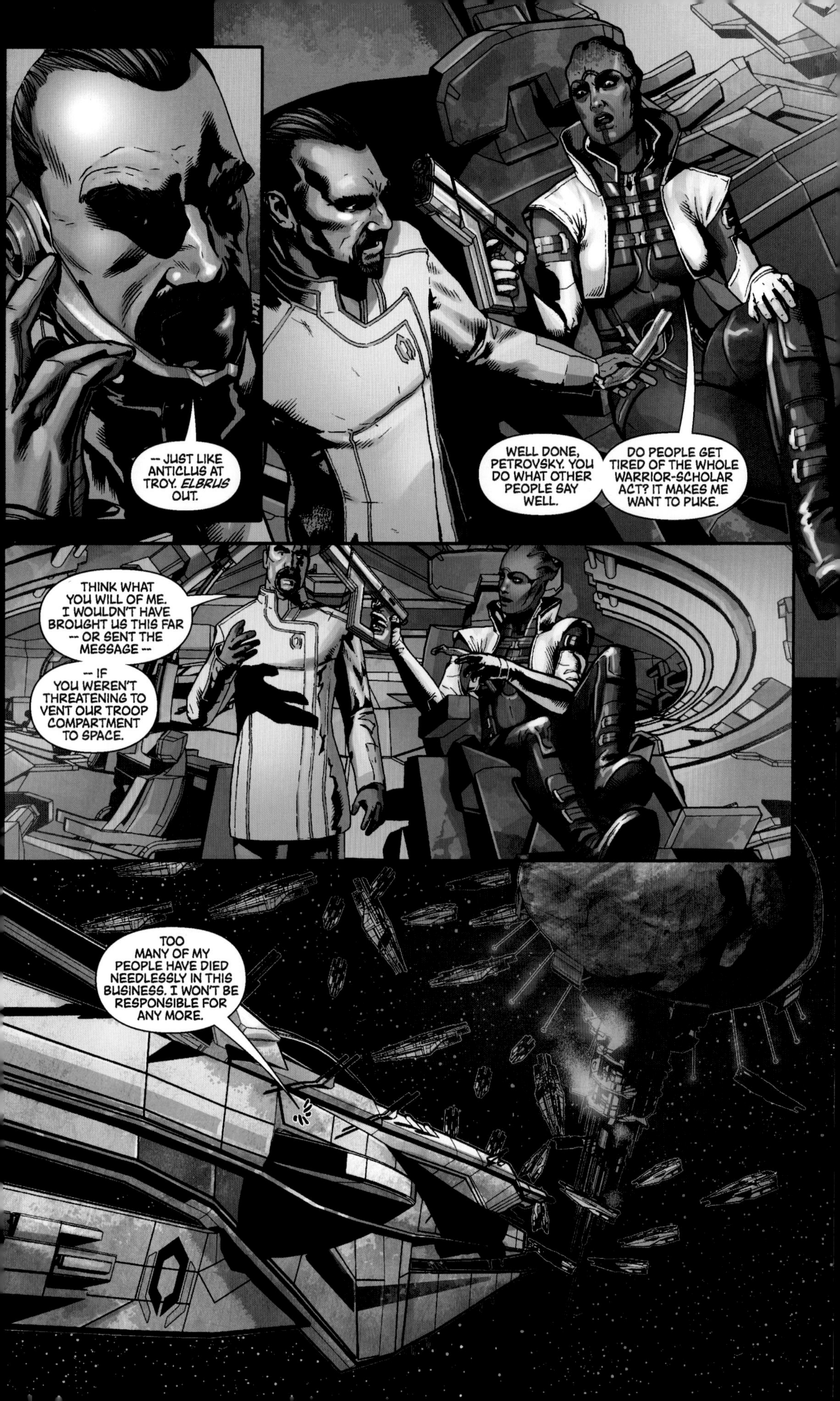
-- JUST LIKE ANTICLUS AT TROY. *ELBRUS* OUT.
WELL DONE, PETROVSKY. YOU DO WHAT OTHER PEOPLE SAY WELL.
DO PEOPLE GET TIRED OF THE WHOLE WARRIOR-SCHOLAR ACT? IT MAKES ME WANT TO PUKE.
THINK WHAT YOU WILL OF ME. I WOULDN'T HAVE BROUGHT US THIS FAR -- OR SENT THE MESSAGE --
-- IF YOU WEREN'T THREATENING TO VENT OUR TROOP COMPARTMENT TO SPACE.
TOO MANY OF MY PEOPLE HAVE DIED NEEDLESSLY IN THIS BUSINESS. I WON'T BE RESPONSIBLE FOR ANY MORE.

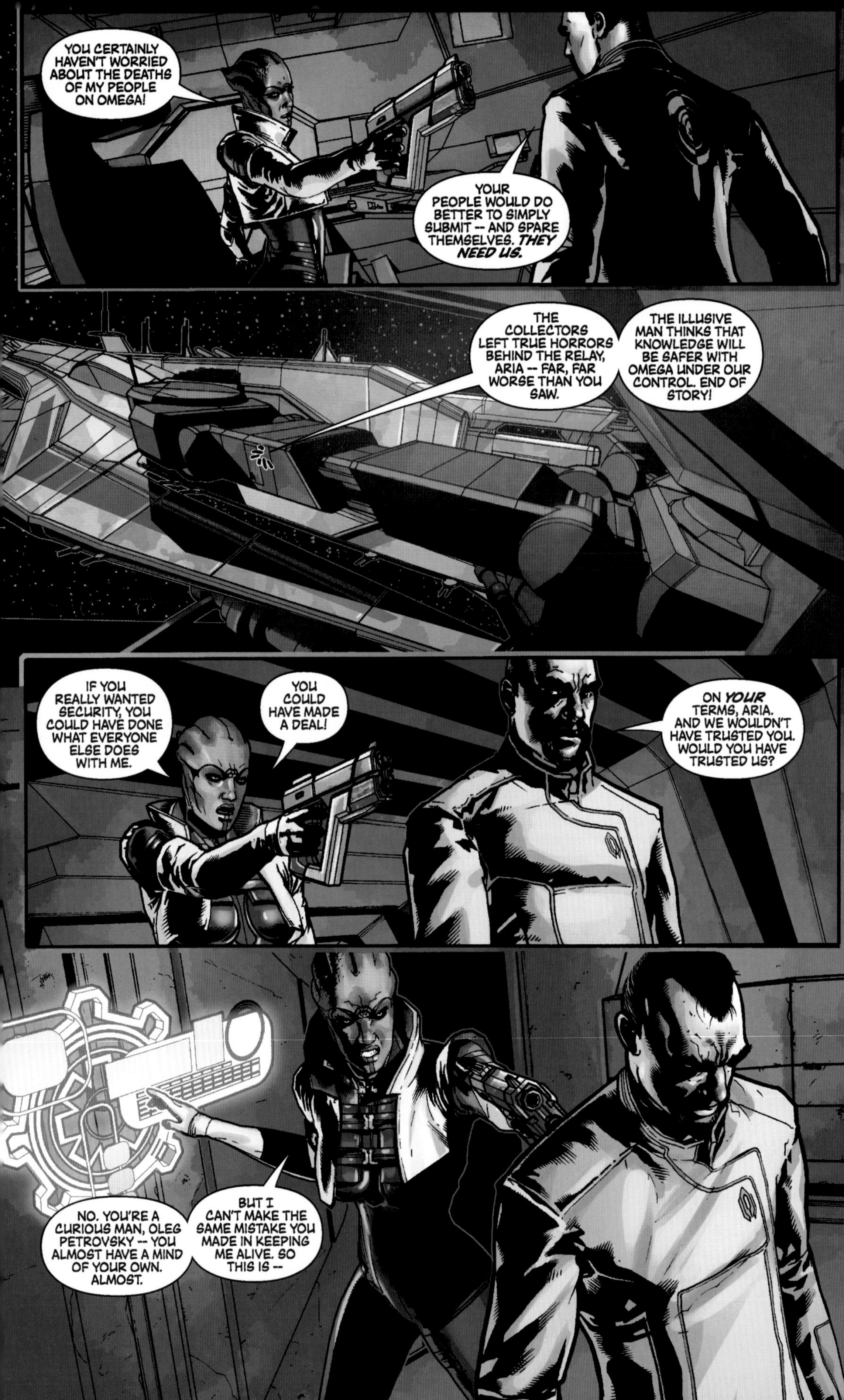
YOU CERTAINLY HAVEN'T WORRIED ABOUT THE DEATHS OF MY PEOPLE ON OMEGA!
YOUR PEOPLE WOULD DO BETTER TO SIMPLY SUBMIT -- AND SPARE THEMSELVES. *THEY NEED US.*
THE COLLECTORS LEFT TRUE HORRORS BEHIND THE RELAY, ARIA -- FAR, FAR WORSE THAN YOU SAW.
THE ILLUSIVE MAN THINKS THAT KNOWLEDGE WILL BE SAFER WITH OMEGA UNDER OUR CONTROL. END OF STORY!
IF YOU REALLY WANTED SECURITY, YOU COULD HAVE DONE WHAT EVERYONE ELSE DOES WITH ME.
YOU COULD HAVE MADE A DEAL!
ON *YOUR* TERMS, ARIA. AND WE WOULDN'T HAVE TRUSTED YOU. WOULD YOU HAVE TRUSTED US?
NO. YOU'RE A CURIOUS MAN, OLEG PETROVSKY -- YOU ALMOST HAVE A MIND OF YOUR OWN. ALMOST.
BUT I CAN'T MAKE THE SAME MISTAKE YOU MADE IN KEEPING ME ALIVE. SO THIS IS --

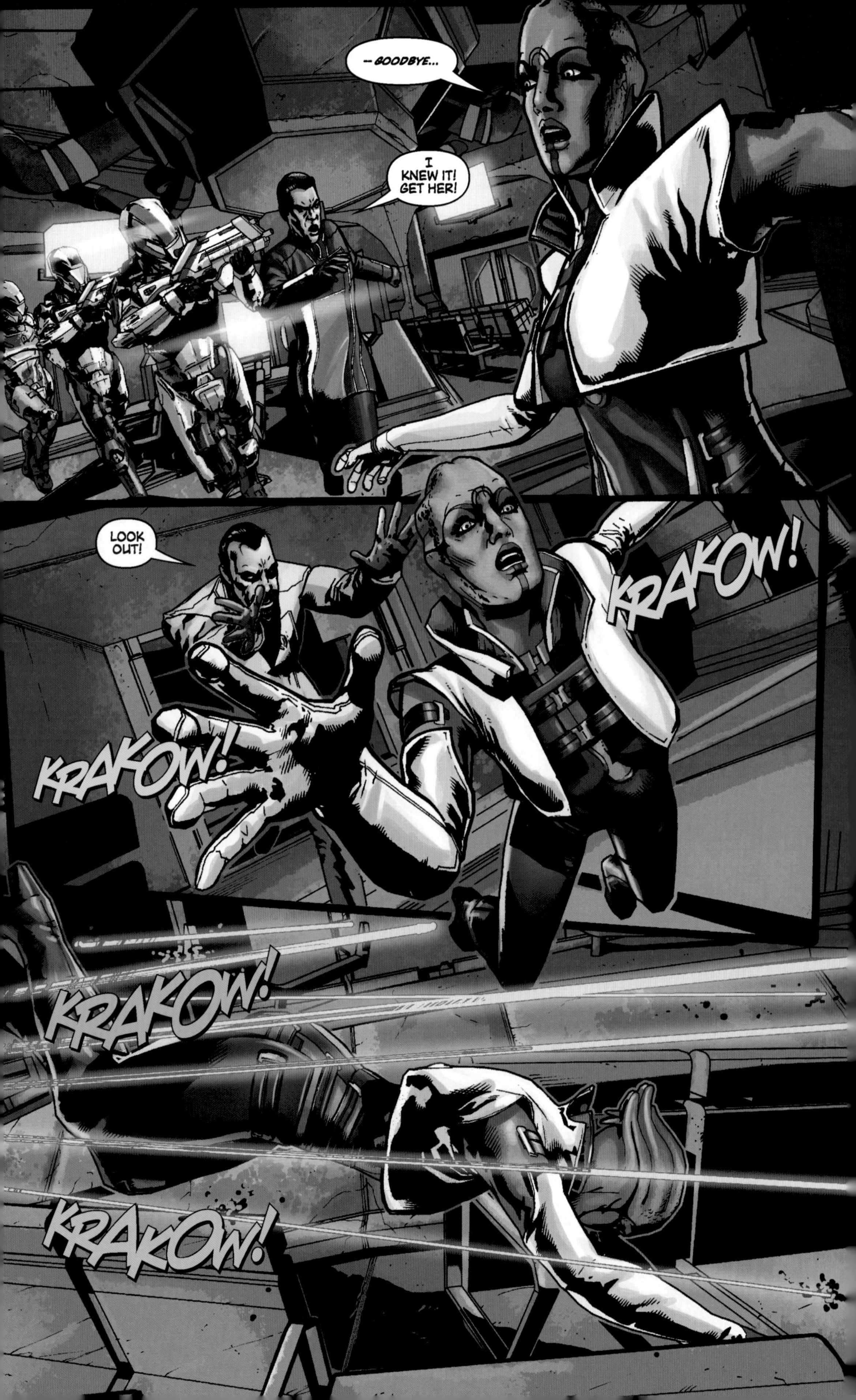
--GOODBYE...
I KNEW IT! GET HER!
LOOK OUT!
KRAKOW!
KRAKOW!
KRAKOW!
KRAKOW!

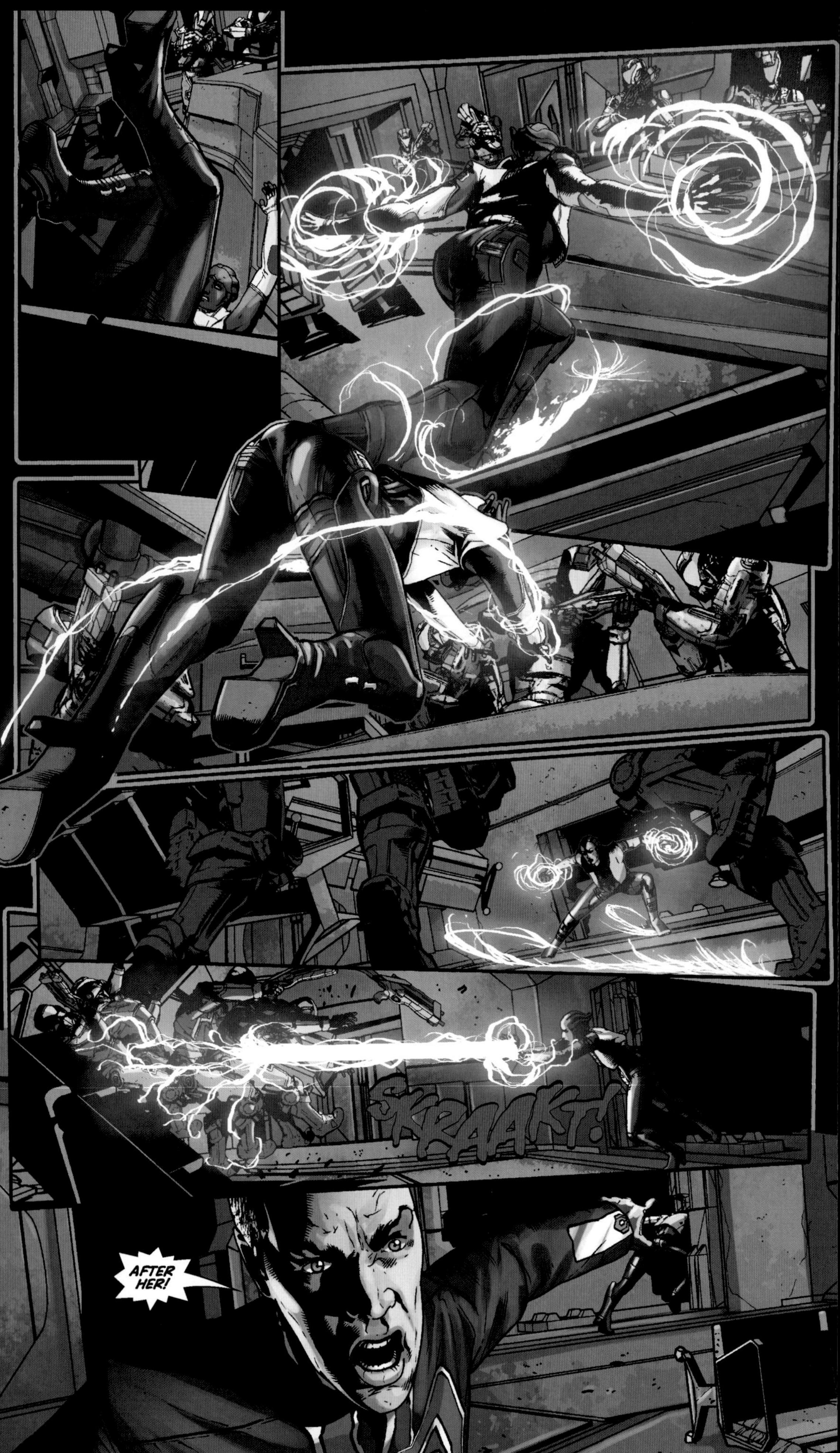
SKRAAKT!
AFTER HER!

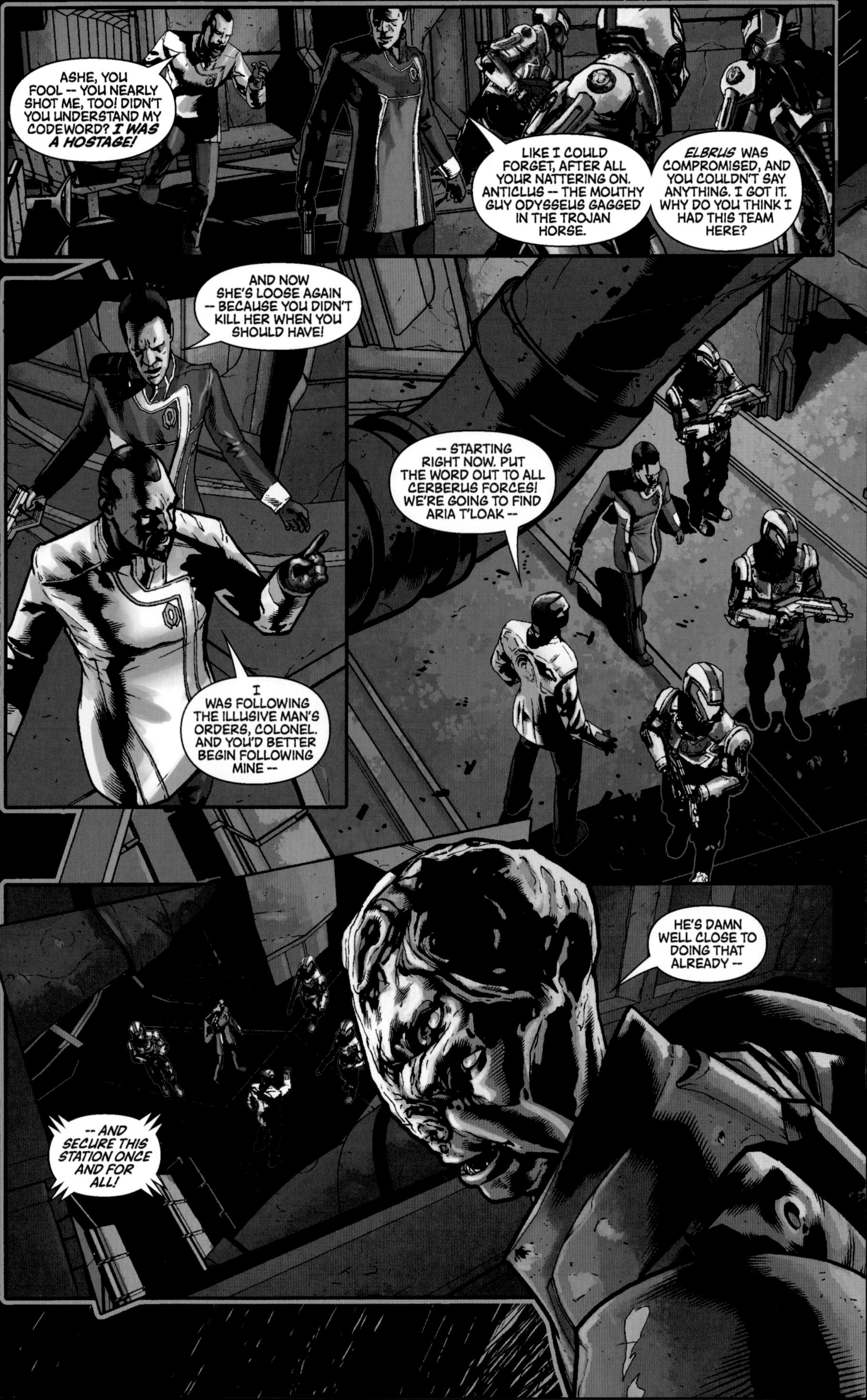
ASHE, YOU FOOL -- YOU NEARLY SHOT ME, TOO! DIDN'T YOU UNDERSTAND MY CODEWORD? *I WAS A HOSTAGE!*
LIKE I COULD FORGET, AFTER ALL YOUR NATTERING ON. ANTICLUS -- THE MOUTHY GUY ODYSSEUS GAGGED IN THE TROJAN HORSE.
ELBRUS WAS COMPROMISED, AND YOU COULDN'T SAY ANYTHING. I GOT IT. WHY DO YOU THINK I HAD THIS TEAM HERE?
AND NOW SHE'S LOOSE AGAIN -- BECAUSE YOU DIDN'T KILL HER WHEN YOU SHOULD HAVE!
I WAS FOLLOWING THE ILLUSIVE MAN'S ORDERS, COLONEL. AND YOU'D BETTER BEGIN FOLLOWING MINE --
-- STARTING RIGHT NOW. PUT THE WORD OUT TO ALL CERBERUS FORCES! WE'RE GOING TO FIND ARIA T'LOAK --
HE'S DAMN WELL CLOSE TO DOING THAT ALREADY --
-- AND SECURE THIS STATION ONCE AND FOR ALL!

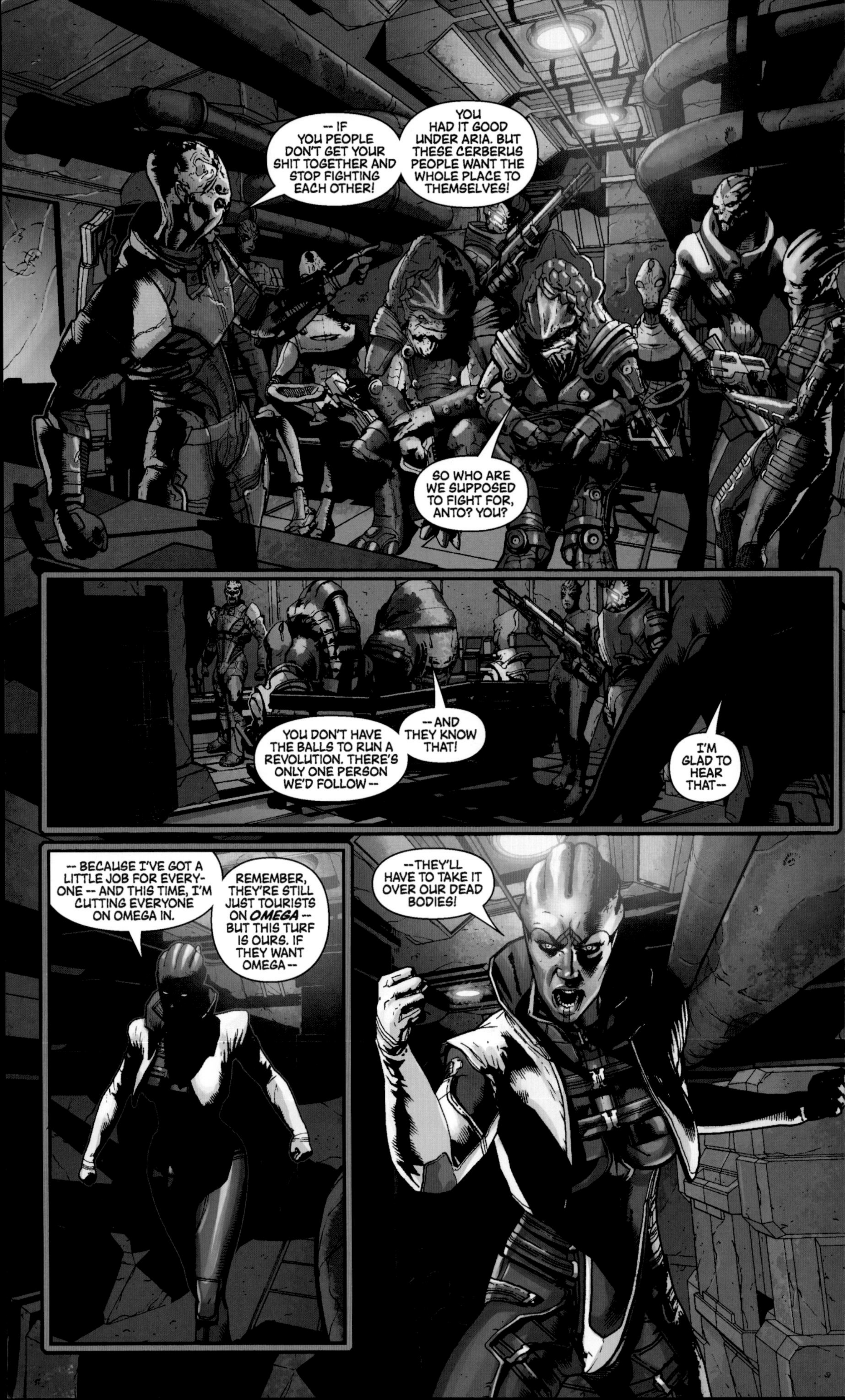
-- IF YOU PEOPLE DON'T GET YOUR SHIT TOGETHER AND STOP FIGHTING EACH OTHER!
YOU HAD IT GOOD UNDER ARIA. BUT THESE CERBERUS PEOPLE WANT THE WHOLE PLACE TO THEMSELVES!
SO WHO ARE WE SUPPOSED TO FIGHT FOR, ANTO? YOU?
YOU DON'T HAVE THE BALLS TO RUN A REVOLUTION. THERE'S ONLY ONE PERSON WE'D FOLLOW --
-- AND THEY KNOW THAT!
I'M GLAD TO HEAR THAT--
-- BECAUSE I'VE GOT A LITTLE JOB FOR EVERY-ONE -- AND THIS TIME, I'M CUTTING EVERYONE ON OMEGA IN.
REMEMBER, THEY'RE STILL JUST TOURISTS ON ***OMEGA*** -- BUT THIS TURF IS OURS. IF THEY WANT OMEGA --
--THEY'LL HAVE TO TAKE IT OVER OUR DEAD BODIES!

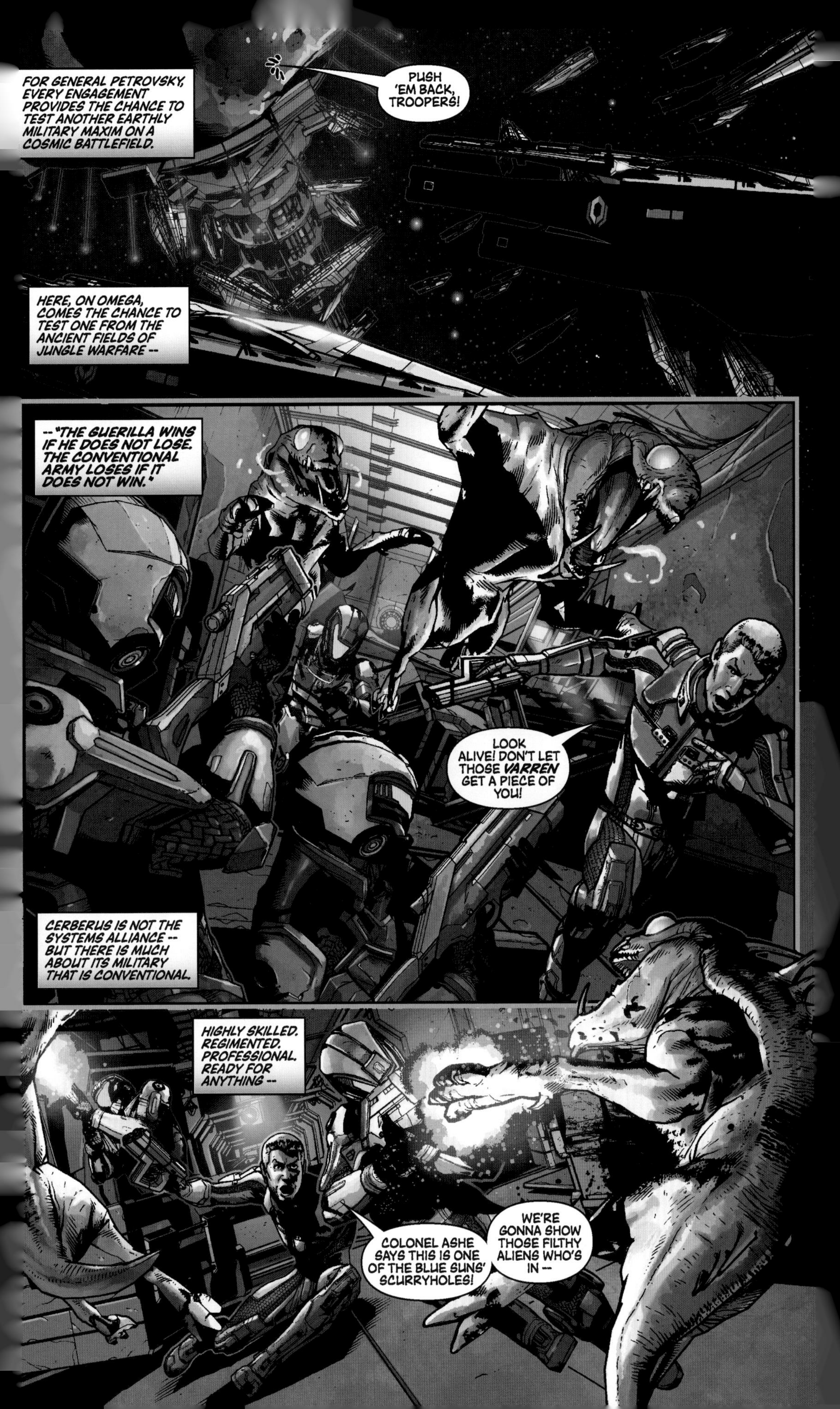
FOR GENERAL PETROVSKY, EVERY ENGAGEMENT PROVIDES THE CHANCE TO TEST ANOTHER EARTHLY MILITARY MAXIM ON A COSMIC BATTLEFIELD.
PUSH 'EM BACK, TROOPERS!
HERE, ON OMEGA, COMES THE CHANCE TO TEST ONE FROM THE ANCIENT FIELDS OF JUNGLE WARFARE --
-- "THE GUERILLA WINS IF HE DOES NOT LOSE. THE CONVENTIONAL ARMY LOSES IF IT DOES NOT WIN."
LOOK ALIVE! DON'T LET THOSE VARREN GET A PIECE OF YOU!
CERBERUS IS NOT THE SYSTEMS ALLIANCE -- BUT THERE IS MUCH ABOUT ITS MILITARY THAT IS CONVENTIONAL.
HIGHLY SKILLED. REGIMENTED. PROFESSIONAL. READY FOR ANYTHING --
COLONEL ASHE SAYS THIS IS ONE OF THE BLUE SUNS' SCURRYHOLES!
WE'RE GONNA SHOW THOSE FILTHY ALIENS WHO'S IN --

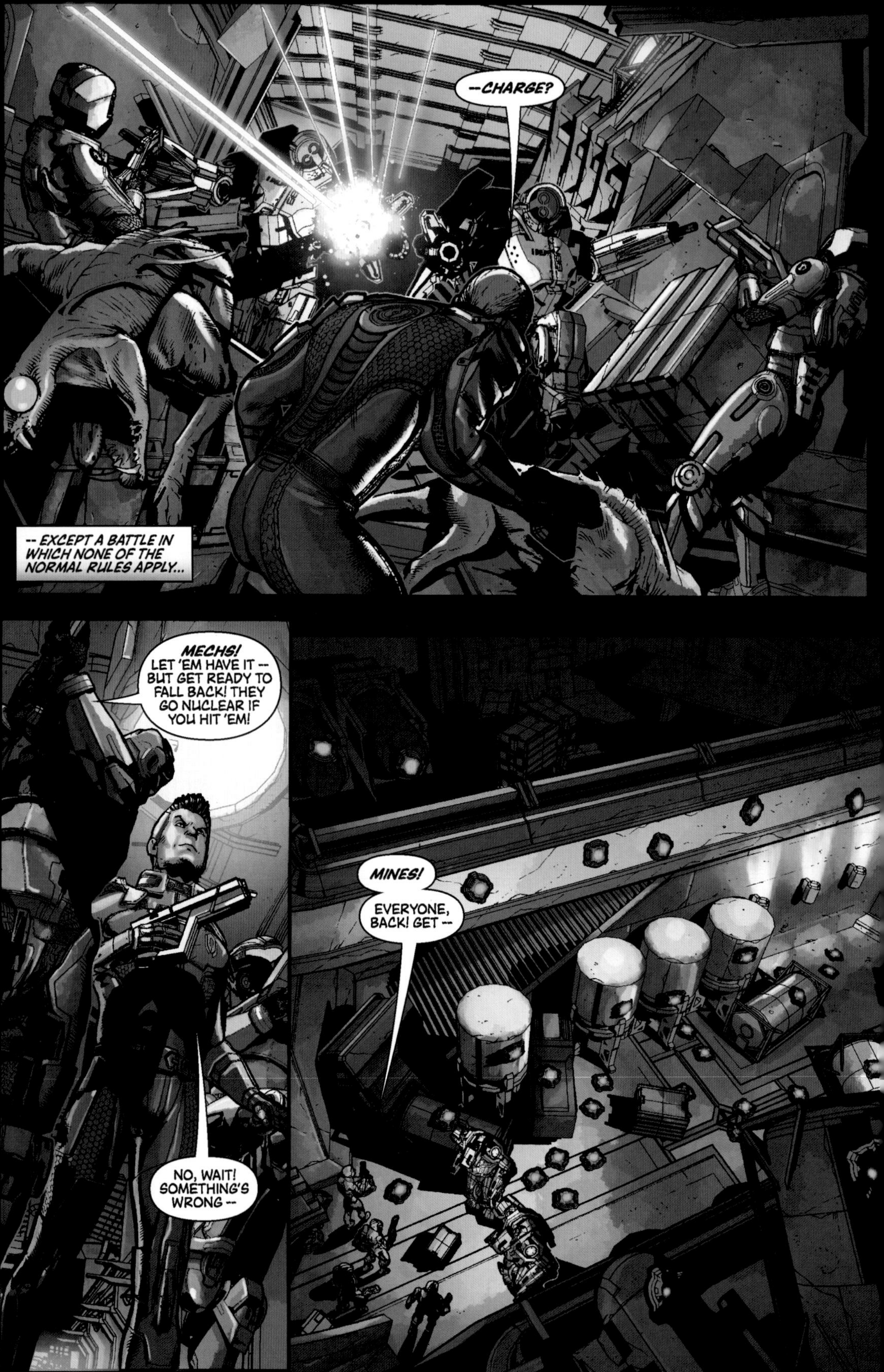
--CHARGE?
-- EXCEPT A BATTLE IN WHICH NONE OF THE NORMAL RULES APPLY...
MECHS! LET 'EM HAVE IT -- BUT GET READY TO FALL BACK! THEY GO NUCLEAR IF YOU HIT 'EM!
NO, WAIT! SOMETHING'S WRONG --
MINES!
EVERYONE, BACK! GET --

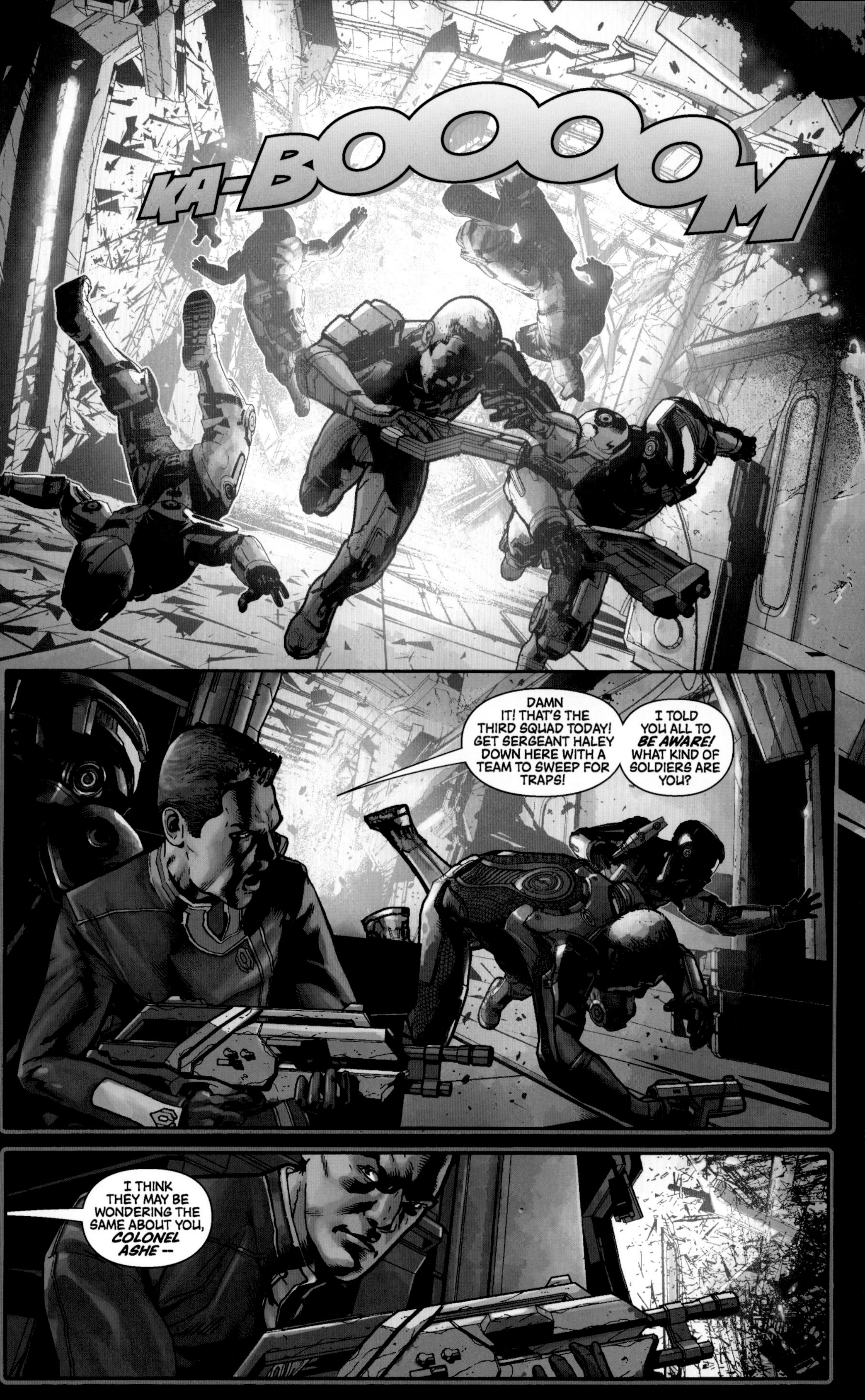
KA-BOOOOOM
DAMN IT! THAT'S THE THIRD SQUAD TODAY! GET SERGEANT HALEY DOWN HERE WITH A TEAM TO SWEEP FOR TRAPS!
I TOLD YOU ALL TO *BE AWARE!* WHAT KIND OF SOLDIERS ARE YOU?
I THINK THEY MAY BE WONDERING THE SAME ABOUT YOU, *COLONEL ASHE* --

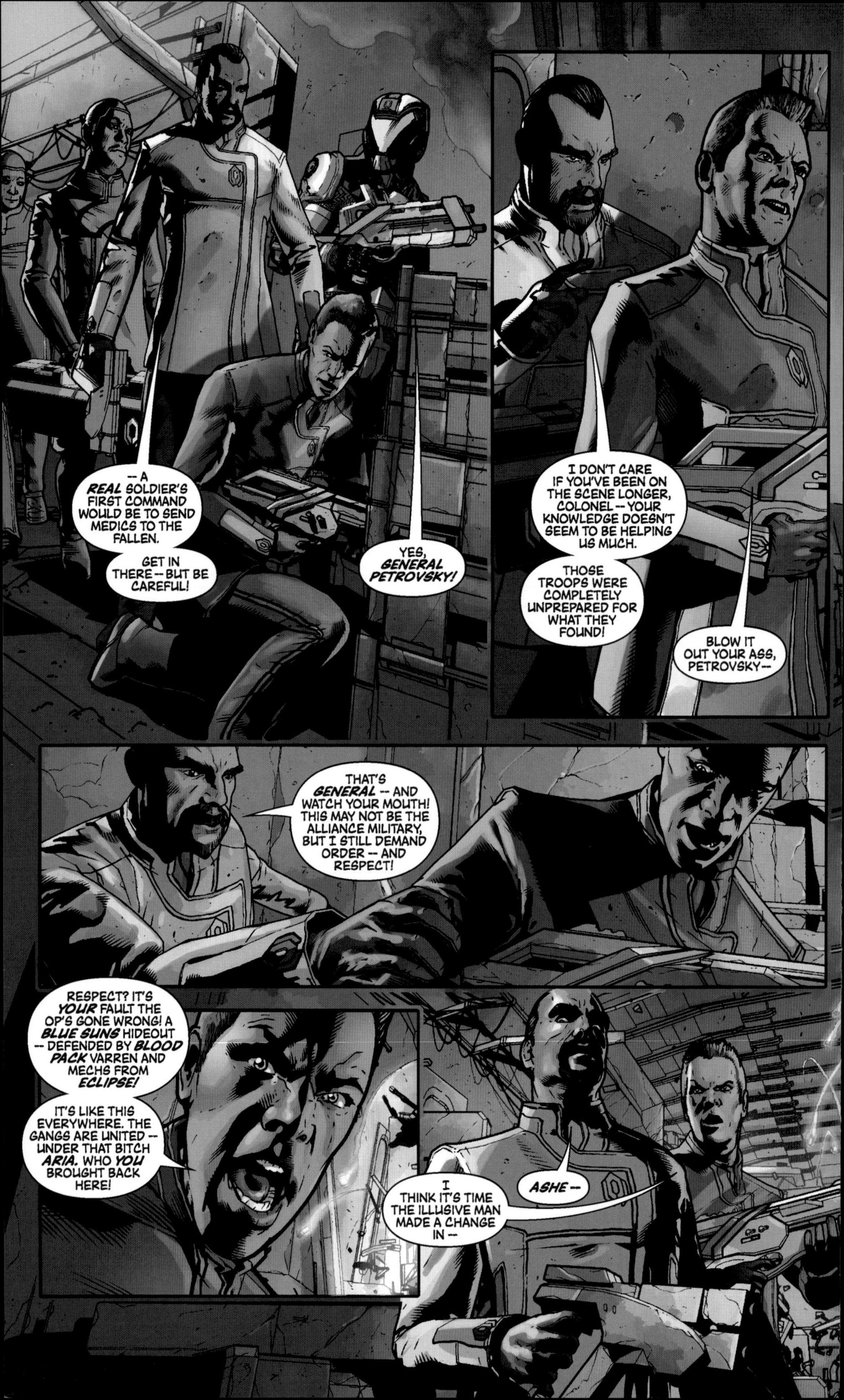
-- A REAL SOLDIER'S FIRST COMMAND WOULD BE TO SEND MEDICS TO THE FALLEN.
GET IN THERE -- BUT BE CAREFUL!
YES, GENERAL PETROVSKY!
I DON'T CARE IF YOU'VE BEEN ON THE SCENE LONGER, COLONEL -- YOUR KNOWLEDGE DOESN'T SEEM TO BE HELPING US MUCH.
THOSE TROOPS WERE COMPLETELY UNPREPARED FOR WHAT THEY FOUND!
BLOW IT OUT YOUR ASS, PETROVSKY--
THAT'S GENERAL -- AND WATCH YOUR MOUTH! THIS MAY NOT BE THE ALLIANCE MILITARY, BUT I STILL DEMAND ORDER -- AND RESPECT!
RESPECT? IT'S YOUR FAULT THE OP'S GONE WRONG! A BLUE SUNS HIDEOUT -- DEFENDED BY BLOOD PACK VARREN AND MECHS FROM ECLIPSE!
IT'S LIKE THIS EVERYWHERE. THE GANGS ARE UNITED -- UNDER THAT BITCH ARIA. WHO YOU BROUGHT BACK HERE!
ASHE --
I THINK IT'S TIME THE ILLUSIVE MAN MADE A CHANGE IN --

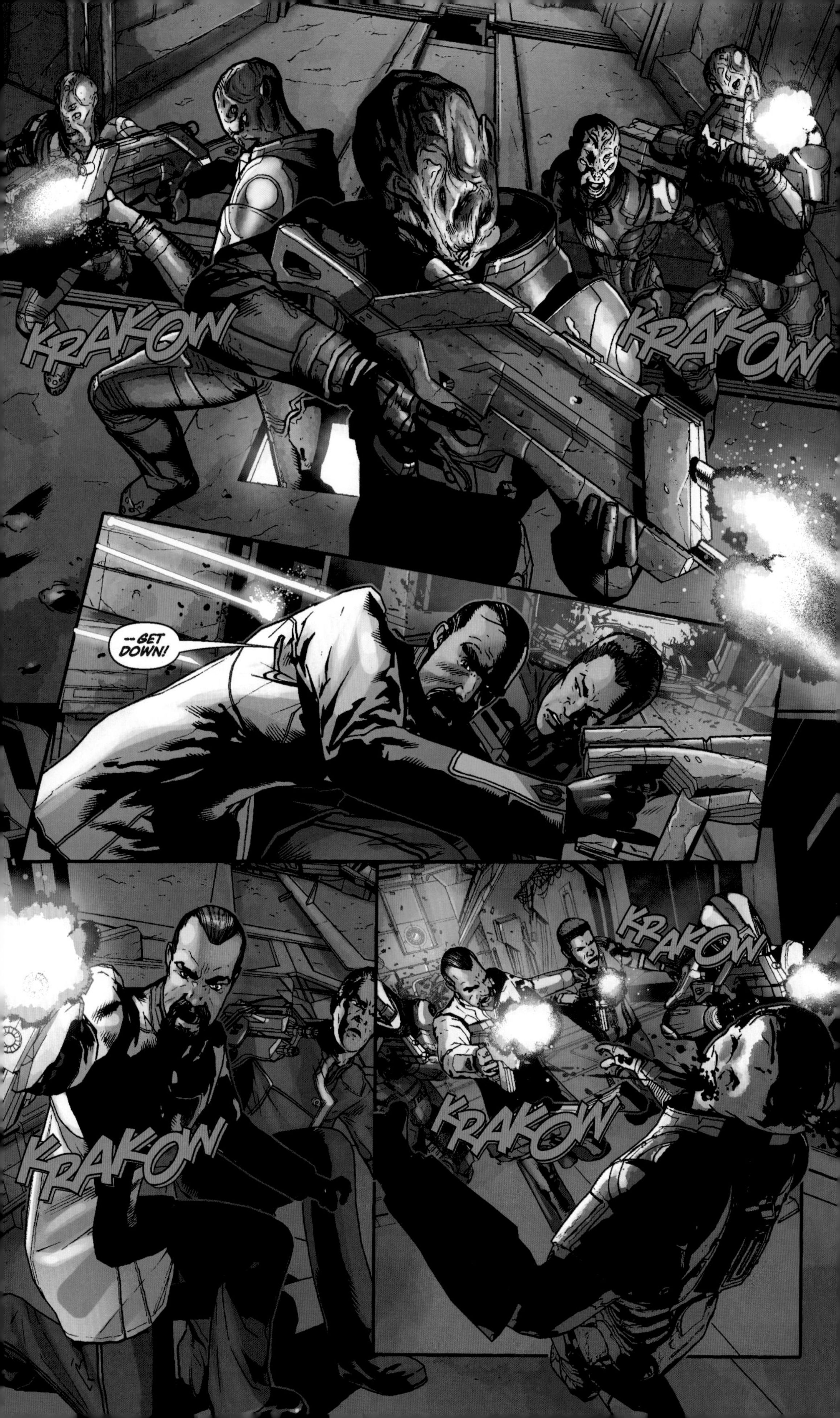
KRAKOW
KRAKOW
--GET DOWN!
KRAKOW
KRAKOW
KRAKOW

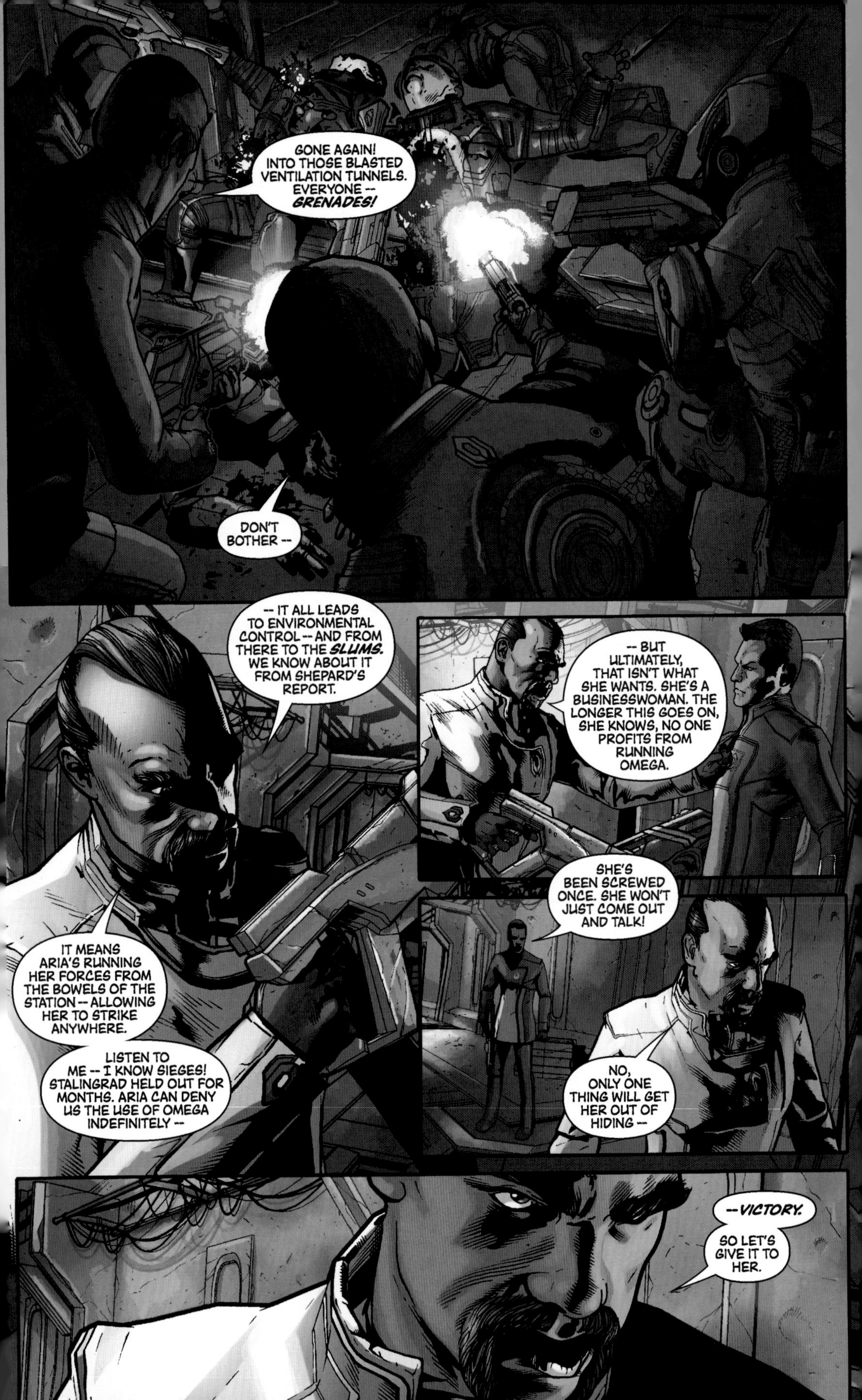
GONE AGAIN! INTO THOSE BLASTED VENTILATION TUNNELS. EVERYONE -- *GRENADES!*
DON'T BOTHER --
-- IT ALL LEADS TO ENVIRONMENTAL CONTROL -- AND FROM THERE TO THE *SLUMS.* WE KNOW ABOUT IT FROM SHEPARD'S REPORT.
IT MEANS ARIA'S RUNNING HER FORCES FROM THE BOWELS OF THE STATION -- ALLOWING HER TO STRIKE ANYWHERE.
LISTEN TO ME -- I KNOW SIEGES! STALINGRAD HELD OUT FOR MONTHS. ARIA CAN DENY US THE USE OF OMEGA INDEFINITELY --
-- BUT ULTIMATELY, THAT ISN'T WHAT SHE WANTS. SHE'S A BUSINESSWOMAN. THE LONGER THIS GOES ON, SHE KNOWS, NO ONE PROFITS FROM RUNNING OMEGA.
SHE'S BEEN SCREWED ONCE. SHE WON'T JUST COME OUT AND TALK!
NO, ONLY ONE THING WILL GET HER OUT OF HIDING --
-- *VICTORY.*
SO LET'S GIVE IT TO HER.

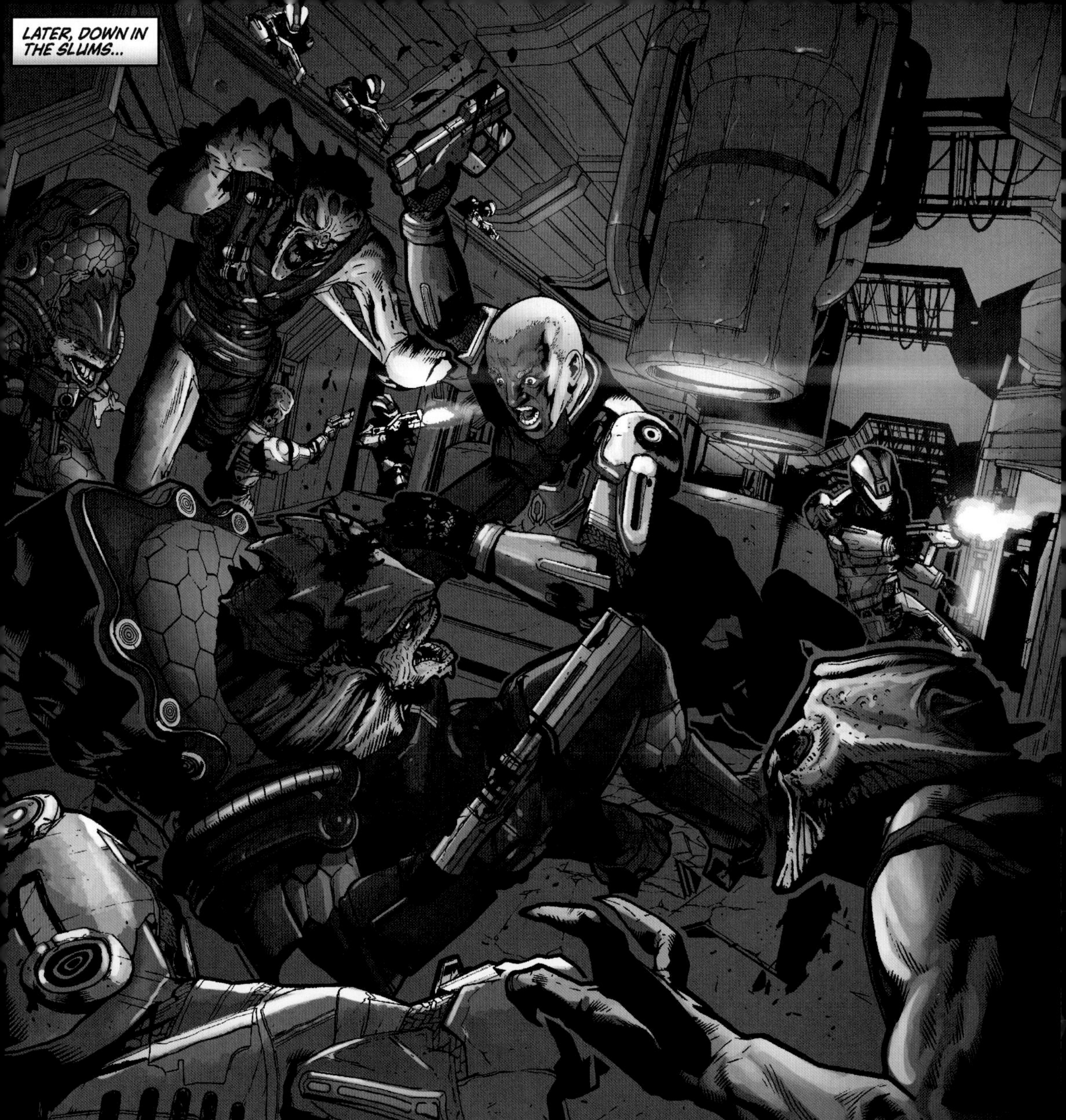
LATER, DOWN IN THE SLUMS...

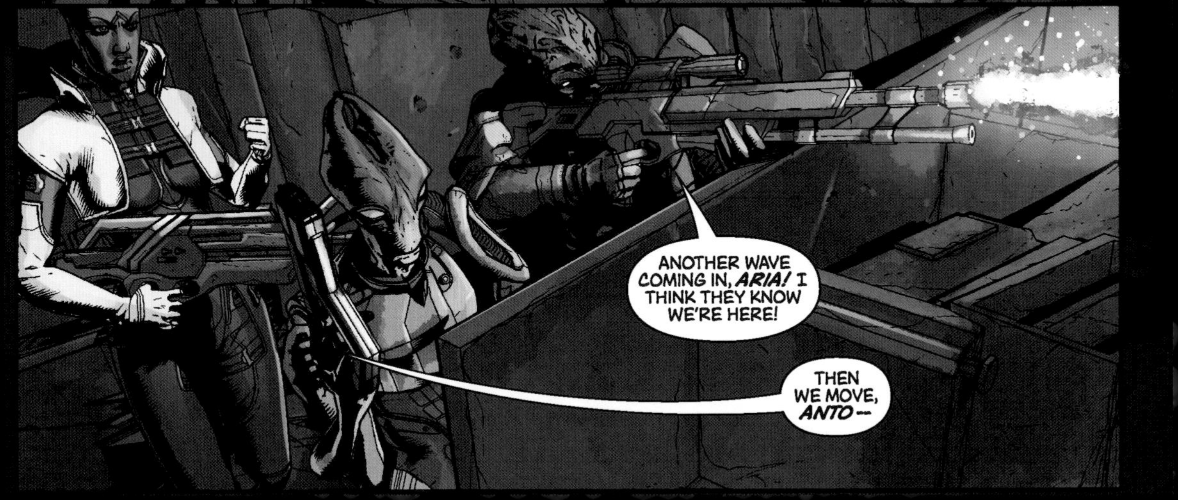
ANOTHER WAVE COMING IN, ARIA! I THINK THEY KNOW WE'RE HERE!
THEN WE MOVE, ANTO--

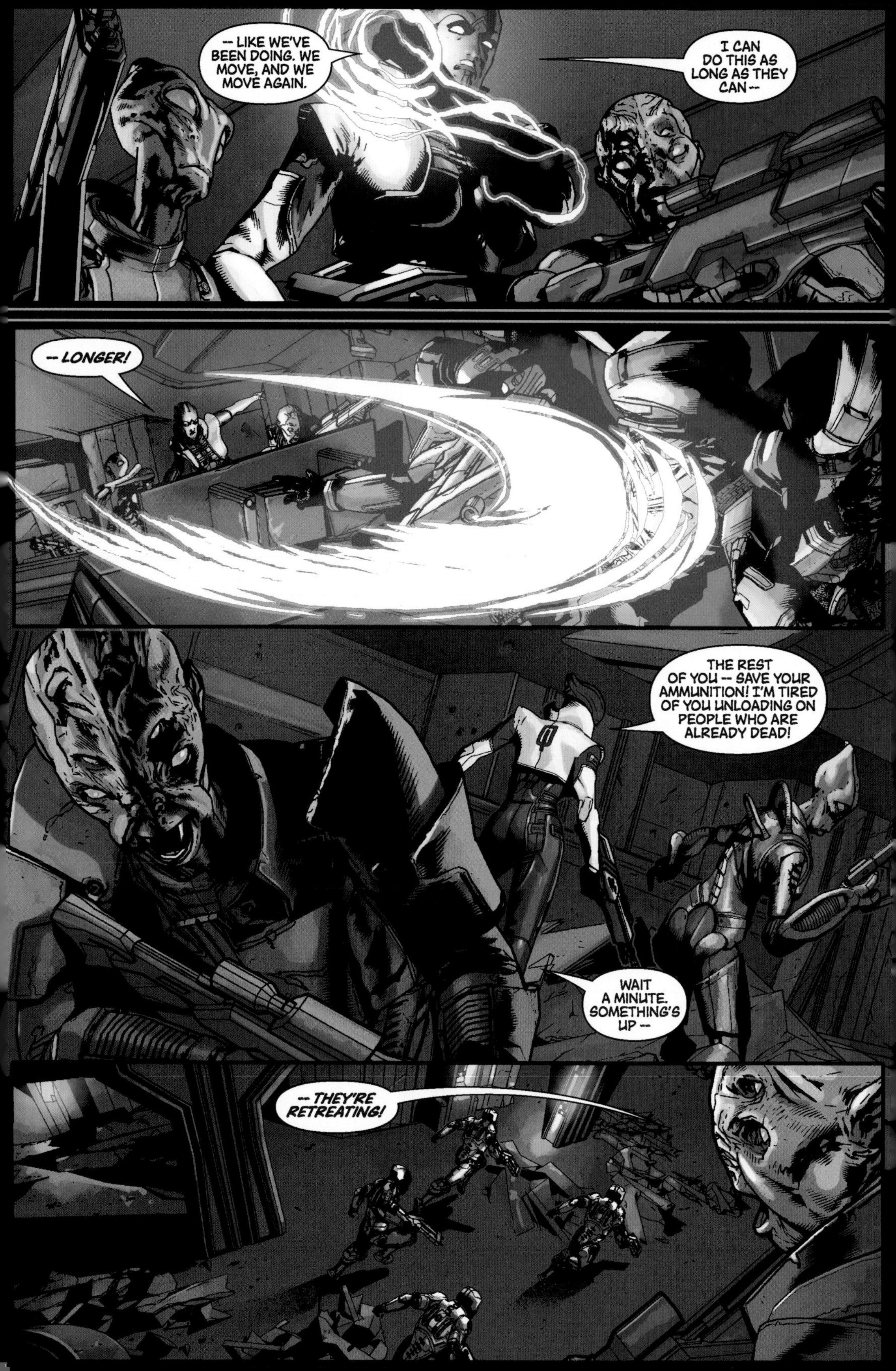
-- LIKE WE'VE BEEN DOING. WE MOVE, AND WE MOVE AGAIN.
I CAN DO THIS AS LONG AS THEY CAN --
-- LONGER!
THE REST OF YOU -- SAVE YOUR AMMUNITION! I'M TIRED OF YOU UNLOADING ON PEOPLE WHO ARE ALREADY DEAD!
WAIT A MINUTE. SOMETHING'S UP --
-- THEY'RE RETREATING!

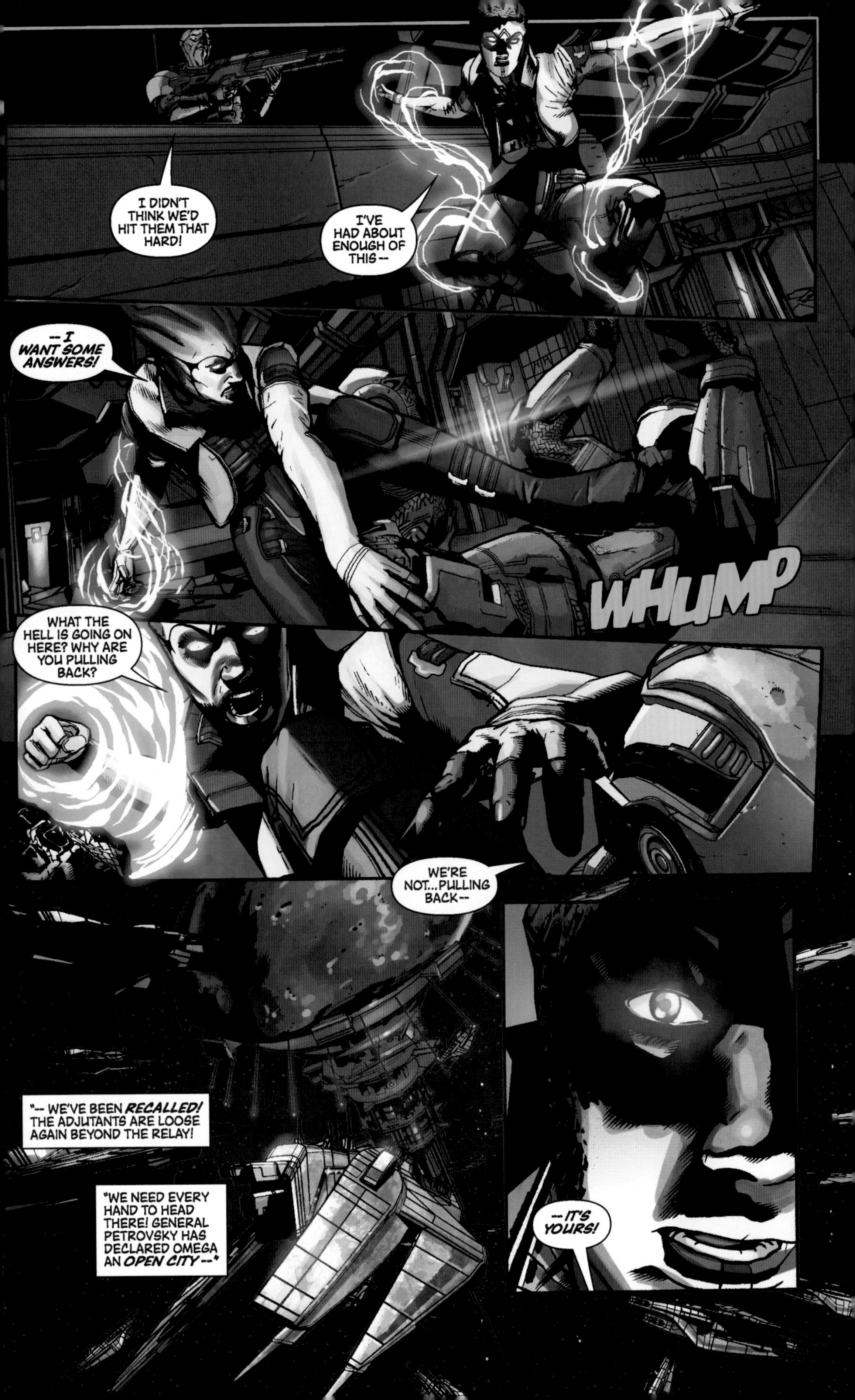

I DIDN'T THINK WE'D HIT THEM THAT HARD!
I'VE HAD ABOUT ENOUGH OF THIS --
-- I WANT SOME ANSWERS!
WHUMP
WHAT THE HELL IS GOING ON HERE? WHY ARE YOU PULLING BACK?
WE'RE NOT...PULLING BACK--
"-- WE'VE BEEN RECALLED! THE ADJUTANTS ARE LOOSE AGAIN BEYOND THE RELAY!
"WE NEED EVERY HAND TO HEAD THERE! GENERAL PETROVSKY HAS DECLARED OMEGA AN OPEN CITY --"
-- IT'S YOURS!

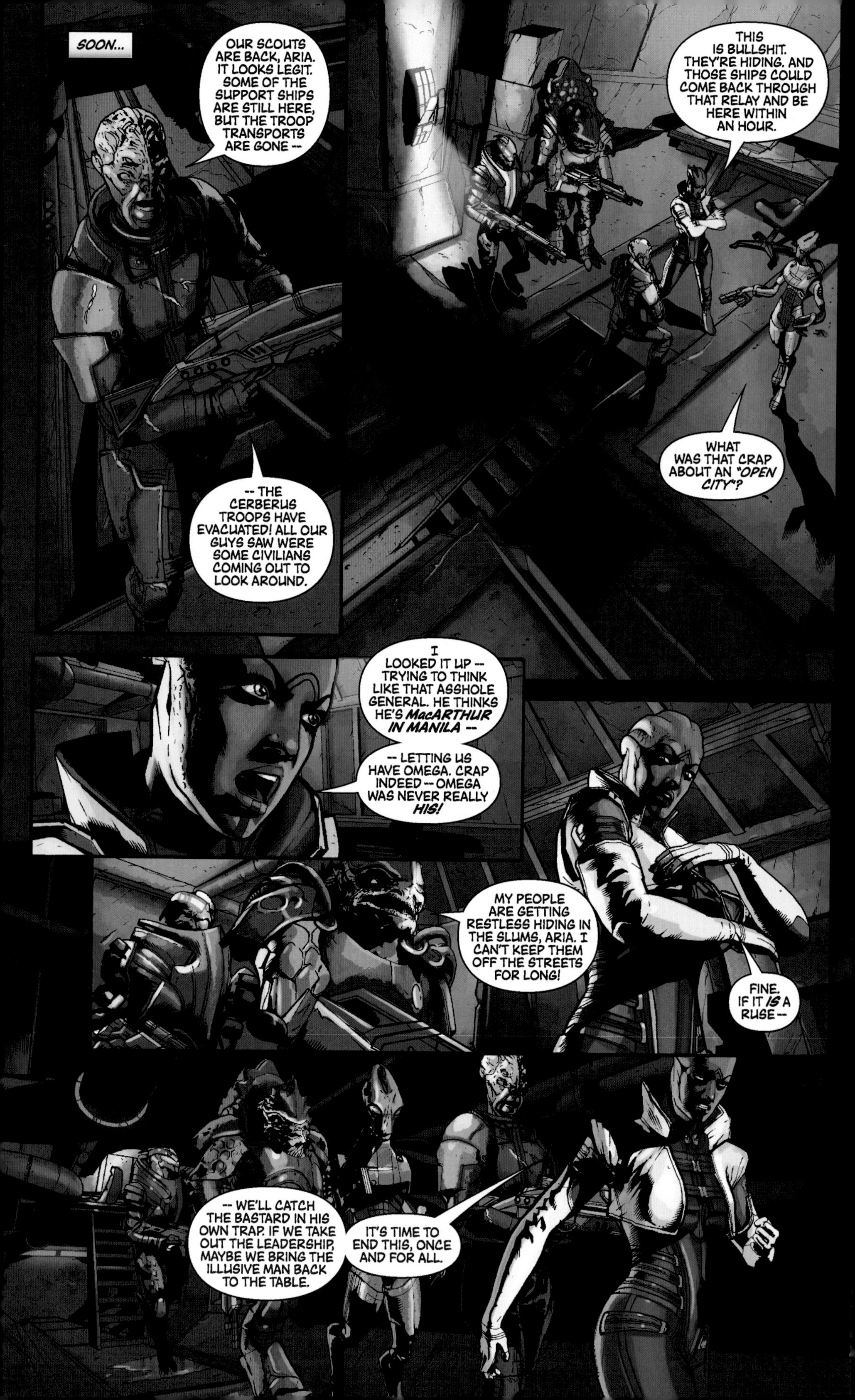
SOON...
OUR SCOUTS ARE BACK, ARIA. IT LOOKS LEGIT. SOME OF THE SUPPORT SHIPS ARE STILL HERE, BUT THE TROOP TRANSPORTS ARE GONE --
-- THE CERBERUS TROOPS HAVE EVACUATED! ALL OUR GUYS SAW WERE SOME CIVILIANS COMING OUT TO LOOK AROUND.
THIS IS BULLSHIT. THEY'RE HIDING. AND THOSE SHIPS COULD COME BACK THROUGH THAT RELAY AND BE HERE WITHIN AN HOUR.
WHAT WAS THAT CRAP ABOUT AN "OPEN CITY"?
I LOOKED IT UP -- TRYING TO THINK LIKE THAT ASSHOLE GENERAL. HE THINKS HE'S MacARTHUR IN MANILA --
-- LETTING US HAVE OMEGA. CRAP INDEED -- OMEGA WAS NEVER REALLY HIS!
MY PEOPLE ARE GETTING RESTLESS HIDING IN THE SLUMS, ARIA. I CAN'T KEEP THEM OFF THE STREETS FOR LONG!
FINE. IF IT IS A RUSE --
-- WE'LL CATCH THE BASTARD IN HIS OWN TRAP. IF WE TAKE OUT THE LEADERSHIP, MAYBE WE BRING THE ILLUSIVE MAN BACK TO THE TABLE.
IT'S TIME TO END THIS, ONCE AND FOR ALL.

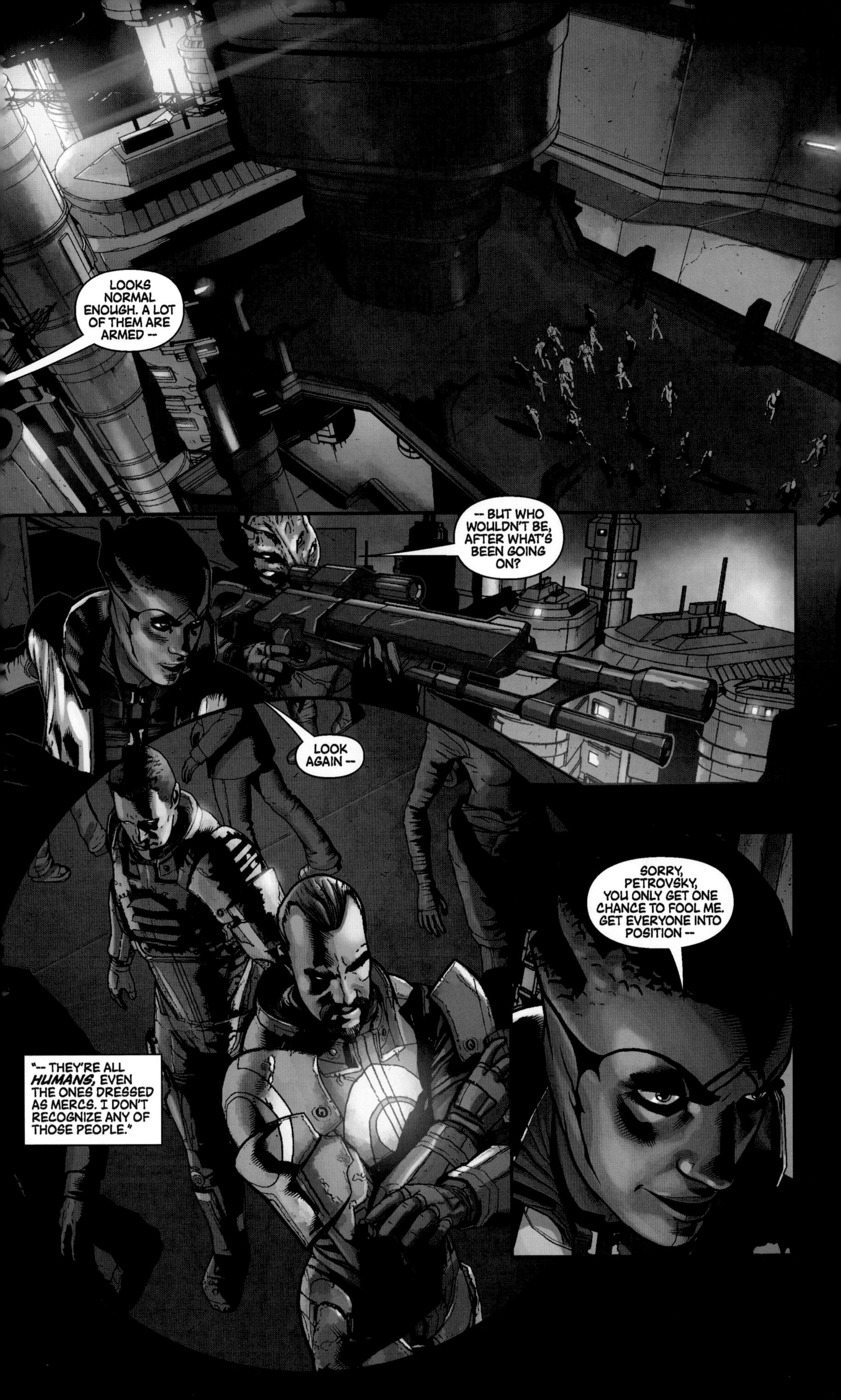
LOOKS NORMAL ENOUGH. A LOT OF THEM ARE ARMED --
-- BUT WHO WOULDN'T BE, AFTER WHAT'S BEEN GOING ON?
LOOK AGAIN --
"-- THEY'RE ALL *HUMANS,* EVEN THE ONES DRESSED AS MERCS. I DON'T RECOGNIZE ANY OF THOSE PEOPLE."
SORRY, PETROVSKY, YOU ONLY GET ONE CHANCE TO FOOL ME. GET EVERYONE INTO POSITION --

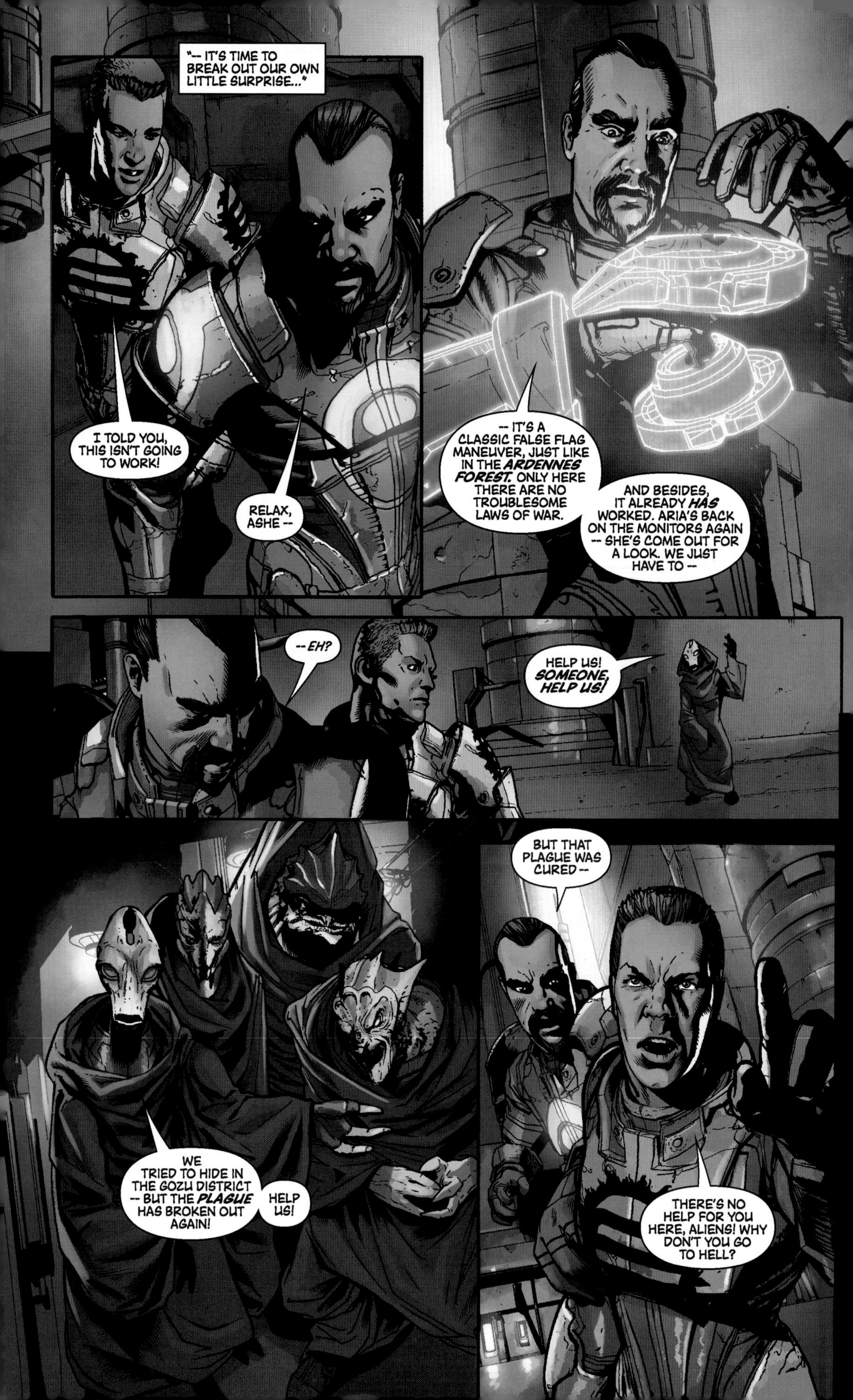
"-- IT'S TIME TO BREAK OUT OUR OWN LITTLE SURPRISE..."
I TOLD YOU, THIS ISN'T GOING TO WORK!
RELAX, ASHE --
-- IT'S A CLASSIC FALSE FLAG MANEUVER, JUST LIKE IN THE *ARDENNES FOREST.* ONLY HERE THERE ARE NO TROUBLESOME LAWS OF WAR.
AND BESIDES, IT ALREADY *HAS* WORKED. ARIA'S BACK ON THE MONITORS AGAIN -- SHE'S COME OUT FOR A LOOK. WE JUST HAVE TO --
-- *EH?*
HELP US! *SOMEONE, HELP US!*
WE TRIED TO HIDE IN THE GOZU DISTRICT -- BUT THE *PLAGUE* HAS BROKEN OUT AGAIN!
HELP US!
BUT THAT PLAGUE WAS CURED --
THERE'S NO HELP FOR YOU HERE, ALIENS! WHY DON'T YOU GO TO HELL?

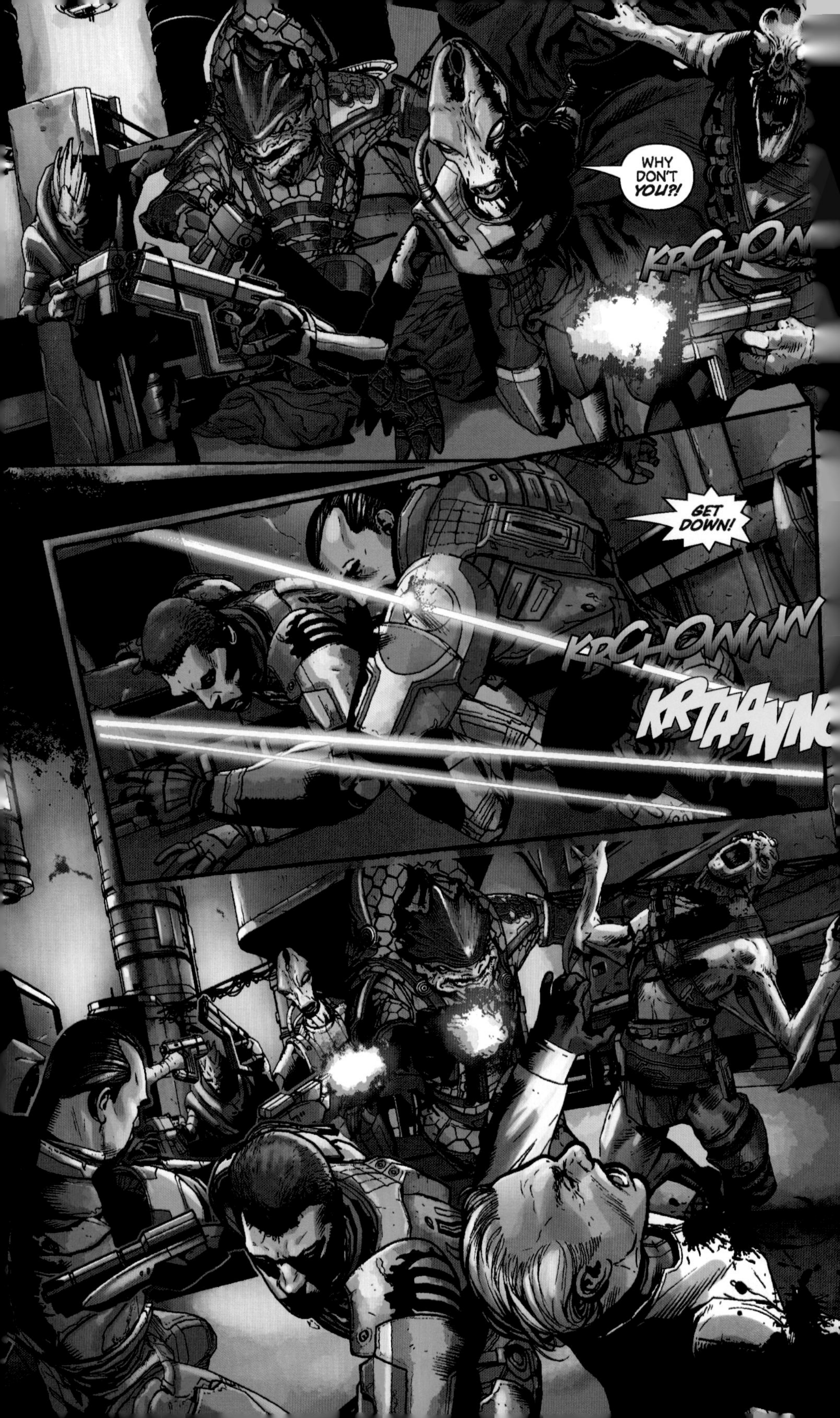
WHY DON'T YOU?!
KRCHOW
GET DOWN!
KRCHOWWW
KRTAANN

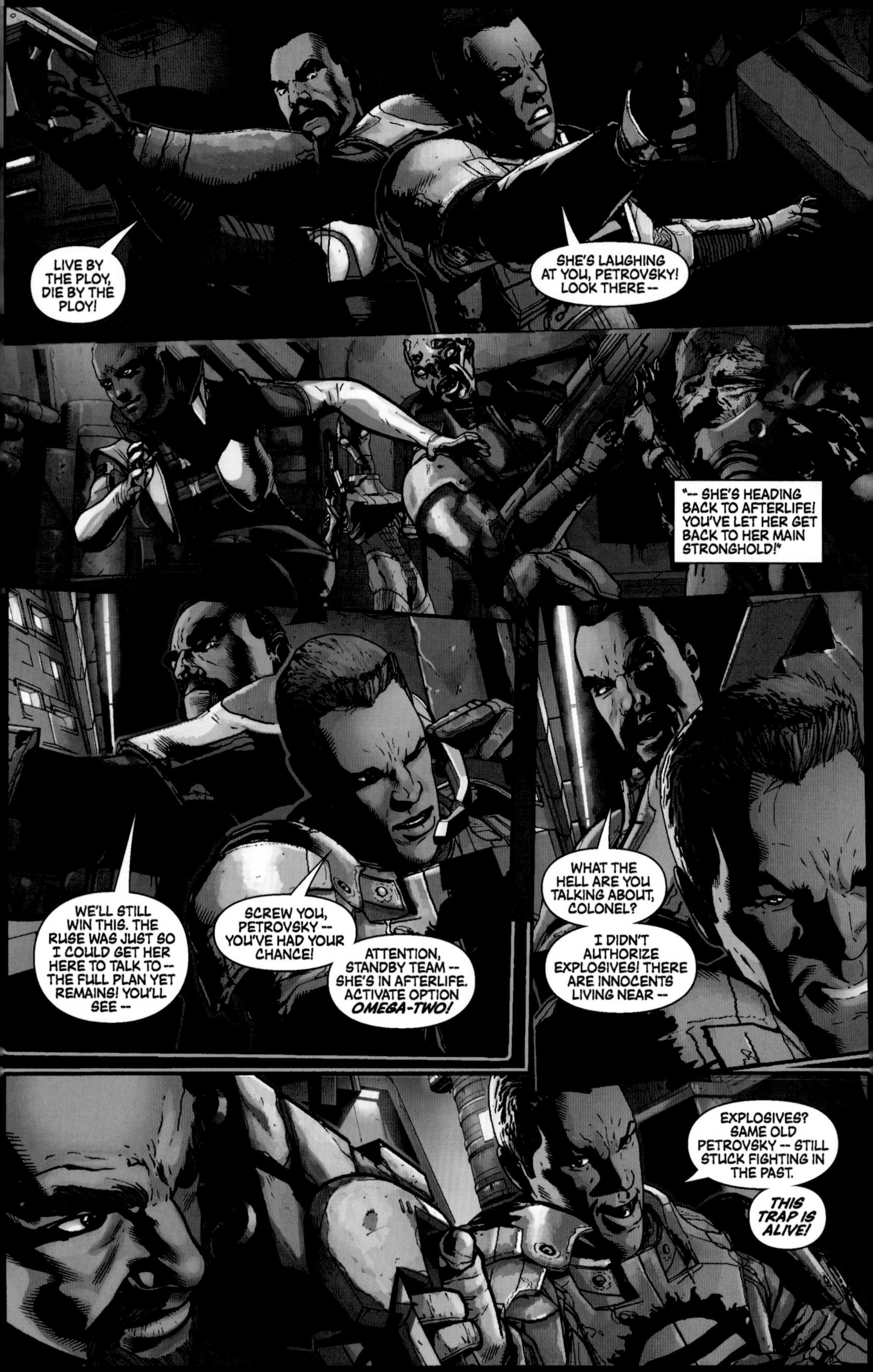
LIVE BY THE PLOY, DIE BY THE PLOY!
SHE'S LAUGHING AT YOU, PETROVSKY! LOOK THERE --
"-- SHE'S HEADING BACK TO AFTERLIFE! YOU'VE LET HER GET BACK TO HER MAIN STRONGHOLD!"
WE'LL STILL WIN THIS. THE RUSE WAS JUST SO I COULD GET HER HERE TO TALK TO -- THE FULL PLAN YET REMAINS! YOU'LL SEE --
SCREW YOU, PETROVSKY -- YOU'VE HAD YOUR CHANCE!
ATTENTION, STANDBY TEAM -- SHE'S IN AFTERLIFE. ACTIVATE OPTION OMEGA-TWO!
WHAT THE HELL ARE YOU TALKING ABOUT, COLONEL?
I DIDN'T AUTHORIZE EXPLOSIVES! THERE ARE INNOCENTS LIVING NEAR --
EXPLOSIVES? SAME OLD PETROVSKY -- STILL STUCK FIGHTING IN THE PAST.
THIS TRAP IS ALIVE!

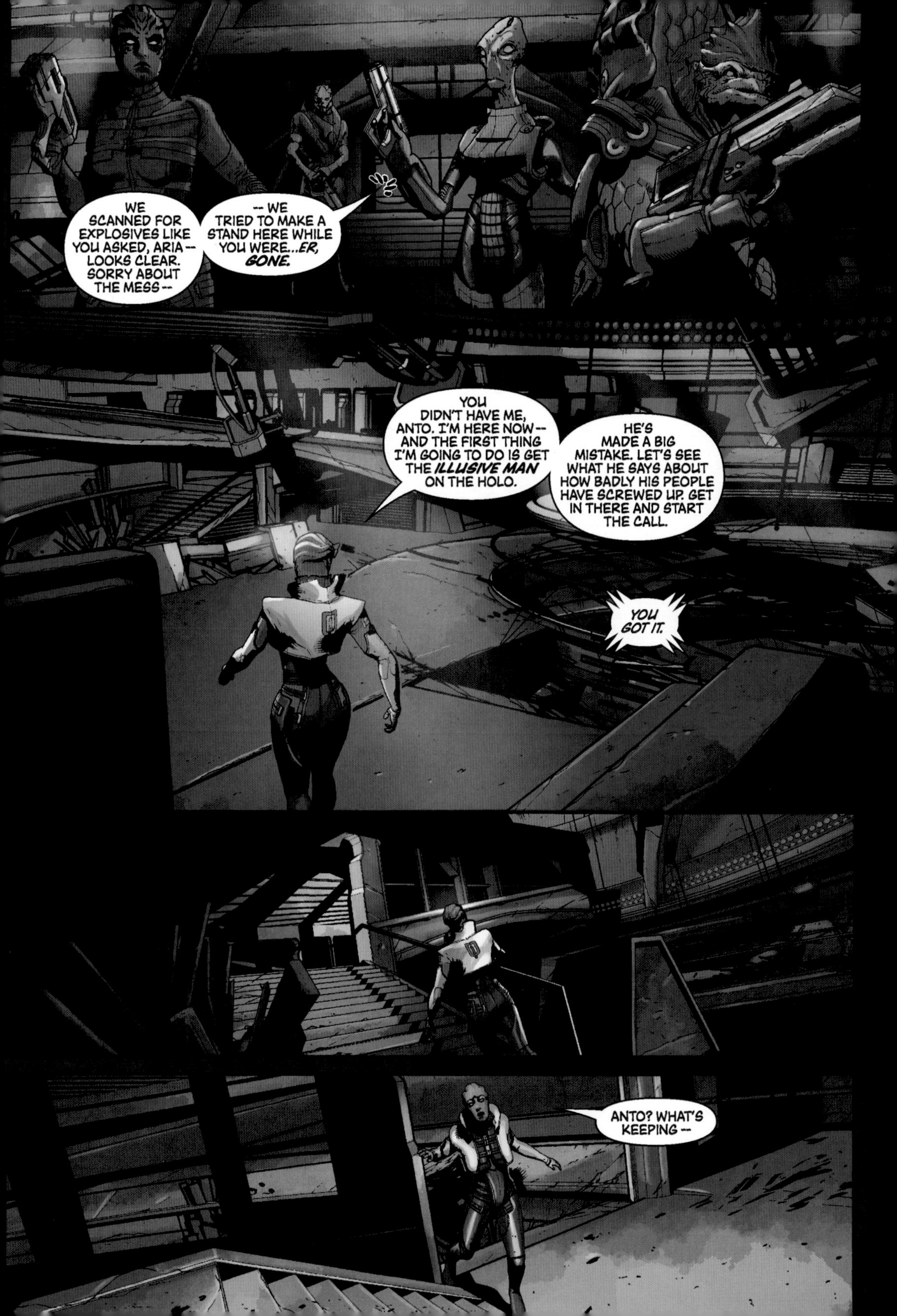
WE SCANNED FOR EXPLOSIVES LIKE YOU ASKED, ARIA -- LOOKS CLEAR. SORRY ABOUT THE MESS --
-- WE TRIED TO MAKE A STAND HERE WHILE YOU WERE... ER, GONE.
YOU DIDN'T HAVE ME, ANTO. I'M HERE NOW -- AND THE FIRST THING I'M GOING TO DO IS GET THE ILLUSIVE MAN ON THE HOLO.
HE'S MADE A BIG MISTAKE. LET'S SEE WHAT HE SAYS ABOUT HOW BADLY HIS PEOPLE HAVE SCREWED UP. GET IN THERE AND START THE CALL.
YOU GOT IT.
ANTO? WHAT'S KEEPING --

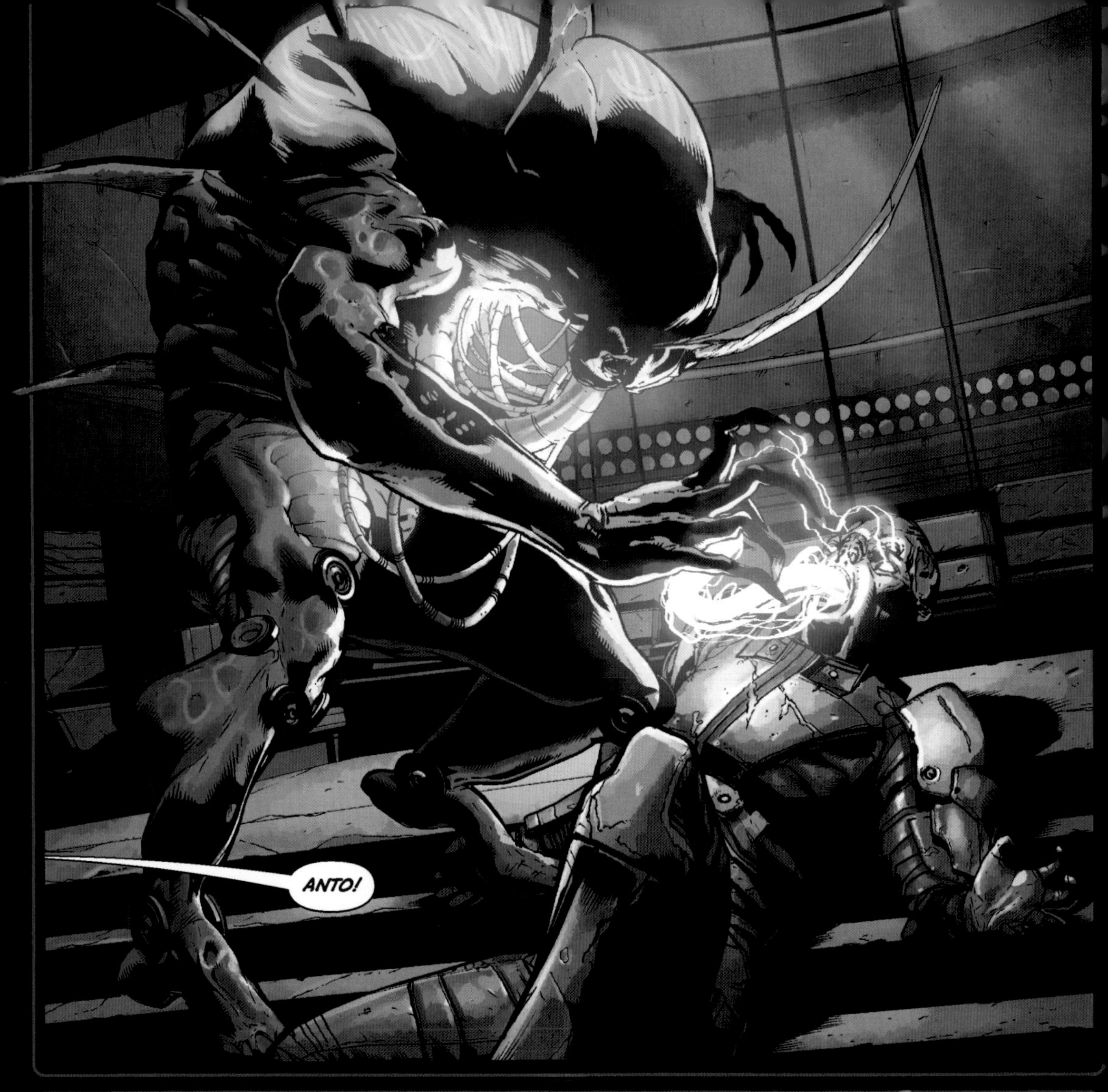
ANTO!
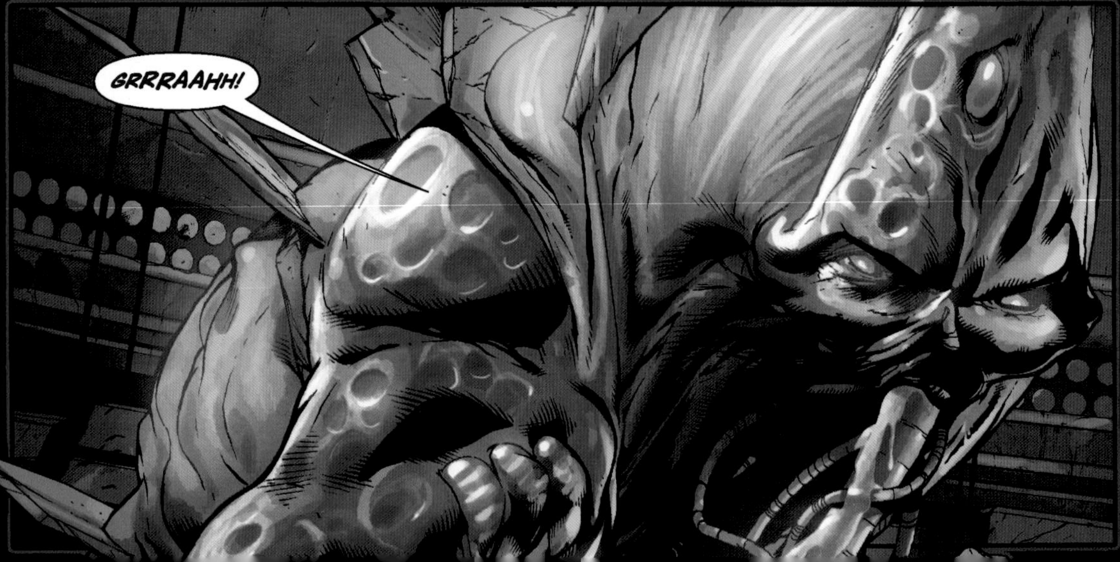
GRRRAAHH!

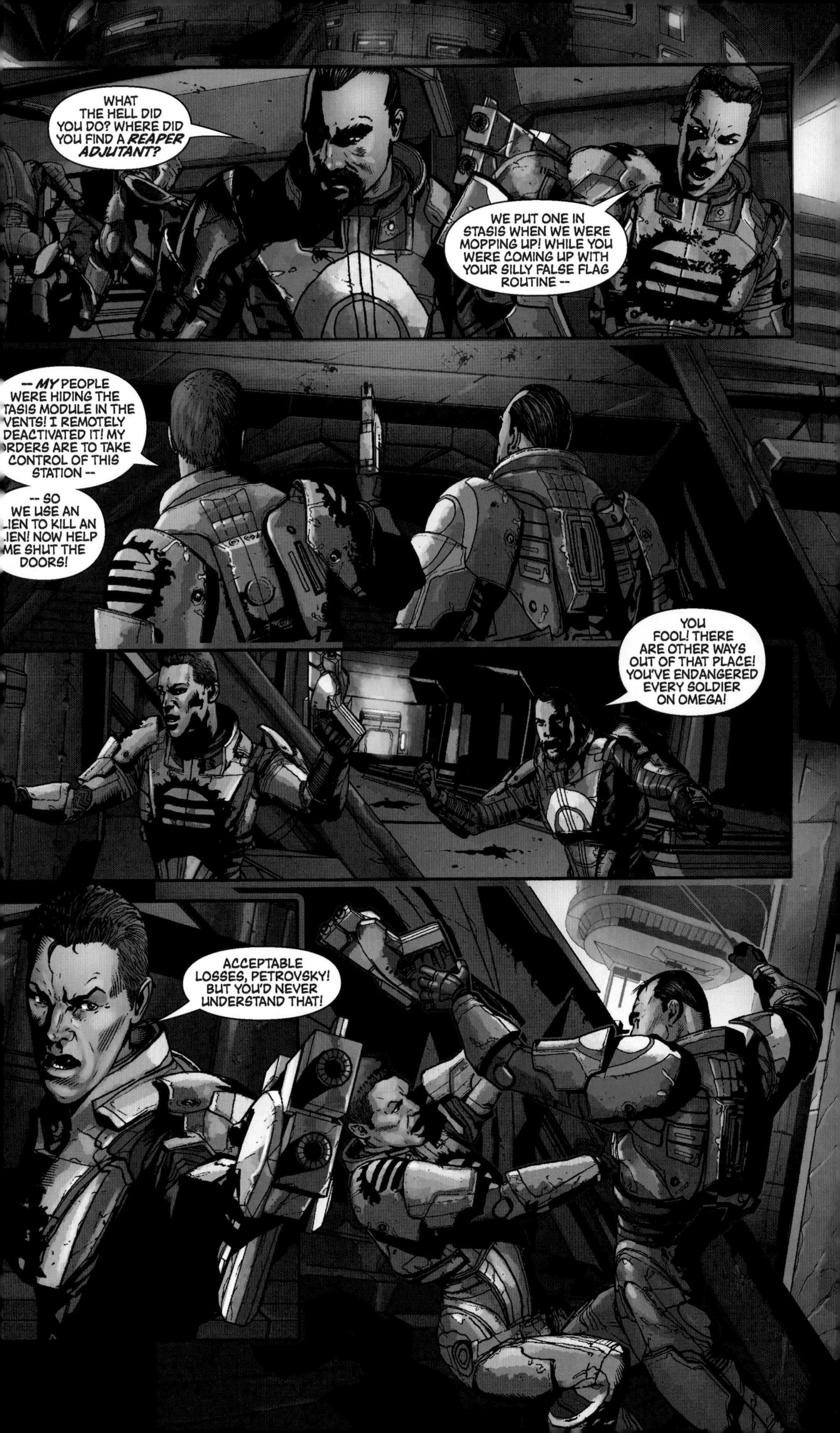
WHAT THE HELL DID YOU DO? WHERE DID YOU FIND A *REAPER ADJUTANT?*
WE PUT ONE IN STASIS WHEN WE WERE MOPPING UP! WHILE YOU WERE COMING UP WITH YOUR SILLY FALSE FLAG ROUTINE --
-- *MY* PEOPLE WERE HIDING THE TASIS MODULE IN THE VENTS! I REMOTELY DEACTIVATED IT! MY RDERS ARE TO TAKE CONTROL OF THIS STATION --
-- SO WE USE AN LIEN TO KILL AN LIEN! NOW HELP ME SHUT THE DOORS!
YOU FOOL! THERE ARE OTHER WAYS OUT OF THAT PLACE! YOU'VE ENDANGERED EVERY SOLDIER ON OMEGA!
ACCEPTABLE LOSSES, PETROVSKY! BUT YOU'D NEVER UNDERSTAND THAT!

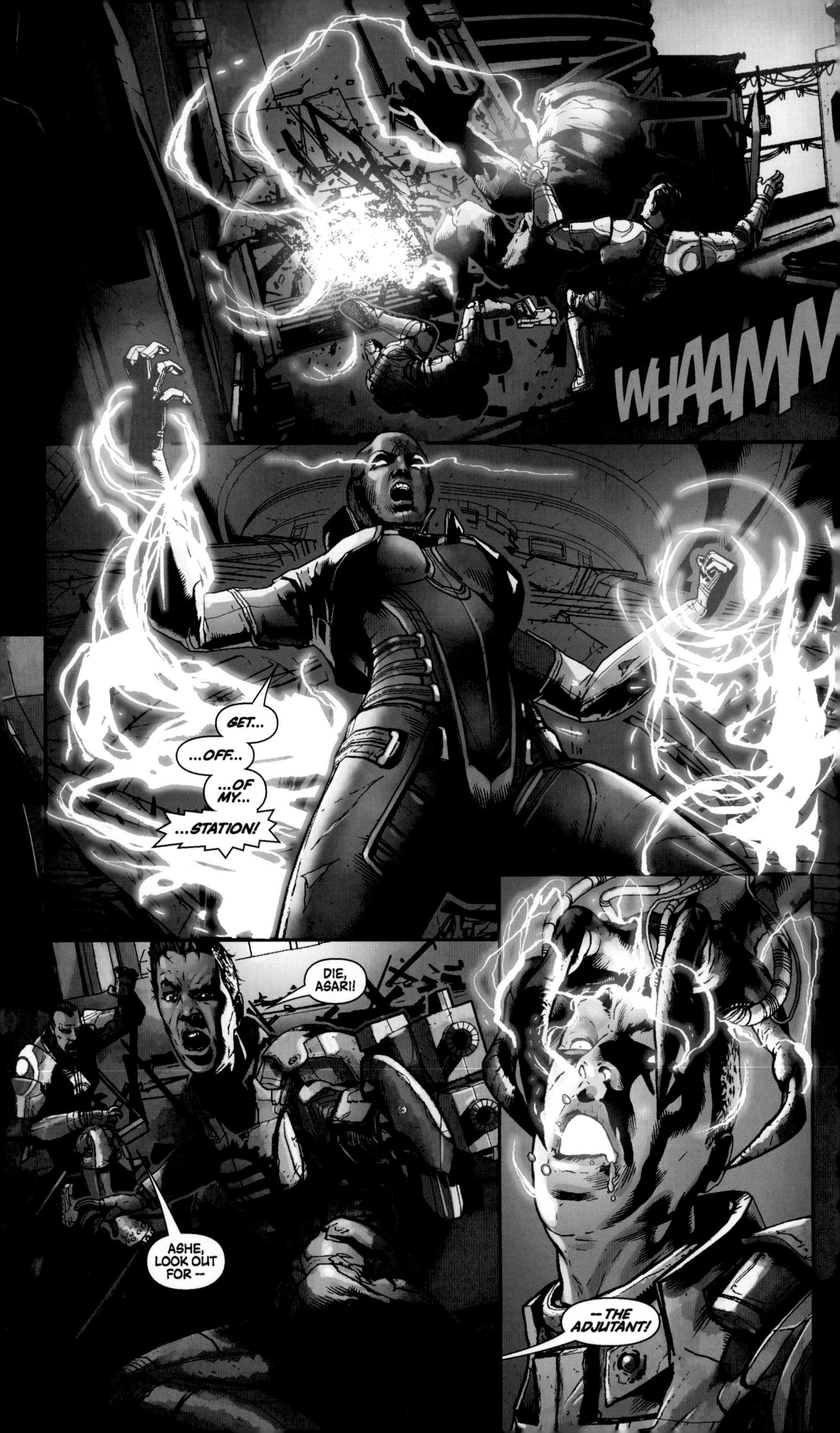
WHAAMM
GET...
...OFF...
...OF MY...
...STATION!
DIE, ASARI!
ASHE, LOOK OUT FOR --
-- THE ADJUTANT!

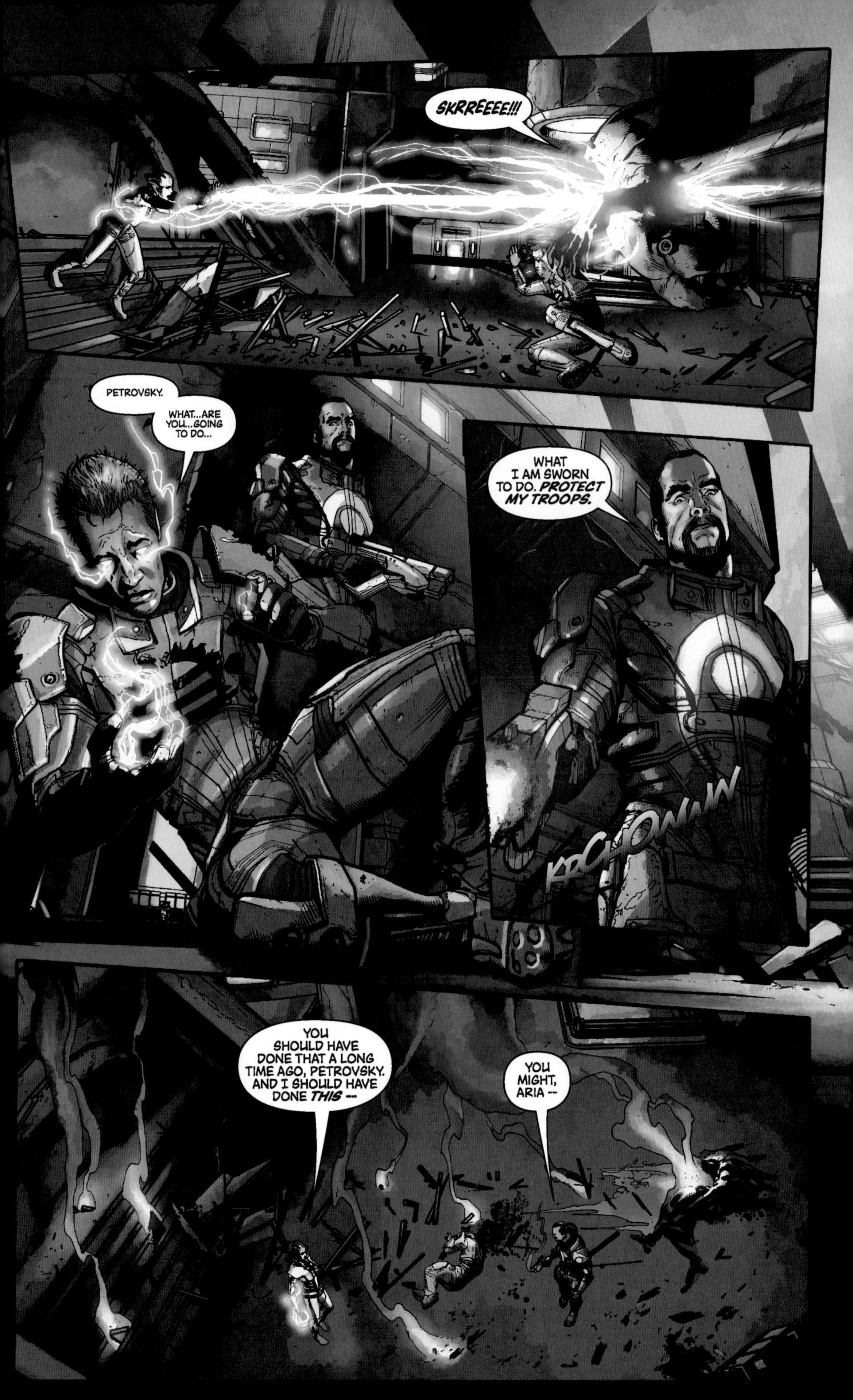
SKRREEEE!!!
PETROVSKY.
WHAT...ARE YOU...GOING TO DO...
WHAT I AM SWORN TO DO. PROTECT MY TROOPS.
KRCHOWW
YOU SHOULD HAVE DONE THAT A LONG TIME AGO, PETROVSKY. AND I SHOULD HAVE DONE THIS --
YOU MIGHT, ARIA --

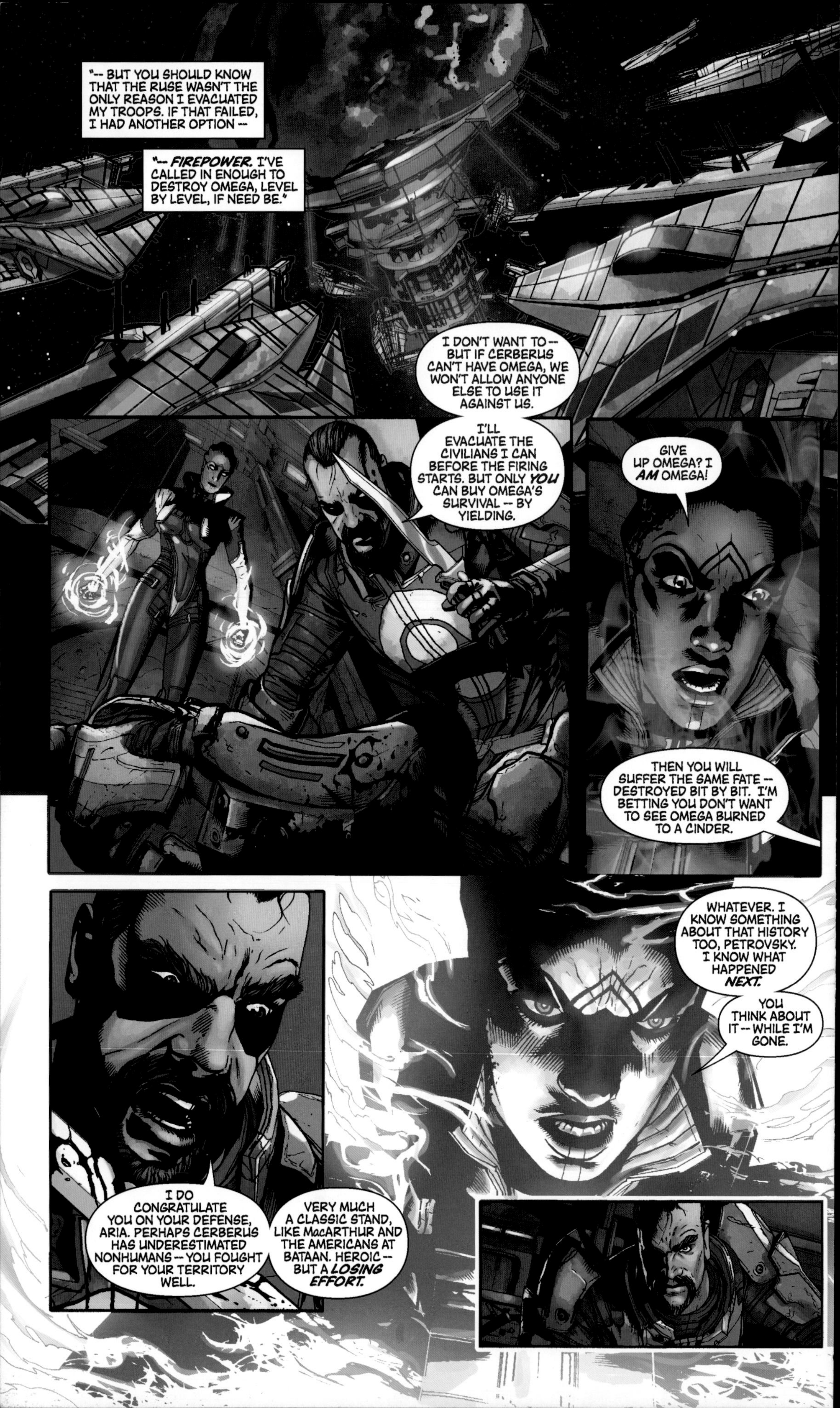
"-- BUT YOU SHOULD KNOW THAT THE RUSE WASN'T THE ONLY REASON I EVACUATED MY TROOPS. IF THAT FAILED, I HAD ANOTHER OPTION --
"-- FIREPOWER. I'VE CALLED IN ENOUGH TO DESTROY OMEGA, LEVEL BY LEVEL, IF NEED BE."
I DON'T WANT TO -- BUT IF CERBERUS CAN'T HAVE OMEGA, WE WON'T ALLOW ANYONE ELSE TO USE IT AGAINST US.
I'LL EVACUATE THE CIVILIANS I CAN BEFORE THE FIRING STARTS. BUT ONLY YOU CAN BUY OMEGA'S SURVIVAL -- BY YIELDING.
GIVE UP OMEGA? I AM OMEGA!
THEN YOU WILL SUFFER THE SAME FATE -- DESTROYED BIT BY BIT. I'M BETTING YOU DON'T WANT TO SEE OMEGA BURNED TO A CINDER.
I DO CONGRATULATE YOU ON YOUR DEFENSE, ARIA. PERHAPS CERBERUS HAS UNDERESTIMATED NONHUMANS -- YOU FOUGHT FOR YOUR TERRITORY WELL.
VERY MUCH A CLASSIC STAND, LIKE MacARTHUR AND THE AMERICANS AT BATAAN. HEROIC -- BUT A LOSING EFFORT.
WHATEVER. I KNOW SOMETHING ABOUT THAT HISTORY TOO, PETROVSKY. I KNOW WHAT HAPPENED NEXT.
YOU THINK ABOUT IT -- WHILE I'M GONE.

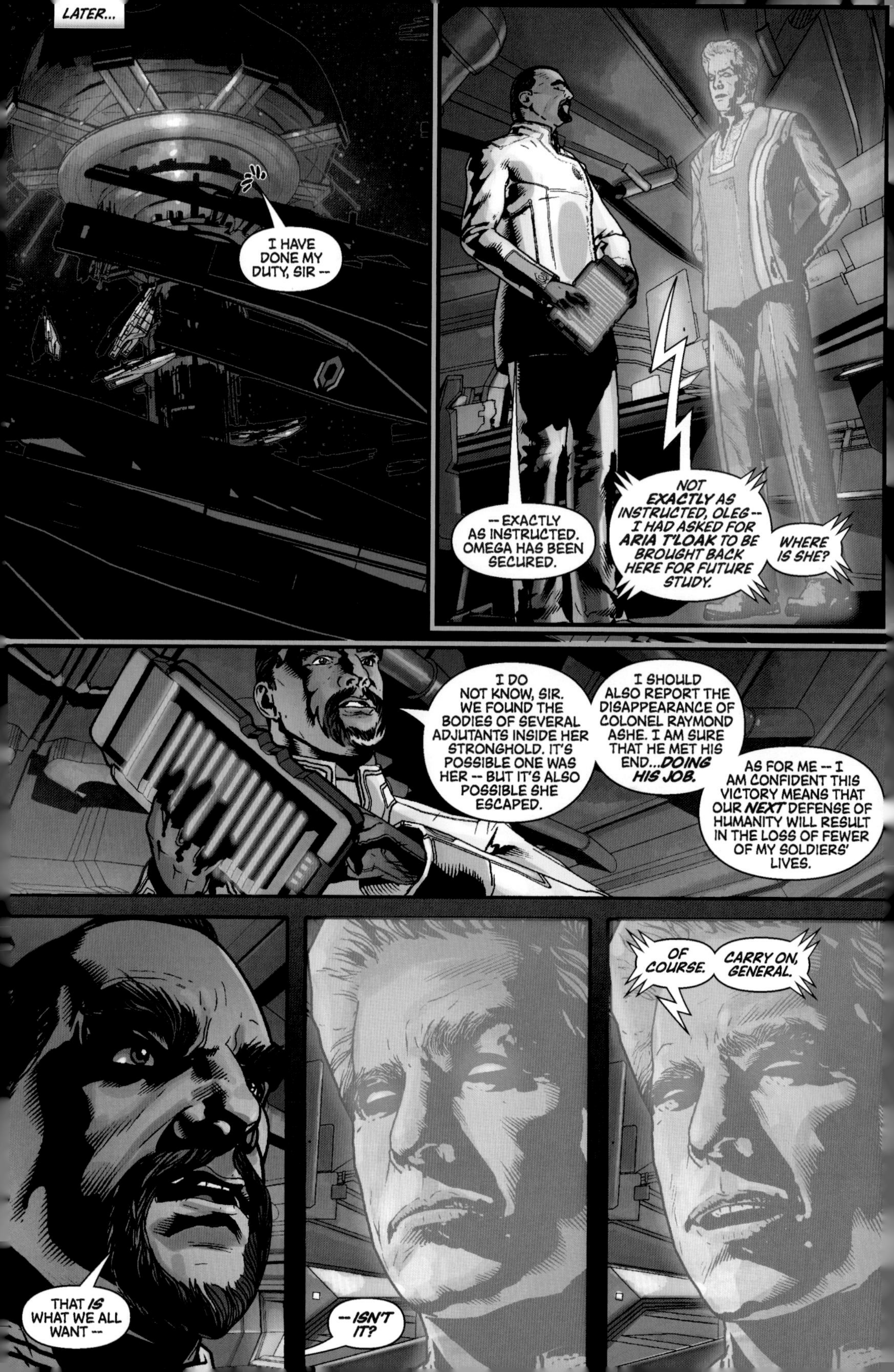
LATER...
I HAVE DONE MY DUTY, SIR --
-- EXACTLY AS INSTRUCTED. OMEGA HAS BEEN SECURED.
NOT *EXACTLY* AS INSTRUCTED, OLEG -- I HAD ASKED FOR **ARIA T'LOAK** TO BE BROUGHT BACK HERE FOR FUTURE STUDY.
WHERE IS SHE?
I DO NOT KNOW, SIR. WE FOUND THE BODIES OF SEVERAL ADJUTANTS INSIDE HER STRONGHOLD. IT'S POSSIBLE ONE WAS HER -- BUT IT'S ALSO POSSIBLE SHE ESCAPED.
I SHOULD ALSO REPORT THE DISAPPEARANCE OF COLONEL RAYMOND ASHE. I AM SURE THAT HE MET HIS END...**DOING HIS JOB.**
AS FOR ME -- I AM CONFIDENT THIS VICTORY MEANS THAT OUR **NEXT** DEFENSE OF HUMANITY WILL RESULT IN THE LOSS OF FEWER OF MY SOLDIERS' LIVES.
THAT **IS** WHAT WE ALL WANT --
-- **ISN'T IT?**
OF COURSE.
CARRY ON, GENERAL.

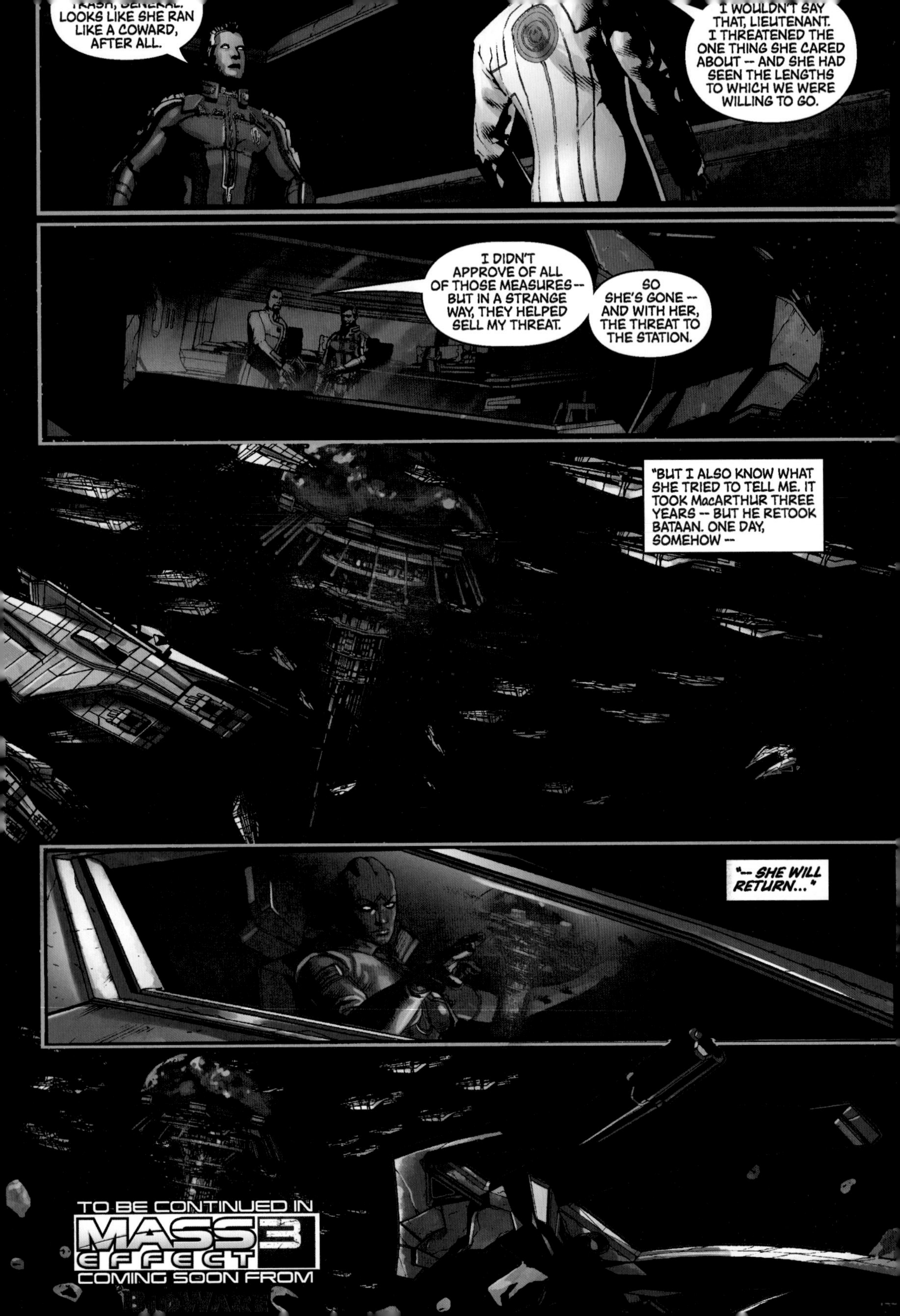
LOOKS LIKE SHE RAN LIKE A COWARD, AFTER ALL.
I WOULDN'T SAY THAT, LIEUTENANT. I THREATENED THE ONE THING SHE CARED ABOUT -- AND SHE HAD SEEN THE LENGTHS TO WHICH WE WERE WILLING TO GO.
I DIDN'T APPROVE OF ALL OF THOSE MEASURES -- BUT IN A STRANGE WAY, THEY HELPED SELL MY THREAT.
SO SHE'S GONE -- AND WITH HER, THE THREAT TO THE STATION.
"BUT I ALSO KNOW WHAT SHE TRIED TO TELL ME. IT TOOK MacARTHUR THREE YEARS -- BUT HE RETOOK BATAAN. ONE DAY, SOMEHOW --
"-- SHE WILL RETURN..."
TO BE CONTINUED IN
MASS EFFECT 3
COMING SOON FROM

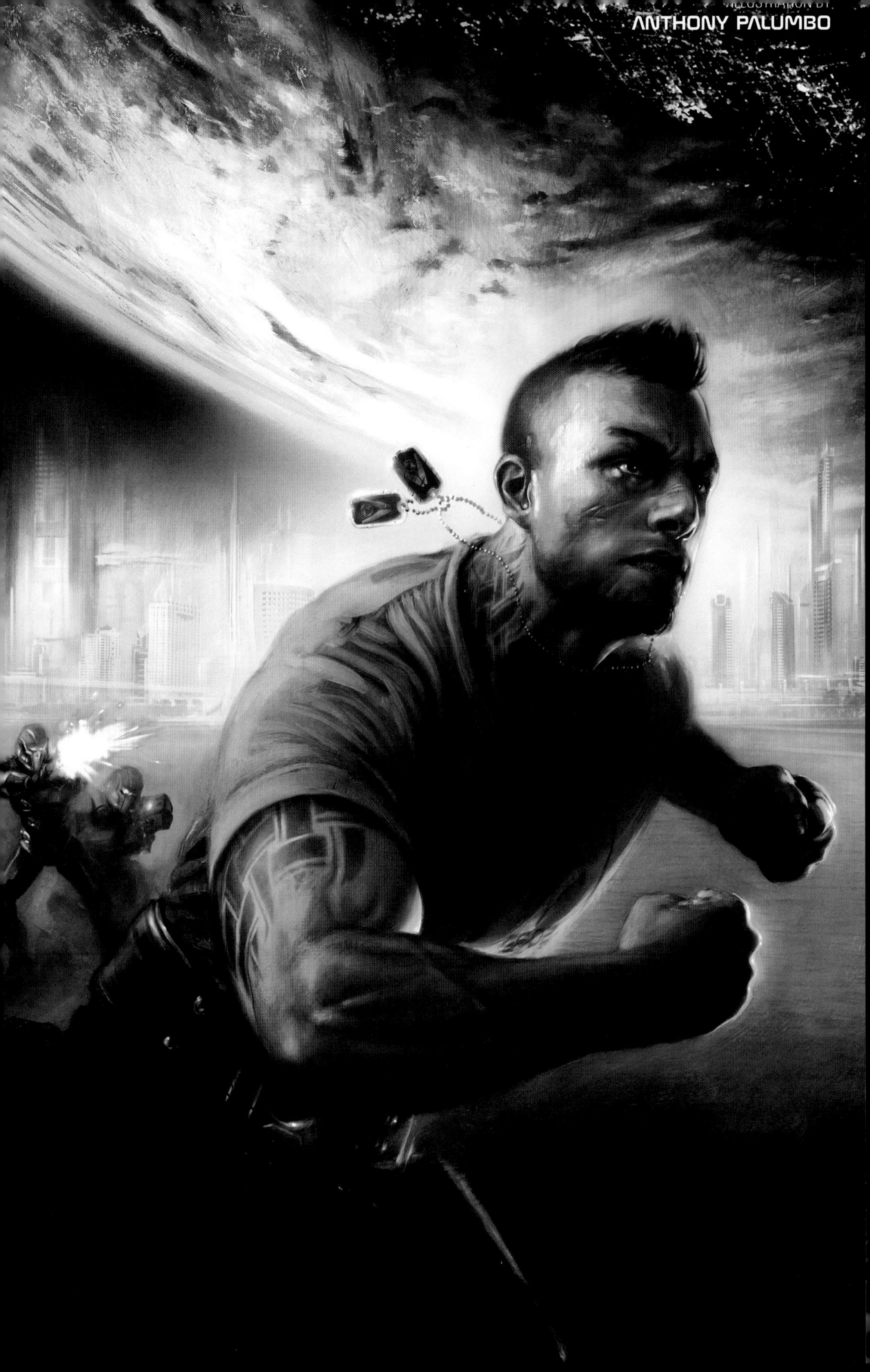
ILLUSTRATION BY
ANTHONY PALUMBO

HOMEWORLDS: JAMES VEGA

SCRIPT
MAC WALTERS

ART
EDUARDO FRANCISCO

COLORS
MICHAEL ATIYEH

LETTERING
MICHAEL HEISLER

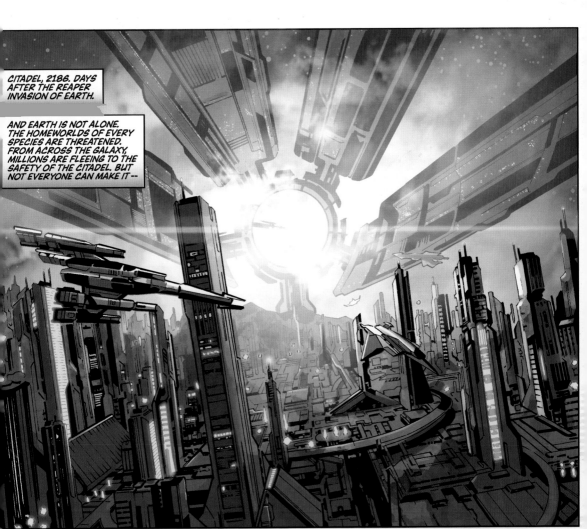

CITADEL, 2186. DAYS AFTER THE REAPER INVASION OF EARTH.

AND EARTH IS NOT ALONE. THE HOMEWORLDS OF EVERY SPECIES ARE THREATENED. FROM ACROSS THE GALAXY, MILLIONS ARE FLEEING TO THE SAFETY OF THE CITADEL, BUT NOT EVERYONE CAN MAKE IT --

-- AND THOSE WHO HAVE MADE IT ARE DESPERATE TO FIND OUT NEWS OF THEIR LOVED ONES.

THEIR FAMILIES.

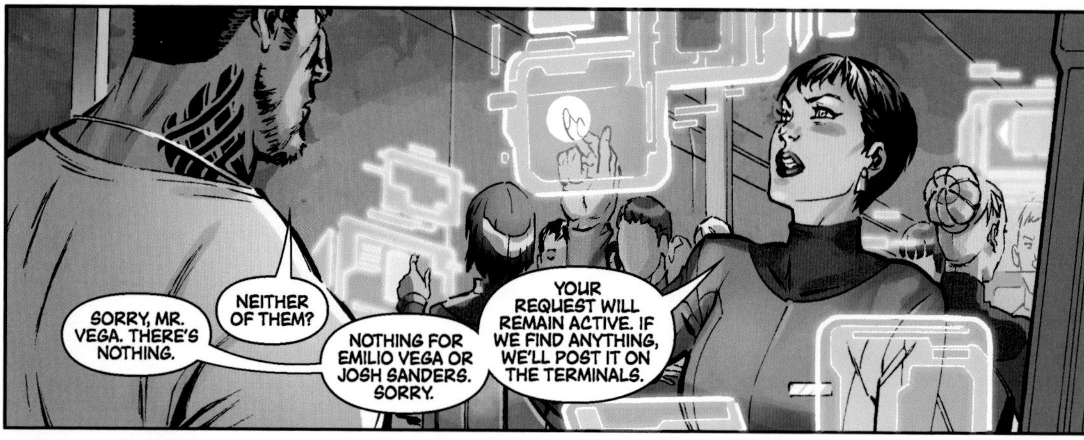
SORRY, MR. VEGA. THERE'S NOTHING.
NEITHER OF THEM?
NOTHING FOR EMILIO VEGA OR JOSH SANDERS. SORRY.
YOUR REQUEST WILL REMAIN ACTIVE. IF WE FIND ANYTHING, WE'LL POST IT ON THE TERMINALS.
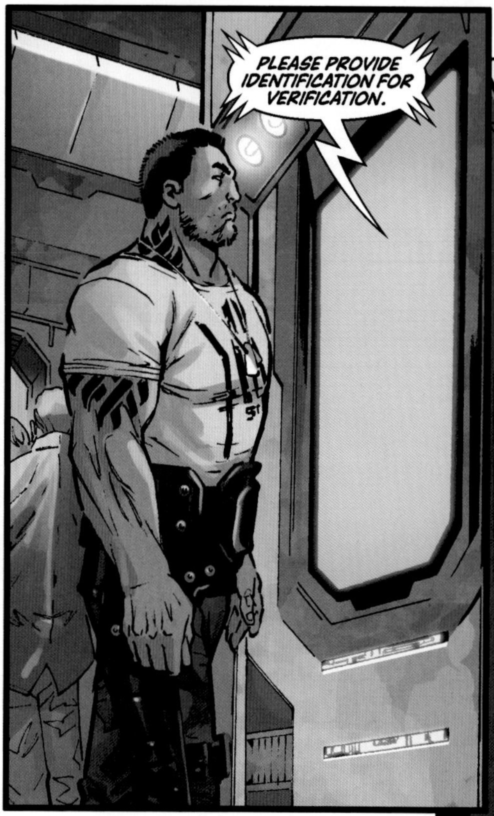
PLEASE PROVIDE IDENTIFICATION FOR VERIFICATION.
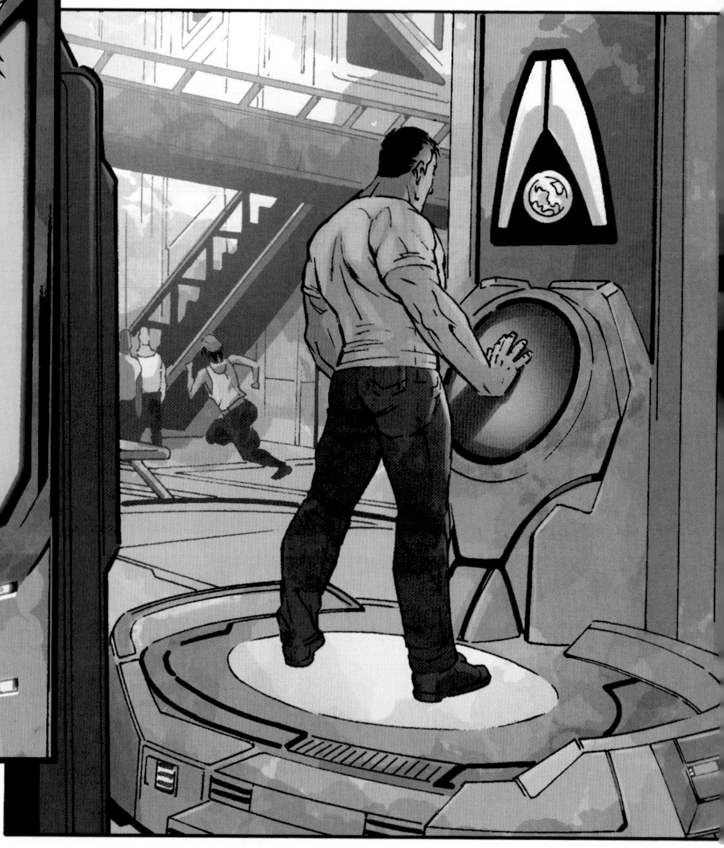
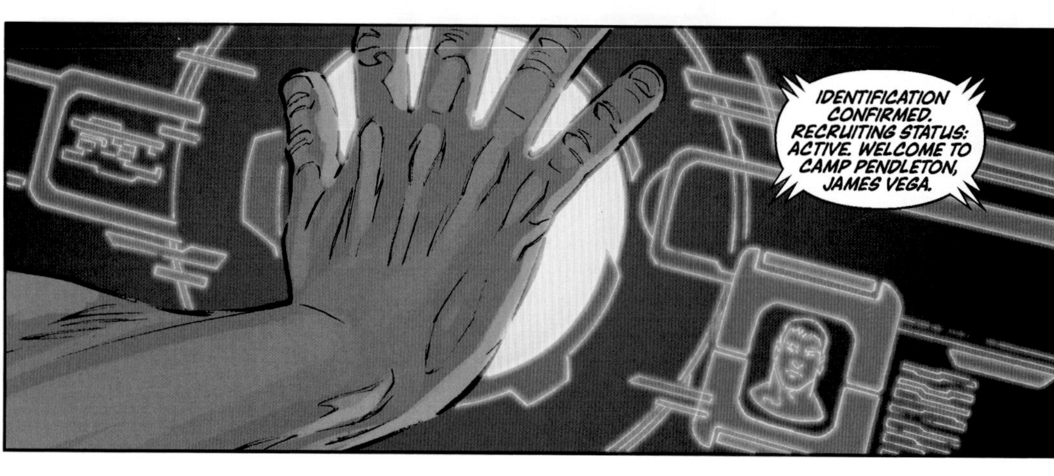
IDENTIFICATION CONFIRMED. RECRUITING STATUS: ACTIVE. WELCOME TO CAMP PENDLETON, JAMES VEGA.

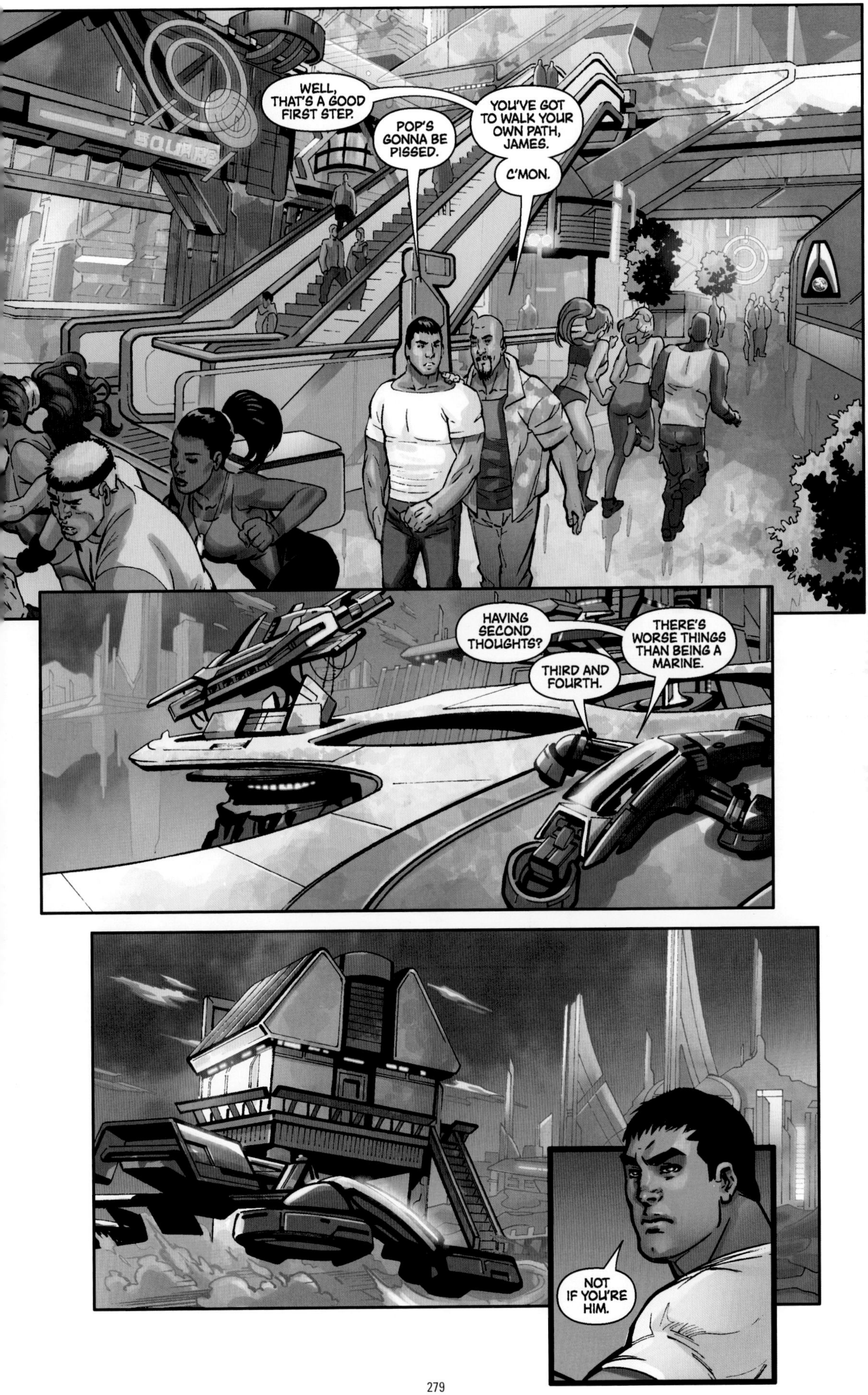
WELL, THAT'S A GOOD FIRST STEP.
POP'S GONNA BE PISSED.
YOU'VE GOT TO WALK YOUR OWN PATH, JAMES.
C'MON.
HAVING SECOND THOUGHTS?
THIRD AND FOURTH.
THERE'S WORSE THINGS THAN BEING A MARINE.
NOT IF YOU'RE HIM.

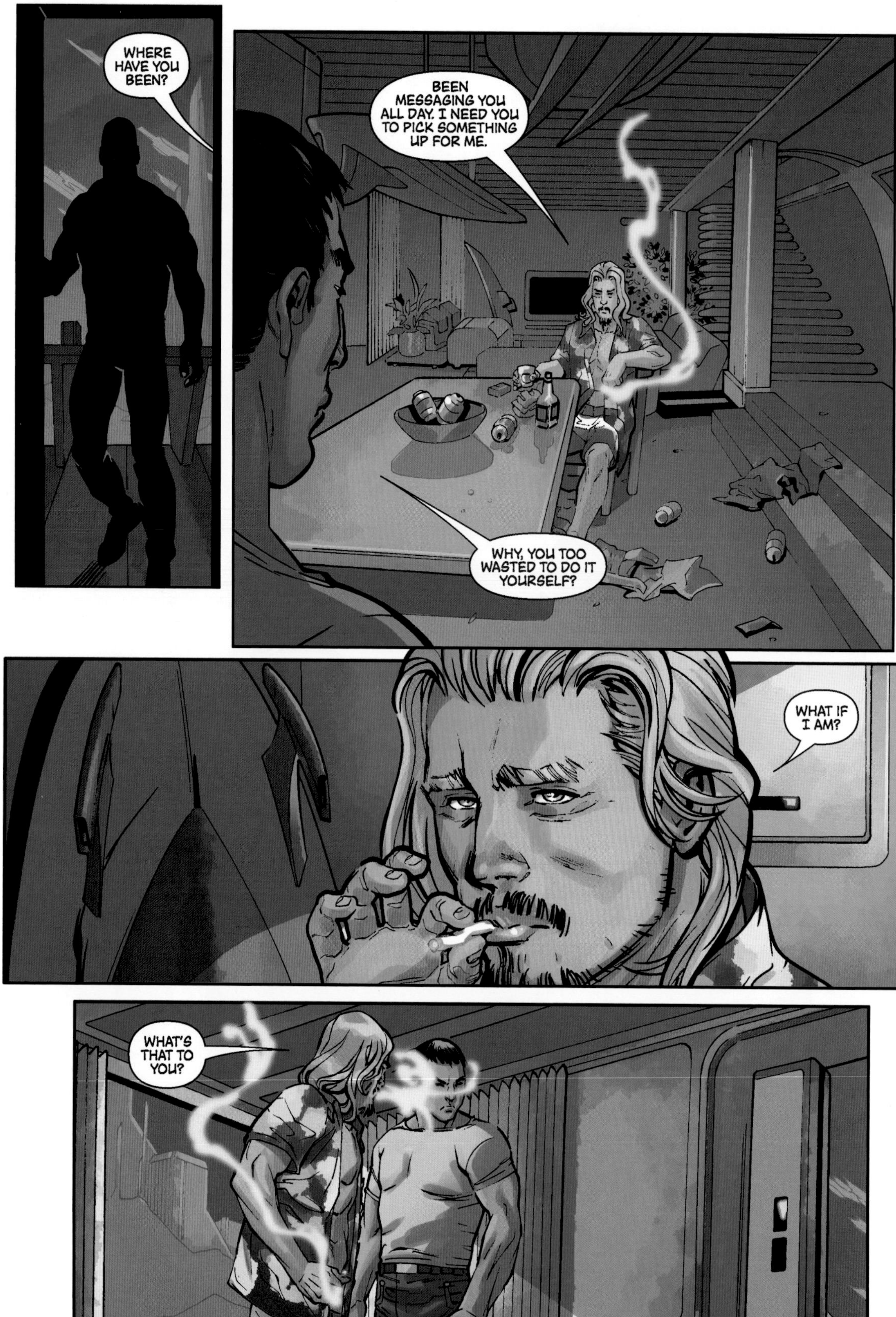
WHERE HAVE YOU BEEN?
BEEN MESSAGING YOU ALL DAY. I NEED YOU TO PICK SOMETHING UP FOR ME.
WHY, YOU TOO WASTED TO DO IT YOURSELF?
WHAT IF I AM?
WHAT'S THAT TO YOU?

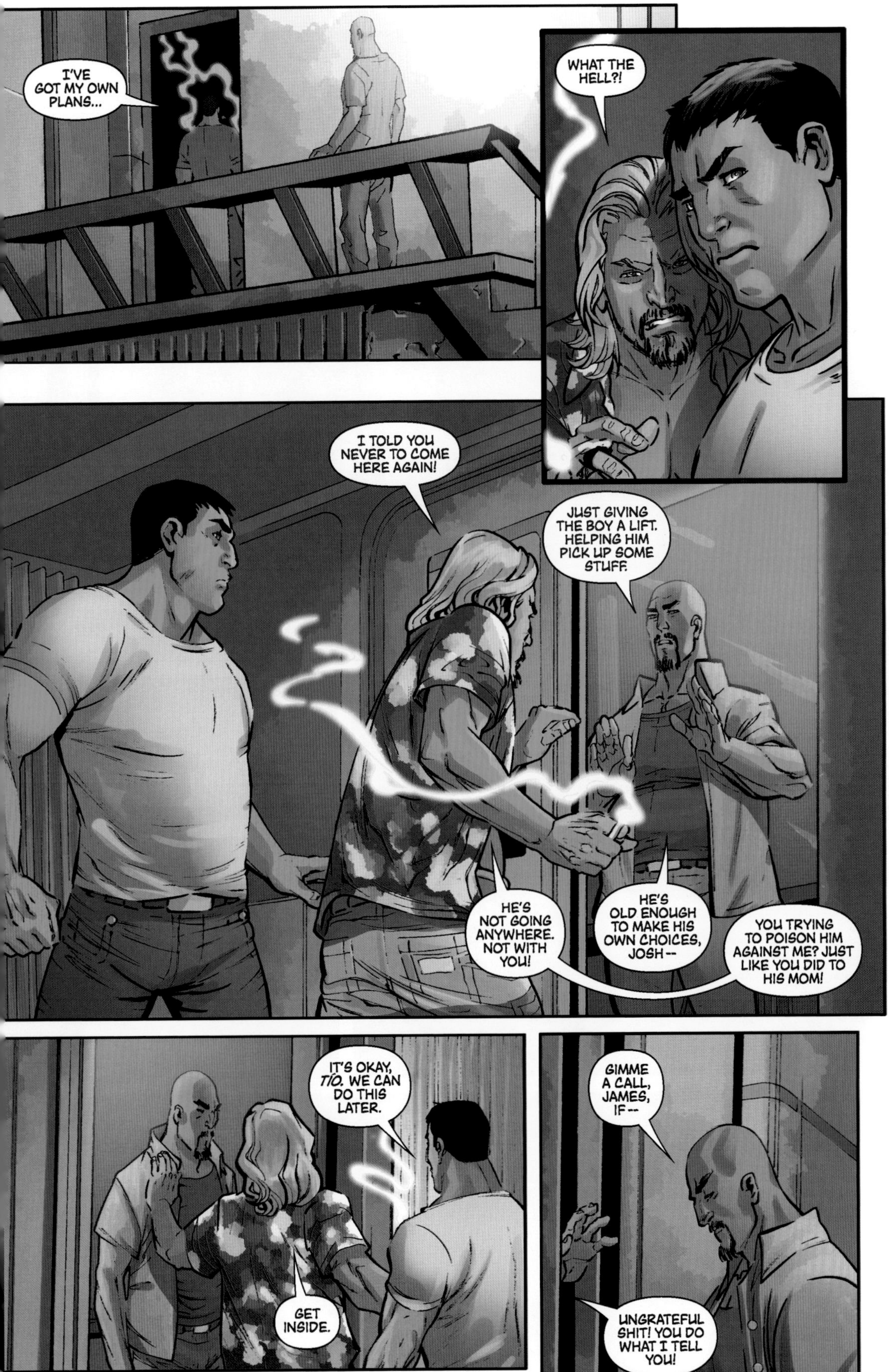
I'VE GOT MY OWN PLANS...
WHAT THE HELL?!
I TOLD YOU NEVER TO COME HERE AGAIN!
JUST GIVING THE BOY A LIFT. HELPING HIM PICK UP SOME STUFF.
HE'S NOT GOING ANYWHERE. NOT WITH YOU!
HE'S OLD ENOUGH TO MAKE HIS OWN CHOICES, JOSH--
YOU TRYING TO POISON HIM AGAINST ME? JUST LIKE YOU DID TO HIS MOM!
IT'S OKAY, *TÍO.* WE CAN DO THIS LATER.
GET INSIDE.
GIMME A CALL, JAMES, IF--
UNGRATEFUL SHIT! YOU DO WHAT I TELL YOU!

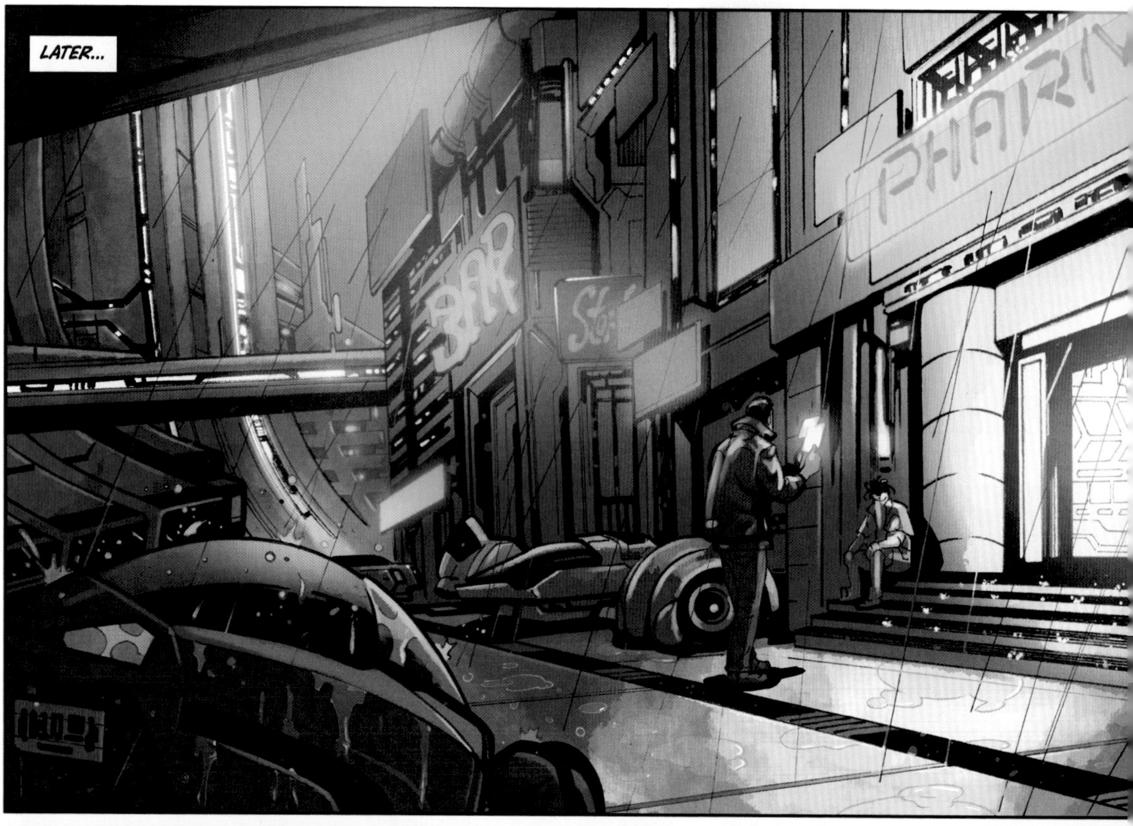
LATER...

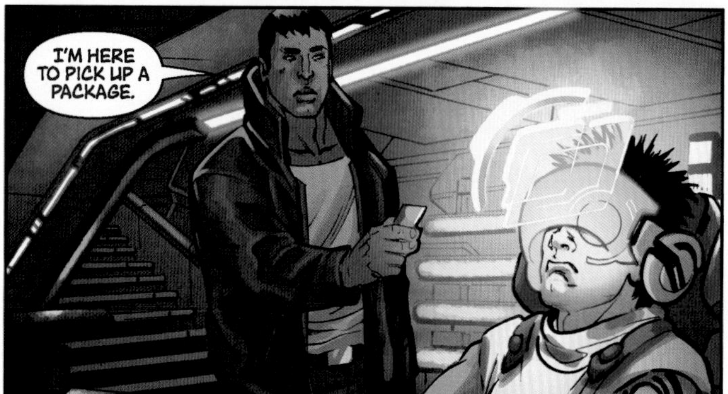
I'M HERE TO PICK UP A PACKAGE.

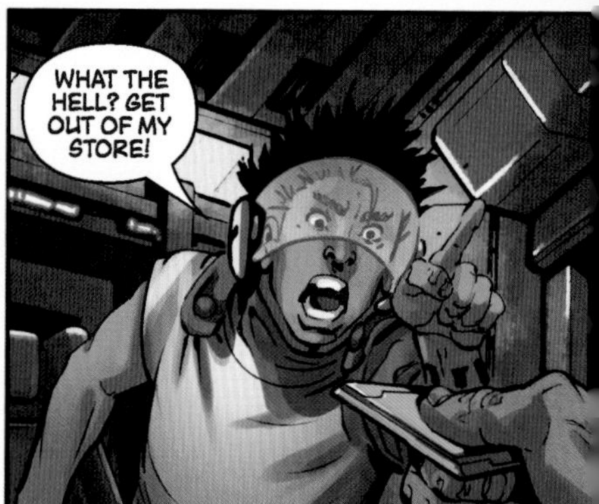
WHAT THE HELL? GET OUT OF MY STORE!

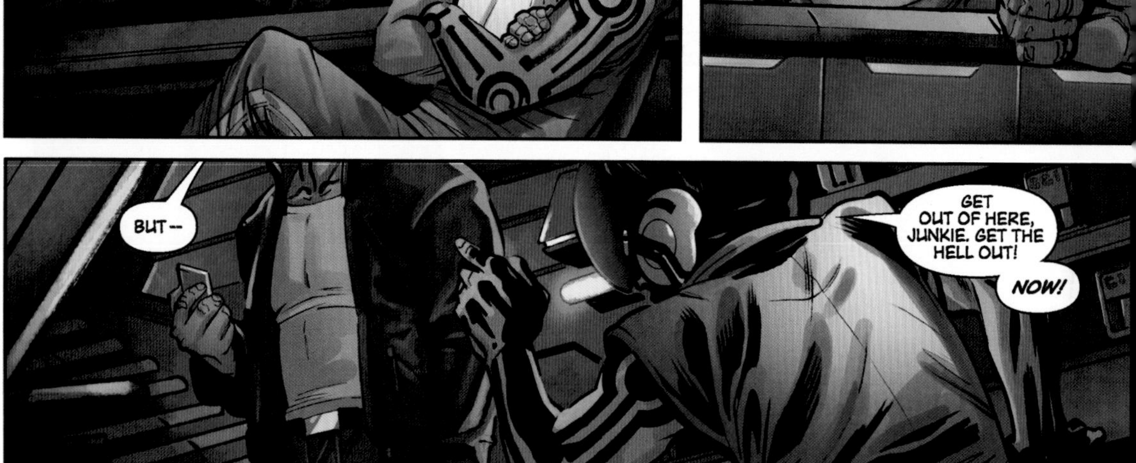
BUT --
GET OUT OF HERE, JUNKIE. GET THE HELL OUT!
NOW!

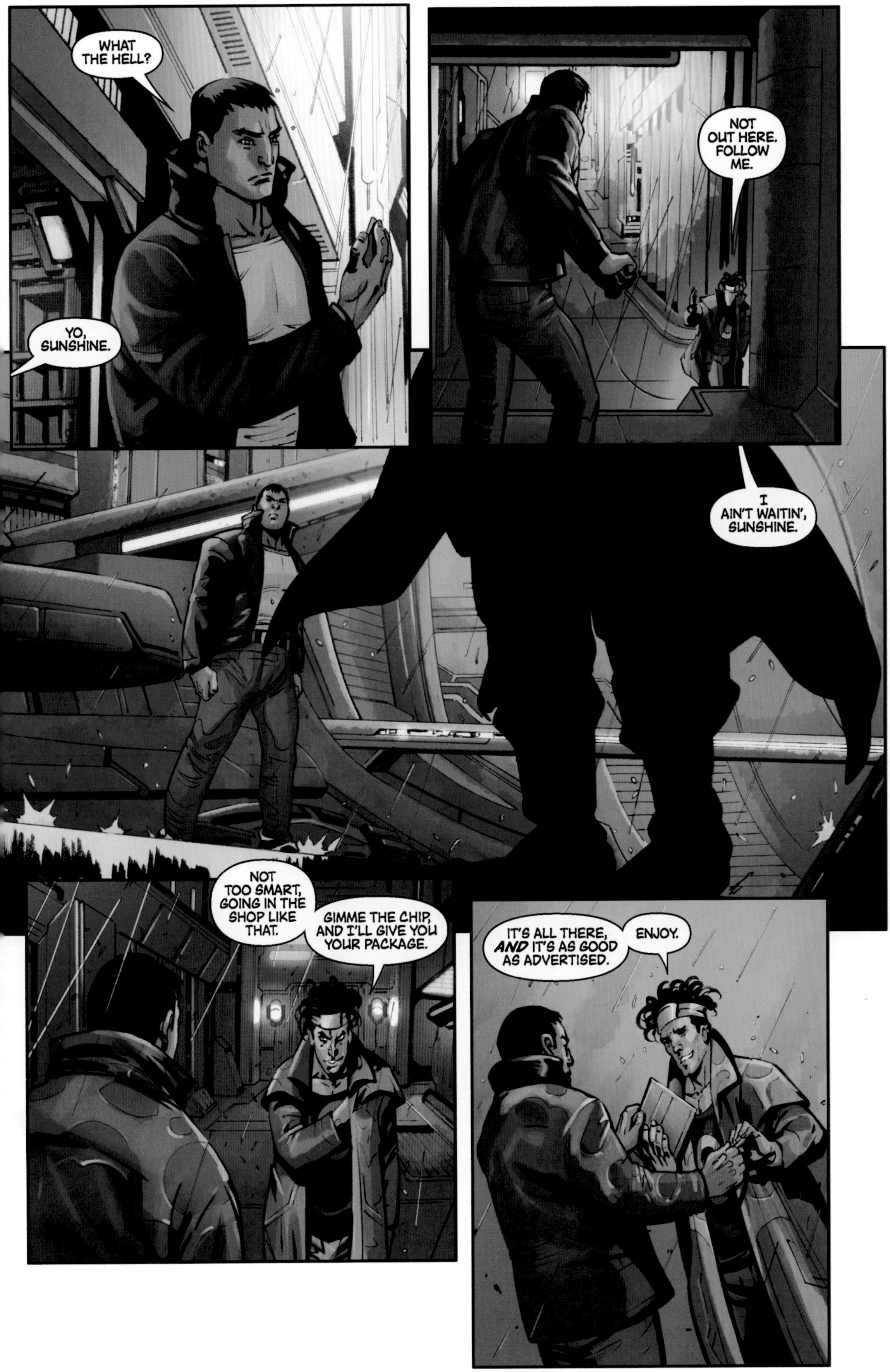
WHAT THE HELL?
YO, SUNSHINE.
NOT OUT HERE. FOLLOW ME.
I AIN'T WAITIN', SUNSHINE.
NOT TOO SMART, GOING IN THE SHOP LIKE THAT.
GIMME THE CHIP, AND I'LL GIVE YOU YOUR PACKAGE.
IT'S ALL THERE, ***AND*** IT'S AS GOOD AS ADVERTISED.
ENJOY.

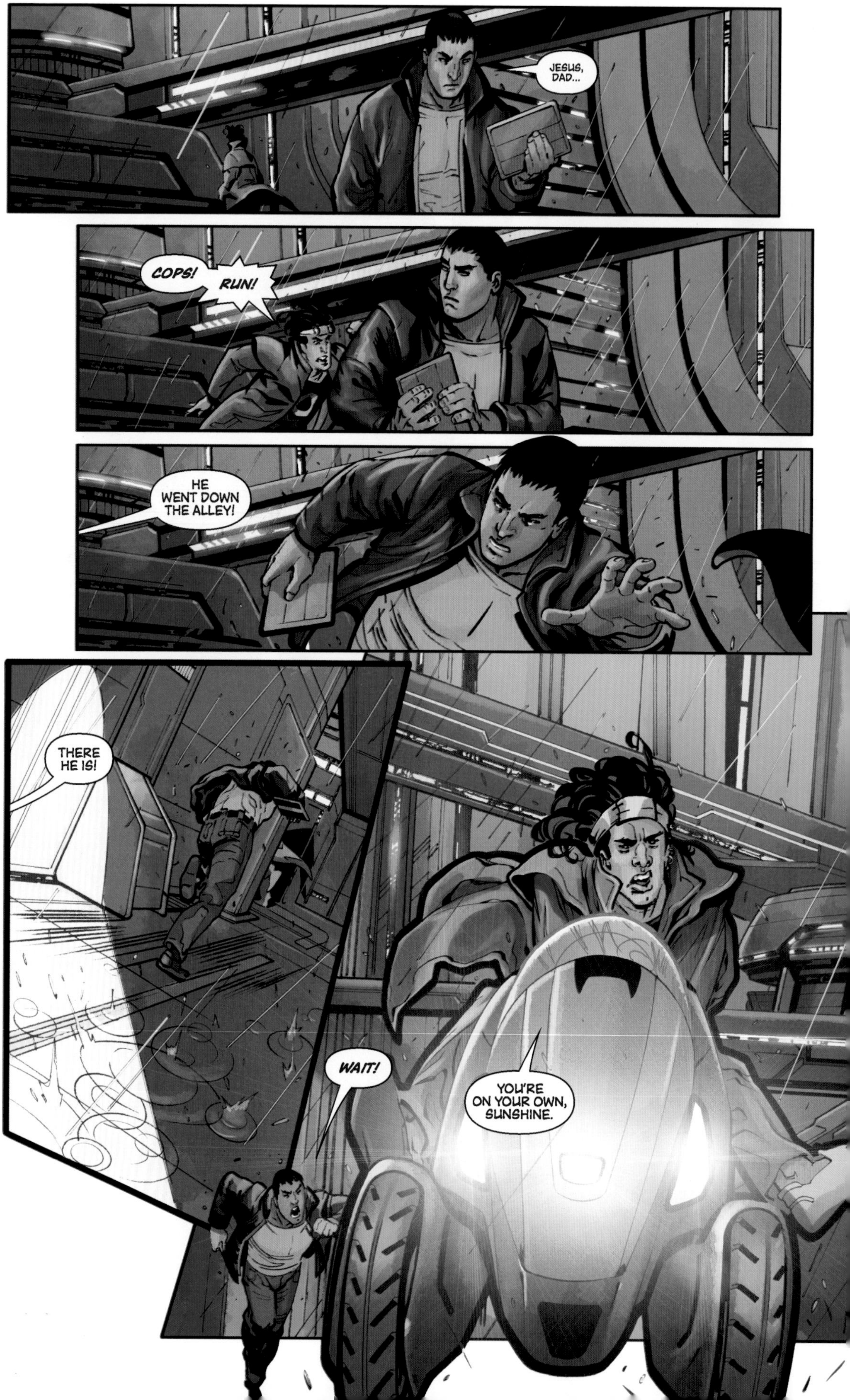
JESUS, DAD...
COPS!
RUN!
HE WENT DOWN THE ALLEY!
THERE HE IS!
WAIT!
YOU'RE ON YOUR OWN, SUNSHINE.

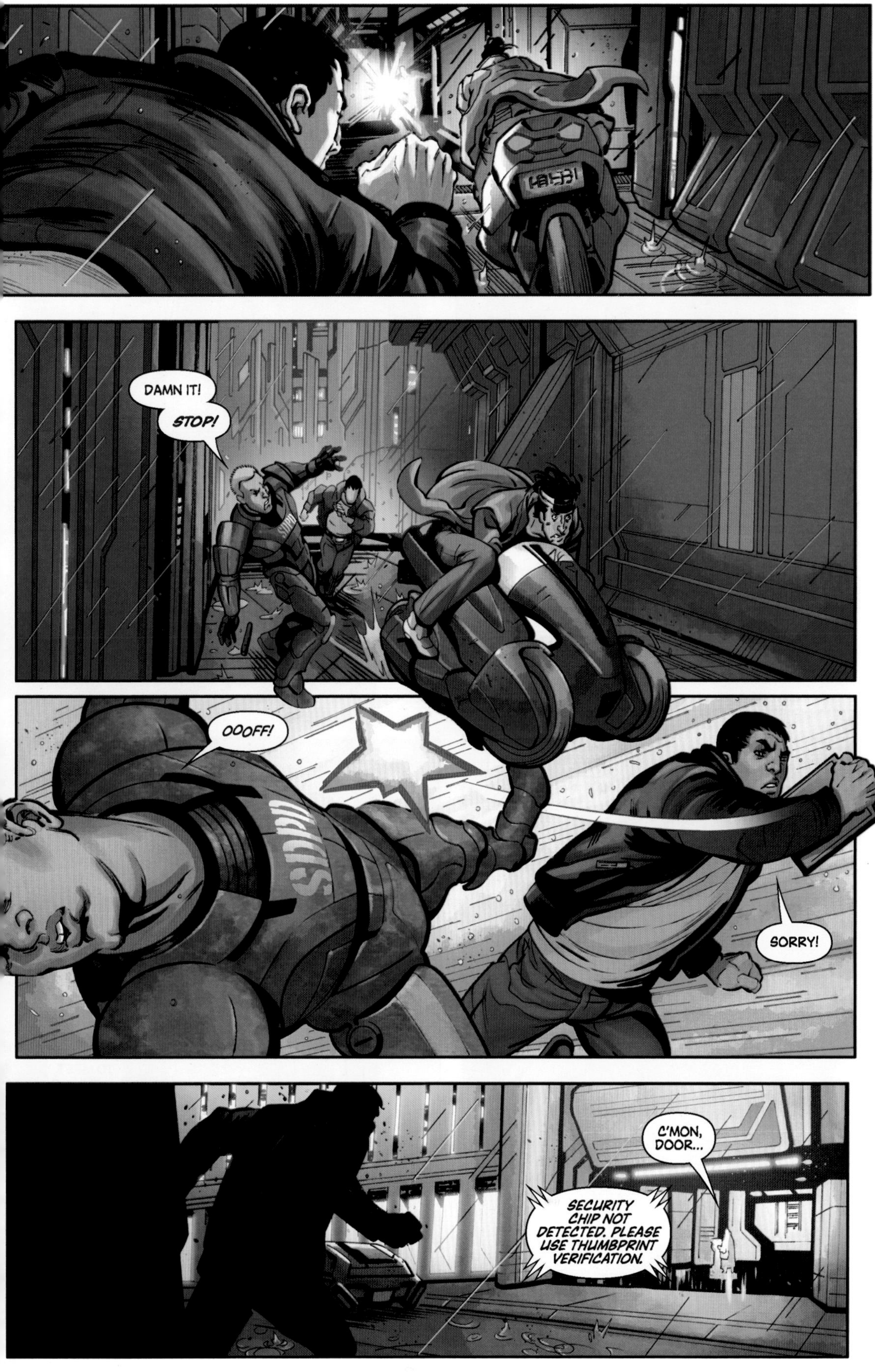
DAMN IT!
STOP!
OOOFF!
SORRY!
C'MON, DOOR...
SECURITY CHIP NOT DETECTED. PLEASE USE THUMBPRINT VERIFICATION.

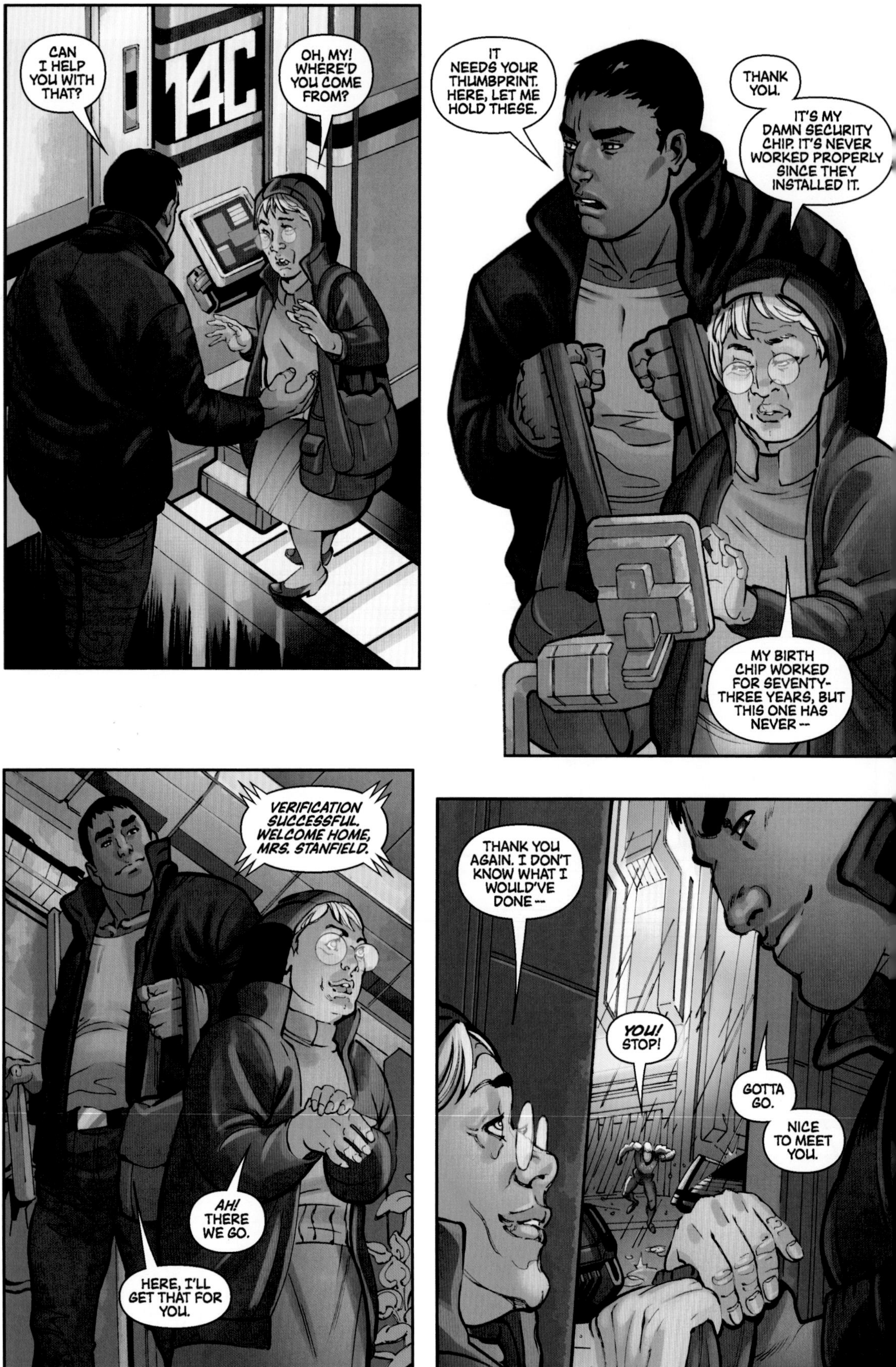
CAN I HELP YOU WITH THAT?
OH, MY! WHERE'D YOU COME FROM?
IT NEEDS YOUR THUMBPRINT. HERE, LET ME HOLD THESE.
THANK YOU.
IT'S MY DAMN SECURITY CHIP. IT'S NEVER WORKED PROPERLY SINCE THEY INSTALLED IT.
MY BIRTH CHIP WORKED FOR SEVENTY-THREE YEARS, BUT THIS ONE HAS NEVER --
VERIFICATION SUCCESSFUL. WELCOME HOME, MRS. STANFIELD.
AH! THERE WE GO.
HERE, I'LL GET THAT FOR YOU.
THANK YOU AGAIN. I DON'T KNOW WHAT I WOULD'VE DONE --
YOU! STOP!
GOTTA GO.
NICE TO MEET YOU.

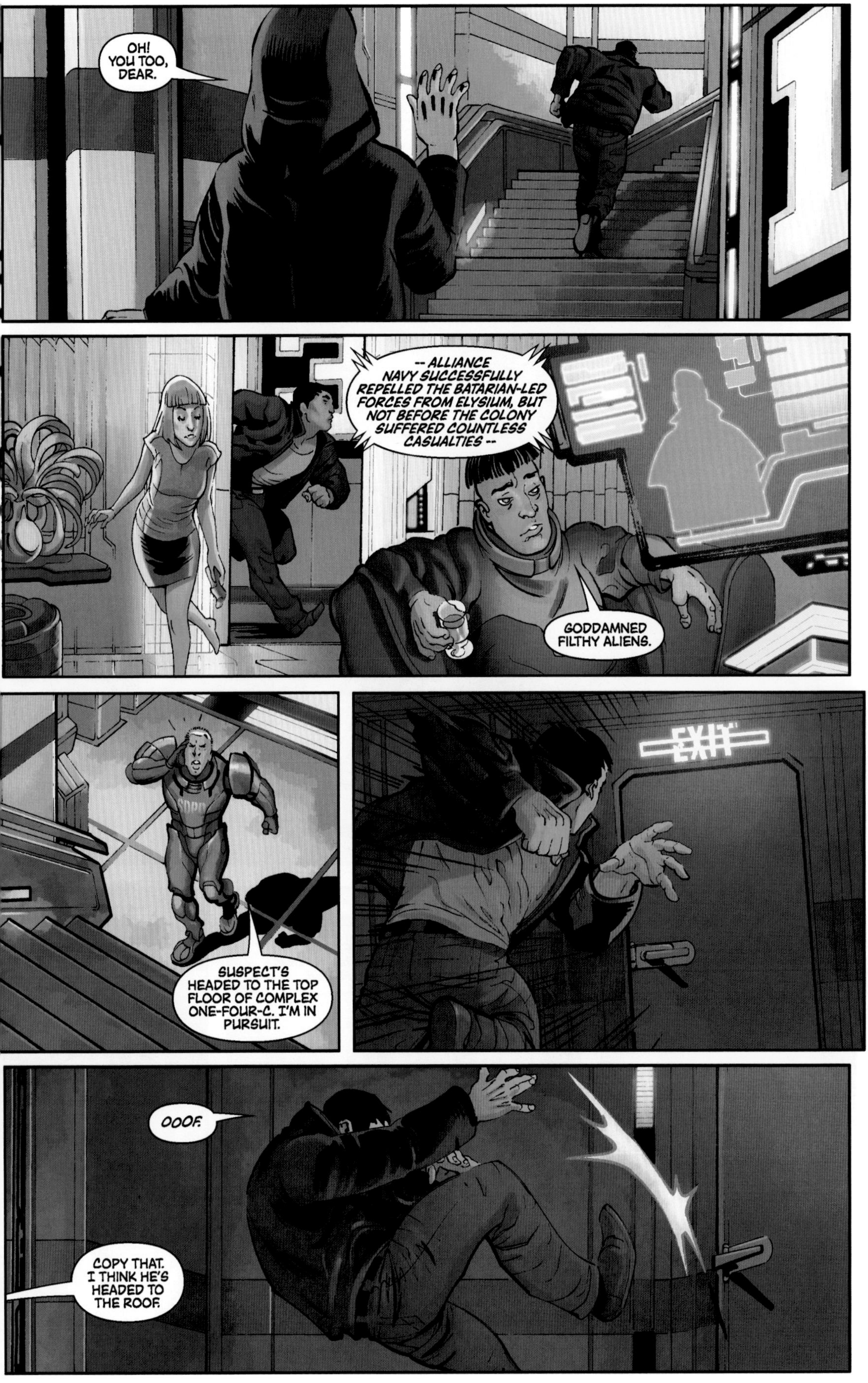
OH! YOU TOO, DEAR.
-- ALLIANCE NAVY SUCCESSFULLY REPELLED THE BATARIAN-LED FORCES FROM ELYSIUM, BUT NOT BEFORE THE COLONY SUFFERED COUNTLESS CASUALTIES --
GODDAMNED FILTHY ALIENS.
SUSPECT'S HEADED TO THE TOP FLOOR OF COMPLEX ONE-FOUR-C. I'M IN PURSUIT.
EXIT
OOOF.
COPY THAT. I THINK HE'S HEADED TO THE ROOF.

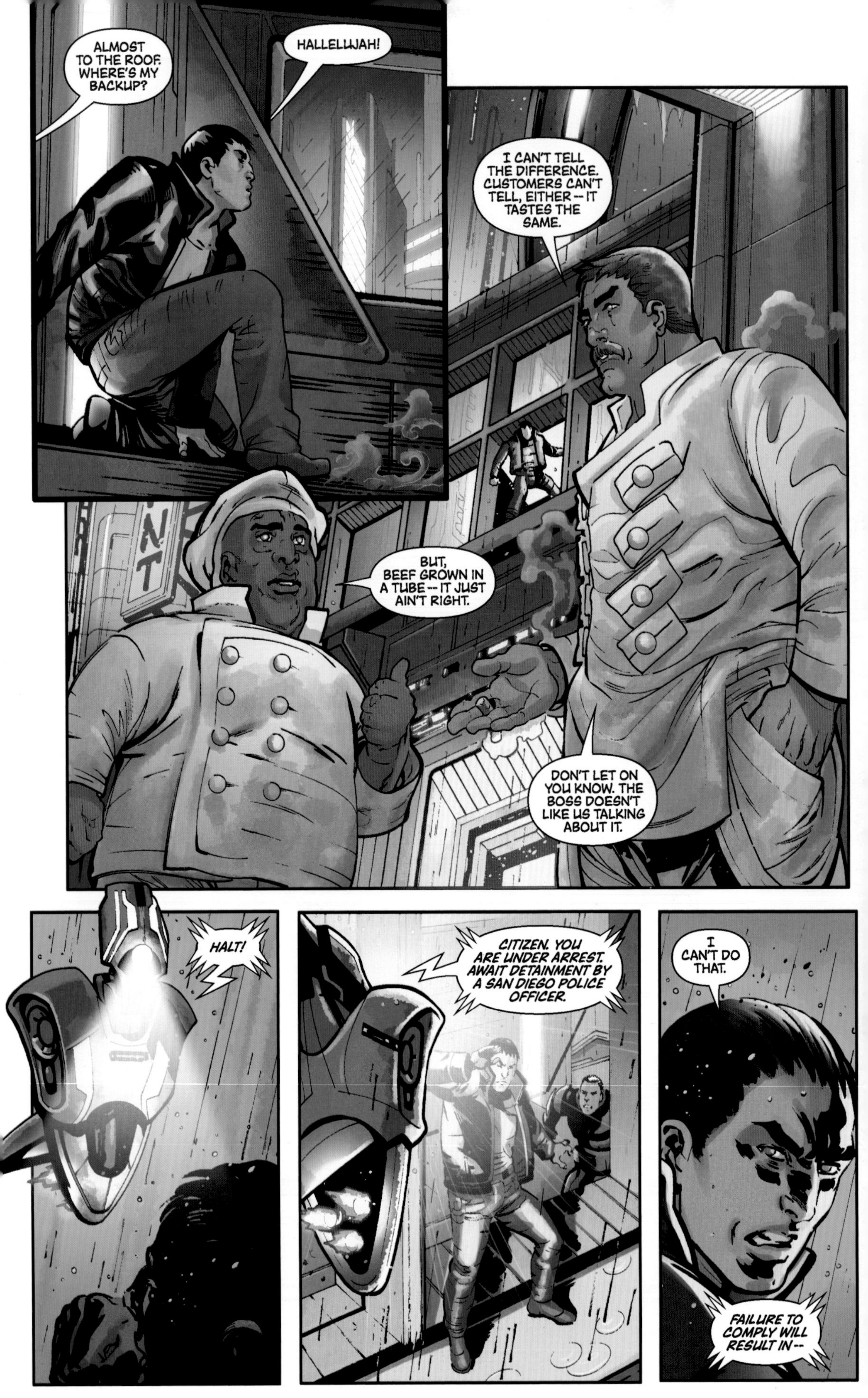

ALMOST TO THE ROOF. WHERE'S MY BACKUP?
HALLELUJAH!
I CAN'T TELL THE DIFFERENCE. CUSTOMERS CAN'T TELL, EITHER -- IT TASTES THE SAME.
BUT, BEEF GROWN IN A TUBE -- IT JUST AIN'T RIGHT.
DON'T LET ON YOU KNOW. THE BOSS DOESN'T LIKE US TALKING ABOUT IT.
HALT!
CITIZEN. YOU ARE UNDER ARREST. AWAIT DETAINMENT BY A SAN DIEGO POLICE OFFICER.
I CAN'T DO THAT.
FAILURE TO COMPLY WILL RESULT IN --

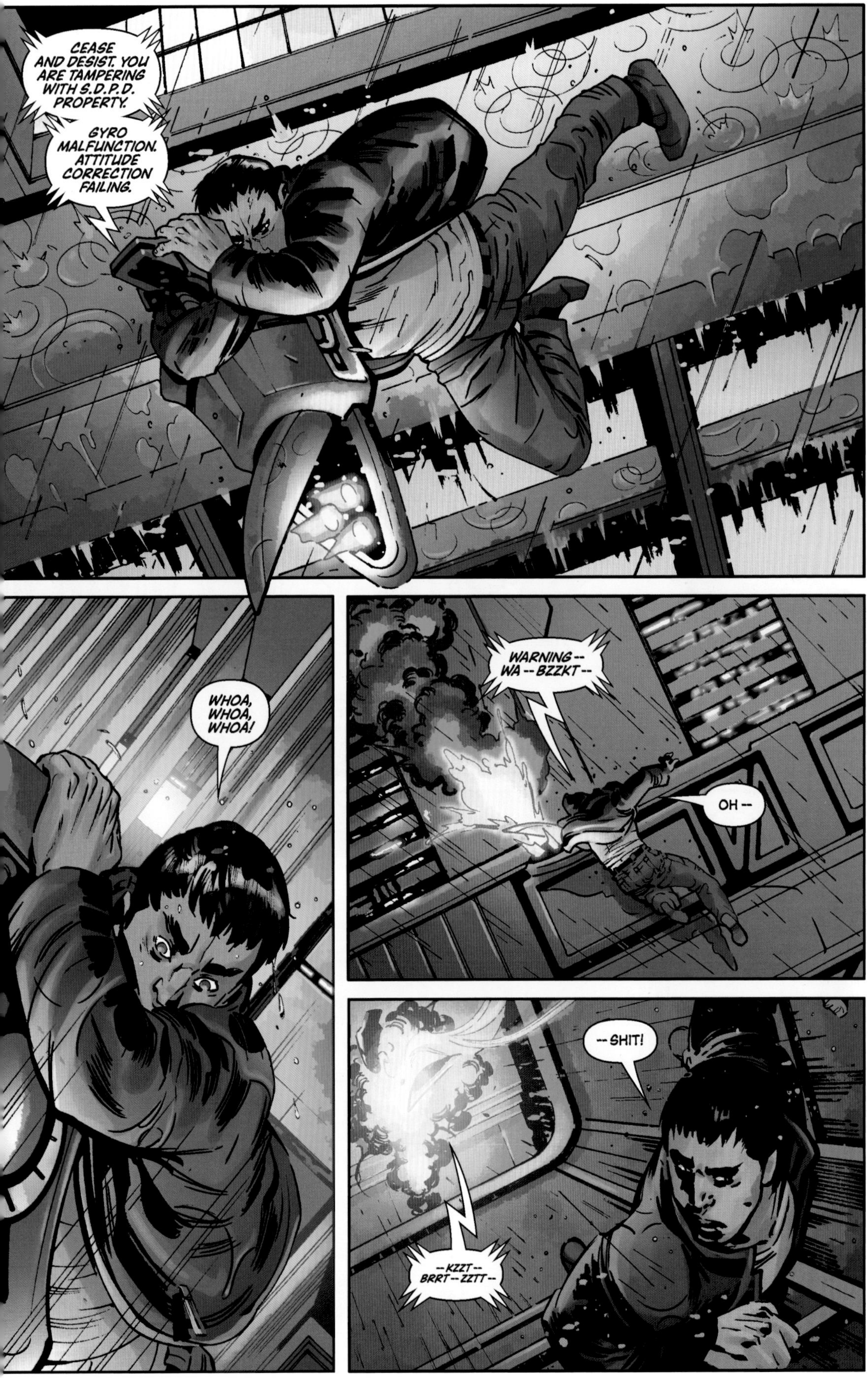
CEASE AND DESIST. YOU ARE TAMPERING WITH S.D.P.D. PROPERTY.
GYRO MALFUNCTION. ATTITUDE CORRECTION FAILING.
WHOA, WHOA, WHOA!
WARNING -- WA -- BZZKT --
OH --
-- SHIT!
-- KZZT -- BRRT -- ZZTT --

WEEOO WEEOO WEEOO

NUMBER TWO, NO MAYO, EXTRA ONIONS. BASKET OF FRIES.

ORDER UP.

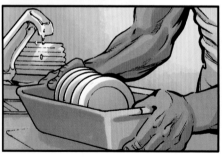

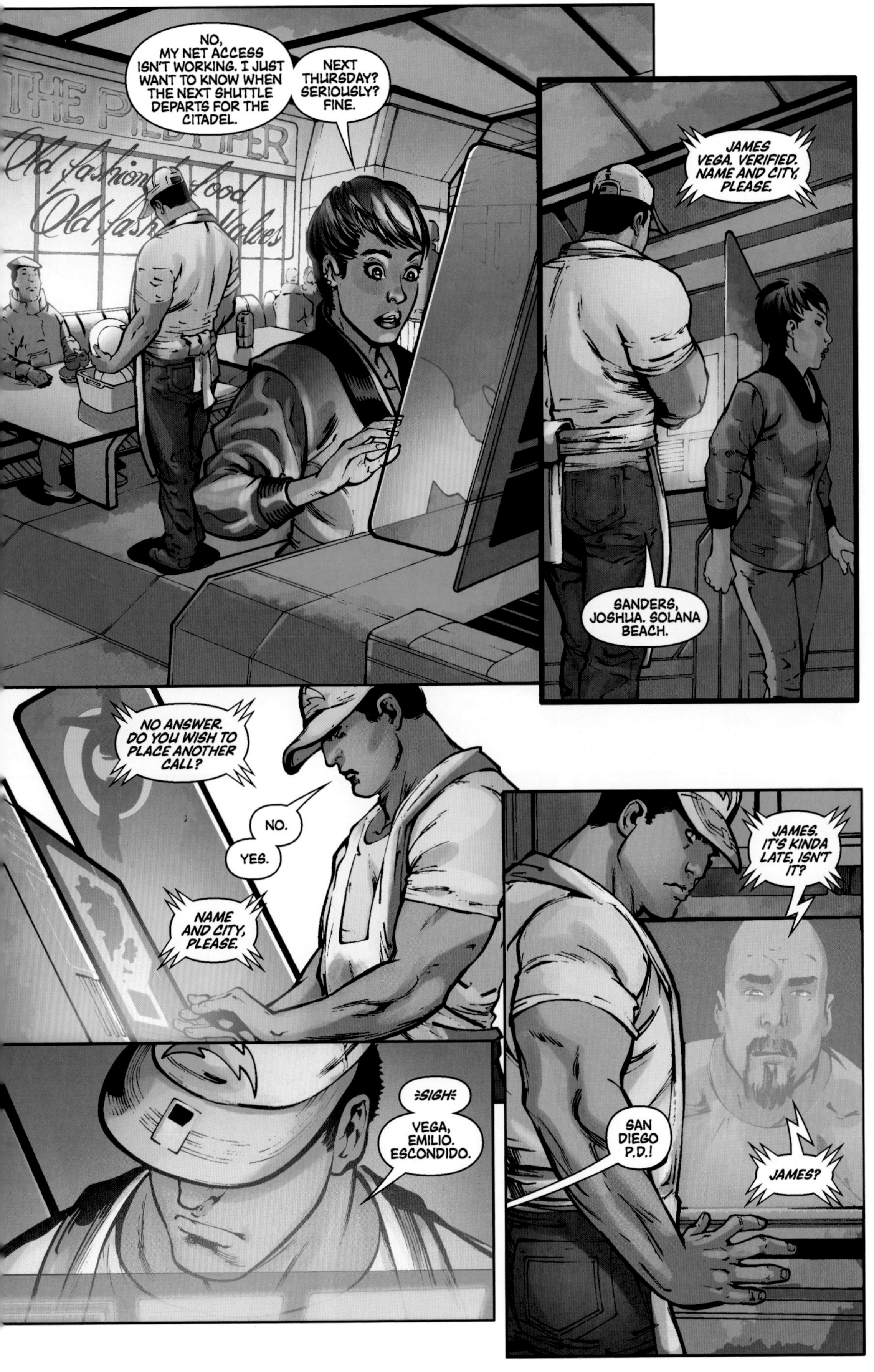
NO, MY NET ACCESS ISN'T WORKING. I JUST WANT TO KNOW WHEN THE NEXT SHUTTLE DEPARTS FOR THE CITADEL.
NEXT THURSDAY? SERIOUSLY? FINE.
JAMES VEGA. VERIFIED. NAME AND CITY, PLEASE.
SANDERS, JOSHUA. SOLANA BEACH.
NO ANSWER. DO YOU WISH TO PLACE ANOTHER CALL?
NO.
YES.
NAME AND CITY, PLEASE.
=SIGH=
VEGA, EMILIO. ESCONDIDO.
JAMES. IT'S KINDA LATE, ISN'T IT?
SAN DIEGO P.D.!
JAMES?

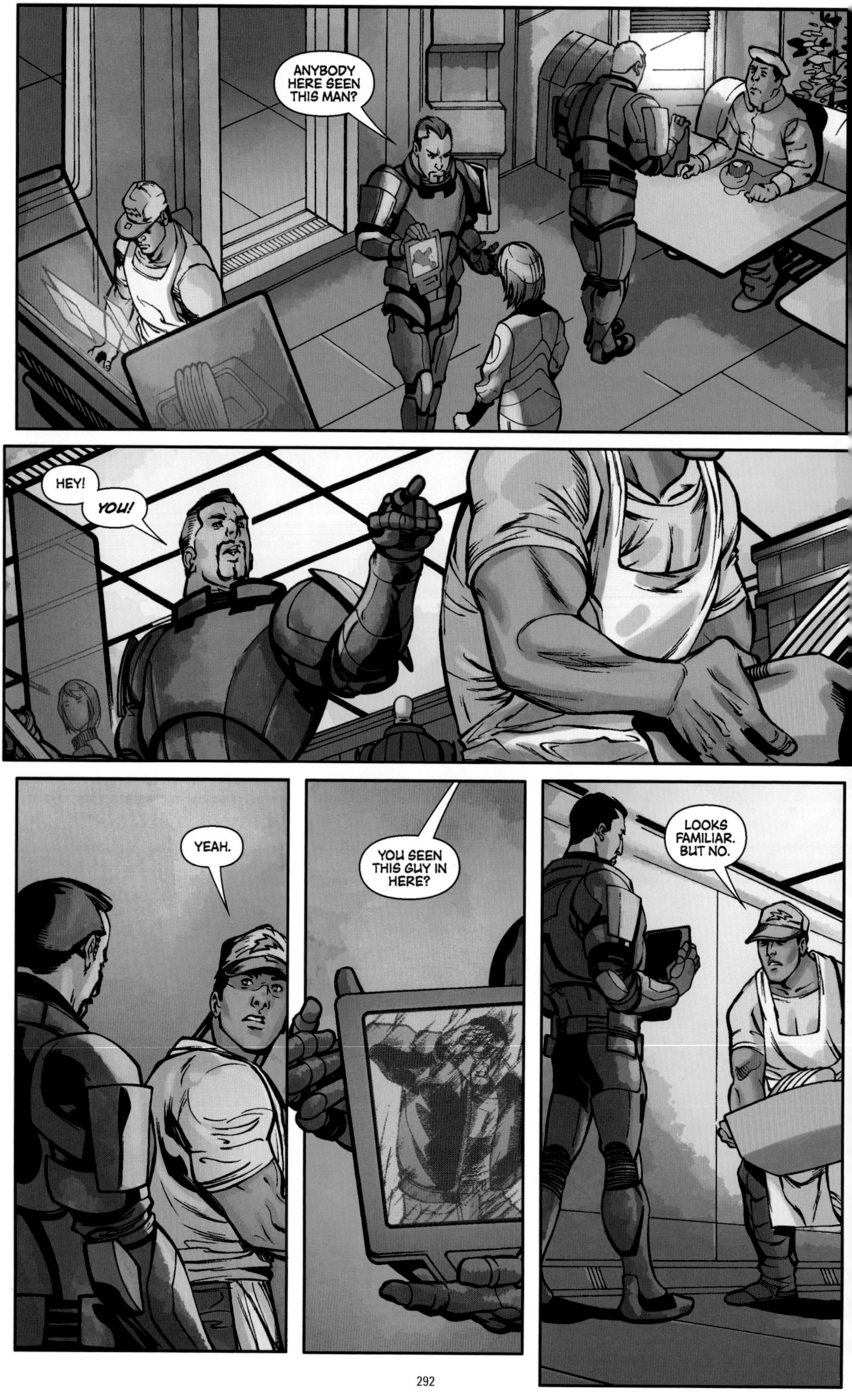
ANYBODY HERE SEEN THIS MAN?
HEY!
YOU!
YEAH.
YOU SEEN THIS GUY IN HERE?
LOOKS FAMILIAR. BUT NO.

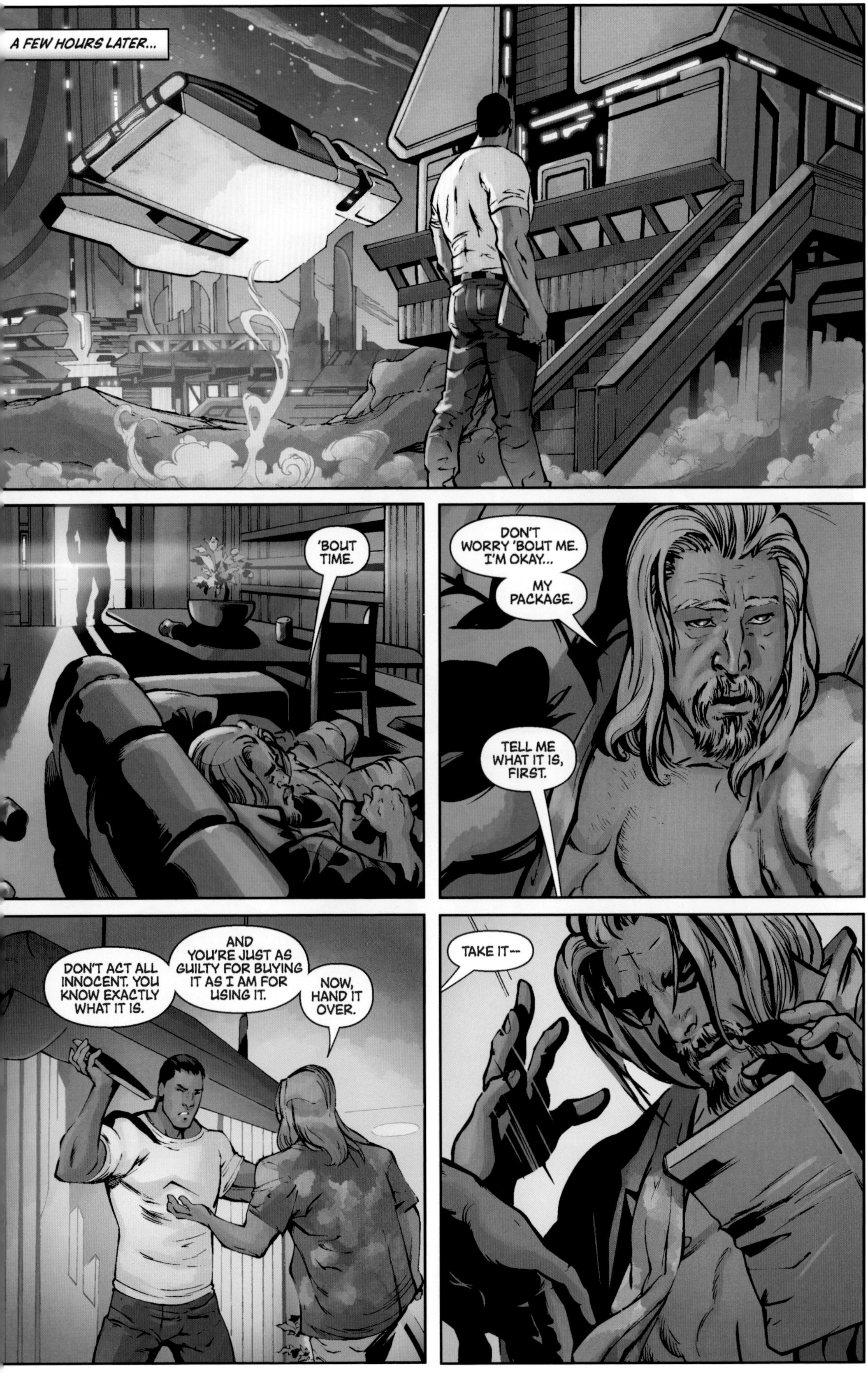
A FEW HOURS LATER...
'BOUT TIME.
DON'T WORRY 'BOUT ME. I'M OKAY...
MY PACKAGE.
TELL ME WHAT IT IS, FIRST.
DON'T ACT ALL INNOCENT. YOU KNOW EXACTLY WHAT IT IS.
AND YOU'RE JUST AS GUILTY FOR BUYING IT AS I AM FOR USING IT.
NOW, HAND IT OVER.
TAKE IT--

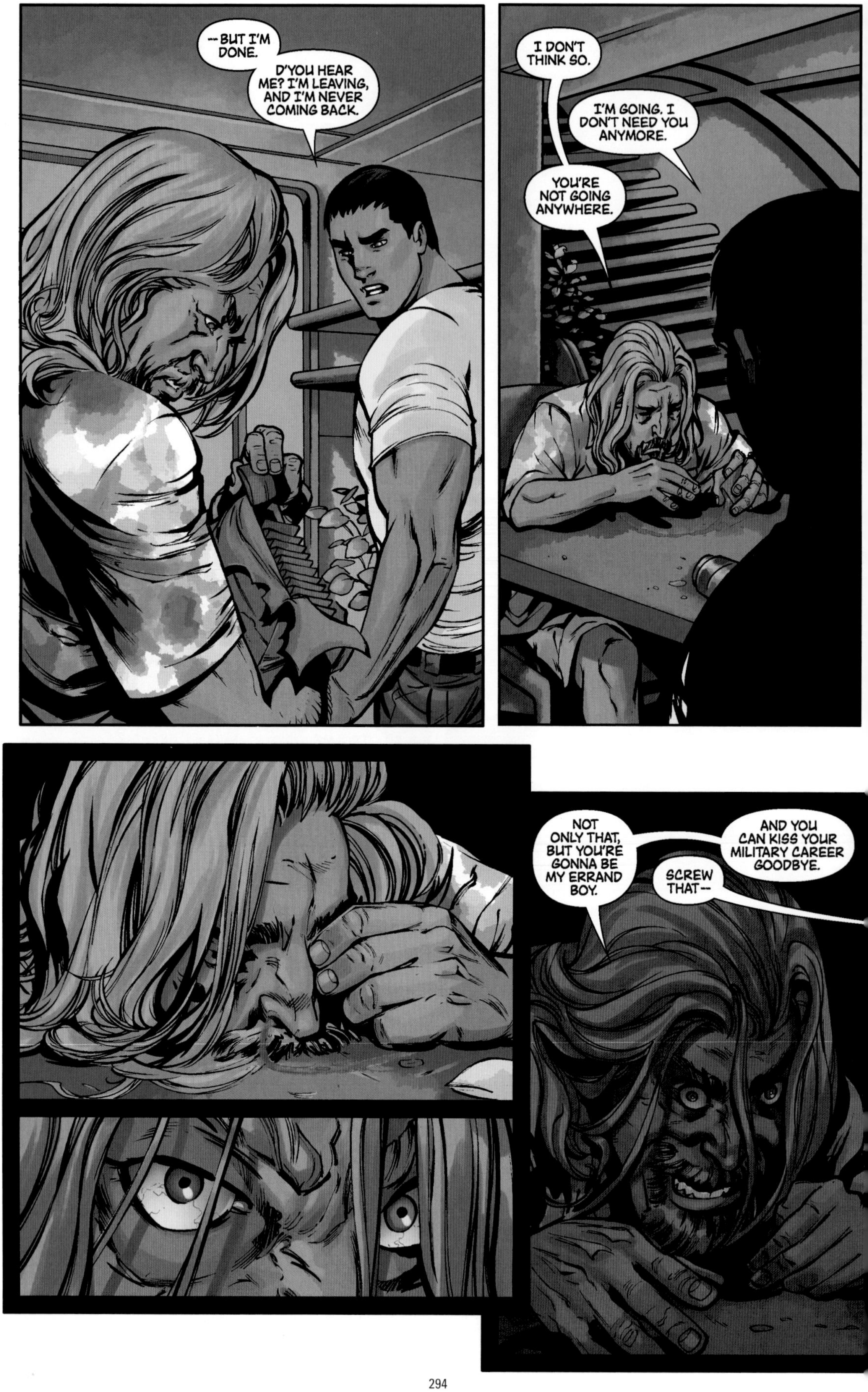
--BUT I'M DONE.
D'YOU HEAR ME? I'M LEAVING, AND I'M NEVER COMING BACK.
I DON'T THINK SO.
I'M GOING. I DON'T NEED YOU ANYMORE.
YOU'RE NOT GOING ANYWHERE.
NOT ONLY THAT, BUT YOU'RE GONNA BE MY ERRAND BOY.
AND YOU CAN KISS YOUR MILITARY CAREER GOODBYE.
SCREW THAT--

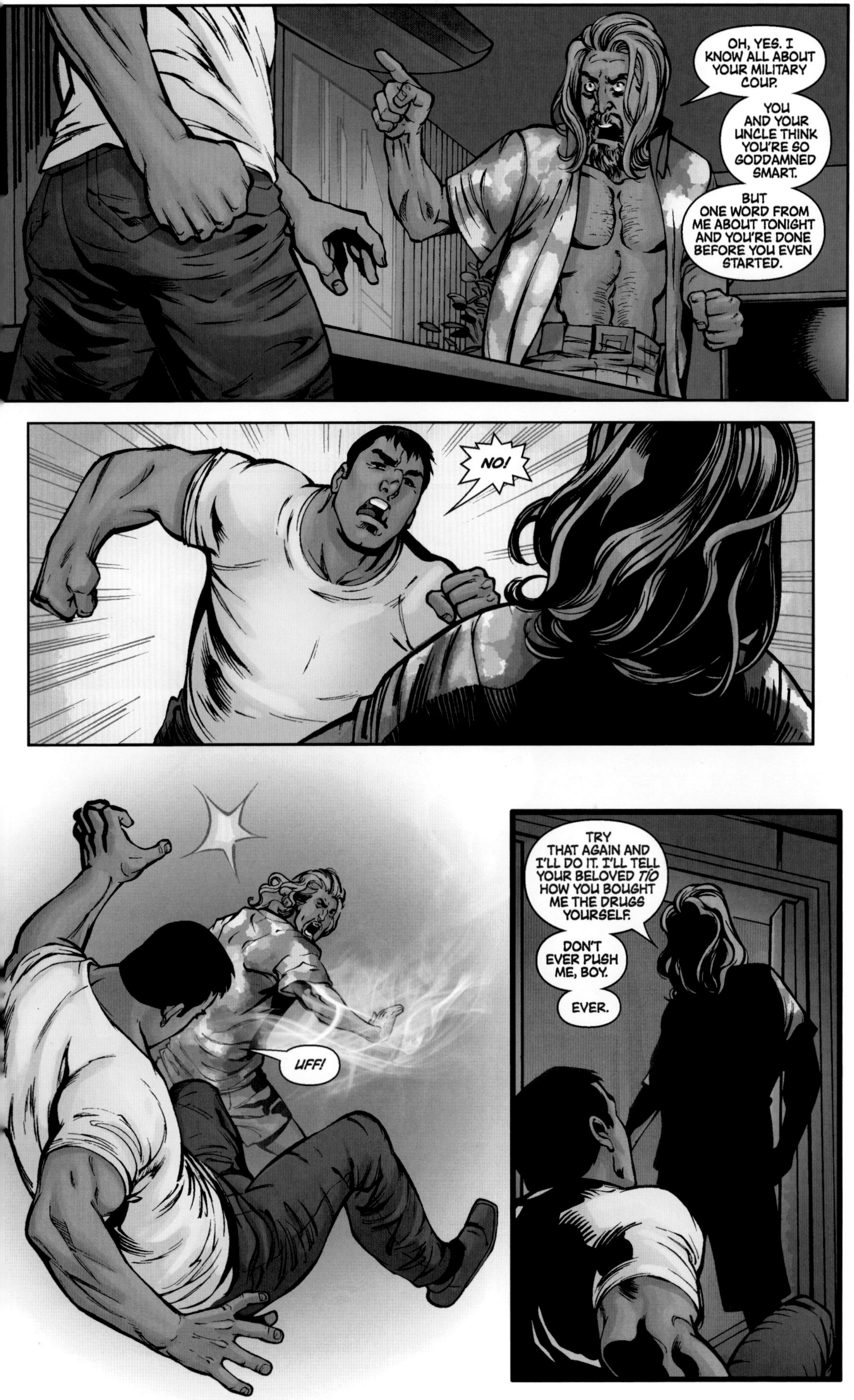
OH, YES. I KNOW ALL ABOUT YOUR MILITARY COUP.
YOU AND YOUR UNCLE THINK YOU'RE SO GODDAMNED SMART.
BUT ONE WORD FROM ME ABOUT TONIGHT AND YOU'RE DONE BEFORE YOU EVEN STARTED.
NO!
UFF!
TRY THAT AGAIN AND I'LL DO IT. I'LL TELL YOUR BELOVED *TÍO* HOW YOU BOUGHT ME THE DRUGS YOURSELF.
DON'T EVER PUSH ME, BOY.
EVER.

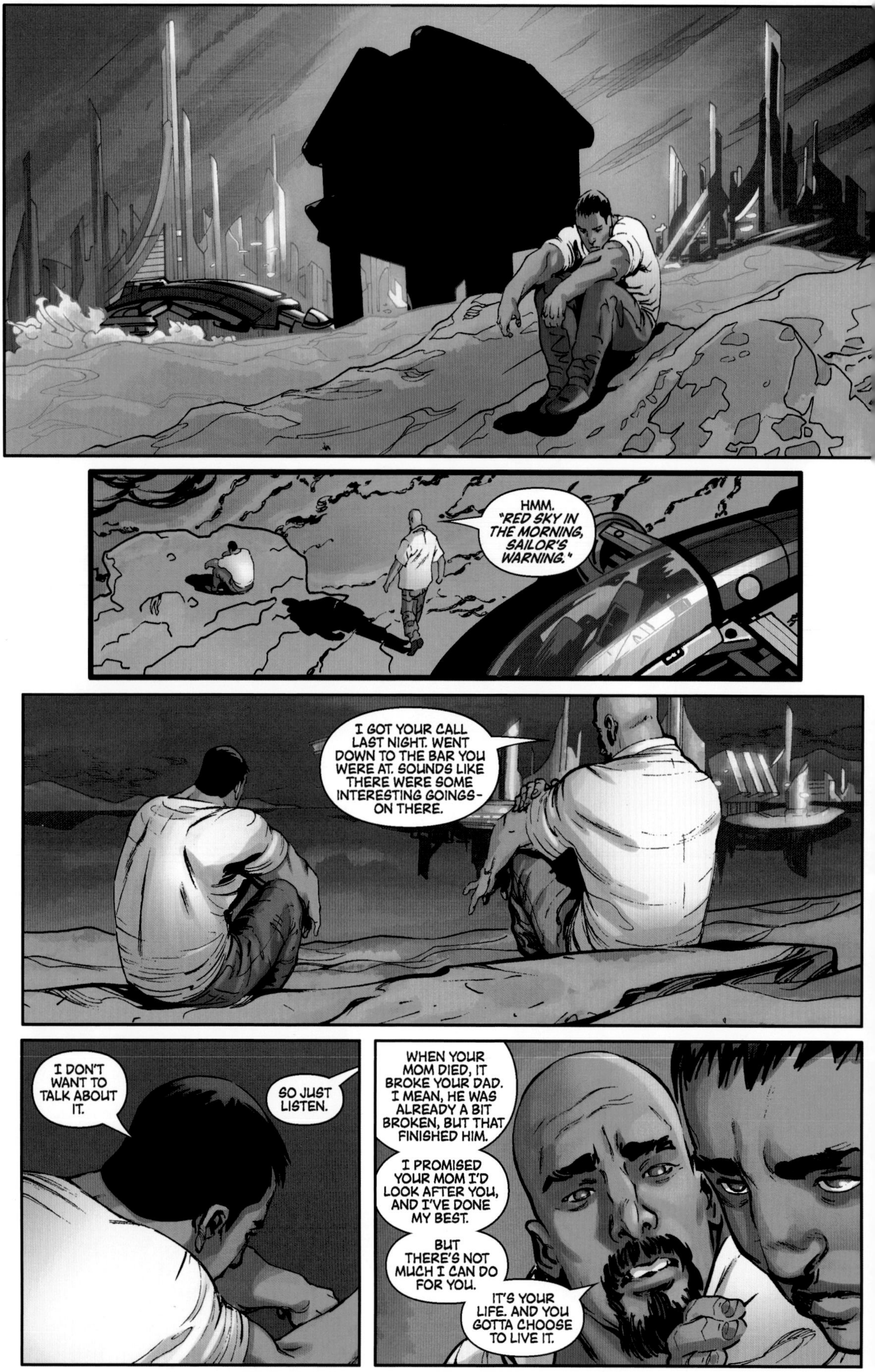
HMM. "RED SKY IN THE MORNING, SAILOR'S WARNING."
I GOT YOUR CALL LAST NIGHT. WENT DOWN TO THE BAR YOU WERE AT. SOUNDS LIKE THERE WERE SOME INTERESTING GOINGS-ON THERE.
I DON'T WANT TO TALK ABOUT IT.
SO JUST LISTEN.
WHEN YOUR MOM DIED, IT BROKE YOUR DAD. I MEAN, HE WAS ALREADY A BIT BROKEN, BUT THAT FINISHED HIM.
I PROMISED YOUR MOM I'D LOOK AFTER YOU, AND I'VE DONE MY BEST.
BUT THERE'S NOT MUCH I CAN DO FOR YOU.
IT'S YOUR LIFE. AND YOU GOTTA CHOOSE TO LIVE IT.

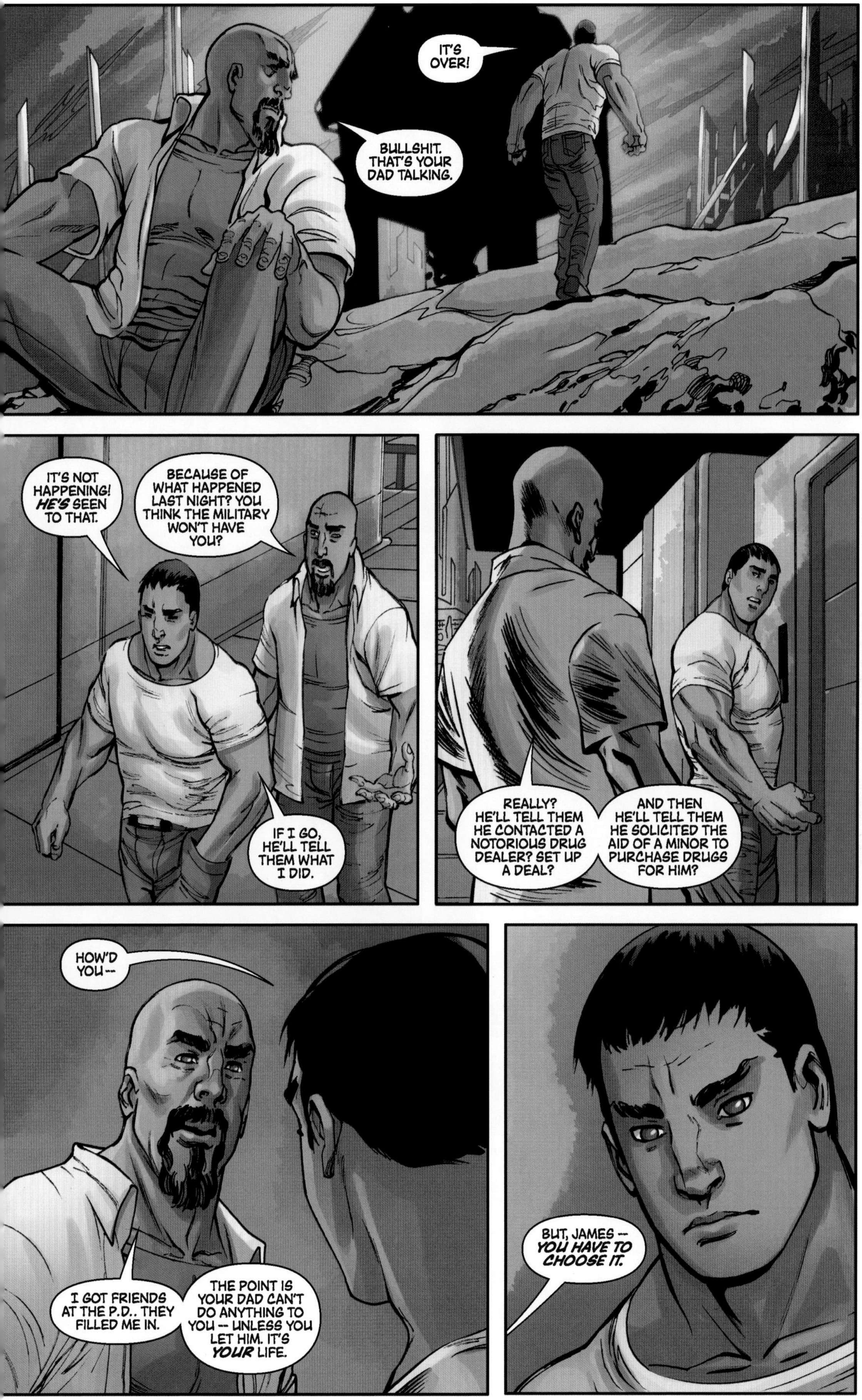
IT'S OVER!
BULLSHIT. THAT'S YOUR DAD TALKING.
IT'S NOT HAPPENING! *HE'S* SEEN TO THAT.
BECAUSE OF WHAT HAPPENED LAST NIGHT? YOU THINK THE MILITARY WON'T HAVE YOU?
IF I GO, HE'LL TELL THEM WHAT I DID.
REALLY? HE'LL TELL THEM HE CONTACTED A NOTORIOUS DRUG DEALER? SET UP A DEAL?
AND THEN HE'LL TELL THEM HE SOLICITED THE AID OF A MINOR TO PURCHASE DRUGS FOR HIM?
HOW'D YOU --
I GOT FRIENDS AT THE P.D.. THEY FILLED ME IN.
THE POINT IS YOUR DAD CAN'T DO ANYTHING TO YOU -- UNLESS YOU LET HIM. IT'S *YOUR* LIFE.
BUT, JAMES -- *YOU HAVE TO CHOOSE IT.*

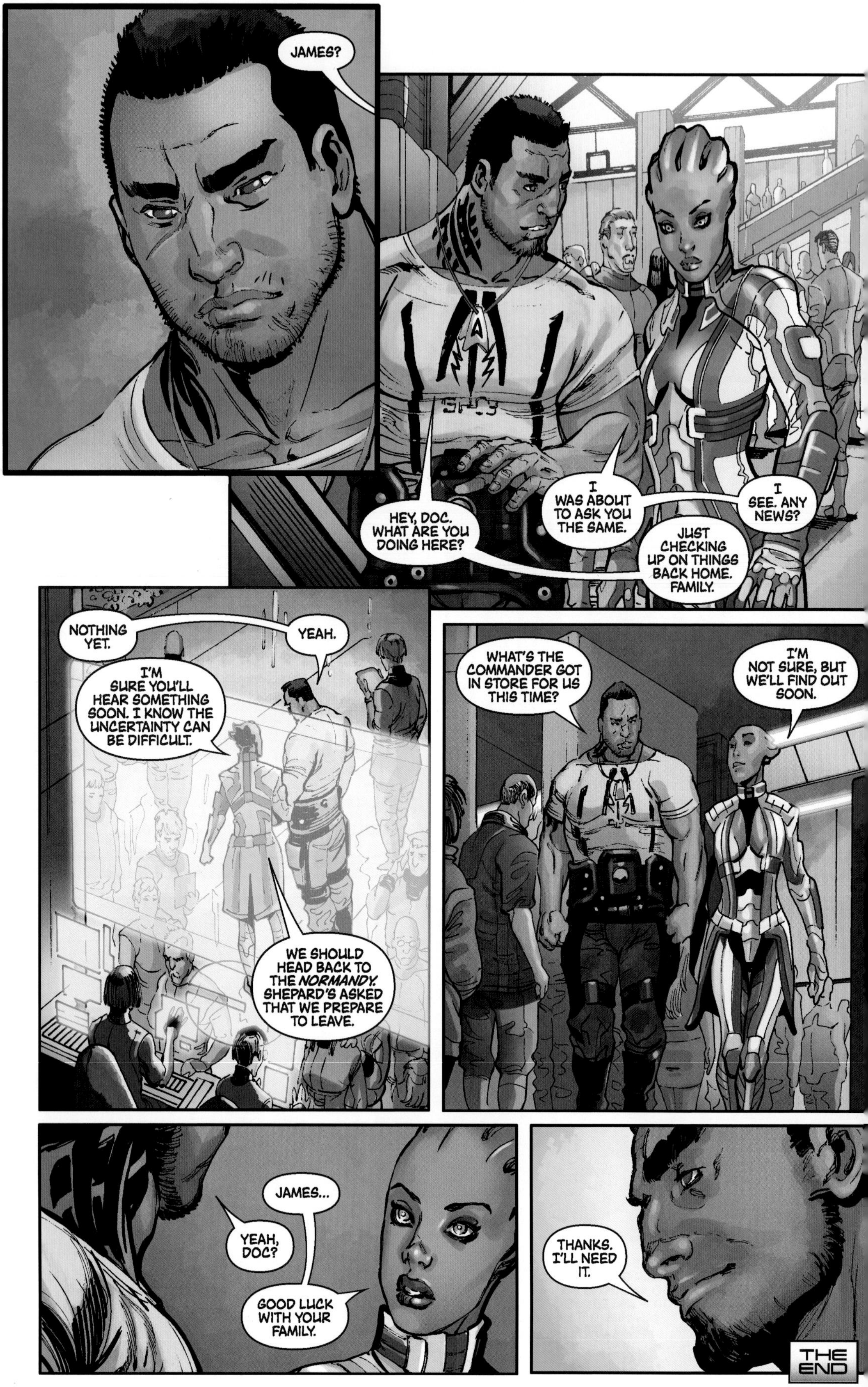
JAMES?
HEY, DOC. WHAT ARE YOU DOING HERE?
I WAS ABOUT TO ASK YOU THE SAME.
JUST CHECKING UP ON THINGS BACK HOME. FAMILY.
I SEE. ANY NEWS?
NOTHING YET.
YEAH.
I'M SURE YOU'LL HEAR SOMETHING SOON. I KNOW THE UNCERTAINTY CAN BE DIFFICULT.
WE SHOULD HEAD BACK TO THE *NORMANDY*. SHEPARD'S ASKED THAT WE PREPARE TO LEAVE.
WHAT'S THE COMMANDER GOT IN STORE FOR US THIS TIME?
I'M NOT SURE, BUT WE'LL FIND OUT SOON.
JAMES...
YEAH, DOC?
GOOD LUCK WITH YOUR FAMILY.
THANKS. I'LL NEED IT.
THE END

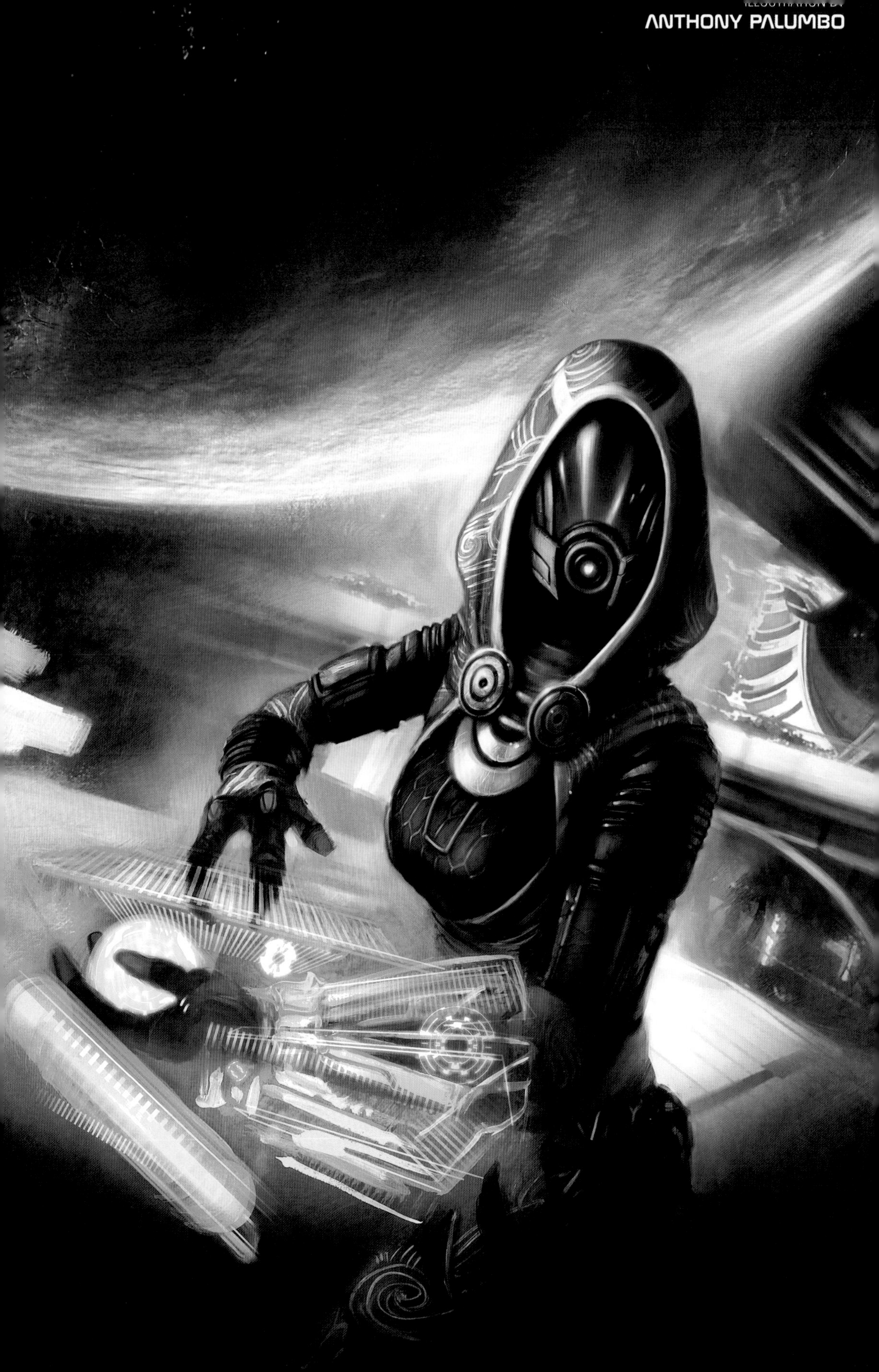
ANTHONY PALUMBO

HOMEWORLDS: TALI'ZORAH NAR RAYYA

STORY
MAC WALTERS AND PATRICK WEEKES

SCRIPT
JEREMY BARLOW

PENCILS
CHRIS STAGGS

INKS
MARC DEERING AND CHRIS STAGGS

COLORS
MICHAEL ATIYEH

LETTERING
MICHAEL HEISLER

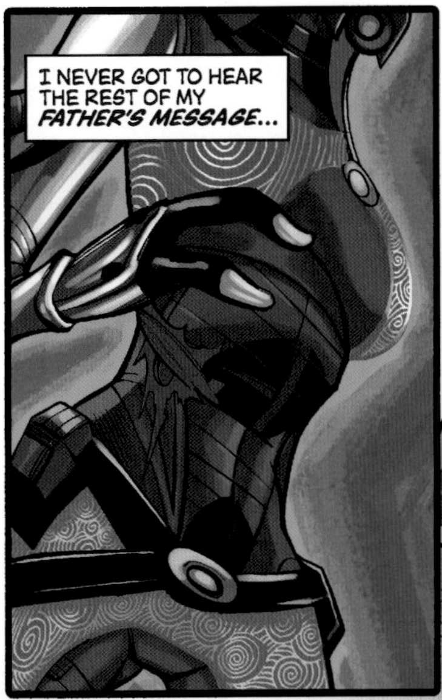
I NEVER GOT TO HEAR THE REST OF MY FATHER'S MESSAGE...

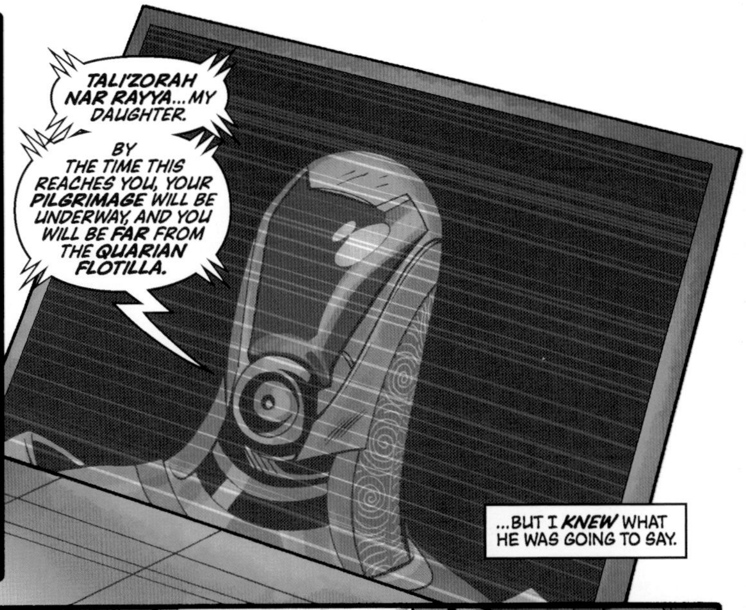
TALI'ZORAH NAR RAYYA... MY DAUGHTER.
BY THE TIME THIS REACHES YOU, YOUR PILGRIMAGE WILL BE UNDERWAY, AND YOU WILL BE FAR FROM THE QUARIAN FLOTILLA.
...BUT I KNEW WHAT HE WAS GOING TO SAY.

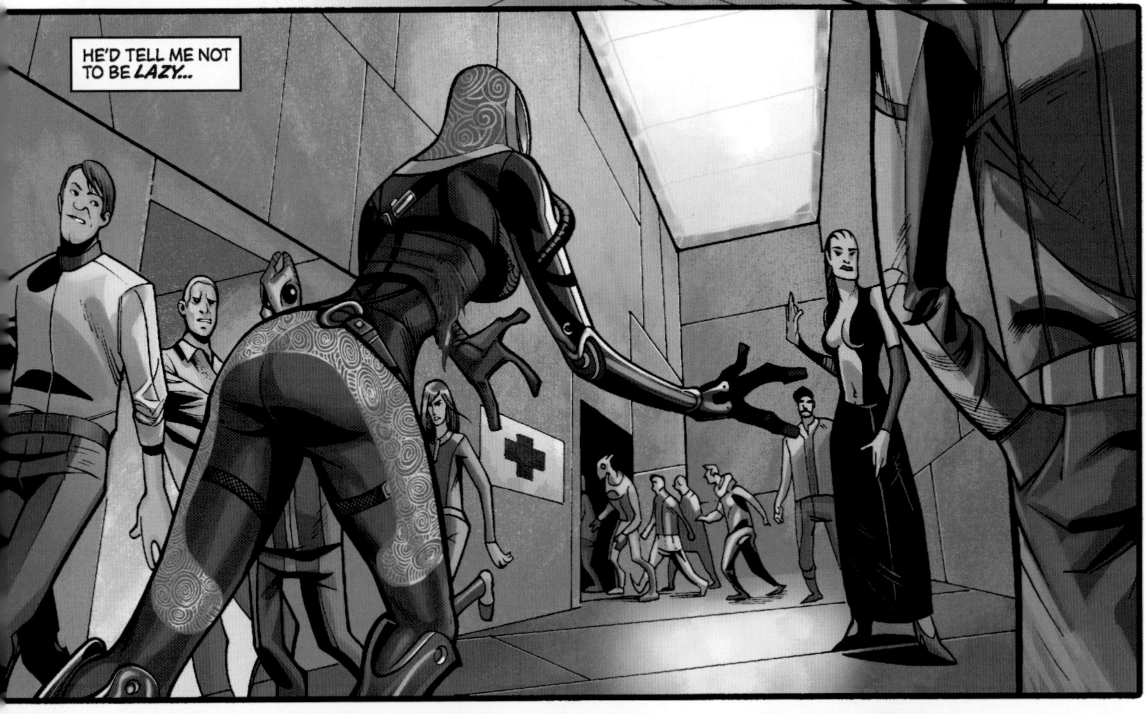
HE'D TELL ME NOT TO BE LAZY...

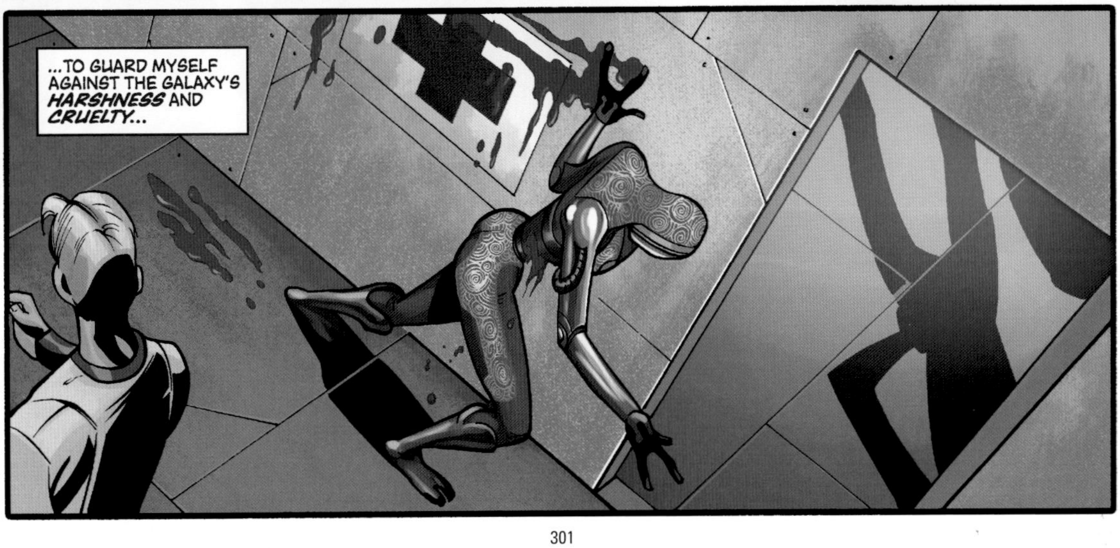
...TO GUARD MYSELF AGAINST THE GALAXY'S HARSHNESS AND CRUELTY...

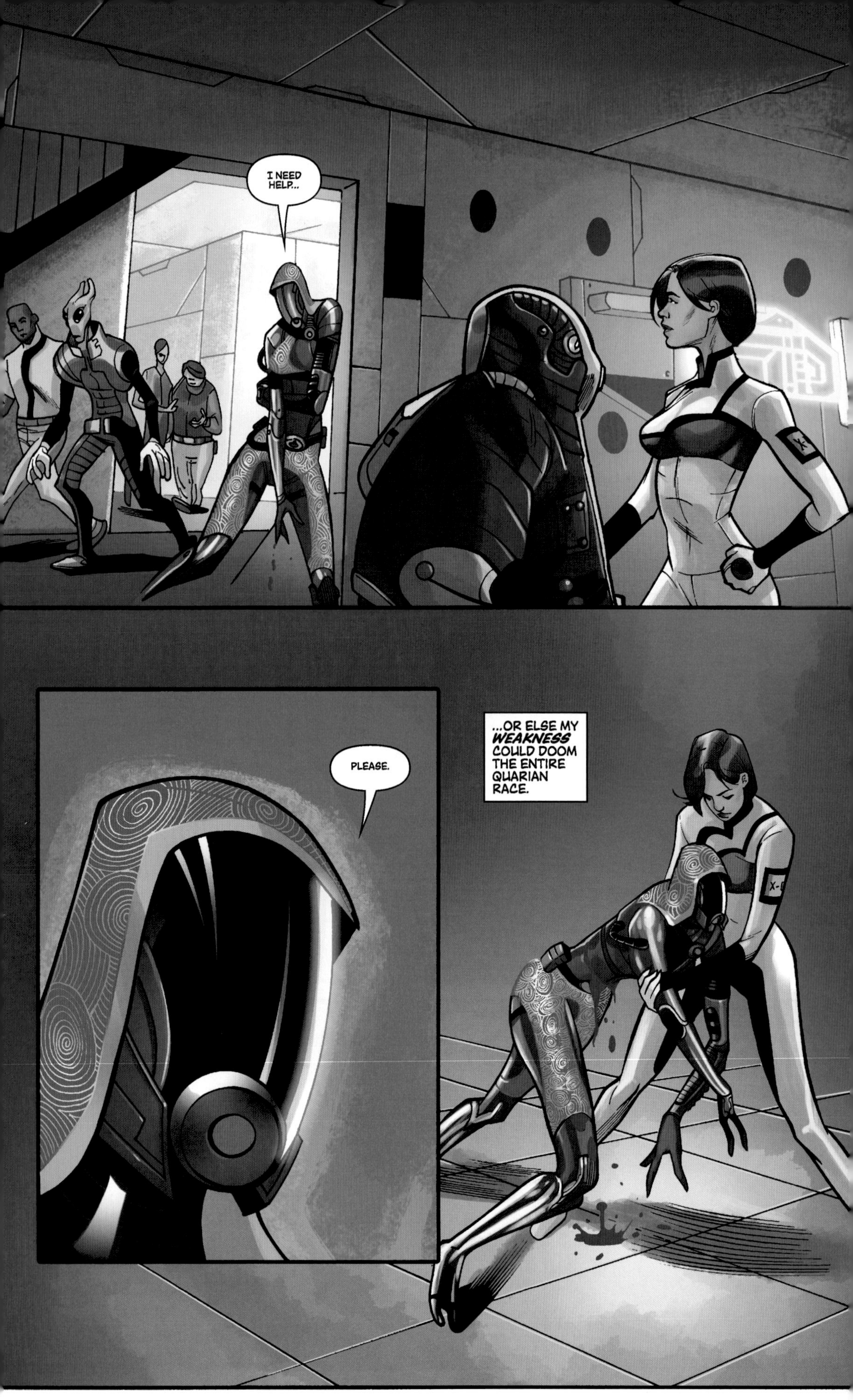
I NEED HELP...
PLEASE.
...OR ELSE MY *WEAKNESS* COULD DOOM THE ENTIRE QUARIAN RACE.

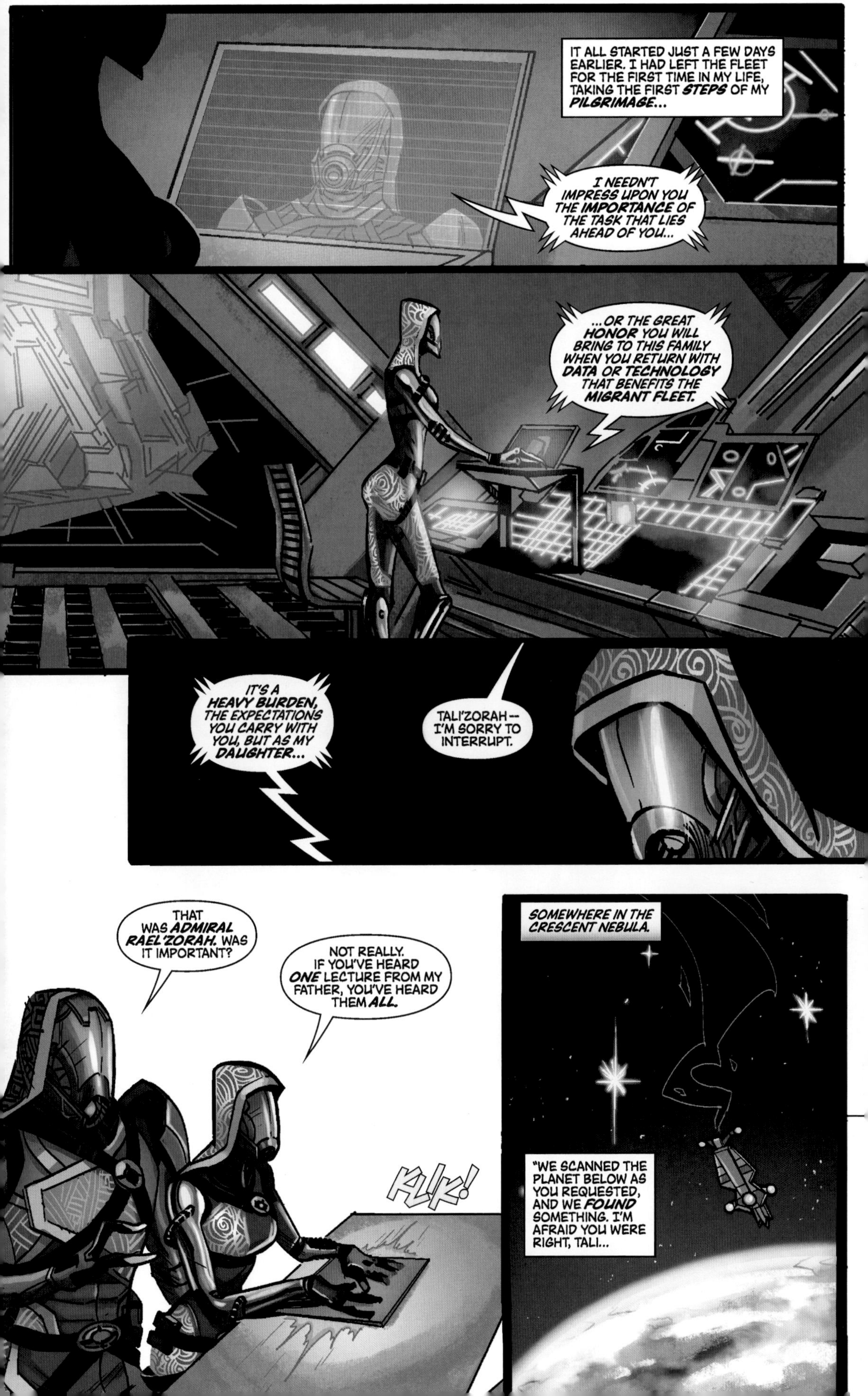
IT ALL STARTED JUST A FEW DAYS EARLIER. I HAD LEFT THE FLEET FOR THE FIRST TIME IN MY LIFE, TAKING THE FIRST STEPS OF MY PILGRIMAGE...
I NEEDN'T IMPRESS UPON YOU THE IMPORTANCE OF THE TASK THAT LIES AHEAD OF YOU...
...OR THE GREAT HONOR YOU WILL BRING TO THIS FAMILY WHEN YOU RETURN WITH DATA OR TECHNOLOGY THAT BENEFITS THE MIGRANT FLEET.
IT'S A HEAVY BURDEN, THE EXPECTATIONS YOU CARRY WITH YOU, BUT AS MY DAUGHTER...
TALI'ZORAH -- I'M SORRY TO INTERRUPT.
THAT WAS ADMIRAL RAEL'ZORAH. WAS IT IMPORTANT?
NOT REALLY. IF YOU'VE HEARD ONE LECTURE FROM MY FATHER, YOU'VE HEARD THEM ALL.
KLIK!
SOMEWHERE IN THE CRESCENT NEBULA.
"WE SCANNED THE PLANET BELOW AS YOU REQUESTED, AND WE FOUND SOMETHING. I'M AFRAID YOU WERE RIGHT, TALI...

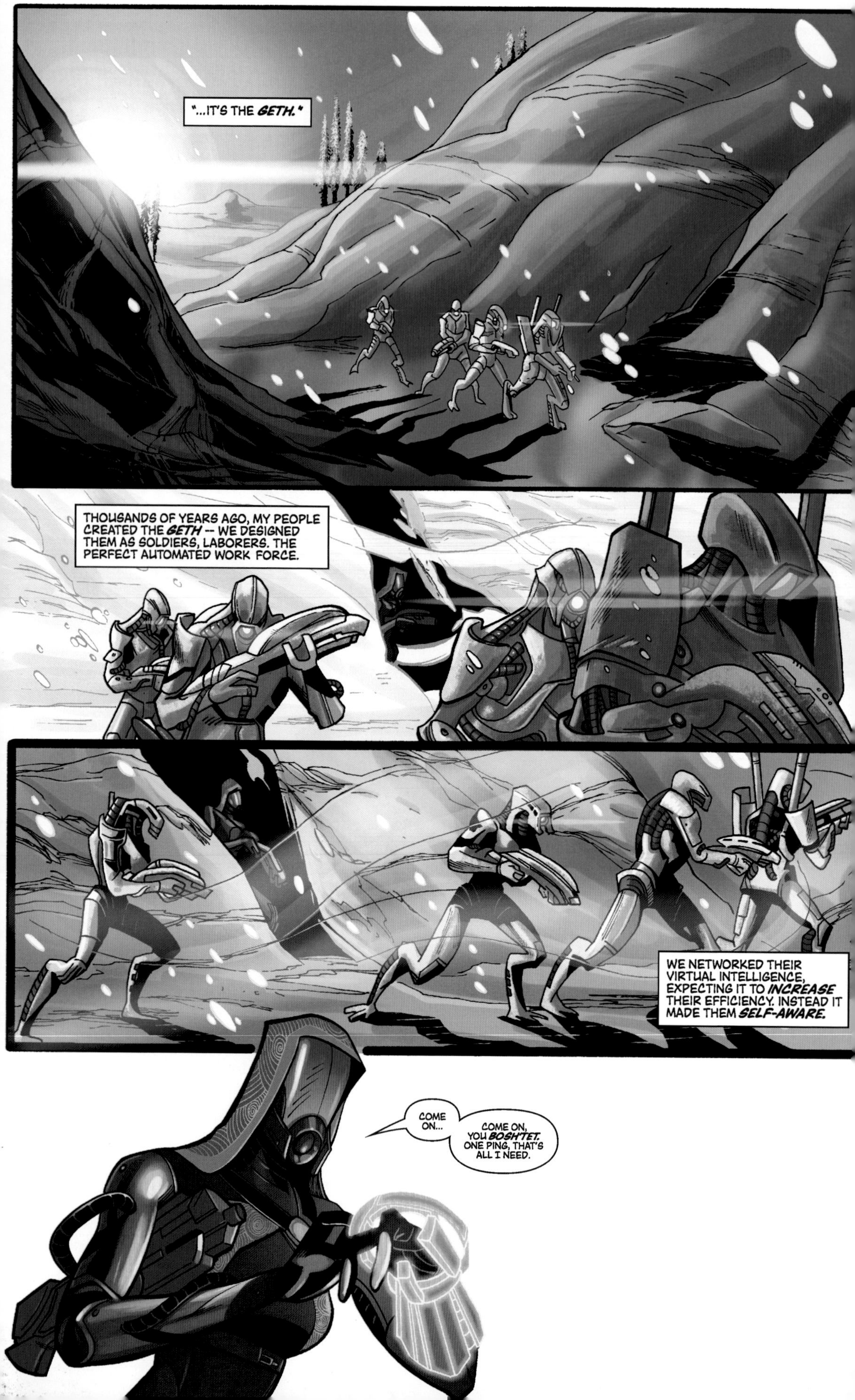
"...IT'S THE *GETH.*"
THOUSANDS OF YEARS AGO, MY PEOPLE CREATED THE *GETH* -- WE DESIGNED THEM AS SOLDIERS, LABORERS. THE PERFECT AUTOMATED WORK FORCE.
WE NETWORKED THEIR VIRTUAL INTELLIGENCE, EXPECTING IT TO *INCREASE* THEIR EFFICIENCY. INSTEAD IT MADE THEM *SELF-AWARE.*
COME ON...
COME ON, YOU *BOSH'TET.* ONE PING, THAT'S ALL I NEED.

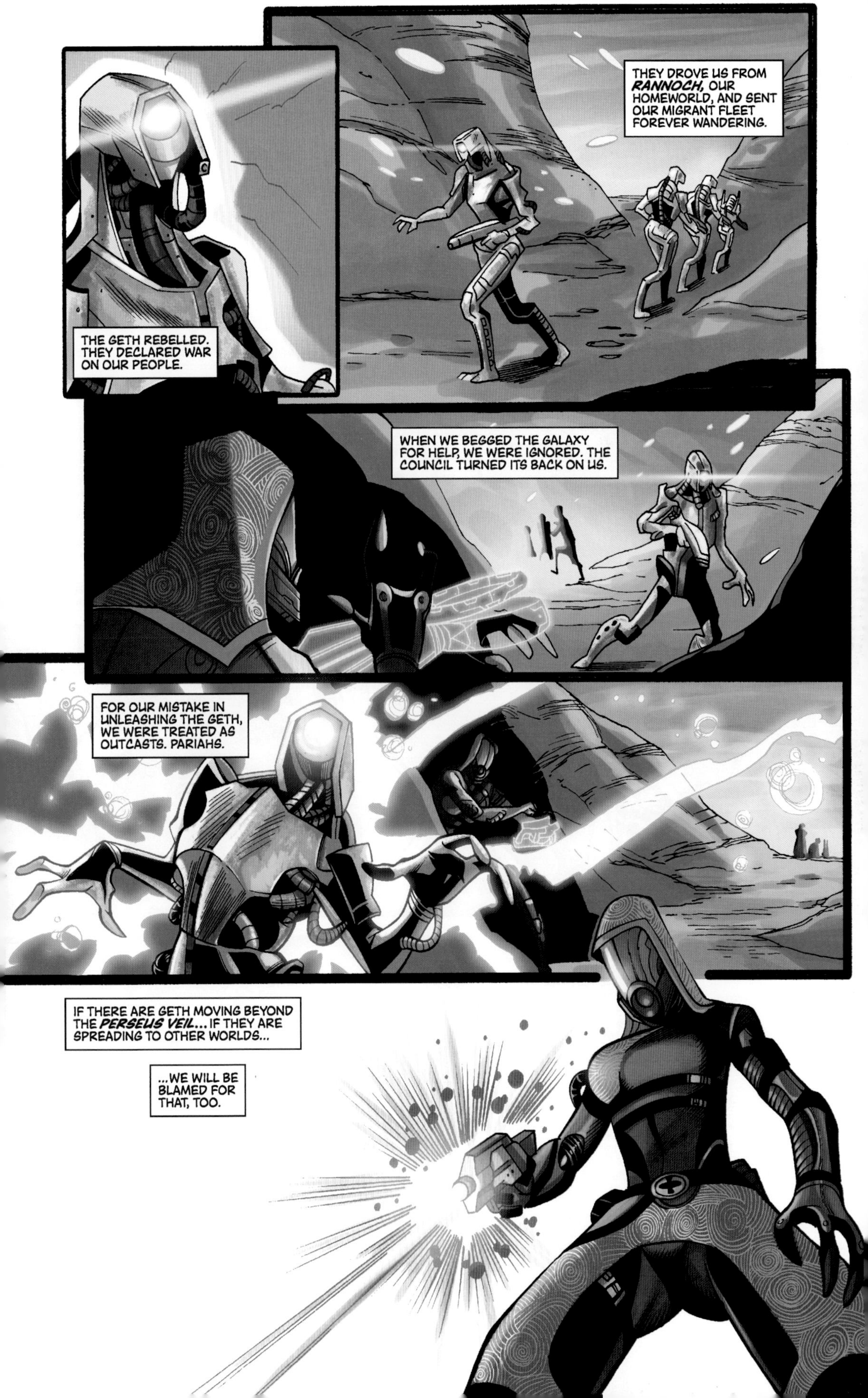
THE GETH REBELLED. THEY DECLARED WAR ON OUR PEOPLE.
THEY DROVE US FROM *RANNOCH,* OUR HOMEWORLD, AND SENT OUR MIGRANT FLEET FOREVER WANDERING.
WHEN WE BEGGED THE GALAXY FOR HELP, WE WERE IGNORED. THE COUNCIL TURNED ITS BACK ON US.
FOR OUR MISTAKE IN UNLEASHING THE GETH, WE WERE TREATED AS OUTCASTS. PARIAHS.
IF THERE ARE GETH MOVING BEYOND THE *PERSEUS VEIL*... IF THEY ARE SPREADING TO OTHER WORLDS...
...WE WILL BE BLAMED FOR THAT, TOO.

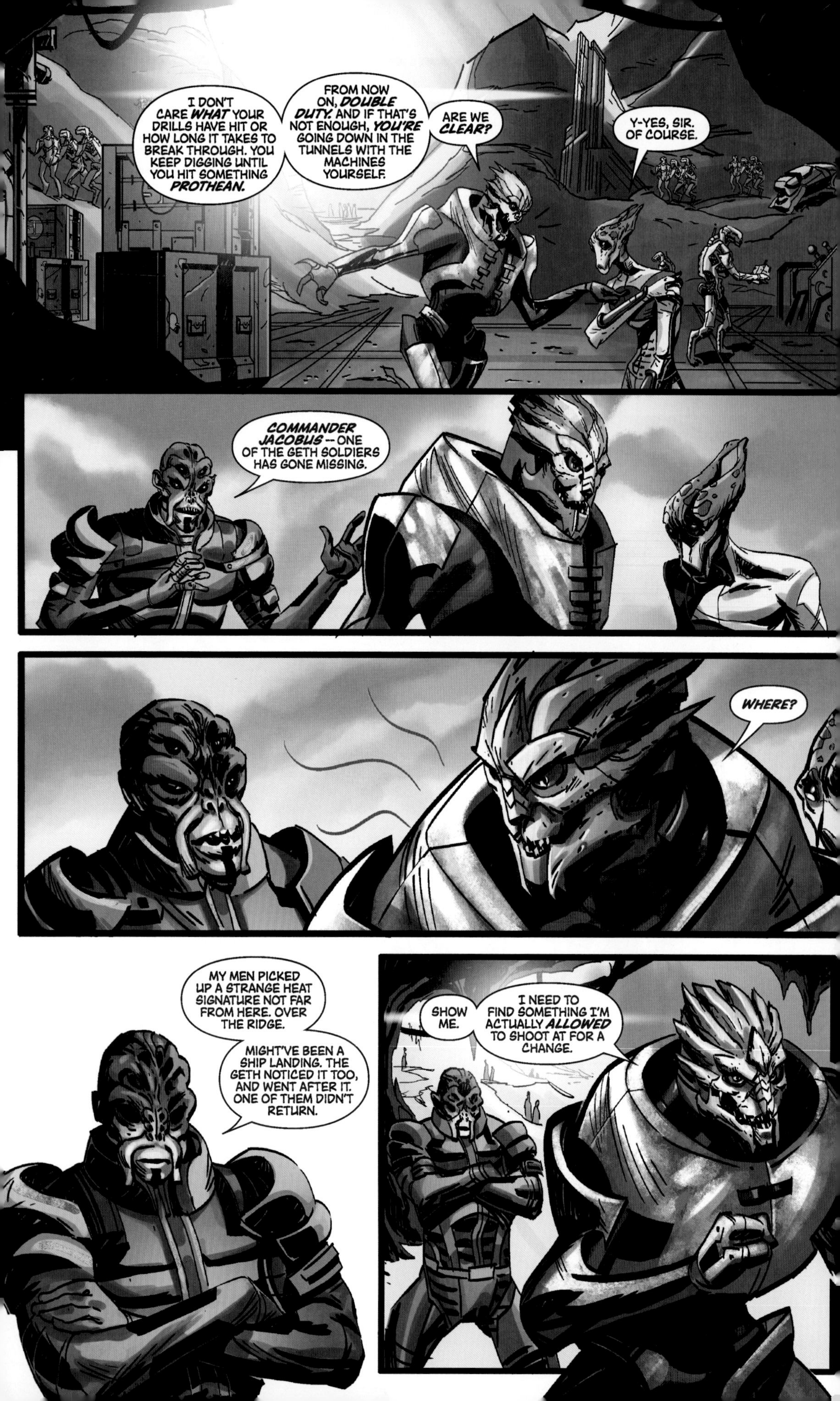
I DON'T CARE WHAT YOUR DRILLS HAVE HIT OR HOW LONG IT TAKES TO BREAK THROUGH. YOU KEEP DIGGING UNTIL YOU HIT SOMETHING PROTHEAN.
FROM NOW ON, DOUBLE DUTY. AND IF THAT'S NOT ENOUGH, YOU'RE GOING DOWN IN THE TUNNELS WITH THE MACHINES YOURSELF.
ARE WE CLEAR?
Y-YES, SIR. OF COURSE.
COMMANDER JACOBUS -- ONE OF THE GETH SOLDIERS HAS GONE MISSING.
WHERE?
MY MEN PICKED UP A STRANGE HEAT SIGNATURE NOT FAR FROM HERE. OVER THE RIDGE.
MIGHT'VE BEEN A SHIP LANDING. THE GETH NOTICED IT TOO, AND WENT AFTER IT. ONE OF THEM DIDN'T RETURN.
SHOW ME.
I NEED TO FIND SOMETHING I'M ACTUALLY ALLOWED TO SHOOT AT FOR A CHANGE.

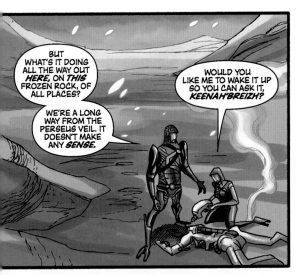

BUT WHAT'S IT DOING ALL THE WAY OUT *HERE*, ON *THIS* FROZEN ROCK, OF ALL PLACES?

WE'RE A LONG WAY FROM THE PERSEUS VEIL. IT DOESN'T MAKE ANY *SENSE*.

WOULD YOU LIKE ME TO WAKE IT UP SO YOU CAN ASK IT, *KEENAH'BREIZH?*

I'D RATHER WE *GOT OUT OF HERE* AND *FORGOT* ABOUT THIS.

YOU ASKED FOR PASSAGE TO *ILLIUM* — YOU NEVER MENTIONED THAT YOUR PILGRIMAGE INCLUDED PICKING A *FIGHT* WITH THE GETH.

IF WE CAN ACCESS ITS *MEMORY CORE* BEFORE IT SELF-PURGES, WE MIGHT BE ABLE TO FIND OUT *WHY* THEY'RE --

EDEN PRIME WAS A MAJOR VICTORY. THE BEACON HAS BROUGHT US ONE STEP CLOSER TO FINDING THE CONDUIT.

AND ONE STEP CLOSER TO THE RETURN OF THE *REAPERS*...

WHAT *WAS* THAT?

NONE OF IT MAKES SENSE TO ME, BUT I'VE SEEN ENOUGH TO KNOW THAT IT'S *TROUBLE.*

STAY HERE AND STUDY IT IF YOU WANT. BUT MY SHIP IS LEAVING. *NOW.*

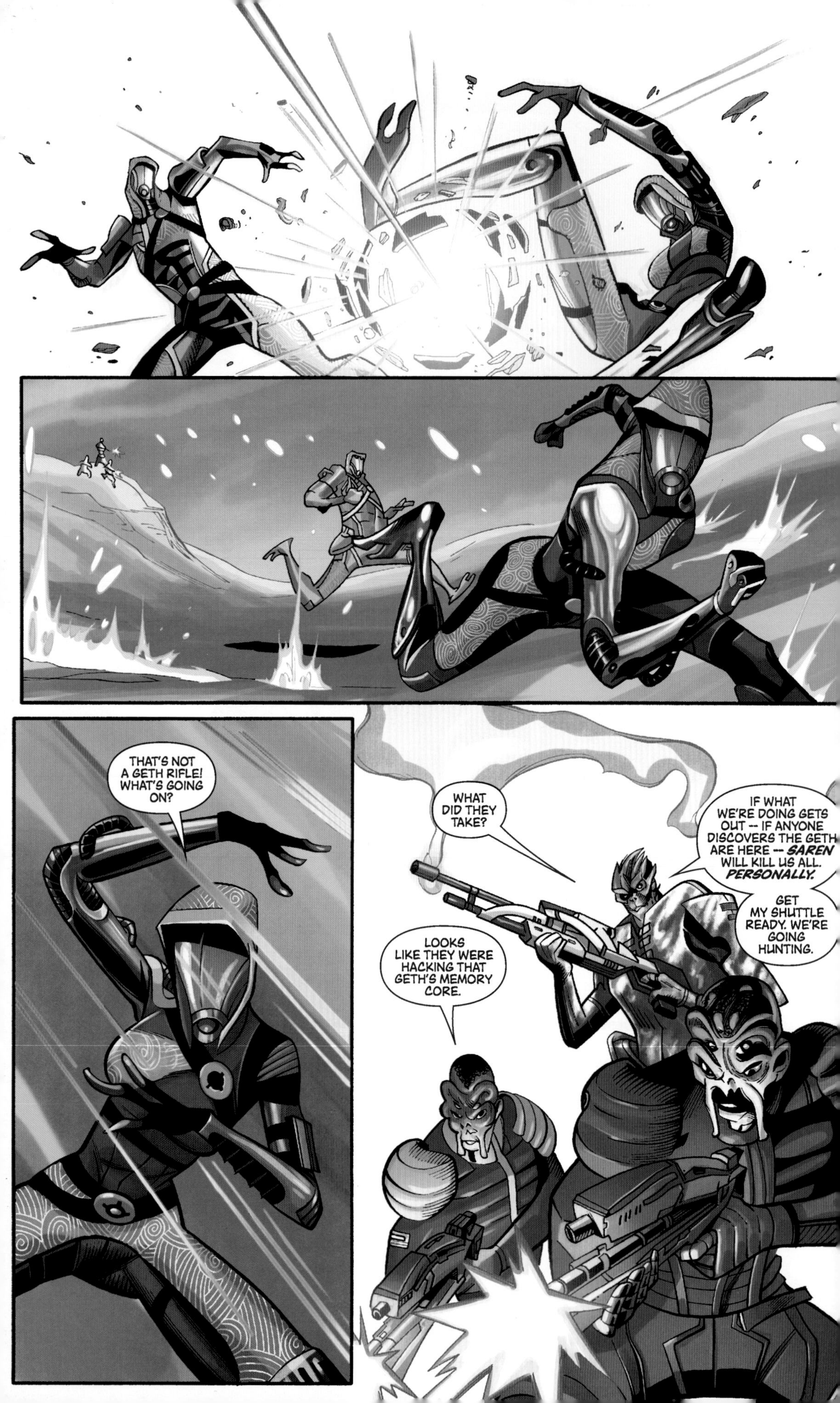
THAT'S NOT A GETH RIFLE! WHAT'S GOING ON?
WHAT DID THEY TAKE?
LOOKS LIKE THEY WERE HACKING THAT GETH'S MEMORY CORE.
IF WHAT WE'RE DOING GETS OUT -- IF ANYONE DISCOVERS THE GETH ARE HERE -- ***SAREN*** WILL KILL US ALL. ***PERSONALLY.***
GET MY SHUTTLE READY. WE'RE GOING HUNTING.

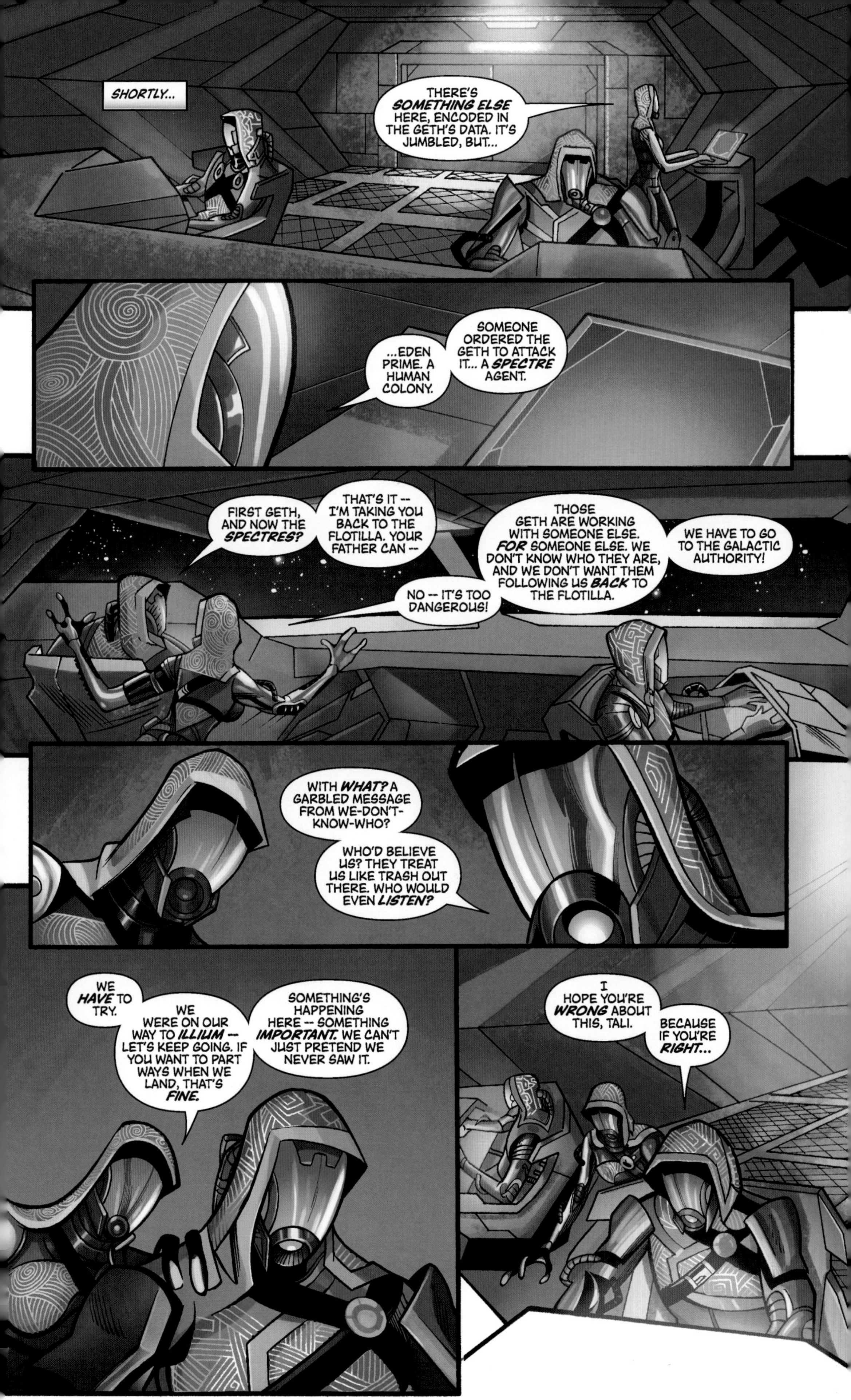
SHORTLY...
THERE'S SOMETHING ELSE HERE, ENCODED IN THE GETH'S DATA. IT'S JUMBLED, BUT...
...EDEN PRIME. A HUMAN COLONY.
SOMEONE ORDERED THE GETH TO ATTACK IT... A SPECTRE AGENT.
FIRST GETH, AND NOW THE SPECTRES?
THAT'S IT -- I'M TAKING YOU BACK TO THE FLOTILLA. YOUR FATHER CAN --
NO -- IT'S TOO DANGEROUS!
THOSE GETH ARE WORKING WITH SOMEONE ELSE. FOR SOMEONE ELSE. WE DON'T KNOW WHO THEY ARE, AND WE DON'T WANT THEM FOLLOWING US BACK TO THE FLOTILLA.
WE HAVE TO GO TO THE GALACTIC AUTHORITY!
WITH WHAT? A GARBLED MESSAGE FROM WE-DON'T-KNOW-WHO?
WHO'D BELIEVE US? THEY TREAT US LIKE TRASH OUT THERE. WHO WOULD EVEN LISTEN?
WE HAVE TO TRY.
WE WERE ON OUR WAY TO ILLIUM -- LET'S KEEP GOING. IF YOU WANT TO PART WAYS WHEN WE LAND, THAT'S FINE.
SOMETHING'S HAPPENING HERE -- SOMETHING IMPORTANT. WE CAN'T JUST PRETEND WE NEVER SAW IT.
I HOPE YOU'RE WRONG ABOUT THIS, TALI.
BECAUSE IF YOU'RE RIGHT...

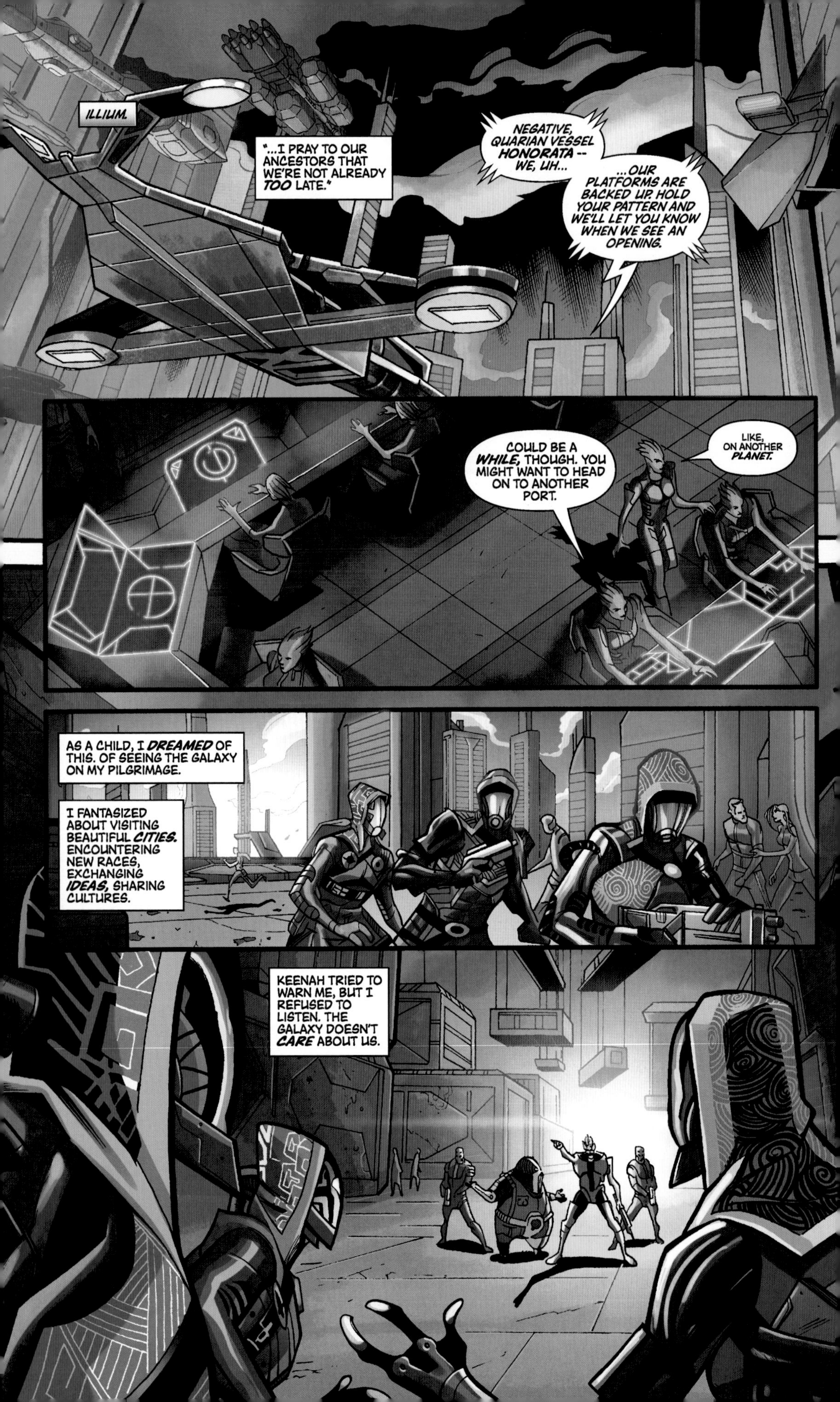
ILLIUM.
"...I PRAY TO OUR ANCESTORS THAT WE'RE NOT ALREADY TOO LATE."
NEGATIVE, QUARIAN VESSEL HONORATA -- WE, UH...
...OUR PLATFORMS ARE BACKED UP. HOLD YOUR PATTERN AND WE'LL LET YOU KNOW WHEN WE SEE AN OPENING.
COULD BE A WHILE, THOUGH. YOU MIGHT WANT TO HEAD ON TO ANOTHER PORT.
LIKE, ON ANOTHER PLANET.
AS A CHILD, I DREAMED OF THIS. OF SEEING THE GALAXY ON MY PILGRIMAGE.
I FANTASIZED ABOUT VISITING BEAUTIFUL CITIES. ENCOUNTERING NEW RACES, EXCHANGING IDEAS, SHARING CULTURES.
KEENAH TRIED TO WARN ME, BUT I REFUSED TO LISTEN. THE GALAXY DOESN'T CARE ABOUT US.

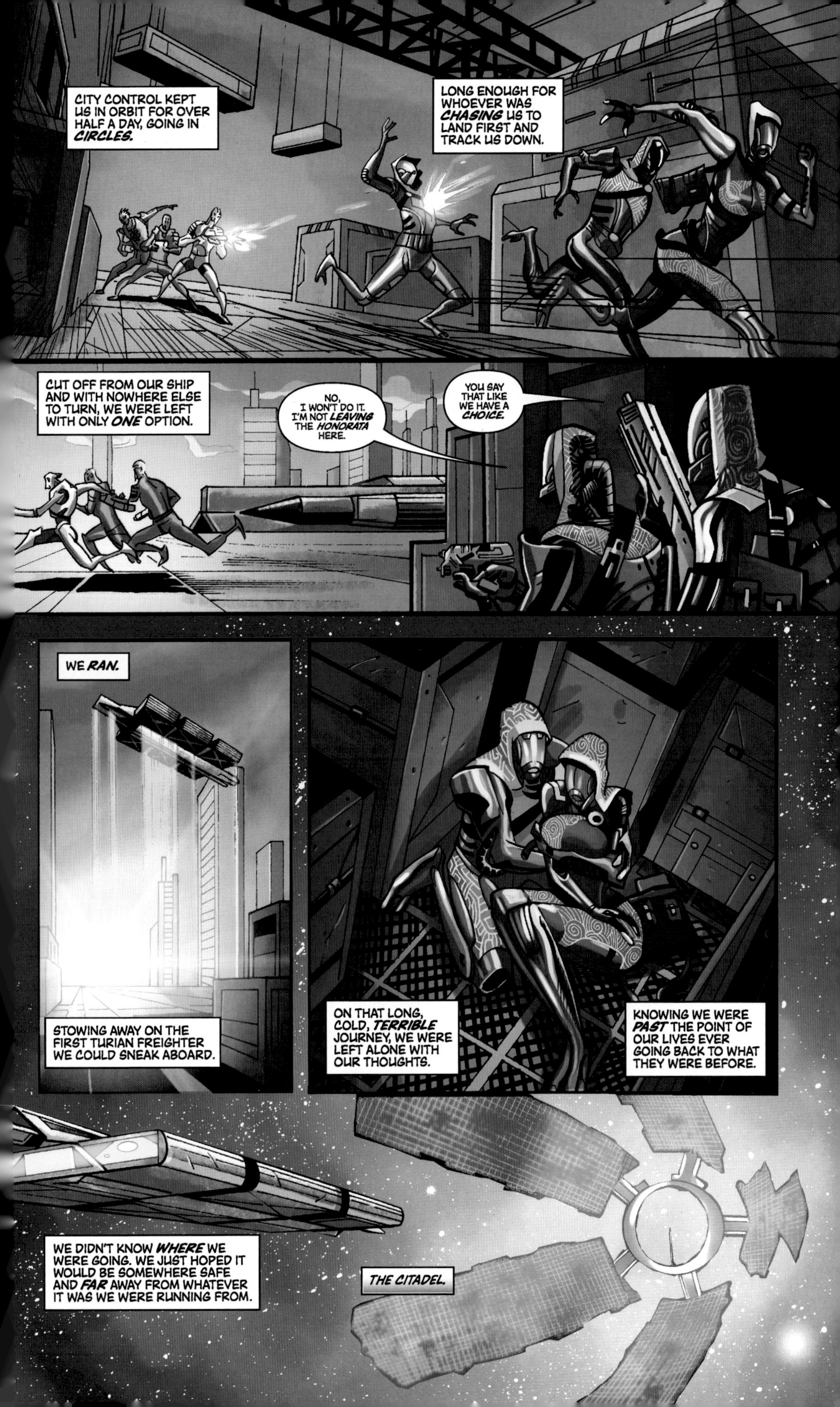
CITY CONTROL KEPT US IN ORBIT FOR OVER HALF A DAY, GOING IN *CIRCLES.*
LONG ENOUGH FOR WHOEVER WAS *CHASING* US TO LAND FIRST AND TRACK US DOWN.
CUT OFF FROM OUR SHIP AND WITH NOWHERE ELSE TO TURN, WE WERE LEFT WITH ONLY *ONE* OPTION.
NO, I WON'T DO IT. I'M NOT *LEAVING* THE *HONORATA* HERE.
YOU SAY THAT LIKE WE HAVE A *CHOICE.*
WE *RAN.*
STOWING AWAY ON THE FIRST TURIAN FREIGHTER WE COULD SNEAK ABOARD.
ON THAT LONG, COLD, *TERRIBLE* JOURNEY, WE WERE LEFT ALONE WITH OUR THOUGHTS.
KNOWING WE WERE *PAST* THE POINT OF OUR LIVES EVER GOING BACK TO WHAT THEY WERE BEFORE.
WE DIDN'T KNOW *WHERE* WE WERE GOING. WE JUST HOPED IT WOULD BE SOMEWHERE SAFE AND *FAR* AWAY FROM WHATEVER IT WAS WE WERE RUNNING FROM.
THE CITADEL.

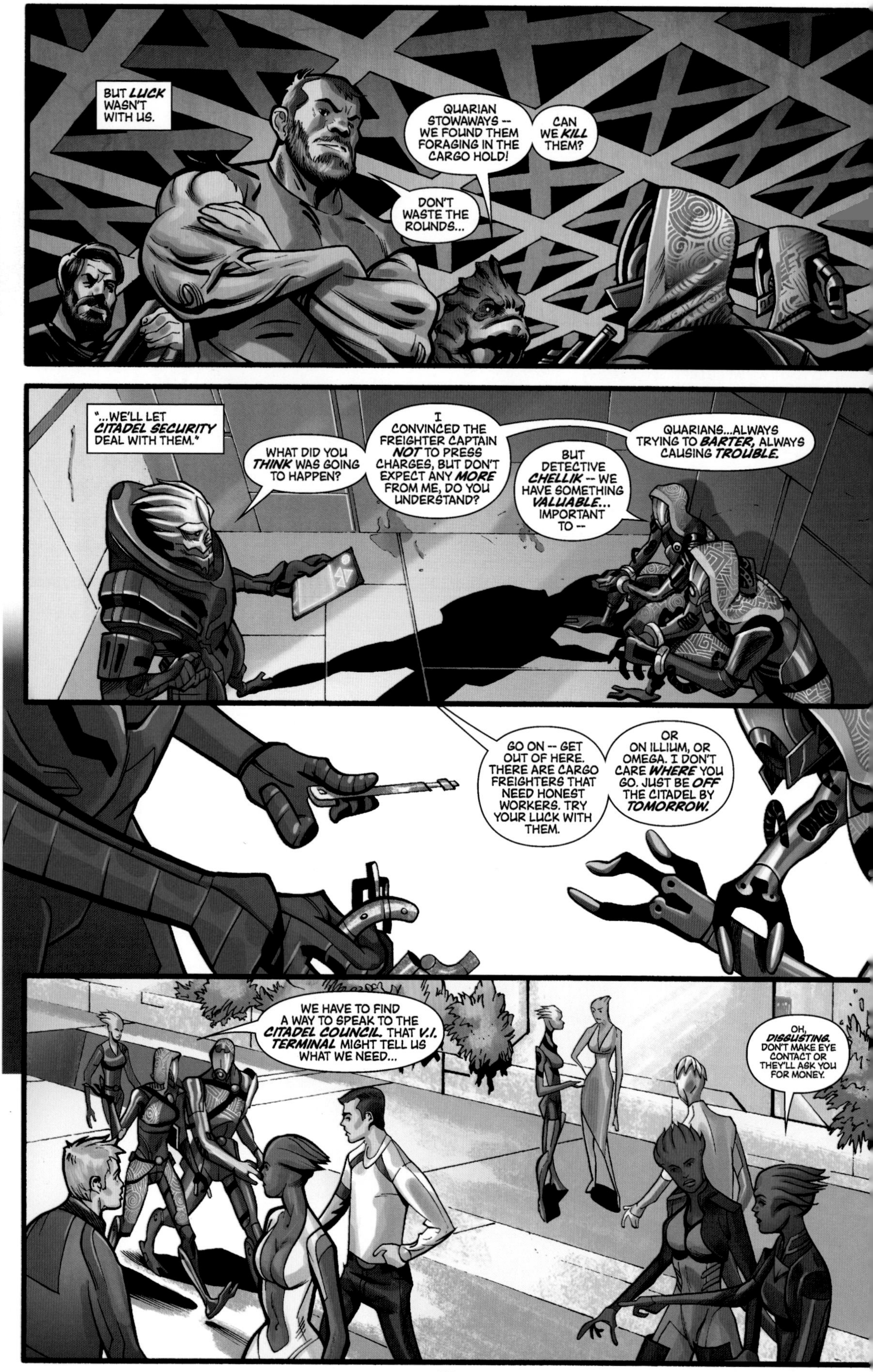

BUT LUCK WASN'T WITH US.
QUARIAN STOWAWAYS -- WE FOUND THEM FORAGING IN THE CARGO HOLD!
CAN WE KILL THEM?
DON'T WASTE THE ROUNDS...
"...WE'LL LET CITADEL SECURITY DEAL WITH THEM."
WHAT DID YOU THINK WAS GOING TO HAPPEN?
I CONVINCED THE FREIGHTER CAPTAIN NOT TO PRESS CHARGES, BUT DON'T EXPECT ANY MORE FROM ME, DO YOU UNDERSTAND?
BUT DETECTIVE CHELLIK -- WE HAVE SOMETHING VALUABLE... IMPORTANT TO --
QUARIANS...ALWAYS TRYING TO BARTER, ALWAYS CAUSING TROUBLE.
GO ON -- GET OUT OF HERE. THERE ARE CARGO FREIGHTERS THAT NEED HONEST WORKERS. TRY YOUR LUCK WITH THEM.
OR ON ILLIUM, OR OMEGA. I DON'T CARE WHERE YOU GO. JUST BE OFF THE CITADEL BY TOMORROW.
WE HAVE TO FIND A WAY TO SPEAK TO THE CITADEL COUNCIL. THAT V.I. TERMINAL MIGHT TELL US WHAT WE NEED...
OH, DISGUSTING. DON'T MAKE EYE CONTACT OR THEY'LL ASK YOU FOR MONEY.

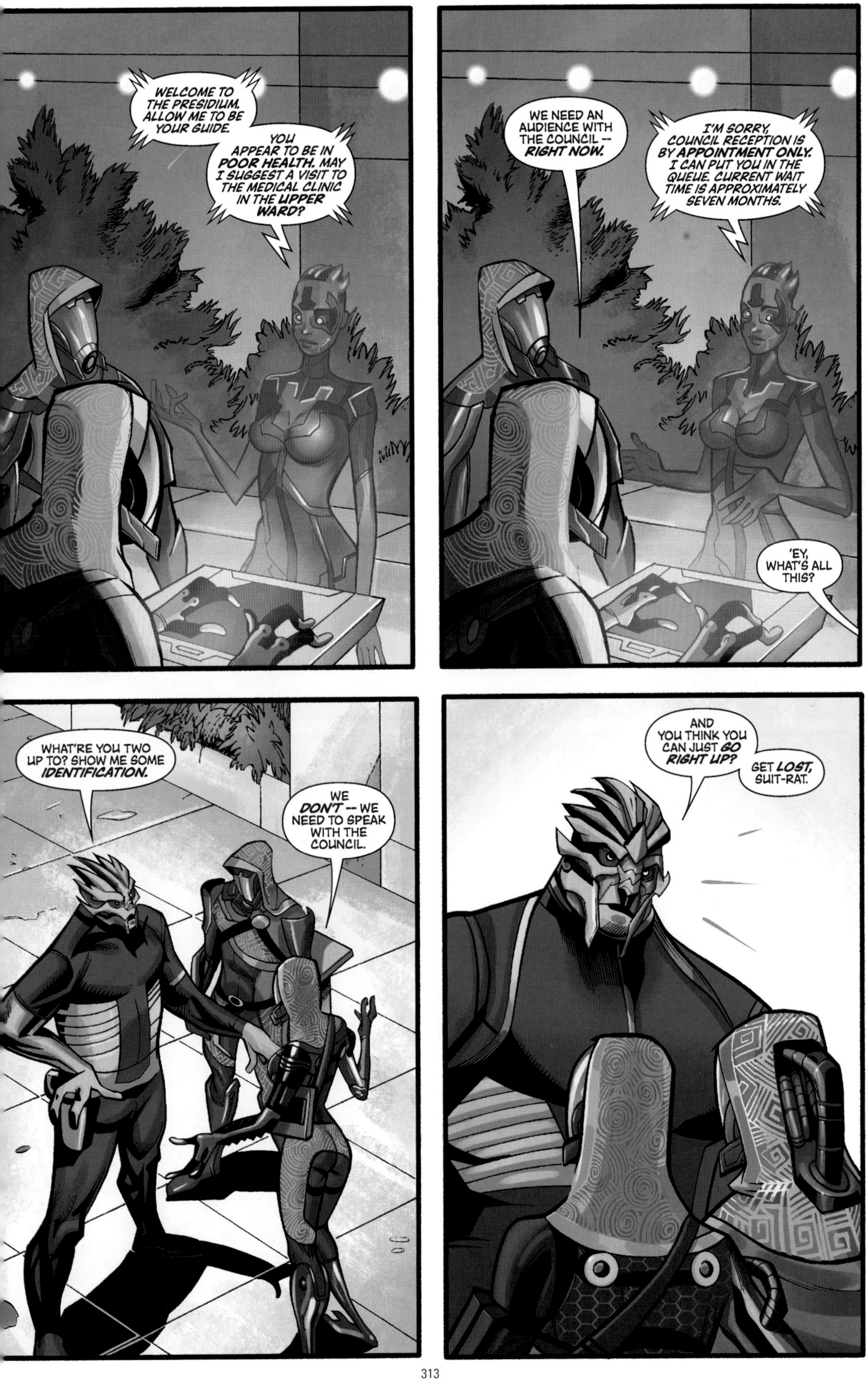
WELCOME TO THE PRESIDIUM. ALLOW ME TO BE YOUR GUIDE.
YOU APPEAR TO BE IN POOR HEALTH. MAY I SUGGEST A VISIT TO THE MEDICAL CLINIC IN THE UPPER WARD?
WE NEED AN AUDIENCE WITH THE COUNCIL -- RIGHT NOW.
I'M SORRY, COUNCIL RECEPTION IS BY APPOINTMENT ONLY. I CAN PUT YOU IN THE QUEUE. CURRENT WAIT TIME IS APPROXIMATELY SEVEN MONTHS.
'EY, WHAT'S ALL THIS?
WHAT'RE YOU TWO UP TO? SHOW ME SOME IDENTIFICATION.
WE DON'T -- WE NEED TO SPEAK WITH THE COUNCIL.
AND YOU THINK YOU CAN JUST GO RIGHT UP?
GET LOST, SUIT-RAT.

TALI, STOP. LET'S THINK THIS THROUGH A MINUTE. WE --

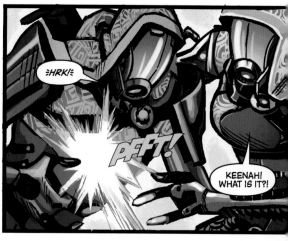

≡HRK!≡

PFFT!

KEENAH! WHAT IS IT?!

AAGH!

PFFT!

COME ON! DON'T STOP NOW -- WE HAVE TO KEEP MOVING!

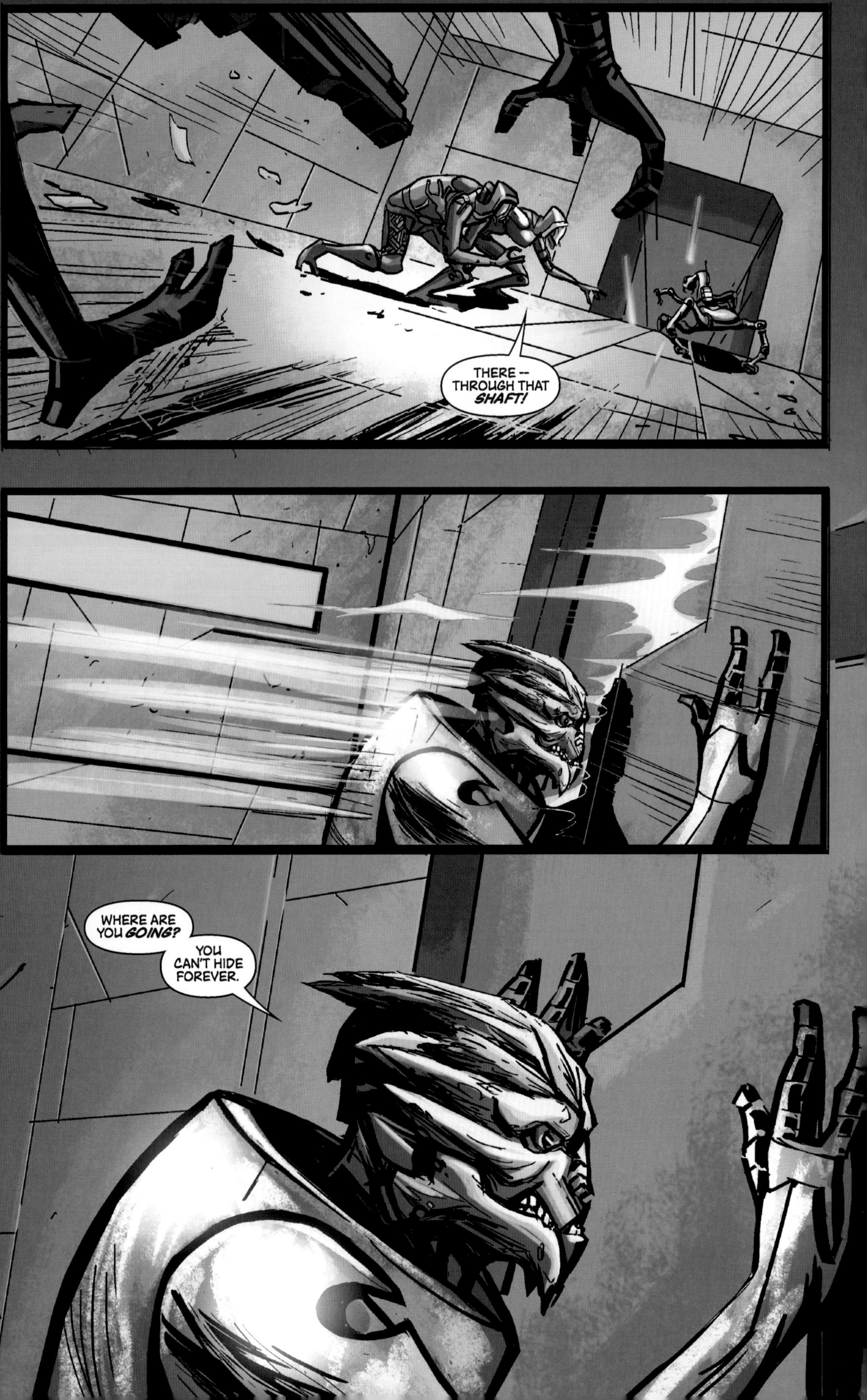
THERE -- THROUGH THAT SHAFT!
WHERE ARE YOU GOING?
YOU CAN'T HIDE FOREVER.

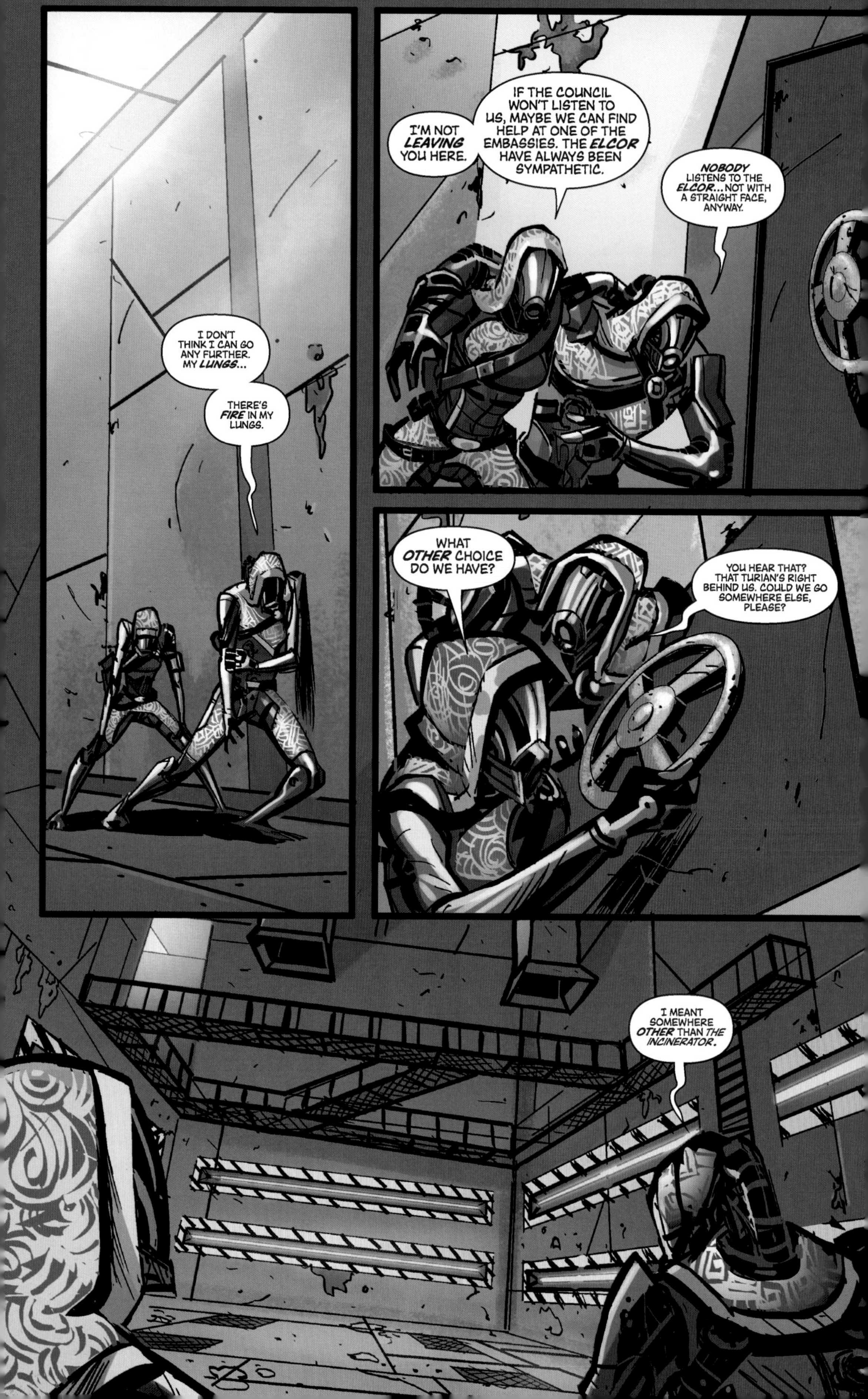
I DON'T THINK I CAN GO ANY FURTHER. MY LUNGS...
THERE'S FIRE IN MY LUNGS.
I'M NOT LEAVING YOU HERE.
IF THE COUNCIL WON'T LISTEN TO US, MAYBE WE CAN FIND HELP AT ONE OF THE EMBASSIES. THE ELCOR HAVE ALWAYS BEEN SYMPATHETIC.
NOBODY LISTENS TO THE ELCOR...NOT WITH A STRAIGHT FACE, ANYWAY.
WHAT OTHER CHOICE DO WE HAVE?
YOU HEAR THAT? THAT TURIAN'S RIGHT BEHIND US. COULD WE GO SOMEWHERE ELSE, PLEASE?
I MEANT SOMEWHERE OTHER THAN THE INCINERATOR.

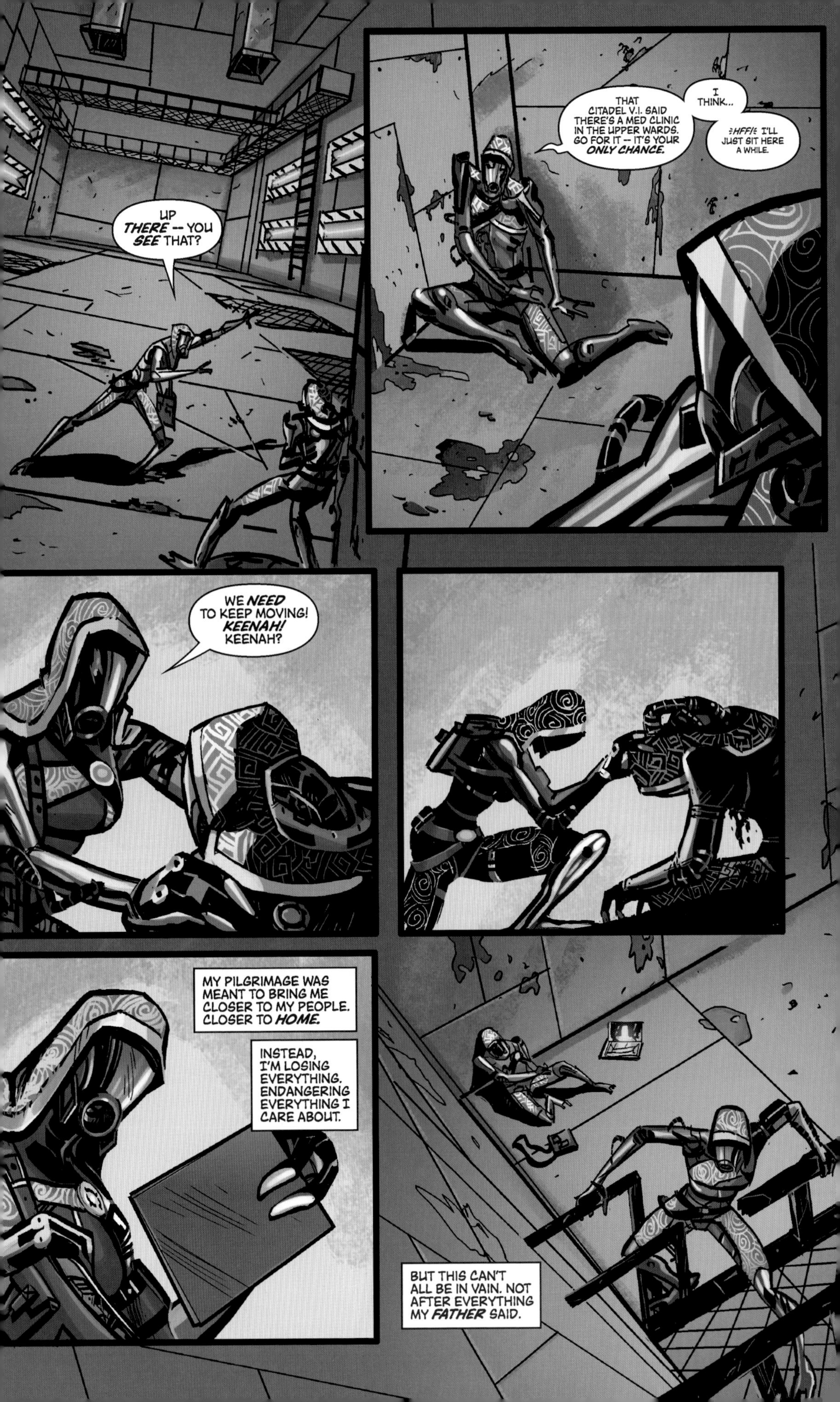
UP THERE -- YOU SEE THAT?
THAT CITADEL V.I. SAID THERE'S A MED CLINIC IN THE UPPER WARDS. GO FOR IT -- IT'S YOUR ONLY CHANCE.
I THINK...
≑HFF!≑ I'LL JUST SIT HERE A WHILE.
WE NEED TO KEEP MOVING! KEENAH! KEENAH?
MY PILGRIMAGE WAS MEANT TO BRING ME CLOSER TO MY PEOPLE. CLOSER TO HOME.
INSTEAD, I'M LOSING EVERYTHING. ENDANGERING EVERYTHING I CARE ABOUT.
BUT THIS CAN'T ALL BE IN VAIN. NOT AFTER EVERYTHING MY FATHER SAID.

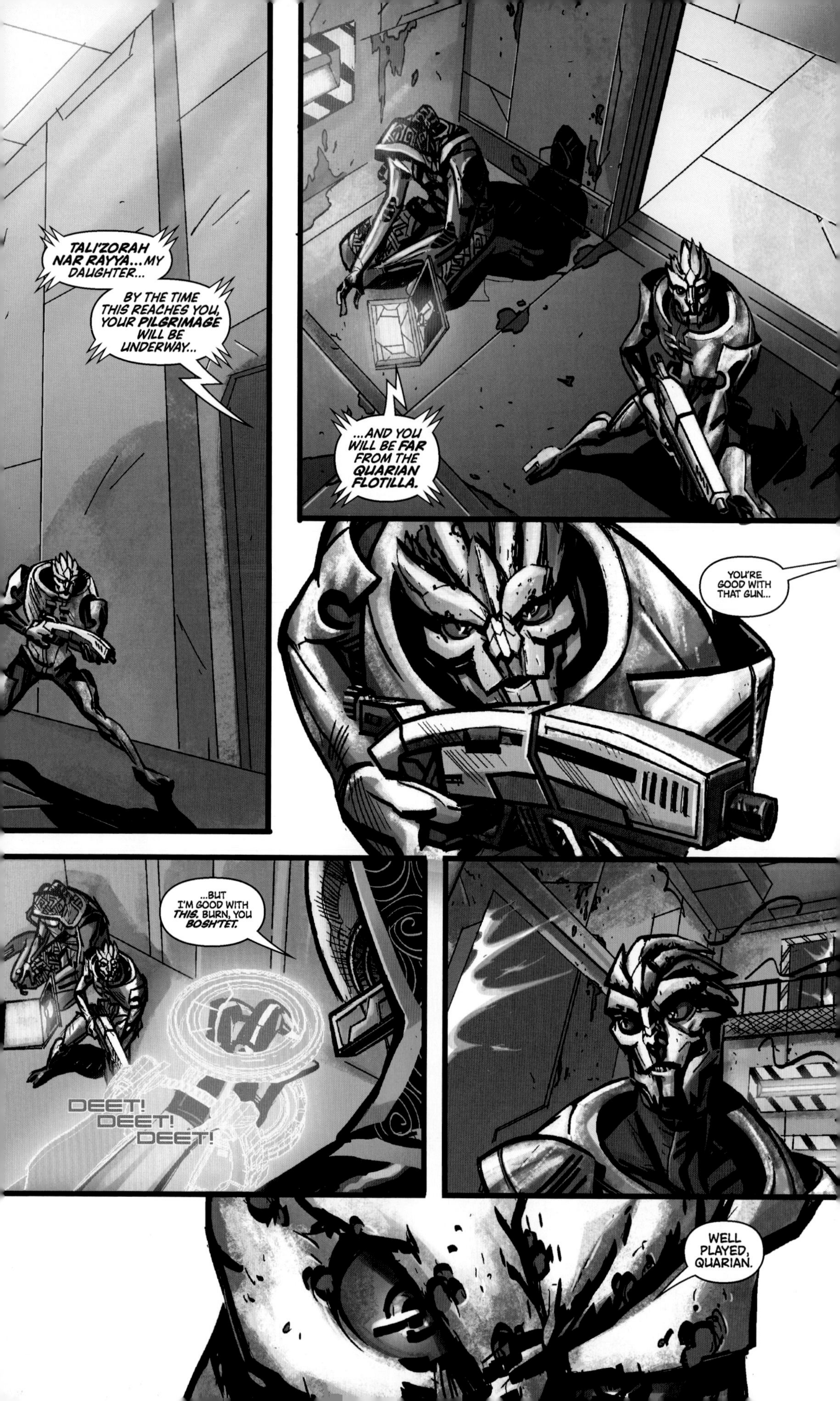
TALI'ZORAH NAR RAYYA... MY DAUGHTER...
BY THE TIME THIS REACHES YOU, YOUR PILGRIMAGE WILL BE UNDERWAY...
...AND YOU WILL BE FAR FROM THE QUARIAN FLOTILLA.
YOU'RE GOOD WITH THAT GUN...
...BUT I'M GOOD WITH THIS. BURN, YOU BOSH'TET.
DEET! DEET! DEET!
WELL PLAYED, QUARIAN.

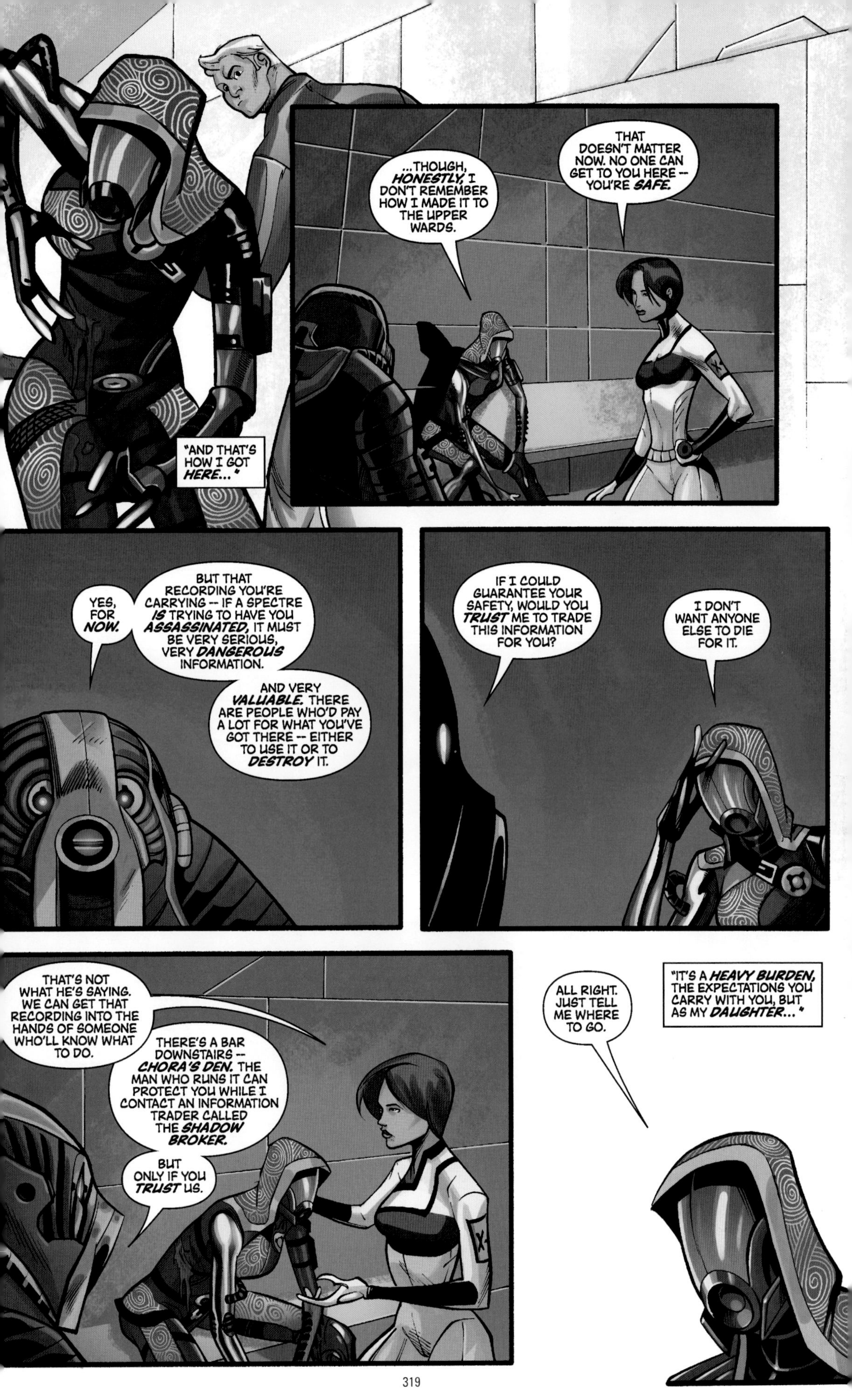

"AND THAT'S HOW I GOT HERE..."
...THOUGH, HONESTLY, I DON'T REMEMBER HOW I MADE IT TO THE UPPER WARDS.
THAT DOESN'T MATTER NOW. NO ONE CAN GET TO YOU HERE -- YOU'RE SAFE.
YES, FOR NOW.
BUT THAT RECORDING YOU'RE CARRYING -- IF A SPECTRE IS TRYING TO HAVE YOU ASSASSINATED, IT MUST BE VERY SERIOUS, VERY DANGEROUS INFORMATION.
AND VERY VALUABLE. THERE ARE PEOPLE WHO'D PAY A LOT FOR WHAT YOU'VE GOT THERE -- EITHER TO USE IT OR TO DESTROY IT.
IF I COULD GUARANTEE YOUR SAFETY, WOULD YOU TRUST ME TO TRADE THIS INFORMATION FOR YOU?
I DON'T WANT ANYONE ELSE TO DIE FOR IT.
THAT'S NOT WHAT HE'S SAYING. WE CAN GET THAT RECORDING INTO THE HANDS OF SOMEONE WHO'LL KNOW WHAT TO DO.
THERE'S A BAR DOWNSTAIRS -- CHORA'S DEN. THE MAN WHO RUNS IT CAN PROTECT YOU WHILE I CONTACT AN INFORMATION TRADER CALLED THE SHADOW BROKER.
BUT ONLY IF YOU TRUST US.
ALL RIGHT. JUST TELL ME WHERE TO GO.
"IT'S A HEAVY BURDEN, THE EXPECTATIONS YOU CARRY WITH YOU, BUT AS MY DAUGHTER..."

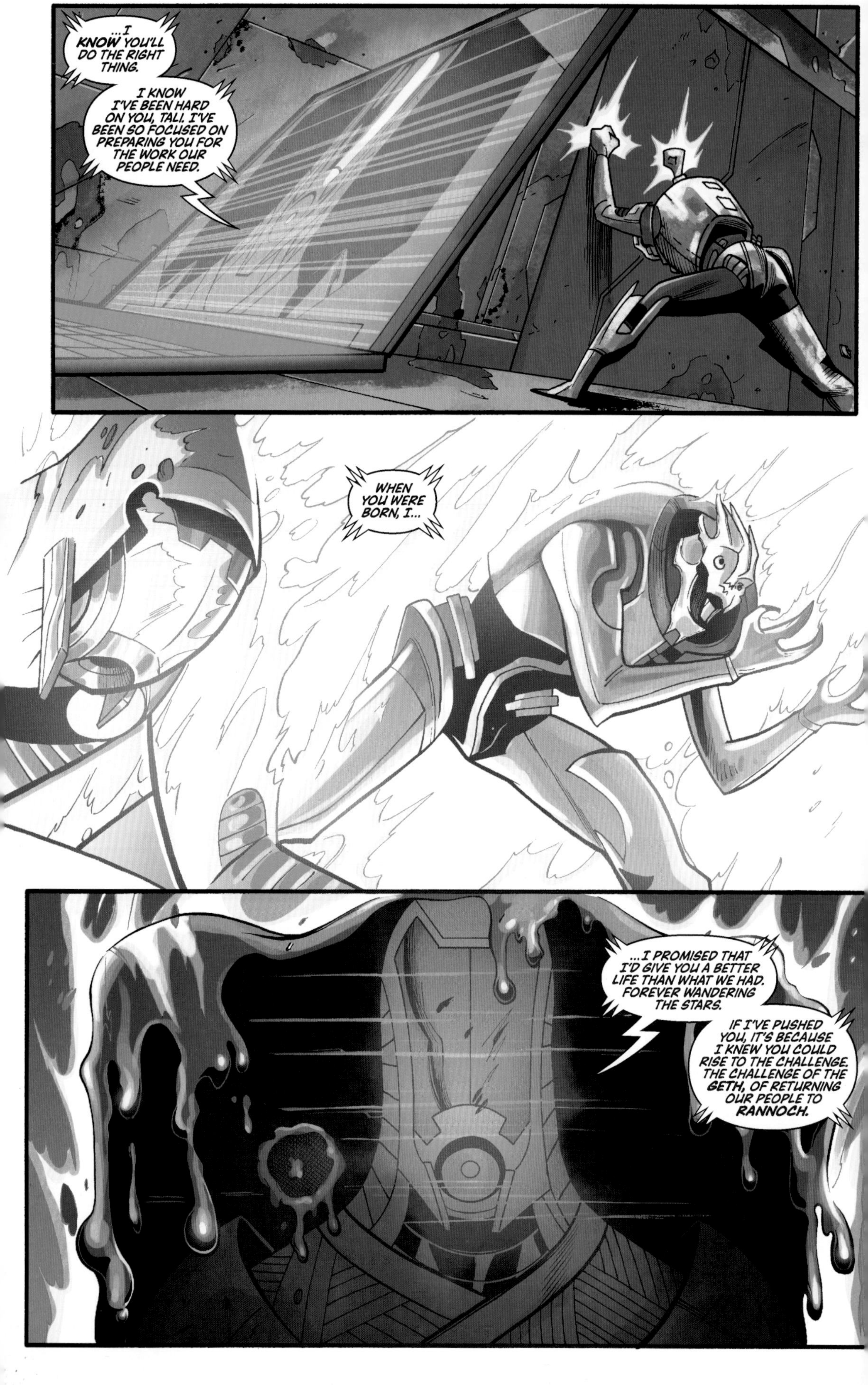
...I KNOW YOU'LL DO THE RIGHT THING.
I KNOW I'VE BEEN HARD ON YOU, TALI. I'VE BEEN SO FOCUSED ON PREPARING YOU FOR THE WORK OUR PEOPLE NEED.
WHEN YOU WERE BORN, I...
...I PROMISED THAT I'D GIVE YOU A BETTER LIFE THAN WHAT WE HAD. FOREVER WANDERING THE STARS.
IF I'VE PUSHED YOU, IT'S BECAUSE I KNEW YOU COULD RISE TO THE CHALLENGE. THE CHALLENGE OF THE GETH, OF RETURNING OUR PEOPLE TO RANNOCH.

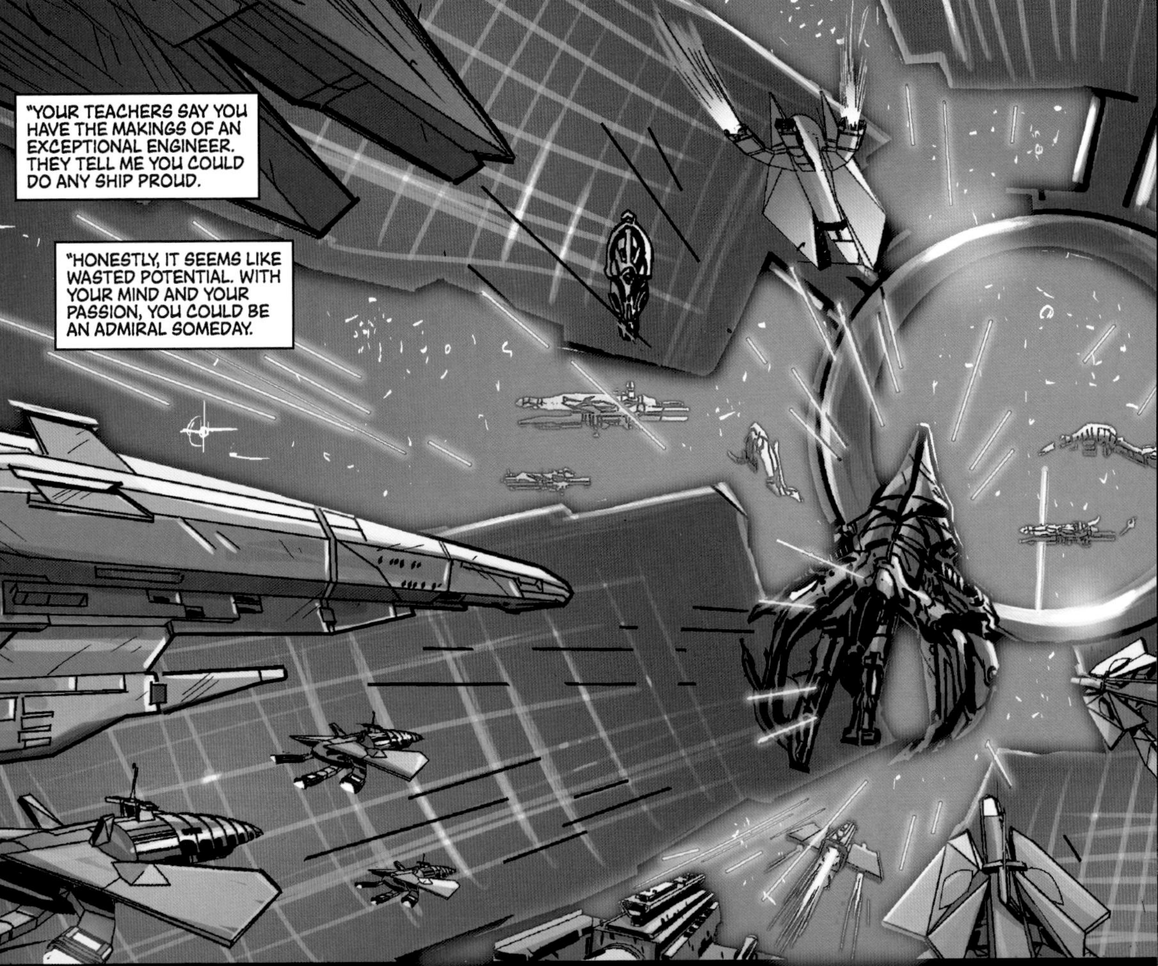
"YOUR TEACHERS SAY YOU HAVE THE MAKINGS OF AN EXCEPTIONAL ENGINEER. THEY TELL ME YOU COULD DO ANY SHIP PROUD.
"HONESTLY, IT SEEMS LIKE WASTED POTENTIAL. WITH YOUR MIND AND YOUR PASSION, YOU COULD BE AN ADMIRAL SOMEDAY.
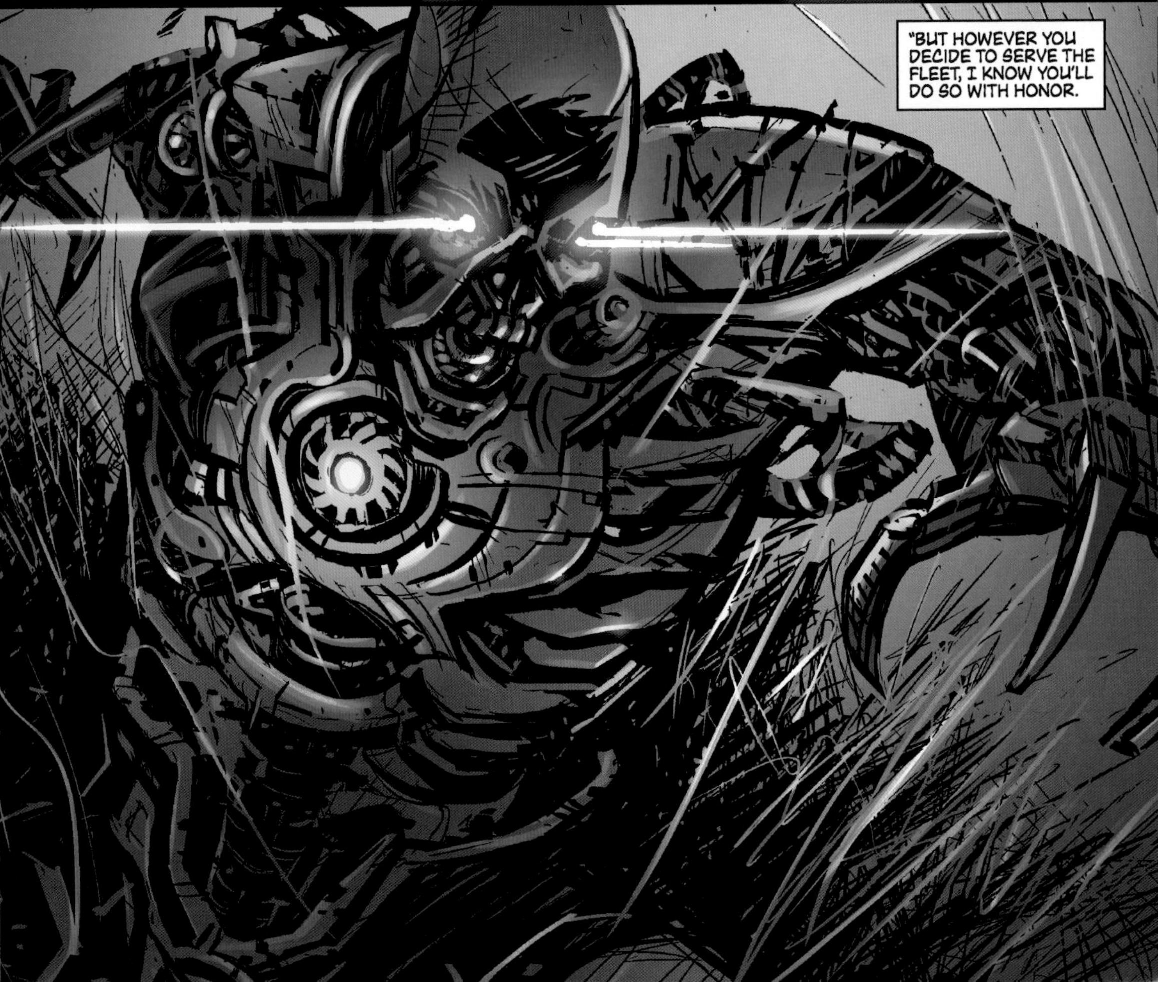
"BUT HOWEVER YOU DECIDE TO SERVE THE FLEET, I KNOW YOU'LL DO SO WITH HONOR.

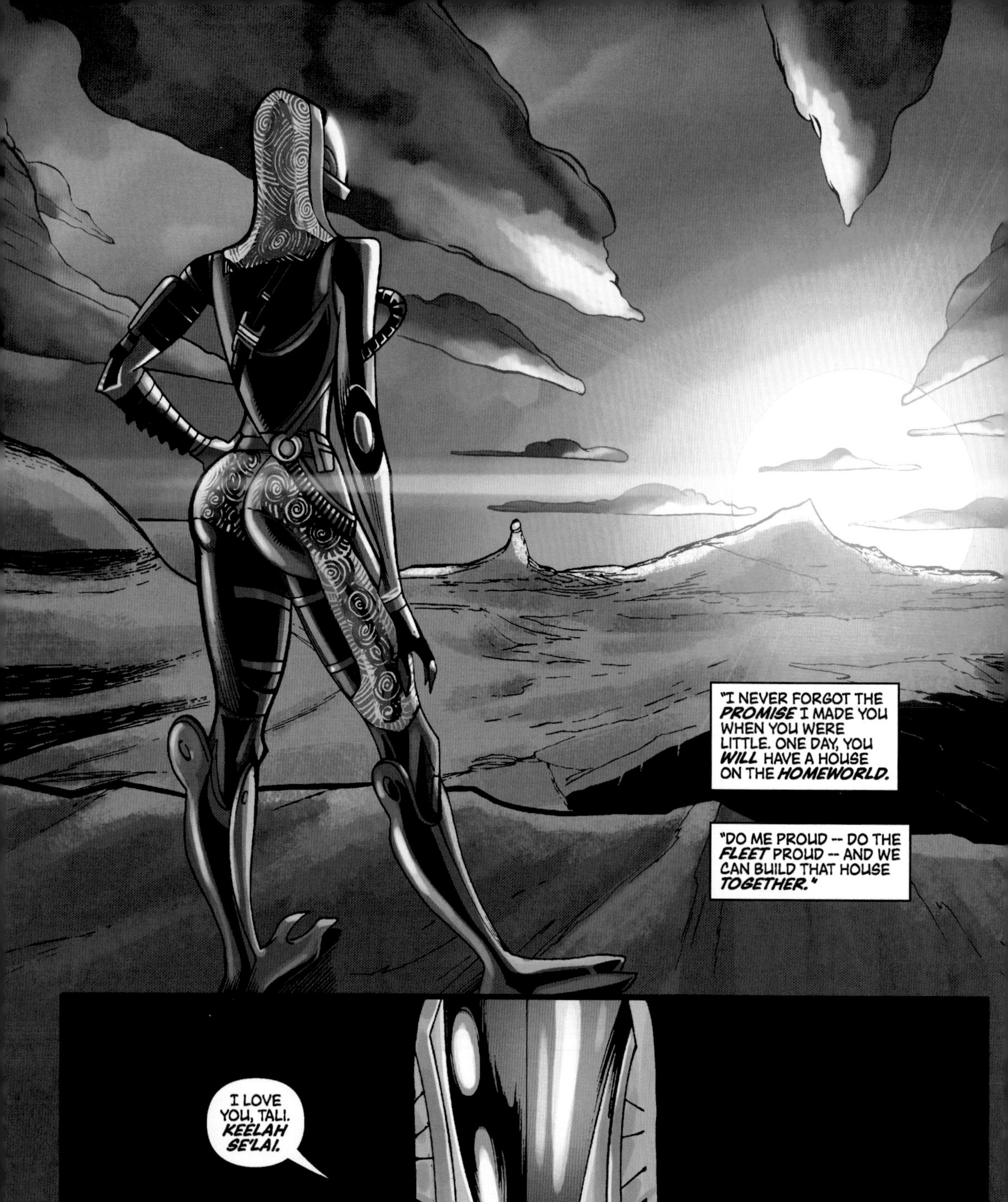
"I NEVER FORGOT THE PROMISE I MADE YOU WHEN YOU WERE LITTLE. ONE DAY, YOU WILL HAVE A HOUSE ON THE HOMEWORLD.
"DO ME PROUD -- DO THE FLEET PROUD -- AND WE CAN BUILD THAT HOUSE TOGETHER."

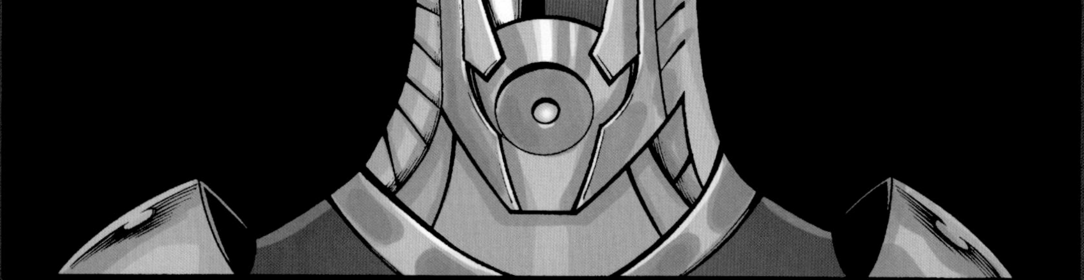
I LOVE YOU, TALI. KEELAH SE'LAI.

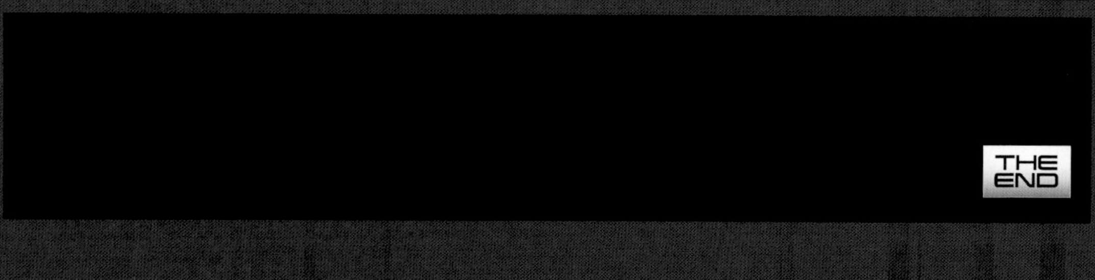
THE END

ILLUSTRATION BY
ANTHONY PALUMBO

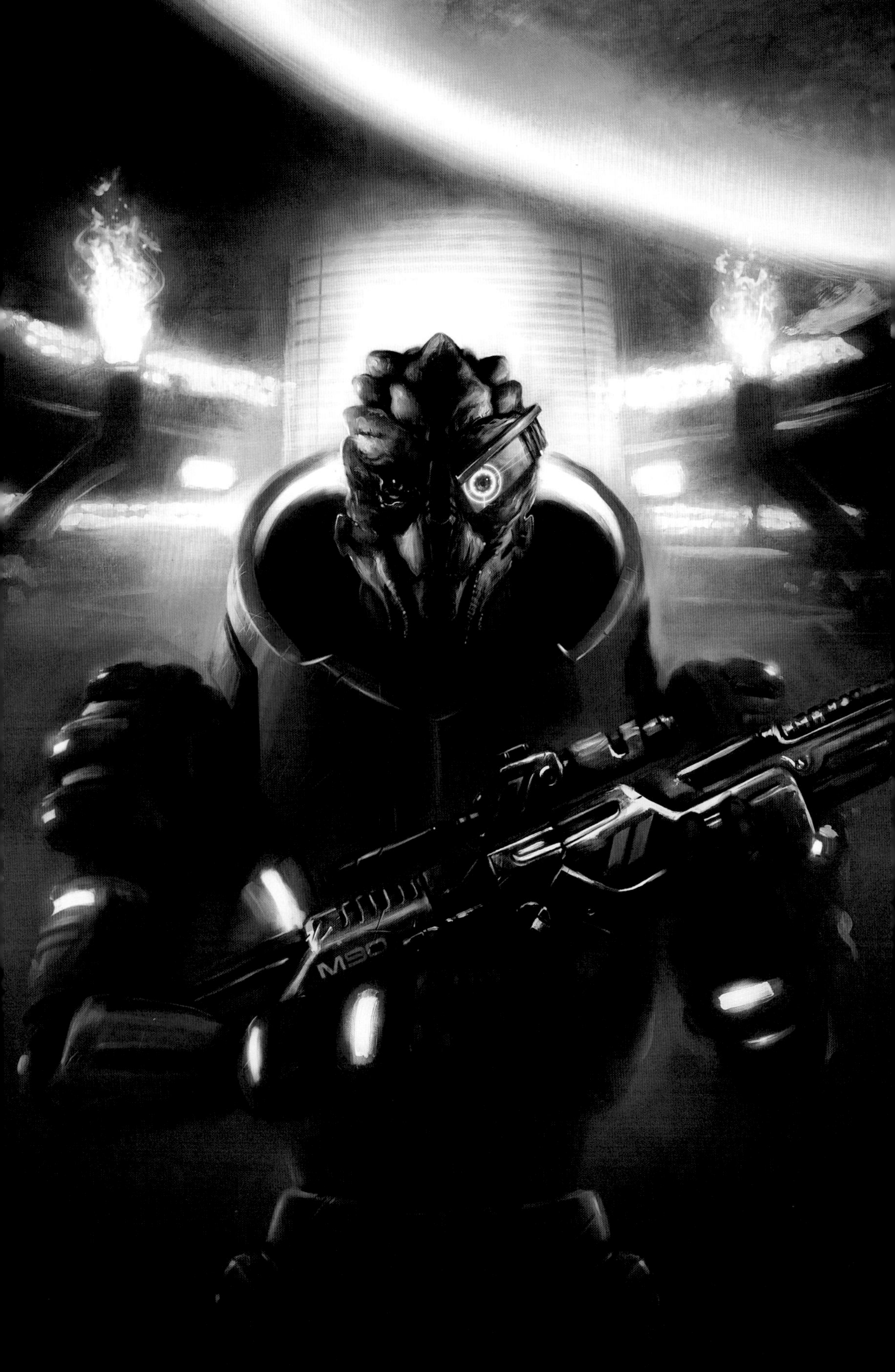
M90

HOMEWORLDS: GARRUS VAKARIAN

STORY
MAC WALTERS AND JOHN DOMBROW

SCRIPT
JEREMY BARLOW

ART
GARRY BROWN

COLORS
MICHAEL ATIYEH

LETTERING
MICHAEL HEISLER

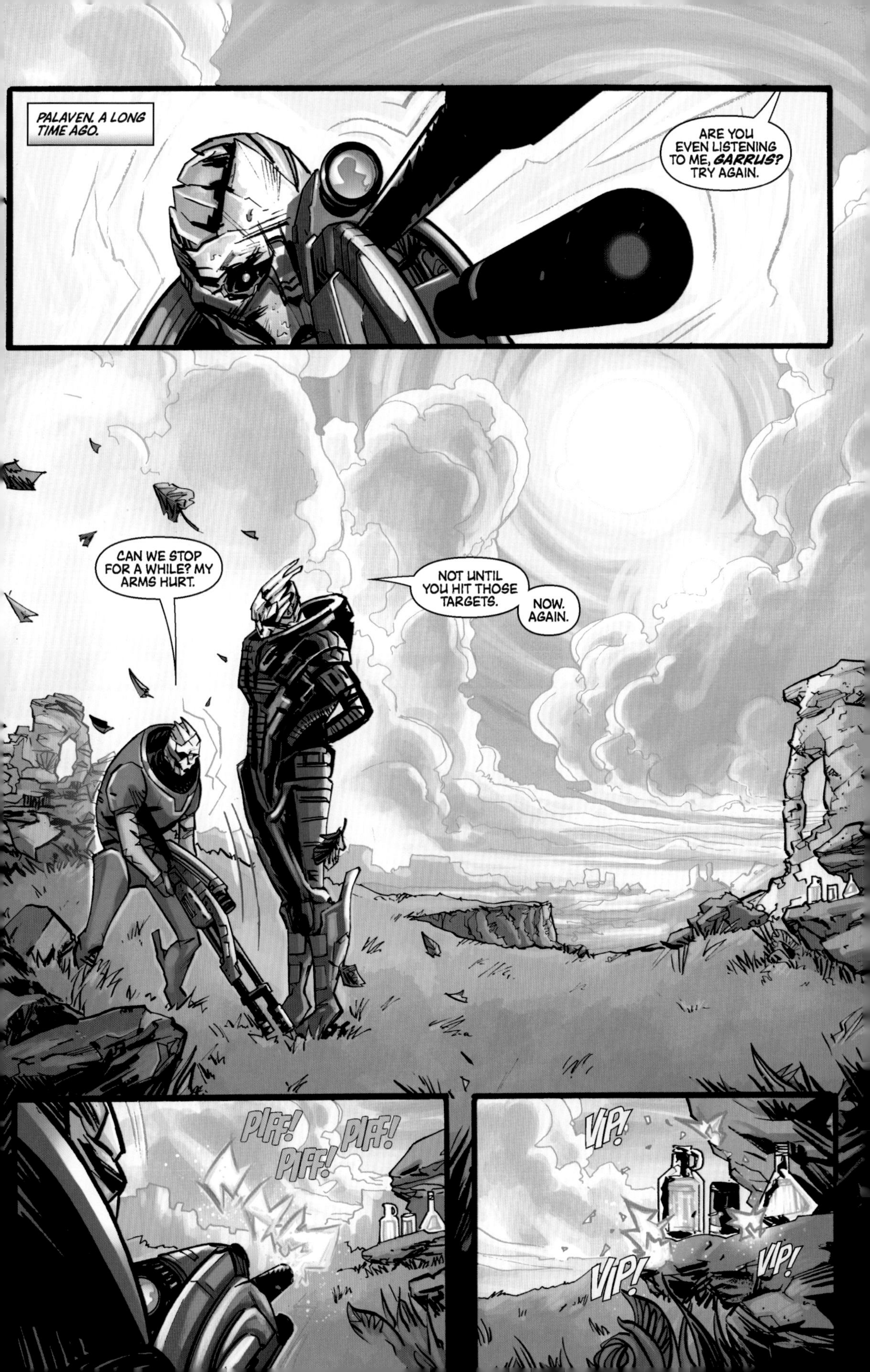
PALAVEN. A LONG TIME AGO.
ARE YOU EVEN LISTENING TO ME, GARRUS? TRY AGAIN.
CAN WE STOP FOR A WHILE? MY ARMS HURT.
NOT UNTIL YOU HIT THOSE TARGETS.
NOW. AGAIN.
PIFF!
PIFF!
PIFF!
VIP!
VIP!
VIP!

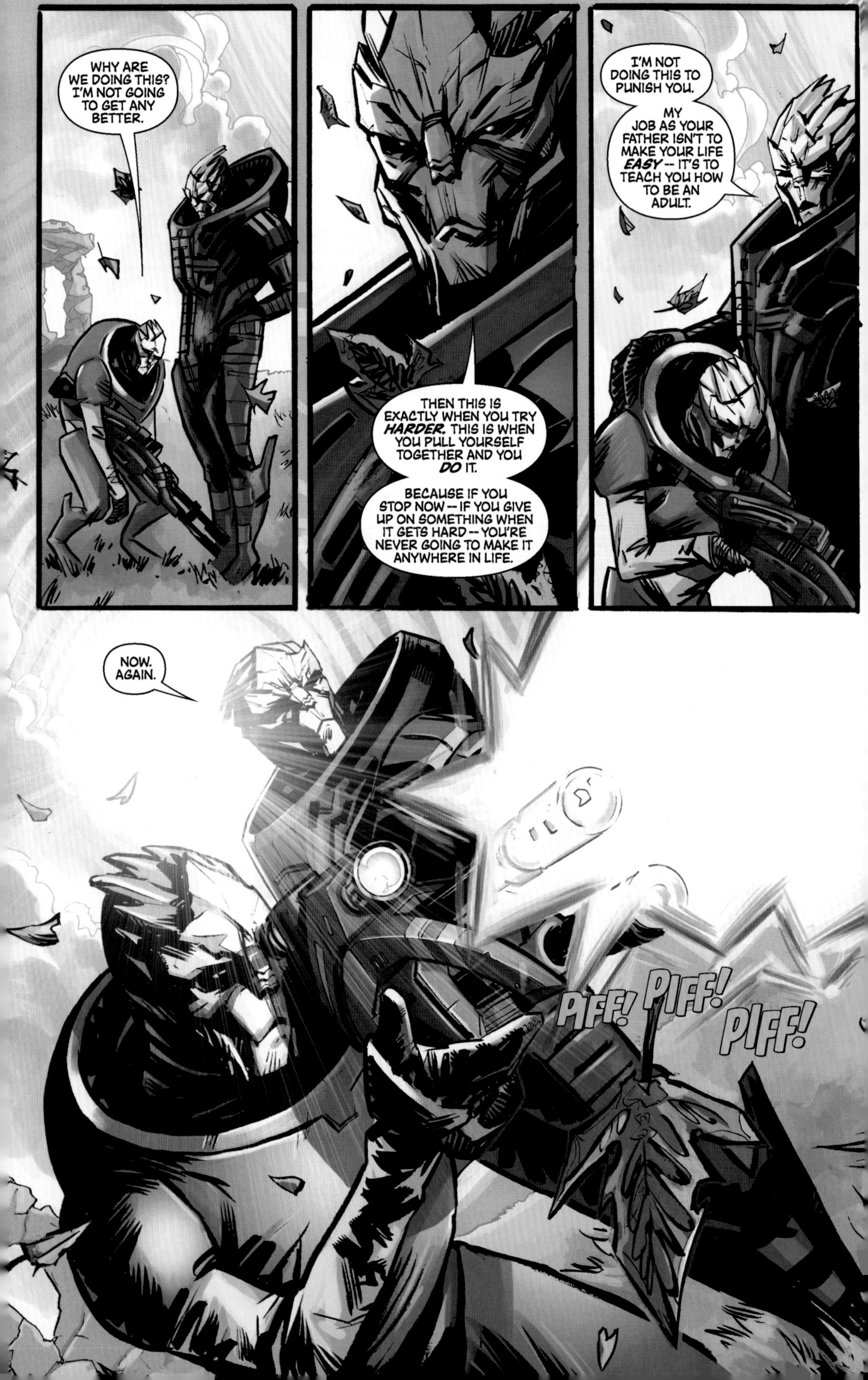
WHY ARE WE DOING THIS? I'M NOT GOING TO GET ANY BETTER.
THEN THIS IS EXACTLY WHEN YOU TRY HARDER. THIS IS WHEN YOU PULL YOURSELF TOGETHER AND YOU DO IT.
BECAUSE IF YOU STOP NOW -- IF YOU GIVE UP ON SOMETHING WHEN IT GETS HARD -- YOU'RE NEVER GOING TO MAKE IT ANYWHERE IN LIFE.
I'M NOT DOING THIS TO PUNISH YOU.
MY JOB AS YOUR FATHER ISN'T TO MAKE YOUR LIFE EASY -- IT'S TO TEACH YOU HOW TO BE AN ADULT.
NOW. AGAIN.
PIFF! PIFF! PIFF!

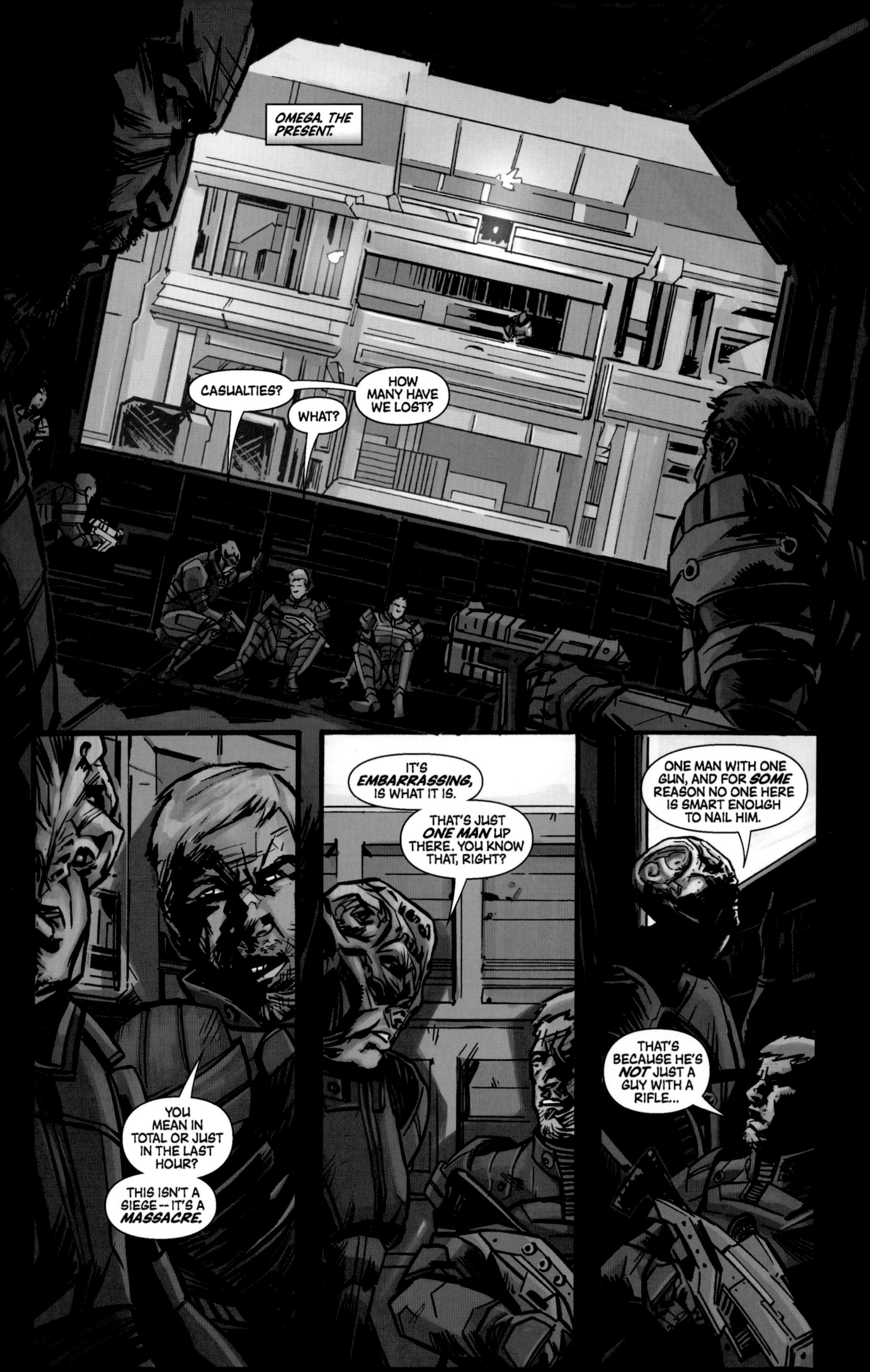
OMEGA. THE PRESENT.
CASUALTIES?
WHAT?
HOW MANY HAVE WE LOST?
YOU MEAN IN TOTAL OR JUST IN THE LAST HOUR?
THIS ISN'T A SIEGE -- IT'S A MASSACRE.
IT'S EMBARRASSING, IS WHAT IT IS.
THAT'S JUST ONE MAN UP THERE. YOU KNOW THAT, RIGHT?
ONE MAN WITH ONE GUN, AND FOR SOME REASON NO ONE HERE IS SMART ENOUGH TO NAIL HIM.
THAT'S BECAUSE HE'S NOT JUST A GUY WITH A RIFLE...

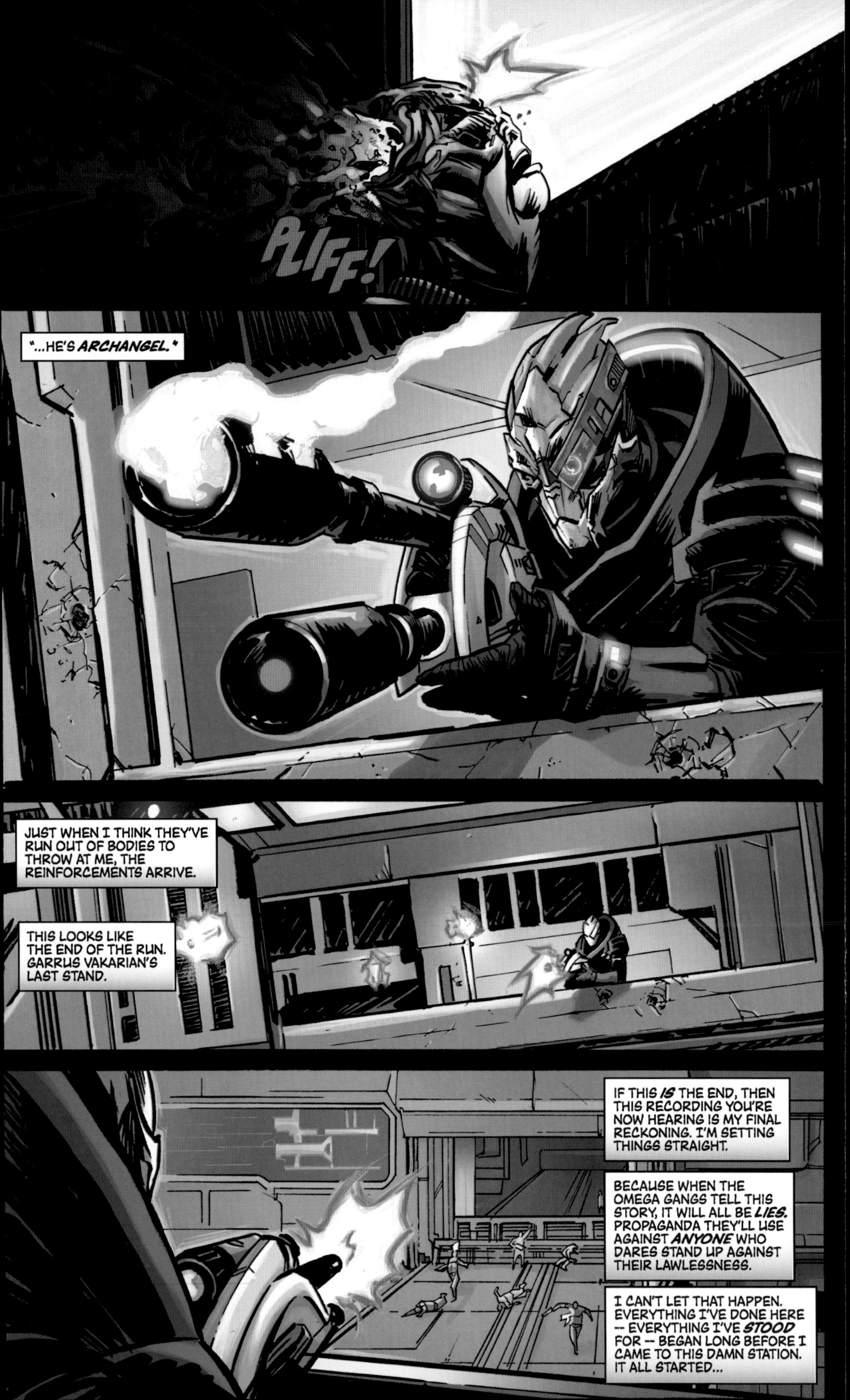
PLIFF!
"...HE'S *ARCHANGEL.*"
JUST WHEN I THINK THEY'VE RUN OUT OF BODIES TO THROW AT ME, THE REINFORCEMENTS ARRIVE.
THIS LOOKS LIKE THE END OF THE RUN. GARRUS VAKARIAN'S LAST STAND.
IF THIS *IS* THE END, THEN THIS RECORDING YOU'RE NOW HEARING IS MY FINAL RECKONING. I'M SETTING THINGS STRAIGHT.
BECAUSE WHEN THE OMEGA GANGS TELL THIS STORY, IT WILL ALL BE *LIES.* PROPAGANDA THEY'LL USE AGAINST *ANYONE* WHO DARES STAND UP AGAINST THEIR LAWLESSNESS.
I CAN'T LET THAT HAPPEN. EVERYTHING I'VE DONE HERE -- EVERYTHING I'VE *STOOD* FOR -- BEGAN LONG BEFORE I CAME TO THIS DAMN STATION. IT ALL STARTED...

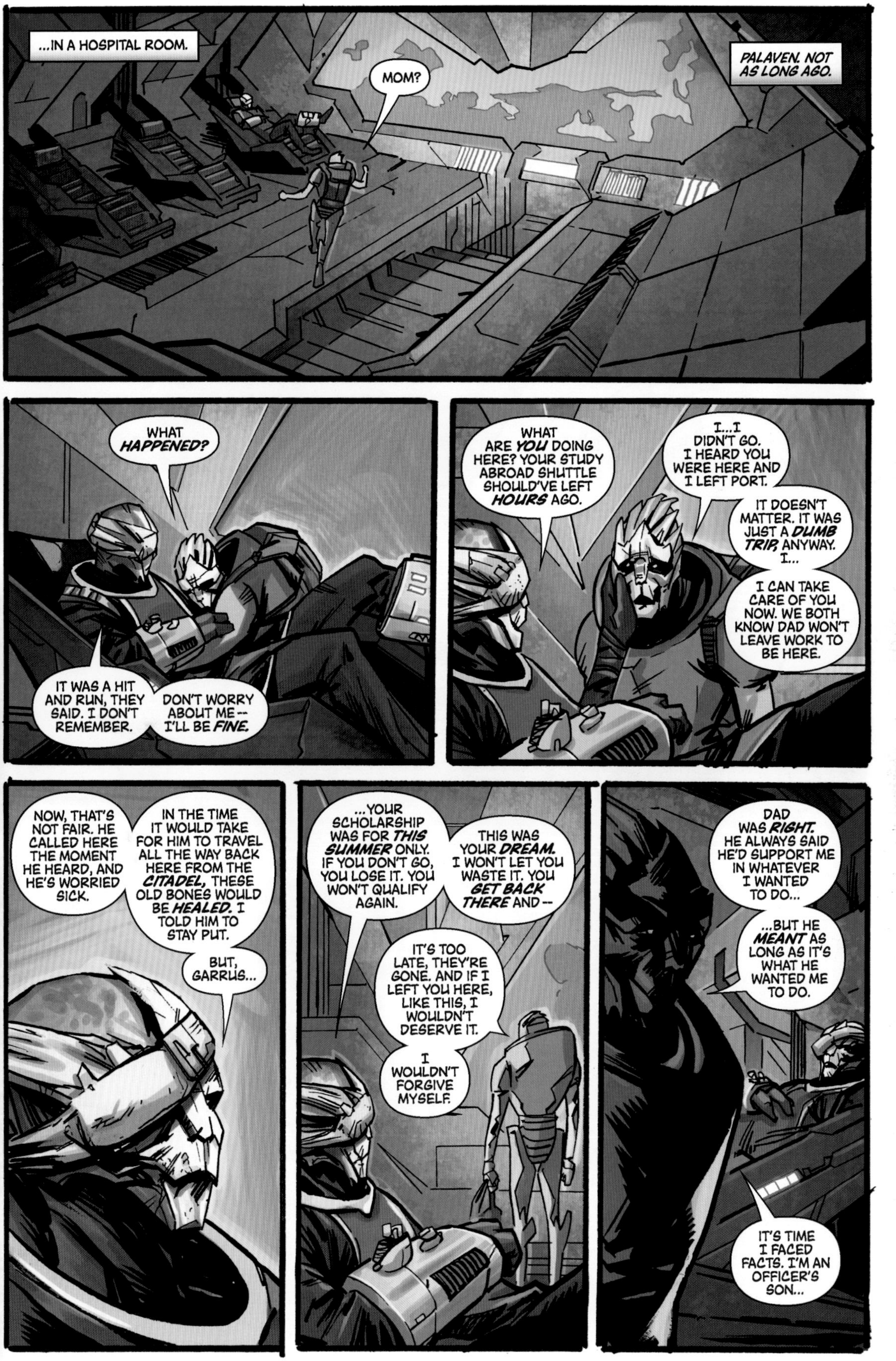

...IN A HOSPITAL ROOM.
PALAVEN. NOT AS LONG AGO.
MOM?
WHAT HAPPENED?
IT WAS A HIT AND RUN, THEY SAID. I DON'T REMEMBER.
DON'T WORRY ABOUT ME -- I'LL BE FINE.
WHAT ARE YOU DOING HERE? YOUR STUDY ABROAD SHUTTLE SHOULD'VE LEFT HOURS AGO.
I...I DIDN'T GO. I HEARD YOU WERE HERE AND I LEFT PORT.
IT DOESN'T MATTER. IT WAS JUST A DUMB TRIP, ANYWAY. I...
I CAN TAKE CARE OF YOU NOW. WE BOTH KNOW DAD WON'T LEAVE WORK TO BE HERE.
NOW, THAT'S NOT FAIR. HE CALLED HERE THE MOMENT HE HEARD, AND HE'S WORRIED SICK.
IN THE TIME IT WOULD TAKE FOR HIM TO TRAVEL ALL THE WAY BACK HERE FROM THE CITADEL, THESE OLD BONES WOULD BE HEALED. I TOLD HIM TO STAY PUT.
BUT, GARRUS...
...YOUR SCHOLARSHIP WAS FOR THIS SUMMER ONLY. IF YOU DON'T GO, YOU LOSE IT. YOU WON'T QUALIFY AGAIN.
THIS WAS YOUR DREAM. I WON'T LET YOU WASTE IT. YOU GET BACK THERE AND --
IT'S TOO LATE, THEY'RE GONE. AND IF I LEFT YOU HERE, LIKE THIS, I WOULDN'T DESERVE IT.
I WOULDN'T FORGIVE MYSELF.
DAD WAS RIGHT. HE ALWAYS SAID HE'D SUPPORT ME IN WHATEVER I WANTED TO DO...
...BUT HE MEANT AS LONG AS IT'S WHAT HE WANTED ME TO DO.
IT'S TIME I FACED FACTS. I'M AN OFFICER'S SON...

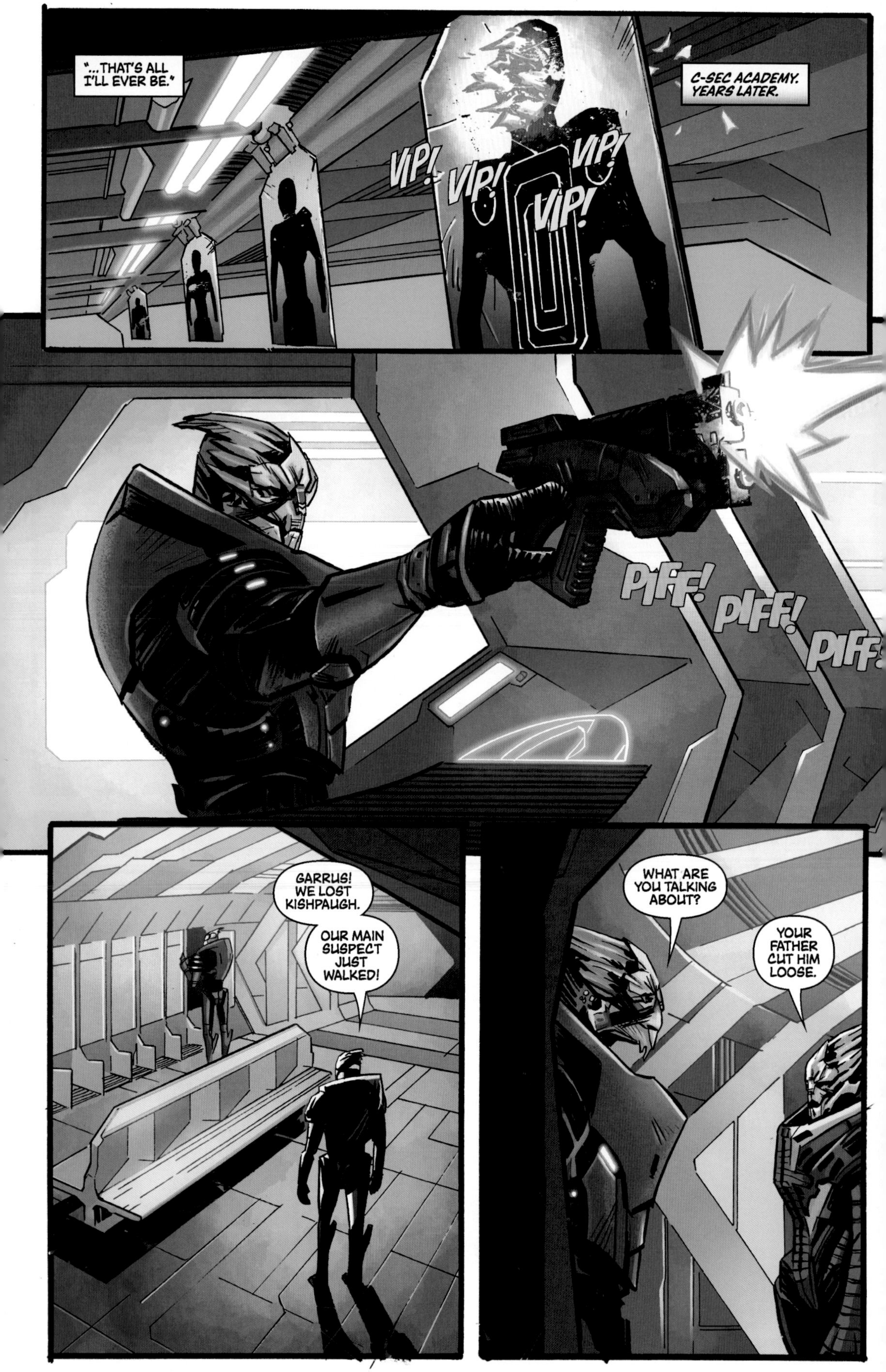

"...THAT'S ALL I'LL EVER BE."
C-SEC ACADEMY. YEARS LATER.
VIP!
VIP!
VIP!
VIP!
PIFF!
PIFF!
PIFF!
GARRUS! WE LOST KISHPAUGH.
OUR MAIN SUSPECT JUST WALKED!
WHAT ARE YOU TALKING ABOUT?
YOUR FATHER CUT HIM LOOSE.

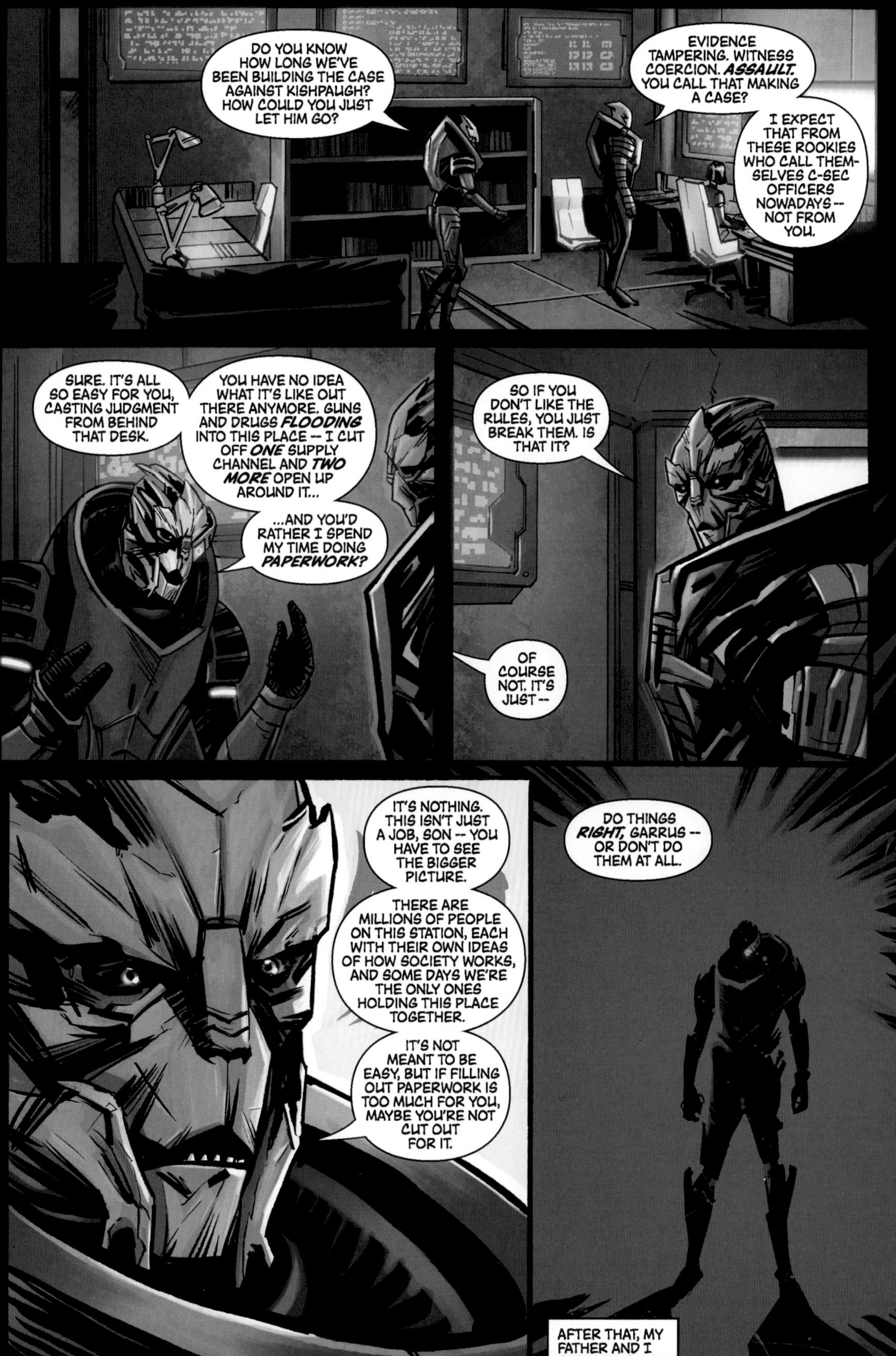
DO YOU KNOW HOW LONG WE'VE BEEN BUILDING THE CASE AGAINST KISHPAUGH? HOW COULD YOU JUST LET HIM GO?
EVIDENCE TAMPERING. WITNESS COERCION. *ASSAULT.* YOU CALL THAT MAKING A CASE?
I EXPECT THAT FROM THESE ROOKIES WHO CALL THEMSELVES C-SEC OFFICERS NOWADAYS -- NOT FROM YOU.
SURE. IT'S ALL SO EASY FOR YOU, CASTING JUDGMENT FROM BEHIND THAT DESK.
YOU HAVE NO IDEA WHAT IT'S LIKE OUT THERE ANYMORE. GUNS AND DRUGS *FLOODING* INTO THIS PLACE -- I CUT OFF *ONE* SUPPLY CHANNEL AND *TWO MORE* OPEN UP AROUND IT...
...AND YOU'D RATHER I SPEND MY TIME DOING *PAPERWORK?*
SO IF YOU DON'T LIKE THE RULES, YOU JUST BREAK THEM. IS THAT IT?
OF COURSE NOT. IT'S JUST --
IT'S NOTHING. THIS ISN'T JUST A JOB, SON -- YOU HAVE TO SEE THE BIGGER PICTURE.
THERE ARE MILLIONS OF PEOPLE ON THIS STATION, EACH WITH THEIR OWN IDEAS OF HOW SOCIETY WORKS, AND SOME DAYS WE'RE THE ONLY ONES HOLDING THIS PLACE TOGETHER.
IT'S NOT MEANT TO BE EASY, BUT IF FILLING OUT PAPERWORK IS TOO MUCH FOR YOU, MAYBE YOU'RE NOT CUT OUT FOR IT.
DO THINGS *RIGHT,* GARRUS -- OR DON'T DO THEM AT ALL.
AFTER THAT, MY FATHER AND I STEERED CLEAR OF EACH OTHER.

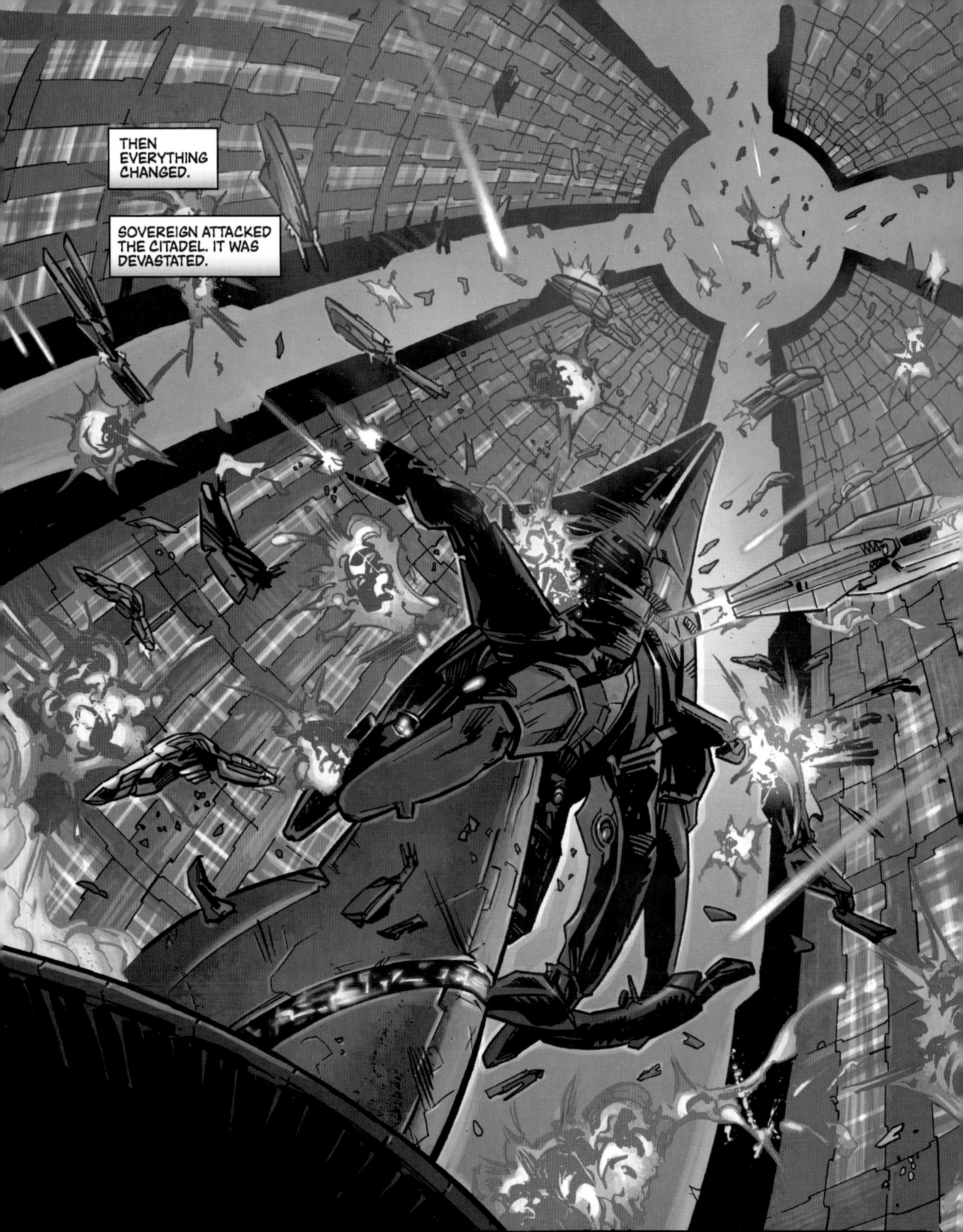
THEN EVERYTHING CHANGED.
SOVEREIGN ATTACKED THE CITADEL. IT WAS DEVASTATED.
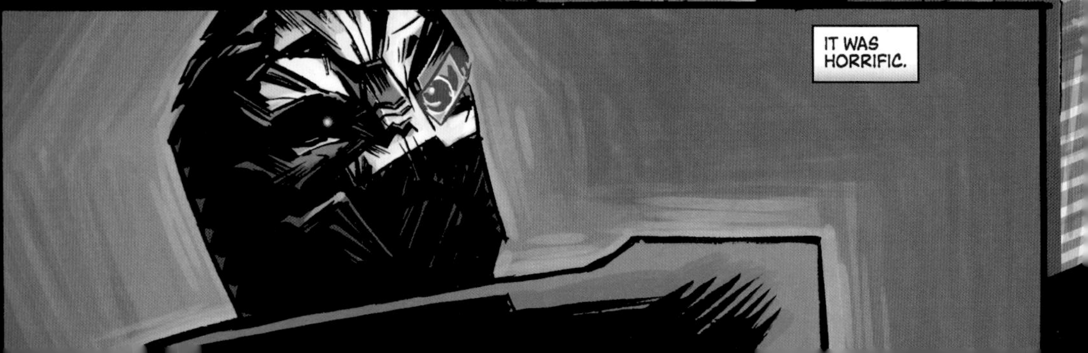
IT WAS HORRIFIC.

AT THE TIME, IT WAS HARD TO SEE A WAY FORWARD.

THE CITADEL WOULD BE REPAIRED, BUT HOW COULD LIFE EVER GO BACK TO WHAT IT WAS BEFORE?

...ISSUED AN *OFFICIAL STATEMENT* REGARDING THE ATTACK, COMMENDING THE *BRAVERY* OF THOSE FIRST RESPONDERS, AND *ASSURING* THE PUBLIC THE THREAT HAS *PASSED...*

IT TURNS OUT, VERY EASILY.

IT TURNS OUT, IT'S EASIER TO PRETEND A TRAGEDY NEVER HAPPENED -- THAT A PROBLEM NEVER EXISTED -- THAN TO DEAL WITH IT DIRECTLY.

EASIER FOR *SOME.* FED UP WITH ALL THE CITADEL'S *RED TAPE,* I TOOK MATTERS INTO MY OWN HANDS.

YOU *CAN'T* DO THIS TO ME. YOU'RE *C-SEC!*

NOT ANYMORE, *KISHPAUGH.* I'M FREE TO BREAK THE LAW JUST LIKE *YOU,* AND I'M *LOOKING* FOR A REASON TO DO IT.

THAT POISON YOU PUSH -- WHERE DO YOU GET IT? WHO'S YOUR SUPPLIER?

OMEGA. IT ALL COMES FROM OMEGA.

YOU DON'T WANT TO WORK WITH US ANYMORE, THAT'S *FINE.*

BUT YOU KEEP PUSHING THE *LINE* LIKE THIS, VAKARIAN, AND I'LL LOCK YOU UP *MYSELF,* YOU HEAR ME?

LOUD AND CLEAR. DON'T WORRY -- I'M NOT YOUR PROBLEM ANYMORE...

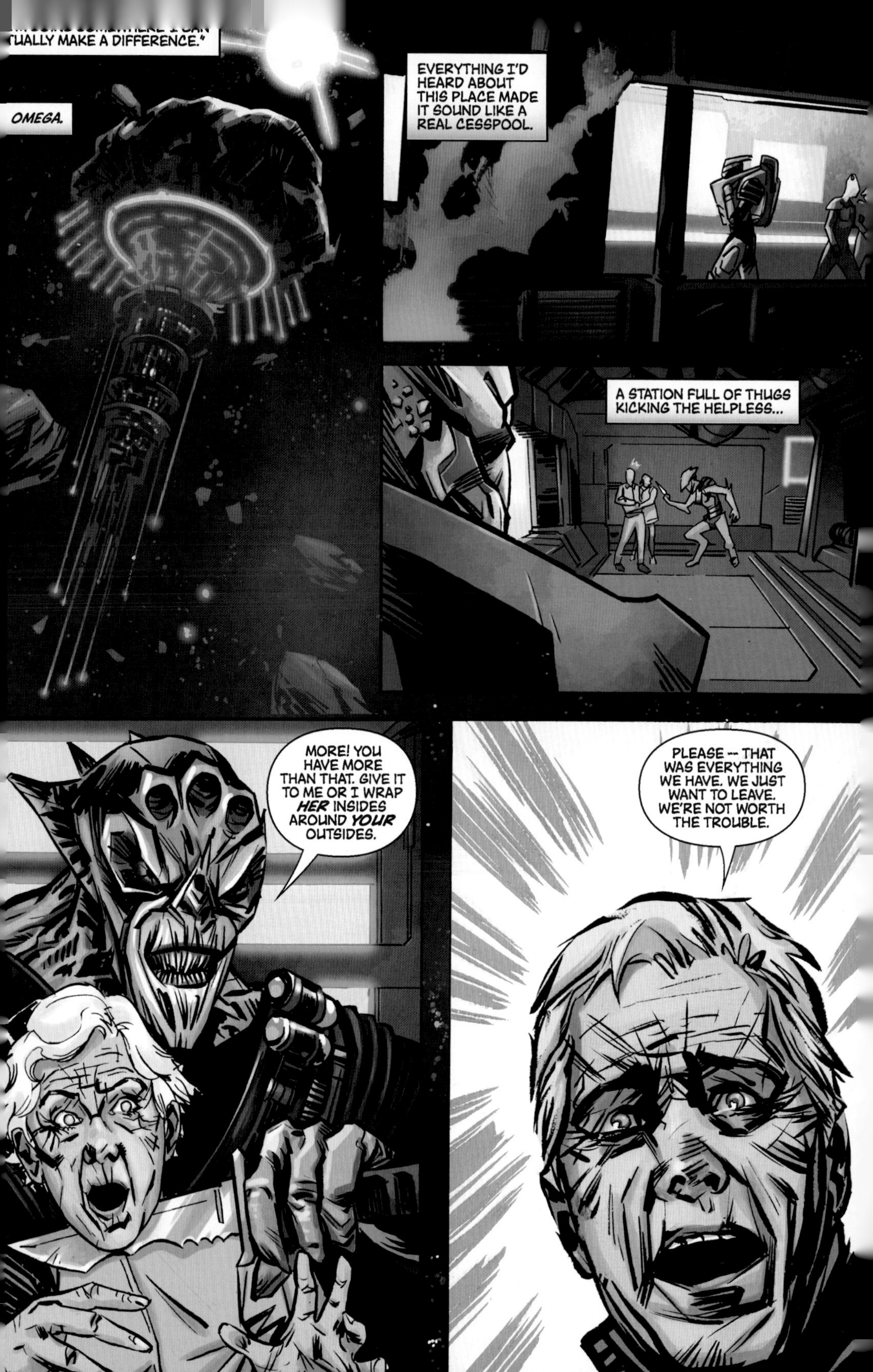
TUALLY MAKE A DIFFERENCE."
OMEGA.
EVERYTHING I'D HEARD ABOUT THIS PLACE MADE IT SOUND LIKE A REAL CESSPOOL.
A STATION FULL OF THUGS KICKING THE HELPLESS...
MORE! YOU HAVE MORE THAN THAT. GIVE IT TO ME OR I WRAP *HER* INSIDES AROUND *YOUR* OUTSIDES.
PLEASE -- THAT WAS EVERYTHING WE HAVE. WE JUST WANT TO LEAVE. WE'RE NOT WORTH THE TROUBLE.

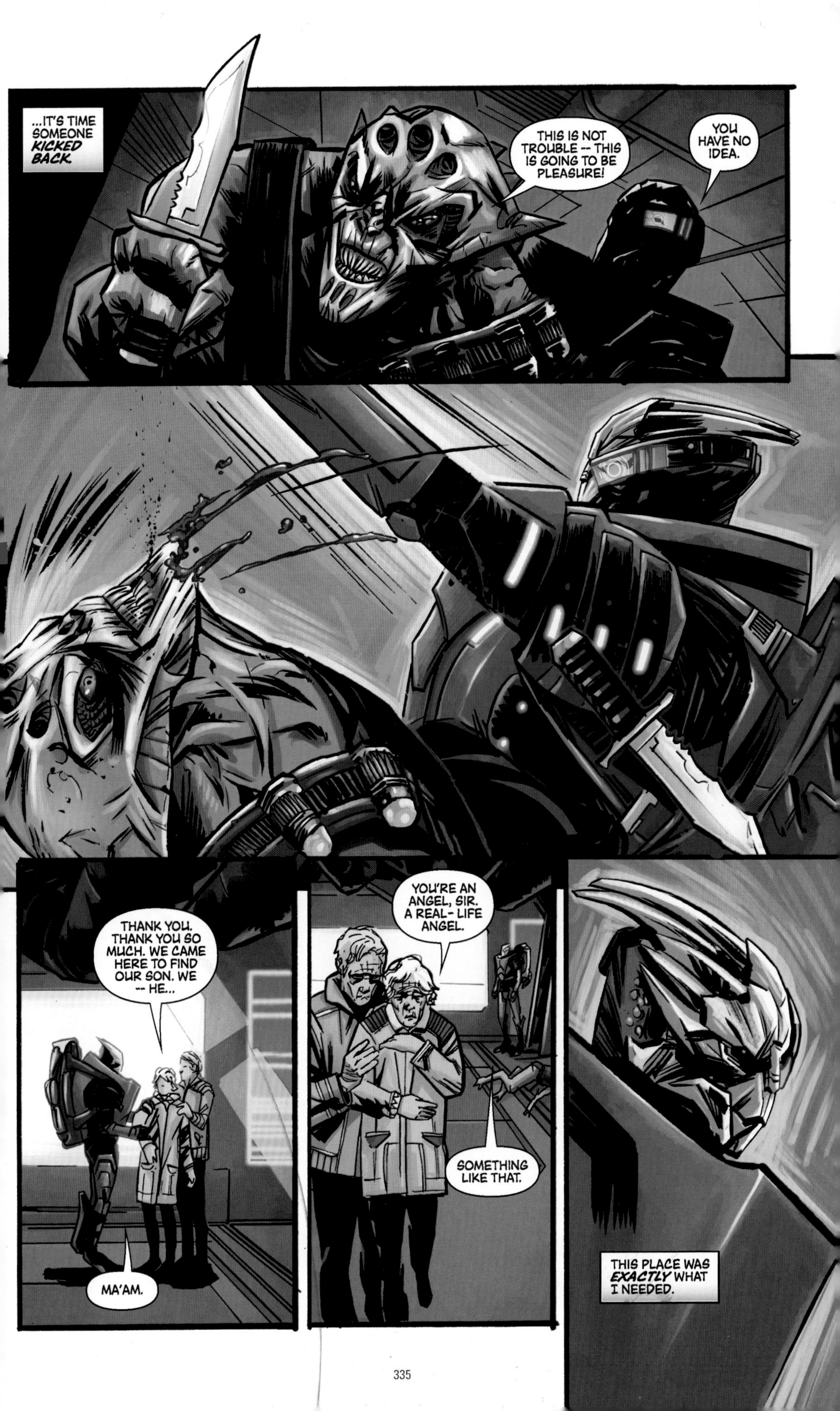
...IT'S TIME SOMEONE *KICKED BACK.*
THIS IS NOT TROUBLE -- THIS IS GOING TO BE PLEASURE!
YOU HAVE NO IDEA.
THANK YOU. THANK YOU SO MUCH. WE CAME HERE TO FIND OUR SON. WE -- HE...
MA'AM.
YOU'RE AN ANGEL, SIR. A REAL-LIFE ANGEL.
SOMETHING LIKE THAT.
THIS PLACE WAS *EXACTLY* WHAT I NEEDED.

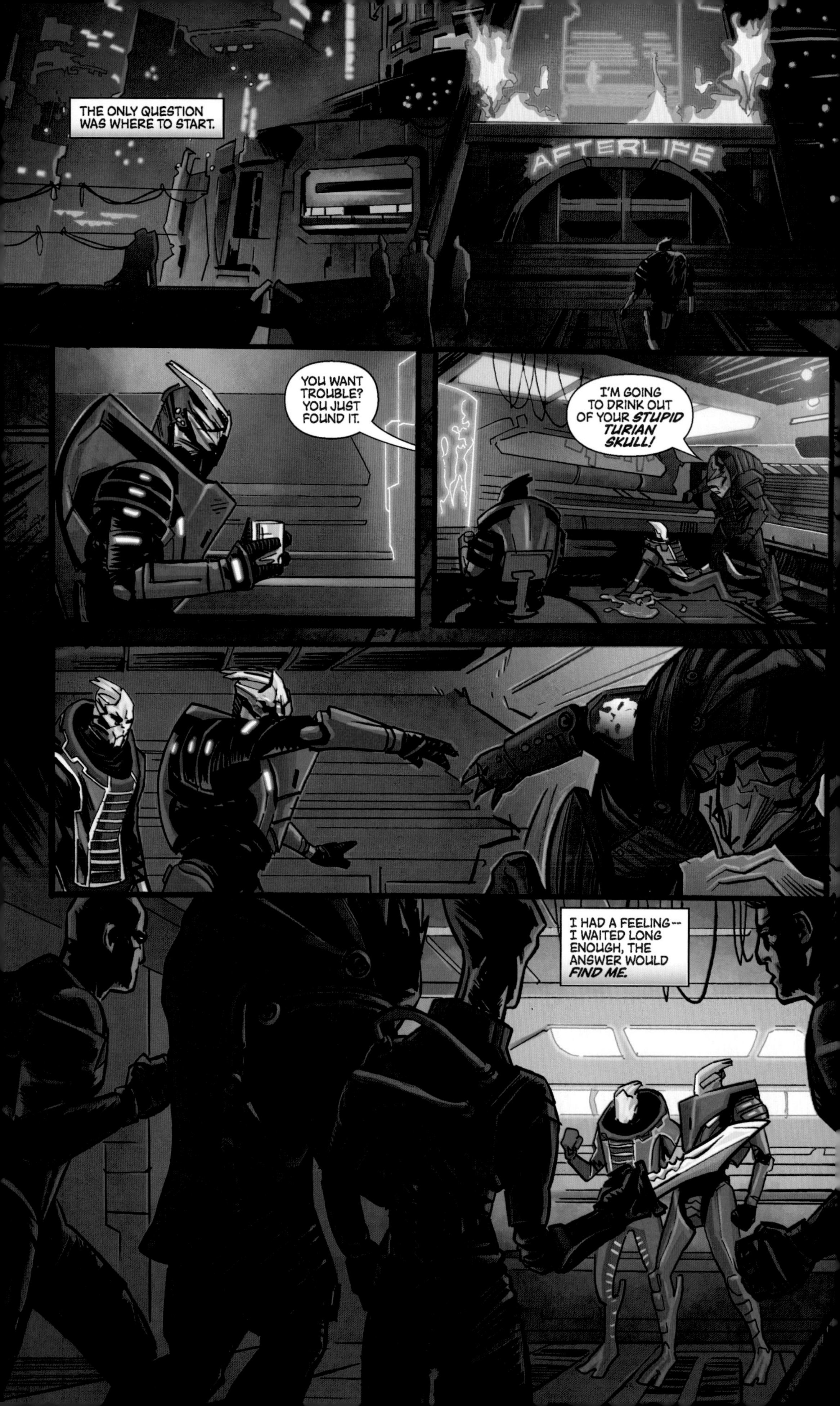

THE ONLY QUESTION WAS WHERE TO START.
AFTERLIFE
YOU WANT TROUBLE? YOU JUST FOUND IT.
I'M GOING TO DRINK OUT OF YOUR *STUPID TURIAN SKULL!*
I HAD A FEELING-- I WAITED LONG ENOUGH, THE ANSWER WOULD *FIND ME.*

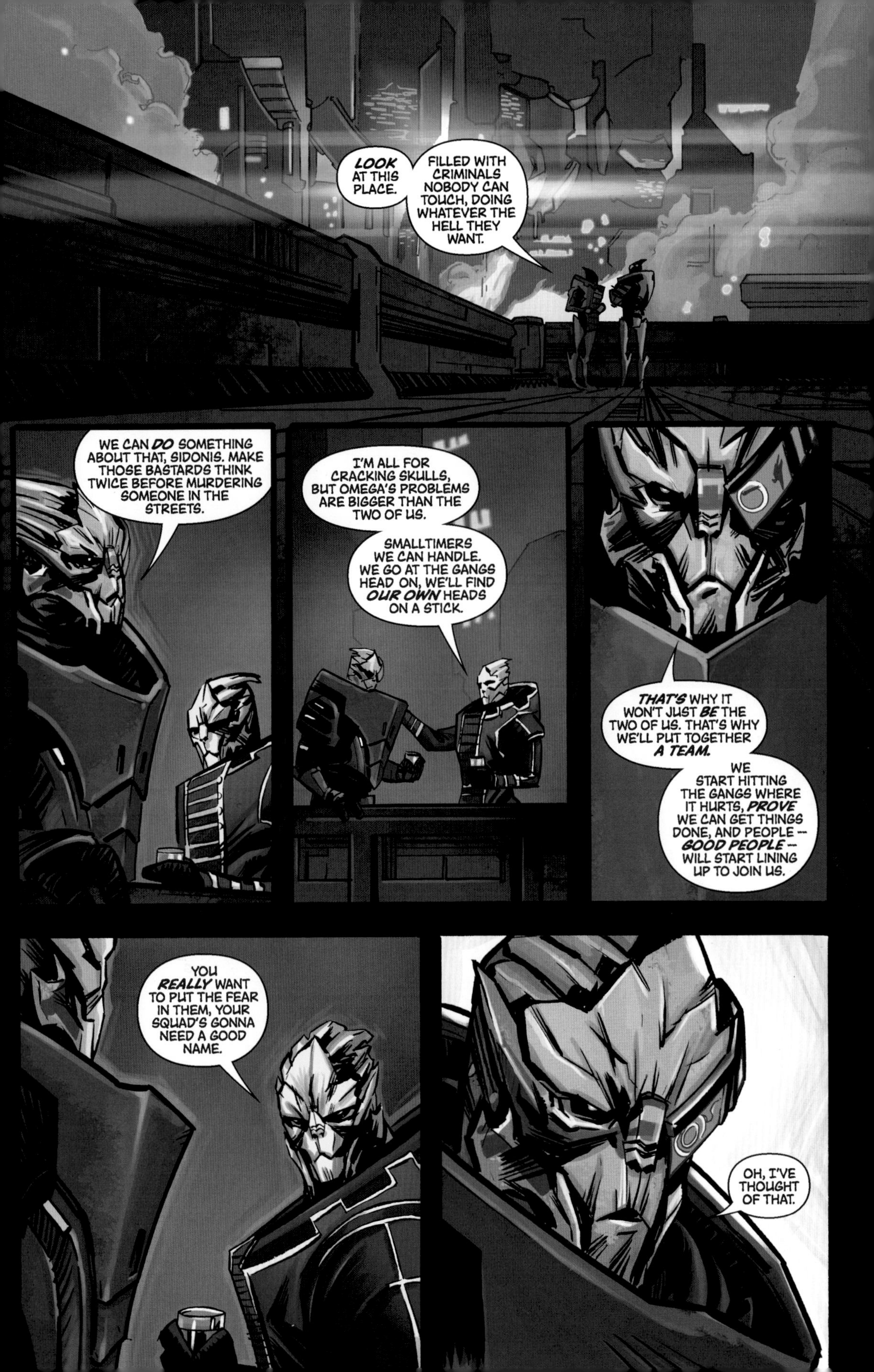
LOOK AT THIS PLACE.
FILLED WITH CRIMINALS NOBODY CAN TOUCH, DOING WHATEVER THE HELL THEY WANT.
WE CAN DO SOMETHING ABOUT THAT, SIDONIS. MAKE THOSE BASTARDS THINK TWICE BEFORE MURDERING SOMEONE IN THE STREETS.
I'M ALL FOR CRACKING SKULLS, BUT OMEGA'S PROBLEMS ARE BIGGER THAN THE TWO OF US.
SMALLTIMERS WE CAN HANDLE. WE GO AT THE GANGS HEAD ON, WE'LL FIND OUR OWN HEADS ON A STICK.
THAT'S WHY IT WON'T JUST BE THE TWO OF US. THAT'S WHY WE'LL PUT TOGETHER A TEAM.
WE START HITTING THE GANGS WHERE IT HURTS, PROVE WE CAN GET THINGS DONE, AND PEOPLE -- GOOD PEOPLE -- WILL START LINING UP TO JOIN US.
YOU REALLY WANT TO PUT THE FEAR IN THEM, YOUR SQUAD'S GONNA NEED A GOOD NAME.
OH, I'VE THOUGHT OF THAT.

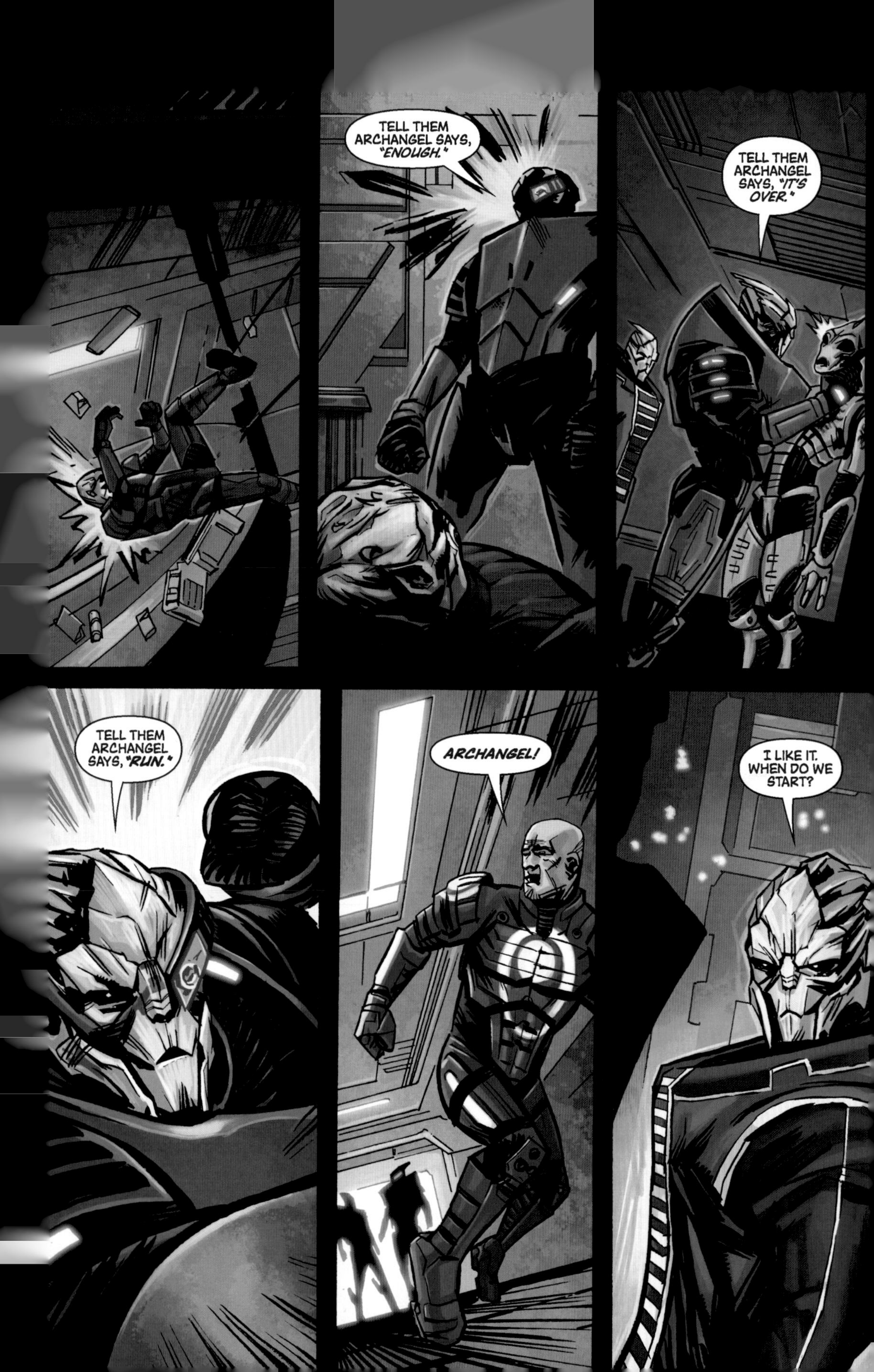
TELL THEM ARCHANGEL SAYS, "ENOUGH."
TELL THEM ARCHANGEL SAYS, "IT'S OVER."
TELL THEM ARCHANGEL SAYS, "RUN."
ARCHANGEL!
I LIKE IT. WHEN DO WE START?

ONCE WORD SPREAD, FORMING THE SQUAD DIDN'T TAKE LONG.

MOSTLY MERCS WHO WANTED TO ATONE. SECURITY CONSULTANTS TIRED OF PLAYING BY THE RULES. EX-MILITARY OPERATIVES, FORMER C-SEC AGENTS. THE USUAL.

EVENTUALLY THERE WERE *TWELVE* OF US, INCLUDING ME.

HAD A SALARIAN EXPLOSIVES EXPERT.

PRETTY SURE HE'D SPENT TIME IN THE SPECIAL TASKS GROUP.

DEET!

FWOOOM

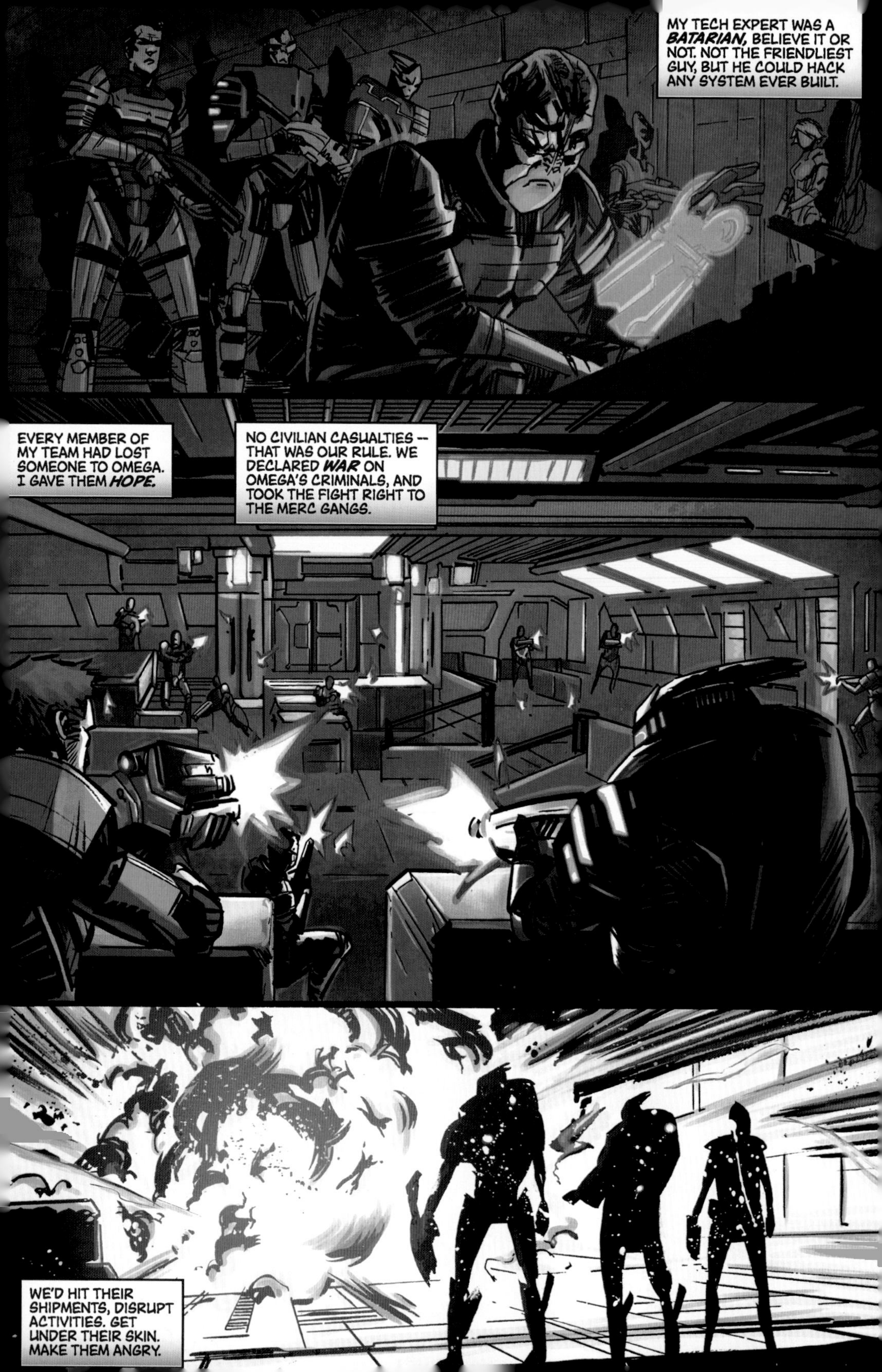
MY TECH EXPERT WAS A ***BATARIAN,*** BELIEVE IT OR NOT. NOT THE FRIENDLIEST GUY, BUT HE COULD HACK ANY SYSTEM EVER BUILT.
EVERY MEMBER OF MY TEAM HAD LOST SOMEONE TO OMEGA. I GAVE THEM ***HOPE.***
NO CIVILIAN CASUALTIES -- THAT WAS OUR RULE. WE DECLARED ***WAR*** ON OMEGA'S CRIMINALS, AND TOOK THE FIGHT RIGHT TO THE MERC GANGS.
WE'D HIT THEIR SHIPMENTS, DISRUPT ACTIVITIES. GET UNDER THEIR SKIN. MAKE THEM ANGRY.

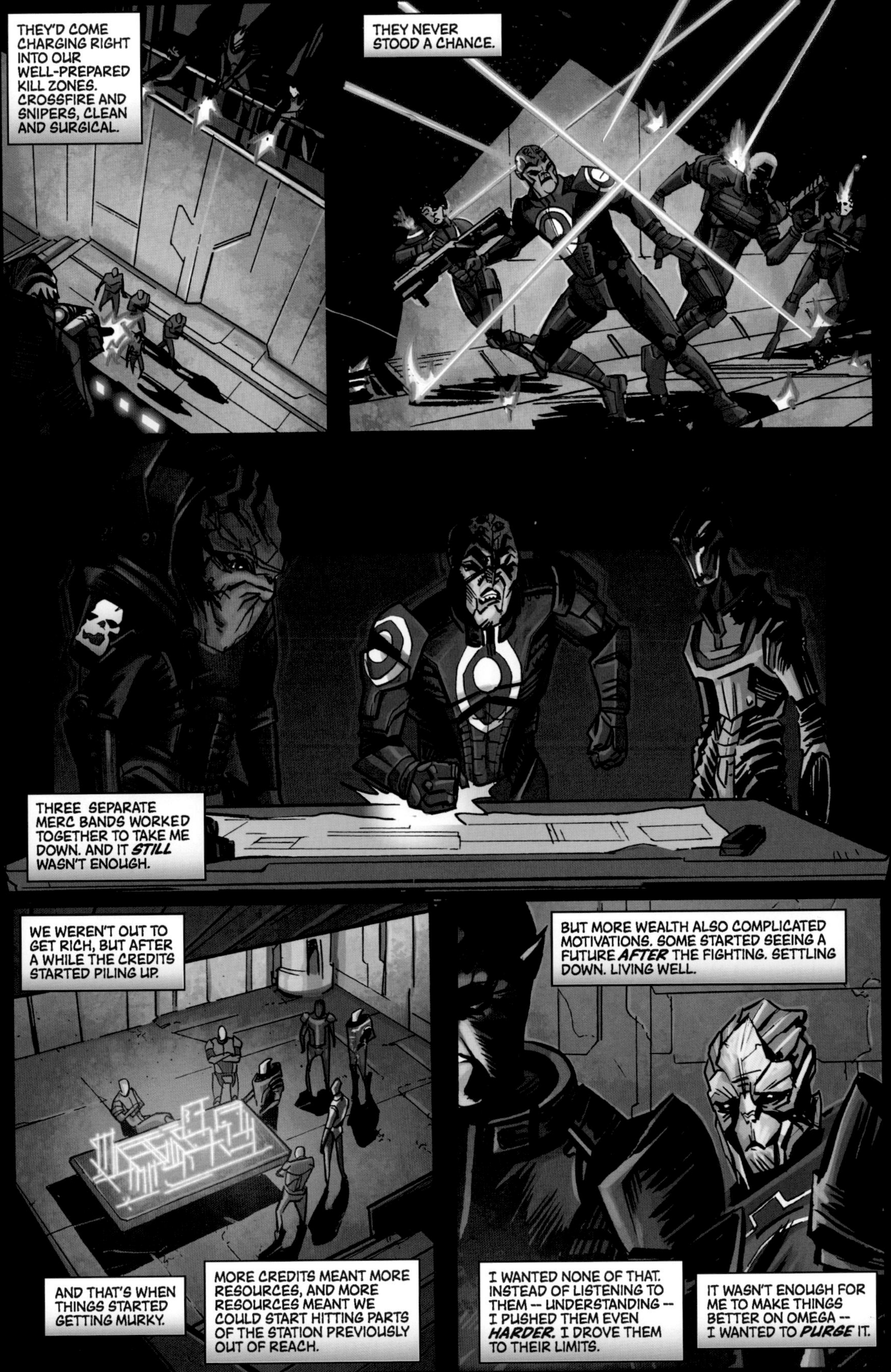
THEY'D COME CHARGING RIGHT INTO OUR WELL-PREPARED KILL ZONES. CROSSFIRE AND SNIPERS, CLEAN AND SURGICAL.
THEY NEVER STOOD A CHANCE.
THREE SEPARATE MERC BANDS WORKED TOGETHER TO TAKE ME DOWN. AND IT STILL WASN'T ENOUGH.
WE WEREN'T OUT TO GET RICH, BUT AFTER A WHILE THE CREDITS STARTED PILING UP.
AND THAT'S WHEN THINGS STARTED GETTING MURKY.
MORE CREDITS MEANT MORE RESOURCES, AND MORE RESOURCES MEANT WE COULD START HITTING PARTS OF THE STATION PREVIOUSLY OUT OF REACH.
BUT MORE WEALTH ALSO COMPLICATED MOTIVATIONS. SOME STARTED SEEING A FUTURE AFTER THE FIGHTING. SETTLING DOWN. LIVING WELL.
I WANTED NONE OF THAT. INSTEAD OF LISTENING TO THEM -- UNDERSTANDING -- I PUSHED THEM EVEN HARDER. I DROVE THEM TO THEIR LIMITS.
IT WASN'T ENOUGH FOR ME TO MAKE THINGS BETTER ON OMEGA -- I WANTED TO PURGE IT.

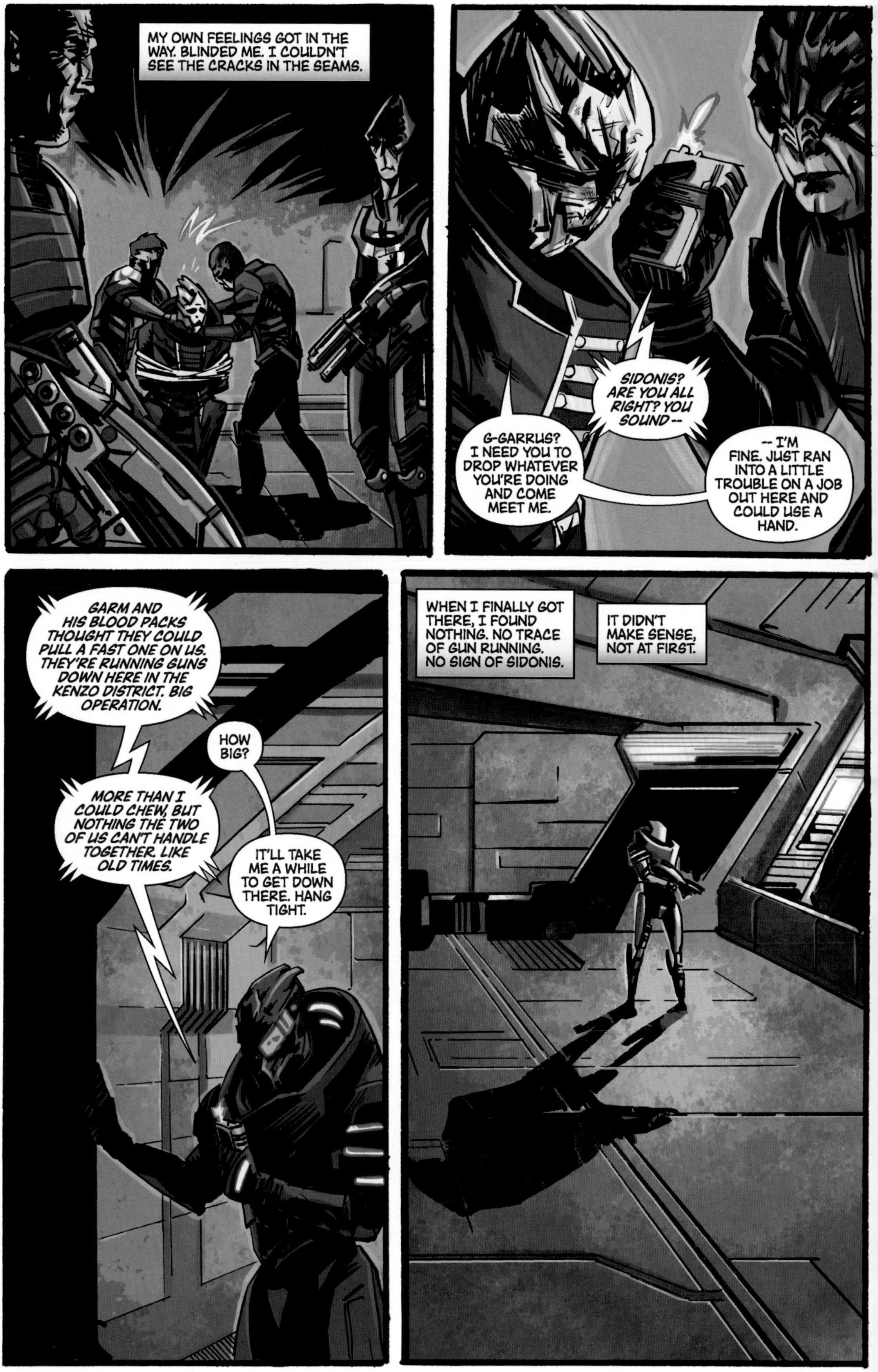
MY OWN FEELINGS GOT IN THE WAY. BLINDED ME. I COULDN'T SEE THE CRACKS IN THE SEAMS.
G-GARRUS? I NEED YOU TO DROP WHATEVER YOU'RE DOING AND COME MEET ME.
SIDONIS? ARE YOU ALL RIGHT? YOU SOUND --
-- I'M FINE. JUST RAN INTO A LITTLE TROUBLE ON A JOB OUT HERE AND COULD USE A HAND.
GARM AND HIS BLOOD PACKS THOUGHT THEY COULD PULL A FAST ONE ON US. THEY'RE RUNNING GUNS DOWN HERE IN THE KENZO DISTRICT. BIG OPERATION.
HOW BIG?
MORE THAN I COULD CHEW, BUT NOTHING THE TWO OF US CAN'T HANDLE TOGETHER. LIKE OLD TIMES.
IT'LL TAKE ME A WHILE TO GET DOWN THERE. HANG TIGHT.
WHEN I FINALLY GOT THERE, I FOUND NOTHING. NO TRACE OF GUN RUNNING. NO SIGN OF SIDONIS.
IT DIDN'T MAKE SENSE, NOT AT FIRST.

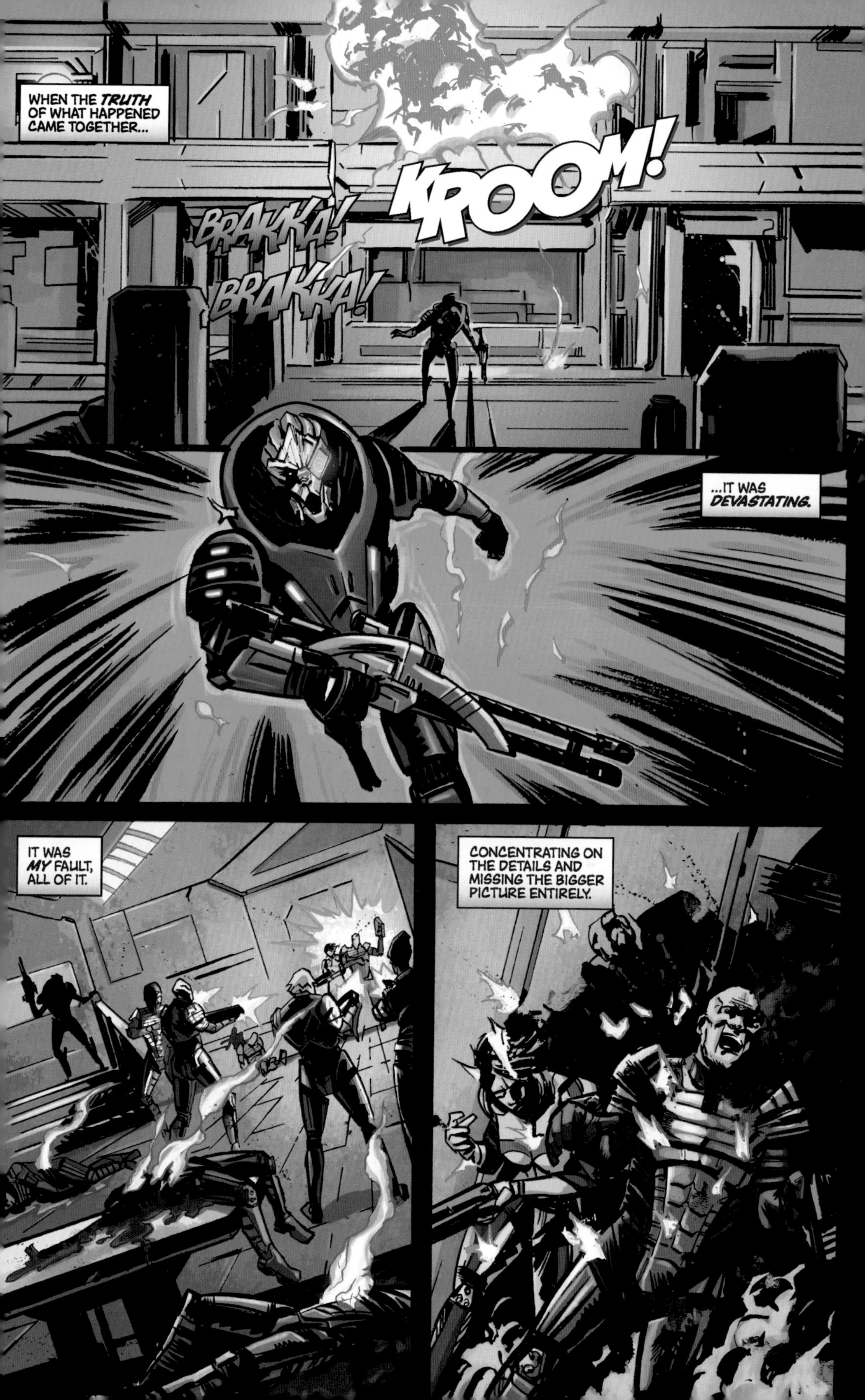
WHEN THE TRUTH OF WHAT HAPPENED CAME TOGETHER...
BRAKKA!
BRAKKA!
KROOM!
...IT WAS DEVASTATING.
IT WAS MY FAULT, ALL OF IT.
CONCENTRATING ON THE DETAILS AND MISSING THE BIGGER PICTURE ENTIRELY.

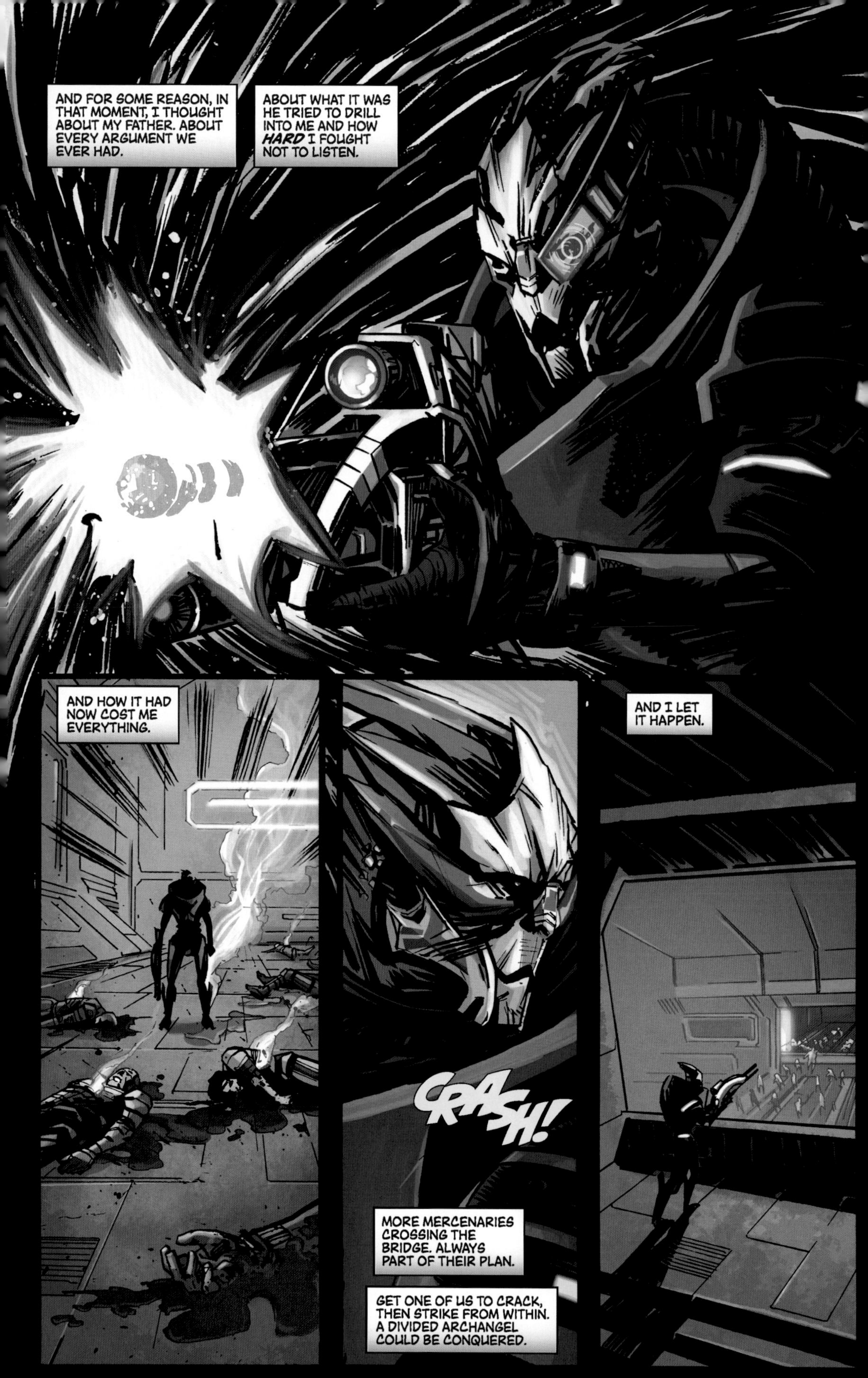
AND FOR SOME REASON, IN THAT MOMENT, I THOUGHT ABOUT MY FATHER. ABOUT EVERY ARGUMENT WE EVER HAD.
ABOUT WHAT IT WAS HE TRIED TO DRILL INTO ME AND HOW HARD I FOUGHT NOT TO LISTEN.
AND HOW IT HAD NOW COST ME EVERYTHING.
AND I LET IT HAPPEN.
CRASH!
MORE MERCENARIES CROSSING THE BRIDGE. ALWAYS PART OF THEIR PLAN.
GET ONE OF US TO CRACK, THEN STRIKE FROM WITHIN. A DIVIDED ARCHANGEL COULD BE CONQUERED.

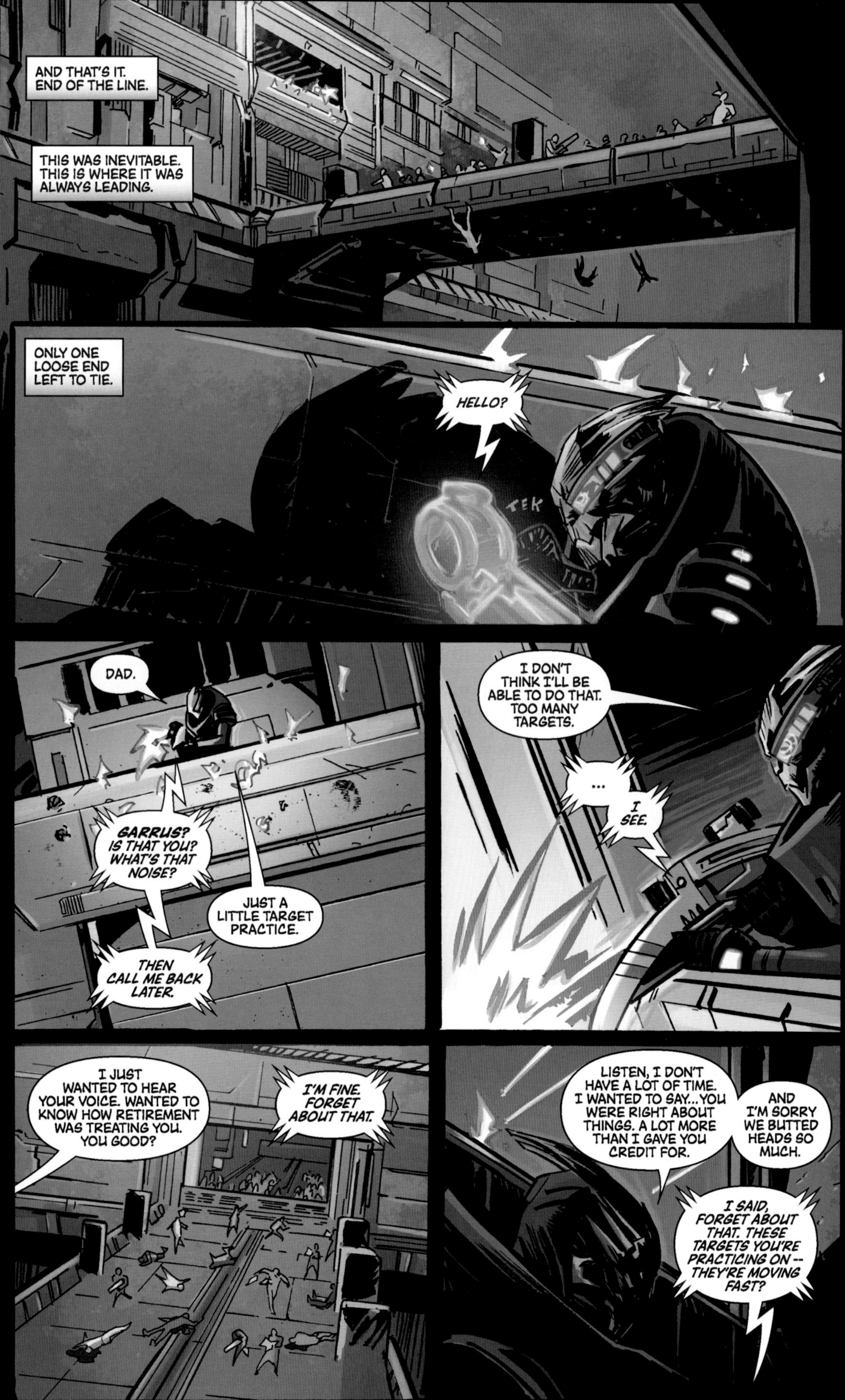
AND THAT'S IT. END OF THE LINE.
THIS WAS INEVITABLE. THIS IS WHERE IT WAS ALWAYS LEADING.
ONLY ONE LOOSE END LEFT TO TIE.
HELLO?
TEK
DAD.
GARRUS? IS THAT YOU? WHAT'S THAT NOISE?
JUST A LITTLE TARGET PRACTICE.
THEN CALL ME BACK LATER.
I DON'T THINK I'LL BE ABLE TO DO THAT. TOO MANY TARGETS.
...
I SEE.
I JUST WANTED TO HEAR YOUR VOICE. WANTED TO KNOW HOW RETIREMENT WAS TREATING YOU. YOU GOOD?
I'M FINE. FORGET ABOUT THAT.
LISTEN, I DON'T HAVE A LOT OF TIME. I WANTED TO SAY... YOU WERE RIGHT ABOUT THINGS. A LOT MORE THAN I GAVE YOU CREDIT FOR.
AND I'M SORRY WE BUTTED HEADS SO MUCH.
I SAID, FORGET ABOUT THAT. THESE TARGETS YOU'RE PRACTICING ON -- THEY'RE MOVING FAST?

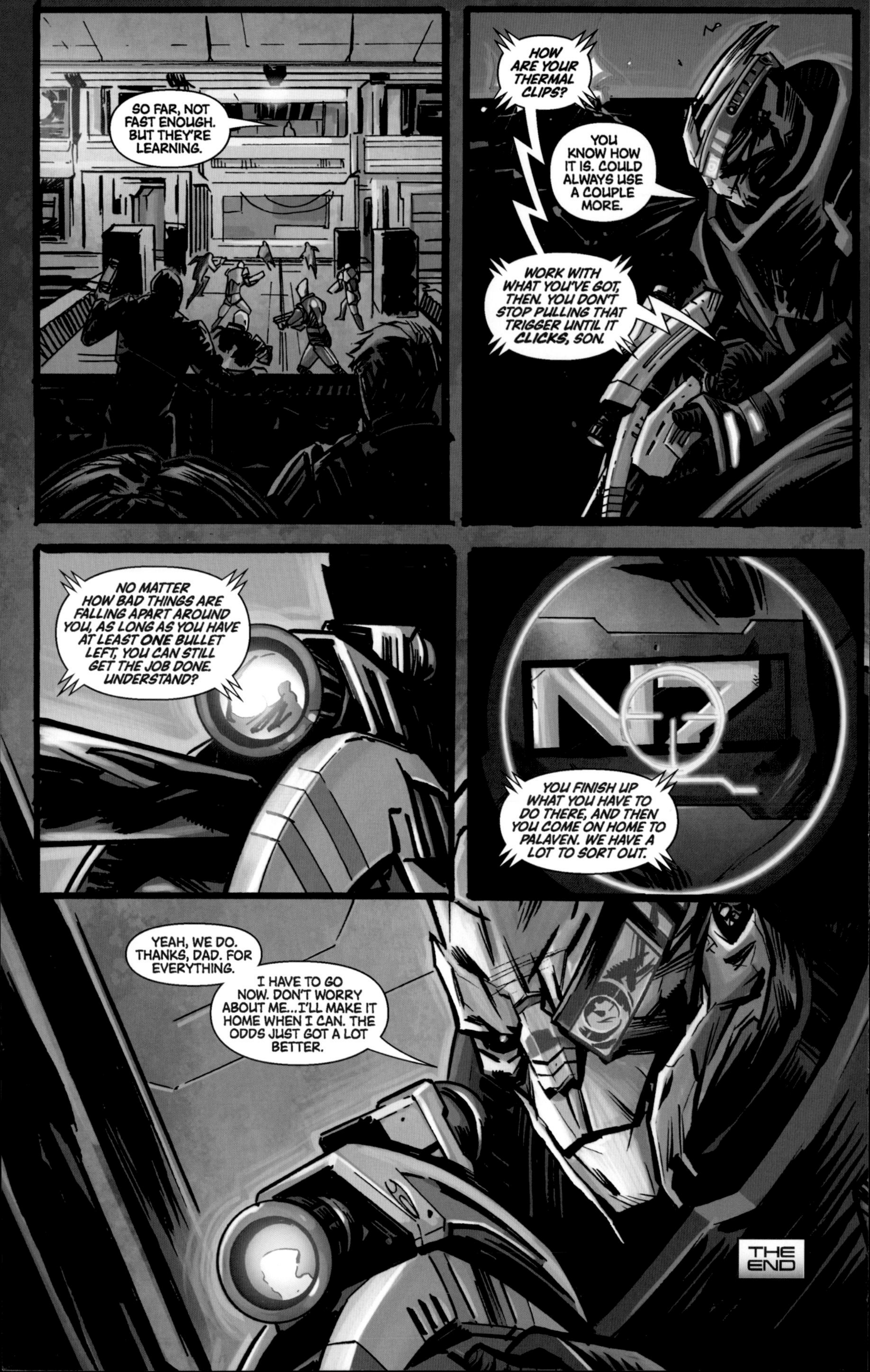
SO FAR, NOT FAST ENOUGH. BUT THEY'RE LEARNING.
HOW ARE YOUR THERMAL CLIPS?
YOU KNOW HOW IT IS. COULD ALWAYS USE A COUPLE MORE.
WORK WITH WHAT YOU'VE GOT, THEN. YOU DON'T STOP PULLING THAT TRIGGER UNTIL IT CLICKS, SON.
NO MATTER HOW BAD THINGS ARE FALLING APART AROUND YOU, AS LONG AS YOU HAVE AT LEAST ONE BULLET LEFT, YOU CAN STILL GET THE JOB DONE. UNDERSTAND?
N7
YOU FINISH UP WHAT YOU HAVE TO DO THERE, AND THEN YOU COME ON HOME TO PALAVEN. WE HAVE A LOT TO SORT OUT.
YEAH, WE DO. THANKS, DAD. FOR EVERYTHING.
I HAVE TO GO NOW. DON'T WORRY ABOUT ME...I'LL MAKE IT HOME WHEN I CAN. THE ODDS JUST GOT A LOT BETTER.
THE END

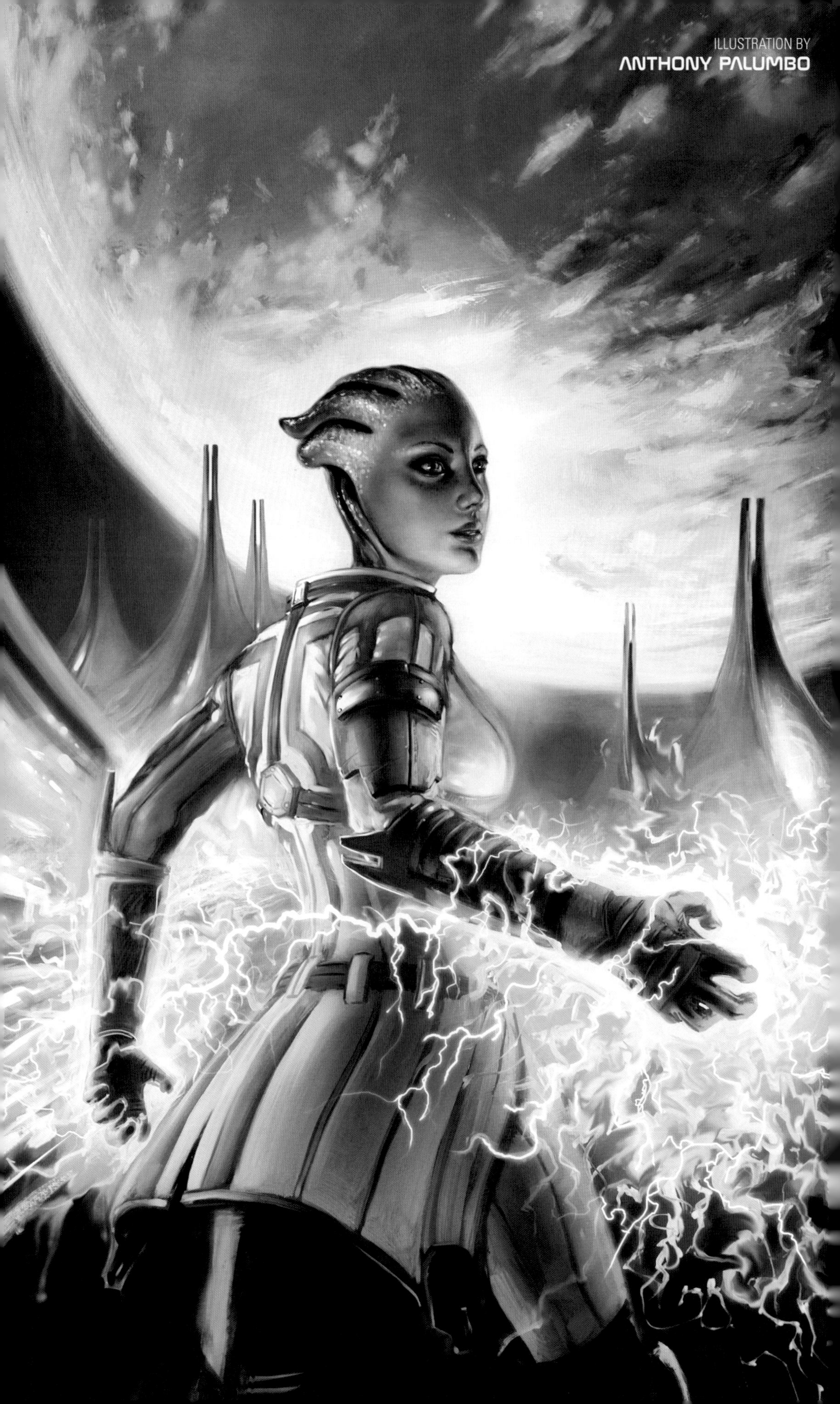
ILLUSTRATION BY
ANTHONY PALUMBO

HOMEWORLDS: LIARA T'SONI

STORY
MAC WALTERS AND
SYLVIA FEKETEKUTY

SCRIPT
JEREMY BARLOW

ART
OMAR FRANCIA

COLORS
MICHAEL ATIYEH

LETTERING
MICHAEL HEISLER

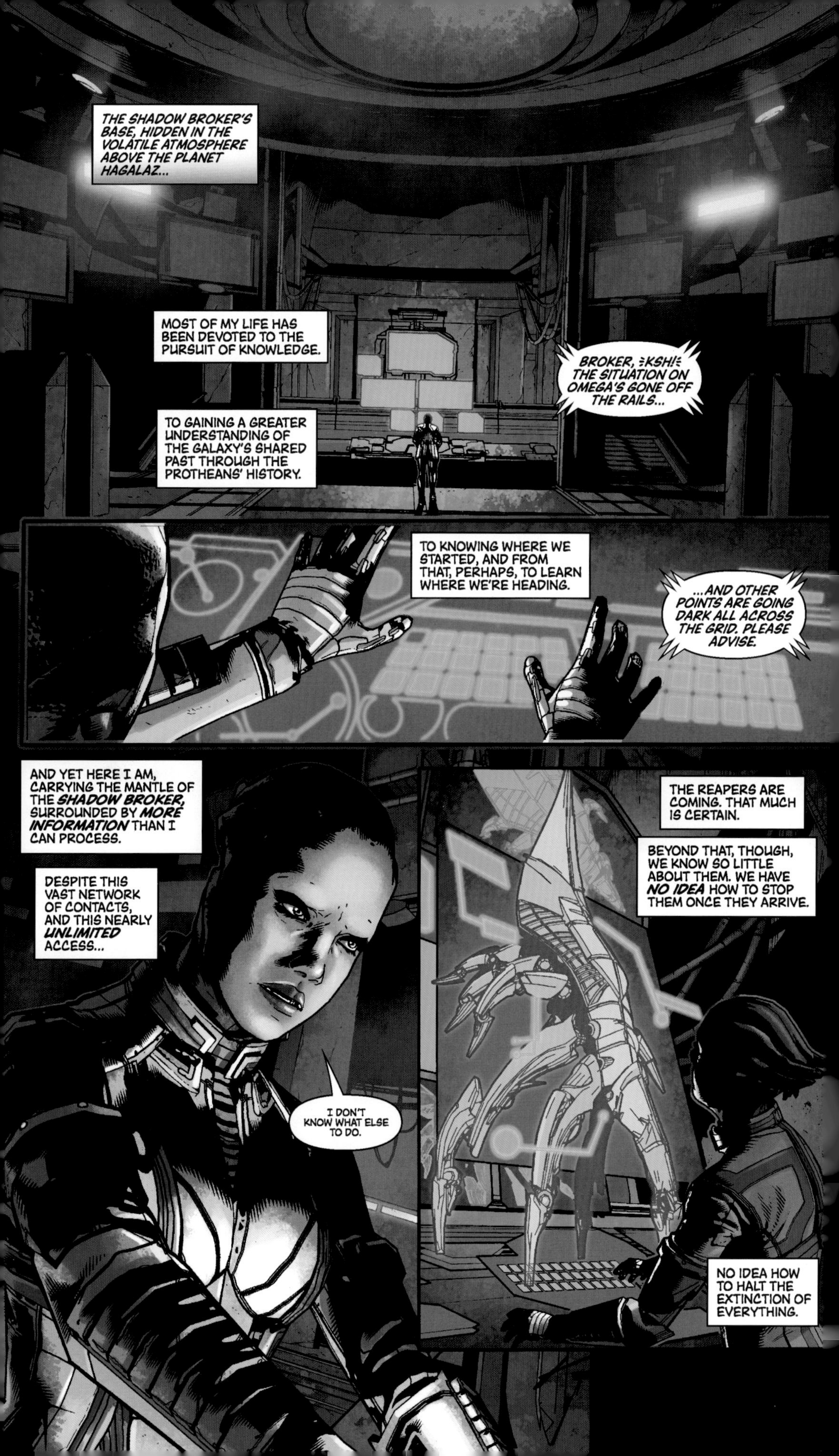
THE SHADOW BROKER'S BASE, HIDDEN IN THE VOLATILE ATMOSPHERE ABOVE THE PLANET HAGALAZ...
MOST OF MY LIFE HAS BEEN DEVOTED TO THE PURSUIT OF KNOWLEDGE.
TO GAINING A GREATER UNDERSTANDING OF THE GALAXY'S SHARED PAST THROUGH THE PROTHEANS' HISTORY.
BROKER, =KSH!= THE SITUATION ON OMEGA'S GONE OFF THE RAILS...
TO KNOWING WHERE WE STARTED, AND FROM THAT, PERHAPS, TO LEARN WHERE WE'RE HEADING.
...AND OTHER POINTS ARE GOING DARK ALL ACROSS THE GRID. PLEASE ADVISE.
AND YET HERE I AM, CARRYING THE MANTLE OF THE SHADOW BROKER, SURROUNDED BY MORE INFORMATION THAN I CAN PROCESS.
DESPITE THIS VAST NETWORK OF CONTACTS, AND THIS NEARLY UNLIMITED ACCESS...
I DON'T KNOW WHAT ELSE TO DO.
THE REAPERS ARE COMING. THAT MUCH IS CERTAIN.
BEYOND THAT, THOUGH, WE KNOW SO LITTLE ABOUT THEM. WE HAVE NO IDEA HOW TO STOP THEM ONCE THEY ARRIVE.
NO IDEA HOW TO HALT THE EXTINCTION OF EVERYTHING.

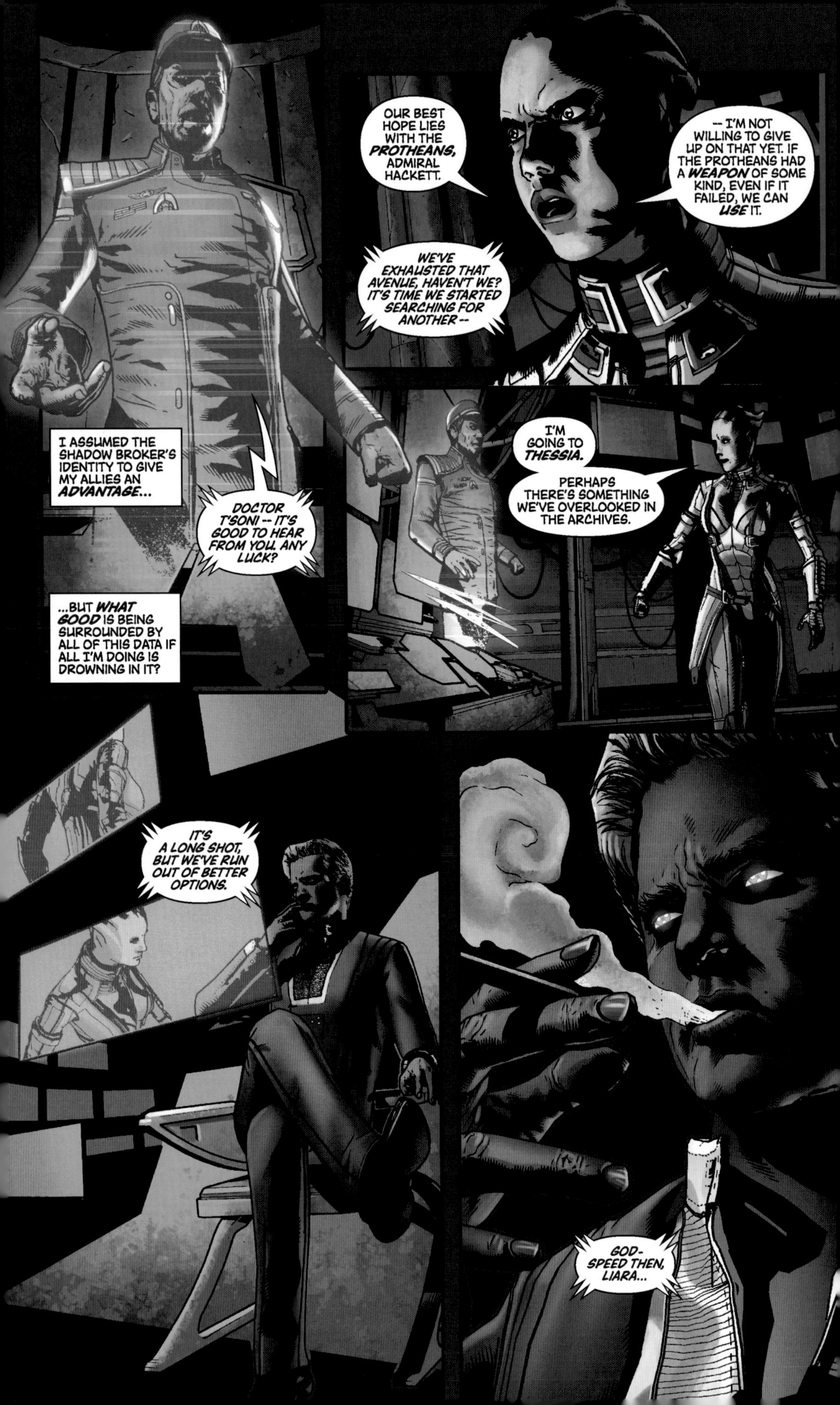

I ASSUMED THE SHADOW BROKER'S IDENTITY TO GIVE MY ALLIES AN ADVANTAGE...
DOCTOR T'SONI -- IT'S GOOD TO HEAR FROM YOU. ANY LUCK?
...BUT WHAT GOOD IS BEING SURROUNDED BY ALL OF THIS DATA IF ALL I'M DOING IS DROWNING IN IT?
OUR BEST HOPE LIES WITH THE PROTHEANS, ADMIRAL HACKETT.
-- I'M NOT WILLING TO GIVE UP ON THAT YET. IF THE PROTHEANS HAD A WEAPON OF SOME KIND, EVEN IF IT FAILED, WE CAN USE IT.
WE'VE EXHAUSTED THAT AVENUE, HAVEN'T WE? IT'S TIME WE STARTED SEARCHING FOR ANOTHER --
I'M GOING TO THESSIA.
PERHAPS THERE'S SOMETHING WE'VE OVERLOOKED IN THE ARCHIVES.
IT'S A LONG SHOT, BUT WE'VE RUN OUT OF BETTER OPTIONS.
GOD-SPEED THEN, LIARA...

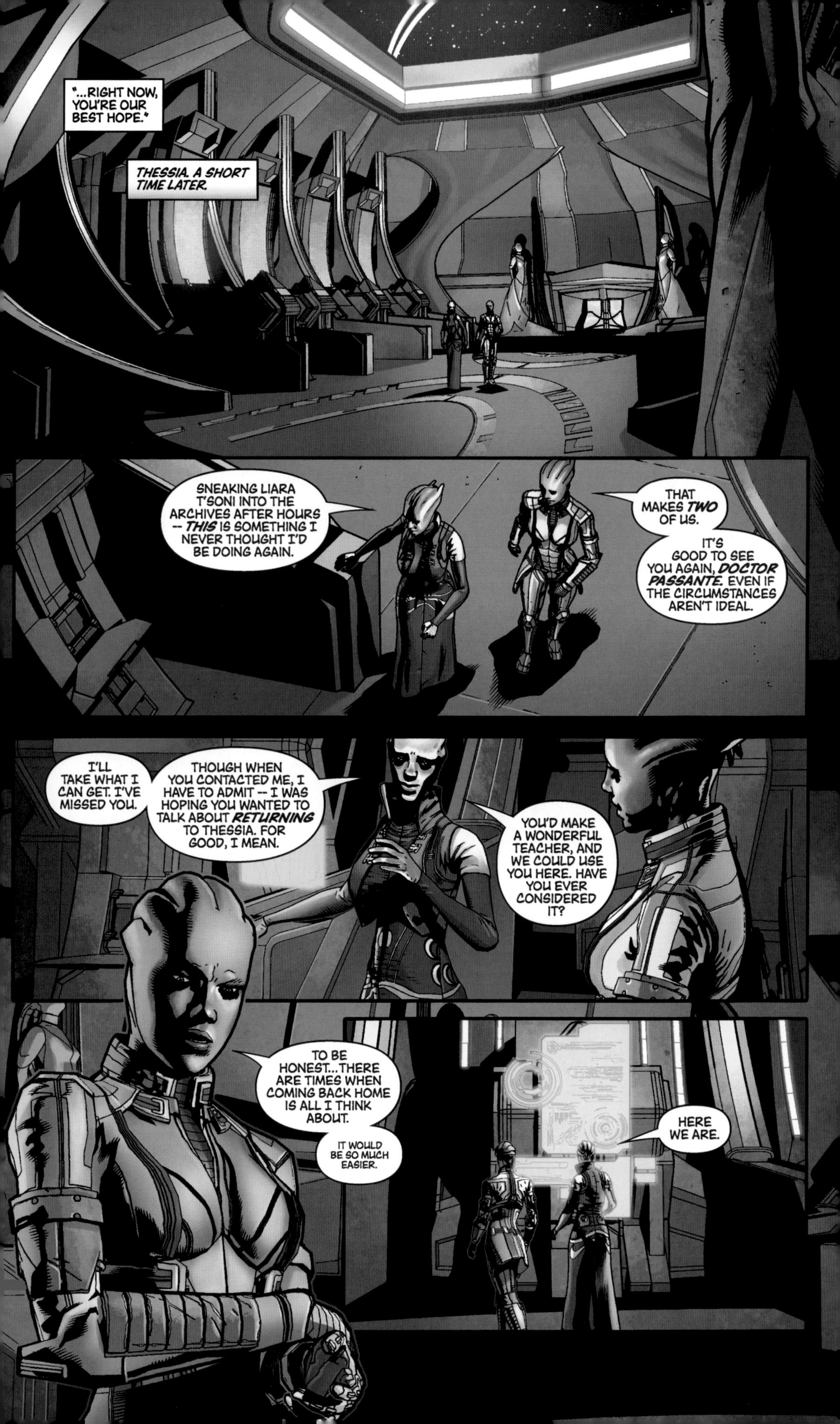

"...RIGHT NOW, YOU'RE OUR BEST HOPE."
THESSIA. A SHORT TIME LATER.
SNEAKING LIARA T'SONI INTO THE ARCHIVES AFTER HOURS -- *THIS* IS SOMETHING I NEVER THOUGHT I'D BE DOING AGAIN.
THAT MAKES *TWO* OF US.
IT'S GOOD TO SEE YOU AGAIN, *DOCTOR PASSANTE.* EVEN IF THE CIRCUMSTANCES AREN'T IDEAL.
I'LL TAKE WHAT I CAN GET. I'VE MISSED YOU.
THOUGH WHEN YOU CONTACTED ME, I HAVE TO ADMIT -- I WAS HOPING YOU WANTED TO TALK ABOUT *RETURNING* TO THESSIA. FOR GOOD, I MEAN.
YOU'D MAKE A WONDERFUL TEACHER, AND WE COULD USE YOU HERE. HAVE YOU EVER CONSIDERED IT?
TO BE HONEST...THERE ARE TIMES WHEN COMING BACK HOME IS ALL I THINK ABOUT.
IT WOULD BE SO MUCH EASIER.
HERE WE ARE.

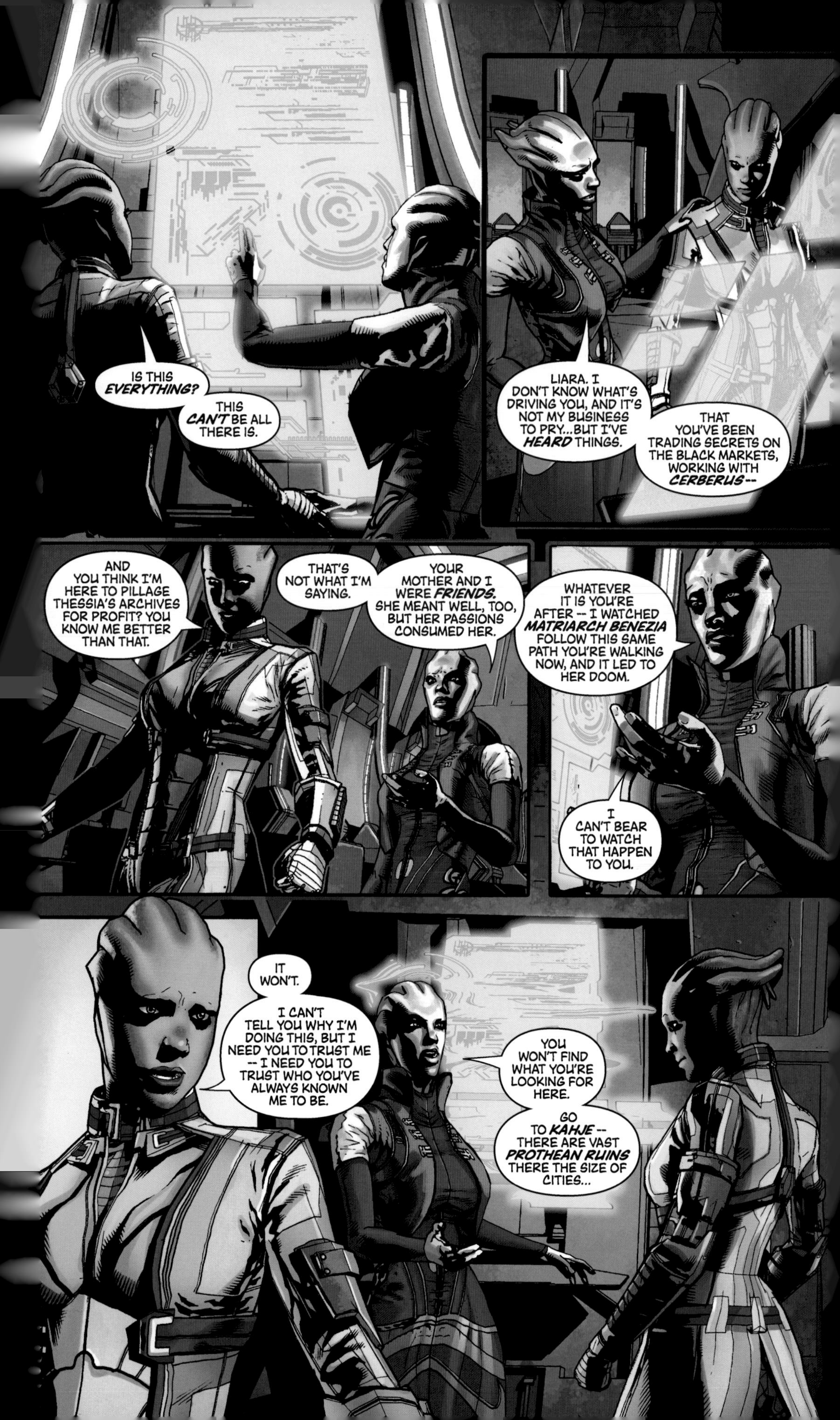
IS THIS EVERYTHING?
THIS CAN'T BE ALL THERE IS.
LIARA. I DON'T KNOW WHAT'S DRIVING YOU, AND IT'S NOT MY BUSINESS TO PRY...BUT I'VE HEARD THINGS.
THAT YOU'VE BEEN TRADING SECRETS ON THE BLACK MARKETS, WORKING WITH CERBERUS--
AND YOU THINK I'M HERE TO PILLAGE THESSIA'S ARCHIVES FOR PROFIT? YOU KNOW ME BETTER THAN THAT.
THAT'S NOT WHAT I'M SAYING.
YOUR MOTHER AND I WERE FRIENDS. SHE MEANT WELL, TOO, BUT HER PASSIONS CONSUMED HER.
WHATEVER IT IS YOU'RE AFTER -- I WATCHED MATRIARCH BENEZIA FOLLOW THIS SAME PATH YOU'RE WALKING NOW, AND IT LED TO HER DOOM.
I CAN'T BEAR TO WATCH THAT HAPPEN TO YOU.
IT WON'T.
I CAN'T TELL YOU WHY I'M DOING THIS, BUT I NEED YOU TO TRUST ME -- I NEED YOU TO TRUST WHO YOU'VE ALWAYS KNOWN ME TO BE.
YOU WON'T FIND WHAT YOU'RE LOOKING FOR HERE.
GO TO KAHJE -- THERE ARE VAST PROTHEAN RUINS THERE THE SIZE OF CITIES...

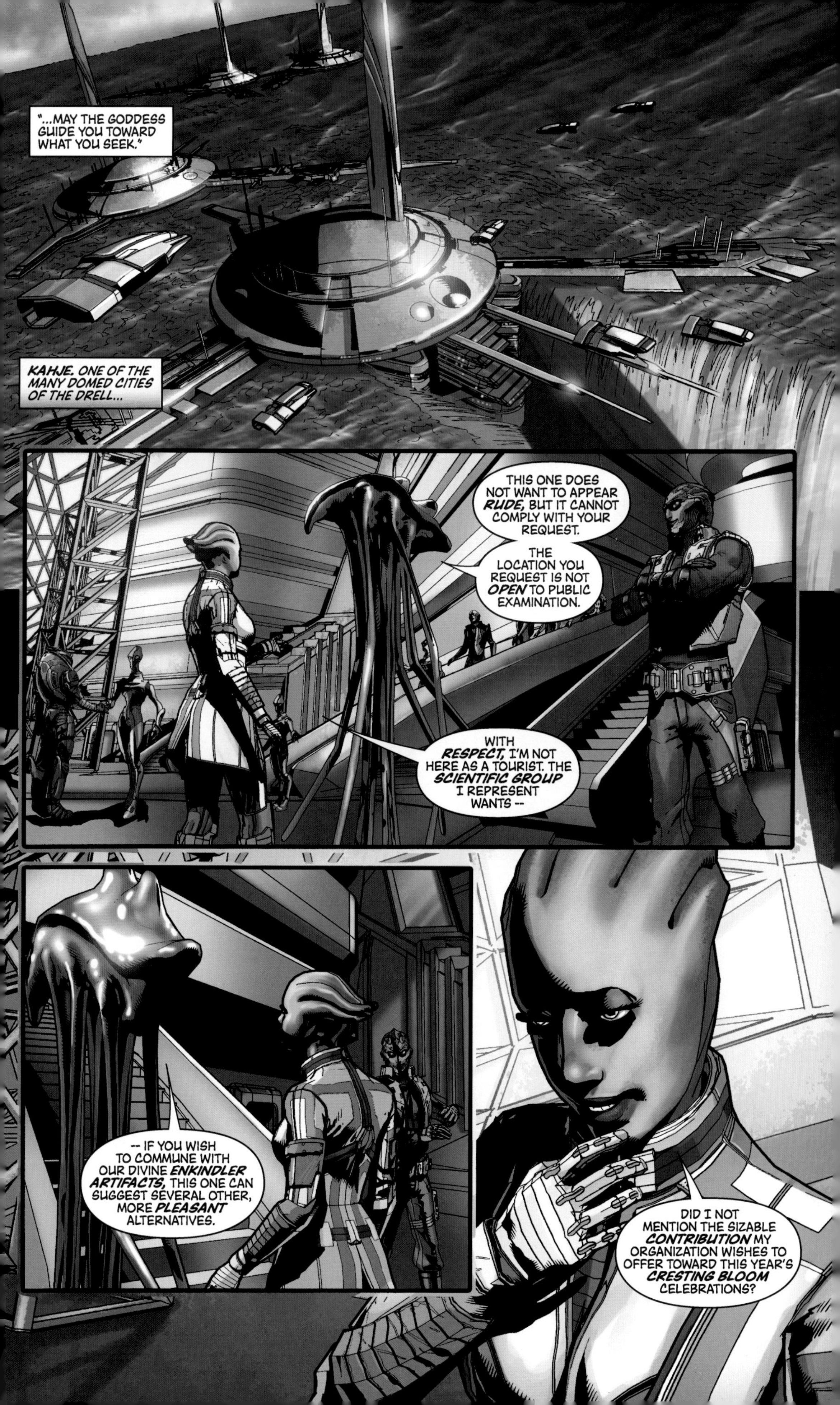

"...MAY THE GODDESS GUIDE YOU TOWARD WHAT YOU SEEK."
KAHJE. ONE OF THE MANY DOMED CITIES OF THE DRELL...
THIS ONE DOES NOT WANT TO APPEAR RUDE, BUT IT CANNOT COMPLY WITH YOUR REQUEST.
THE LOCATION YOU REQUEST IS NOT OPEN TO PUBLIC EXAMINATION.
WITH RESPECT, I'M NOT HERE AS A TOURIST. THE SCIENTIFIC GROUP I REPRESENT WANTS --
-- IF YOU WISH TO COMMUNE WITH OUR DIVINE ENKINDLER ARTIFACTS, THIS ONE CAN SUGGEST SEVERAL OTHER, MORE PLEASANT ALTERNATIVES.
DID I NOT MENTION THE SIZABLE CONTRIBUTION MY ORGANIZATION WISHES TO OFFER TOWARD THIS YEAR'S CRESTING BLOOM CELEBRATIONS?

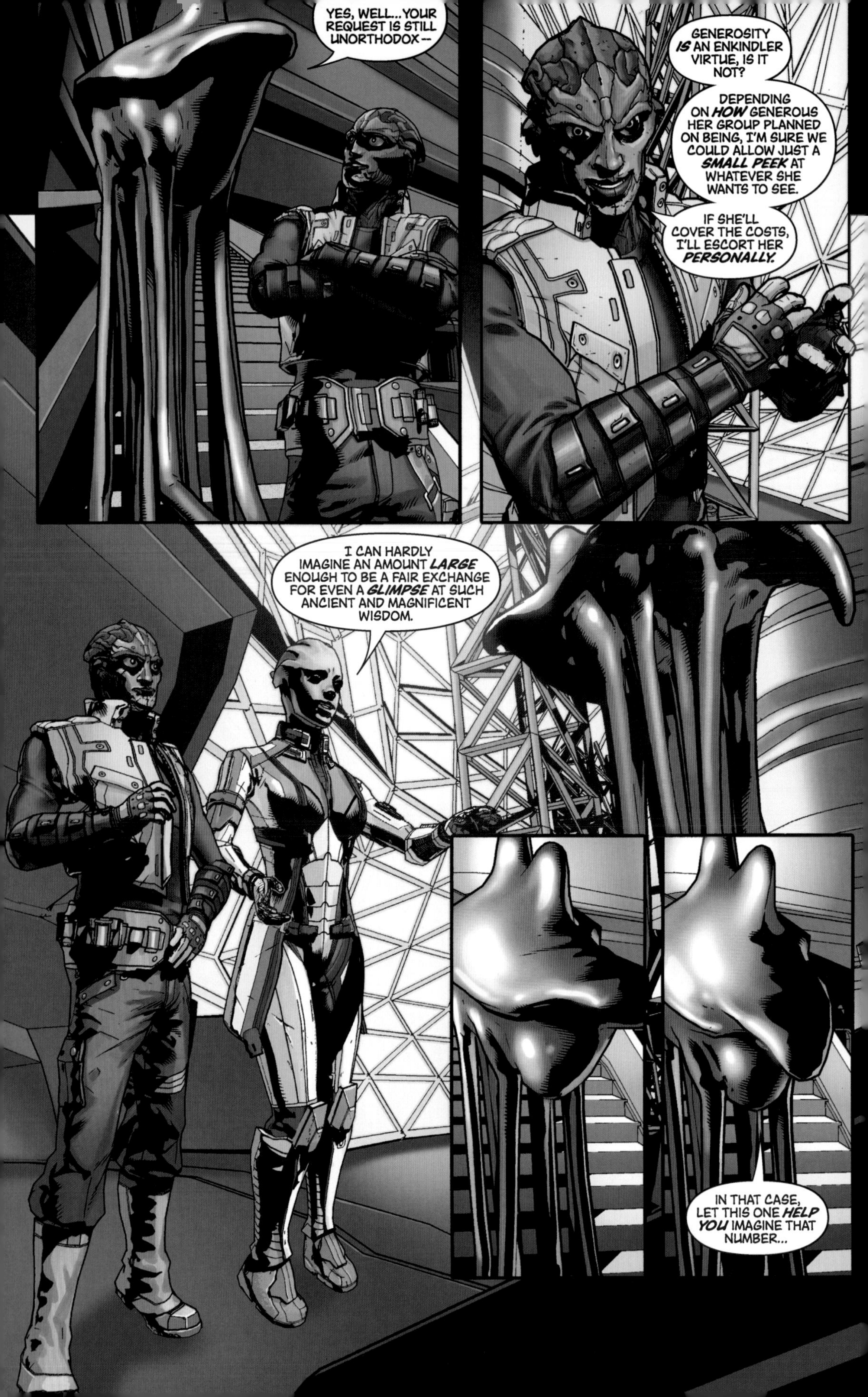
YES, WELL... YOUR REQUEST IS STILL UNORTHODOX --
GENEROSITY *IS* AN ENKINDLER VIRTUE, IS IT NOT?
DEPENDING ON *HOW* GENEROUS HER GROUP PLANNED ON BEING, I'M SURE WE COULD ALLOW JUST A *SMALL PEEK* AT WHATEVER SHE WANTS TO SEE.
IF SHE'LL COVER THE COSTS, I'LL ESCORT HER *PERSONALLY.*
I CAN HARDLY IMAGINE AN AMOUNT *LARGE* ENOUGH TO BE A FAIR EXCHANGE FOR EVEN A *GLIMPSE* AT SUCH ANCIENT AND MAGNIFICENT WISDOM.
IN THAT CASE, LET THIS ONE *HELP YOU* IMAGINE THAT NUMBER...

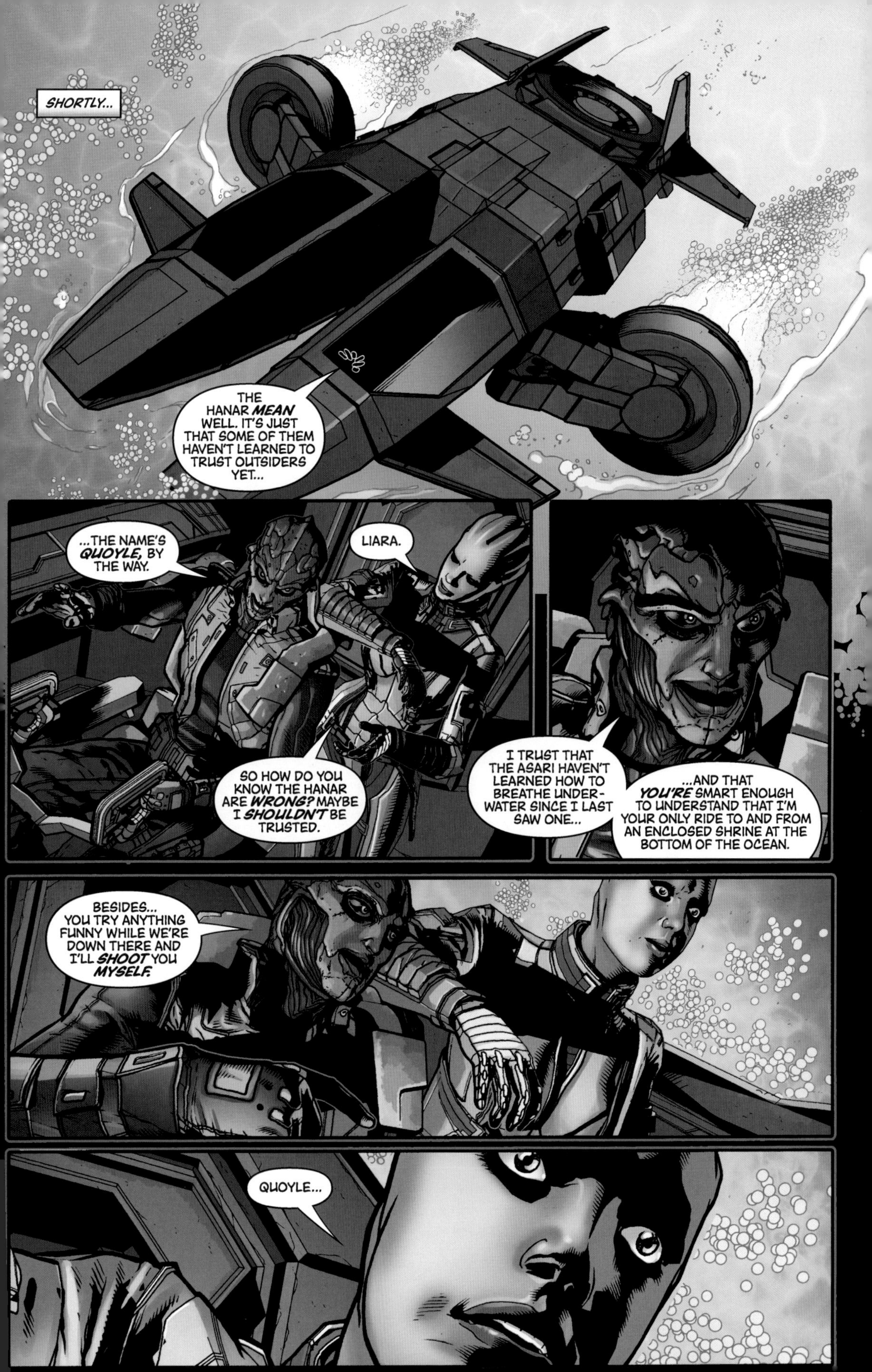
SHORTLY...
THE HANAR *MEAN* WELL. IT'S JUST THAT SOME OF THEM HAVEN'T LEARNED TO TRUST OUTSIDERS YET...
...THE NAME'S *QUOYLE*, BY THE WAY.
LIARA.
SO HOW DO YOU KNOW THE HANAR ARE *WRONG?* MAYBE I *SHOULDN'T* BE TRUSTED.
I TRUST THAT THE ASARI HAVEN'T LEARNED HOW TO BREATHE UNDER-WATER SINCE I LAST SAW ONE...
...AND THAT *YOU'RE* SMART ENOUGH TO UNDERSTAND THAT I'M YOUR ONLY RIDE TO AND FROM AN ENCLOSED SHRINE AT THE BOTTOM OF THE OCEAN.
BESIDES... YOU TRY ANYTHING FUNNY WHILE WE'RE DOWN THERE AND I'LL *SHOOT* YOU *MYSELF.*
QUOYLE...

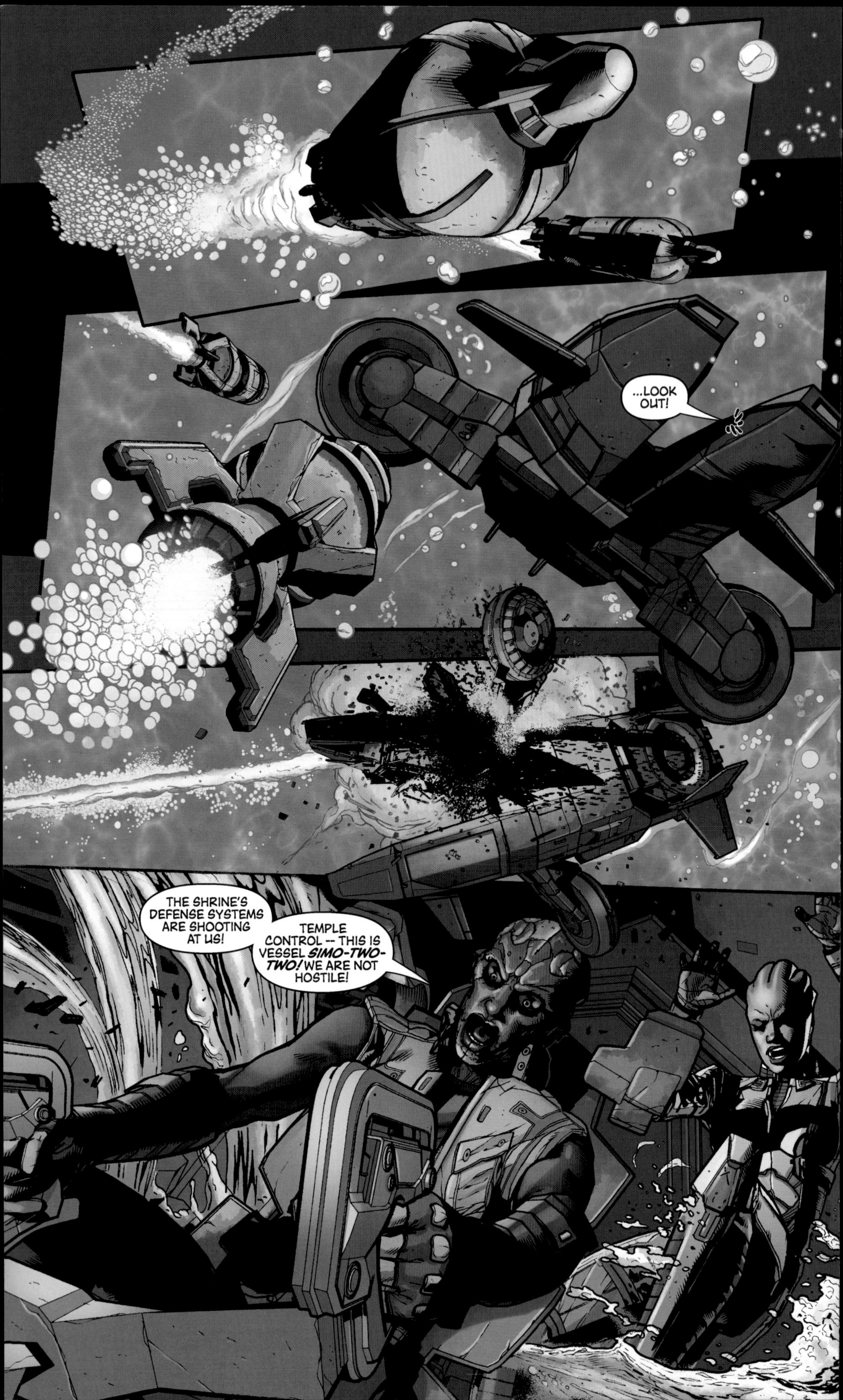
...LOOK OUT!
THE SHRINE'S DEFENSE SYSTEMS ARE SHOOTING AT US!
TEMPLE CONTROL -- THIS IS VESSEL *SIMO-TWO-TWO!* WE ARE NOT HOSTILE!

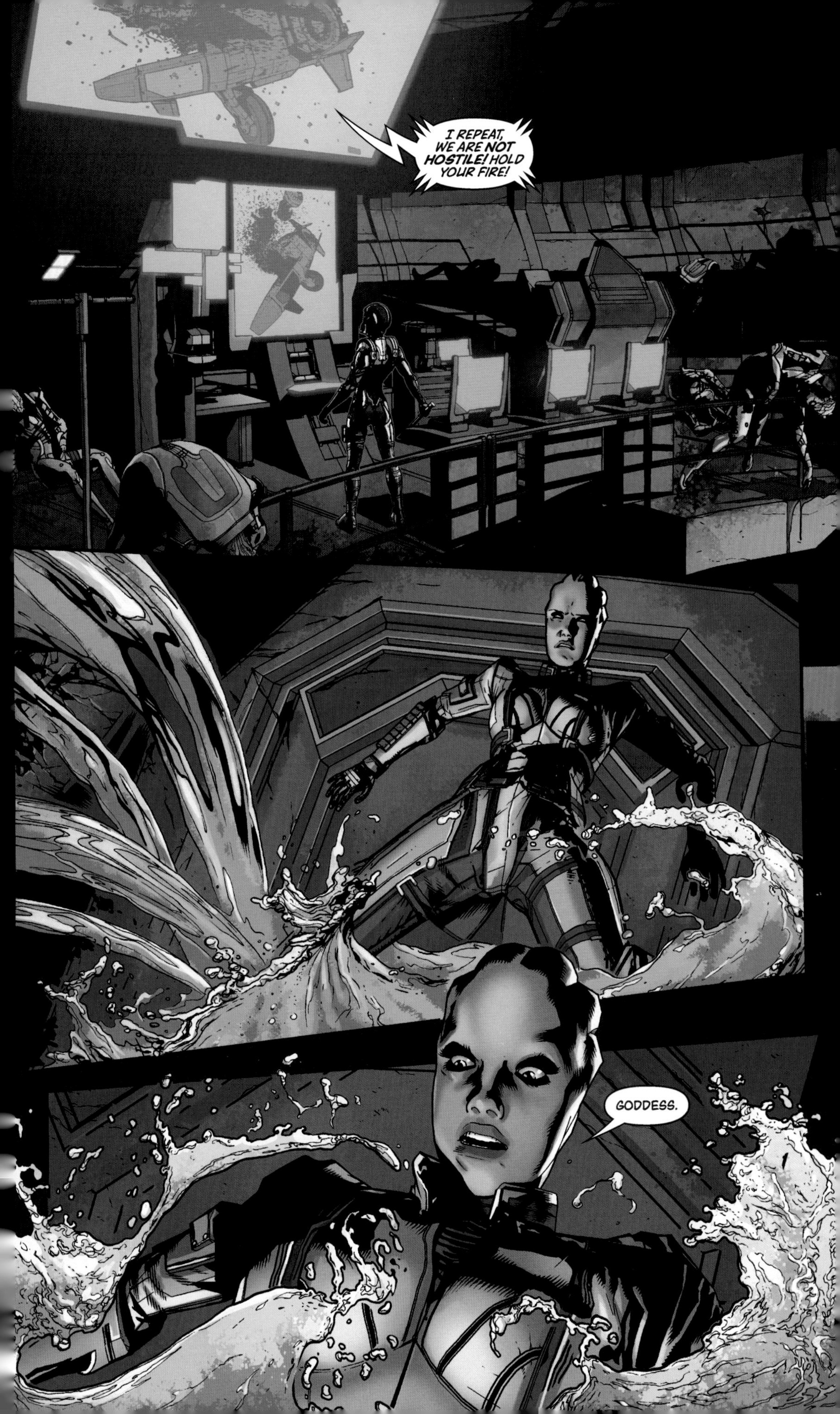
I REPEAT, WE ARE NOT HOSTILE! HOLD YOUR FIRE!
GODDESS.

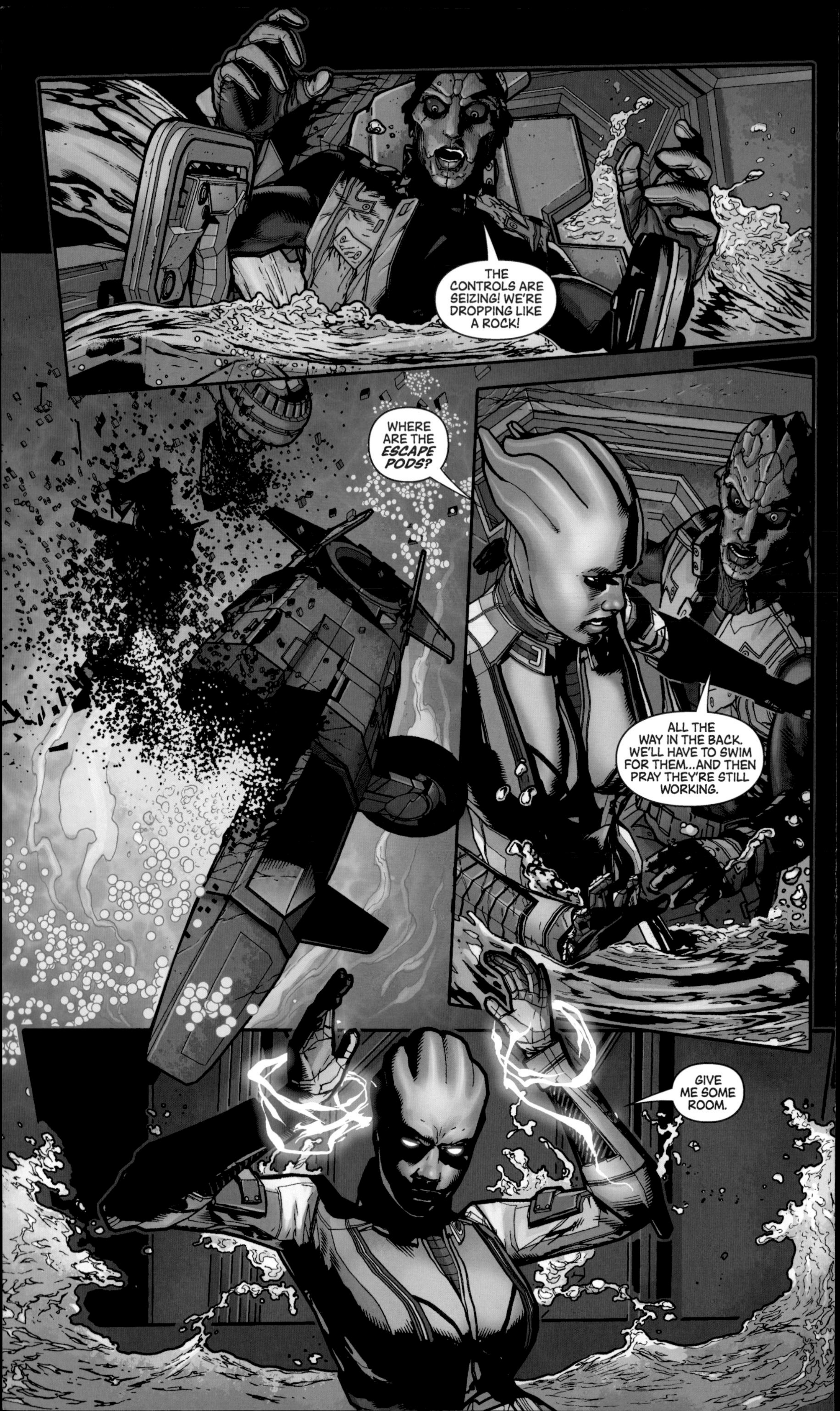
THE CONTROLS ARE SEIZING! WE'RE DROPPING LIKE A ROCK!
WHERE ARE THE *ESCAPE PODS?*
ALL THE WAY IN THE BACK. WE'LL HAVE TO SWIM FOR THEM...AND THEN PRAY THEY'RE STILL WORKING.
GIVE ME SOME ROOM.

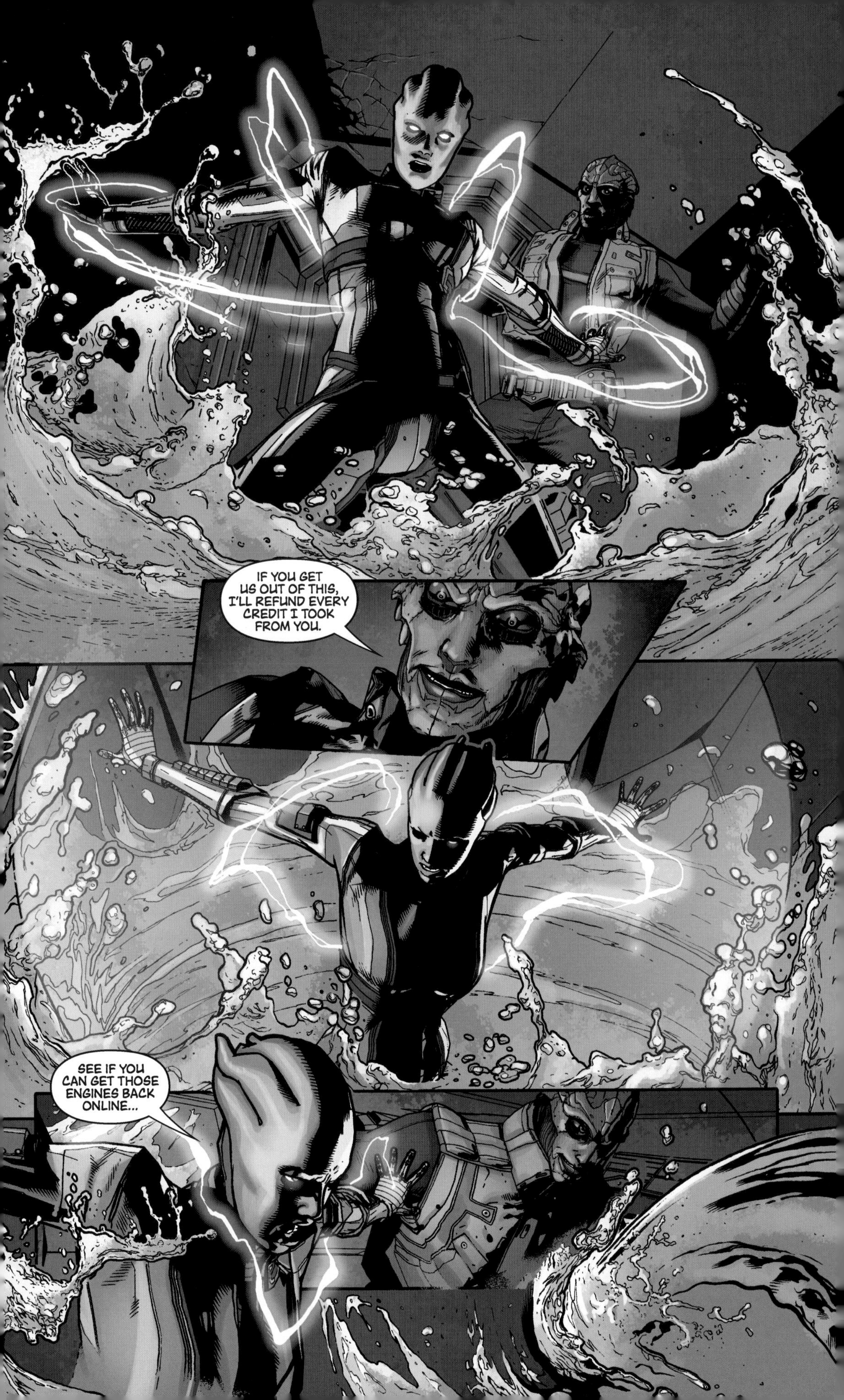
IF YOU GET US OUT OF THIS, I'LL REFUND EVERY CREDIT I TOOK FROM YOU.
SEE IF YOU CAN GET THOSE ENGINES BACK ONLINE...

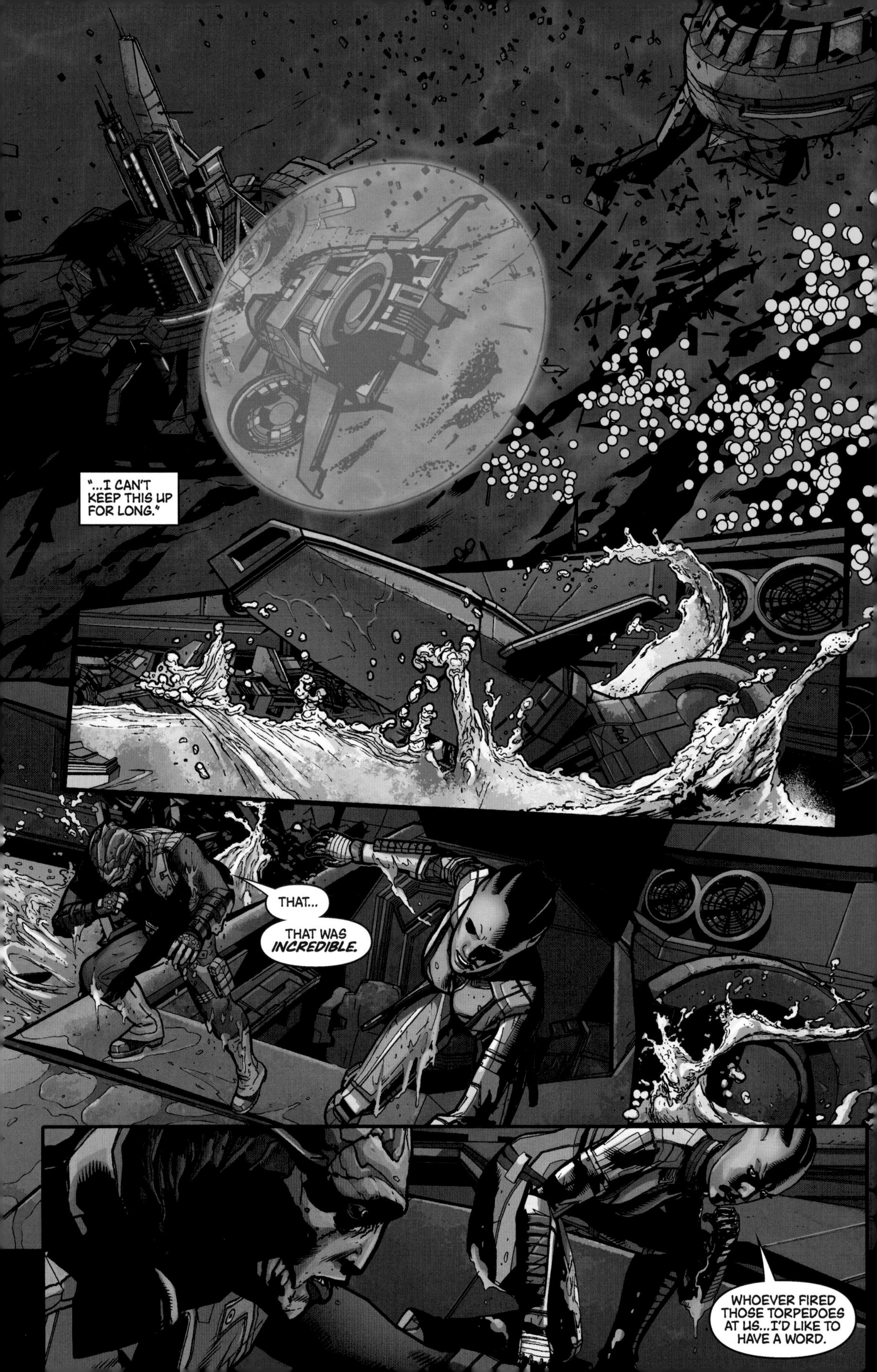
"...I CAN'T KEEP THIS UP FOR LONG."
THAT...
THAT WAS *INCREDIBLE.*
WHOEVER FIRED THOSE TORPEDOES AT US...I'D LIKE TO HAVE A WORD.

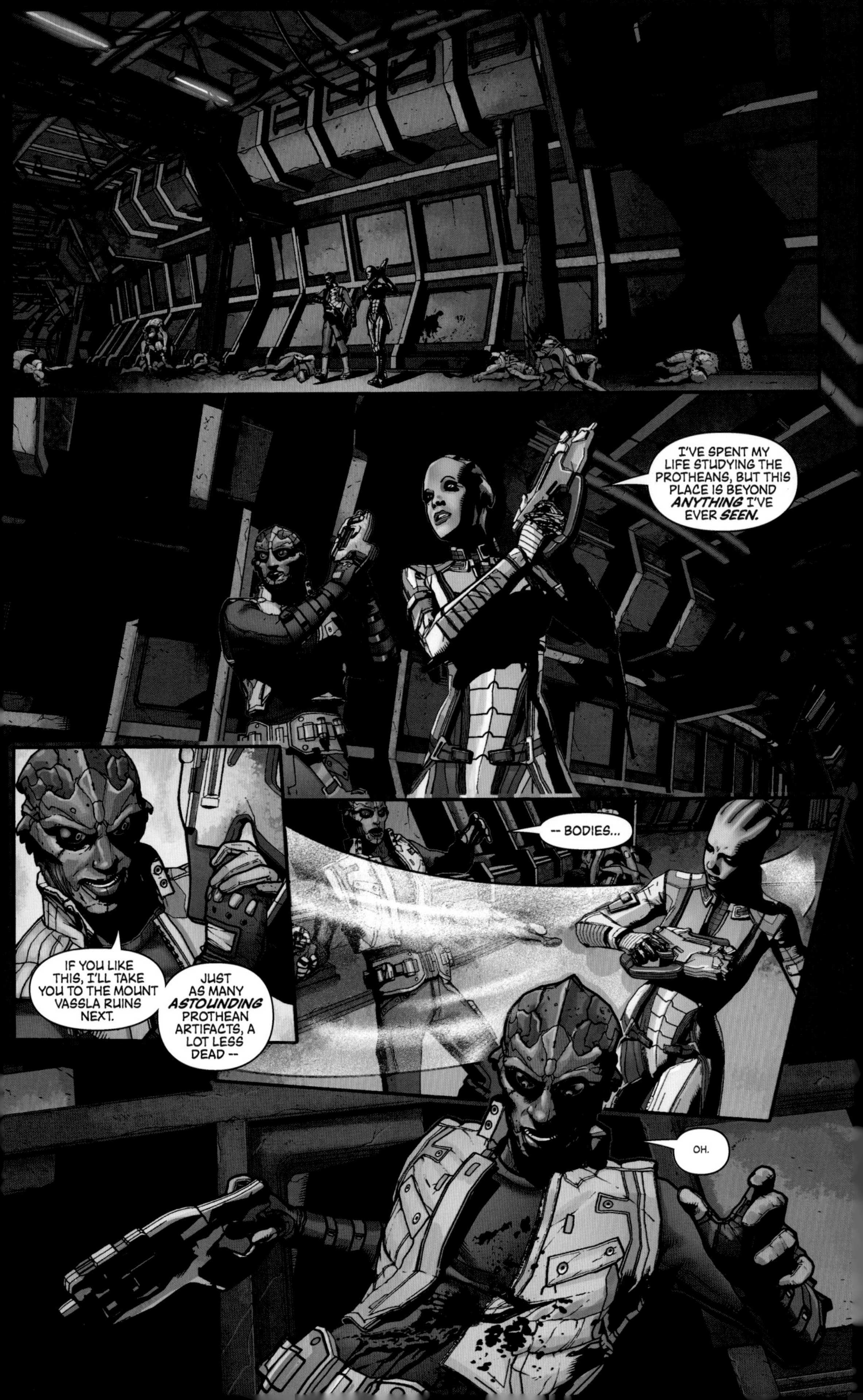
I'VE SPENT MY LIFE STUDYING THE PROTHEANS, BUT THIS PLACE IS BEYOND ANYTHING I'VE EVER SEEN.
IF YOU LIKE THIS, I'LL TAKE YOU TO THE MOUNT VASSLA RUINS NEXT.
JUST AS MANY ASTOUNDING PROTHEAN ARTIFACTS, A LOT LESS DEAD --
-- BODIES...
OH.

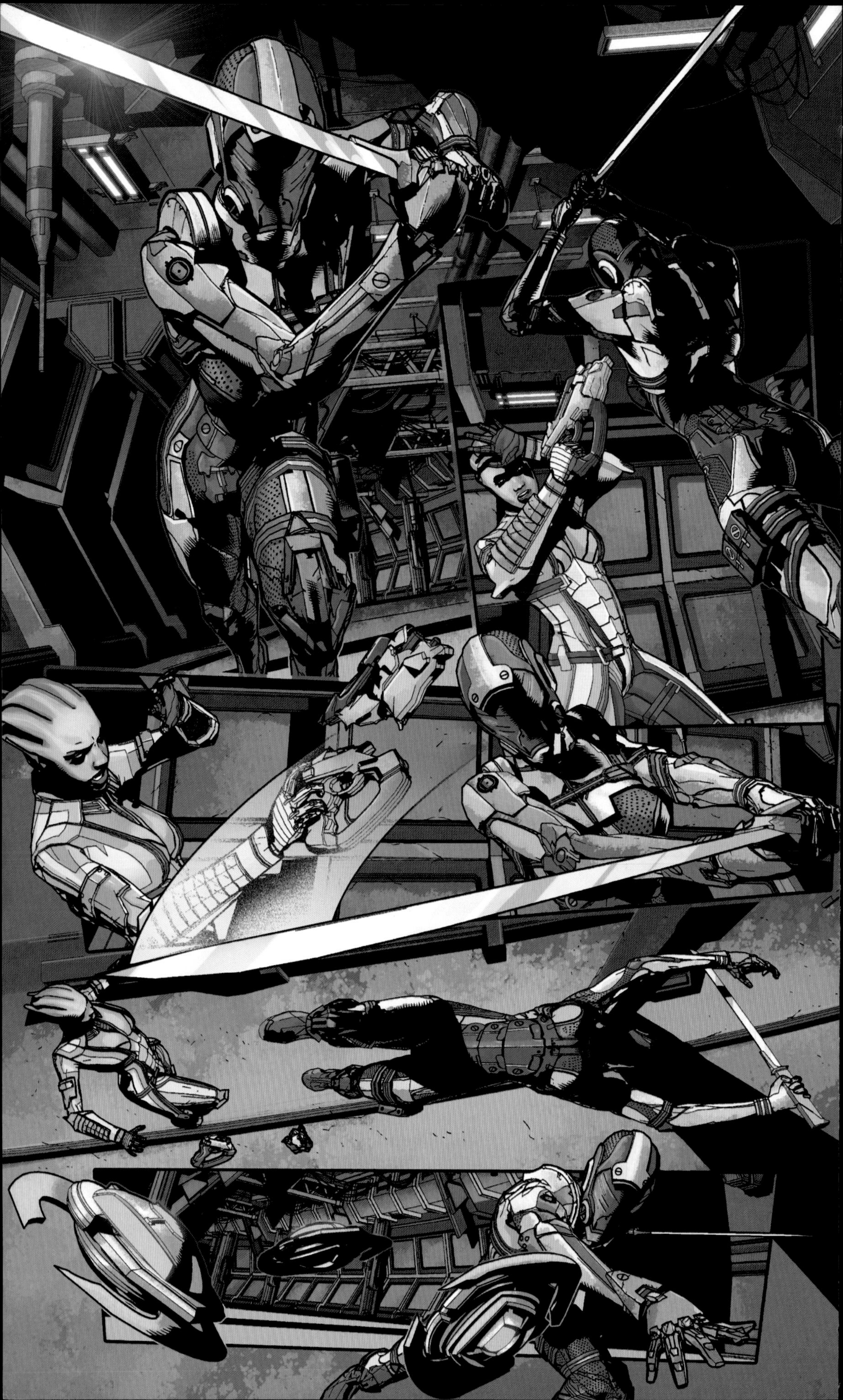

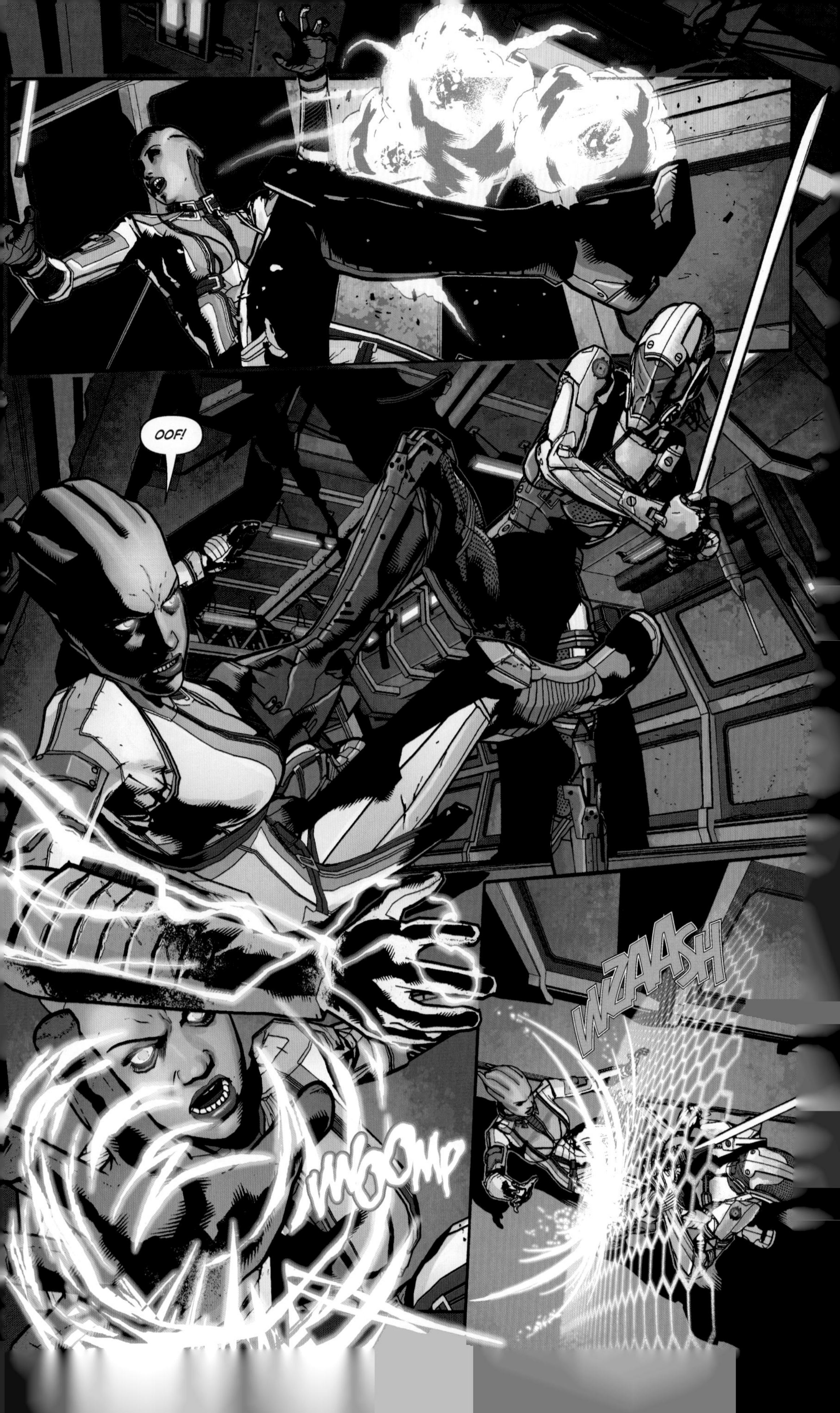
OOF!
WHOOMP
WZAASH

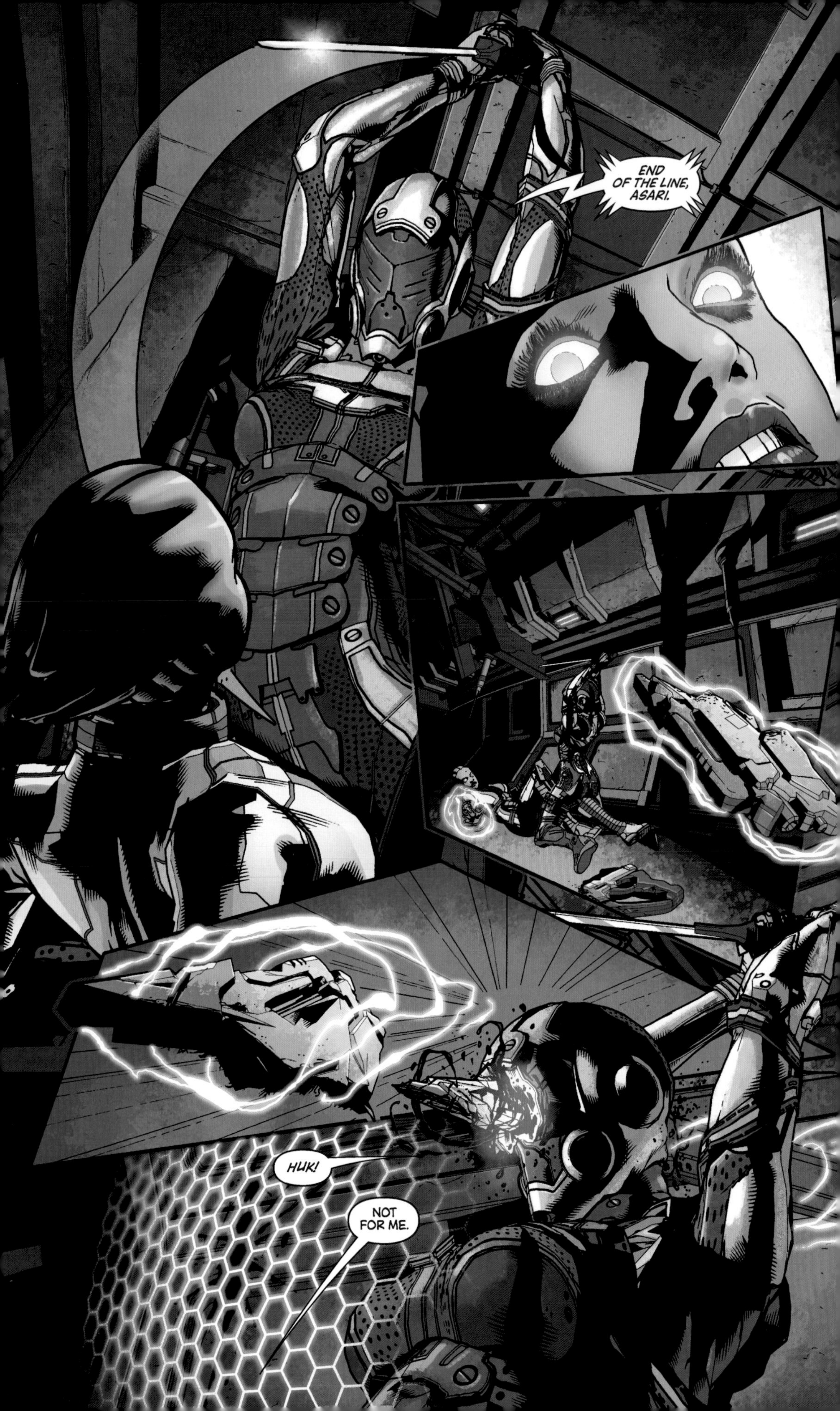
END OF THE LINE, ASARI.
HUK!
NOT FOR ME.

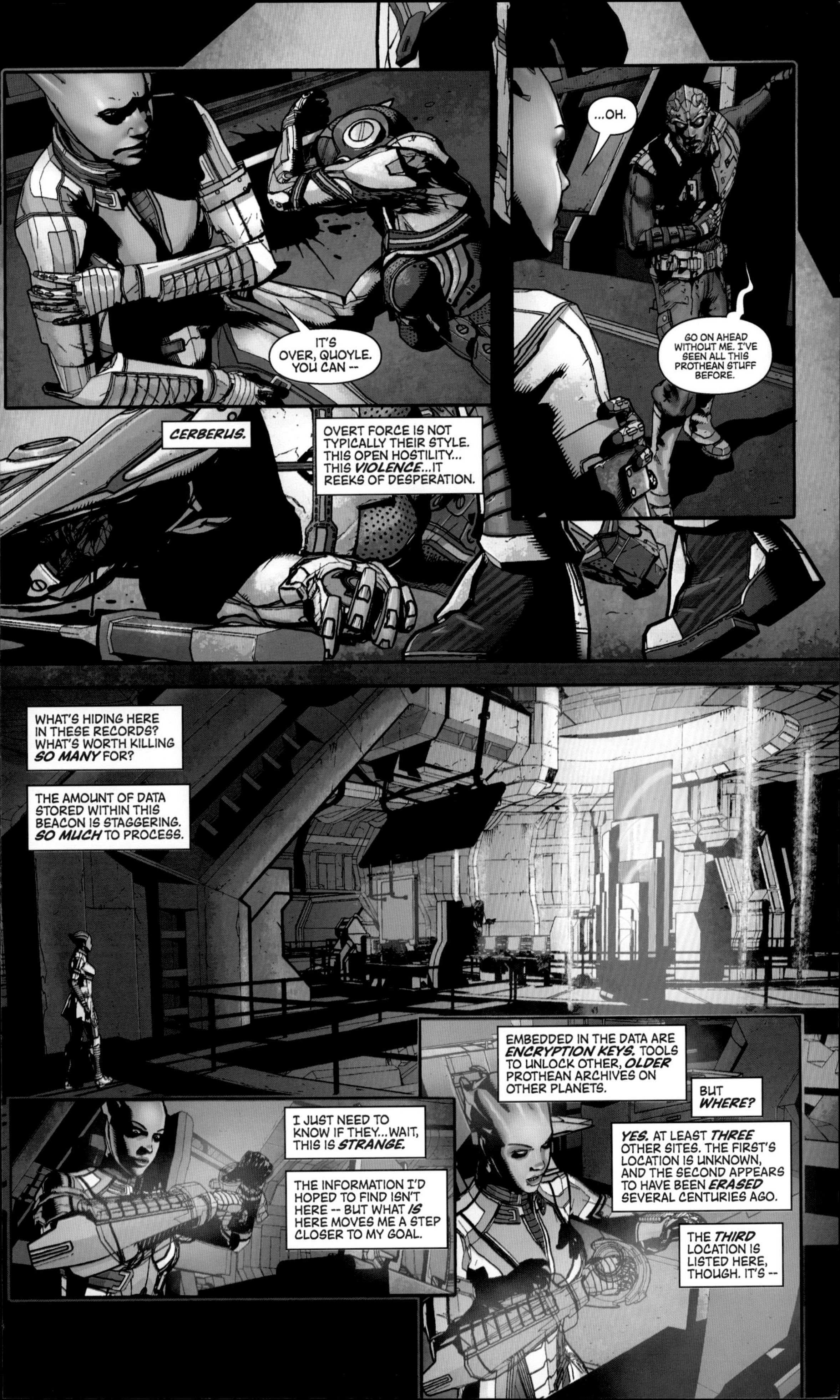

IT'S OVER, QUOYLE. YOU CAN --
...OH.
GO ON AHEAD WITHOUT ME. I'VE SEEN ALL THIS PROTHEAN STUFF BEFORE.
CERBERUS.
OVERT FORCE IS NOT TYPICALLY THEIR STYLE. THIS OPEN HOSTILITY... THIS VIOLENCE...IT REEKS OF DESPERATION.
WHAT'S HIDING HERE IN THESE RECORDS? WHAT'S WORTH KILLING SO MANY FOR?
THE AMOUNT OF DATA STORED WITHIN THIS BEACON IS STAGGERING. SO MUCH TO PROCESS.
I JUST NEED TO KNOW IF THEY...WAIT, THIS IS STRANGE.
THE INFORMATION I'D HOPED TO FIND ISN'T HERE -- BUT WHAT IS HERE MOVES ME A STEP CLOSER TO MY GOAL.
EMBEDDED IN THE DATA ARE ENCRYPTION KEYS. TOOLS TO UNLOCK OTHER, OLDER PROTHEAN ARCHIVES ON OTHER PLANETS.
BUT WHERE?
YES. AT LEAST THREE OTHER SITES. THE FIRST'S LOCATION IS UNKNOWN, AND THE SECOND APPEARS TO HAVE BEEN ERASED SEVERAL CENTURIES AGO.
THE THIRD LOCATION IS LISTED HERE, THOUGH. IT'S --

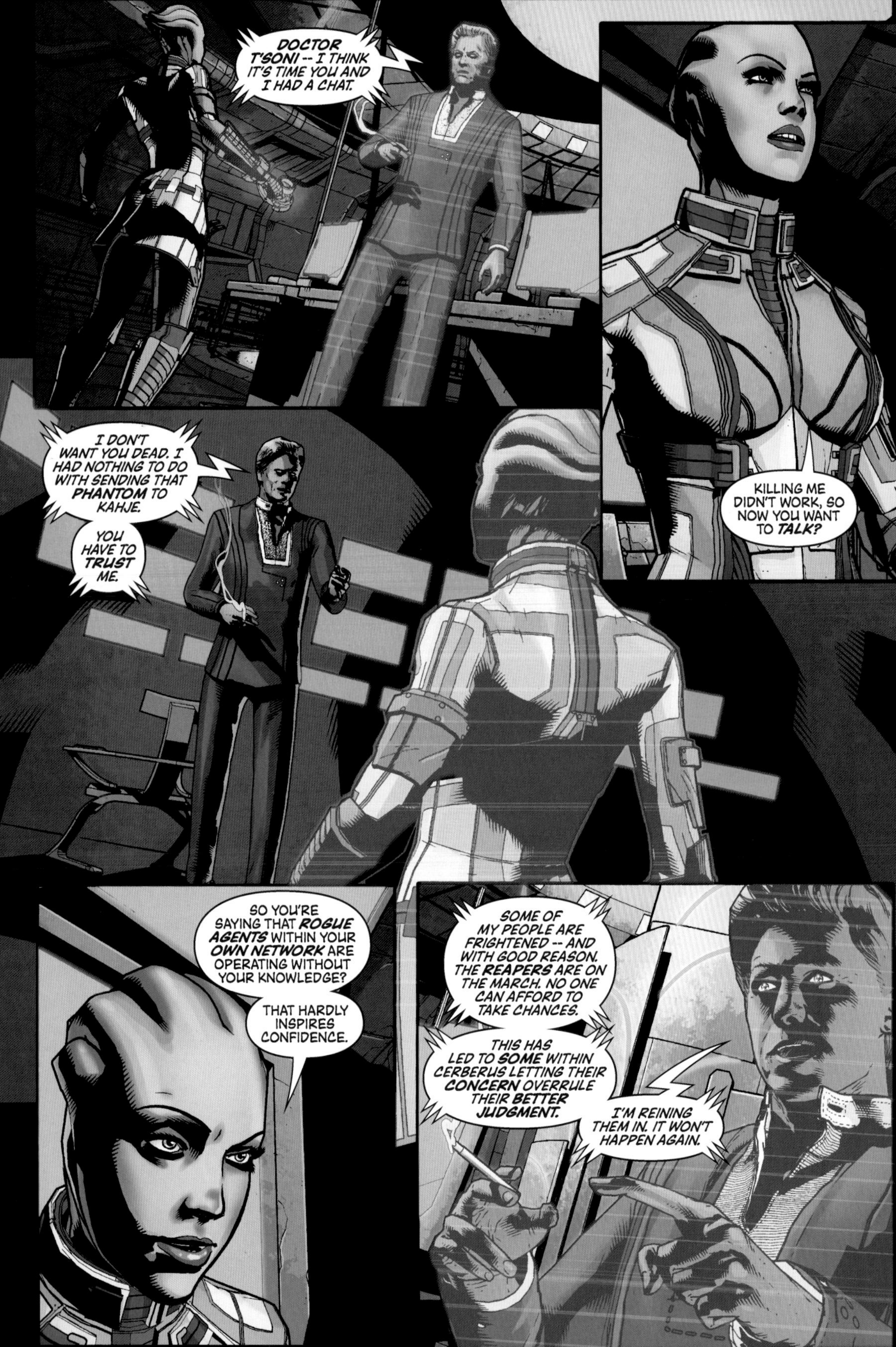
DOCTOR T'SONI -- I THINK IT'S TIME YOU AND I HAD A CHAT.
KILLING ME DIDN'T WORK, SO NOW YOU WANT TO TALK?
I DON'T WANT YOU DEAD. I HAD NOTHING TO DO WITH SENDING THAT PHANTOM TO KAHJE.
YOU HAVE TO TRUST ME.
SO YOU'RE SAYING THAT ROGUE AGENTS WITHIN YOUR OWN NETWORK ARE OPERATING WITHOUT YOUR KNOWLEDGE?
THAT HARDLY INSPIRES CONFIDENCE.
SOME OF MY PEOPLE ARE FRIGHTENED -- AND WITH GOOD REASON. THE REAPERS ARE ON THE MARCH. NO ONE CAN AFFORD TO TAKE CHANCES.
THIS HAS LED TO SOME WITHIN CERBERUS LETTING THEIR CONCERN OVERRULE THEIR BETTER JUDGMENT.
I'M REINING THEM IN. IT WON'T HAPPEN AGAIN.

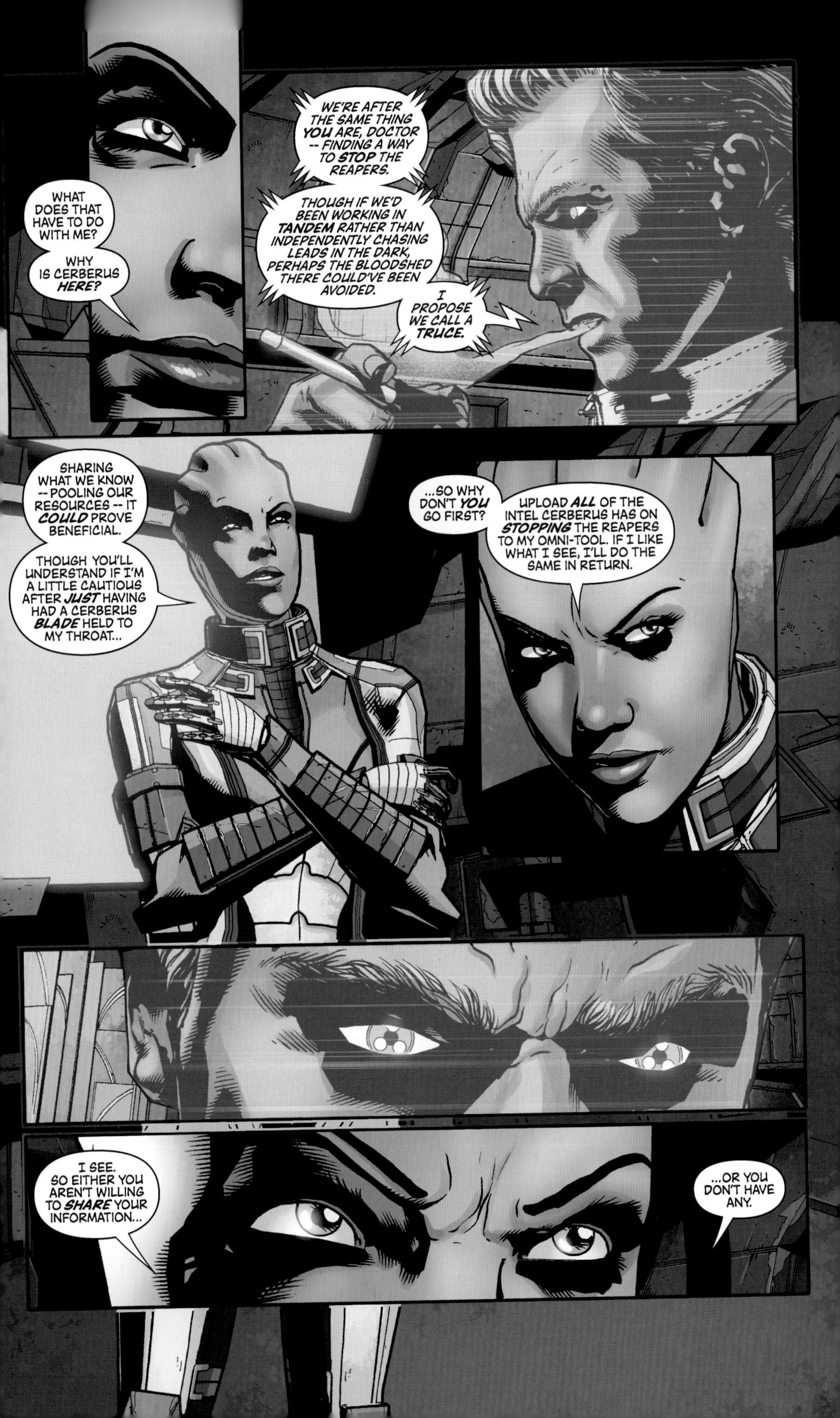

WHAT DOES THAT HAVE TO DO WITH ME?
WHY IS CERBERUS HERE?
WE'RE AFTER THE SAME THING YOU ARE, DOCTOR -- FINDING A WAY TO STOP THE REAPERS.
THOUGH IF WE'D BEEN WORKING IN TANDEM RATHER THAN INDEPENDENTLY CHASING LEADS IN THE DARK, PERHAPS THE BLOODSHED THERE COULD'VE BEEN AVOIDED.
I PROPOSE WE CALL A TRUCE.
SHARING WHAT WE KNOW -- POOLING OUR RESOURCES -- IT COULD PROVE BENEFICIAL.
THOUGH YOU'LL UNDERSTAND IF I'M A LITTLE CAUTIOUS AFTER JUST HAVING HAD A CERBERUS BLADE HELD TO MY THROAT...
...SO WHY DON'T YOU GO FIRST?
UPLOAD ALL OF THE INTEL CERBERUS HAS ON STOPPING THE REAPERS TO MY OMNI-TOOL. IF I LIKE WHAT I SEE, I'LL DO THE SAME IN RETURN.
I SEE. SO EITHER YOU AREN'T WILLING TO SHARE YOUR INFORMATION...
...OR YOU DON'T HAVE ANY.

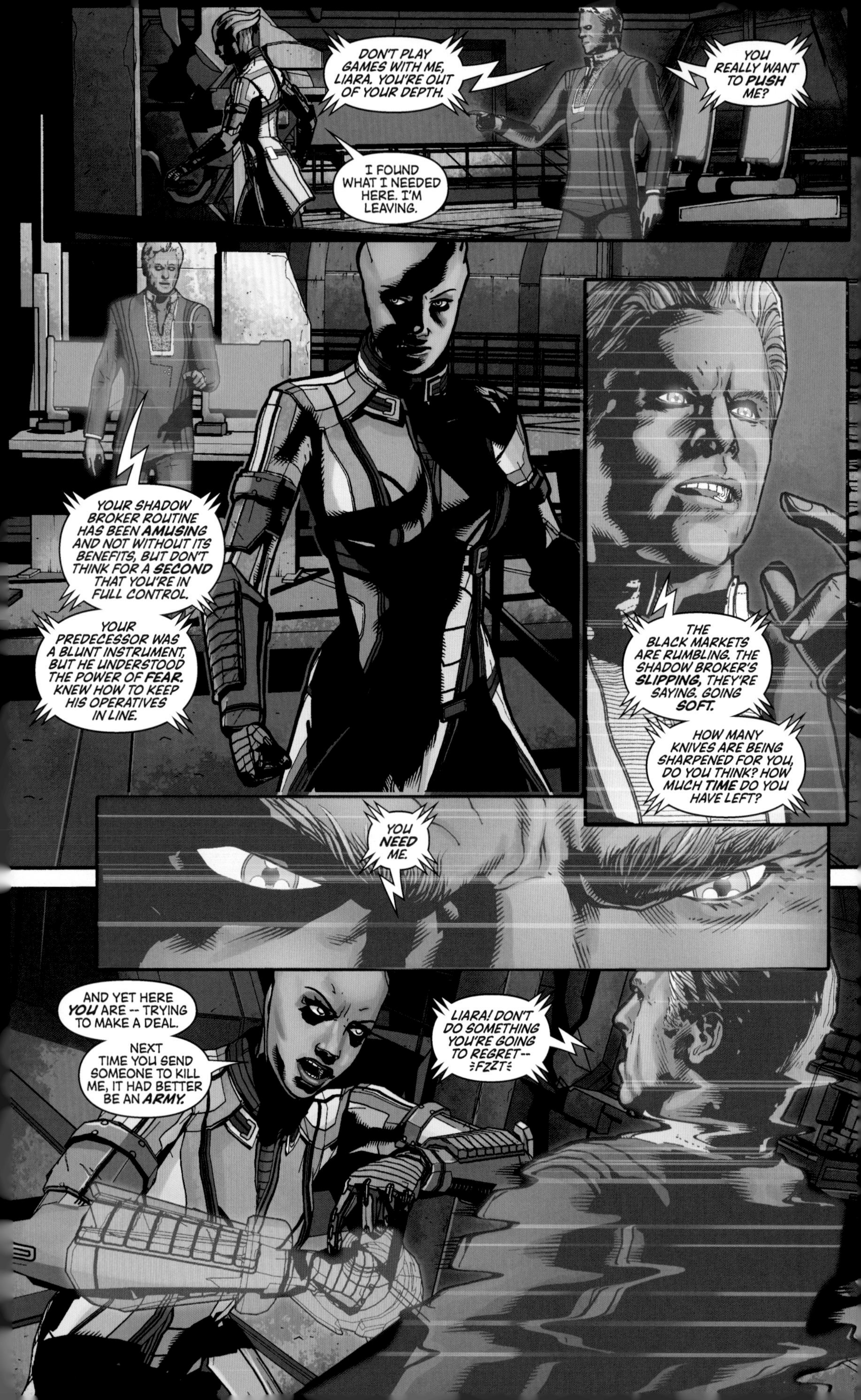
DON'T PLAY GAMES WITH ME, LIARA. YOU'RE OUT OF YOUR DEPTH.
YOU REALLY WANT TO PUSH ME?
I FOUND WHAT I NEEDED HERE. I'M LEAVING.
YOUR SHADOW BROKER ROUTINE HAS BEEN AMUSING AND NOT WITHOUT ITS BENEFITS, BUT DON'T THINK FOR A SECOND THAT YOU'RE IN FULL CONTROL.
YOUR PREDECESSOR WAS A BLUNT INSTRUMENT, BUT HE UNDERSTOOD THE POWER OF FEAR. KNEW HOW TO KEEP HIS OPERATIVES IN LINE.
THE BLACK MARKETS ARE RUMBLING. THE SHADOW BROKER'S SLIPPING, THEY'RE SAYING. GOING SOFT.
HOW MANY KNIVES ARE BEING SHARPENED FOR YOU, DO YOU THINK? HOW MUCH TIME DO YOU HAVE LEFT?
YOU NEED ME.
AND YET HERE YOU ARE -- TRYING TO MAKE A DEAL.
NEXT TIME YOU SEND SOMEONE TO KILL ME, IT HAD BETTER BE AN ARMY.
LIARA! DON'T DO SOMETHING YOU'RE GOING TO REGRET--
FZZT

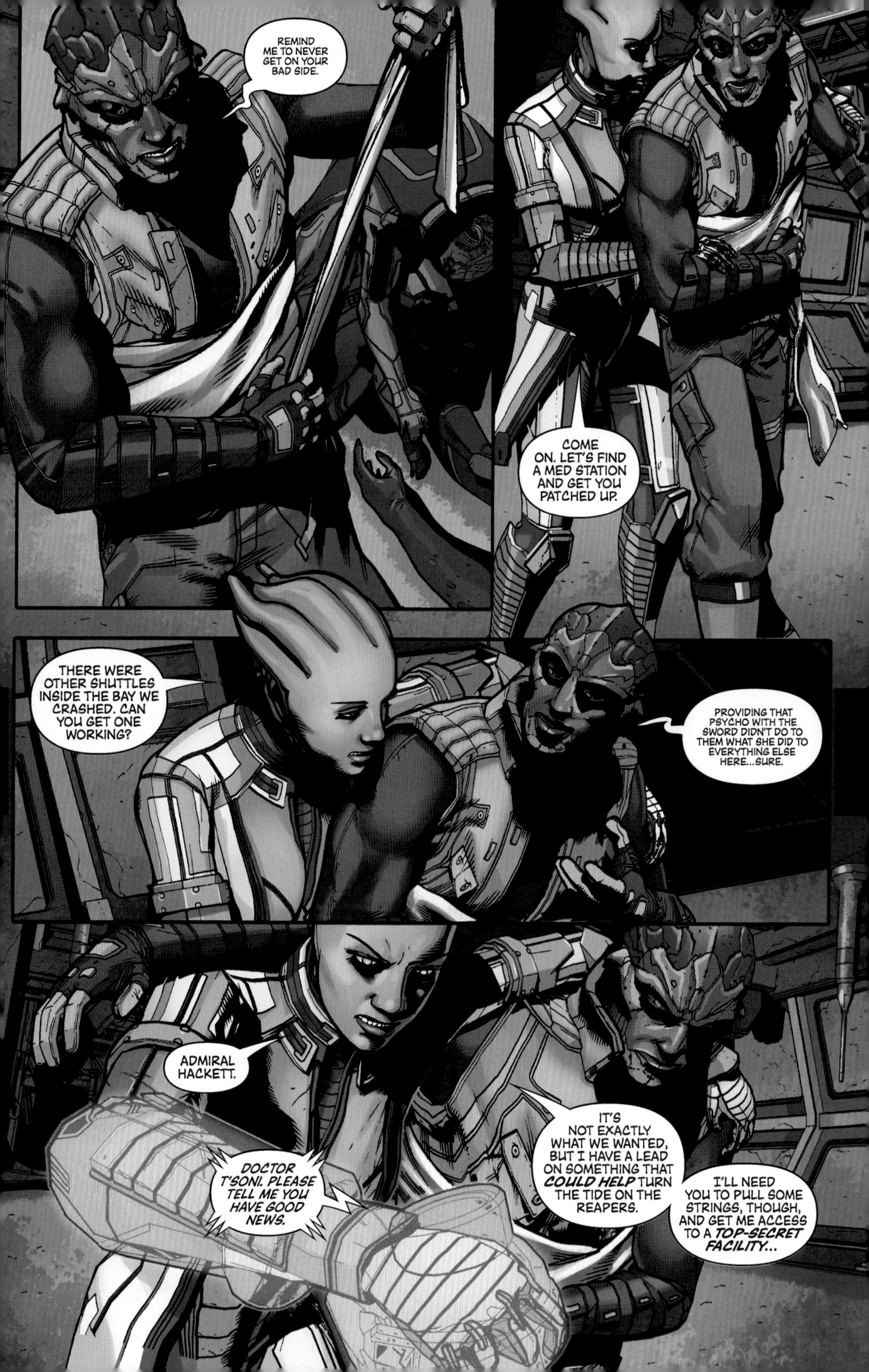
REMIND ME TO NEVER GET ON YOUR BAD SIDE.
COME ON. LET'S FIND A MED STATION AND GET YOU PATCHED UP.
THERE WERE OTHER SHUTTLES INSIDE THE BAY WE CRASHED. CAN YOU GET ONE WORKING?
PROVIDING THAT PSYCHO WITH THE SWORD DIDN'T DO TO THEM WHAT SHE DID TO EVERYTHING ELSE HERE...SURE.
ADMIRAL HACKETT.
DOCTOR T'SONI. PLEASE TELL ME YOU HAVE GOOD NEWS.
IT'S NOT EXACTLY WHAT WE WANTED, BUT I HAVE A LEAD ON SOMETHING THAT COULD HELP TURN THE TIDE ON THE REAPERS.
I'LL NEED YOU TO PULL SOME STRINGS, THOUGH, AND GET ME ACCESS TO A TOP-SECRET FACILITY...

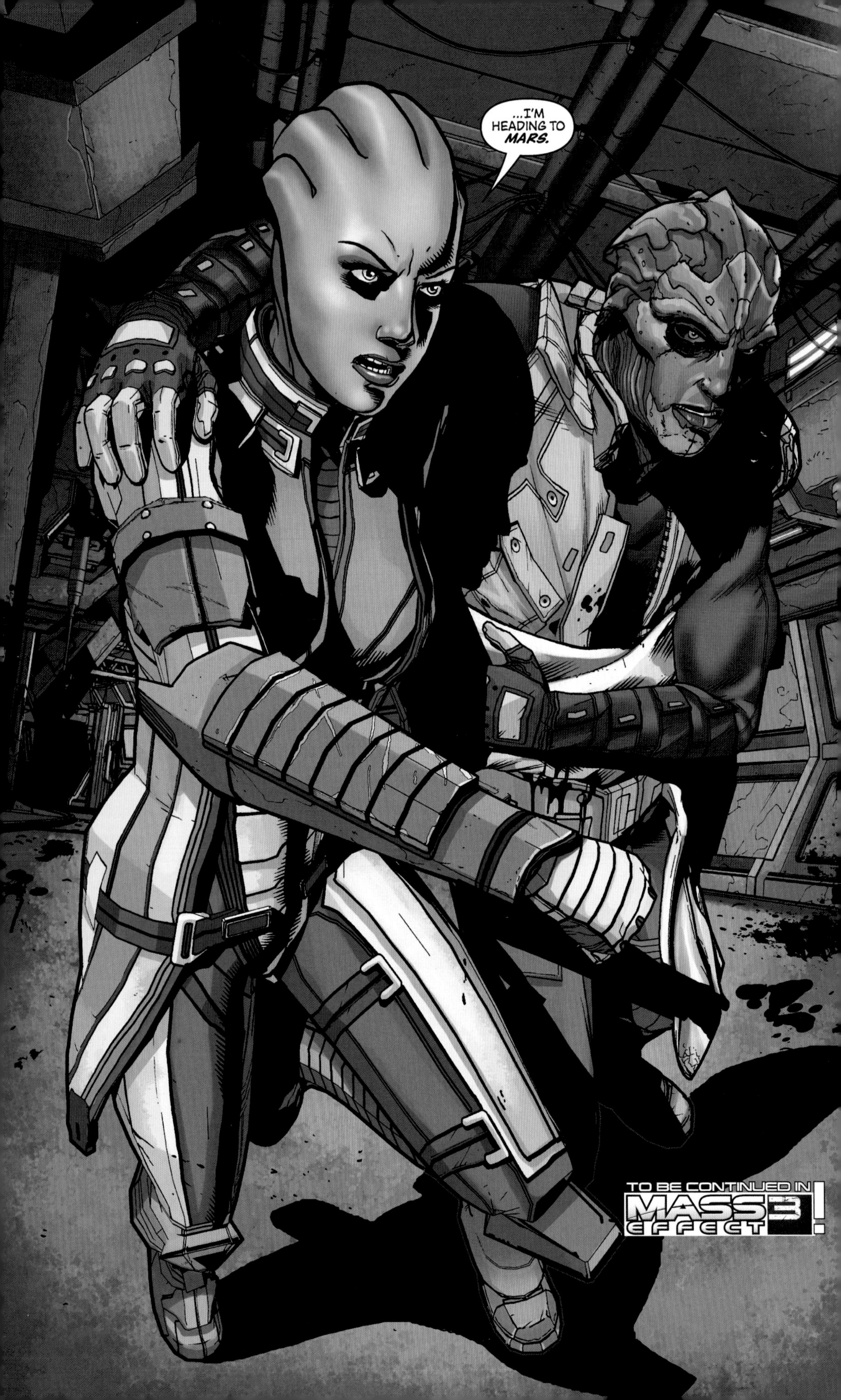
...I'M HEADING TO MARS.
TO BE CONTINUED IN MASS EFFECT 3!

BEN HUEN

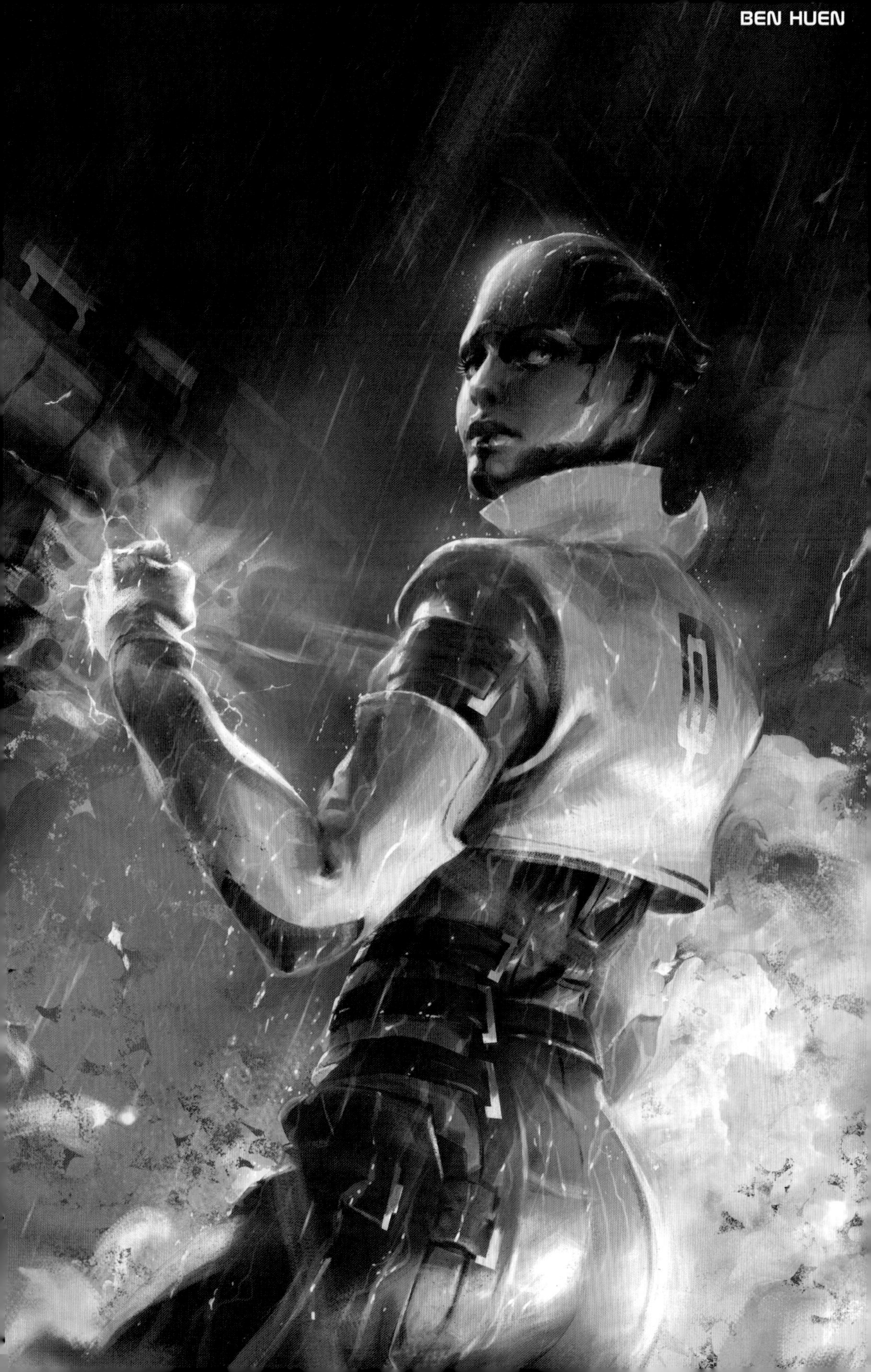

INCURSION

SCRIPT
MAC WALTERS

ART
EDUARDO FRANCISCO

COLORS
MICHAEL ATIYEH

LETTERING
MICHAEL HEISLER

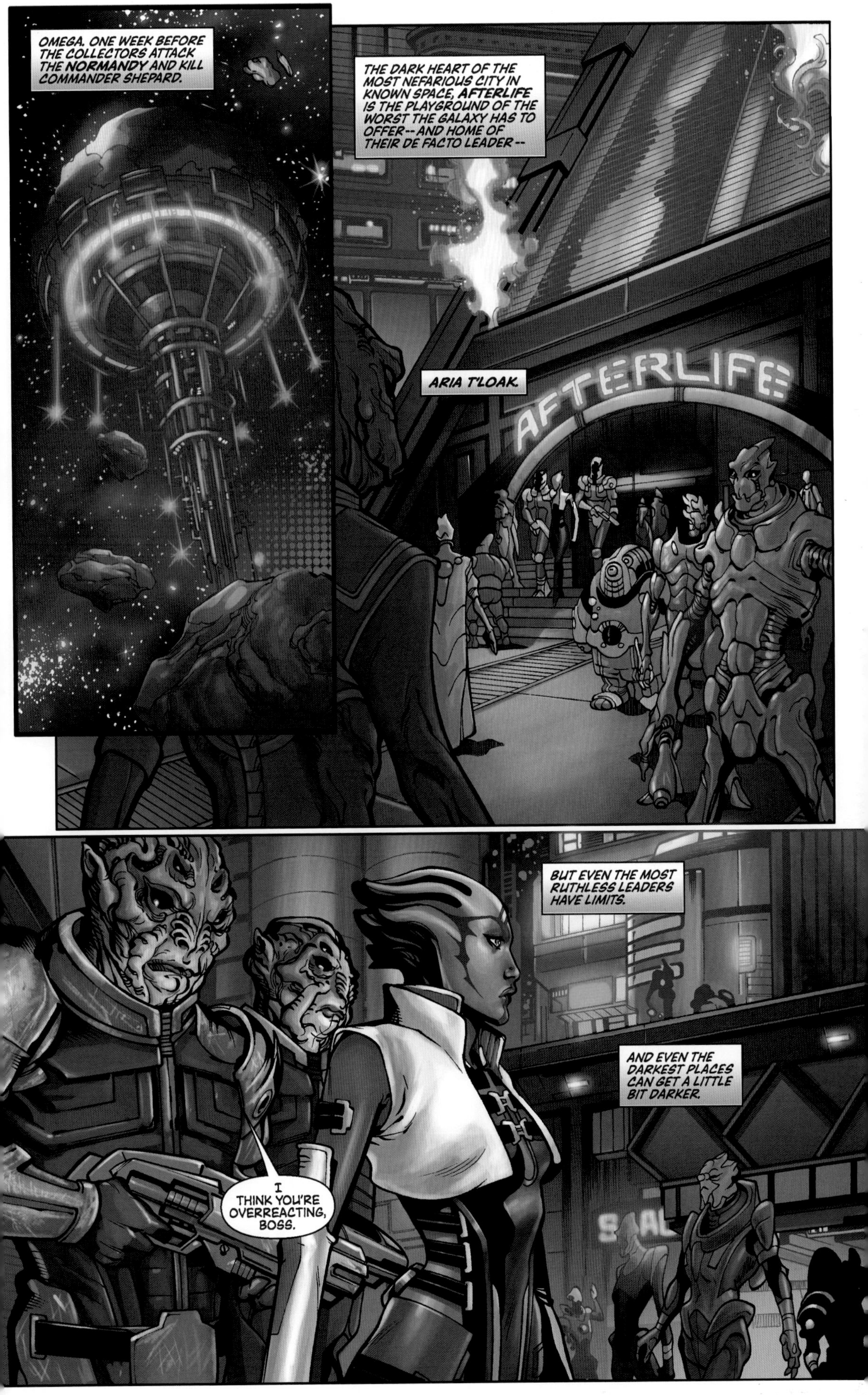
OMEGA. ONE WEEK BEFORE THE COLLECTORS ATTACK THE NORMANDY AND KILL COMMANDER SHEPARD.
THE DARK HEART OF THE MOST NEFARIOUS CITY IN KNOWN SPACE, AFTERLIFE IS THE PLAYGROUND OF THE WORST THE GALAXY HAS TO OFFER-- AND HOME OF THEIR DE FACTO LEADER--
ARIA T'LOAK.
AFTERLIFE
BUT EVEN THE MOST RUTHLESS LEADERS HAVE LIMITS.
AND EVEN THE DARKEST PLACES CAN GET A LITTLE BIT DARKER.
I THINK YOU'RE OVERREACTING, BOSS.

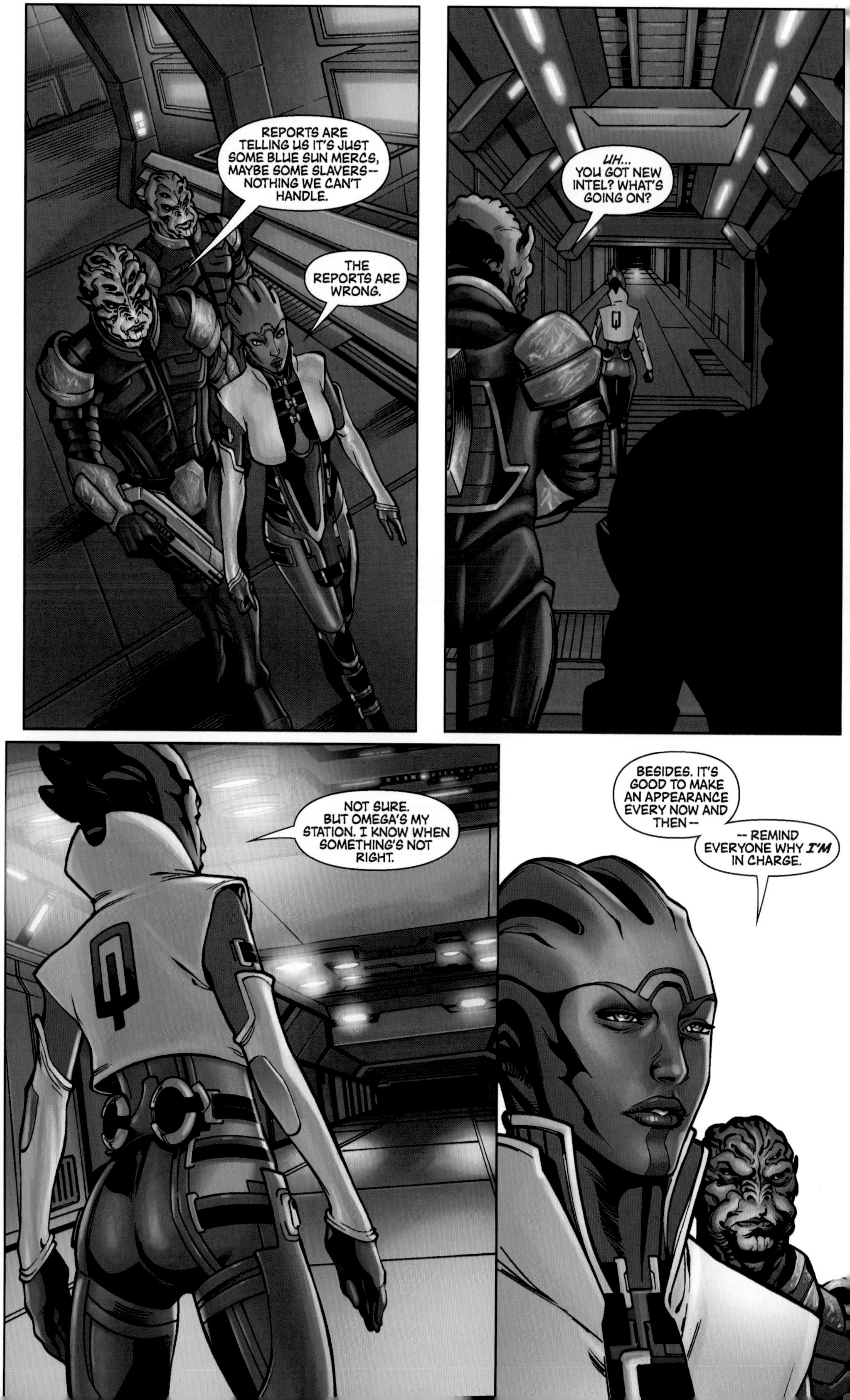
REPORTS ARE TELLING US IT'S JUST SOME BLUE SUN MERCS, MAYBE SOME SLAVERS-- NOTHING WE CAN'T HANDLE.
THE REPORTS ARE WRONG.
UH... YOU GOT NEW INTEL? WHAT'S GOING ON?
NOT SURE. BUT OMEGA'S MY STATION. I KNOW WHEN SOMETHING'S NOT RIGHT.
BESIDES. IT'S GOOD TO MAKE AN APPEARANCE EVERY NOW AND THEN --
-- REMIND EVERYONE WHY I'M IN CHARGE.

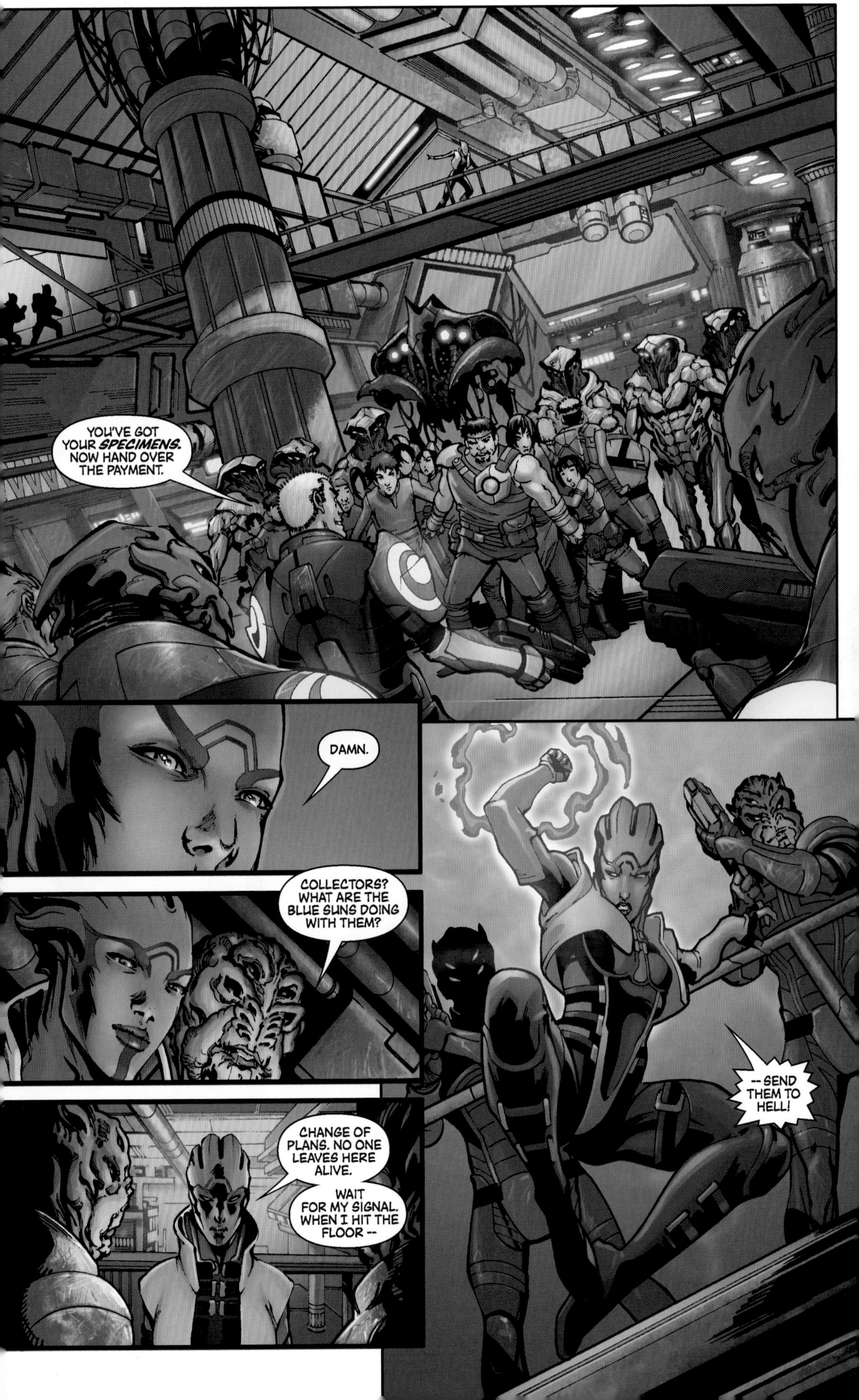
YOU'VE GOT YOUR *SPECIMENS.* NOW HAND OVER THE PAYMENT.
DAMN.
COLLECTORS? WHAT ARE THE BLUE SUNS DOING WITH THEM?
CHANGE OF PLANS. NO ONE LEAVES HERE ALIVE.
WAIT FOR MY SIGNAL. WHEN I HIT THE FLOOR --
-- SEND THEM TO HELL!

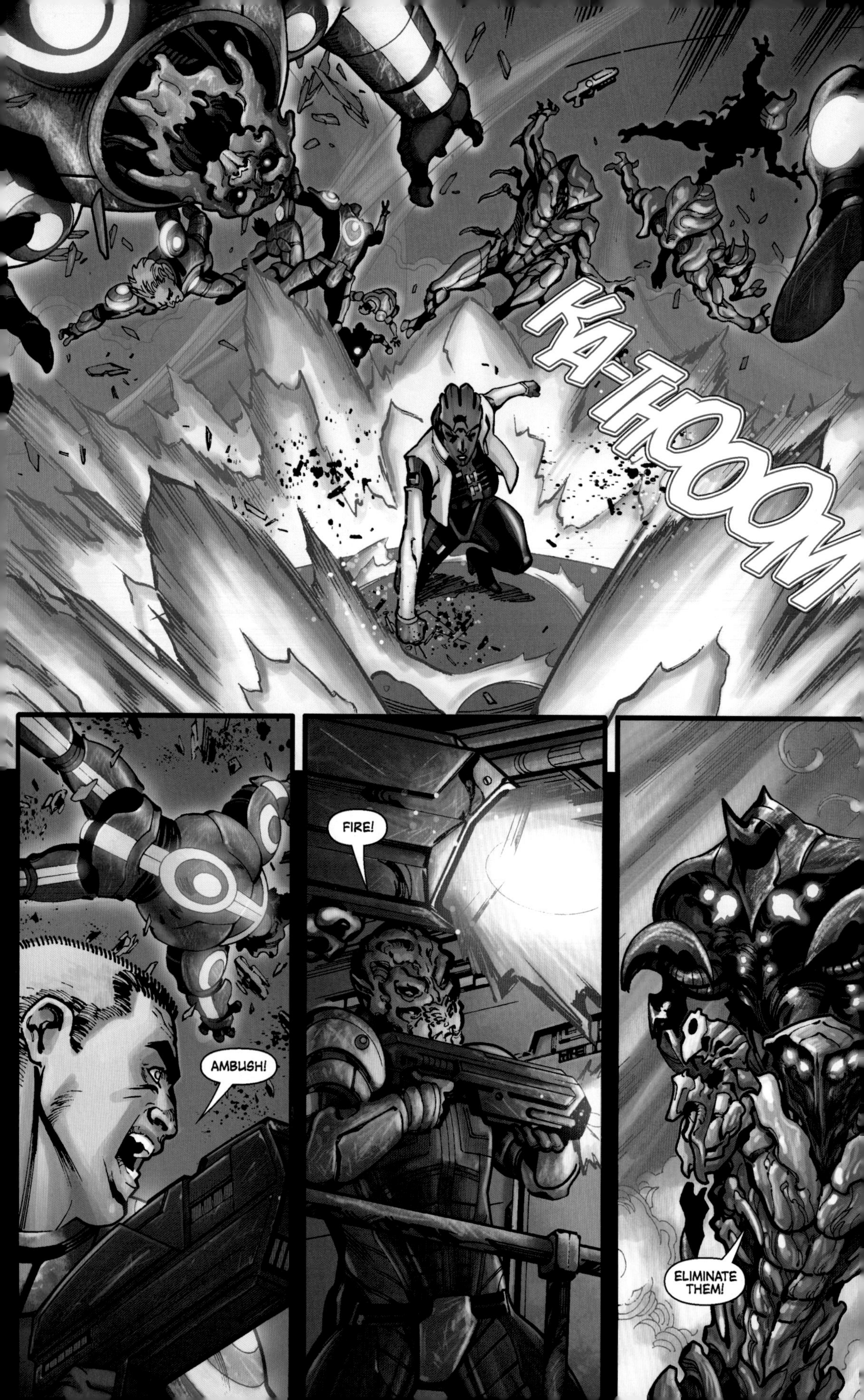
KA-THOOOM
AMBUSH!
FIRE!
ELIMINATE THEM!

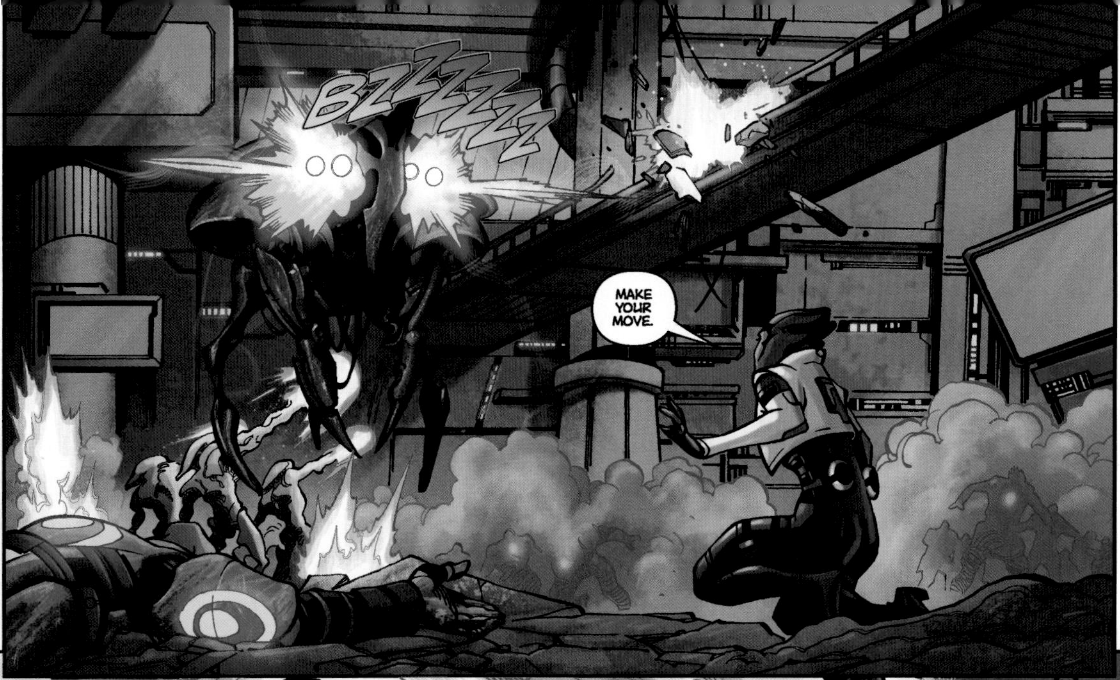
BZZZZZZZ
MAKE YOUR MOVE.
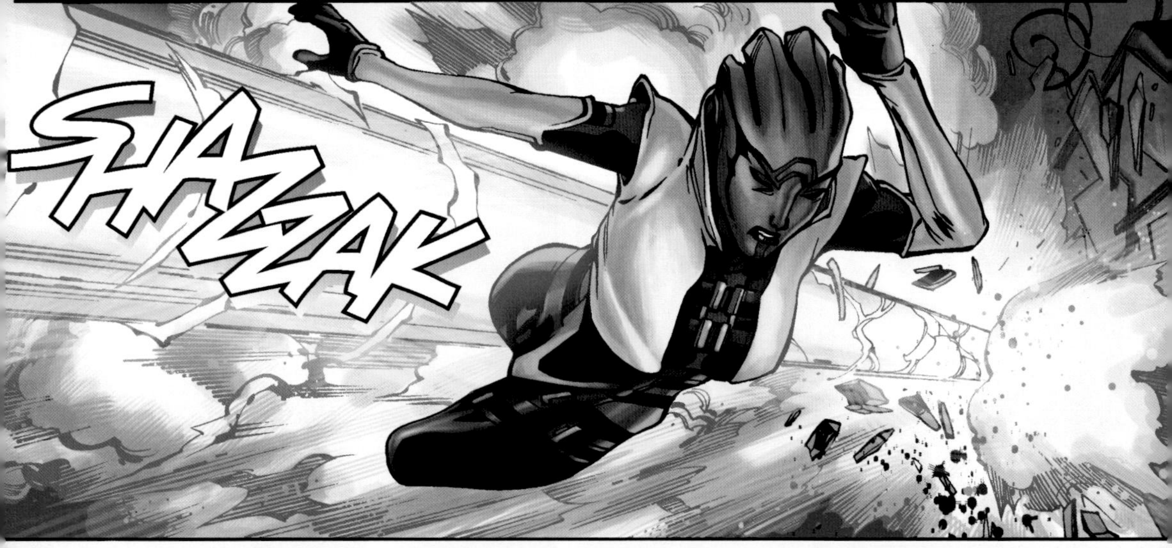
SHAZZAK
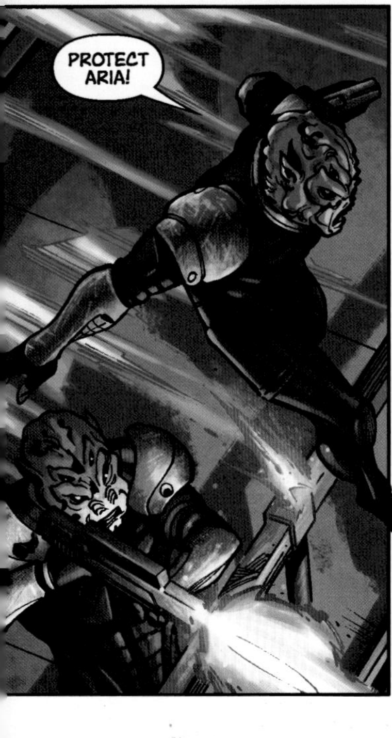
PROTECT ARIA!
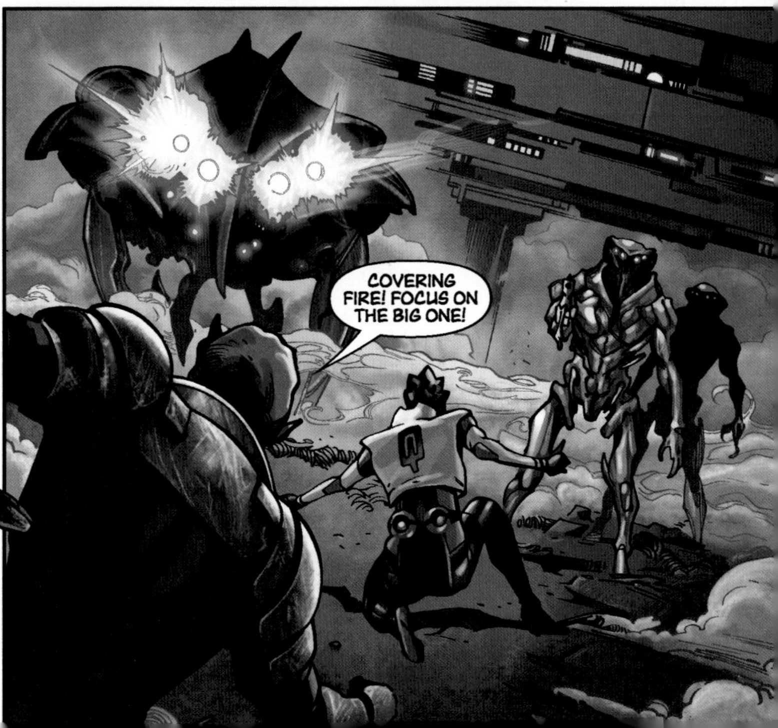
COVERING FIRE! FOCUS ON THE BIG ONE!

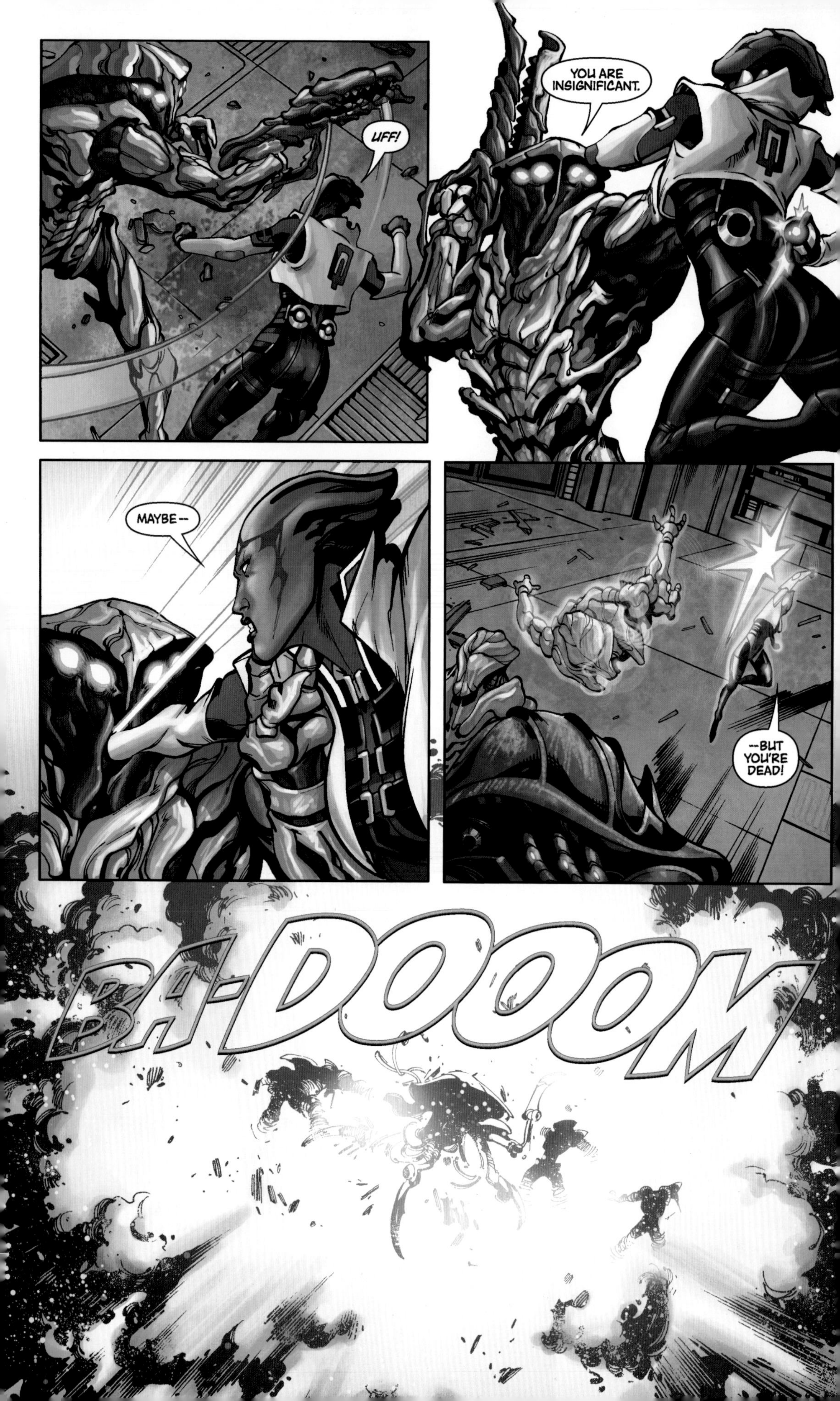
UFF!
YOU ARE INSIGNIFICANT.
MAYBE--
--BUT YOU'RE DEAD!
BA-DOOOM

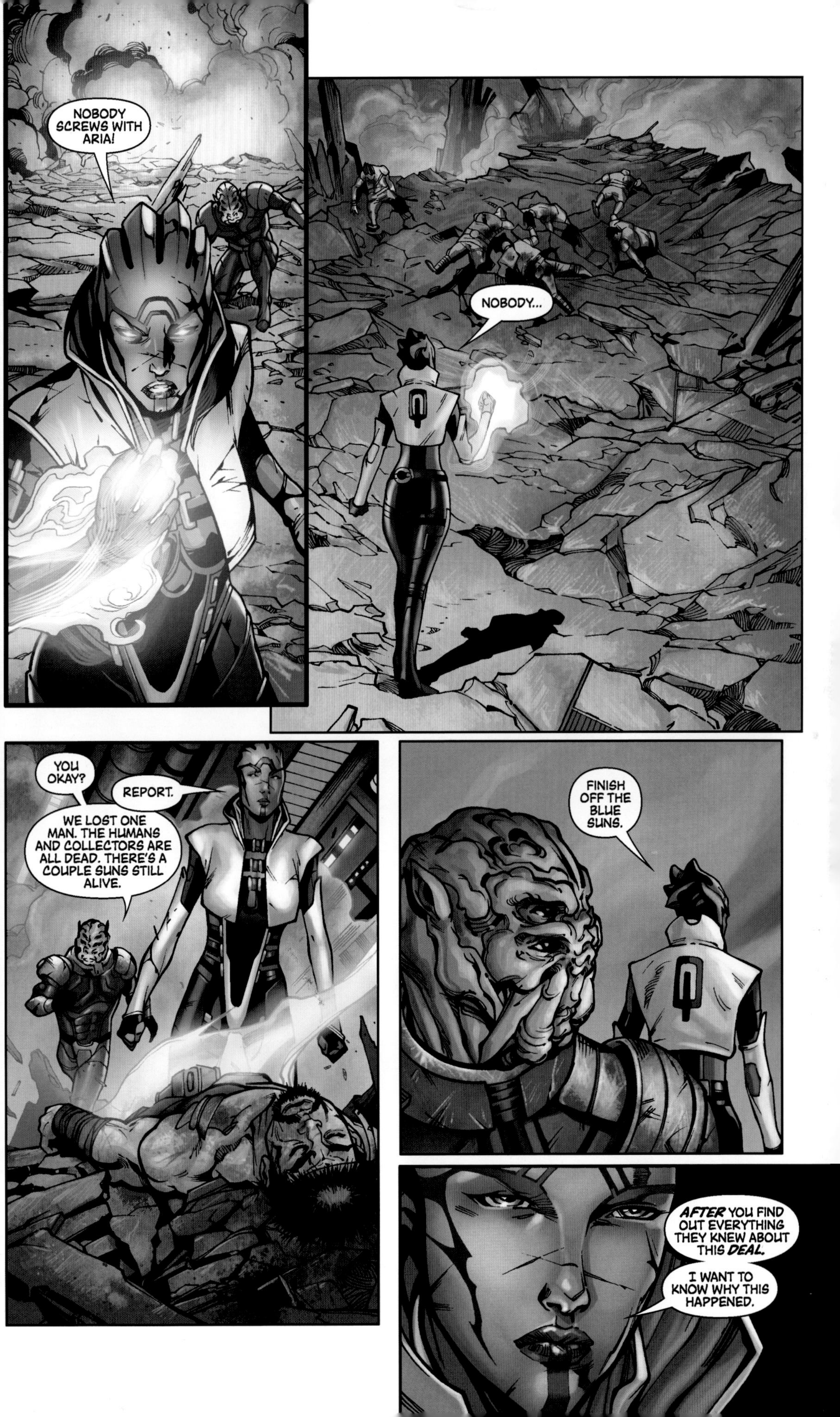
NOBODY SCREWS WITH ARIA!
NOBODY...
YOU OKAY?
REPORT.
WE LOST ONE MAN. THE HUMANS AND COLLECTORS ARE ALL DEAD. THERE'S A COUPLE SUNS STILL ALIVE.
FINISH OFF THE BLUE SUNS.
AFTER YOU FIND OUT EVERYTHING THEY KNEW ABOUT THIS DEAL.
I WANT TO KNOW WHY THIS HAPPENED.

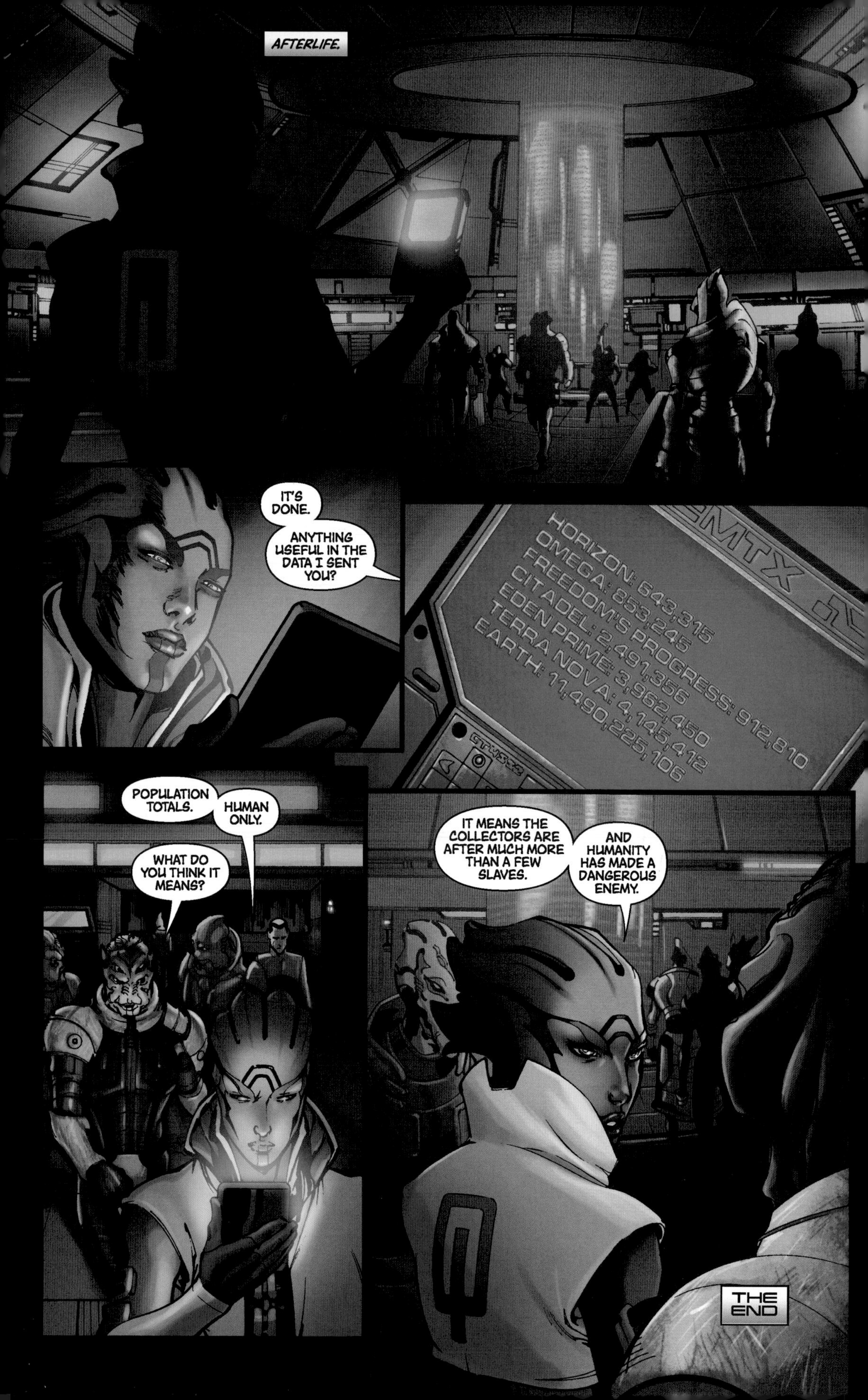
AFTERLIFE.
IT'S DONE.
ANYTHING USEFUL IN THE DATA I SENT YOU?
HORIZON: 643,315
OMEGA: 853,245
FREEDOM'S PROGRESS: 912,810
CITADEL: 2,491,356
EDEN PRIME: 3,962,450
TERRA NOVA: 4,145,412
EARTH: 11,490,225,106
POPULATION TOTALS.
HUMAN ONLY.
WHAT DO YOU THINK IT MEANS?
IT MEANS THE COLLECTORS ARE AFTER MUCH MORE THAN A FEW SLAVES.
AND HUMANITY HAS MADE A DANGEROUS ENEMY.
THE END

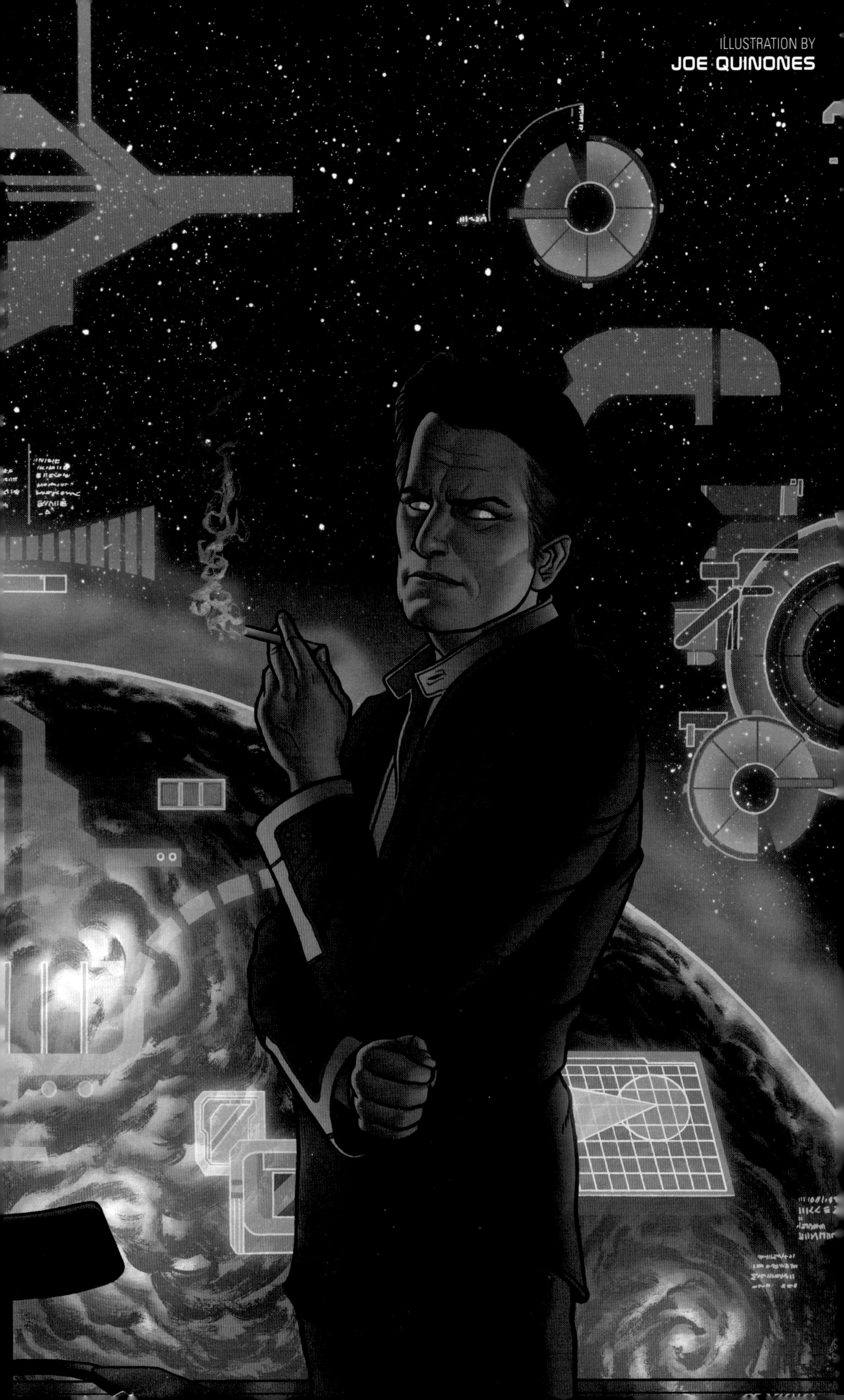
ILLUSTRATION BY
JOE QUINONES

INQUISITION

SCRIPT
MAC WALTERS

ART
JEAN DIAZ

COLORS
MICHAEL ATIYEH

LETTERING
MICHAEL HEISLER

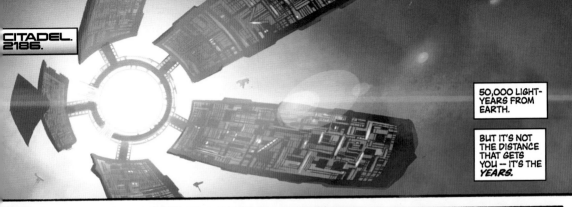

50,000 LIGHT-YEARS FROM EARTH.

BUT IT'S NOT THE DISTANCE THAT GETS YOU -- IT'S THE *YEARS.*

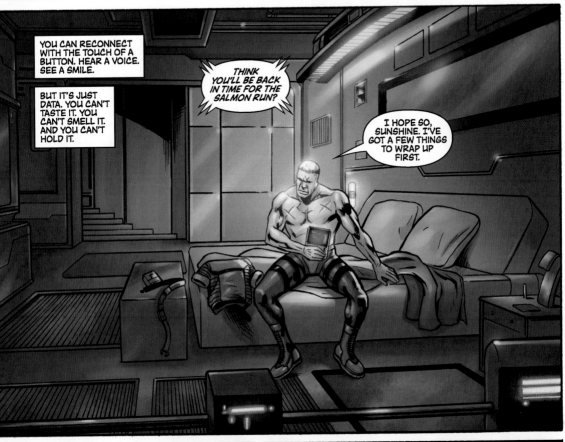

YOU CAN RECONNECT WITH THE TOUCH OF A BUTTON. HEAR A VOICE. SEE A SMILE.

BUT IT'S JUST DATA. YOU CAN'T TASTE IT. YOU CAN'T SMELL IT. AND YOU CAN'T HOLD IT.

THINK YOU'LL BE BACK IN TIME FOR THE SALMON RUN?

I HOPE SO, SUNSHINE. I'VE GOT A FEW THINGS TO WRAP UP FIRST.

OKAY, DAD. CALL ME WHEN YOU'RE HEADING OUT. LOVE YOU.

LOVE YOU TOO. I'LL SEE YOU *SOON.*

AND WITH EACH DAY EVERYTHING -- AND EVERYONE -- DRIFTS A LITTLE BIT FURTHER AWAY.

EVTX

CAPTAIN BAILEY:

THERE IS A MATTER I NEED TO DISCUSS WITH YOU. PLEASE COME BY MY OFFICE AT YOUR EARLIEST CONVENIENCE.

COUNCILOR DONNEL UDINA

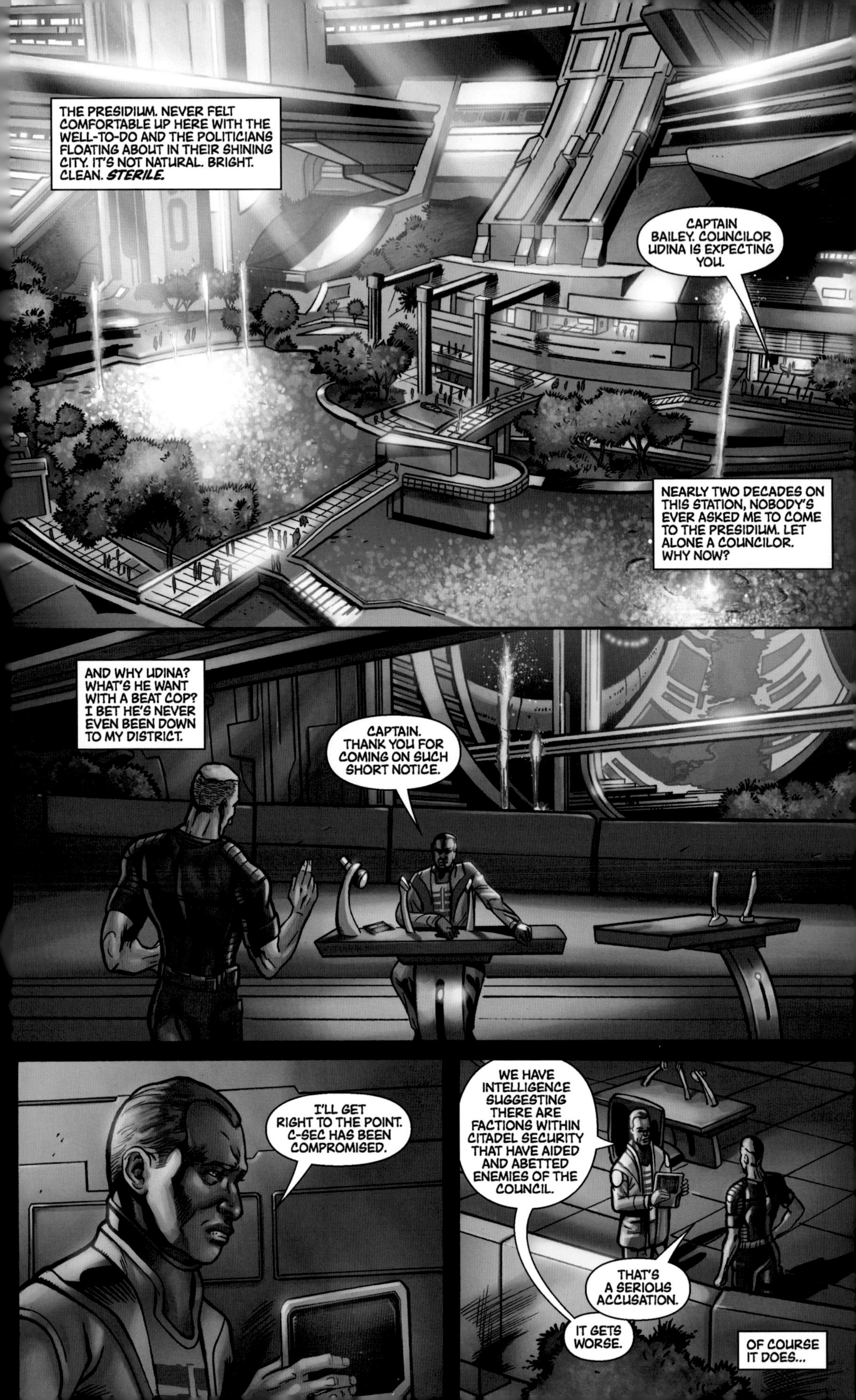
THE PRESIDIUM. NEVER FELT COMFORTABLE UP HERE WITH THE WELL-TO-DO AND THE POLITICIANS FLOATING ABOUT IN THEIR SHINING CITY. IT'S NOT NATURAL. BRIGHT. CLEAN. *STERILE.*
CAPTAIN BAILEY. COUNCILOR UDINA IS EXPECTING YOU.
NEARLY TWO DECADES ON THIS STATION, NOBODY'S EVER ASKED ME TO COME TO THE PRESIDIUM. LET ALONE A COUNCILOR. WHY NOW?
AND WHY UDINA? WHAT'S HE WANT WITH A BEAT COP? I BET HE'S NEVER EVEN BEEN DOWN TO MY DISTRICT.
CAPTAIN. THANK YOU FOR COMING ON SUCH SHORT NOTICE.
I'LL GET RIGHT TO THE POINT. C-SEC HAS BEEN COMPROMISED.
WE HAVE INTELLIGENCE SUGGESTING THERE ARE FACTIONS WITHIN CITADEL SECURITY THAT HAVE AIDED AND ABETTED ENEMIES OF THE COUNCIL.
THAT'S A SERIOUS ACCUSATION.
IT GETS WORSE.
OF COURSE IT DOES...

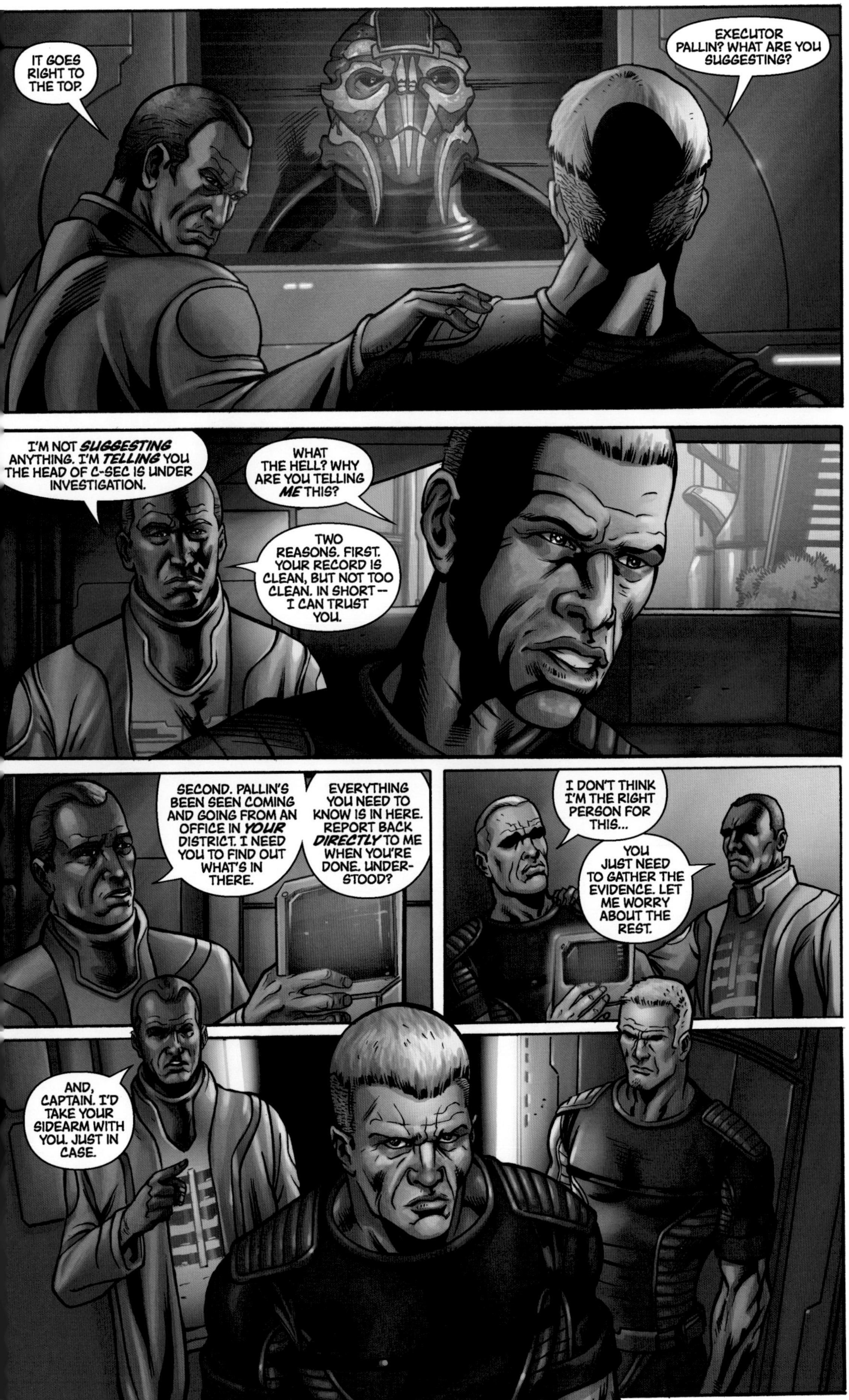
IT GOES RIGHT TO THE TOP.
EXECUTOR PALLIN? WHAT ARE YOU SUGGESTING?
I'M NOT *SUGGESTING* ANYTHING. I'M *TELLING* YOU THE HEAD OF C-SEC IS UNDER INVESTIGATION.
WHAT THE HELL? WHY ARE YOU TELLING *ME* THIS?
TWO REASONS. FIRST. YOUR RECORD IS CLEAN, BUT NOT TOO CLEAN. IN SHORT -- I CAN TRUST YOU.
SECOND. PALLIN'S BEEN SEEN COMING AND GOING FROM AN OFFICE IN *YOUR* DISTRICT. I NEED YOU TO FIND OUT WHAT'S IN THERE.
EVERYTHING YOU NEED TO KNOW IS IN HERE. REPORT BACK *DIRECTLY* TO ME WHEN YOU'RE DONE. UNDER-STOOD?
I DON'T THINK I'M THE RIGHT PERSON FOR THIS...
YOU JUST NEED TO GATHER THE EVIDENCE. LET ME WORRY ABOUT THE REST.
AND, CAPTAIN. I'D TAKE YOUR SIDEARM WITH YOU. JUST IN CASE.

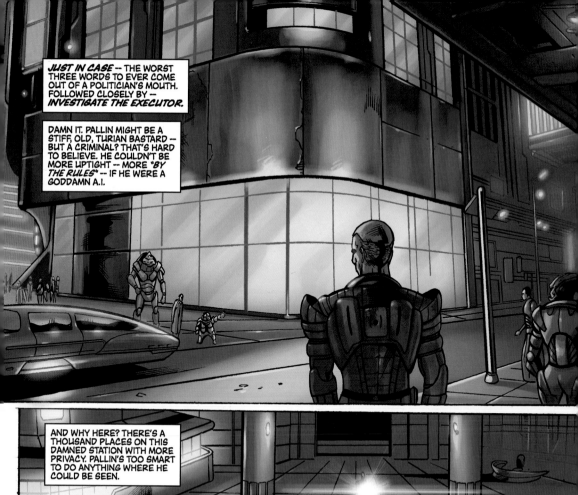

JUST IN CASE -- THE WORST THREE WORDS TO EVER COME OUT OF A POLITICIAN'S MOUTH. FOLLOWED CLOSELY BY -- *INVESTIGATE THE EXECUTOR.*

DAMN IT. PALLIN MIGHT BE A STIFF, OLD, TURIAN BASTARD -- BUT A CRIMINAL? THAT'S HARD TO BELIEVE. HE COULDN'T BE MORE UPTIGHT -- MORE *"BY THE RULES"* -- IF HE WERE A GODDAMN A.I.

AND WHY HERE? THERE'S A THOUSAND PLACES ON THIS DAMNED STATION WITH MORE PRIVACY. PALLIN'S TOO SMART TO DO ANYTHING WHERE HE COULD BE SEEN.

OR MAYBE NOT.

LOOKS LIKE YOU BOYS WERE AFTER THE SAME THING AS ME.

AND WHAT EXACTLY ARE YOU AFTER, CAPTAIN?

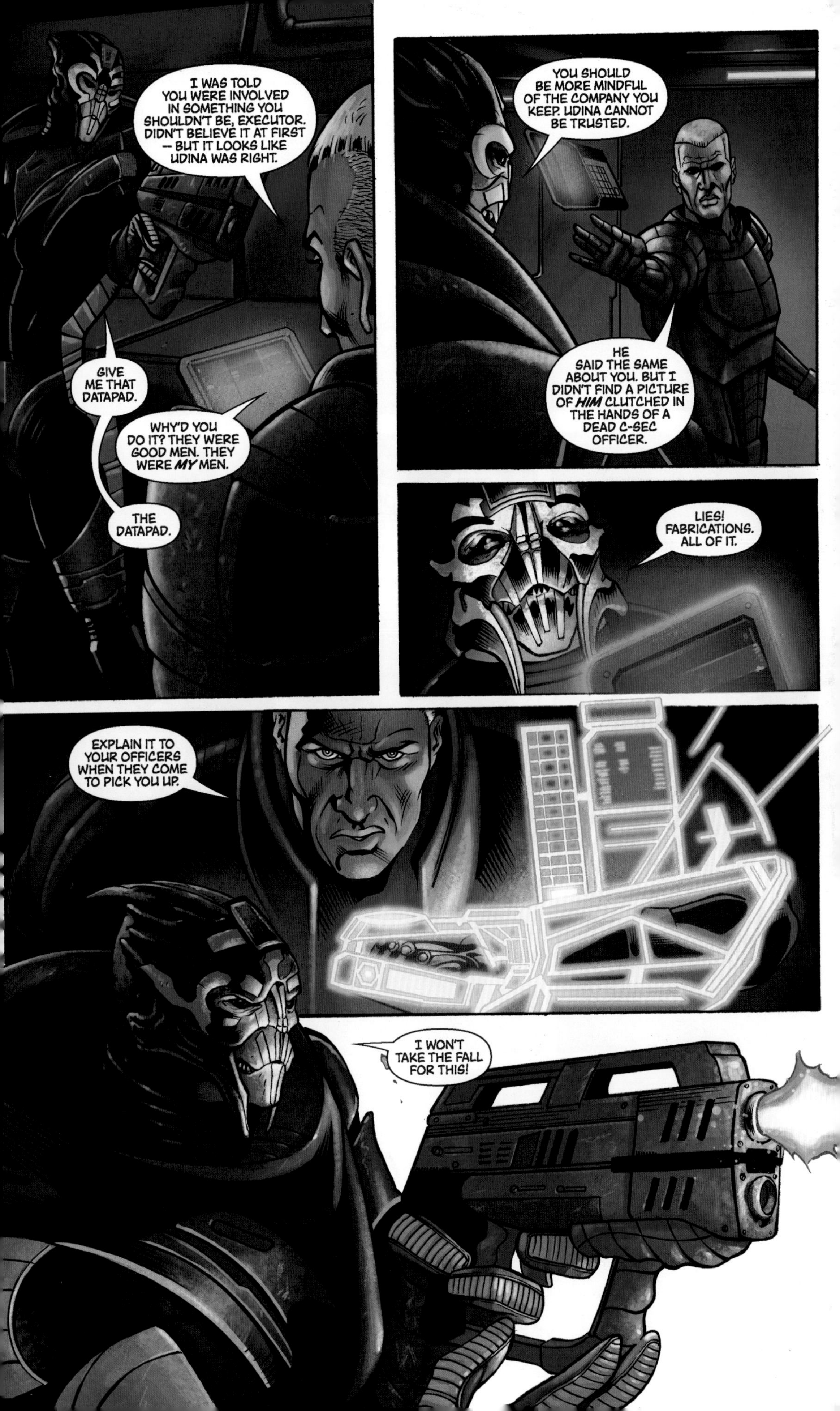
I WAS TOLD YOU WERE INVOLVED IN SOMETHING YOU SHOULDN'T BE, EXECUTOR. DIDN'T BELIEVE IT AT FIRST -- BUT IT LOOKS LIKE UDINA WAS RIGHT.
GIVE ME THAT DATAPAD.
WHY'D YOU DO IT? THEY WERE GOOD MEN. THEY WERE *MY* MEN.
THE DATAPAD.
YOU SHOULD BE MORE MINDFUL OF THE COMPANY YOU KEEP. UDINA CANNOT BE TRUSTED.
HE SAID THE SAME ABOUT YOU. BUT I DIDN'T FIND A PICTURE OF ***HIM*** CLUTCHED IN THE HANDS OF A DEAD C-SEC OFFICER.
LIES! FABRICATIONS. ALL OF IT.
EXPLAIN IT TO YOUR OFFICERS WHEN THEY COME TO PICK YOU UP.
I WON'T TAKE THE FALL FOR THIS!

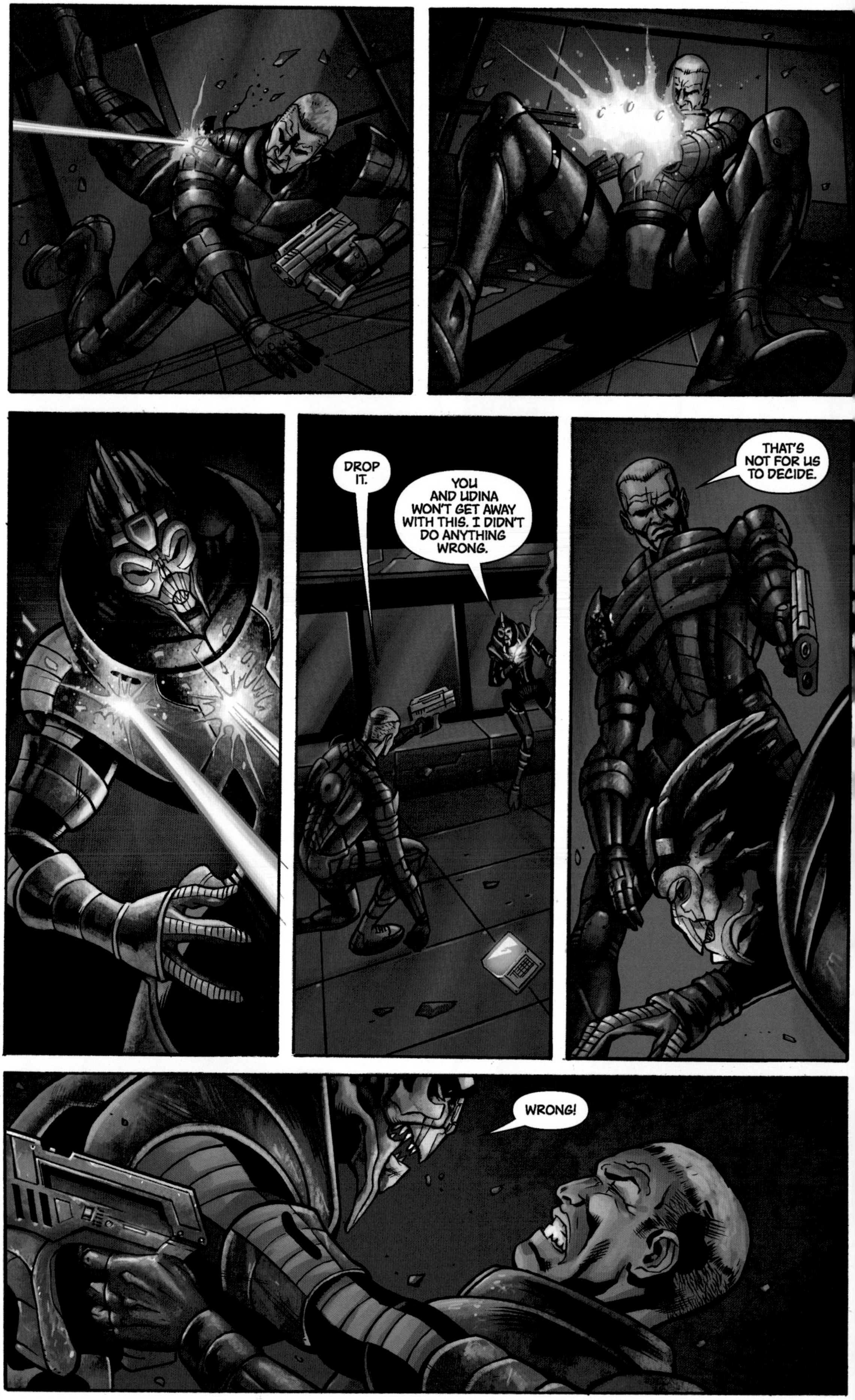
DROP IT.
YOU AND UDINA WON'T GET AWAY WITH THIS. I DIDN'T DO ANYTHING WRONG.
THAT'S NOT FOR US TO DECIDE.
WRONG!

NOBODY DECIDES MY FATE BUT *ME.*

NOBODY.

KRCHOMMM!

FATE... IS A BITCH, EXECUTOR.

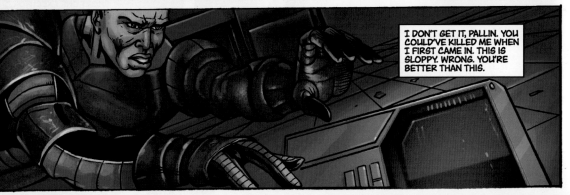

I DON'T GET IT, PALLIN. YOU COULD'VE KILLED ME WHEN I FIRST CAME IN. THIS IS SLOPPY. WRONG. YOU'RE BETTER THAN THIS.

AT LEAST I THOUGHT YOU WERE.

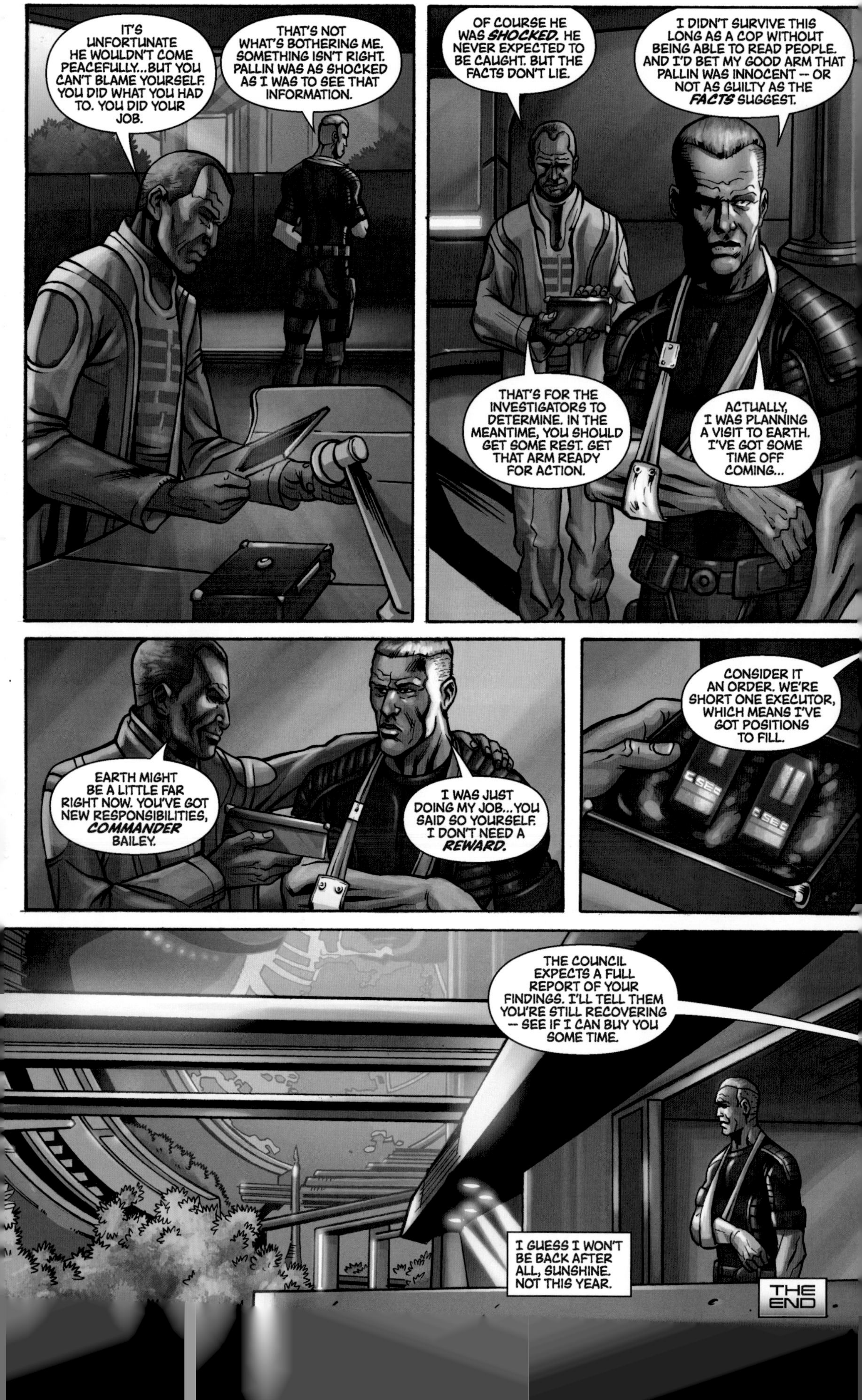
IT'S UNFORTUNATE HE WOULDN'T COME PEACEFULLY...BUT YOU CAN'T BLAME YOURSELF. YOU DID WHAT YOU HAD TO. YOU DID YOUR JOB.
THAT'S NOT WHAT'S BOTHERING ME. SOMETHING ISN'T RIGHT. PALLIN WAS AS SHOCKED AS I WAS TO SEE THAT INFORMATION.
OF COURSE HE WAS SHOCKED. HE NEVER EXPECTED TO BE CAUGHT. BUT THE FACTS DON'T LIE.
I DIDN'T SURVIVE THIS LONG AS A COP WITHOUT BEING ABLE TO READ PEOPLE. AND I'D BET MY GOOD ARM THAT PALLIN WAS INNOCENT -- OR NOT AS GUILTY AS THE FACTS SUGGEST.
THAT'S FOR THE INVESTIGATORS TO DETERMINE. IN THE MEANTIME, YOU SHOULD GET SOME REST. GET THAT ARM READY FOR ACTION.
ACTUALLY, I WAS PLANNING A VISIT TO EARTH. I'VE GOT SOME TIME OFF COMING...
EARTH MIGHT BE A LITTLE FAR RIGHT NOW. YOU'VE GOT NEW RESPONSIBILITIES, COMMANDER BAILEY.
I WAS JUST DOING MY JOB...YOU SAID SO YOURSELF. I DON'T NEED A REWARD.
CONSIDER IT AN ORDER. WE'RE SHORT ONE EXECUTOR, WHICH MEANS I'VE GOT POSITIONS TO FILL.
C-SEC
C-SEC
THE COUNCIL EXPECTS A FULL REPORT OF YOUR FINDINGS. I'LL TELL THEM YOU'RE STILL RECOVERING -- SEE IF I CAN BUY YOU SOME TIME.
I GUESS I WON'T BE BACK AFTER ALL, SUNSHINE. NOT THIS YEAR.
THE END

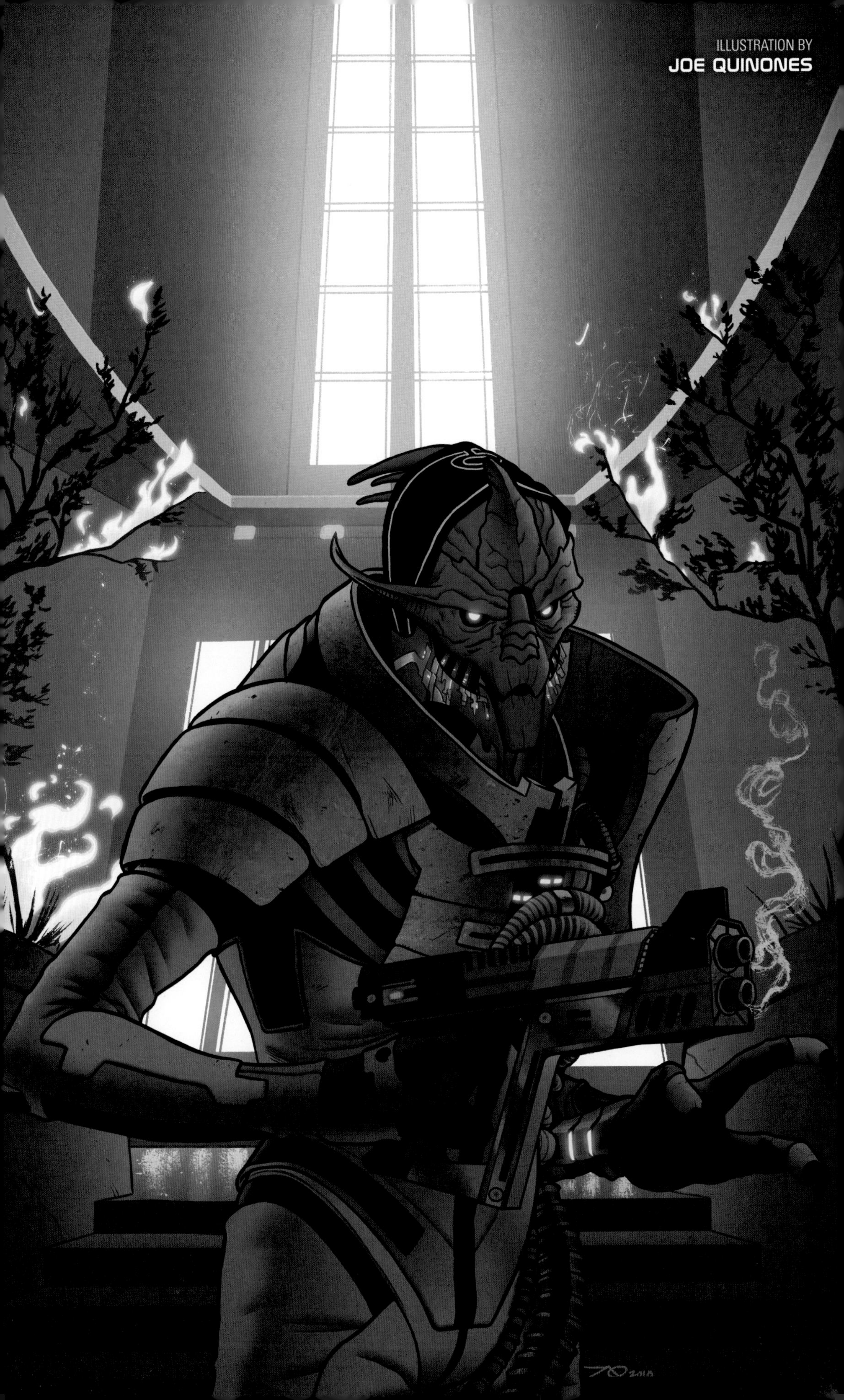

ILLUSTRATION BY
JOE QUINONES

CONVICTION

SCRIPT
MAC WALTERS

ART
EDUARDO FRANCISCO

COLORS
MICHAEL ATIYEH

LETTERING
MICHAEL HEISLER

SOMEWHERE DEEP IN THE HEART OF OMEGA. DAYS AFTER THE ANNIHILATION OF A BATARIAN SYSTEM BY COMMANDER SHEPARD.

-- WHILE THE CITADEL COUNCIL SCRAMBLES TO DENOUNCE THE SO-CALLED TERRORIST ACTS ALLEGEDLY CARRIED OUT BY COMMANDER SHEPARD, BATARIAN OFFICIALS ARE DEMANDING RETRIBUTION.

COUNCILOR UDINA HAS PUBLICLY DENIED THAT THE HUMAN ALLIANCE HAD ANYTHING TO DO WITH THE DESTRUCTION OF THE MASS RELAY...

IT'S YOUR BET, HUMAN!

-- BATARIAN LEADERS ARE CALLING FOR SHEPARD'S HEAD --

ZZSSAT!

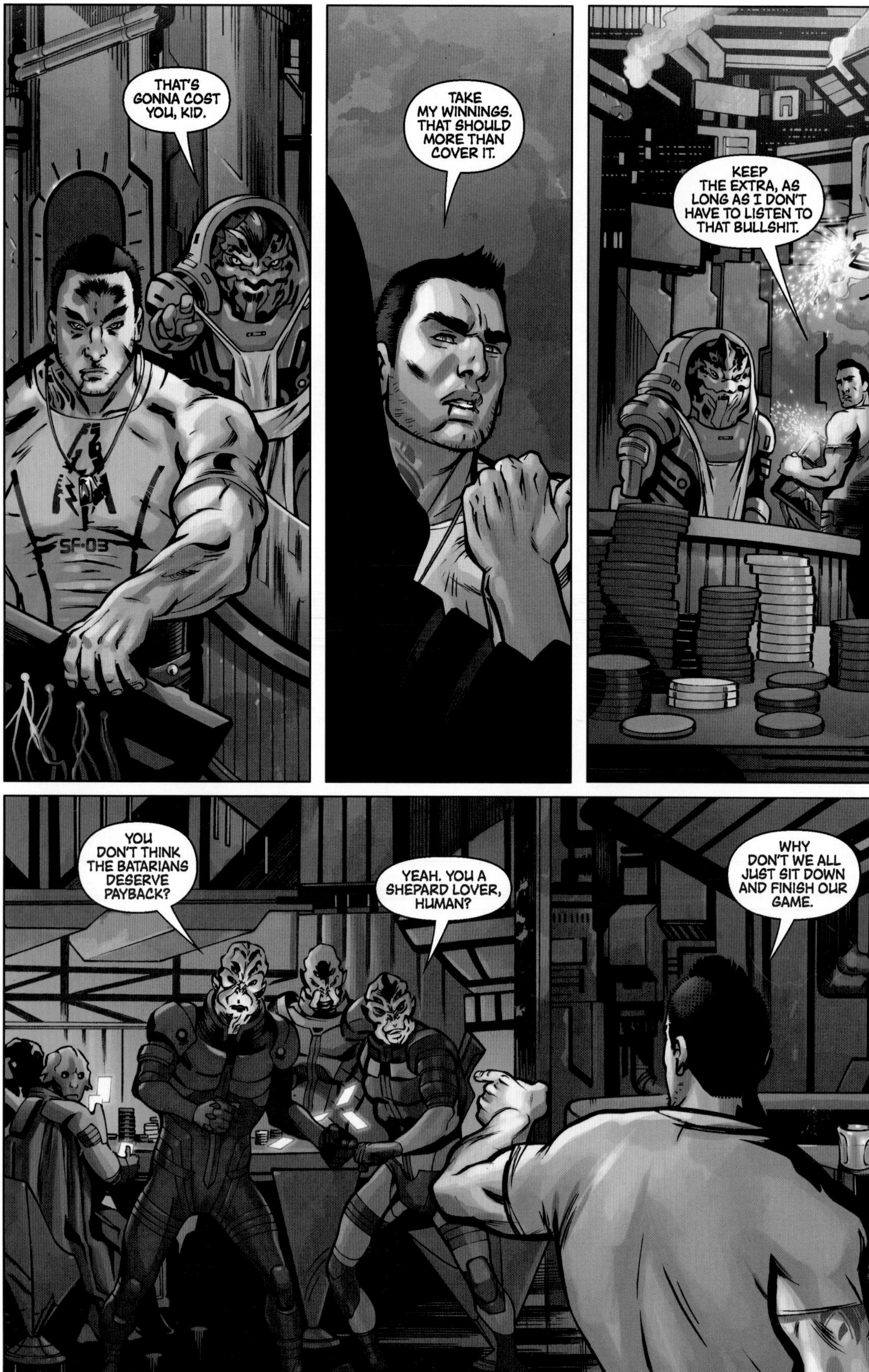
THAT'S GONNA COST YOU, KID.
SF-03
TAKE MY WINNINGS. THAT SHOULD MORE THAN COVER IT.
KEEP THE EXTRA, AS LONG AS I DON'T HAVE TO LISTEN TO THAT BULLSHIT.
YOU DON'T THINK THE BATARIANS DESERVE PAYBACK?
YEAH. YOU A SHEPARD LOVER, HUMAN?
WHY DON'T WE ALL JUST SIT DOWN AND FINISH OUR GAME.

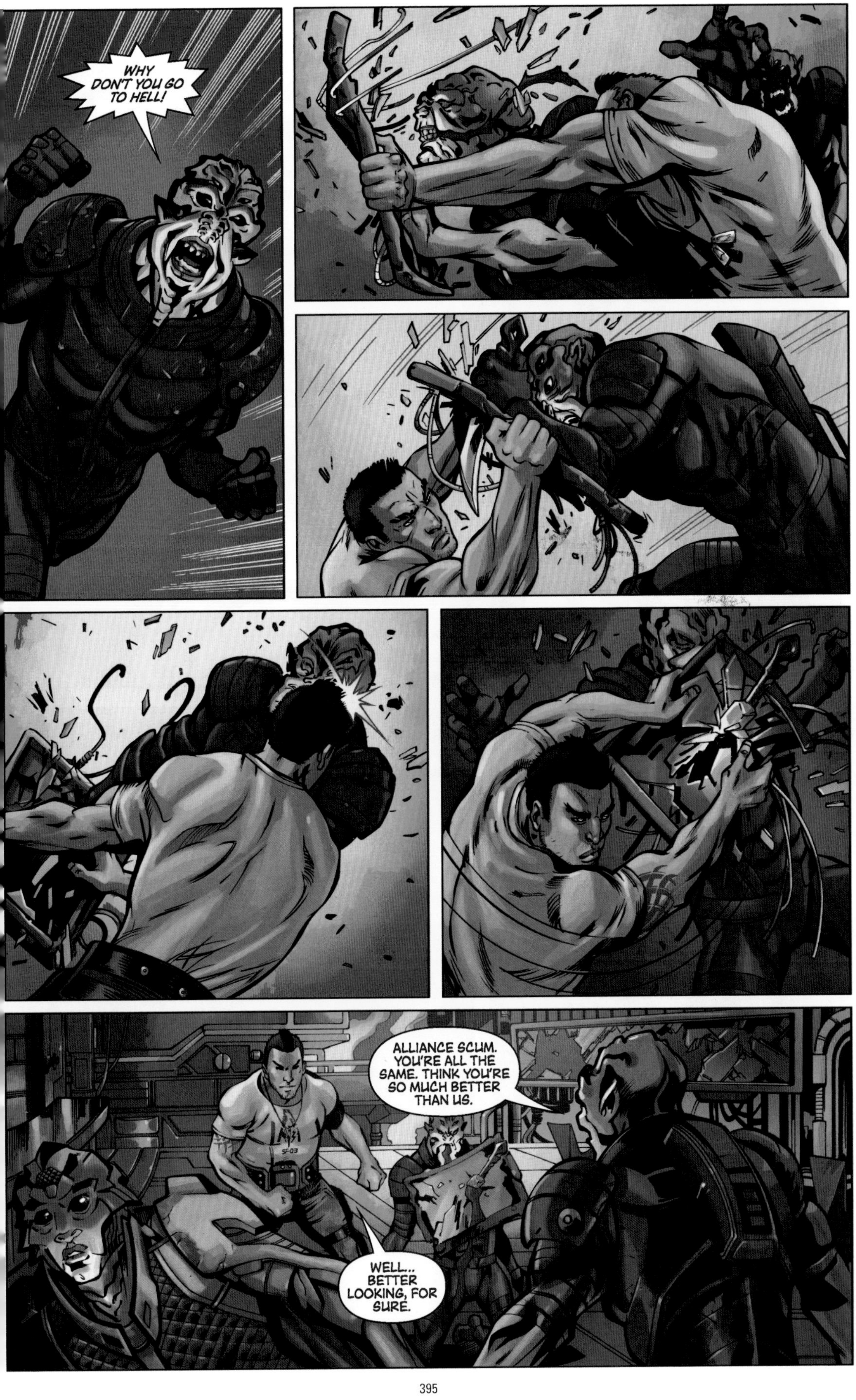
WHY DON'T YOU GO TO HELL!
ALLIANCE SCUM. YOU'RE ALL THE SAME. THINK YOU'RE SO MUCH BETTER THAN US.
WELL... BETTER LOOKING, FOR SURE.

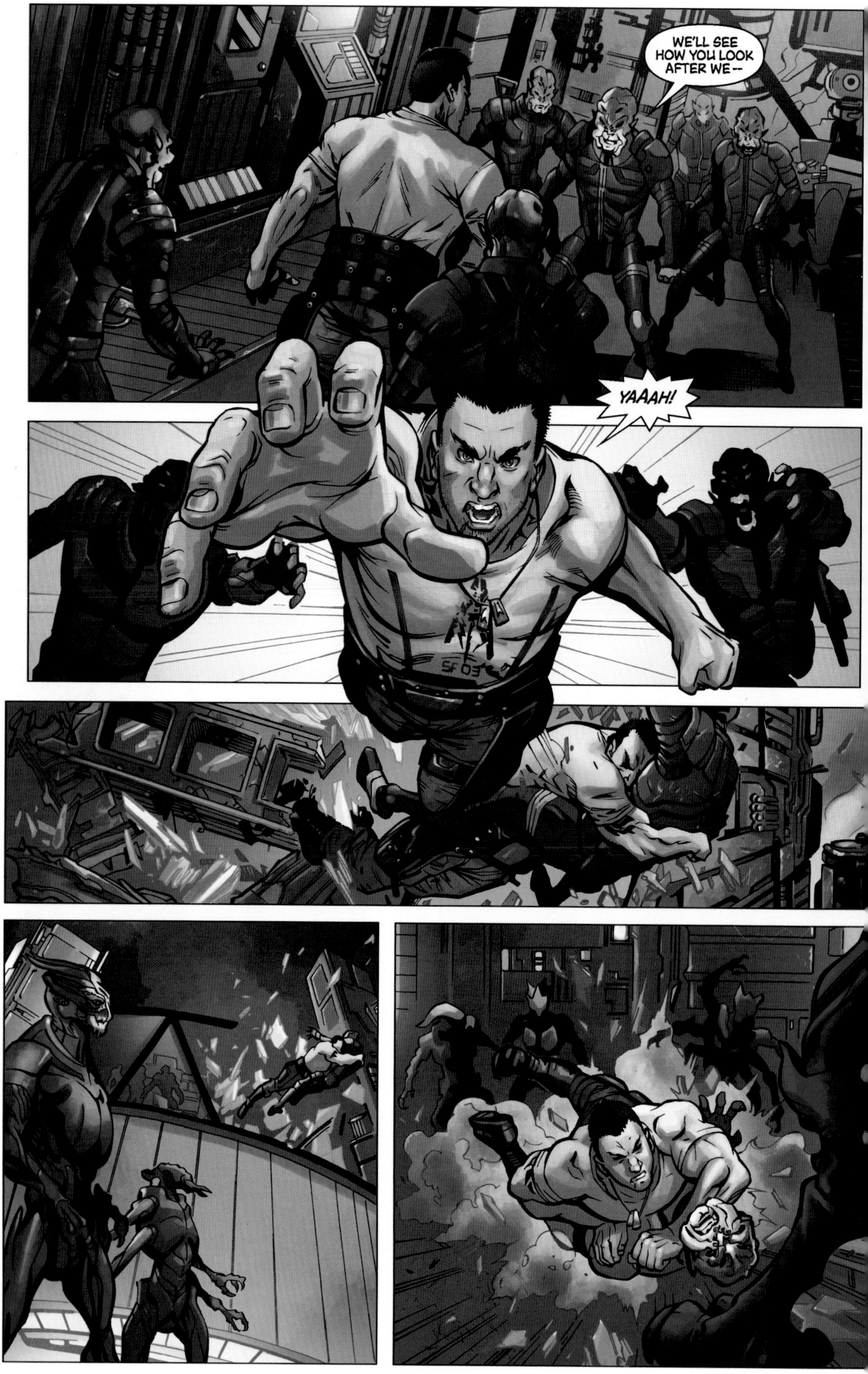
WE'LL SEE HOW YOU LOOK AFTER WE --
YAAAH!

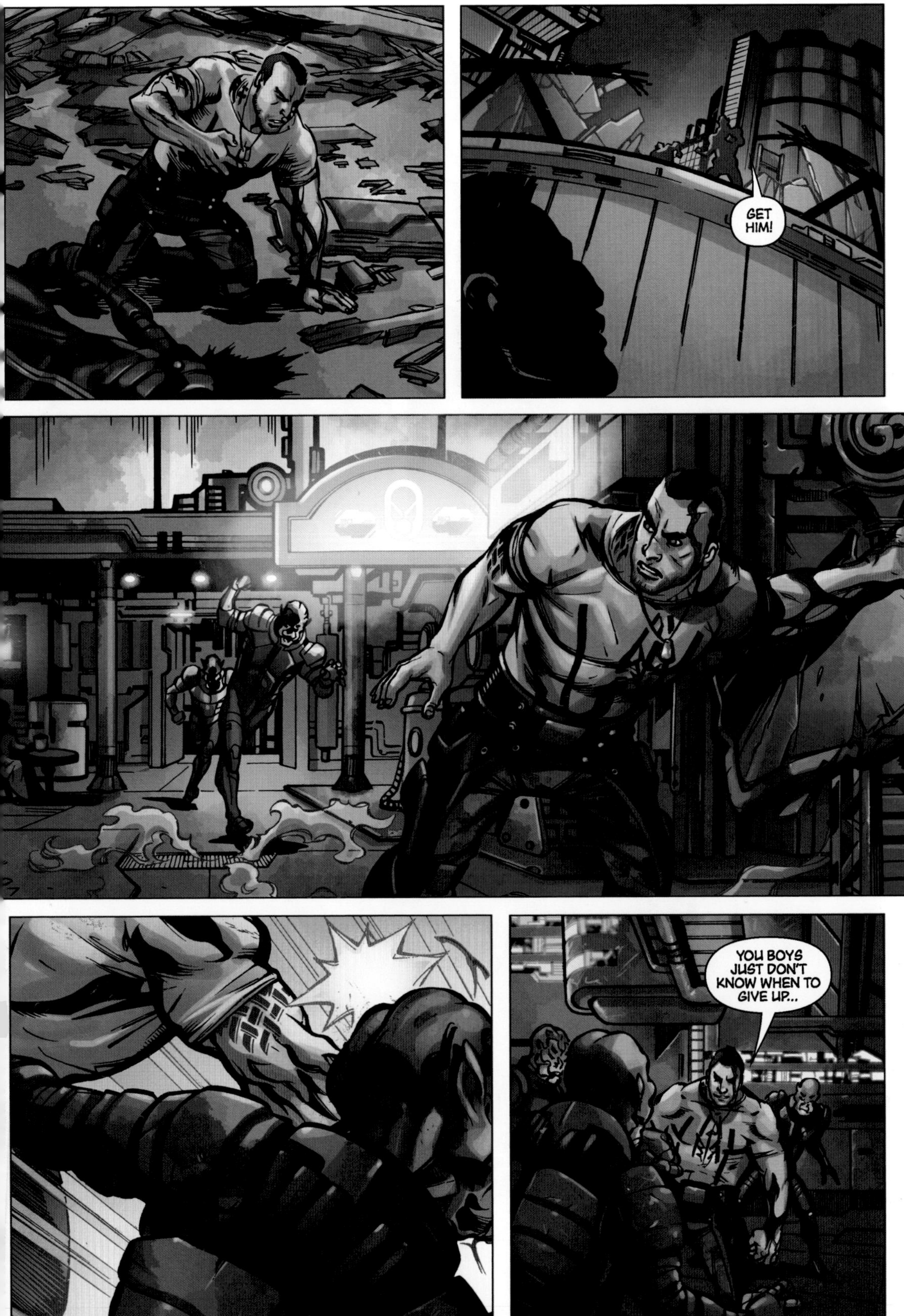
GET HIM!
YOU BOYS JUST DON'T KNOW WHEN TO GIVE UP...

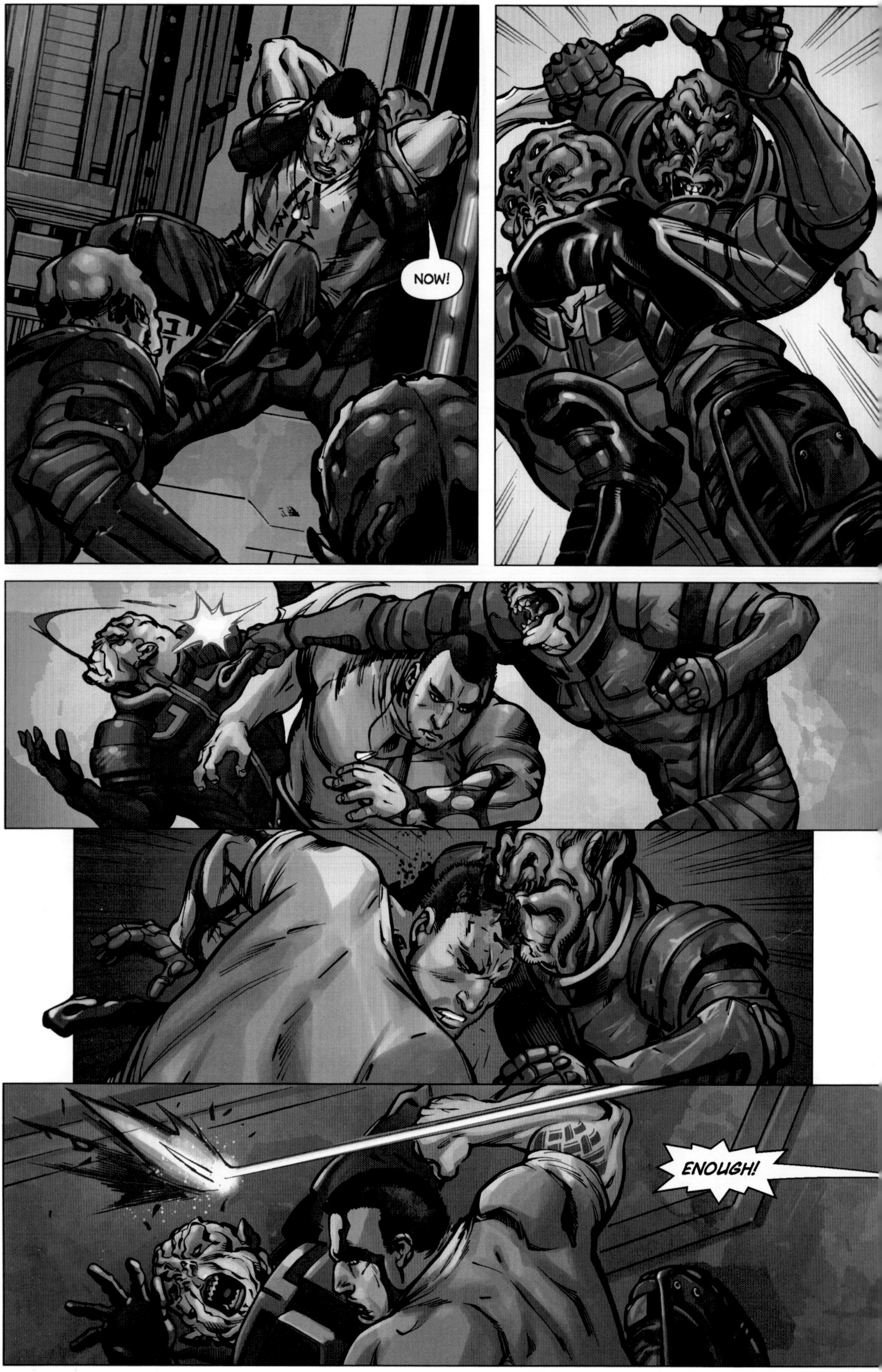
NOW!
ENOUGH!

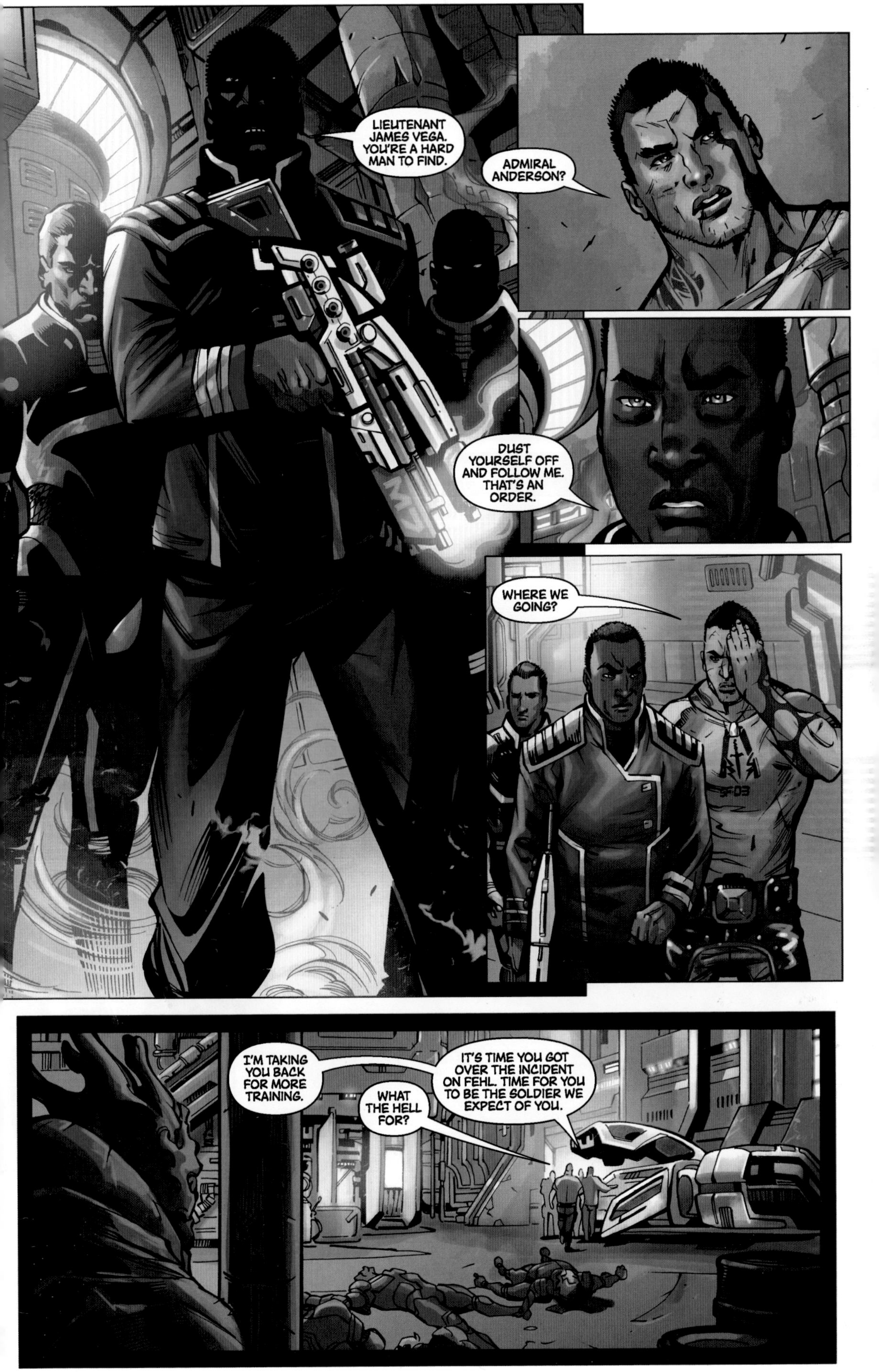
LIEUTENANT JAMES VEGA. YOU'RE A HARD MAN TO FIND.
ADMIRAL ANDERSON?
DUST YOURSELF OFF AND FOLLOW ME. THAT'S AN ORDER.
WHERE WE GOING?
I'M TAKING YOU BACK FOR MORE TRAINING.
WHAT THE HELL FOR?
IT'S TIME YOU GOT OVER THE INCIDENT ON FEHL. TIME FOR YOU TO BE THE SOLDIER WE EXPECT OF YOU.

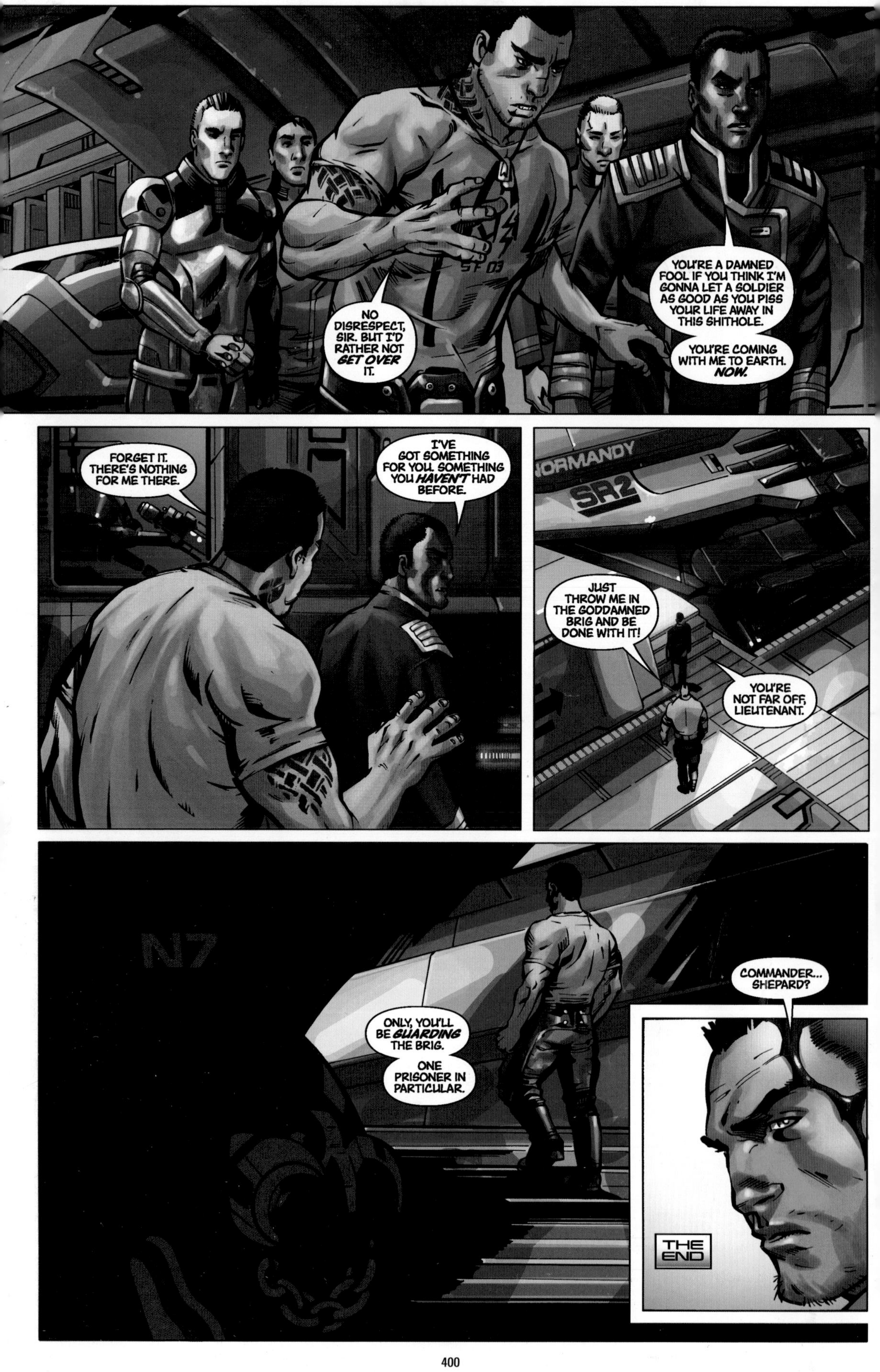
NO DISRESPECT, SIR. BUT I'D RATHER NOT *GET OVER* IT.
YOU'RE A DAMNED FOOL IF YOU THINK I'M GONNA LET A SOLDIER AS GOOD AS YOU PISS YOUR LIFE AWAY IN THIS SHITHOLE.
YOU'RE COMING WITH ME TO EARTH. *NOW.*
FORGET IT. THERE'S NOTHING FOR ME THERE.
I'VE GOT SOMETHING FOR YOU. SOMETHING YOU *HAVEN'T* HAD BEFORE.
NORMANDY
SR2
JUST THROW ME IN THE GODDAMNED BRIG AND BE DONE WITH IT!
YOU'RE NOT FAR OFF, LIEUTENANT.
N7
ONLY, YOU'LL BE *GUARDING* THE BRIG.
ONE PRISONER IN PARTICULAR.
COMMANDER... SHEPARD?
THE END